Studies in Renaissance Literature

Volume 42

LOCALIZING CHRISTOPHER MARLOWE

Studies in Renaissance Literature

ISSN 1465-6310

General Editors
Brooke Conti
Jane Grogan
Ramona Wray

Studies in Renaissance Literature offers investigations of topics in English literature focussed in the sixteenth and seventeenth centuries; its scope extends from early Tudor writing, including works reflecting medieval concerns, to the Restoration period. Studies exploring the interplay between the literature of the English Renaissance and its cultural history are particularly welcomed.

Proposals or queries should be sent in the first instance to the editors, or to the publisher, at the addresses given below; all submissions receive prompt and informed consideration.

Professor Brooke Conti, Cleveland State University, English Department, Rhodes Tower, Cleveland, OH 44115, USA

Professor Jane Grogan, University College Dublin, School of English, Drama and Film, Newman Building, Belfield, Dublin 4, Ireland

Professor Ramona Wray, Queen's University Belfast, School of Arts, English and Languages, University Square, Belfast, BT7 1NN

Boydell & Brewer Limited, PO Box 9, Woodbridge, Suffolk, IP12 3DF

Previously published volumes in this series are listed at the back of this volume

LOCALIZING CHRISTOPHER MARLOWE

His Life, Plays and Mythology, 1575–1593

Arata Ide

D. S. BREWER

© Arata Ide 2023

All Rights Reserved. Except as permitted under current legislation
no part of this work may be photocopied, stored in a retrieval system,
published, performed in public, adapted, broadcast,
transmitted, recorded or reproduced in any form or by any means,
without the prior permission of the copyright owner

The right of Arata Ide to be identified as
the author of this work has been asserted in accordance with
sections 77 and 78 of the Copyright, Designs and Patents Act 1988

First published 2023
D. S. Brewer, Cambridge

ISBN 978-1-84384-693-2

D. S. Brewer is an imprint of Boydell & Brewer Ltd
PO Box 9, Woodbridge, Suffolk IP12 3DF, UK
and of Boydell & Brewer Inc.
668 Mt Hope Avenue, Rochester, NY 14620–2731, USA
website: www.boydellandbrewer.com

A catalogue record for this title is available
from the British Library

The publisher has no responsibility for the continued existence or accuracy of URLs
for external or third-party internet websites referred to in this book, and does not
guarantee that any content on such websites is, or will remain, accurate or appropriate

This publication is printed on acid-free paper

For my late parents

CONTENTS

List of Illustrations	ix
Acknowledgements	xii
List of Abbreviations	xiv
Timeline	xvi
Note for the Reader	xxi
Introduction	1

PART I: LIFE

1.	Matthew Parker and the Norwich–Corpus Connection	33
2.	Marlowe in the Community of Canterbury Scholars	64
3.	The Origin of the Rumour against Marlowe	89
4.	Marlowe and the Privy Council	114

PART II: PLAYS

5.	Dido, Elizabeth I, and the University Playwrights	149
6.	Tamburlaine's Prophetic Oratory and the English Holy War	175
7.	*The Jew of Malta* and the Diabolic Power of Theatrics	207
8.	Ramism, Thomas Nashe, and the 'New Sects of Singularitie'	238

PART III: MYTHS

9.	Robert Greene on Marlowe's Atheism	267
10.	The Genesis of the Marlowe Myth	296
	Conclusion	335

Contents

Appendix 1: Transcript of the plan in Norfolk Record Office, NRS 23372, Z99   348

Appendix 2: Transcript of the plan in Corpus Christi College Archives, CCCC08/28   350

Appendix 3: Transcript and translation of the John Marley vs Nevell Hayes case   352

Appendix 4: List of Foundation Scholars of Corpus Christi College, 1573–87   354

Bibliography   364

Index   399

ILLUSTRATIONS

1. The supplicat of Thomas Nashe: CUA, Supplicats, 1585–86, no. 83. Reproduced by kind permission of the Syndics of Cambridge University Library.   137

2. The supplicat of Gabriel Harvey: CUA, Supplicats, 1569–70, no. 9. Reproduced by kind permission of the Syndics of Cambridge University Library.   137

3. The supplicat of Nicholas Faunt: CUA, Supplicats, 1575–76, no. 109. Reproduced by kind permission of the Syndics of Cambridge University Library.   138

4. The supplicat of Christopher Marlowe: CUA, Supplicats, 1583–84, no. 199. Reproduced by kind permission of the Syndics of Cambridge University Library.   138

5. The supplicats of the scholars at Corpus Christi College: CUA, Supplicats, 1583–84, no. 194 (Edward Elwin), no. 195 (Thomas Lewgar), no. 196 (Abraham Tilman), no. 197 (Simon Thaxter), and no. 198 (Thomas Driver). Reproduced by kind permission of the Syndics of Cambridge University Library.   139

6. Nicholas Bacon's Plan of Corpus Christi College, 1577, 'The number of those that be Lodged in the Colleg & how & in what chambers they be lodged', left half. NRO, NRS 23372, Z99. Reproduced by kind permission of Norfolk Record Office.   140

7. Bacon's plan, right half. NRO, NRS 23372, Z99. Reproduced by kind permission of Norfolk Record Office.   141

8. Matthew Parker's Plan of Corpus Christi College, 1574–75. CCCA, CCCC08/28, recto. Reproduced by kind permission of The Parker Library, Corpus Christi College, Cambridge.   142

9. Corpus Christi College, plan of the college site, 1576, first verso of the document endorsed as 'The annuall revenuewes and exspences of Benet Colledge in Cambridge'. NRO, NRS 23372, Z99. Reproduced by kind permission of Norfolk Record Office.   143

Illustrations

10. Parker's plan, verso. Reproduced by kind permission of The Parker Library, Corpus Christi College, Cambridge.   144

11. Manwood's monument in the parish church of St Stephen, Canterbury. © Arata Ide.   144

12. Samuel Foxe's account of Englishmen whom he encountered at Padua. BL, Lansdowne MS 679, fol. 44v. © The British Library. All Rights Reserved.   145

13. Foxe's handwritten 'Martin'. BL, Lansdowne MS 679, fol. 44v (detail). © The British Library. All Rights Reserved.   146

14. Foxe's handwritten 'Italicis'. BL, Lansdowne MS 679, fol. 49r (detail). © The British Library. All Rights Reserved.   146

15. Foxe's handwritten 'etiam'. BL, Lansdowne MS 679, fol. 73v (detail). © The British Library. All Rights Reserved.   146

16. Foxe's handwritten 'Martini'. BL, Lansdowne MS 679, fol. 44r (detail). © The British Library. All Rights Reserved.   146

17. 'Ring of Pikes' in Thomas Styward, *The Pathwaie to Martiall Discipline* (London, 1581), p. 68. RB 14636, The Huntington Library, San Marino, California.   167

18. Captain Thomas Smith and young citizens in the funeral procession of Sir Philip Sidney, depicted in Thomas Lant, *Sequitur Celebritas & Pompa Funeris* (London, 1588), fol. 24. BL, General Reference Collection 74/C.20.f.12. © The British Library. All rights Reserved.   178

19. 'Duke' Joshua portrayed in Richard Lloyd, *A Briefe Discourse of the Most Renowned Actes and Right Valiant Conquests of Those Puisant Princes, Called the Nine Worthies* (London, 1584), sig. B1r. Bodleian Library, Mal. 649 (1). By permission of The Bodleian Libraries, University of Oxford.   183

20. Plan of Dover Harbour, perhaps drawn by John Hill in 1595. BL, Cotton MS Augustus, I.i.46. © The British Library. All Rights Reserved.   231

21. The 'cross wall' of the great pent in Dover Harbour. BL, Cotton MS Augustus, I.i.46 (detail). © The British Library. All Rights Reserved.   232

22. The scribal copy of the Baines Note. BL, Harley MS 6853, fol. 307r (detail). © The British Library. All Rights Reserved.   309

The author and publisher are grateful to all the institutions and individuals listed for permission to reproduce the materials in which they hold copyright. Every effort has been made to trace the copyright holders; apologies are offered for any omission, the publisher will be pleased to add any necessary acknowledgement in subsequent editions.

ACKNOWLEDGEMENTS

It has taken me a long time to complete my biographical project of Christopher Marlowe. While it gradually took shape, I have been helped and supported by a number of friends, acquaintances, and colleagues, some of whom, to my regret, I am no longer able to meet and thank in person. For reasons of space, and due to my limited faculty of memory, it is not possible to include here all those to whom I have been indebted in various ways over the decades, but before I begin, I extend my heartfelt gratitude to all of them.

In the first stages of this project, I spent much of my research time in Cambridge University Library and Parker Library at Corpus Christi College, where I was kindly assisted and supported by their tirelessly supportive librarians and archivists. It is my pleasure to express my especial thanks to Elisabeth Leedham-Green. Her presence was a guiding light for me when researching in the college archives, and all of her observations on the university students and fellows in Tudor Cambridge have given me great inspiration and insight into their everyday lives. I am deeply grateful for her valuable suggestions on the earlier drafts of Introduction and Part 1. I am also indebted to Catherine P. Hall, who first drew my attention to the Matthew Parker's college plan of Corpus Christi; and to Gill Cannell and Lucy Hughes, who were gracious hosts at Parker Library. I also owe thanks to the librarians and archivists of the Bodleian Library, British Library, the Canterbury Cathedral Archives and Library, the English Faculty Library at Oxford University, the Guildhall Library (London), Keio University Library, Lambeth Palace Library, the UK National Archives, and the Norfolk Record Office.

My project would not have been possible without the pioneering work of Marlowe's biographers, specifically the work of Constance B. Kuriyama. I extend my sincere thanks to her for her interest in my articles, and for her warm encouragement and valuable suggestions. I am also grateful to Janet Clare, Hester Higton, Martin Ingram, Emrys Lloyd Jones, Akiko Kusunoki, Jeremy Lowe, Peter Roberts, Paul Whitfield White, the anonymous readers of *Early Theatre*, *Reformation*, *Studies in English Literature 1500–1900*, *Studies in Philology*, and *Transactions of Cambridge Bibliographical Society*, for having kindly read and commented on sections or the whole of my manuscript at its earlier stages. Of course, I am solely responsible for all remaining errors and faults.

Acknowledgements

I am deeply grateful to the Series Editors of Studies in Renaissance Literature at Boydell & Brewer – Brooke A. Conti, Jane Grogan, and Ramona Wray – for their kind interest in my project, and especially to the anonymous reader for reading my early bulky manuscript with scrupulous care and for providing insightful pointers and advice to reframe my project in a more ambitious form. Also, I would like to thank Elizabeth McDonald, the commissioning editor, for supporting my project with enthusiasm, and for her patient guidance with thoughtful feedback; to Caroline Palmer, the editorial director, for tactfully forwarding my first email to Elizabeth; and to all the staff of Boydell & Brewer for seeing this book through to publication.

It has been my great pleasure to have been trained under Yasuo Tamaizumi, Member of the Japan Academy, and to have engaged in friendly competition with the studious scholars who gather at his workshop on English Renaissance literature. He has always been generous in giving me warm encouragement and keen insights into how to read English literary texts. Also, I would like to thank Takehiko Fukunaga, poet and novelist, and Kenji Ohba, former president of Meiji Gakuin University, for first motivating me, as an undergraduate student, to pursue my studies in English Renaissance literature.

I will forever remain indebted to my generous and intellectually stimulating colleagues at Keio University: Keiko Kawachi, Takayuki Tatsumi, Takami Matsuda, Ippei Inoue, Hisayo Ogushi, Isamu Takahashi, Ryuichi Hotta, Noriyuki Harada, Mitsushige Sato, Nobuya Takahashi, and Satoko Tokunaga. I am also grateful to my seminar students at Keio University for urging me to look out for trendy new things; and to my friends, Masanobu Endo, Yojiro Matsuura, Satoru Mizutani, Koichi Otani, and Naoto Tanabe, who have readily understood the significance of my project and given me moral support. Last but not least, I am truly thankful to my wife, Keiko, for her continual and patient support in completing this book. My own research was largely undertaken at the expense of my wife and children, who deserve my gratitude and apologies. And my greatest thanks are due to my late parents, Sadaji and Kikuko, for their love, prayers, and care, and for bringing me up in difficult circumstances, and in whose memory I dedicate this book.

The Grants-in-Aid for Scientific Research of the Japan Society of the Promotion of Science (JSPS) enabled me to conduct research in the UK and to carry out this project. I was supported by JSPS KAKENHI Grant Numbers JP20K00422, JP17K02516, JP25370304. It should also be noted with gratitude that the publication of this book was funded by the Fukuhara Memorial Fund for the Studies of English and American Literature, and also by the Keio University Fukuzawa Memorial Fund.

Arata Ide
Mita, Tokyo

ABBREVIATIONS

AC	*Archaeologia Cantiana*
APC	John Roche Dasent (ed.), *Acts of the Privy Council of England: New Series* (32 vols, London, 1890–1907)
BL	British Library
CCAL	Canterbury Cathedral Archives and Library
CCCA	Corpus Christi College Archives
CUA	Cambridge University Archives
EHR	*English Historical Review*
ELH	*English Literary History*
ELR	*English Literary Renaissance*
JEH	*Journal of Ecclesiastical History*
JEGP	*Journal of English and German Philology*
HLQ	*Huntington Library Quarterly*
LPL	Lambeth Palace Library
MLR	*Modern Language Review*
MRDE	*Medieval and Renaissance Drama in England*
N&Q	*Notes and Queries*
NRO	Norfolk Record Office
ODNB	*The Oxford Dictionary of National Biography* (Oxford, 2004)
PMLA	*Publications of the Modern Language Association of America*
RES	*Review of English Studies*

Abbreviations

REED   Records of Early English Drama

SEL   *Studies in English Literature 1500–1900*

SP   State Papers (UK)

SQ   *Shakespeare Quarterly*

STC   A. W. Pollard and G. R. Redgrave, *A Short-Title Catalogue of Books Printed in England, Scotland and Ireland and of English Books Printed Abroad, 1475–1640*, 2nd edn rev. and enlarged by W. A. Jackson, F. S. Ferguson, and K. F. Pantzer (3 vols, London, 1986–91)

TCBS   *Transactions of Cambridge Bibliographical Society*

TNA   The National Archives (UK)

TIMELINE

1558	Robert Greene christened at St George, Tombland, Norwich (11 July)
1564	Marlowe christened at St George's Church, Canterbury (26 February)
	Edward Halliwell's *Dido* performed before Elizabeth I at King's College, Cambridge (7 August)
1569	Mathew Parker, Archbishop of Canterbury, orders his secretary, John Josselin, to draw up a *Historiola Collegii Corporis Christi*
1572	Nicholas Faunt admitted to Gonville and Caius College (29 January)
	Nathaniel Woodes presented to the living of South Walsham, Norfolk
1573	Faunt migrates to Corpus Christi College (March)
	Thomas Aldrich resigns mastership of Corpus Christi (16 August)
	Robert Norgate elected master of Corpus Christi (22 August)
1574	Christopher Abbys nominated as Norwich scholar (13 April)
1574–75	Parker's plan of Corpus Christi College drawn up
1575	Parker makes his will, assigning the storehouse to three scholars (5 April)
	Death of Parker (17 May)
	Greene matriculates at St John's College (26 November)
1575–76	Exhibition given to Greene by a warrant signed by the mayor and some of the aldermen of Norwich
1577	Sir Nicholas Bacon's plan of Corpus Christi College drawn up

Timeline

1578	Faunt employed by Sir Francis Walsingham as a foreign agent (by September)
	Sir Roger Manwood installed as Lord Chief Baron of the Exchequer (17 November)
	Marlowe enrolled as scholar of the King's School, Canterbury (December)
1579	Thomas Harris elected fellow of Corpus Christi College in place of Richard Willoughbye (28 April)
	Christopher Abbys elected fellow of Corpus Christi (28 April)
	Richard Baines arrives at the English seminary at Rheims (4 July)
1580	Marlowe arrives at Corpus Christi College (December)
	Arrival of the seminary priests in England, headed by Edmund Campion and Robert Persons
1581	Marlowe matriculates at Cambridge (17 March)
1582	Baines imprisoned for seeking to poison the well of the seminary (May)
	Marlowe absent from Cambridge (July–August)
	Tobias Bland, bachelor of Corpus Christi College, publishes a libel against Master Robert Norgate and Sir Francis Walsingham
1583	Disastrous collapse of scaffolding at Paris Garden (13 January)
	Reginald Scot participates in constructing waterproofed walls of Dover harbour (March–July)
	Marlowe absent from Cambridge (April–June)
	William Gager's *Dido* performed at Christ Church, Oxford (12 June)
	John Whitgift appointed Archbishop of Canterbury (14 August)
	Robert Dallington publishes *A Booke of Epitaphes Made vpon the Death of the Right Worshipfull Sir William Bvttes*, to which at least three fellows and seven scholars of Corpus Christi College contribute eulogies
1584	Marlowe receives his BA (12 April)
	Marlowe absent from Cambridge (July–December)

Timeline

	Samuel Foxe, eldest son of the martyrologist John Foxe, reaches Padua (13 October)
	Richard Willoughbye, a former fellow of Corpus Christi College, is elected *consiliarius* of the English Nation at the university of Padua
	Reginald Scot publishes *The Discouerie of Witchcraft*
1585	Gager's *Meleager* is performed at Christ Church, Oxford (12 January)
	Marlowe absent from Cambridge (May–mid-June, mid-July–September)
	Marlowe with his father and relatives signs Katherine Benchkin's will in Canterbury (19 August)
1587	Funeral of Sir Philip Sidney (16 February)
	Marlowe granted 'grace' for an MA (31 March)
	Marlowe gives a deposition supporting the allegation of Richard Gee, a victualler (April)
	Privy Council drafts a letter to the Cambridge authorities to preserve Marlowe's reputation (29 May)
	Death of Robert Norgate, master of Corpus Christi College (2 November)
	John Copcot elected master of Corpus Christi (6 November)
	Philip Gawdy, a law student at Clifford's Inn, refers to *2 Tamburlaine* in a letter to his father (16 November)
1588	Greene refers to 'that Atheist *Tamburlan*' in the preface to *Perimedes the Blacksmith* (entry in Stationers' Register 29 March)
	Expulsion of Anthony Hickman, a fellow, from Corpus Christi College (May)
	Defeat of the Spanish Armada (July)
1589	Marlowe and the poet Thomas Watson involved in a swordfight in Hog Lane, London, with William Bradley, an innkeeper's son. Bradley killed on the spot. Marlowe and Watson detained on suspicion of murder (18 September)
	Marlowe released on bail of £40 (1 October)

Timeline

	Thomas Walsingham II, son of Thomas and Audley Walsingham, born
1590	Death of Sir Francis Walsingham (6 April)
	Tamburlaine the Great published by Richard Jones
1591	William Hacket, prophet, executed near Cheapside cross (28 July)
	Proclamation titled *A Declaration of Great Troubles Pretended against the Realme by a Number of Seminarie Priests and Jesuists* issued (18 October)
1592	Sir Robert Sidney reports that Marlowe arrested in Vlissingen for counterfeiting money (26 January)
	All plays forbidden in and around London (23 June–December)
	Richard Verstegan publishes *An Aduertisement Written to a Secretarie of My L. Treasurer's of Ingland*, containing a passage about Sir Walter Raleigh's school of atheism (August)
	Death of Robert Greene (3 September)
	Marlowe involved in a street fight with William Corkine, a tailor, in Canterbury (15 September)
	Entry for *Greene's Groatsworth of Wit* recorded in Stationers' Register 'vppon the perill of Henrye Chettle' (20 September)
	Death of Sir Roger Manwood (14 December)
1592–93	Plague rampant; burials registered in city and liberties of London total 10,775
1593	Warrant issued for Richard Cholmeley's arrest (19 March)
	John Greenwood and Henry Barrow, separatists, hanged at Tyburn (6 April)
	Marlowe stays at Thomas Walsingham's house in Scadbury, taking refuge from the plague (May)
	Xenophobic libel pasted up on the wall of the Dutch Church cemetery in Austin Friars (5 May)
	Thomas Kyd arrested on suspicion of the libel (12 May)
	Privy Council issues a warrant for Marlowe's arrest (18 May)
	Marlowe appears before the Privy Council and is ordered to give his daily attendance (20 May)

Timeline

	Possible date for receipt of Baines Note by Privy Council (26 May)
	Marlowe killed by Ingram Frizer at the house of Eleanor Bull in Deptford (30 May)
	Entry for *The Second Report of Doctor Iohn Faustus* recorded in Stationers' Register (16 November)
	John Fineaux matriculates at Trinity College, Cambridge
1594	Publication of *Dido, Queen of Carthage* and *Edward II*, both displaying Marlowe's name on their title pages
1597	Elizabeth I stays at Scadbury and dubs Thomas Walsingham a knight (20–21 July)
	Thomas Beard describes Marlowe's death as God's punishment for his atheism in *The Theatre of Gods Judgements*
1598	*Hero and Leander* published, with dedication to Sir Thomas Walsingham by Edward Blount

NOTE FOR THE READER

All quotations from contemporary manuscript and printed books retain original spelling, punctuation, and capitalization. However, the use of vv (w), ye (the), and yt (that) has been modernized. All instances of the long s have been silently emended and abbreviated words have been extended with the supplied letters in brackets. For quotations from Latin, abbreviated words have been extended with the supplied letters in italics for readability. For the sake of clarity and consistency, signature numbers are rendered in Arabic numerals throughout. Long titles have been curtailed. Dates are given in Old Style (i.e. according to the Julian Calendar), except that the year is reckoned to begin on 1 January. Biblical citations are from *The Geneva Bible: A Facsimile of the 1560 Edition*, intro. Lloyd E. Berry (Madison, 1969).

INTRODUCTION

How might a biographer today challenge the established narrative of Marlowe studies? As several literary scholars, including Ian Donaldson and John Carey, have argued, biography, no longer able to resort to the old methodologies, now aims for increasing scholarly sophistication by taking the approach of rehabilitating the author and establishing their output within their contemporary cultural system.[1] Historians, too, now give more prominent attention to the usefulness of critical biography. Jacques Le Goff, a leading historian of the Annales School, and Giovanni Levi, one of the pioneers of microhistory, are highly sensitive to what sociology, the history of mentalities, political science, and symbolic and interpretive anthropology have all contributed to our understanding of the individual as a historical agent.[2] In other words, a biographer can reconstruct the value systems of the specific social and cultural locale within which the individual was deeply integrated as an agent, and elucidate how the meanings of the texts that they produced were generated within complex systems of beliefs and values.

At the same time, however, we must bear in mind that the fundamental starting point of any Marlowe biography must be the Socratic axiom 'Knowledge of ignorance is the beginning of wisdom'. It is in vain, an illusion, to seek to reconstruct a complete figure of Marlowe, the man, from the extremely limited volume of his biographical documents. He 'exists' only as a slender collection of textual fragments; we know next to nothing about his life. Few biographical documents survive, other than his birth record in the parish register, a handful of injury and pecuniary cases in court records, mandates of, and reports to, the Privy Councillors, the coroner's

---

[1] See, for instance, Ian Donaldson, 'Matters of Life and Death: The Return of Biography', *Australian Book Review*, 286 (2006), 23–9; John Carey, 'Is the Author Dead? Or, the Mermaids and the Robot', in Takashi Kozuka and J. R. Mulryne (eds), *Shakespeare, Marlowe, Jonson: New Directions in Biography* (Aldershot, 2006), pp. 43–54; and Richard Wilson, *Will Power: Essays on Shakespearean Authority* (Detroit, 1993), p. 18.

[2] Jacques Le Goff, 'The Whys and Ways of Writing a Biography: The Case of Saint Louis', *Exemplaria*, 1:1 (1989), 207–26; Giovanni Levi, 'On Microhistory', in Peter Burke (ed.), *New Perspectives on Historical Writing*, 2nd edn (Cambridge, 2001), pp. 97–119; and Giovanni Levi, 'The Uses of Biography', in Hans Renders and Binne de Hann (eds), *Theoretical Discussions of Biography: Approaches from History, Microhistory, and Life Writing*, rev. and augmented edn (Leiden, 2014), pp. 61–74.

examination of his death, and a few hearsay accounts of his religious beliefs. Moreover, the evidence is fragmentary, discontinuous, and contradictory. There are far fewer residual biographical documents than there are for Shakespeare; thus, the task is still too difficult for Marlowe's biographers to fully reconstruct his whole life.

For these reasons, those who attempt to write a full biography of Marlowe must run the risk of spinning hypothetical scenarios to construct a putative 'truth' of his life, and of filling documentary lacunas with contextual information and material derived from his literary works; and they must also confront the considerable temptation to equate conjecture with fact. Often, they fall prey to developing 'circular arguments of considerable ingenuity' based on many speculations, or to committing 'biographical and critical fallacies [that] hide a more complex truth'.[3]

Localizing Christopher Marlowe shares with Marlowe biographers the conviction that it is essential to enter into new research projects of discovery in the archives, and that the author-centred approach through historical materials is indispensable to understanding him and his literary output. However, I neither intend nor am competent to write another full biography of Marlowe. It seems that the preferable approach, once we take into account the great array of major biographies already published, should *not* be to conjure up another whole portrait of Marlowe by putting forward supposed 'facts' based upon a very few reliable documents, embellished by many speculations. Rather it should be to offer new readings about these fragmentary documents, whether reliable or legendary, as well as about Marlowe's literary output, based on the locally and temporally specific contexts of those documents, drawn with historical veracity. In other words, not to tell the 'historical truth' of Marlowe's life, but rather to examine with *historical truthfulness* these surviving documents through which we can see the important facets of his social experience; to reassemble Marlowe, even if the reconstructed portrait is not a fully rounded one, solely by means of these fragments and their interpretations.

My aim, therefore, in *Localizing Christopher Marlowe*, is to place Marlowe at the centre of my research and to reassess his individual and collective experiences by using hitherto overlooked sources pertaining and peripheral to his life. Admittedly, Marlowe was not the sole originator of his identity; he was located in the temporal and spatial processes of his subjective

---

[3] J. A. Downie, 'Marlowe: Facts and Fictions', in J. A. Downie and J. T. Parnell (eds), *Constructing Christopher Marlowe* (Cambridge, 2000), pp. 13–29, at p. 16; Lukas Erne, 'Biography, Mythography, and Criticism: The Life and Works of Christopher Marlowe', *Modern Philology*, 103:1 (2005), 28–50, at p. 28. Regarding the risk of too much speculation, see also J. A. Downie, 'Marlowe, May 1593, and the "Must-Have" Theory of Biography', *RES*, NS, 58: 235 (2007), 245–67.

construction. At the same time, however, he was not a textual and cultural zombie. The cultural and other value systems within the boundaries of his local experience naturally transformed him into an agent for various interests and with multiple responsibilities, but they also motivated him to deploy a variety of constructive and creative strategies to fashion himself and produce his literary output with agentic capability. This way of thinking encourages us to bring back into focus an acute sense of a life lived through actual events and within the social spheres of everyday existence.

REDUCING THE SCALE: A PORTRAIT OF MARLOWE

The local communities with which Marlowe was intimately involved and with which he shared mutual interests and affinities can be fairly confidently located to specific times and places: Canterbury, where he was born and spent his early formative years; Cambridge, his *alma mater*, which provided him with cultural capital from 1580 to 1587; and the theatrical circles of London, where he made his living by writing plays intensively between 1587 and 1590. These locales are the potential areas to target for investigation. It was William Urry, cathedral and city archivist at Canterbury, who first took the initiative to localize the early life of Marlowe by exploring exhaustively the archival documents and reconstructing the tightly knit local community of the playwright's birthplace in his *Christopher Marlowe and Canterbury*. Andrew Butcher, the editor of Urry's posthumous work and himself a medieval historian of note, was acutely aware of the significance of Urry's prosopographical approach to the local community members, in enabling us 'to assess the collective experience of Marlowe and his contemporaries and to begin to set limits to the ways in which the individual might absorb and express that collective experience'. He also foresaw the possibility that 'the biography of the decentralized author' would play an important role when examining social entities that are contextually and temporally specific, such as family and neighbourhood, educational institutes, aristocratic households, theatrical syndicates, and so forth.[4]

In Part I, I focus on the social community of Cambridge, more particularly of Corpus Christi College, which might be, for a biographer of Marlowe, a minor section or even a footnote in his life story. Limiting our attention to the microscopic world of the college community and its system of values will not, in truth, enable us to venture into the current thriving business of biography, but this does not necessarily mean that we are only exploring a niche part of Marlowe scholarship. Rather, the approach of localization

---

[4] William Urry, *Christopher Marlowe and Canterbury*, ed. with an introduction by Andrew Butcher (London, 1988), pp. xvii, xxxi, and xl.

may be fruitful, especially when applied to the close-knit community of which Marlowe is known to have been a member and where he spent six years following his upbringing in the city of Canterbury. The significance of focusing our attention on the surviving evidence of the playwright's university life can be well attested by the fact that it has been well rehearsed and highlighted ever since the first wave of Marlovian biography: G. C. Moore Smith, Leslie Hotson, C. F. Tucker Brooke, Frederick S. Boas, and John Bakeless.[5] The long line of prominent biographers who devote considerable space to exploring the subject eloquently shows that it can be one of the main arenas of investigation.

Although the biographers of Marlowe have given us important insights into the intellectual and cultural milieu of his university, some crucial areas of research, such as the college networks that connected patrons and clients and the politico-religious attitudes they shared, have remained unexplored. Since the scholarly turn towards exploring the complex interactions between politics and social class that emerged in the 1980s, critics have focused on Marlowe's involvement with state power in new ways, frequently acknowledging the crucial importance of his network of Cambridge friends during his career in the intelligence service under Sir Francis Walsingham.[6] Considering that Marlowe was only active as an intelligencer and playwright for six years after leaving Cambridge, it is a reasonable assumption that some of his important contacts with figures in the political domain, as well as in the theatre, may have been made during his six and a half years of university life. At the same time, it was the financially and politically intricate relationships of Corpus Christi College that bred the defamatory rumour that Marlowe went to the English seminary at Rheims, the training school for militant Catholic missionaries. The social sphere of his college experience is therefore the spatio-temporal-cultural locale on which our principal focus should be fixed.

[5] G. C. Moore Smith, 'Marlowe at Cambridge', *Modern Language Review*, 4:2 (1909), 167-77; J. Leslie Hotson, *The Death of Christopher Marlowe* (1925; repr. New York, 1967), pp. 57-64; C. F. Tucker Brooke, *The Life of Marlowe and* The Tragedy of Dido Queen of Carthage (1930; repr. New York, 1966); Frederick S. Boas, *Christopher Marlowe: A Biographical and Critical Study* (Oxford, 1940); John Bakeless, *The Tragicall History of Christopher Marlowe* (2 vols, Cambridge, 1942).

[6] For example, see Constance Brown Kuriyama, 'Marlowe's Nemesis: The Identity of Richard Baines', in Kenneth Friedenreich, Roma Gill, and Constance B. Kuriyama (eds), *'A Poet and a Filthy Play-maker': New Essays on Christopher Marlowe* (New York, 1988), pp. 343-60; and Constance Brown Kuriyama, *Christopher Marlowe: A Renaissance Life* (Ithaca, 2002), pp. 85-6, 98-105; Charles Nicholl, *The Reckoning: The Murder of Christopher Marlowe* (London, 1992), pp. 119-20; Roy Kendall, 'Richard Baines and Christopher Marlowe's Milieu', *ELR,* 24:3 (1994), 507-52; Park Honan, *Christopher Marlowe: Poet and Spy* (Oxford, 2005), pp. 125-32.

Introduction

It must be admitted, however, that the close investigation of the social world of the college has not been brought thoroughly up to date, and so it would be well worth trying to reduce our scale: to observe the details of the specific locale and its community that surely cultivated a sense of belonging in Marlowe on the basis of his living quarters and his friendships, and to recover the collective experiences of the social groups or small communities with which we know he was personally and financially involved. Adopting this micro-biographical approach, which bears similarities to the work of the micro-historians, I share the conviction of Roger Chartier that 'It is on this reduced scale, and probably only on this scale, that we can understand, without deterministic reduction, the relationships between systems of beliefs, of values and representations on one side, and social affiliations on another'.[7] This approach necessitates, as a matter of convenience, narrowing the chronological scope of my study to the period from 1575, when Matthew Parker's scholarship – which gave Marlowe the opportunity to enter Corpus Christi College – was established, up to the playwright's death in 1593.

At the same time, the scarcity of documents about Marlowe demands a detailed analysis of the college and its distinct sociocultural systems. If the terrain of research is sufficiently well focused, as Carlo Ginzburg and Carlo Poni argue, 'the individual documentary series can transcend time and space in a way that permits us to find the same individual or group of individuals in different social contexts'.[8] That is to say, we can compensate for the scarcity of documentary evidence about Marlowe by gathering together a variety of neglected documents left in the college archives concerning his college fellows, peers, seniors, and juniors. In fact, research into these archival sources enables us to grasp the details of the sociocultural system within which their lived experiences are articulated; to illustrate the complexity of social relationships through their shared alliances and affinities, and through the sometimes intense frictions among the college communities; and, consequently, to shed light upon Marlowe's own experiences and literary activities as embedded in his social context.

As a clear example, by localizing Marlowe in the social and cultural context of Corpus Christi College we can dispel the aura of the global icon derived from the portrait of a twenty-one-year-old young man, dated 1585,

---

[7] Roger Chartier, 'Intellectual History or Sociocultural History? The French Trajectories', in Dominick LaCapra and Steven L. Kaplan (eds), *Modern European Intellectual History: Reappraisals and New Perspectives* (Ithaca, 1982), pp. 13–46, at p. 32.

[8] Carlo Ginzburg and Carlo Poni, 'The Name and the Game: Unequal Exchange and the Historiographic Marketplace', in Edward Muir and Guido Ruggiero (eds), *Microhistory and the Lost Peoples of Europe*, trans. Eren Branch (Baltimore, 1991), pp. 1–10, at p. 5.

hanging in the college hall. The sitter, 'bravely clad', with a degree of magnificence, has been said to be the college alumnus Christopher Marlowe. Until recently, the portrait was supposed to have been discovered in the Master's Lodge, a part of Corpus's 'New Court', built in the 1820s. However, based on the testimony of Peter Hall, a former student of the college, Park Honan discloses that it was actually found in 'the main locale of the Parker scholars, on the east side of the Old Court'; and he describes the circumstances of its discovery.[9] In 1952, Mr Hall happened to move into the room on the first floor at the south-east corner of the old court. Shortly afterwards, his bedroom, located in the roof-space above his main room, underwent renovation 'in order to install a more modern fire', whereupon workmen 'found two planks of oak underneath the old fire'. On these two planks, Mr Hall saw the portrait split in two.

Undoubtedly, this testimony has made an extremely valuable contribution to our understanding of the portrait's origin. Honan aligns himself with the conventional narrative, purporting to be able to identify the sitter as Marlowe and so appearing to take a step closer to solving the riddle of the portrait. Admittedly, no other candidate for the sitter than Marlowe has been proposed for over fifty years; and, since almost all the Parker scholars sought a career in the Church, few members of the college are likely to have been so fortunate (or ostentatious) as to have their own portrait. The accumulation of this indirect evidence encourages Honan to ask: 'If the sitter was not Marlowe, who else could he be?'. He affirms that Marlowe 'had funds to dress fashionably, and an artist's motive for having himself painted in 1585', and suggests that he subsequently 'left the painting behind or gave it to a fellow scholar'.[10]

Was this the face that a painter portrayed in memory of a scholar obtaining his BA? If that were the case, Marlowe could well have had a concealed source of income ample enough to hire a portrait painter. His personal finances might have been improved either by being engaged in espionage and playwriting or by obtaining support from a generous patron as early as 1585. However, these are ill-founded conjectures.[11] It seems unlikely that Marlowe had achieved such celebrity as a poet (let alone as a spy) by that time. A close look at the state of the average scholar's finances in the archives reveals the difficulties they faced in order to survive. Even a self-financing pensioner often had to pawn essential commodities to scrape

---

[9] Honan, *Christopher Marlowe*, p. 113.

[10] *Ibid.*, pp. 116–17.

[11] For the argument regarding the difficulty of identification, see Thomas Healy, 'Marlowe's Biography', in Emily C. Bartels and Emma Smith (eds), *Christopher Marlowe in Context* (Cambridge, 2013), pp. 334–45, at p. 335; A. D. Wraight and Virginia F. Stern, *In Search of Christopher Marlowe: A Pictorial Biography* (Chichester, 1993), pp. 68–9; and Downie, 'Marlowe: Facts and Fictions', p. 16.

a living. The financial circumstances of Parker scholars, in particular, were so closely monitored by the tutors and the foundation administrators that showy extravagance was discouraged. Marlowe, who had to be supported by a Parker scholarship for the full six years, must have been no exception.

Moreover, if we assume, as Honan does, that the room where the portrait was found is vital to our understanding of who the sitter is, it remains unexplained why the painting had been kept, not in 'the stoare house' possibly assigned to Marlowe along with two other John Parker scholars, but in the roof-space of the room at the south-east corner of the college. John Parker's father, Matthew, the Archbishop of Canterbury, had himself assigned particular chambers to particular scholars. As a consequence, several rooms were taken up mostly by scholars who came from the same town or province. The plan of Corpus Christi College that Honan consulted was drawn up to show the widespread geographical allocation of scholars' rooms around 1575, when the new scholarship was founded by John Parker according to his father's will. The lower chamber at the south-east corner in question was one of the strongholds of the 'Norwich scholars', most of whom came from Norwich and entered holy orders. In the middle chamber lodged a 'Norwich fellow', who was elected by the mayor, aldermen, and commonalty of Norwich, in charge of the instruction of the Norwich scholars. It would seem unlikely, therefore, that the portrait of a young dramatist of the college would have been bequeathed to this Norwich-based community and retained among them.[12] For now, however, we must leave uncertain the identity of the sitter, and content ourselves with Edward Blount's adumbrative, but affectionate, description of Marlowe: 'albeit the eye there taketh his ever farewell of that beloved object, yet the impression of the man, that hath been dear unto us' is 'living an afterlife in our memory'.[13] Blount saw the image of the playwright in his mind's eye, not in a portrait.

REINVESTIGATING DOCUMENTS: MARLOWE'S 'SUPPLICAT'

Narrowing the focus of our observation and integrating Marlowe into the context of local common practice draws our attention to the necessity of reinvestigating documents in the university archives that might contribute to our image of the man, while forcing us to relinquish the mythologizing

---

[12] Predictably enough, several academic members of Corpus Christi College are also negative about identifying the subject of the portrait as Marlowe. See Oliver Rackham, 'The Pseudo-Marlowe Portrait: A Wish Fulfilled?', *The Letter*, 93 (Corpus Christi College, Cambridge, Michaelmas, 2014), 31–3; Peter R. Roberts, 'Christopher Marlowe at Corpus, 1580–87', *Pelican: The Magazine of Corpus Christi College Cambridge*, 26 (Easter, 2014), 22–31.

[13] Christopher Marlowe, *Hero and Leander*, in Millar MacLure (ed.), *The Poems, The Revels Plays* (London, 1968), p. 3.

icon of the playwright. I would like to give a small but illustrative instance here by focusing on a slip of manuscript paper called a 'supplicat': a certificate produced in the process of the degree conferment. After a candidate for a BA had successfully undergone the university's examinations, the praelector of his college submitted a supplicat in which he certified to the university regent house that the candidate had qualified for the final interview with the vice-chancellor and the senate, which was usually held during the week preceding Ash Wednesday.[14] In the supplicat, the candidate, or 'questionist', stated in a formula that he had been present for the requisite number of terms, had duly attended lectures, and had performed other exercises required by the university statutes.[15] The praelector subscribed his name (often alongside those of the examiners who took part in the admission of questionists) to give assurance of the candidate's suitability for the BA. If successful in the final interview, the questionist became a 'determiner', and was pronounced shortly after by the proctor to be ready to commence (i.e. receive) the BA. After the nine terms following the commencement, the bachelor was entitled to proceed to the MA degree through similar formalities, and produced the document of supplicat for the MA.

It was often the case that, in preparing a supplicat, a scribe copied the Latin text of the set formula with the addition of the candidate's name. No wonder then that, as the scribal production of supplicats was yearly routine work, we can find some ready-made supplicats where the blanks were filled in later with the name of the candidate.[16] It may have been convenient for a student close to graduation and busy with job searching or other miscellaneous duties to ask a scribe to make a clean copy of his document. However, a considerable number of candidates who qualified for the formality of the final interview wrote out the set formula themselves. This is understandable because drawing up the supplication for oneself did not cost anything, and, indeed, was something that might happen only once in a lifetime. To copy one's autographed self-recommendation letter to the university regent house in graceful and distinctive handwriting could provide the means and opportunity to express the feelings of achievement and self-respect that the candidate had striven for after several years of rigorous college life.

[14] For the common practice concerning the procedure of the senate's examining the 'questionist', see C. Bowie Millican's succinct description in 'The Supplicats for Spenser's Degrees', *HLQ*, 2:4 (1939), 467–70. See also George Peacock, *Observations on the Statutes of the University of Cambridge* (London, 1841), appendices A and B.

[15] For documentary information about the 'supplicats', see John Venn and J. A. Venn (eds), *The Book of Matriculations and Degrees: 1544–1659* (Cambridge, 1913), pp. xii–xiii.

[16] For instance, see CUA, Supplicats, 1568–69, no. 1, Robert Wright, B.A. (Christ's), no. 2, Thomas Newell, B.A. (Pembroke), and no. 47, Richard Robinson, M.A. (Trinity).

Introduction

'Personality is expressed even in the most disciplined writing', as Alfred Fairbank points out, because 'handwriting involves not only hand, eye, and brain (and pen, paper, and the flow of ink) but the will of the writer and his attitude to his writing'.[17] Moreover, to borrow Jonathan Gibson's phrase, the italic signature by which the writer demonstrated his identity in his supplicat 'simply stands in lieu of its writer's presence: it is more like an object (a seal, say) than a sentence'.[18]

It is natural, therefore, that a questionist's neat, scrupulous handwriting breathes life into an otherwise merely monotonous formula on a little slip of paper, conveying the author's spirit so vigorously as to urge us to imagine his personality behind the letters. John Palmer of Trinity College, for example, in submitting his supplicat to the regent house, made a pointed display of his astonishing penmanship, producing the finest italic script, which, by the middle of the sixteenth century, had become 'the writing of ceremony of the well-educated man', customarily employed as a suitable ceremonial hand in formal letters concerning university matters and in diplomatic correspondence.[19] Palmer's later attempt to procure a fellowship by sending beautifully written letters to William Cecil, the chancellor of Cambridge University, prompts us to imagine that his calligraphic skill in italic script was put to good use to win promotion for himself in the university.[20]

Similarly, Thomas Nashe produced his autographed supplicat (figure 1) as meticulously and dexterously as when he contributed the calligraphic Latin verses on Ecclesiasticus for a presentation copy when elected to a Lady Margaret scholarship in 1585 (probably before he was eighteen).[21] Gabriel Harvey, later Nashe's great enemy and himself a proud scholar,

---

[17] Alfred Fairbank and Bruce Dickins, *The Italic Hand in Tudor Cambridge* (London, 1962), p. 17. For a full discussion on the early modern English practice of italic script, see James Daybell, *The Material Letter in Early Modern England: Manuscript Letters and the Culture and Practices of Letter-Writing* (Basingstoke, 2012), pp. 86–90; Jonathan Gibson, 'From Palatino to Cresci: Italian Writing Books and the Italic Scripts of Early Modern English Letters', in James Daybell and Andrew Gordon (eds), *Cultures of Correspondence in Early Modern Britain* (Philadelphia, 2016), pp. 29–47.

[18] Gibson, 'From Palatino to Cresci', p. 40.

[19] Wilfrid Blunt, *Sweet Roman Hand: Five Hundred Years of Italic Cursive Script* (London, 1952), p. 22.

[20] CUA, Supplicats, 1579–80, no. 67. For Palmer's letter to Cecil to procure a fellowship, see BL, Lansdowne MS 33 (38), fol. 74 (1581); and BL, Lansdowne MS 36 (48), fol. 113 (1582). H. R. Woudhuysen points out that 'skilled penmen must usually have been able to find work from companies and important institutions on a salaried or piecemeal basis'; see his *Sir Philip Sidney and the Circulation of Manuscripts 1558–1640* (Oxford, 1996), p. 76.

[21] CUA, Supplicats, 1585–86, no. 83. For Nashe's holograph manuscript, see W. W. Greg (ed.), *English Literary Autographs 1550–1650, Part 1: Dramatists* (Oxford, 1925), no.

provided in the supplicat for his BA (figure 2) a display of his (unfortunately immature) italic hand, in which he wrote out a letter to John Young, Master of Pembroke and later Bishop of Rochester, seeking his support – both to pursue an MA degree and for his struggle against his baiting enemies within the college.[22] Nashe later gave ironic praise of Harvey's 'faire capitall Romane hand', smirking that it was better than that of a 'magistrall scribe, that holds all his liuing by setting school-boies copies'.[23] Finally, Nicholas Faunt, a senior to Marlowe at King's School and Corpus Christi College and later the secretary of Sir Francis Walsingham, made fair copies in his delicate italic hand, such as the one that we find in the stipendiary book of the treasurer of Canterbury cathedral concerning his receipt of the quarterly allowance as a King's scholar (figure 3).[24]

What concerns us here is Marlowe's supplicat for his BA (figure 4), where the formula is written out in a distinctive italic hand, somewhat lacking in expertise but apparently affected for that particular occasion to display the writer's self-esteem with a degree of formality.[25] It would be easy to deny the biographical validity of the document on the basis of its singularity, where it becomes conspicuous by comparison to the only surviving autograph that Marlowe subscribed: appended to the will of his friend's mother Katherine Benchkin.[26] That would explain why the distinctive italic hand has been neglected so far by Marlovian scholarship. However, since the signature to Benchkin's will is written in an ordinary secretary hand, the difference in handwriting styles prevents us from attempting to make a comparison between these two signatures. The candidacy for the MA gave Marlowe another occasion to produce his supplicat, which survives and is written in a secretary hand. Unfortunately, the formula in the supplicat for the MA seems to have been copied by a slipshod scribe, who also took on the task of drawing up the supplicat of Thomas Lewgar, another candidate for the MA at Corpus Christi.[27] The scribe carelessly left out the line 'post finalem eius determinatione[m]' from both of these documents,

---

XX; and Ronald B. McKerrow (ed.), *The Works of Thomas Nashe*, 2nd edn, rev. F. P. Wilson (5 vols, Oxford, 1958), vol. 3, pp. 298–9.

[22] CUA, Supplicats, 1569–70, no. 9. For Harvey's letters in his early italic hand, see BL, MS Sloane 93, fols 2–34; for his signature, see fols 86v, 92r.

[23] Thomas Nashe, *Haue with You to Saffron-Walden*, in McKerrow and Wilson (eds), *Works of Nashe*, vol. 3, p. 60.

[24] CUA, Supplicats, 1575–76, no. 109. For Faunt's autograph signature, see CCAL, MS DCc MA 40, fols 399r, 404v, and 408v.

[25] CUA, Supplicats, 1583–84, no. 199.

[26] Kent History and Library Centre, PRC 16/36, reproduced in Honan, *Christopher Marlowe*, p. 108.

[27] CUA, Supplicats, 1586–87, no. 65 (Marlowe) and no. 64 (Lewgar).

Introduction

later adding it to the top margin in the copy of Lewgar's supplicat, and interpolating it between the first and the second lines in that of Marlowe's. Not only these additions but also that of the omitted 'omnibus' in the line 'cu[m] omnibus oppositionibus responsionibus' in the former document, along with the correction of the spelling of 'omnibus' in the latter, suggest that these supplicats are not holographs. Taken together, these considerations would suggest that, while the holographic identification of Marlowe's supplicat for the BA cannot be proved without more convincing evidence, its singularity and uniqueness do not necessarily diminish the value of the document as a biographical component nor deny the possibility that Marlowe produced the document himself.

My purpose here is not to prove that the surviving BA supplicat is another autograph of Marlowe, but to suggest that the slip of his supplicat ceases to be an inorganic or lifeless document specifically owing to its singularity and uniqueness and should be considered one of the most important constituent parts – more reliable and attractive than the portrait of the anonymous young man – that shape the patchy biography we have of Marlowe as a cultural construct. This is significant when considered in the light of the specific local context of human relations and common practices within the college community of the time. Six supplicats survive for questionists at Corpus Christi College who obtained a BA degree in 1583–84: Edward Elwin, Thomas Lewgar, Abraham Tilman, Simon Thaxter, Thomas Driver, and Christopher Marlowe.[28] These supplicats are all written in different hands and subscribed by the college fellow and praelector of that academic year, Thomas Harris, in his neat italic script. What is interesting in terms of handwriting is the fact that only two of these questionists, Tilman and Marlowe, submitted their supplicats in an italic script. Tilman's gracefully written supplicat displays a similar level of formality to his italic scripted signature in the Audit Book (figure 5, the supplicate in the middle).[29]

The fact that Marlowe and Tilman prepared their supplicats in an italic script may be more than coincidence, for both came from King's School, Canterbury and were obviously closely acquainted. It is quite probable that the shared comradeship and value system nurtured in the same local communities for years worked to influence such formal acts as preparing the slip of a manuscript for a momentous event in their lives.

---

[28] CUA, Supplicats, 1583–84, no. 194 (Edward Elwin), no. 195 (Thomas Lewgar), no. 196 (Abraham Tilman), no. 197 (Simon Thaxter), and no. 198 (Thomas Driver).

[29] Abraham Tilman, elected fellow on 6 July 1587. For his italic signature, see CCCA, CCCC02/B/5, Audit Book 1578–90, fols 10v and 11r in 1587. All references to the College Archives are to numbers supplied by ArchiveSearch, the online listing of archival holdings established by the University of Cambridge: see <https://archive-search.lib.cam.ac.uk> [accessed 11 November 2022].

In a brief memorial note, Benjamin Charier, their junior at King's School and Corpus Christi, names and commemorates Tilman as the 'Queenes scholler in Canterburye', the title of which suggests feelings of respect and reverence for Tilman among his contemporaries at King's School.[30] Rivalry with and/or respect for this honourable peer from the same school, as well as his own ambition and pride, might have motivated Marlowe to ask a scribe to copy the set formula in a ceremonial script – or, more likely, to write it out himself.

Thus, the flat and insipid formula of the supplicat, so far neglected by biographers, can, when embedded in the local and contemporary prosopographical contexts, shed some new light on Marlowe's own experiences lived in the complexity of his social relationships. His italic-scripted supplicat is a modest illustration of this complexity, but there is no doubt that the college clusters and personal relationships are significant from a variety of angles, specifically in reconstructing Marlowe within the intellectual and cultural community of the college, and in recovering the collective experiences shared among those alongside whom he was obliged to eat and sleep. As is suggested in Alan Bray's description of the tomb shared by two men, John Finch and Thomas Baines, in the chapel of Christ's College, Cambridge, many cases of homosocial relationships developed from the close ties between 'chamberers' or 'chummers' (or, as the word survives in modern English, 'chums'): young men sharing chambers at the universities or at the Inns of Court.[31] In order to investigate the college social clusters and the ways in which such chamberers wove intricate networks through the propinquity of their daily living, and to explore their homosocial, political affiliations, and conflicts, we have to realize that there survive more archival documents of university matters – peripheral as well as relevant to Marlowe – than we have hitherto imagined. The total quantity of these documents is not large, but I believe that there are enough for us to launch our own micro-biography project on Marlowe.

THE MICROSCOPIC WORLD OF THE COLLEGE COMMUNITY

Matthew Parker, the Archbishop of Canterbury from 1559 to 1575, instructed his Latin secretary, John Josselin (or Joscelyn), to draw up a *Historiola Collegii Corporis Christi* 'at his own desire, and for his own use' around

---

[30] For the memorial note of Benjamin Charier, see Chapter 2, pp. 74–5.
[31] Alan Bray, *The Friend* (Chicago, 2003), pp. 140–6. Martin Ingram kindly drew my attention to the episode in Bray's book and gave a valuable suggestion on 'chums'. For more information on students' camaraderie, see also Alexandra Shepard, *Meanings of Manhood in Early Modern England* (Oxford, 2003), pp. 93–126.

Introduction

1569.[32] Parker's aim seems to have been to make a detailed catalogue, rather than to describe the history of the college itself, and also to enumerate the benevolent acts of the college's benefactors to that date. Unsurprisingly, the *Historiola* concludes with a panegyric on Parker's sizeable endowments for founding Norwich scholarships in 1567 and 1569 for the schoolboys of his native town. It may have been this self-promotion that encouraged Parker's enemies to obtain a copy of it, render it into English, and print it overseas with satirical notes in the margins.[33] What is unique to the *Historiola*, however, is its meticulous account of the college buildings, particularly of the chambers as they existed around that time. Josselin precisely specifies on whose request and at whose expense these chambers were decorated – the windows glazed; the floors, walls, and ceilings plastered; new chimneys, garrets, and studies added – without failing to mention Parker's generous donations towards refurbishments of the Master's Lodge and a number of other chambers where he had once boarded as a scholar, fellow, and master. This curious list might suggest Parker's vainglorious ostentation, but what matters to us is his desire to remind the Norwich scholars 'of their benefactor and through him of their common local origins'.[34]

It may have been this desire that motivated Parker to pay assiduous attention to the Norwich scholars' lodgings and to assign them 'the three lower Chambers on the *East*-Side of the Quadrangle'.[35] One of these chambers still contained memories of his younger days, for Josselin reports that 'The ceiling of the ground-floor room under the Library was plastered by Matthew Parker, when Scholar and Bible-clerk'.[36] Moreover, the archbishop made arrangements that certain books donated to the college should 'remayne within the vnder chamber of the x[th] chamber on the Easte side for the com[m]on vse of all vj. Norwiche schollers'. Many domestic implements, including coverlets of tapestry and a table and chairs, were also furnished 'w[th]in the vnder chamber of the ix[th] tenthe and xj[th] Chambers on the Easte side, for the vse of certeine Norwiche schollers newe founded in Corpus

---

[32] John Josselin, *Historiola Collegii Corporis Christi*, ed. John Willis Clark (Cambridge, 1880), pp. v and 40. For Josselin's collaboration with Parker, see May McKisack, *Medieval History in the Tudor Age* (Oxford, 1971), pp. 45–8.

[33] *The Life off the 70. Archbishopp off Canterbury Presently Sittinge Englished* (Zurich, 1574).

[34] Victor Morgan, with a contribution by Christopher Brooke, *A History of the University of Cambridge, Volume II, 1546–1750* (Cambridge, 2004), p. 215.

[35] Robert Masters, *The History of the College of Corpus Christi* (Cambridge, 1753–55), p. 201.

[36] Josselin, *Historiola*, p. 26. The translated quotation is from Robert Willis and John Willis Clark, *The Architectural History of the University of Cambridge and of the Colleges of Cambridge and Eton* (4 vols, Cambridge, 1886), vol. 1, p. 253.

christi college In Cambridge'.[37] The rooms were assigned to these scholars with the intention that they would imitate their benefactor's religious devotion, as well as his affection for the *alma mater*, and pass them down to succeeding generations. A private chamber with a refurbished interior or containing donated objects could function as an external commemoration of the local benefactors through whose charity the daily lives of the scholars were maintained. Each chamber had its own history to be told.

Parker's enthusiasm and administrative circumspection were shared with his old college friend Sir Nicholas Bacon, the Lord Keeper, who created a foundation for six perpetual scholarships in 1577.[38] Some of the documents relating to the college, which are now in the possession of Norfolk Record Office and shelf-marked as NRS 23372, Z99, bear the traces of Bacon's scrupulous attentiveness to his own scholars and their assigned living space. The documents, loosely bundled together, consist of about thirty sheets of paper pertaining to Corpus Christi College, dating from the sixteenth to the eighteenth centuries. At least ten of them can be dated to the latter half of the sixteenth century and are more or less connected with the Bacon foundation at the college.[39] What we should focus on here is the plan captioned 'The number of those that be Lodged in the Colleg & how & in what chambers they be lodged' (figures 6 and 7), in which we find a drawing of the quadrangle with eleven chambers (including a chamber over the buttery) and the detached pensionary. Each unit of accommodation has three storeys, designated as 'the vpp[er] chamb[e]r', 'middle chamb[e]r', and

[37] CCCA, CCCC07/18, Parker Register formerly Small Parker Book 13, pp. 144–5.
[38] For Bacon's commitment to education, see J. M. Anderson, *The Honorable Burden of Public Office: English Humanists and Tudor Politics in the Sixteenth Century* (New York, 2010), pp. 107–14.
[39] Although NRS 23372, Z99 is by no means unknown to scholars who have studied the history of the university, the bundle of documents has never been closely examined. H. C. Porter first mentioned the document in his *Reformation and Reaction in Tudor Cambridge* (Cambridge, 1958), pp. 50–1. He consulted photographs of NRO, NRS 23372, Z99 in the Parker Library. The document he used is titled 'Thexercyses in benenet [*sic*] colledge from the begynyng of the terme vntill the ending' and was later transcribed by Richard F. Hardin in his article 'Marlowe and the Fruits of Scholarism', *Philological Quarterly*, 63:3 (1984), 387–400. Morgan makes reference to another document, 'The annuall revenuewes and exspences of Benet Colledge in Cambridge', contained in NRS 23372, Z99, when discussing the close relationship between the college and Norwich magnates. See Victor Morgan, 'Cambridge University and "the Country"', in Lawrence Stone (ed.), *The University in Society: Oxford and Cambridge from the 14th to the Early 19th Century* (Princeton, 1975), pp. 183–245, at p. 203. For the nature and formation of these documents, see my article 'Corpus Christi College, Cambridge in 1577: Reading the Social Space in Sir Nicholas Bacon's College Plan', *TCBS*, 15:2 (2013), 279–328.

Introduction

'lower chamb[e]r', all of which are crammed together with the names of the college residents.[40]

In mapping out his new scholarship project, Bacon had the ideal role model in Parker, who had established the Norwich scholarships (funded by municipal financial resources) in 1567 and 1569, the Canterbury scholarships in 1569, and the Parker scholarships in 1575; the last funded by his bequeathed property. Parker's method of assessing the living conditions of his scholars can be discerned in a similar plan to that drawn up for Bacon, now in the possession of Corpus Christi College Archives (figure 8).[41] This document, though bearing an inscription by a later hand, 'Cir[ca]. an[no]. 1576', can be dated earlier, namely to late 1574 or early 1575, when Parker was preparing to establish the new scholarships. The pensionary is omitted from the plan, and all the scholars, except those funded by Parker and other foundations, are also left out. The fellows are mentioned not by name but in terms of numbers, such as 'a fellowe', in a similar way to that used for the survey of the college site (figure 9). Thus, just as in the case of the plan intended for Bacon, the compiler of Parker's plan seems to have considered the archbishop's best interests and to have chosen to include information immediately relevant to him. It is likely, therefore, that this plan was drawn up at Parker's request as background information to help him allocate space for his new scholars.

This assumption can be supported by another plan, on the verso (figure 10), which was roughly drawn up but contains more detailed information about each chamber.[42] In the storehouse shown on this plan there is an interesting inscription: 'for iij schollers' (see Chamber 4 in Appendix 2). These occupants of the storehouse were the first scholars of the new foundation that Parker established in 1575. What the compiler suggests here is that the storehouse should be set aside for these scholars; moreover, it is clear that the plan itself was produced to help in arranging the details of the scholarships around that time.

It was two years later that the more detailed plan of the court was created for Bacon.[43] Preliminary discussions concerning the foundation seem to

---

[40] See Appendix 1 for its transcription.

[41] CCCA, CCCC08/28 (Miscellaneous Documents 1480–1700, no. 138r). This plan is transcribed by Willis in his edition of Josselin's *Historiola* and reproduced in Darryll Grantley and Peter Roberts (eds), *Christopher Marlowe and English Renaissance Culture* (Aldershot, 1996).

[42] CCCA, CCCC08/28 (Miscellaneous Documents 1480–1700, no. 138v). See Appendix 2 for its transcription.

[43] Judging from the distinctive handwriting, the compiler seems to have been Robert Norgate, the master of the college (private correspondence with Elisabeth Leedham-Green, who declared the author 'definitely Norgate').

have taken place between him and the college delegates by then, given the following entry in the college account of 1577: 'It[e]m for the expenses of the Mr of the Colledg Mr Kett & Mr Chevers to Gorrambury & so to London befor east[e]r Mr Kett & Mr Chevers attending at the Court the East[e]r tyme to speake & confer w[i]th my L. Kep[er] about his foundacion.'[44] It may have been on such occasions that the insiders' reports, including the plan, were closely consulted. There is no telling why Bacon's plan was more detailed than Parker's. It may be the case that meticulous preparations were necessary because the increase in the number of students had made it difficult for Bacon to assign three lower 'raunginge' rooms to the six new scholars; it may also be due to Bacon's keen 'eye for detail' and his interest in building activities.[45]

What this plan provides is detailed information about room allocation, but only covering a limited period. Who lived where and with whom might seem trivial and insignificant, but it was not so, at least for Matthew Parker and Sir Nicholas Bacon. As a result of their particular college experiences, they may have been well aware of a sort of 'homophilic' tendency described by a number of sociologists: social similarity and propinquity generate strong ties between individuals.[46] That is, college members of similar age and/or place of birth would naturally have communicated with each other more frequently and have become more emotionally attached while living in the same chamber for several years; this closeness would have strengthened their comradeship and helped them to form strong social ties, which would in turn have made a considerable contribution to their benefactors' cause. Each chamber on the plan enables us, therefore, to identify a socially, psychologically, or politically affiliated cluster around the branch that stemmed from the students' financial patrons, and to make assumptions about how the college members, by making efficient use of their durable ties, allied themselves to other local or courtly magnates as well. In this

---

[44] CCCA, CCCC02/B/4, Audit Book 1550–80, fol. 7v of the account in 1577 (3a Trimestri of 1577). See also Audit Book 1550–80, fol. 3r of the account in 1577 (1a Trimestri of 1577).

[45] Patrick Collinson, 'Sir Nicholas Bacon and the Elizabethan *Via Media*', in *Godly People: Essays on English Protestantism and Puritanism* (London, 1983), pp. 135–53, at p. 145. For Bacon's building activities, see Hassell Smith, 'The Gardens of Sir Nicholas and Sir Francis Bacon: An Enigma Resolved and a Mind Explored', in Anthony Fletcher and Peter Roberts (eds), *Religion, Culture and Society in Early Modern Britain: Essays in Honour of Patrick Collinson* (Cambridge, 1994), pp. 125–60.

[46] Leon Festinger, Stanley Schachter, and Kurt Bach, *Social Pressures in Informal Groups: A Study of Human Factors in Housing* (1950; repr. Stanford, 1963); Miller McPherson, Lynn Smith-Lovin, and James M. Cook, 'Birds of a Feather: Homophily in Social Networks', *Annual Review of Sociology*, 27:1 (2001), 415–44; and Ray Reagans, 'Close Encounters: Analyzing How Social Similarity and Propinquity Contribute to Strong Network Connections', *Organization Science*, 22:4 (2011), 835–49.

Introduction

respect, the plan is undoubtedly extremely valuable, given that the importance of social networks linking local communities, the university, and the court is now becoming more widely accepted by historians.[47]

To localize Christopher Marlowe within the context of the college community, I begin in Chapter 1 with this important document, which shows how rooms were allocated in the first half of 1577, three years before Marlowe came to Corpus Christi. As can be detected in Parker's assignment of chambers according to the category of scholarship, the chambers were allocated not at random but according to specific rules and measures. This residential allocation brought about the segmentation of the college community into several regional units, with scholars who came from a similar locality clustered together. What this plan shows is a symbolic microcosm of the social communications and identities that gave meaning to their lives. The document therefore seems vital for understanding how the college members constructed their community during Marlowe's time.

Accordingly, Chapters 1 and 2 reconstruct the social relationships among the college fellows and students by consulting college archival materials and concentrating on several compartments of the quadrangle. Chapter 1 focuses on the cluster of Norwich students at the south-east corner under the strict tutelage of Norwich fellows; Chapter 2 turns to that composed of Canterbury students, mainly from King's School, including Marlowe. These chapters will therefore reveal the mutual interdependence of the students who allied themselves with other adjacent chamberers, with magnates of municipal corporations, and with government officials at court.

A deep understanding of local politics and affiliations at the college will enable us to outline the characteristics of a particular group of students, the value systems shared by them, and the ways in which these poor students survived throughout their college lives by the alliances they developed. Chapter 1 will contribute to our understanding of the mindset, literary tastes, and collective zeal that those Norwich chamberers on the east side of the court either participated in or reacted against, and will explore the prevailing social norms that governed the relationships among Norwich fellows and scholars who were funded by the mayor and aldermen of Norwich. By way of illustration, I draw attention to Nathaniel Woodes,

---

[47] The interrelationship between local benefactors and students at Cambridge is well documented in Morgan, 'Cambridge University and "the Country"'. See also Warren Boutcher, 'Pilgrimage to Parnassus: Local Intellectual Traditions, Humanist Education and the Cultural Geography of Sixteenth-Century England', in Yun Lee Too and Niall Livingstone (eds), *Pedagogy and Power: Rhetorics of Classical Learning* (Cambridge, 1998), pp. 110–47; John Craig, *Reformation, Politics and Polemics: The Growth of Protestantism in East Anglian Market Towns 1500–1610* (Aldershot, 2001), pp. 64–132; and Matthew Reynolds, *Godly Reformers and Their Opponents in Early Modern England: Religion in Norwich, c. 1560–1643* (Woodbridge, 2005), pp. 39–62.

whom we know to have been a minister in Norwich and, more significantly, the author of the play *The Conflict of Conscience*, and to Robert Greene, another Cambridge playwright hailing from Norwich, who had a long-time enmity towards Marlowe. Placing these two men and their literary output within this specific local context will reveal not only the significance of the networks set up through the close relationship between Norwich and Corpus Christi but also the features of religious enthusiasm and the political agendas shared among the Norwich-based aldermen, fellows, and scholars throughout the 1570s and early 1580s. We can then get a clearer view of what impression an advancement-oriented scholar like Marlowe, with good political connections and humanist ambitions, could make on those of his college contemporaries who wished to pursue a career in holy orders as ministers of local churches.

Giving us a glimpse of the everyday lives of fellows and scholars just as vivid as the plan of the college are the Act Books in the Cambridge University Archives, which contain a wide range of office and lawsuits conducted in the university court or 'the vice-chancellor's court'.[48] The jurisdiction of the university was administered by the vice-chancellor's court or, 'unless the proctors or taxors of the University, or any of them, or a master of arts, or one of superior degree, be one of the litigants', by the commissary's court.[49] Each week during term time, both courts sat in the university consistory located on the east side of the Schools Quadrangle, 'although extra sessions were also frequently convened in the judges' college rooms'.[50] The university had jurisdiction over legal matters, and over suits involving scholars or privileged persons of the university as one of the parties, and so the details of these pleas, depositions, crimes, and so on can give vital clues to understanding the complex relationships within university society. Chapter 2 therefore guides us through these documents, both to trace the trail of Marlowe and to examine his local associations with college members. Highlighting a neglected document related to Marlowe's friendship with his

---

[48] For essential information on the Act Books, as well as on the history and business of the vice-chancellor's court, see Heather Peek and Catherine Hall, *Archives of the University of Cambridge* (Cambridge, 1962), pp. 48–52; Dorothy M. Owen, *Cambridge University Archives: A Classified List* (Cambridge, 1998), pp. 65–130; and, more recently and better informed, Jacqueline Cox, 'Trials and Tribulations: The Cambridge University Courts, 1540–1660', *TCBS*, 15:4 (2015), 595–623.

[49] *The Statutes of Queen Elizabeth for the University of Cambridge. Translated from the Original Latin Statutes, Which Were Published by Mr. George Dyer, in 'The Privileges of the University of Cambridge', London, 1824* (London, 1838), chap. 48, p. 33.

[50] Willis and Clark, *Architectural History*, vol. 3, p. 22. See also Alexandra Shepard, 'Legal Learning and the Cambridge University Courts, c. 1560–1640', *Journal of Legal History*, 19:1 (1998), 62–74, at p. 64.

needy Canterbury friends, I draw attention to their collegiate experience through the eyes of a poor scholar, and investigate, with the help of several documents in the Act Books, the network of contacts the playwright developed, to show the indispensability of local connections between ordinary scholars. This will also demonstrate the relevance of Constance Brown Kuriyama's argument concerning Marlowe's relationship with John Benchkin, a native of Canterbury and student of the college: 'Contrary to the impression left by part of the evidence that Marlowe must have been a gifted sociopath, there are a number of indications, both during the university period and after, that he was perfectly capable of normal sociability and friendship.'[51]

At the same time, what should not be forgotten is that, while some evidence for Marlowe's sociability is extant, there is indirect evidence indicating hostile feelings towards him among university students, which can be detected in the Privy Council's letter to the university authorities demanding that they suppress the defamatory rumour that Marlowe 'was determined to haue gone beyond the seas to Reames and there to remaine'.[52] This rumour has often been regarded as evidence of his anti-social tendencies and lack of religious orthodoxy. However, after examining the relationships among the Canterbury scholars, and treating the Privy Council's letter as another document concerning college matters relating to Marlowe, I consider in Chapter 3 the nature of this rumour and the possibilities for friction in the closed and tight-knit society of the college by outlining the characteristics of a particular group of students and the system of values they shared, and explore the way in which Marlowe allied himself to local or courtly magnates and the social milieu of the college community that led some of its members to defame him for retracting his MA degree.

In Chapter 4 I assess how and to what extent Marlowe came under the patronage and protection of the Privy Council – in particular, of Sir Francis Walsingham – and speculate about what kind of 'good service' he did for Walsingham and his allies in the council. At the same time, I examine how his activities under the council's patronage put him in a difficult financial situation throughout his life. Uncovering Walsingham's protégés in and around Corpus Christi College renders the assumptions about Marlowe's local connection with Walsingham more convincing and offers us a vital perspective on his literary output during and after his college years. Local readings of his plays from this perspective will therefore form the main topic in Part II.

---

[51] Constance B. Kuriyama, 'Second Selves: Marlowe's Cambridge and London Friendships', in John Pitcher (ed.), *MRDE, Vol. 14* (Cranbury, NJ, 2001), pp. 86–104, at p. 87.
[52] John Roche Dasent (ed.), *Acts of the Privy Council of England* (32 vols, London, 1890–1907), vol. 15, p. 141.

LOCALIZING CHRISTOPHER MARLOWE

I am not intending to supplement this restricted but detailed approach with the colourful attributes commonly assigned to Marlowe: 'spy', 'traitor', 'atheist', 'sociopath', 'brawler', 'sodomite', 'tobacco smoker', 'counterfeiter', 'rakehell', and so on. Admittedly, his distinctive character can be detected early on, from his college years, in his exceptional connection with the Privy Council, as well as in his risky choice of a literary or humanist career. It might be convenient for the sake of argument to portray the whole of his life and activities as being in line with the slanderous picture painted by Robert Greene, Richard Baines, Thomas Kyd, and several godly moralists, and to understand his plays from their perspectives. However, as Stephen Orgel points out, 'the transgressive Marlowe is largely a posthumous phenomenon'.[53] As I argue in later chapters, slanderous reports and accounts of Marlowe's deviant social behaviour were produced as a result of the feverish craze for heresy-hunting in the 1590s and were gradually amplified into several urban legends after his death.[54] Keith M. Botelho points out that, 'Rather than think that this rumored life takes us away from the "true" story of Marlowe's career, it is essential to see that rumor and news as well as uncertainty and skepticism *do* constitute the story'.[55] The Marlovian myth may be used as evidence for the cultural process of demonization and popular interest in him at the time when these accounts were made, but should not be treated as biographically crucial 'facts' for understanding his opinions, personality, and/or literary activities. It is essential, therefore, for us to become fully aware of, and remain aloof from, the strong cultural impetus to mythologize or demonize Marlowe, which demands that we place uncritical confidence in the grand narrative. Adopting a critical attitude seems to be important because, as Lukas Erne argues, 'Such resistance to biographical stereotypes may well lead to fruitful reexaminations of Marlowe's plays. Once we stop pretending we know Marlowe once and for all, Marlowe studies may well have exciting times ahead'.[56]

Just as Marlowe was located in his own temporal, spatial, and cultural process of self-construction, his literary works should similarly be

---

[53] Stephen Orgel, *The Authentic Shakespeare and Other Problems of the Early Modern Stage* (New York, 2002), p. 375.

[54] I have used the words 'gossip', 'rumour', and 'urban (or contemporary) legend' almost exactly according to the definitions in Nicholas DiFonzo and Prashant Bordia, 'Rumor, Gossip and Urban Legends', *Diogenes*, 54:1 (2007), 19–35.

[55] Keith M. Botelho, *Renaissance Earwitnesses: Rumor and Early Modern Masculinity* (New York, 2009), p. 29, emphasis in original.

[56] Erne, 'Biography, Mythography, and Criticism', p. 50. See also Healy, 'Marlowe's Biography', p. 337.

Introduction

understood closely and strictly within the specific temporal and spatial circumstances that transformed him into an agent working to advance the various interests and responsibilities of his patrons and audiences, and we should ask how these circumstances motivated him to produce those works with agentic capability, though what we know about him only permits us to reconstruct a fragment of the cultural politics of Elizabethan literature. Placing Marlowe in the social and cultural context of Corpus Christi College, Cambridge and of the theatrical city of London encourages us to use techniques for analysis that have a close affinity to what Leah S. Marcus calls 'localization' or 'local reading'. To paraphrase her argument, localization allows us to be aware of the cultural otherness of what we thought we understood, to circumvent the overfamiliarity of the traditional Renaissance Marlowe, and to clear up several prejudices of which we have not been conscious concerning his life.[57] It offers a slightly altered (though admittedly provisional) way of understanding the playwright and his plays and, above all, puts an end to the boundless process of mythologizing Marlowe.

As the methodology I apply in *Localizing Christopher Marlowe* prevents us from examining all his works, in Part II I highlight the three plays *Dido, Queen of Carthage*, *Tamburlaine the Great*, and *The Jew of Malta*, which are considered to have been written during and immediately after his college days and before 1590, when Sir Francis Walsingham died, in full awareness of the political necessities, frustrations, obsessions, and anxieties shared by Walsingham and his associates. This analysis will explain the dynamics of patronage that compelled Marlowe to endorse and promote his patron's politico-religious stance – dexterously, with some critical detachment – and the ways in which the local systems of beliefs and values correlating with shifts in political circumstances were consciously or unconsciously worked into his plays.

After the earlier chapters' exploration of the complex relationships and literary interests, the confrontations and comradeships, among the college members at Corpus Christi, Chapter 5 examines the role of the academic drama, which underwent considerable change in the 1570s and 1580s – from being a humanist medium of learning to becoming a political, satirical medium for promoting closer social ties within a particular group or faction. I then focus on several amateur university playwrights, exploring their ingenious ways of representing Elizabeth; and I track down the voices of anxiety and discontent among the aspiring intellectuals in their plays. Focusing on *Dido, Queen of Carthage*, I consider the play from the perspective of what I call the 'heliotropic tendency' towards allying with

---

[57] Leah Marcus, *Puzzling Shakespeare: Local Reading and Its Discontents* (Berkeley, 1988), p. 40.

the militarist faction of Leicester and Walsingham prevalent in Cambridge at that time.

Chapter 6 highlights the moment when Marlowe encountered the theatrical culture of London against the backdrop of the mobilization led by Walsingham, and shows how the 'prophetic' oratory of *Tamburlaine the Great* perfectly fulfilled the fervent desire for chivalric honour among the populace. Central to this chapter are the political and religious aspects of his 'prophetic' oratory used to mobilize the military mindset of Londoners in conjunction with inflammatory contemporary preaching. The play, while written to comply with the urgent request of the Privy Council, represented and obliquely commented on the workings of the holy war discourse driven by the power of the dominant ideology, and demonstrated Marlowe's position as a Parker scholar inclined to take holy orders gave him precise knowledge of, and critical insight into, the divine legitimization of war.

What a university scholar gained from his extremely difficult, impecunious life was not only 'cultural capital' – the social assets that gave him advantages for promotion in a stratified society – but also the measures to make good use of it for surviving financial hardships after having launched himself into the world.[58] Following on from the narrative of Chapters 2 and 4, which tracks Marlowe's financial conditions in and after Cambridge by referring to the circumstantial evidence and examining the self-protective measures he took to survive, Chapter 7 moves on to consider Barabas's theatrical power to thrive in the critical situation of Malta, a beleaguered isle, and shows that *The Jew of Malta* shared the prevailing anxiety about Machiavellian strangers who purportedly had exceptional powers of theatrics. The play also reflects Marlowe's own attitude towards the power of theatrics as a practical strategy to survive the national crisis. His intellectual probing leads us to find in the play a similar orientation to that in Reginald Scot's *The Discouerie of Witchcraft*: things that seem to happen by divine power can be created by the power of theatrics. After examining the intellectual bent among Marlowe's local associates – in particular, those who had been involved in the construction of Dover harbour in the 1580s – I suggest the possibility that Marlowe had a rapport with their empirical attitude that may have encouraged him to cast doubt on the authenticity of political and religious discourses in terms of fiction making: an attitude that may have naturally become a strong incentive for his enemies to invent and then attack his 'monstrous opinions', so troublesome to the authorities.

---

[58] For the notion of 'cultural capital', especially 'in the institutionalized state', see Pierre Bourdieu, 'The Forms of Capital', in John G. Richardson (ed.), *Handbook of Theory and Research for the Sociology of Education* (New York, 1986), pp. 241–58.

Introduction

Giving our consideration to these three plays within their locally and temporally specific contexts enables us to see that it is inappropriate to seek in Marlowe's dramatic works evidence of those characteristics that his enemies carped at in demonizing him. Rather, what we should keep in mind in understanding the colourful attributes of Marlowe as an 'atheist' is the fact that a flood of poisonous discourses permeated society, leading to the invention of a variety of heretical monsters in the 1590s. Naturally, the object of our concern is not just the puritan radicals severely lashed by the pens of anti-Martinists, but also those who were reported by hearsay and condemned as 'atheists' in the process of heresy-hunting in the 'ugly decade'.[59] This juxtaposition does not mean that the demonization of 'puritans' and 'atheists' constituted different social phenomena. In fact, they were closely linked, and together made up the religious heresy syndrome of the decade that was set against the backdrop of the upheaval of war, epidemics, and economic collapse. It also needs to be stressed that it was this heresy syndrome that encouraged the emergence of Marlowe as an 'atheist'. This can be clearly seen when we pay attention, as Michael Hunter does, to the significance of 'a juxtaposition not hitherto noted': to the fact that the reports or gossip concerning Marlowe's atheism are preserved among the papers of Sir John Puckering, Lord Keeper of the Great Seal, along with examinations of several puritan radicals that were carried out at the same time.[60]

This juxtaposition is noteworthy, for it urges us to see the process of constructing Marlowe's 'atheism' in the context of the polemic enthusiasm created by the production of schismatic discourses and writings about them, and the suppression of heresy on the initiative of Richard Bancroft, a leading member of the Ecclesiastical Commission, and Puckering himself. Admittedly, the detection of atheists around 1593 was the by-product of a series of investigations into religious deviants and libellers, but the 'atheist' Marlowe and those puritan radicals had distinctive traits in common: their monstrous identities were invented using literary strategies and the imagination of polemicists, writers, and intelligencers; that is, they were constituted not merely of what they and their opponents wrote but also of gossips, rumour, hearsay, and news reports that were more fictitious than factual. The emergence of their monstrous reputations in turn spread

---

[59] Patrick Collinson, 'Ecclesiastical Vitriol: Religious Satire in the 1590s and the Invention of Puritanism', in John Guy (ed.), *The Reign of Elizabeth I: Court and Culture in the Last Decade* (Cambridge, 1995), pp. 150–70, at p. 153. David Loewenstein has also emphasized 'the nastiness of the nineties' in *Treacherous Faith: The Specter of Heresy in Early Modern English Literature and Culture* (Oxford, 2013), pp. 5 and 165.

[60] Michael Hunter, 'The Problem of "Atheism" in Early Modern England', *Transactions of the Royal Historical Society*, 5th ser., 35 (1985), 135–57, at p. 136.

prejudice against their literary outputs, leading to further gossip, contemporary legends, and caricatured stage characters, which cast a dark shadow over the next few decades.

Chapter 8 therefore acts as a bridge to the chapters in Part III that deal with the Marlowe myth, and turns our attention to these poisonous discourses in the 1590s that intensified the religious suppression of 'heretics' and encouraged polemical enthusiasm for inventing a variety of religious monsters. In order to elucidate that complicated process, I first discuss the disputatious atmosphere of the university, which would often act as a politico-religious catalyst and transform an ambitious, destitute youth – whether conservative or radical – into a contentious polemicist. I then focus on Thomas Nashe, who was one of those caught up in the febrile atmosphere at Cambridge and who transplanted its heated temperament into the print culture of London, reviling Martin Marprelate and what Nashe considered the contemporary 'absurditie' in the arts. I end the chapter by examining how Marlowe – and *Tamburlaine* as his towering creation – cut a conspicuous figure as an instigator of prophetic oratory declaiming 'mighty lines' and became a powerful source of inspiration and enthusiasm for religious radicals, as well as for the discontented populace.

The portrait that *Localizing Christopher Marlowe* attempts to paint is not that of Marlowe as representative of the 'overreaching' Renaissance man, let alone the biased caricature that his enemies tried to work up. Rather, its chapters encourage us to imagine Marlowe as an aspiring, sociable person, just like other university adolescents; a destitute scholar seeking the patronage of local magnates and the Privy Council, and trying to make the most of his cultural assets to survive; a social critic acquainted with the power of theatrics in all its aspects; and an unprecedented playwright who sent a huge shockwave through English culture in the 1590s and was, hence, invented, largely by his enemies, as an 'atheist'.

LOCALIZING THE MARLOWE MYTH

> O barbarous! Do you bring the words of these hellish spiders against me? If they, like unnatural villains, used those words, shall I be charged with them?
>
> Walter Raleigh, 1603

At his trial at Winchester in November 1603, Sir Walter Raleigh was accused of a conspiracy to overthrow the new regime of James I and was found guilty of treason on hearsay evidence. He made an urgent appeal to the prosecution to produce at least two lawful witnesses at the time of his arraignment, saying 'let my accuser come face to face and be deposed'. In the early modern legal system, although much debate as to the sufficiency of witnesses in number and kind was underway, there was as yet no notion of absolute need to call a witness to the stand as one of the primary sources of proof. Chief Justice John Popham refused to produce the accuser, on the ground that 'Where no circumstances do concur to make a matter probable, then an accuser may be heard: but so many circumstances agreeing and confirming the accusation in this case, the accuser is not to be produced'.[61] That is to say, hearsay evidence was admissible even in state trials for treason and was usable, though not alone sufficient, in confirmation of other testimony.[62] No wonder Raleigh, having neither right nor opportunity for cross-examination in his own defence, censured the way in which Edward Coke, the attorney general, skilfully and ruthlessly manipulated hearsay witnesses as 'barbarous'.

The tragic case of Raleigh clearly demonstrates the tyrannical leverage of hearsay evidence at that time. Naturally, the 'spectre of heresy', resurgent in the early 1590s, drove the powerful legal and political machinery used to accuse and demonize supposed religious deviants.[63] The explosive publication of anti-heretical, anti-Catholic polemics in the late sixteenth century and the climate of intense religious anxiety, conflict, and demonization readily stimulated the imagination of the populace, as well as of witnesses avid to promote their own interests, to produce 'impossible Fictions' invented with 'undeserved abuse', of the kind that the imprisoned Robert Southwell bitterly complained about.[64] In examining Jesuits, 'atheists', and other social dissidents, it was extremely common for the 'facts' to be based on hearsay, gossip, rumours, and sometimes fragmentary literary discourses.

What we know about the heretical utterances and subversive activities of Marlowe is primarily based on unsubstantiated hearsay reports of three untrustworthy witnesses, Richard Cholmeley, Richard Baines, and Thomas Kyd, all of whom were obviously motivated, immediately before and after Marlowe's death, by the desire to gain their own advantage or to avoid criminal prosecution by smearing Marlowe's reputation. Cholmeley's disparaging remark that the primary members of the Privy Council, as well as Marlowe, were all atheists and Machiavellians urges us to doubt its credibility and biographical value. Baines had become notorious in print as early as the 1580s for his dissembling tricks at the English College in Rheims and

---

[61] David Jardine, *Criminal Trials* (2 vols, London, 1832–35), vol. 1, pp. 427–8.
[62] John H. Wigmore, 'The History of the Hearsay Rule', *Harvard Law Review*, 17:7 (1904), 437–58, at p. 443.
[63] For the construction of heretics in the 1590s, see Loewenstein, *Treacherous Faith*, pp. 157–76.
[64] Robert Southwell, *An Humble Supplication to Her Maiestie*, ed. R. C. Bald (Cambridge, 1953), p. 28.

for his recantation immediately afterwards in a French prison cell. The fact that he and Marlowe accused each other of the intent to go to the enemy or to Rome before Robert Sidney, the governor of Vlissingen, suggests the obvious animosity between the two and the malicious intent of Baines's allegations. Finally, Kyd's letter to Sir John Puckering concerning Marlowe's 'atheistic' beliefs was an attempt to clear himself from suspicion of atheism and xenophobic libel after several episodes of severe torture.[65]

Moreover, it has been well attested that almost all the 'monstrous' opinions attributed to Marlowe originated from readily available literary sources and should be considered not as Marlowe's own way of thinking but rather as the familiar features of what ordinary people thought a dangerous atheist blasphemer or anyone of his mindset was like.[66] Even those charges whose origin seems difficult to trace, such as 'St John the Evangelist was bedfellow to Christe, that he leaned always in his bosum, that he used him as the synners of Sodoma', can be explained. Mario DiGangi points out that, 'Traditional exegesis and iconography permitted homoerotic interpretations of certain figures, most notably David (when paired with Jonathan), St Sebastian and the disciple John (both of whom are paired with Jesus). These traditions were well known to Renaissance English writers'.[67] It would be problematic, therefore, to employ those hearsay reports as sufficient evidence of the religious opinions of Marlowe himself. David Riggs is right in saying, 'While these sensational utterances cried out for retribution, they lead us away from the flesh-and-blood Christopher Marlowe and into the symbolic universe of Elizabethan morality'.[68]

Admittedly, we can find in their reports several references to actual persons. Marlowe's attempt to persuade 'men of quallitie', including Matthew Roydon, to defect to Scotland, and his initiation into John Poole's method of counterfeiting coins in Newgate Prison, allow us to make conjectures about the sphere of his political activities and factional contacts. This might then encourage us to assume that these hearsay reports are not all necessarily false and to treat them as potential evidence for writing a biography of Marlowe. As J. B. Steane remarks: 'it seems to me absurd, in the present state of our knowledge, to dismiss all of

---

[65] *Thomas Kyd: Facts and Problems* (Oxford, 1967), pp. 26–32.
[66] Paul H. Kocher, 'Backgrounds for Marlowe's Atheist Lecture', in Baldwin Maxwell, W. D. Briggs, Francis R. Johnson, and E. N. S. Thompson (eds), *Renaissance Studies in Honor of Hardin Craig* (Stanford, 1941), pp. 112–32, provides a detailed discussion of the literary sources for Baines's note, though inappropriately (it seems) concluding that the atheist argument recorded in the note is that of Marlowe 'clearly enough'.
[67] Mario DiGangi, *The Homoerotics of Early Modern Drama* (Cambridge, 1997), p. 20.
[68] David Riggs, *The World of Christopher Marlowe* (London, 2004), p. 76.

these Elizabethan rumours and accusations as "the Marlowe myth".[69] At the same time, however, the difficulty of regarding these reports as reliable testimony places us in a dilemma: to what extent can we assume that they reflect Marlowe's actual behaviour and mindset? Insufficient evidence survives to corroborate them, so in practice one would have to construct a tentative portrait of the playwright by picking and choosing some passages that one prefers and reading his plays from that perspective. Thus, the arbitrary choice taken from hearsay evidence to construct the portrait of what we want Marlowe to be like only allows us to see an illusory contour that does not exist intrinsically; and so we run the risk of being censured (as the attorney general was by Raleigh) as 'barbarous' for manipulating hearsay witnesses for our own purposes.

G. Kitson Clark has argued for the efficiency of the rules that lawyers have worked out over many centuries for the treatment of evidence in the field of historical studies, saying that

> those who research into history, and those who use history, ought to consider very carefully the rules which a court of law imposes on the evidence brought before it: such rules as the exclusion of hearsay evidence, the need for corroboration, or the duty to hear both sides to a conflict.[70]

Although deriving from his capacious study of nineteenth-century society, Clark's suggestion concerning the virtue of the hearsay rule ought to be taken seriously when examining those malicious reports against Marlowe. In particular, when we have neither sufficient corroboration nor opportunities to cross-examine the witnesses, it is all the more important to observe the hearsay rule and appraise carefully whether those reports disadvantageous to Marlowe have any validity to substantiate the claim against the accused. Such strong resistance to using hearsay evidence as a convenient source of inventing 'facts' about the playwright should effectively prevent us from biographical fallacies.

Excluding the hearsay evidence does not imply, however, that those statements uttered by his enemies are worthless as historical documents. Rather, they have high validity, *not* in revealing the religious or political opinions of Marlowe himself, but in tracing the development of how prejudice, gossip, and hearsay demonized the suspect as a heretic. They then help us to understand what fragments of contemporary discourses were

---

[69] J. B. Steane (ed.), *Christopher Marlowe: The Complete Plays* (Aylesbury, 1969), p. 15. For a similar attitude, see David Wootton, 'New Histories of Atheism', in Michael Hunter and David Wootton (eds), *Atheism from the Reformation to the Enlightenment* (Oxford, 1992), pp. 13–53, at pp. 18–21, 30–1.

[70] G. Kitson Clark, *The Critical Historian* (New York, 1967), p. 16.

mobilized to create this atheist monster and fabricate this series of urban legends about him. Even Francis Meres's ridiculous statement that Marlowe was 'stabd to death by a bawdy Seruingman, a riuall of his in his lewde loue' may be regarded, as John Archer argues, as 'a vestige of the contemporary gossip that associated an excessive sexuality with Marlowe and his way of life'.[71] In short, we can learn from their malicious reports not what Marlowe was actually like, but what they *wanted* Marlowe to be like.

The most important question to ask, therefore, seems to be exactly the one that Nicholas Davidson proposes: 'If the charges made against Marlowe by Baines and Kyd were neither exceptional nor new, [...] we need to ask why they were presented to the authorities only in the spring of 1593.'[72] I would like to add another: why did the target of the charges have to be Marlowe? To be more precise, by looking at the charges against Marlowe as one of the constituents of the social process that produced the religious deviant and his contemporary legend, we are able to direct our focus mainly at the myth-making function of literary discourses in their specific spatial, temporal, and cultural contexts. What I propose in Part III, then, is a modest endeavour: a sketch of this whole process, by probing into the allegations of Cholmeley, Baines, and Kyd, and then a widening of the scope to examine the literary discourses on 'atheists' produced in the 1590s, such as the political and moral pamphlets riddled with accusations and personal attacks, the popular plays featuring a blasphemous character, and the local gossip circulated among the populace.

How and why, then, did Marlowe come to be represented as a religious deviant or a 'sociopath' abruptly around 1593? In Chapter 9, I argue that, to answer these questions, it is necessary to locate Robert Greene's first remarks on *Tamburlaine* and Marlowe within a specific set of cultural and social circumstances, and to examine what literary and sociocultural context fomented the earliest and extraordinary criticisms made by him in *Perimedes* (1588). I therefore consider what cultivated Greene's negative attitude towards Marlowe in *Perimedes* by reappraising the social context and the design of his conversion narratives: *A Looking-Glass for London and England* (c.1588), *The Repentance of Robert Greene* (1592), and *Greene's Groatsworth of Wit* (1592), highlighting their relationships with Greene's invectives against Marlowe. At the same time, through addressing his occasional mental recourse to the locality of Norwich and

---

[71] Francis Meres, *Palladis Tamia* (London, 1598), fol. 287r. John Michael Archer, *Sovereignty and Intelligence: Spying and Court Culture in the English Renaissance* (Stanford, 1993), p. 68.

[72] Nicholas Davidson, 'Christopher Marlowe and Atheism', in Darryll Grantley and Peter Roberts (eds), *Christopher Marlowe and English Renaissance Culture* (Aldershot, 1996), pp. 129–47, at p. 139.

its puritan environment on the basis of the archival findings about the connection between Greene, the prominent benefactors of Norwich, and the Norwich fellows of Corpus Christi College, I suggest the possibility that his prejudice against and exhortation to Marlowe originated from the local factional rivalries within the university. This will reveal how the urban legend of Marlowe may have got started, and how it reached its full development later on.

Chapter 10, based on the analysis of Greene's narratives and his prejudice against Marlowe, looks at how the slanderous discourse about Raleigh's school of atheism and its conjurer master, which Robert Persons had invented in his *Elizabethae Angliae Reginae Haeresim Caluinianam Propugnantis, Saeuissimum in Catholicos sui Regni Edictum* (1592), came into existence and was (mis)understood by readers, and then appropriated, reworked, and put to entirely new uses by informers and moral polemicists against Marlowe. The consequent malicious reports of Cholmeley, Baines, and Kyd will be reconsidered as some of the constituent parts of the process of constructing atheist monsters. At the same time, it is necessary to see how Marlowe's sudden (and unfortunately timely) death allowed and even encouraged his contemporaries to understand the incident, which may have confirmed suspicions about his atheism and debauchery – and the belief that he had suffered divine retribution – within a providential, moral framework, thereby recasting the characters of his plays within the Greeneian quasi-biographical perspective.

This enquiry into the cultural phenomena produced by Marlowe's death and demonization will naturally lead us to recognize the social function of theatre to construct 'reality' from fictitious, imaginative discourses of or about him. In fact, the motifs and ideas of his plays infiltrated popular conceptions of what constituted an atheist, a serious threat to society, giving rise to moral gossiping about the playwright and his Faustus-like atheist disciples; they even inspired several contemporary legends of the devil's appearance during the performance of *Doctor Faustus*. Closely examining those legends gives us fresh light on a contested arena of society where the power of theatrics to create 'reality' from illusion for audiences under social stresses collided violently with campaigns against theatre that might incur divine retribution. The result was a set of legends that were produced against the backdrop of the heresy craze and the appearance of the plague, rampant around 1593.

Thus, the localization of the Marlowe myth will show more than we might expect about how 'Marlowe' was constructed by multi-layered literary discourses, both his own and those of his enemies, discourses that worked on the imagination of his contemporaries, and even of far more recent generations, strongly enough to produce a variety of Marlowe myths.

We know next to nothing about Marlowe. What we do know, however, is enough to reconstruct a cross-section of the culture and politics of Renaissance drama, with Marlowe as its pivotal agent.

Part I

LIFE

Chapter 1

MATTHEW PARKER AND THE NORWICH–CORPUS CONNECTION

The chamber plans of Corpus Christi that we are going to examine in this chapter are a visual and spatial representation of the college's social space and show how it served as a hub of communications, propelling members to affiliate with others, both inside and outside their communities, and to expand their factional networks into the intellectual layers of society. What we find in these plans is a kind of microcosm of the social nuclei that spread dendrites of personal and political interconnections to cells in other colleges, cities, provinces, and the royal court. This micro-level understanding of local politics and affiliations provides insight into how university scholars came to have a rapport with local magnates and to be engaged in working for them, and what political agendas they had to support in return for patronage.

THE FORMATION OF CLUSTERS IN THE COLLEGE COMMUNITY

It was a common feature of universities in the later sixteenth century that the influx of so many students caused a 'serious crisis of accommodation'.[1] Corpus Christi College was no exception. Although the total membership was reported to amount to only thirty-two in 1564, numbers had shot up to more than ninety in less than a decade.[2] The refurbishment of a disused building into the pensionary in 1569 was obviously one of the measures employed to deal with the problem, which was of great urgency.[3] Moreover,

---

[1] Lawrence Stone, 'The Size and Composition of the Oxford Student Body 1580–1910', in Lawrence Stone (ed.), *The University in Society: Oxford and Cambridge from the 14th to the Early 19th Century* (Princeton, 1975), pp. 3–110, at p. 17.
[2] H. P. Stokes, *Corpus Christi* (London, 1898), pp. 67–8.
[3] Robert Willis and John Willis Clark, *The Architectural History of the University of Cambridge and of the Colleges of Cambridge and Eton* (4 vols, Cambridge, 1886), vol. 1, p. 260.

the college delegates complained in 1579 that the college had no convenient place for divine service, 'by reason that the number of Fellowes, Schollers and Students in the same Colledge be so muche encreased and daily do encrease'.[4] Judging from Bacon's plan of 1577, the college seems to have been unable to afford sufficient living space to keep up with the marked increase. By then, the three-storey building was closely packed with 107 college members: the master, eleven fellows, and eighty-four students in the court, together with one fellow and ten students in the pensionary.

The high density of residents seems to have been further exacerbated by the unavailability of one particular chamber on the east side of the court. This chamber, under the Old Library (Chamber 11 in Parker's plan of 1575), had disappeared by the time of Bacon's plan of 1577. The general overview of the college (figure 9) gives an important clue as to the reason for its disappearance. In the south-east corner, where Chamber 11 had previously been, we can find a drawing of a spacious L-shaped room, which suggests that the chamber was converted into a part of the Master's Lodge. Robert Masters, the college historian, possibly depending on the Chapter Book, dates the refurbishment of this chamber to 1618, saying: 'the Chamber next the Dining-Room, which had been the old Library, was now appropriated to the Master, lest the Society when assembled upon business in the latter, should be overheard.'[5] It seems, however, that the chamber had been appropriated rather earlier, at least by 1577. When Philip Nichols, one of the fellows, brought a suit in 1580 against Robert Norgate, the master, for his mismanagement of the college finances, Nichols, along with several other fellows, complained about Norgate's lavish spending on the renovation. In the 'Articles, whereupon the Fellows of Corpus Christi College have just occasion to complain against the Master of that College', they claimed that 'The now Mr hath expended in repairing of his owne house in the Towne, and his lodgyng in the Colledge above one hundre[d] m[ar]kes as appereth by his owne accomptes'.[6]

---

[4] Robert Masters, *The History of the College of Corpus Christi* (Cambridge, 1753–55), Appendix, p. 83.

[5] *Ibid.*, p. 136. For Masters's evidence dating the refurbishment to 1618, see CCCA, CCCC01/C/1, Chapter Book 1, p. 136 (15 November 1619). I am greatly indebted to Elisabeth Leedham-Green, who kindly directed my attention to the entry. This entry, though dated 1619, describes the rearrangement of rooms to avoid eavesdropping. The Chapter Book is transcribed by Elisabeth Leedham-Green in <https://www.corpus.cam.ac.uk/sites/default/files/downloads/chapter-book-1.pdf> [accessed 11 November 2022].

[6] TNA, SP, 12/141, fol. 77v (17 August 1580).

Overcrowding did not necessarily mean confusion, however: Bacon's plan clearly sets out the overall pattern of the room allocation. Almost all the lower chambers were occupied by the students for whom the college ensured stable sources of funding. The college fellows lived in the middle chamber, where it was possible to get a little more privacy and sunshine, though the increase in membership made it necessary for several fellows to share their rooms with the pupils they looked after.[7] Each upper chamber, or garret, built above and accessed by stairs within the respective fellow's room, was crammed with four students on average. Very rarely was any student in receipt of a foundation grant, and so they had to secure assistance from their parents or patrons. Some of these students worked their way through their degree by performing menial service. Some, with good prospects, waited for their opportunity to obtain a scholarship; others, with degrees, planned the next stage of their careers in or outside the university. Wealthy fellow-commoners seem not to have predominated as much as we might suppose; there were never more than six fellow-commoners, almost all of whom were allocated to the newly refurbished and more sparsely inhabited pensionary.

A comparison between the two plans of 1575 and 1577 helps us to understand more clearly the common practices of the college members as they moved in and out. Let us consider first the way in which rooms were assigned when the turnover of students receiving fellowships took place. Almost all the cases are easy to understand, for succession to a fellowship normally meant succession to the chamber. Thomas Gooch, an Archbishop Parker's Foundation fellow, provides a typical example. He obtained his fellowship in 1569 and, as we learn from Parker's plan of 1575, occupied the first floor of Chamber 9. When he relinquished his fellowship in 1575, he gave up his chamber to John Thaxter, whose name can be found in Chamber 9 of Bacon's plan. Another example occurs on the first floor of Chamber 7, which Moses Fowler, a college foundation fellow, inherited (along with his fellowship) from Samuel Bird in 1576.

A seemingly singular case is that of Philip Nichols, whose name appears on the ground floor in Chamber 7 of Bacon's plan. Although it seems unusual for the ground-floor room to be allocated to a fellow, this case was actually a natural consequence of following the common practice. Nichols inherited his fellowship and chamber in 1576 from John Scot, a fellow of the first college foundation, who, according to Parker's plan of 1575, had

---

[7] Requests from parents, as well as the increase in membership, compelled several fellows to share their rooms with their pupils. See, for instance, Ruth Hughey (ed.), *The Correspondence of Lady Katherine Paston, 1603–1627* ([Norwich], 1941), pp. 70, 78.

resided in Chamber 11. However, the same chamber was appropriated, as mentioned above, by the master of the college, which may have prevented Nichols from using the chamber and necessitated his remaining on the ground floor of Chamber 7, possibly as an emergency measure. Thus, the practice of turnover seems to have been settled even under such peculiar circumstances, though this inconvenience might have given Nichols one good reason to bring proceedings against the college master.

Matthew Parker assigned to five funded scholars from Norwich the three lower chambers on the east side. According to Bacon's plan of 1577, however, these five scholars (Henry Golding, John Dix, Henry Gold, Thomas Plombe, and Christopher Abbys) were living in just two chambers (9 and 10) on the east side. The reason we cannot find the third lower chamber allotted to them is, of course, because Chamber 11 had been appropriated by the college master. Parker's plan shows Abbys occupying the ground floor of Chamber 11 with Thomas Corbet, a Bible clerk from Essex. After the chamber was appropriated, Abbys moved into the lower floor of Chamber 10 to live with other Norwich scholars, while Corbet moved into Chamber 2. Abbys's removal to Chamber 10 may have been due to his (or his tutor's) respect for Parker's intention. At the same time, this arrangement was possibly worked out at Abbys's own request, because sharing the room with scholars and fellows of a similar background would have made him feel at home, and would have reduced the daily stresses of his life. Thus, the two ground-floor chambers on the east side were occupied by the Norwich scholars, under the eye of John Thaxter and Henry Aldrich, fellows who also came from that city and who were in close contact with several 'godly' magnates.[8]

Parker's design for allocating chambers according to foundation groups seems to have functioned well, at least among the Norwich members on the east side. This was not always the case, however, with some of the other chambers. In 1569, Parker appropriated three lower chambers on the north side for five scholars from Canterbury, and what we discover in his plan of 1575 almost precisely corresponds to his directions.[9] Four of the scholars (Nicholas Faunt, Philip Nichols, Moses Fowler, and Timothy Cotton) were living in the lower chambers of the north side; only William Lawse, a newcomer, lived in Chamber 1, on the west side. By 1577, however, they seem to have been no longer bound by Parker's initial policy. Certainly, we

---

[8] The term 'godly' is used throughout this book in the sense that Collinson explains it as 'the appellation preferred by those sixteenth-century Englishmen whose unsympathetic neighbours called them "puritans", "precisians", and, with an equally derogatory intent, "saints" and "scripture men"'. See Patrick Collinson, *Godly People: Essays on English Protestantism and Puritanism* (London, 1983), p. 1.

[9] John Lamb, *Masters' History of the College of Corpus Christi* (London, 1831), p. 103.

can find in Bacon's plan Brian Exton and Robert Stone from King's School in Canterbury, who succeeded Fowler and Cotton, in Chamber 8 at the north-east corner. Lawse had stayed on in Chamber 1, now with Richard Manwaring, a new successor to Nichols. This change of residence was by no means unique, because Samuel Beadle, a carpenter's son from the parish of St George in Canterbury and successor to Faunt, joined Christopher Pashley from Canterbury in Chamber 4, on the west side. These changes, which took place over several years, may have been due to the homophilic tendency taht prompted scholars native to a similar place to gather in clusters, unconcerned about the founder's policy.

Let us now pay closer attention to the ground floor of Chamber 4, which was assigned 'for iij schollers' by Parker's will, drawn up on 5 April 1575.[10] The archbishop established a new foundation of scholarships out of the annuity from his estate at Lambeth, and laid down the general requirement that these scholars should be from three different regions: 'The 1st of these is to be taken out of *Canterbury* School, being a Native of the City, the 2d out of that at *Aylsham*, being born there, and the 3d in like manner from *Wymondham*'.[11] They were to be accommodated in 'that roome or chamber in the said Colledge late called a storehouse now repaired and finished for that purpose at the cost and charges of the said John Parker in accomplishment likewise of the will of the said most reverend father'.[12] The Audit Book of the college shows that these new Parker scholars were Christopher Pashley from Canterbury, Robert Thexton from Aylsham, and James Poynter from Wymondham.[13] According to Bacon's plan, however, we find that it was Samuel Beadle, rather than Thexton, who was set up in the storehouse, while Thexton was accommodated in Chamber 6, on the north side. In 1575, Chamber 6 was occupied by Thomas Harris, a college foundation scholar from Norfolk, and Nicholas Faunt, a Canterbury scholar from King's School and a future secretary of Sir Francis Walsingham. Since Faunt passed on his scholarship to Beadle in 1577, the vacancy in the chamber should naturally have been taken up by Beadle, but it seems that the transfer, either authorized or unauthorized, was made between Thexton and Beadle, as a consequence of which Thexton relocated to Chamber 6, while Beadle took up residence in the storehouse. Thus, the storehouse on the north-west corner came to be occupied by the

---

[10] See Appendix 2; and John Strype, *The Life and Acts of Matthew Parker* (3 vols, Oxford, 1821), vol. 3, pp. 336–7.

[11] Masters, *History of Corpus Christi*, p. 203.

[12] CCCA, CCCC02/M/14/57. The citation revealing the agreement (dated 12 April 1580) is from John Bakeless, *The Tragicall History of Christopher Marlowe* (2 vols, Cambridge, MA, 1942), vol. 1, p. 65.

[13] CCCA, CCCC02/B/4, Audit Book, fol. 4r of the account in 1575.

two scholars from King's School (Beadle and Pashley) and may have been congenial to those from Canterbury.

Another replacement occurred on the ground floor of Chamber 5, where Henry Sutterton and William Norgate, both scholars in receipt of college foundations, were living in 1575. The plan of 1577 shows that Sutterton, after having relinquished his post to Richard Braborne in 1576,[14] took up provisional residence on the second floor of Chamber 10, looking to pursue his next career outside the university, while Norgate, who was the brother of Robert Norgate, the college master, and who came from Aylsham, joined Thexton (from the same town) in Chamber 6. Since the chamber also housed Thomas Harris from Norfolk on the ground floor, and Francis Kett, a fellow from Wymondham, upstairs, the 'local' atmosphere may have made it congenial for scholars from Norfolk. Norgate's departure from Chamber 5 produced a chain reaction: the vacancy was filled by John Temple, again from Norfolk, who had formerly lodged in Chamber 1. These moves contributed to the development of the Norfolk cluster on the north side, and, at the same time, enabled Richard Manwaring, who had succeeded Nichols (Chamber 7) as a Canterbury scholar in 1577, to join Lawse, another scholar from Canterbury, in Chamber 1. Manwaring's move was possibly welcomed by Nichols, as well as by Lawse, because Nichols became a fellow in that year but was unable to relocate from Chamber 7 to the first floor of Chamber 11, as mentioned above.

These movements, allowing scholars with regional ties to group together, may have made life difficult for Bacon – who required that 'the three lower Chambers raunginge on the weste side of the Courte' be assigned to his Suffolk scholars and that this allocation should be brought to early fruition – because Chambers 1 and 4, on the west side, had been newly occupied by the scholars from Canterbury. However, Chambers 2 and 3 were obviously convenient enough for establishing a foothold for building a pro-Baconian cluster, for the first floors of these chambers had only three college-funded scholars in all, although their privileges had to be carefully considered. Two of them, fortunately, had already obtained their BA and were to leave the college shortly. Moreover, the fellows Sophonius Smith and Henry Lewes, both of whom came from Suffolk, took up their quarters on the first floor of Chambers 1 and 2 to keep an eye on Bacon's scholars. In fact, Smith took charge of James and Edmund Bacon – respectively the nephew and grandson of the Lord Keeper – in October 1584.[15] It seems natural, there-

---

[14] This Braborne is possibly the same person as Richard Brabon, the tutor of Sir Robert Drury. See R. C. Bald, *Donne and the Drurys* (Cambridge, 1959), p. 19.

[15] Robert Rosenthal, *Papers of Sir Nicholas Bacon in the University of Chicago Library* (Chicago, 1989), p. 339. James Bacon was the son of James, the brother of the Lord Keeper, who died in 1573. See A. Hassell Smith, Gillian M. Baker, and R. W. Kenny

fore, for Bacon to have taken advantage of the situation and to have targeted the west side of the court.

By tracing the scholars' movements in this way, we can see that like-minded scholars were likely to flock together, contrary to their patrons' initial residential allocations in some cases, moving near to those who originated from a similar locality. The network connectivity sustained by native places or schools seems to have been the undercurrent that promoted these instances of chamber-moving within the college. At the same time, it appears that the segmentation of the college community into several regional units was reinforced by changing and swapping rooms, and Nicholas Bacon gave further impetus to this growing trend through the establishment of his foundation in 1577.

THE CHAMBERS ON THE EAST SIDE AND THE NORWICH RADICALS

Let us now focus closely on several social clusters that will be particularly important in reconstructing the local networks of the college community. This section profiles several Norwich fellows and scholars (Chambers 9 and 10 in Bacon's plan), giving a good understanding of the vicissitudes of religious contestation in the 1570s in which they were engaged to a greater or lesser extent within the college. It is appropriate to begin with two fellows who lived on Parker's foundation and were situated on the first floor of these chambers: John Thaxter and Henry Aldrich, both from the city of Norwich. These two 'Norwich fellows' were to be funded by Archbishop Parker's source of revenue and elected out of the five Norwich scholars by the college authorities.

As we have seen, Thaxter succeeded Thomas Gooch, one of the Norwich fellows, who had vacated his fellowship in 1575. Despite this apparently normal line of succession, however, curiously enough Parker's plan of 1574–75 shows that 'Sr Thaxter fellow' remained on the ground floor of Chamber 2 rather than moving to the first floor of Chamber 9, which Gooch continued to occupy. Naturally, one fellowship was not shared between these two fellows, and it is unlikely that Master Norgate mistakenly gave Thaxter the new title as fellow while leaving the name of 'Mr Gooch' as residing in the chamber where the new fellow should have been admitted. This apparently puzzling situation demonstrates how precisely these plans reflect the complicated situation of the college personnel changes. According to the Chapter Book, Thaxter had already

---

(eds), *The Papers of Nathaniel Bacon of Stiffkey, Volume I: 1556–1577* (Norwich, 1979), p. 100.

been admitted as a fellow on 19 May 1574, funded by the increase in college revenues from 1544 to 1569. Soon after, however, on 30 April 1575, he resigned his fellowship and then, by consent of the college master and several fellows (namely Richard Willoughbye, Robert Sayer, and Henry Yemes), was elected to the Parker fellowship on the same day '*vice* Gooch by benefit of having the master's vote'.[16] It is difficult to know the exact cause of this irregular procedure of replacement, but what seems obvious is that the college authorities were extraordinarily cautious and even high-handed in choosing the Norwich fellows.

Another irregularity in choosing Parker's Norwich fellow can be seen in an account which Robert Masters gives concerning a dispute between John Thaxter and Thomas Plombe in 1579:

> the former (upon *Henry Aldrich*'s having sent a Resignation of his Fellowship,) gave up that he before held in expectation of the Society's choosing him into Mr. *Aldrich*'s Place, which they accordingly did, and he was immediately admitted to it; but soon after this was over, it was said Mr. *Aldrich* had recalled his Resignation, and that by Letter before this new Election was made, whereupon there seems to have been a fresh Election in favour of *Plumbe*, at the time that the Fellowship was of course void; however this Revocation having not been notified to the Society before the first Election, the Visitors were of [the] opinion it was of no weight; and accordingly gave their Determination in favour of the former.[17]

Thomas Plombe (or Plumbe) was the BA Norwich scholar under Aldrich's charge, as we can see in Chamber 10. The reason why Thaxter, who had already been Parker's Norwich fellow, had to be reassigned to Aldrich's post is obscure, but it is not so difficult to imagine that the dispute was the product of contested manoeuvring behind closed doors over the choice of successor to the Norwich fellowship. The college master and his henchmen seem to have attempted to prevent Aldrich's active intervention in choosing the new Norwich fellow and to have been wary of taking control of the personnel management themselves. As a consequence of this trouble, Christopher Abbys was admitted and elected as fellow in place of Aldrich on 28 April 1579.

Admittedly, the college authorities had good reason to be as cautious and circumspect as could be in their choice of Norwich fellows because of their desire to suppress the influence of religious radicals, who had gained momentum under the mastership of Thomas Aldrich (1570–73), the second son of John Aldrich – the mayor and leading godly alderman

---

[16] CCCA, CCCC01/C/1, Chapter Book 1 (Liber Actorum in Collegio Corporis Christi), pp. 11–12. The quotation is from the transcriptions of the Chapter Books.

[17] Masters, *History of Corpus Christi*, p. 116.

of Norwich – and elder brother of Henry. Since John Aldrich enjoyed a close intimacy with Thomas Parker, the brother of Matthew, Archbishop of Canterbury, these local family contacts surely led Matthew Parker in 1569 to recommend Thomas Aldrich, a fellow of Trinity not more than thirty years of age at the time, to the mastership of Corpus Christi.[18] Parker wrote to William Cecil on 8 March 1570 to the effect, 'I know [Thomas Aldrich] to be an honest young man, learned in all the tongues, and also in French and Italian, and is I trust like to do service in the realm hereafter'.[19] However, Aldrich's radical tendencies escaped Parker's notice. Aldrich had been in full sympathy with the Presbyterian movement led by Thomas Cartwright, his colleague at Trinity, who was then in the eye of the storm in Cambridge. The attitude of the university authorities towards Cartwright hints at the great enthusiasm for radicalism then among fellows and students: 'The youth of the University, which is at this time very toward in learning, doth frequent his Lectures in great numbers; and therefore in danger to be poisoned by him with love of contention and liking of novelties.'[20] Aldrich was definitely among those 'poisoned by him' for his anti-intellectualistic attitude, 'as an head precisian in despising of the degrees of the university, and a great maintainer of Mr. Cartwright', which made him refuse, in contravention of the Corpus Christi statutes, to proceed to the degree of bachelor of divinity in January 1573.[21]

To settle the fierce college dispute over the matter, Parker advised the master Aldrich to resign, but was stung to fury by the stubborn defiance of Aldrich and some of his college colleagues. Parker complained to Queen Elizabeth about their impudence in a letter dated 15 June 1573:

> they say in jest that I am pope of Lambeth and of Benet College [the original name for Corpus Christi], and that I am out of all credit and of no reputation, and that they will sue to some great man of the council to accept [Aldrich] as chaplain, to outface me, and to beard mine authority.[22]

---

[18] Matthew Reynolds, *Godly Reformers and Their Opponents in Early Modern England: Religion in Norwich, c. 1560–1643* (Woodbridge, 2005), p. 47. For biographical information on mayors and aldermen of Norwich, I am indebted to Basil Cozens-Hardy and Ernest A. Kent, *The Mayors of Norwich 1403 to 1835* (Norwich, 1938).

[19] John Bruce and Thomas Thomason Perowne (eds), *Correspondence of Matthew Parker* (Cambridge, 1853), p. 358.

[20] John Strype, *The History of the Life and Acts of the Most Reverend Father in God, Edmund Grindal* (Oxford, 1821), p. 240.

[21] Thomas Aldrich's name can be found in the petitions on behalf of Thomas Cartwright in 1570. See John Strype, *Annals of the Reformation* (4 vols, Oxford, 1824), vol. 2, part 2, pp. 412–17. For further details of this affair, see Lamb, *Masters' History*, pp. 123–8; and H. C. Porter, *Reformation and Reaction in Tudor Cambridge* (Cambridge, 1958), pp. 149–55.

[22] Bruce and Perowne (eds), *Correspondence of Matthew Parker*, p. 429.

As H. C. Porter argues, several letters sent from Corpus Christi to Burghley reveal 'the internal balance of power in the college'.[23] The fellows of the pro-Aldrich faction were Henry Aldrich and Thomas Robartes, a Welsh fellow, who later went to Norwich to become the leader of the Presbyterian movement; three more fellows were then elected under Aldrich's mastership: Adam Longworth, John Scot, and Henry Lewes.[24] Parker bitterly complained about Aldrich's insolence, saying: 'The childish maliciousness for his vain tales, and his with his brother's ingratitude to me, besides their manifest precisianship, is too intolerable.' Moreover, the archbishop directed the brunt of his anger at the pro-Aldrich fellows who made their living out of Parker's fellowship: 'Some of those five fellowes hath and do now live of my purse daily'.[25] The opposing faction consisted of Robert Norgate, the succeeding college master and related to Matthew Parker by marriage;[26] Richard Fletcher, a client of Parker and later Bishop of London; and three more fellows, Robert Sayer, Richard Willoughbye, and Thomas Gooch,[27] all of whom became involved two years later in the abovementioned irregular procedure in choosing Thaxter as Parker fellow.

Under the mastership of Aldrich, religious radicalism linked Corpus Christi College with Norwich more closely than ever. Matthew Reynolds pertinently terms the relationship 'the Aldrich–Parker–Corpus Christi connection'.[28] In fact, the Aldrich brothers and Robert Willan (fellow from 1563 to 1570), all avowed supporters of Thomas Cartwright, were from Norwich. Young 'precisian' enthusiasts of the college who had been shaped by radical thinking, such as Thomas Robartes, were attracted to the city. Nathaniel Woodes, whom we now know as the author of the play *The Conflict of Conscience*, was undoubtedly another of those enthusiasts. He obtained his BA in 1570–71 and his MA in 1574 at Corpus and was collated to the living of South Walsham near Norwich via the Corpus–Norwich connection.[29] John Martin, Woodes's classmate, who was ordained deacon at Norwich on 17 October 1571 (the same day as Woodes's ordination), is named in the lists of clergy in the archdeaconry of Norwich who refused

---

[23] Porter, *Reformation and Reaction*, p. 151.
[24] BL, Lansdowne MS 17 (70), fol. 153. For the puritan movement in Norwich led by Thomas Robartes and John More, see Patrick Collinson, *The Elizabethan Puritan Movement* (1967; repr. Oxford, 1990), pp. 127 and 141.
[25] Bruce and Perowne (eds), *Correspondence of Matthew Parker*, pp. 436 and 438.
[26] Stephen Wright, 'Norgate, Robert (d. 1587)', in *ODNB*.
[27] BL, Lansdowne MS 17 (75), fol. 163.
[28] See Reynolds, *Godly Reformers*, pp. 47, 88–9.
[29] For Nathaniel Woodes's *The Conflict of Conscience* and the milieu of Norwich puritanism, see my article, 'Nathaniel Woodes, Foxeian Martyrology, and the Radical Protestants of Norwich in the 1570s', *Reformation*, 13 (2008), 103–32.

to wear the surplice.[30] The most interesting case is that of Robert Harrison, who, having obtained his MA from Corpus in 1572, became the master of Aylsham Grammar School on the recommendation of John Aldrich and Stephen Lymbert, the master of Norwich School.[31] Harrison's nonconformity brought trouble soon after and caused him to be dismissed. Nevertheless, this future separatist enjoyed the confidence of influential aldermen well enough to be offered the mastership of the Great Hospital in the city, where Robert Browne, another religious radical and classmate of Woodes, joined him to set up a Congregational church in 1580.[32] Browne later reminisced about how he came to Norwich: 'While he thus was careful, & besought the Lord to shewe him more comfort of his kingdom & church, then he sawe in Cambrige, he remembred some in Norfolke, whome he hard saie were verie forward.'[33] This statement well demonstrates the strength of the Norwich–Corpus relationship at that time.

NATHANIEL WOODES AND FOXEIAN MARTYROLOGY

Placing Nathaniel Woodes within this specific local context gives us a good perspective on how an ordinary poor scholar at Corpus Christi came to develop a rapport with Norwich magnates during his college years and to engage in writing a play for them. Moreover, it reveals the features of religious enthusiasm, political agendas, and literary tastes shared among the powerful factions of the aldermen and commonalty of the city who had exercised their tremendous leverage to elect Norwich scholars and fellows at Corpus in the 1570s.

It was Celesta Wine who first detected Woodes's close relationship with some of the Norwich magnates.[34] The living of St Mary, South Walsham was annexed in 1251 by Walter Suffield, Bishop of Norwich, to St Giles Hospital (or the Great Hospital) in the city, and was 'potentially one of the hospital's most lucrative holdings.'[35] The advowson and profits of St Mary remained

---

[30] R. A. Houlbrooke (ed.), *The Letter Book of John Parkhurst, Bishop of Norwich* (Norwich, 1974), p. 220.

[31] *Ibid.*, pp. 195–6, 210–11.

[32] For further details, see Albert Peel, *The Brownists in Norwich and Norfolk about 1580* (Cambridge, 1920), pp. 1–6.

[33] Albert Peel and Leland H. Carlson (eds), *The Writings of Robert Harrison and Robert Browne* (London, 1953), p. 405.

[34] Celesta Wine, 'Nathaniel Woodes: Author of the Morality Play *The Conflict of Conscience*', *RES*, OS, 15:60 (1939), 458–63.

[35] On Walter Suffield's appropriation of St Mary, South Walsham, see Carole Rawcliffe, *Medicine for the Soul: The Life, Death, and Resurrection of an English Medieval Hospital St. Giles's, Norwich, c. 1249–1550* (Stroud, 1999), pp. 82–3.

in the possession of the hospital until the dissolution of the monasteries, when the living came under the jurisdiction of the mayor, sheriffs, and commonalty of Norwich in 1547. This is exactly the time that the Great Hospital began supervising the administration of Norwich Grammar School. In other words, the mayor and aldermen, who had kept in close touch with all of the administrative and personnel matters pertaining to the Norwich fellows and scholars at Corpus Christi, had the advowson to collate clergymen, including Woodes, to the benefice of St Mary, South Walsham. Regrettably, while Wine observes the fact that Woodes 'was presented with this living might indicate that he had influential friends among the upper middle class of Norwich', she makes no attempt to pursue this line of prosopographical research.[36] So who were those influential friends and how close were they to Woodes?

On 18 June 1572, Nathaniel Woodes, seeking employment after obtaining his BA, appeared before the justices of the Mayor's Court of Norwich. This was about two weeks before his appointment to the living of St Mary, South Walsham. The following entry can be found in the court record for that day:

> This daye Nathanyell Woodes clarke cam into the courte and reqwestith the favor of Mr Mayor and this howse to haue the vicarage of Southwalsham w[hi]ch dothe app[er]tayne to the hospitall, and he is appoynted to go se it and to make answer of the lyking therof on frydaye next, and vpon his lyking he ys graunted the goodwill of this howse.[37]

The Mayor's Court, which consisted of the mayor and aldermen, met twice a week, usually on Wednesdays and Saturdays. This major legislative body exercised jurisdiction over the city and administered a wide range of legal business, including civil and criminal suits, interrogations, appointment of city officials, and screening of candidates for university scholarships.[38] It was not necessarily unusual, therefore, for Woodes, requesting a presentation to the living of St Mary, to have attended a briefing by the members of the court who held the advowson of the church. What *is* interesting, however, is that they seem to have been extraordinarily generous to Woodes in granting their favour: his appointment appears to have depended solely 'vpon his lyking' of the vicarage. Woodes appeared in court again on Saturday, 21 June:

> This daye Nathaniell woodes clarke according as he was com[m]aunded at the last courte dothe here com and shewe that he lykith of the vicarage of Southwalsham and prayeth the gyfte therof and to haue a presentac[i]on to

---

[36] Wine, 'Nathaniel Woodes', p. 460.
[37] NRO, NCR 16a/9, Mayor's Court Book (13 June 1569–16 June 1576), fol. 252.
[38] William Hudson and John Cottingham Tingey (eds), *The Records of the City of Norwich* (2 vols, Norwich, 1906), vol. 1, pp. cxxvii–cxxx.

whom it ys answeryd that if he will dwell thervpon and promys that if he shall resigne it at enytyme that then he shall resine the same ageyne vnto Mr Mayor for the tyme beying to the vse of the cittie before any other p[er]son then he shall haue it or elles not w[hi]ch he here saythe fully p[ro]myseth to do, and thervpon he is willed to make his presentac[i]on & he shall haue Mr Mayor and the Justices handes theronto.[39]

Woodes's job-hunting went ahead without a hitch. Soon after, on 30 June, he was presented to the living by Robert Suckling, the mayor at that time.[40]

Woodes's commencement of the MA on 8 May 1574 suggests that he had been keeping in touch with the college members even after obtaining his living in South Walsham in 1572 and was therefore well informed about the college dispute between the Aldrich and Parker factions. Considering the strong connection between Corpus and Norwich at that time, his appointment to St Mary's vicarage, with the willing consent of the Mayor's Court, allows us to assume that he sought the support of, or was recruited by, the godly master and fellows with similar ideological interests. On behalf of their younger college associate, the Aldrich brothers and other Corpus men, including Thomas Robartes, were possibly ready to use their influence and provide enough information for Robert Suckling and the aldermen to approve Woodes's appointment to the modest but important benefice. At the same time, Suckling, having been strongly associated with John Aldrich in the Norwich Merchant Adventurers' Company enterprise, may have been sympathetic towards the candidate recommended by Thomas Aldrich and his allies. Suckling probably shared the religious orientation of the Aldriches, for he was one of the leading members of St Andrew's church, a puritan stronghold headed by John More.[41]

Recently, Martin Wiggins has suggested, based on the fact that the roles in *The Conflict of Conscience* are conspicuously all male, that Woodes may have written it during his residence at Corpus Christi and originally intended it for performance at the college, and consequently places the play 'on the junction between Cambridge and South Walsham'.[42] Although we have no evidence in the college archives to support this possibility, it is most likely that the play emerged out of Corpus's cultural milieu in the early 1570s. At the same time, its title page explicitly indicates that Norwich was the author's living (and consequently the play's production) environment,

---

[39] NRO, NCR 16a/9, Mayor's Court Book, fol. 253.
[40] NRO, DN REG/13/19, fol. 179r.
[41] Cozens-Hardy and Kent, *Mayors of Norwich*, pp. 60–1. For radical Protestants at St Andrew's church, see Patrick Collinson, *The Religion of Protestants: The Church in English Society 1559–1625* (Oxford, 1982), pp. 141–5.
[42] Martin Wiggins, *British Drama 1533–1642: A Catalogue* (Oxford, 2012), vol. 2, pp. 75–6.

and there is no reason to question the reliability of this information. Erin Sullivan, by taking such extant evidence into consideration, expands Wiggins's suggestion into a hypothesis that

> Woodes wrote the play in the early 1570s with a university audience in mind, regardless of whether or not a performance ever took place, and that when he returned to it during his time in Norwich his envisioned audience became readers who, in addition to reading the play, might also undertake private performances in their homes.[43]

This elaborate scenario cannot be proven; nevertheless, such a Corpus–Norwich connection does seem to deserve special attention.

Not all radical Protestants were necessarily infected with anti-theatrical prejudice.[44] Rather, early Reformation dramatists were fully aware that a play, just as much as printed pamphlets, and sermons from the pulpit, could be a medium with great potential to disseminate Protestant moral and religious values. Woodes was no doubt one of those who considered drama in this way. The cultural milieu of both the college community and Norwich was benign enough to encourage him to turn his hand to drama, and may even have cultivated his positive attitude towards it. Thomas Aldrich, the college master, explicitly endorsed its pedagogical validity, for in 1567 Aldrich himself, being a fellow of Trinity, collaborated with his colleague Thomas Wilkes to write an academic play for college performance.[45] It seems to be no coincidence that Thomas Cartwright, another fellow of Trinity and (as we have seen) a fervent radical whom Aldrich deeply admired, was active in producing plays and performing disputations. Cartwright was paid three shillings by the college to produce Plautus' *Trinummus* and two shillings for 'his plaie' in 1563/4, and was then appointed as one of the disputants in the philosophy act in 1564 before the queen, arguing against the thesis that 'Monarchy is the best form of government'. He led the agitation again the next year, this time against the surplice.[46]

---

[43] Erin Sullivan, 'Doctrinal Doubleness and the Meaning of Despair in William Perkins's "Table" and Nathaniel Woodes' *The Conflict of Conscience*', *Studies in Philology*, 110:3 (2013), 533–61, at p. 553.

[44] This point is argued by Paul Whitfield White, *Theatre and Reformation: Protestantism, Patronage, and Playing in Tudor England* (Cambridge, 1993), chap. 6. See also, C. E. McGee, 'Puritans and Performers in Early Modern Dorset', *Early Theatre*, 6:1 (2003), 51–66, which complicates 'the familiar story of the rise of Puritanism and the decline of drama'.

[45] Alan Nelson (ed.), *Cambridge*, REED (2 vols, Toronto, 1989), vol. 1, pp. 252–3.

[46] Elizabeth Goldring, Faith Eales, Elizabeth Clarke, and Jayne Elisabeth Archer (eds), *John Nichols's The Progresses and Public Processions of Queen Elizabeth: A New Edition of the Early Modern Sources* (5 vols, Oxford, 2014), vol. 1, p. 410; Nelson (ed.), *Cambridge*, vol. 1, p. 225; Collinson, *Elizabethan Puritan Movement*, p. 112.

Moreover, several godly members of Norwich Municipal Corporation were known as liberal patrons of players. John Aldrich, during his mayoralty, paid rewards to 'Messengers Mynstelles and others', 'the Duke of Norffolkes Players', and 'Mr Bucke for his paynes in makinge and playing an Interlude by the commaundement of Mr Iohn Aldrich then Mayor'.[47] Thomas Sotherton, who belonged to the Grocers' guild, was another munificent patron of players; during his mayoralty in 1565 he sanctioned the performance of the staunchly Calvinistic Grocers' play, which featured the revised version of an earlier 'Adam and Eve' pageant.[48] In February 1576, when Woodes had been in post in South Walsham for almost four years, the Mayor's Court was still generous enough towards 'the hole company of the waytes of this Cittie' to grant them leave to play comedies, interludes, and 'tragedes which shall seme to them mete'.[49] These cultural environments, which were religiously radical but favourably disposed towards dramatic entertainment, may have encouraged Woodes to compose *The Conflict of Conscience*.

The most important feature of the play is that it devotes considerable space to the protagonist's suffering under the persecution of the Cardinal and the Legate. Leslie Mahin Oliver highlights Woodes's debt to John Foxe's *Actes and Monuments*, particularly for the long inquisition scene of Act 4, Scene 1, and points out that 'His trial, occupying most of the act, is, in all probability, a composite of many such trials, or "examinations", as they had been reported by Foxe in the *Acts and Monuments*'.[50] Moreover, it seems that Woodes drew heavily on Foxe for the play's martyrological vision. In collecting and compiling material on the Protestant martyrs, Foxe used the resources of traditional hagiography in order to highlight the providential aspect of these marvellous testimonies, and in this way carefully rehabilitated the cults of the martyr saints.[51] What makes *Actes and Monuments*

---

[47] David Galloway (ed.), *Norwich 1540–1642*, REED (Toronto, 1984), p. 45.

[48] This play was definitely performed. See Galloway (ed.), *Norwich*, pp. 52–3. For the two texts of the Norwich Grocers' play, see John C. Coldewey (ed.), *Early English Drama: An Anthology* (New York and London, 1993), pp. 151–63. For the Grocers' play, see Paul Whitfield White, *Drama and Religion in English Provincial Society, 1485–1660* (Cambridge, 2008), chap. 3. Paul Whitfield White, who directed my attention to Thomas Sotherton's involvement with dramatic productions, suggested that Woodes's play might have been performed in the private houses of local magnates such as Sotherton.

[49] Galloway (ed.), *Norwich*, p. 57.

[50] Leslie Mahin Oliver, 'John Foxe and *The Conflict of Conscience*', *RES*, OS, 25:97 (1949), 1–9, at p. 3.

[51] For Foxe's appropriation of traditional hagiography, see, in particular, Alexandra Walsham, *Providence in Early Modern England* (Oxford, 1999), p. 73; and Susannah Brietz Monta, *Martyrdom and Literature in Early Modern England* (Cambridge, 2005), pp. 53–65. For the appropriation of the saint play by Protestant dramatists,

unique is Foxe's shift of emphasis from the miracles of the saints to their sufferings. Beginning with the testimonies of the primitive Church, he tries to convince his readers that suffering for truth is a guarantee of election, while encouraging them to overcome their own daily afflictions and join with the Church of the elect.[52] Woodes evidently shared this conviction with Foxe, who, as Susannah Brietz Monta observes, 'used martyrs' suffering to help readers dismiss the anxiety predestinarian beliefs might provoke and embrace confident assurance'.[53]

Indeed, *The Conflict of Conscience* shows such a strong affinity with *Actes and Monuments* in this respect that the Foxeian educational stance is evident from the beginning. Philologus, the protagonist, discusses with his friend Mathetes the sufferings of the 'true Church'. He illustrates his point with biblical episodes from Abel to Christ, and then the Apostles:

> *Iames* vnder *Herod*, was headed with the Sworde,
> The rest of the Apostles, did suffer much turmoyle:
> Good *Paul* was murthered by *Nero* his worde:
> *Domitian* deuised a Barrell full of Oyle,
> The body of *Iohn* the Euangelist to boile:
> The Pope at this instant sondrie tormentes procure,
> For such as by Gods holy word will indure.
> By these former stories, two thinges we may learne,
> And profytably recorde in our remembraunce:
> The fyrst is Gods Church from the Diuels to discerne:
> The second to marke, what manyfest resistaunce,
> The Trueth of God hath, and what incombraunce:
> It bringeth vpon them that will it professe,
> Wherfore, they must arme them selues, to suffer distresse.[54]

Woodes reminds the audience of this long martyrological history in order to teach the important moral that those who profess 'the trueth of God' will inevitably suffer persecution and can distinguish themselves by their remarkable acts of resistance. In other words, profession of faith, which entails trials and tribulations, is strong proof of God's election: 'This is the

---

see Peter Happé, 'The Protestant Adaptation of the Saint Play', in Clifford Davidson (ed.), *The Saint Play in Medieval Europe* (Kalamazoo, MI, 1986), pp. 205–40.

[52] For this aspect, see Patrick Collinson, 'John Foxe and National Consciousness', in Christopher Highley and John N. King (eds), *John Foxe and His World* (Aldershot, 2002), pp. 10–34, at p. 25.

[53] Monta, *Martyrdom and Literature*, p. 117. Foxe's attempt to demonstrate martyrs' suffering as consolation for the reader is discussed in full detail by Monta (pp. 14–21).

[54] Nathaniel Woodes, *The Conflict of Conscience 1581*, ed. Herbert Davis and F. P. Wilson, Malone Society Reprints (Oxford, 1952), lines 186–99.

summe of all your talke [...] / That God doth punnish his elect to keepe their faith in ure.'[55] Foxeian martyrology is employed to encourage the audience to have the assurance of faith and identify themselves with the 'true Church' undergoing tribulation. Philologus' great fall from the glory of Protestant heroic martyrdom into the despair of apostasy will bring about the desired educational, as well as dramatic, effect. Even the alternative ending, of Philologus' reconversion, cannot seriously impair this effect.[56] The representation of Philologus as either martyr or anti-martyr is persuasive enough to impress upon the audience the real necessity for martyr-like zeal.

This Foxeian vision of *The Conflict of Conscience* may have been appealing to several aldermen. Foxe came to Norwich in 1560, at the invitation of John Parkhurst, the Bishop of Norwich, and his family stayed there for a few years.[57] This comradeship probably accounts for the martyrologist's insider episodes detailing stories about local celebrities in the first edition of *Actes and Monuments* (1563). In the 1570s, a number of eyewitnesses to Catholic persecutions during Mary's reign still survived. One of those was Thomas Sotherton, the mayor and John Aldrich's brother-in-law. His spiritual agony is sympathetically treated in the section on the burning of Elizabeth Cooper as a heretic on 13 July 1557, around which time the young Sotherton served as sheriff with his brother.[58] Sotherton seems also to have provided Foxe with materials on the martyrdom of Cicely Ormes, the wife of a worsted weaver, who was examined by Michael Dunning, chancellor of the Diocese of Norwich, on 23 July 1557. She was 'very simple', but zealous enough to show contempt for his threats and to dismiss what she had to suffer for her faith: 'Then rose he & red the bloudy sentence of conde[m]natio[n] against her, & so deliuered her to the secular power, the sherifs of the city, master T. Sutterton, & master Leonard Sutterto[n] brethre[n], who immediatly caried her to the Gildhal in Norw. wher she remained vntil her death.'[59]

Moreover, Foxe evidently had an opportunity to learn stories about several residents of Aylsham who seem to have strengthened their sense of

---

[55] *Ibid.*, lines 238–9.
[56] The second issue has an alternative ending in which the messenger joyfully announces the protagonist's reconversion to the Protestant faith. The issue was also given a new title page and a new prologue. Apparently, after the play was published, either the publisher Richard Bradocke or Woodes decided to delete the name of Francis Spira and give the play a 'comic' ending.
[57] J. F. Mozley, *John Foxe and His Book* (1940; repr. New York, 1970), p. 65.
[58] John Foxe, *Actes and Monuments of These Latter and Perillous Dayes* (London, 1563), p. 1603.
[59] *Ibid.*, p. 1618.

solidarity with fellow sufferers in Norwich by sharing their tragic experiences. One of those was Launcelot Thexton, the vicar, who was 'sore persecuted, & hys goodes muche spoyled'.[60] This Launcelot was the father of the very Robert Thexton who had obtained the Parker scholarship for Aylsham School in 1575 and who was accommodated in Chamber 6 at Corpus Christi. Later, Launcelot joined forces with Thomas Peck, the godly mayor, and John Aldrich in inviting Robert Harrison to be the master of Aylsham Grammar School in 1573. It is reported that Thexton and the inhabitants were 'well inclined to preferre thervnto one Robert Harrison graduated master of arte in Cambridge'.[61]

Woodes's ministry (and possibly his literary activities), conducted under the auspices of these godly magnates, would not allow him to forget this collective memory of Catholic persecution under the Marian regime, which was still fresh and shared by living eyewitnesses and their families. Thus, localizing *The Conflict of Conscience* in the context of Norwich in the 1570s enables us to understand both how it was imbued with such strong anti-Catholic sentiments and why it has such an intensely martyrological aspect. We can also recognize what politico-religious convictions and contentious fervour were cultivated, shared, and inflamed not only among the godly municipal authorities but also among the Norwich-oriented radical wing in the community of Corpus Christi during the mastership of Thomas Aldrich. Behind this religious enthusiasm lies the traumatic collective memory and political cautiousness embedded in eyewitness accounts such as those of Sotherton and Thexton, whose sufferings are commemorated in *Actes and Monuments*. The hostility and wariness towards Catholic revitalization supported by Foxeian martyrological discourse were the main factors that had made Norwich the seat of Protestant radicalism, driving some intellectual radicals to link Episcopalian suppression in the 1570s with the Catholic persecution of Protestants in the 1550s. This was the line of thought that the Aldrich brothers, along with other radicals, were following by censuring Matthew Parker, 'pope of Lambeth and of Benet College', and that the new master of Corpus, Robert Norgate, under Parker's guidance, subsequently had to suppress.

ROBERT NORGATE AS MASTER OF CORPUS CHRISTI COLLEGE

Robert Norgate was admitted to the fellowship of Corpus Christi in 1567, the same year that Nathaniel Woodes matriculated, and seems to have been not unconcerned with martyrs and sufferers under the Marian regime, for

---

[60] *Ibid.*, p. 1678.
[61] Houlbrooke (ed.), *Letter Book of Parkhurst*, p. 195.

he himself was born in Aylsham and was possibly a witness of persecution in his formative years. Nevertheless, he kept his distance from the religious agenda advocated by the Norwich-oriented radicals, presumably because of his intramural political position.

Under Norgate's mastership (1573–87), the enthusiastic fervour of the radical generation obviously receded into the background. This was what Matthew Parker had eagerly sought. Parker's affection for the college and enthusiasm for controlling 'precisian' excess seems to have bubbled up so vigorously that he not only assisted Norgate in his promotion to the mastership but also generously presented him to the rectory of Lackingdon in Essex in 1574.[62] This does not necessarily mean, however, that religious radicalism was eradicated from the college under Norgate's mastership. Rather, his administration placed less stress on controlling the religious opinions of fellows and scholars than on the political stability that he could secure by employing coercive and nepotistic measures. This administrative stance, while making Norgate and his henchmen strictly cautious in selecting new fellows and scholars, may have circumstantially allowed a few college members with radical tendencies, such as Robert Browne and John Greenwood, to hatch their unorthodox ideas, as long as they made no waves like the one that had subsided with the resignation of Thomas Aldrich. We might be able to include in this list Francis Kett, the college fellow who had been educated at Corpus Christi under Aldrich's mastership and who was burned alive for his Arian heresy in Norwich 1589.[63]

The mission that the new master had to carry out at Parker's command was to undermine the solidarity of Henry Aldrich and the radical remnants by filling up any vacancy, particularly of Parker's fellowships funded out of his 'purse dayly', with an appropriate, submissive fellow who stood in the moderate, godly middle. What we have seen above regarding the puzzling nature of events when Norgate elected Norwich fellows bears the imprint of such political manoeuvrings. Moreover, the religious leanings of the fellows elected to Norwich fellowships under Norgate plainly show his political intent to bring stability to the administration against factious radicals within the college. It appears that none of these Norwich fellows – John Thaxter, John Dix, and Christopher Abbys – showed any antipathy

---

[62] Masters, *History of Corpus Christi*, p. 129.
[63] There is no knowing when Kett came to adopt the unorthodox opinion of anti-trinitarianism. He dedicated to Queen Elizabeth his *The Glorious and Beautiful Garland of Mans Glorification* in 1585, in which, according to Dewey Wallace, 'hints and suggestions of Kett's later ideas' appear, particularly with regard to millenarianism. See Dewey D. Wallace, 'From Eschatology to Arian Heresy: The Case of Francis Kett', *Harvard Theological Review*, 67:4 (1974), 459–73, at p. 468.

to attaining university degrees, unlike the Aldrich brothers, and in fact all proceeded subsequently to become Bachelors of Divinity.

Thaxter, who was admitted as a fellow on 30 April 1575, seems to have had no objection to conforming to the English Church, given that he maintained a preaching, catechizing, and pastoral ministry. On resigning his fellowship in 1580, he was collated to the comparatively remunerative rectory of Bridgham St Mary, Norfolk,[64] and guided the flock of about a hundred communicants 'by means of the ancient exercise of public catechising, which he has used for six or seven years both at Cambridge and in the country, and which has proved more profitable than "other preachings"'. In a letter to Bassingbourn Gawdy, his patron and local magnate, Thaxter complains that the people have no copy of the catechism in print and cannot understand it, supposedly 'being wholly bent to the toil of manual affairs and the tilth of the ground'. He asks Gawdy to have two small catechisms printed, one for the youth and the other for more advanced students, for their edification, adding that he 'has nothing to say against other catechisms, but "every man's spittle savours best in his own mouth"'.[65]

Considering the fact that all the clergy were strongly encouraged to use 'the most ancient and laudable custom of teaching in the Church of England' on Sunday afternoons, it is possible to regard Thaxter's committed devotion to catechizing both at college and in the parish as demonstrating his allegiance to the politico-religious agenda of the Church.[66] Moreover, he seems to have enjoyed moderate success and financial stability through his church stipend. The mayor and burgesses of Thetford asked him to preach every fortnight in the town, which was at that time without a preacher, and they 'moved diu[er]se of the inhabitantes what they woulde voluntarylye gyve towardes the p[re]cher for his paynes there taken emongest them'. However, Thaxter's perceived wealth seems to have been great enough to provoke John Hillarye, a 'very disorderlye & scanderous' common councillor in Thetford, who refused to contribute towards Thaxter, and who said 'in raylinge mannor' that 'he woulde gyve nothinge neyther needeth the said p[re]cher to come Skippinge thither for lyvinge, for he had lyvinge

---

[64] For the financial resources of the rectory, see Francis Blomefield, *An Essay towards a Topographical History of the County of Norfolk* (11 vols, London, 1805–10), vol. 1, pp. 438–9.

[65] Walter Rye (ed.), *Report on the Manuscripts of the Family of Gawdy* (London, 1885), p. 23.

[66] Praise for the 'ancient and laudable custom' of the catechism was given by James I in his 'Directions concerning Preachers' (1622). See Henry Gee and William John Hardy (eds), *Documents Illustrative of English Church History* (New York, 1896), p. 517.

enoughe'.[67] These accounts concerning Thaxter allow us to imagine him to have been a moderate conformist, seeking, as other highly educated clergymen did, to maintain a decent professional lifestyle by accumulating vacant benefices.

John Dix, who succeeded to the Norwich fellowship in place of Thaxter on 1 October 1580, also followed a successful career, under the ecclesiastical regime of John Whitgift and Richard Bancroft, as a rector of St Bartholomew-by-the-Exchange and St Andrew Undershaft in London, as well as a prebendary of Bristol and St Paul's. In 1613, he bequeathed his five children the sum of more than 300 pounds and gave 'my good freind Mr Doctor Bright Parson of Wigborough in Essex one greeke Testament of Robert Stephen's print covered in black and gilt vppon the leaves as A token of my loue vnto him'.[68] The 'Mr Doctor Bright' whom he remembered with deep affection in his will is Arthur Bright, who was also a prebendary of St Paul's and described by the local parishioners of Wigborough as 'a sufficiente preacher', although 'for the moste parte non residente' and 'verie scandalous for chopinge and changeinge of benefices'.[69]

Dix had his cultural roots in Norwich, though for the latter half of his life he was based in London. As he mentioned his 'naturall Brother Thomas Dix dwellinge in St Georges of Colegate parrishe in Norwitch' in his will, we can trace his family connection with the parish up until his death. The register of St George, Colegate gives the entry of his birth in 1554 as 'John the sonne of Barnabie Dixe and Dorrathie his wife was baptized the xx[th] of December'.[70] After attending Norwich Grammar School, he was admitted to Corpus in 1570. However, it was on 19 May 1574 when he formally obtained the Norwich scholarship; his matriculation at the university was then pushed back to Easter 1575. This unusual gap of five years was possibly due to his father's poor health, for Barnabie Dix was buried on 8 August 1574. During these difficult years, John may have stayed mainly in Norwich with his family while watching out for a scholarship vacancy.

On the waiting lists for Norwich scholarships around 1574 were several other promising students at Norwich School. Christopher Abbys, later the

---

[67] TNA, STAC 5/A2/37. For the information concerning John Hillarye, I am indebted to John Craig, who has described the complicated context of the local conflict at Thetford. See his *Reformation, Politics and Polemics: The Growth of Protestantism in East Anglian Market Towns 1500–1610* (Aldershot, 2001), chap. 5.

[68] TNA, PROB 11/123/221.

[69] For the biographical information on Arthur Bright, see Brett Usher, 'The Fortunes of English Puritanism: An Elizabethan Perspective', in Kenneth Fincham and Peter Lake (eds), *Religious Politics in Post-Reformation England: Essays in Honour of Nicholas Tyacke* (Woodbridge, 2006), pp. 98–112, at p. 105, n. 41.

[70] NRO, MF/RO 44/1.

fellow who replaced Henry Aldrich, was obviously one of those candidates. The mayor and aldermen, in a letter to the college authorities dated 13 April 1574, nominated him as a new scholar, stating that they believed 'Chr[ist]ofer Abbes (who was borne in this cittie & brought vpp at Schole in the same) to be bothe forwarde in lernyng and honest and vertuosly geven, whom we know to haue small or no helpe at all of his parentes to maynteyne and fynde hym at Stody'.[71] This personal profile supports the assumption that Abbys had a good relationship with the magnates of the municipal corporation, and it also suggests that his forwardness in learning may have come to the notice of Stephen Lymbert, the puritan schoolmaster who could offer his students a channel to university. Such a mentor–protégé relationship can be detected in Robert Dallington's *A Booke of Epitaphes Made vpon the Death of the Right Worshipfull Sir William Bvttes*, to which Abbys contributed a Latin eulogy along with Lymbert, his peer John Dix, and several Norwich scholars.[72]

The close connection with local godly figures, however, did not necessarily ignite in Abbys such a fervour of hostility as his predecessor Aldrich had directed towards the archbishop and the established Church. Rather, the initial imperative for guarding against extreme radicalism seems to have set up a restrictive environment directing the Norwich fellows to pursue a policy of religious conformity. In fact, in 1588, after Norgate's death, Abbys, with the assistance and under the instruction of John Copcot, the new college master and ally of John Whitgift, assumed the reins of the college governance and expelled a fellow, Anthony Hickman, against whom Copcot was prejudiced because of Hickman's puritan leanings.[73]

Norgate was shrewd in using these personnel issues to establish his control and often did not hesitate to employ heavy-handed methods. Such tendencies made him a target for his critics, and even for the Norwich fellows, in the 1580s, when his financial mismanagement – particularly of the fund-raising for the construction of the new chapel – became apparent and drove the college to the threshold of bankruptcy.[74] The second half of his mastership was a hard period for the college community. Naturally,

---

[71] CCCA, CCCC04/S/3/3.
[72] Robert Dallington, *A Booke of Epitaphes Made vpon the Death of the Right Worshipfull Sir William Bvttes* (London, 1583), sigs A7v–A8r, B6v–B7v. Dallington, a graduate of Corpus Christi College, compiled this book, to which fellows and scholars of the college contributed eulogies of William Butts, the puritan MP for Norfolk and close friend of the Bacons. See K. J. Höltgen, 'Sir Robert Dallington (1561–1637): Author, Traveler, and Pioneer of Taste', *HLQ*, 47:3 (1984), 147–77.
[73] Lamb, *Masters' History*, p. 138.
[74] Peter Roberts, 'Dr Robert Norgate, Master of Corpus, 1573–87', *Letter of the Corpus Association*, 86 (Michaelmas, 2007), 12–22.

these financial difficulties gave the fellows and scholars an undue degree of influence. In fact, twenty-six bachelors in 1582 and twelve bachelors in 1584 (including Christopher Marlowe), respectively, donated 13*s*. 4*d*. to fund the chapel.[75] Meanwhile, the difficulties that dogged Norgate's mastership brought ongoing division and smouldering discontent into the open.

A significant target of criticism was the master's nepotistic election of fellows. In order to protect the interests of his henchmen and bring new fellows over to his side, thereby gaining political dominance in the college, it was highly convenient for Norgate to arrange the appointment of his brother William, who had just obtained his BA in 1575/6 and was seeking employment as a fellow. In the end, the master's plan turned out well, as he used William to fill the vacancy left by Robert Sayer at Michaelmas 1577. Three years later, however, several fellows of the college complained that Norgate, 'having chosen his brother to reade the humanytie lect[ure], although he have not once redd the same sithens his elecc[i]on, [...] doth suffer hym w[i]thoute expulc[i]on or other punyshemen[t]'.[76] Philip Nichols, one of those voicing their complaint and a representative of the anti-Norgate faction holding the master responsible for the large debt, offered a convincing reason for this situation: that the master 'strayghtway confesseth that he bare w[i]th [William] because he was sick one quarter, w[hi]ch is vntrue, and employed him in the Colledg busines the next quarter: so that he could never once read that lecture'.[77] Norgate himself admitted that 'I employed him in the Colledg busines in sending him to London & oth[e]r places for the Colledg benefite / & when he was at home he helped me w[i]th others of the Fellowes to make streight old rekoninges of the stywards to o[u]r great trouble'.[78] The extant document in the college archives captioned 'The Receytes & expenses which I William Norgate ame to account for about the chapel or otherwise howsoever', covering the period from April 1579 to January 1580, may be one of the products of such 'Colledg busines'.[79] The college master had succeeded, after all, in getting his own way.

This is not the only case that shows the master's political manoeuvring. In a letter to William Cecil of 14 July 1580, five fellows of the college, headed

---

[75] We can find 'Sr Marlin' in the list of donations in 1584. See CCCC06/O/22 (former reference: XXIX A22; Chapel MS K).

[76] TNA, SP, 12/141, fol. 77v. The ambitions of college heads and the administrative pressures that they were under are well illustrated by David Cressy, 'The Death of a Vice-Chancellor: Cambridge, 1632', in Mordechai Feingold (ed.), *History of Universities: Volume XXVI/2* (Oxford, 2012), pp. 92–112.

[77] TNA, SP, 12/143, fol. 116v.

[78] CCCA, CCCC02/M/18/38 (Miscellaneous Documents 1480–1700, no. 159), fol. 2v.

[79] CCCA, CCCC06/O/2.

by John Thaxter, gave Cecil their excuses for failing to elect his protégé to a fellowship, and complained about Norgate's high-handed style in the process:

> The Mr notwithstandinge who had affirmed in open chapter that he was and woulde be indifferente for his parte contrarye to this his worde hathe eyther broken or at leaste wise extreemelye stretched the statute to make one Reade a Felowe as wee suppose againste righte havinge but fowr Fellowes to the election of that Reade when as we five were earnest to pr[e]ferre yo[u]r scoller according to his worthines.[80]

The fellow referred to here is William Read, who was elected in place of Francis Kett on 14 June 1580.

Norgate seems to have been as untroubled about nepotism as Cecil. It is no wonder that he himself obtained the mastership (and possibly his fellowship as well) with the help of Matthew Parker, to whom he became related through marriage. Philip Nichols gives us further inside information about the five fellows' complaints, which were that the master

> chose Mr Reade a pensioner of the house, a rich mans sonn, who hath not had asmuch as report of mean learning, not of those w[hi]ch best favoured him: whose father gave that he might be felowe to Mr Kett xl $^{li.}$ as the report went, and Mr Kett denied not; and promised to lend monie to the Colledge.[81]

Although we should not accept this statement at face value, the decision of Norgate and his cronies may well have been strongly affected by pecuniary considerations, which were widely prevalent in universities and also among government officials.[82] In fact, it is difficult not to conclude that Read's father made a further donation of £10 towards Norgate's chapel project with an ulterior motive.[83] It is fair, however, to consider the claim of the master, who had meticulously prepared his defence:

> I w[i]th a sufficient nomb[e]r of the fellowes vpon lett[e]rs commendatory; fro[m] the right Honorable my Lord Treasurer, the Earle of Sussex, Sr Chr[ist]ofer Hatton, Sr James Crofts, Sr Fraunces Walsingh[a]m & Mr Doctor Wilson, of one Mr Read mast[e]r of Arts did elect & admitt the

---

[80] TNA, SP, 12/108, fol. 130r. This document is misidentified as being from 1576 but can definitely be dated to 1580, as it contains the signatures of the fellows incumbent in that year: John Thaxter, Moses Fowler, Philip Nichols, Thomas Harris, and Nicholas Bate.
[81] TNA, SP, 12/143, fol. 115v.
[82] Morgan, *History of the University of Cambridge*, pp. 353–8.
[83] Masters, *History of Corpus Christi*, p. 212.

sayd Mr Read in respect of his woorthines, into a Felloweship of this Colledg lawefullye according to the statute.[84]

These documents not only suggest that Norgate, though poor in management skills, was a man of political astuteness, but also eloquently illustrate how the strength of factional networks pervaded every aspect of daily college life. In the 1580s, almost all the fellows at Corpus had been involved to a greater or lesser degree in political infighting, which was first caused by radicalism within the college and then by the financial mismanagement and political interests of the college master. Norgate's undisguised favouritism naturally created dissatisfaction among the college fellows, some of whom took aggressive measures in response, such as lodging objections against the master with the university authorities and trying to evict his supporters from the college. It was this strained atmosphere that permeated the faculty in the college where Marlowe studied and lived.

ROBERT GREENE AND THE GODLY FACTION OF NORWICH

One final important player associated with the Norwich faction was Robert Greene, who, although he was a scholar at St John's College, had long-term links to the local network of Norwich old boys at Corpus Christi and had easy access to their sources of information. As we will see in Chapter 9, Greene constructed his narrative identity by recourse to Norwich puritanism in *The Repentance of Robert Greene* (1592) and became the mythmaker of Marlowe's 'atheism'. It is therefore worth exploring the possible origins of his prejudice against and rivalry with Marlowe in the network of Norwich relationships that formed across Cambridge in the 1570s.

In *Repentance*, Greene offers a brief sketch of his parents: 'I neede not make long discourse of my parentes, who for their grauitie and honest life [were] well knowne and esteemed amongst their neighbors; namely, in the Cittie of Norwitch, where I was bred and borne.' According to him, his highly regarded father was genuinely enthusiastic about his own child's education: 'my Father had care to haue mee in my Non-age brought vp at schoole, that I might through the studie of good letters grow to be a frend to my self, a profitable member to the common-welth, and a comfort to him in his age.'[85] The school that Greene refers to is undoubtedly Norwich Grammar School, which was then affiliated with the Great Hospital under the supervision of the Mayor and Court of Aldermen.

---

[84] TNA, SP, 12/143, fol. 114r. See also CCCA, CCCC02/M/18/38 (Miscellaneous Document 1480–1700, no. 159), fol. 1r–v.

[85] Alexander B. Grosart (ed.), *The Life and Complete Works in Prose and Verse of Robert Greene* (15 vols, 1881–6; repr. New York, 1964), vol. 12, p. 171.

The Great Hospital's account rolls, now in the Norfolk Record Office, provide a vivid image of both the finances and the administration of the hospital at that time.[86] They chronicle the annual revenues from rectories, manors, and other properties, as well as disbursements for rents, salaries, rewards, and repair work. Because the hospital provided funds for operating the school and for scholarships, the accounts also include payments to the schoolmaster and the usher (assistant master) of the grammar school, and the annuity to Corpus Christi College out of the manors belonging to the hospital. Moreover, the Great Hospital, occasionally at the request of local magnates, gave financial support to poor students of the school to study at Cambridge.

The school was granted five scholarships at Corpus Christi College and six at Gonville and Caius College. Obtaining one of these scholarships was the best way for a candidate to secure his livelihood, but it was a difficult route to follow even for a very talented candidate, as the number of scholarships was vastly insufficient for an institution with more than ninety children.[87] Since scholarships were to be held for at least a few years, they were not always vacant. Stephen Lymbert, the master of the school, and Greene's family were neighbours in the parish of St George, Tombland in 1571, and so Lymbert might have encouraged young Greene to go on to the university.[88] Greene could have been named, as were John Dix and Christopher Abbys, in the waiting list for Norwich scholarships, but seems to have been left out, presumably because of his relatively junior status. Since his seniors and classmates had occupied all five scholarships for Norwich schoolboys by 1574, Greene had to give up his hopes of obtaining a scholarship at Corpus Christi. Fortunately, however, the exhibition from the Great Hospital and possibly his local connections opened the way to St John's College in the following year.

Greene was provided with an unusual allowance to study in Cambridge. The entry can be found only once, in the account roll of 1575–76: 'It[e]m

[86] The history of the Great Hospital's administration is well documented by Carole Rawcliffe in her *Medicine for the Soul*, pp. 65–102, 215–39. See also Ellie Phillips, 'Account Rolles of the Great Hospital, Norwich, 1549–50 and 1570–71', in Ellie Phillips and Isla Fay (eds), *Health and Hygiene in Early-Modern Norwich* (Norwich, 2013), pp. 1–104.

[87] For these scholarships, see H. W. Saunders, *A History of the Norwich Grammar School* (Norwich, 1932), pp. 169–73; Masters, *History of Corpus Christi*, pp. 200–1; John Venn, *Biographical History of Gonville and Caius College 1349–1897* (3 vols, Cambridge, 1897), vol. 3, p. 227.

[88] Under the heading of St George Tombland in parochial assessments of weekly payments to the poor from 1570 to 1571 we can find both 'Mr Limberd' and Greene's father receiving alms. See NRO, NCR 20c/2, 'The Mayor's Booke of the Poore', 1570–71.

in Reward gyven to Robert Grene the soone of Robert Grene Sadler toward his exhibic[i]on at Cambridge as by A warrant sygned by M[aste]r Mayor and certeyne Justyces maye appeere — xx^s.'[89] This document reveals how the Great Hospital gave pecuniary assistance to Robert Greene, a saddler's son, on the command of William Ferrour, the mayor at that time, and some prominent aldermen of the Mayor's Court. The 'reward' came in a timely manner for Greene to matriculate at St John's on 26 November 1575. But why did he attend that college, which had no connection with Norwich Grammar School? This question once led Kenneth Mildenberger to hypothesize that one Robert Greene, who matriculated at Corpus Christi in Easter 1573, was actually the writer, who later migrated to St John's in 1575. As Johnstone Parr points out, however, 'there was never a need to matriculate *twice*'.[90] Moreover, it is improbable that the son of a humble saddler would matriculate at Corpus Christi at the age of fourteen. Hence, the Robert Greene at Corpus is likely to have been a different person.

Greene's entrance to St John's certainly seems to be anomalous, but not so 'curious' as to undermine his identification as the saddler's boy in the document. It is noteworthy, though, that scholarship vacancies were rare at this time. All five scholarships to Corpus Christi were occupied by either Greene's seniors (Henry Gold, Henry Golding, and Thomas Plombe) or his classmates (Christopher Abbys and John Dix). It was in the Easter term of 1578 that Henry Golding turned over his position to William Becket, another waiting candidate.[91] The situation at Gonville and Caius College may have been similar, for at least six students from Norwich Grammar School matriculated from 1571 to 1574, and no entry from Norwich can be found between May 1574 and April 1576.[92] No doubt a rush of applicants deprived Greene of a good opportunity. He thus had to seek an alternative, entering as a sizar; that is, an undergraduate member who earns his living by performing menial services for the college and with the help of parent and benefactor assistance. It may have been desirable for him to matriculate

---

[89] NRO, NCR 24a/48, God's House Collector and Receiver's Annual Accounts, June 1575–June 1576, fol. 10v. I first drew attention to this document in 'Robert Greene Nordovicensis, the Saddler's Son', *N&Q*, 53:4 (2006), 432–6. John Churton Collins identified Robert Greene as the son of the saddler in the parish in *The Plays and Poems of Robert Greene* (2 vols, Oxford, 1905), vol. 1, pp. 12, 13–14. Later, Brenda Richardson, 'Robert Greene's Yorkshire Connexions: A New Hypothesis', *Yearbook of English Studies*, 10 (1980), 160–80, argued for the possibility that Greene was the son of the cordwainer-turned-innkeeper and spent his formative years in Yorkshire.

[90] Kenneth Mildenberger, 'Robert Greene at Cambridge', *Modern Language Notes*, 66:8 (1951), 546–9; Johnston Parr, 'Robert Greene and His Classmates at Cambridge', *PMLA*, 77:5 (1962), 536–43, at p. 542, emphasis in original.

[91] CCCA, Audit Book 1550–80, 3a trimestri of 1578.

[92] Venn, *Biographical History*, vol. 1, pp. 68–85.

at Corpus or Caius, where many childhood friends had boarded. Nevertheless, which college he was forwarded to was contingent upon the channels provided by the local networks of his schoolteachers and benefactors. In fact, the aldermen John Aldrich and Robert Suckling sent their sons to Trinity College.

It was not only because Greene successfully appealed to his schoolteachers and benefactors on account of his talents that the Great Hospital decided to give him financial support. In the local network of the community, ties of friendship between patron and client were often woven tightly within the political or religious commitments they shared.[93] The special allowance for Greene from the hospital also suggests that some influential aldermen and/or schoolteachers involved in its administration felt an ideological affinity with or sympathy towards his family. In fact, the relationship between Greene's father and the aldermen of the hospital seems to have been long-standing and congenial. They leased the hospital's property in Tombland to Greene's father at four shillings for a year's 'ferme'; that is, the fixed yearly rent:

> Of Robert Grene Sadler for the whoalle yeres ferme of A piece of an old hows adioyneng to the charnell and p[ar]cell of the same letten to hym by Indenture from My[chael]m[a]s 1564 for xxx yeres This beeyng the xixth yere of his terme And he to paye yerely therefor at our Ladye and Mychaellmas — iiij^s.[94]

This act may be aligned with Greene's own description that his parents were respected for 'their grauitie and honest life'. Although there is no conclusive proof that Greene's family was known to William Ferrour, the mayor, we can argue that Greene was acquainted, at the very least, with some of the aldermen who were influential in the hospital's decisions, such as Thomas Sotherton and Francis Rugge, his relative and an alderman of East Wymer Ward, to which Greene's parish of St George, Tombland belonged.

Both Sotherton and Rugge were also members of St Andrew's church, where Greene received divine inspiration. On his deathbed, Greene recalled a few people to whom he felt a special obligation. Along with his parents

---

[93] On the close politico-religious relationship, see A. Hassell Smith, *County and Court: Government and Politics in Norfolk 1558–1603* (Oxford, 1974), pp. 201–28; Victor Morgan, 'Cambridge University and "the Country"', in Lawrence Stone (ed.), *The University in Society: Oxford and Cambridge from the 14th to the Early 19th Century*, (Princeton, 1975), pp. 183–245; and Craig, *Reformation, Politics and Polemics*, pp. 114–32.

[94] NRO, NCR 24a/55 (1582-3), fol. 4r. Another entry detailing the lease to Greene's father in 1570–71 is transcribed by Ellie Phillips in Phillips and Fay (eds), *Health and Hygiene in Early-Modern Norwich*, p. 52.

and his wife, a minister from his native city is specifically mentioned in his *Repentance*:

> And this inward motion I receiued in Saint Andrews Church in the Cittie of Norwich, at a Lecture or Sermon then preached by a godly learned man, whose doctrine, and the maner of whose teaching, I liked wonderfull well: yea (in my conscience) such was his singlenes of hart, and zeale in his doctrine, that he might haue conuerted [me] the most monster [sinner] of the world.[95]

This godly minister was undoubtedly John More, 'the Apostle of Norwich'.[96] More was appointed as minister of St Andrew's around 1573. Although it is impossible to reconstruct the precise circumstances of his collation, it cannot have been realized without the friendly assistance of Thomas Sotherton, an influential puritan alderman who had held the advowson of the church and who was, as noted above, one of the eyewitnesses whom John Foxe mentions in *Actes and Monuments*.[97] William Burton gives evidence in a sermon that the puritan congregation at St Andrew's was so devout that it earned a local nickname, 'Saint *Andrewes* birds', for its early morning devotion to preaching, psalm-singing, and prayer.[98]

In January 1574, just after John More's arrival, his brother Miles obtained the post of assistant master of Norwich Grammar School.[99] As in John's case, this employment seems to have been offered to Miles under the auspices of the puritan aldermen of the church, for Thomas Sotherton himself was one of the surveyors of the Great Hospital from 1573 to 1574. Sotherton's sizeable influence over the hospital administration can readily be imagined once we become aware that Thomas Layer, his close relative and himself a powerful alderman of St Andrew's, secured the surveyor's post in the same year.[100] We can imagine this newly appointed assistant master at the school setting up university channels for the sake of its poor but highly talented students. It is plausible that Miles More could have exploited his family contacts. His brother John was perfect for the role of

---

[95] Grosart (ed.), *Works of Greene*, vol. 12, p. 175.

[96] For John More, Thomas Sotherton, and their confreres, I am greatly indebted to Reynolds, *Godly Reformers*, pp. 39–85.

[97] See above, pp. 49–50.

[98] William Burton, *A Sermon Preached in the Cathedrall Church in Norwich, the xxi. Day of December, 1589* (London, 1590), sig. G4v.

[99] In his will dated 20 November 1591, John More bequeaths to 'my brother Miles More a ringe of xl^s' and to 'my brothers daughter Ellyn Moore dwellinge w[i]th me xl^s'. See NRO, NCC 371 Andrewes.

[100] Thomas Hawes (ed.), *An Index to Norwich City Officers 1453–1835* (Norwich, 1989), pp. 95 and 142. John Sotherton, Thomas's younger brother, also held the office of surveyor, from 1570 to 1574.

fixer, since he had enjoyed a close connection with influential members of the university. John matriculated at Christ's College in May 1560 and held the college fellowship from 1568 to 1572. Moreover, from around 1575 he happened to have a close connection with St John's, as his former classmate and teaching colleague at Christ's was the master of the college at that time.

This worthy friend was John Still, who matriculated at Christ's in November 1559, and who, on resigning from the fellowship with More in 1572, held the mastership of St John's from 1574 to 1577. Since both Still and More put their signatures to the petitions for Thomas Cartwright in 1570, it is likely that they shared sympathy for radical Protestants during their days at Christ's College.[101] These petitions also contain the names of Edmund Chapman, later prebendary of Norwich (1569–76), and, as we have seen, Thomas Aldrich, nephew of Thomas Sotherton and the Master of Corpus Christi. Thus, the networks of the new usher of Norwich Grammar School and the puritan faction of St Andrew's could have forwarded Robert Greene to St John's with an extraordinary pension from the budget of the Great Hospital. Greene's last panegyric may have been an acknowledgement of his indebtedness to John More and the godly members of St Andrew's. Finally, these networks show that young Robert Greene probably grew up in an environment far more religiously radical than we might originally have expected.

A promising young student on a full or partial scholarship would have been financially and educationally monitored by the municipal council authorities and encouraged to share the religious and political orientation of his benefactors. To ensure that newcomers measured up to their expectations, the college fellows and senior students of common local origins kept their eyes on them and guided them. The resulting networks provided not only the city magnates but also the fellows and students with local communication channels through which both direct and hearsay information was freely passed on and shared. When Greene, with his stipend from the Great Hospital, came to Cambridge in 1575, his seniors and classmates from Norwich Grammar School gathered in a cluster at Corpus Christi College. Henry Aldrich, the fellow in charge of the Norwich scholars, besides being Thomas Sotherton's nephew was the brother-in-law of Francis Rugge. Both John Dix and Christopher Abbys, Greene's senior classmates, were under Aldrich's supervision, and when Greene obtained his BA in 1580, Dix and Abbys secured the fellowships of Corpus. Although resident at St John's as a sizar, Greene was almost certainly connected to this old-boy network, through which a variety of information was channelled from and to him.

---

[101] John Strype, *Annals of the Reformation*, vol. 2, part 2 (Oxford, 1824), pp. 412–17.

Yet this close relationship to established networks might have become the cause of Greene's uneasiness and guilt, because he soon fell short of the benefactors' expectations, as he says: 'at the Vniuersitie of Cambridge, I light amongst wags as lewd as my selfe, with whome I consumed the flower of my youth'.[102] The fact that he was provided only once, in 1575/6, with the exhibition of the Great Hospital might suggest a weakening of his relationship with the radical puritans. We should remember, however, that there were students other than Greene who had only obtained a one-off exhibition. Moreover, his psychological links to Norwich seem to have remained continuous, for, shortly before or after his commencement to MA in 1583, he went back to Norwich and underwent the religious conversion described above. Several biographers believe that Greene quite possibly lived his married life from 1584 to 1586 in Norwich.[103] After their separation, Greene says that his wife 'went into Lincolneshire, and I to London', which points to their residence having initially been at Greene's place of birth.[104]

The intermittent but close association with the godly faction of Norwich seems to have been strong enough to develop Greene's puritan mindset, which we can discern in the autobiographical narrative of his repentance pamphlets. The spiritual advice both of 'a welwiller' living at Aldersgate Street and of his pious, caring friends, who tried to persuade him to abandon his bad course of life and so avoid 'the second death, & the losse of your soule', certainly represents such religious enthusiasm among the godly in Norwich.[105] The old-boy network of Norwich Grammar School provides us with some vivid glimpses into the local context of his conversion narrative in *The Repentance of Robert Greene* and, furthermore, into his defamatory allegations against Marlowe; but this is a point to be more closely considered later, in Chapter 9.

---

[102] Grosart (ed.), *Works of Greene*, vol. 12, p. 172.
[103] See *ibid.*, vol. 1, p. 16, n. 9; and Collins (ed.), *Plays and Poems of Greene*, vol. 1, p. 22.
[104] Grosart (ed.), *Works of Greene*, vol. 12, p. 177.
[105] *Ibid.*, vol. 12, pp. 163–4.

Chapter 2

MARLOWE IN THE COMMUNITY OF CANTERBURY SCHOLARS

'THE STUDENTS SHALL BE BRAVELY CLAD'

> And now suppose, sweet lady, you see me set forth like a poor scholar to the university, not on horseback but in Hobson's waggon, and all my pack contained in less than a little hood-box; my books not above four in number, and those four were very needful ones too.[1]

To a poor newcomer, collegiate life would not necessarily have seemed to be filled with the bliss of adolescence. At college, a little commonwealth in itself, he had to face the harshness of a real world in which social divisions among the student body reflected those of a strongly class-conscious society at large. In the Elizabethan period, sons of the propertied class went up to Oxford and Cambridge in large numbers in search of social advancement. Certainly, as pointed out by Lawrence Stone, the influx of so many wealthy students opened the door for education to the poor more than ever before, because 'the presence of these wealthy Fellow-Commoners meant that a certain amount of personal charity was distributed among the poor students in the Colleges'.[2] Even so, this trickle-down effect must have been very difficult for a poor student to experience on a daily basis and he would consequently have been forced to suppress his mixed feelings of envy and contempt towards wealthier students. He may have salvaged his pride by devoting himself to his classical studies, as can be observed in Thomas Middleton's 'The Ant's Tale', in which the narrator recollects his collegiate days as a 'servitor to some Londoner's son': 'Now as for study and books, I

---

[1] Thomas Middleton, *Father Hubburd's Tales* (London, 1604), ed. Adrian Weiss, in Gary Taylor and John Lavagnino (eds), *Thomas Middleton: The Collected Works* (Oxford, 2007), pp. 149–82, at p. 180.

[2] Lawrence Stone, 'The Educational Revolution in England, 1560–1640', *Past & Present*, 28 (1964), 41–80, at p. 67.

had the use of my young master's, for he was all day a courtier in the tennis-court tossing of balls instead of books, and only holding disputation with the court-keeper how many dozen he was in.'[3]

Salvaged pride could more or less relieve a poor student of the psychological burden of his social inferiority, but not the financial one. Masters and fellows were often lenient with young men in affluent circumstances; in contrast, a poor student was in the disadvantageous position of being economically weak, mercilessly pursued for payment, and, in some cases, even exploited by fellows and creditors. In a letter of admonition addressed to Cambridge in 1587, William Cecil, Lord Burghley, the university chancellor, wrote that he was informed of a 'great complainte of divers both worshipfull and wise parentes':

> that thorowe the great stipendes of tutors and the little paines they doe take in the instructinge and well-governinge of their puples, not onely the poorer sorte are not able to maintaine their children at the Universitie, and the ritcher be soe corrupte with libertie and remissnes, so that the tutour is more afrayed to displease his puple thorowe the desire of greate gaine, the which he haith by his tutorage, then the puple is of his tutour, that their parentes dothe greatly complaine both of the losse of their childrens tyme and of the greatnes of their charges, as well in tutour stipende as in their sumptuous apparrell.[4]

In this acquisitive society, it was imperative for poor scholars to secure assistance from parents or patrons, and they often had to work as menial servants for fellow-commoners. If they fell into more desperate straits and needed to pay for living and school expenses, they were frequently compelled, with bitter unhappiness, to pawn necessaries such as clothes and books.

A good case in point is Stephen Church, who entered King's School, Canterbury in Christmas 1580,[5] and matriculated as a sizar of Corpus Christi in 1584. Considering his schooling, it is highly probable that he was on familiar terms with Marlowe. Church was not as fortunate as his peer in obtaining a scholarship, and got into financial trouble around 1587, when he wrote to Burghley:

> seeinge it hath pleased allmightie god of his good providence to depriue me of myne only Patron Mr Absolon who was my sole & only Patron I had to mayntayne me in the Uniuersitie of Cambridge: whose death is

---

[3] Middleton, *Father Hubburd's Tales*, p. 180.
[4] James Heywood and Thomas Wrights (eds), *Cambridge University Transactions during the Puritan Controversies of the 16th and 17th Centuries* (2 vols, London, 1854), vol. 1, p. 500.
[5] CCAL, MS DCc MA 41, fols 13r.

such a loste vnto me that if it please not allmightie god to rayse me vp some other in his steade I muste be fayne to goe & sell such bookes & other necessaries as I haue to discharge my Tutor beinge in his deett for the space of this 3 quarters of this yeare xls: & so departe to my greate hinderance & vtter discredditt which will be a greate greefe vnto my power Parentes beinge not able to helpe me in this my greate wante & necessitie.[6]

This 'Mr Absolon' can be identified as William Absalon, who was headmaster of King's School (1565–66) and of Sandwich School (1570–72), and master chaplain of the Savoy (1576–86). He was close to leading figures in Canterbury, including Matthew Parker, the Archbishop of Canterbury, and Roger Manwood, the MP for Sandwich. John Lyly, another Canterbury man, probably also knew Absalon well and even studied under his supervision, if, as William Urry suggests, Lyly had attended King's School as a fellow-commoner.[7]

How Church came to be acquainted with Absalon is not clear, but it can be readily imagined that local or school contacts did make a difference. Since means of communication were still underdeveloped in Elizabethan society, information was naturally circulated on a regional basis. In this respect, local connections were much more significant and effective than today for finding patrons, as well as uncovering talented students. Church, who had to wait for an opportunity to get a scholarship, may have found favour with Absalon through his Canterbury contacts, and was subsequently admitted to the college. However, Absalon's death prevented him from raising funds to pay the stipend, leaving him no alternative but to pawn his books and necessaries and to beg the chancellor for some kind of support.

In the famous soliloquy at the beginning of *Doctor Faustus*, Faustus, dreaming of the 'desperate enterprise' he will launch, says, 'I'll have them fill the public schools with silk, / Wherewith the students shall be bravely clad'.[8] What impression would this speech have made on university students? Certainly, on a superficial level, it may have sounded subversive in its call to defy the university dress code forbidding all students but doctors from

---

[6] BL, Lansdowne MS 54 (12), fol. 29r.

[7] For Lyly's attendance at King's School and the Savoy, see Albert Feuillerat, *John Lyly: Contribution a l'histoire de la Renaissance en Angleterre* (Cambridge, 1910), pp. 42–3; D. L. Edwards, *A History of the King's School Canterbury* (London, 1957), pp. 75, 201; and William Urry, 'John Lyly and Canterbury', *Friends of Canterbury Cathedral Annual Report*, 33 (1960), 19–25, at p. 24.

[8] Christopher Marlowe, *Doctor Faustus*, ed. David Bevington and Eric Rasmussen, *The Revels Plays* (Manchester, 1992), A-text, I.i.92–3.

wearing silk.[9] It seems, however, that at a deeper level Faustus promises to emancipate them from their hard life of debt. To a poor student, living under harsh economic circumstances, being 'bravely clad' meant, above all, that he had readily redeemable goods set aside in case of emergency. He could raise cash, where necessary, by pawning his sumptuous clothing.

But in reality it was hardly possible to find a Faustus-like hero: one who would provide rich goods to pay off their debts. Poor students came into contact with townsfolk when they were forced to pawn (often at an extortionate rate) their doublets, gowns, 'knit hoses', featherbeds, sheets, books, and other necessaries to obtain living expenses and stipends to pay their tutors. Small wonder that we sometimes find students accused of failure to pay debts, or tutors appealing on behalf of their pupils against acquisitive traders who had taken security in exchange for pitifully small sums of cash. In fact, Church, presumably having obtained only lukewarm support from Burghley, found himself in deadlock with the college and left the university without taking a degree.

THE BAND OF POOR SCHOLARS

On 5 March 1584, a contentious case arose between a John Marley of Cambridge, gentleman, and a cook named Nevill Hayes, which came before Andrew Perne, the deputy of the vice-chancellor at the vice-chancellor's court.[10] This case originated from a trifling incident when Marley lent his cloak ('toga') to William Austen, a BA of Corpus Christi College. Marley appears to have been acquainted with Austen for some years, and, according to his testimony, he had bought the cloak from Austen's father in Canterbury.[11] Whether Austen borrowed it to get through the cold winter, or as a pledge, we do not know. What is certain is that Austen was in such financial difficulty around this time that he was forced to pawn the cloak to Hayes, with the consent of his friends and tutor. Hayes testified that Austen pledged the cloak to him and his wife for 13s. 4d. in cash and 13s. 4d. worth of food. It

---

[9] See, for example, *ibid.*, p. 116, n. 92.

[10] CUA, Collect. Admin. 6a [Caryl B. 24], Buckle Book, p. 267. For details, see Appendix 3. This case was first discussed in my article 'Christopher Marlowe, William Austen, and the Community of Corpus Christi College', *Studies in Philology*, 104:1 (2007), 56–81.

[11] John Marley cannot be identified. 'John Merlyn', a surgeon in Cambridge who was in litigation over a debt against a James Forester at the commissary's court in 1581, appears frequently. However, this surgeon was French and had previously been at Wisbech. See CUA, Act Books, Comm. Ct. I. 1, fol. 43r, and Comm. Ct. II. 1, fols 17r–18v.

seems, however, that Austen neglected to inform Marley that he had pawned the cloak; or perhaps he had made a secret of the fact that the cloak was borrowed, which caused problems for Austen's associates in due course.

In fact, Austen must have had some difficulty raising funds from the beginning, for, although his matriculation as pensioner took place during the Easter term of 1578, it was only in the Easter term of 1580, two years later, that he became a scholar.[12] Since the bursar's account (Audit Book) preserved in the college archives records not only payments to the scholars but also the source of revenue of each scholarship, we can learn that Austen was a scholar maintained by the revenue of Eastbridge Hospital in Canterbury. This scholarship was founded by Matthew Parker in 1569, with the stipulation that 'The Master of the Hospital and the Dean of *Canterbury* have the nomination of these [scholars], without any other Restrictions, than that the Lads must be of their School and Natives of *Kent*'.[13] According to Marley's testimony, Austen came from Canterbury, but his name cannot be found in any of the surviving cathedral accounts that record the quarterly allowances to King's School scholars; he may have obtained an education at one of the free schools in the city.[14] During the hardship of his first two years he would have had to turn to his parents or some local benefactor for financial help. Even if a patron had lent him support, however, it would not have been enough to secure a stable livelihood. In a similar case, Christopher Goffe of Norwich matriculated as a sizar at Corpus Christi in 1577 and, unable to obtain a scholarship, sold off his 'three pairs of knit hose' for fifteen shillings two years later.[15] It would not have been long before Austen similarly learned about the world the hard way.

After receiving an Eastbridge scholarship in 1580, Austen's living conditions would have been much improved by an allowance of twelve pence per week for commons. In this case, his straitened circumstances in early 1584 are the more puzzling. They may have resulted from the fact that, after receiving his bachelor's degree in 1583, he was rarely resident at the university. According to the Audit Book, he received only three shillings in the Easter term of 1583, two shillings in Michaelmas 1583, nothing in the Lent term of 1583–84 (this time the Audit Book clearly indicates that he was

---

[12] CCCA, CCCC02/B/4, Audit Book 1550–80, 3a trimestri 1580.
[13] Robert Masters, *The History of the College of Corpus Christi* (Cambridge, 1753–55), p. 202.
[14] William Urry provides abundant evidence for the existence of such small free schools in 'Some Forgotten Schools in Tudor Canterbury', in M. H. A. Berry and J. H. Higginson (eds), *Canterbury Chapters: A Kentish Heritage for Tomorrow* (Liverpool, 1976), pp. 98–105.
[15] CUA, Collect. Admin. 6a [Caryl B. 24], Buckle Book, p. 49.

absent), and nothing again in Easter 1584.[16] This may be the reason why we cannot find any testimony by Austen on his own behalf in the court records. It is not uncommon to find such instances of 'absentee' men. In theory, they would have been beginning the next stage of their studies, but in practice they might not have wished to pursue their degrees if they had been offered more congenial employment. Austen was no doubt busy seeking work at that time, and his financial difficulty may have been due to the cost of transportation, lodging, and food.

It is natural to think that Austen's financial hardship would have been closely monitored by his tutor, for, as Mark H. Curtis points out, one of a tutor's most important tasks was to oversee the finances of his pupils, to the extent that 'Some tutors received their scholars' allowances and personally supervised how they spent them'.[17] As William Vaughan, an Oxford graduate and author of *The Golden-Grove, Moralized in Three Bookes* (1600), remarked, one of '[t]he qualities of a good Tutour' should be that 'hee haue an especiall care and respect to his scholers battles, lest that by permitting them to spend what they please, he incurre the displeasure of the parents, and so hazard his credit'.[18] In the litigation over the cloak, therefore, a representative for Austen's tutor, Samuel Beadle (referred to as 'Beale' in the Act Book), appeared at court. Beadle came from King's School, Canterbury and was a Bachelor of Corpus Christi at that time.

The tutor who had to supervise Austen's finances was Robert Thexton, a Master of Arts from Aylsham, presumably three or four years Austen's senior. Beadle testified that Thexton, unable to appear at court because of illness, was definitely Austen's tutor. Although there is no way of knowing what kind of illness Thexton had, he might have been too seriously incapacitated at that time to perform sensitive tasks as a fellow. On 26 February 1583, while a production was being staged at Pembroke Hall, Miles Mosse, a Master of Arts with strong puritan leanings, had struck and injured Thexton's head, shedding blood, an assault for which Mosse was imprisoned in the Tolbooth and fined 3s. 4d.[19] Thexton might have still been suffering from the after-effects of the injury at the time he was required to appear at court,

---

[16] CCCA, CCCC02/B/5, Audit Book 1578–90, 3a trimestri 1583, 1a trimestri 1584, 2a trimestri 1584, and 3a trimestri 1584.

[17] Mark H. Curtis, *Oxford and Cambridge in Transition 1558–1642* (Oxford, 1959), p. 79.

[18] William Vaughan, *The Golden-Groue, Moralized in Three Books* (London, 1600), sig. X5r.

[19] CUA, Collect. Admin. 6a [Caryl B. 24], Buckle Book, p. 228. See also Alan Nelson (ed.), *Cambridge*, REED (2 vols, Toronto, 1989), vol. 1, p. 308. For Mosse's puritan leanings, see John S. Craig, 'The "Cambridge Boies": Thomas Rogers and the "Brethren" in Bury St Edmunds', in Susan Wabuda and Caroline Litzenberger (eds),

and it is probably no mere coincidence that he resigned his fellowship on 26 February 1584, exactly one year after the date of the injury. He was likely not well enough to check on and deal promptly with his pupil's negligence in financial matters, which in turn would have been an important contributing factor in the conflict that arose between Marley and Hayes.

Austen's position as a student may have considerably restricted his sphere of contact to the few townsfolk whom he felt unembarrassed about asking for a loan. Moreover, the master and fellows were no doubt concerned about protecting their students from extortionate moneylenders. It is likely, therefore, that Nevill Hayes and his wife were people with whom Austen and the members of his college were closely acquainted. In fact, Hayes was a cook who belonged to the society of Corpus Christi College, not a professional moneylender.[20] By approaching him, Austen was able to secure financial backing from within the local community. It is easy to imagine that there was financial interdependence and even friendship between the family of the cook and the poor scholars of the college. Such an instance of town–gown interdependence can be observed in a case against the cook of Clare Hall: on 16 August 1576, the proctors of the university took legal proceedings against him for receiving scholars into his house to eat, drink, and spend the night.[21] In spite of a number of extant documents suggesting that there was violent conflict between town and gown, it is necessary, as Alexandra Shepard argues, to be guarded about accepting at face value the contemporary rhetoric on the division between them, instead acknowledging 'the more complex reality of relations' within the community. In particular, the commercial interests of both sides 'were deeply enmeshed, with the university heavily dependent on the town for its provisions and the town likewise reliant on the university for a significant portion of its livelihood'.[22]

Belief and Practice in Reformation England: A Tribute to Patrick Collinson from His Students (Aldershot, 1998), pp. 163–75.

[20] Hayes's name appears for the first time in an entry for 1580 as 'Et pro fe[o]do Nevill Hayes coci superior [...] x^s' (CCCA, CCCC02/B/4, Audit Book 1550–80, la trimestri 1580). Although he was not a moneylender, illegal gambling might have been one of the sources of his income. See Hilton Kelliher, 'Francis Beaumont and Nathan Field: New Records of Their Early Years', in Peter Beal (ed.), *English Manuscript Studies 1100–1700, Volume 8: Seventeenth-Century Poetry, Music and Drama* (London, 2000), pp. 1–42, at pp. 16–17, 36–7.

[21] CUA, Collect. Admin. 13, *Utinam*, fol. 257v. Clare Hall was the original name of Clare College, and not to be confused with the twentieth-century foundation of the same name.

[22] Alexandra Shepard, 'Contesting Communities? "Town" and "Gown" in Cambridge, c. 1560–1640', in Alexandra Shepard and Phil Withington (eds), *Communities in*

Misfortunes never come alone. William Austen was in need again in 1587, a year after he took his Master's degree, when he was served with a claim by Richard Gee, a victualler, for reimbursement of 18*s*. 4*d*. due for victuals.[23] As noted above, he seems to have been seldom resident at the college after obtaining his BA in the spring of 1583, his absence probably caused by having to seek remunerative employment. It was possible for Eastbridge scholars to retain their scholarships for up to six years; in fact, all the Eastbridge scholars of Austen's generation (i.e. Brian Exton, William Lawse, Mark Graceborough, and Benjamin Charier)retained their scholarships for more than three years and still earned Master's degrees. In Austen's case, he held his for four years, until the Easter term of 1584, and then gave it up to Charier, a King's scholar of Canterbury. In the middle of May that year, Austen's name was deleted from the Buttery Book.[24] Since a few students appear in the register even after giving up their scholarships, this deletion implies that Austen was recognized as having left Cambridge and proceeded to the next stage of his life.

However, Austen's name appears again in the Buttery Book in late February 1586, and he is described as 'Mr. Austen' one month later upon obtaining his Master's degree.[25] It is not clear how he was able to get his degree without being resident at the university. However, a university decree of 1608 states that bachelors seeking an MA were 'not so strictly tied to a local commorancy and study in the University and Town of Cambridge', and so we may reasonably assume that he was still hoping to obtain his degree. He may have brought with him the requisite certificates of good conduct signed by 'three preaching ministers' upon returning to university.[26] Austen's relinquishment of the scholarship and his later return may have been due to severe financial difficulties or, more likely, his reluctance to take holy orders. It is not surprising that he fell into debt once again, either before or after earning his Master's degree.

Although Richard Gee cannot be easily identified, it is probable that he was a victualler who had a business relationship with Nevill Hayes, and that Austen had become acquainted with him through this college cook.[27] We

---

Early Modern England: Networks, Place, Rhetoric (Manchester, 2000), pp. 216–34, at p. 228.
[23] CUA, Collect. Admin. 6a [Caryl B. 24], Buckle Book, p. 438 (7 April 1587).
[24] CCCA, CCCC02/S/33, Buttery Book 1582–86, septimana post annuntiationis 7a, 1584.
[25] *Ibid.*, septimana post nativitatis domini 9a, 1585–6, and septimana annuntiationis, 1586.
[26] David Masson, *The Life of John Milton* (7 vols, Cambridge, 1859), vol. 1, pp. 120–1.
[27] The name of Richard Gee can be found as a victualler in CUA, Collect. Admin. 6a [Caryl B. 24], Buckle Book, p. 272.

do not know how often this had happened previously, but Austen apparently visited Gee's house to buy provisions on credit. On this particular occasion, or on a subsequent trip when he was attempting to resolve the matter of the account, Austen asked a close friend to accompany him. He probably did so because, according to a decree of 1570, 'no one dwelling in the University as a pupil shall go into the town, except in company with a friend of the same college, degree, and condition, nor without leave having been first granted by the tutor, or dean, or master of his college'.[28] It would also have been necessary for Austen to ask his friend to become his surety if required. At Gee's house, Austen appended his name to the account book, witnessed by his friend and Gee. Later, however, he was unable to repay his debts on time, which led Gee to lodge a complaint before the vice-chancellor's court on 7 April.

The Act Book contains two testimonies of witnesses on oath, which were recorded either at the vice-chancellor's court or at the preceding hearing.[29] One is the deposition of Gee, testifying that 'ye sum of money w[hi]ch he demaundeth of w[illia]m austen is trew debt, the same austen did writt that yt is vndrwritte[n] to his debt booke'. It would have been quite natural for a tradesman to hold on to evidence in this way; in this case, Gee's self-protective measure seems to have proved effective. The other is the deposition of Austen's friend supporting Gee's allegation:

> Deposic[i]o[n]: chr[ist]of[er] marley in artib[us] bacch[alaureus] Jur[atus] saith that ye subscription to ye debt booke is ye wrytyng or hande of w[illiam] austin, and that he this depone[n]t went to gees howse when austen went thether to make accompte or ende w[i]th gee.

It was a Christopher Marley, Bachelor of Arts, who went to Gee's house with William Austen.

It would be naïve to think that this 'Christofer Marley' is definitely the future playwright from Corpus Christi College, for there was a certain Christopher Morley at Trinity College at about this time.[30] But a comparison of the year of his MA with the date of this document puts this out of the question: Christopher Morley of Trinity obtained his MA in 1586, whereas the depositions of Richard Gee and 'Christofer Marley', Bachelor of Arts, were recorded about a year later. As for Christopher Marlowe of Corpus Christi, the college had furnished him a supplicat to the senate to request

---

[28] James Heywood (ed.), *Collection of Statutes for the University and the Colleges of Cambridge* (London, 1840), chap. 47, p. 31.

[29] CUA, Collect. Admin. 6a [Caryl B. 24], Buckle Book, p. 569.

[30] On Christopher Morley of Trinity College, see J. Leslie Hotson, *The Death of Christopher Marlowe* (1925; repr. New York, 1967), p. 59; and Sukanta Chaudhuri, 'Marlowe, Madrigals, and a New Elizabethan Poet', *RES*, NS, 39:154 (1988), 199–216.

that the degree be conferred, and, on 31 March 1587, a week before the case, the 'grace' for an MA had been granted to him. This does not necessarily mean that Marlowe earned the degree and was officially authorized as a Master of Arts as a matter of course, but rather that the university authorities had certified him as a candidate eligible for the degree. He had to wait until the July commencement to receive it. It was, therefore, appropriate for the vice-chancellor to refer to him as 'artib[us] bacch[alaureus]'.

Moreover, Austen may have sought the support of a companion who came from the same town and who belonged to the same college to accompany him to Gee's house. Marlowe may well have given assistance to Austen, like his own Faustus, who, in response to a request from his fellow scholars, says, 'For that I know your friendship is unfeigned, / And Faustus' custom is not to deny / The just requests of those that wish him well'.[31] The hearing seems to have been settled with Austen being ordered to pay his debt before Whit Sunday (4 June), with Robert Smyth, Master of Arts, acting as a surety. No doubt this Robert Smyth was another close friend of Austen. Since there were many Robert Smyths in Cambridge, it is very difficult to identify him. It is unlikely to be coincidental, however, that there was a Robert Smyth of Corpus Christi whose residence coincides precisely with that of William Austen of the same college.[32]

It was this small but tight-knit college community that enabled William Austen to survive his period of hardship and with which Marlowe was closely involved. What we can thus detect in Marlowe's faithful dealing with his friend is the intimacy of the friendship networks among the scholars from Canterbury, as in the case, too, of the friendship between Marlowe and John Benchkin.[33] Austin Gray supposed that Marlowe 'left Cambridge for good when, in or about February, 1587, he became a government agent. There would be no need for him to return to Cambridge to bargain for or obtain his M.A., if he wanted it'.[34] However, Marlowe was still lingering in Cambridge in April 1587 to be a witness for his college neighbour.

---

[31] Bevington and Rasmussen (eds), A-text, v.i.18–20. For the importance of the community of scholars to Marlowe, see Richard F. Hardin, 'Marlowe and the Fruits of Scholarism', *Philological Quarterly*, 63:3 (1984), 387–400, at p. 396; and Constance B. Kuriyama, 'Second Selves: Marlowe's Cambridge and London Friendships', in John Pitcher (ed.), *MRDE*, Vol. 14 (Cranbury, NJ, 2001), pp. 86–104, at pp. 100–2.

[32] John Venn and John Archibald Venn, *Alumni Cantabrigienses, Part I: From the Earliest Times to 1751* (4 vols, Cambridge, 1922), vol. 4, p. 107.

[33] Kuriyama, 'Second Selves', p. 87.

[34] Austin K. Gray, 'Some Observations on Christopher Marlowe, Government Agent', *PMLA*, 43:3 (1928), 682–700, at p. 684.

THE STOREHOUSE AND MARLOWE'S CHAMBER-FELLOWS

As we saw in Chapter 1, the storehouse (Chamber 4), newly furnished by Parker in 1575, was one of the community nuclei that existed for the benefit of scholars from Canterbury. It was in this chamber that Christopher Marlowe settled in 1581 as a Parker scholar in place of Christopher Pashley. Marlowe's biographers are practically unanimous in their contention that his roommates were Robert Thexton of Aylsham and Thomas Lewgar from Wymondham. This is, in theory, plausible, but in fact does not hold water, for, as Bacon's plan clearly shows, a few years before Marlowe's admission, Thexton had moved into Chamber 6 to join another Aylsham student, while Samuel Beadle was accommodated with Pashley in the storehouse.[35] It is most likely, therefore, that the newcomer Marlowe was to share the chamber with Beadle. As for Thomas Lewgar, who succeeded James Poynter in 1581, we cannot eliminate the possibility that he relinquished his residence to another scholar from Canterbury and moved into another chamber – one which could have provided him with a more congenial environment such as that in Chamber 6, a cluster made up of Wymondham and Aylsham students.

Marlowe was already well acquainted with Beadle and his predecessor, Pashley, because all of them came from the same parish of St George in Canterbury and were alumni of King's School.[36] The age gap among these fellow townsmen was not a serious impediment to their comradeship. The sense of fraternity among Canterbury students from different years can be discerned, for instance, in the memorial note of Benjamin Charier on Abraham Tilman written into the copy of Thomas Cooper's *Thesaurus Linguae Romanae & Britannicae* (1573), now in the possession of the Parker Library.[37] The note (found near the end of the book) reads:

---

[35] See Chapter 1, pp. 37–8.

[36] Samuel Beadle was the son of a carpenter, and Christopher Pashley a tailor's son, both from the parish of St George. See William Urry, *Christopher Marlowe and Canterbury*, ed. with an introduction by Andrew Butcher (London, 1988), p. 42. According to the chapter accounts of Canterbury Cathedral, Beadle attended King's School from Midsummer 1575 to Midsummer 1577, and Pashley from Christmas 1572 to Midsummer 1575. CCAL, DCc TA 7; DCc MA 40, fol. 432v; DCc TA 8 (1576–77); DCc MA 40, fol. 434r.

[37] Corpus Christi College, Parker Library, shelf-mark L.5.14 (previous shelf-mark N.5.1/L.3.6): Thomas Cooper, *Thesaurus Linguae Romanae & Britannicae* (London, 1573). This copy seems to have originally been Tilman's own (as the inventory drawn up in 1590 shows), afterwards being placed into the charge of Charier, as the copy has a brief description, obviously in Charier's hand, on its title page: 'Ibrahamus Tylman possesser / testis Beniamin Charier'. See Elisabeth S. Leedham-Green, *Books in Cambridge Inventories: Book-Lists from Vice-Chancellor's Court Probate*

> Abraham Tilman Borne at Seling neere Fev[er]sham in Kent some time Queenes scholler in Canterburye came to Corpus Chr[ist]i Colledge in Cambridge in the yeare of o[u]r lord 1580. was scholler of the house and afterward fellowe he died in the yeare 1589. Beniamin Charier succeeded him in his fellowship.[38]

With these words, Charier seems to have intended to leave a thumbnail sketch and so honour the memory of his senior at King's School and Corpus Christi. His marginal note offers us a glimpse of their close friendship.

To reconstruct the chamber-based community of Marlowe's associates, it is well worth turning our attention to Beadle, who succeeded Nicholas Faunt as a Canterbury scholar on 13 March 1577 and obtained his BA in 1581.[39] He retained his scholarship until the spring of 1583, and remained at the college even after it expired, probably by turning to his parents or some other local benefactor for financial help; then, in 1584, he proceeded to work towards his MA. A few months before beginning his MA studies, he represented Thexton in a lawsuit at the vice-chancellor's court, as we saw above.

The court record is valuable for shedding some light on the internal relationships between these members. The fact that Thexton, a fellow from Aylsham, was the tutor of William Austen, the Canterbury scholar, might seem unusual, considering the sort of regional associations that usually emerge in the case of the Norwich fellows, who mainly took charge only of Norwich scholars. However, this kind of match, unrelated to regionality, was actually quite common.[40] Although the precise principle on which these relationships worked cannot be known, tutorials seem generally to have been chamber-based, at least as far as we can tell from a list held by the Corpus Christi Archives giving details of tutorial payments to fellows.[41] This list contains the quarterly payments to eleven fellows from 25 March 1576 to 24 June 1577 for convening tutorials for their pupils. However, some of the funded scholars (Thomas Corbet, Christopher Pashely, James Poynter, and Robert Thexton) are unaccountably missing from the list. The document provides the information that several fellows looked after

---

Inventories in the Tudor and Stuart Periods (2 vols, Cambridge, 1986), vol. 1, pp. 481–3, item 32.

[38] Cooper, *Thesaurus Linguae Romanae & Britannicae*, Parker Library copy, sig. Vvvvvv 6v.

[39] CCCA, CCCC01/C/1, Chapter Book 1, p. 15.

[40] William Roberts, the tutor of Lady Katherine Paston's son, is another instance. He came from Wales and was a fellow when Paston's son was resident at Corpus between 1624 and 1627. See Ruth Hughey (ed.), *The Correspondence of Lady Katherine Paston, 1603–1627* ([Norwich], 1941), p. 34.

[41] CCCA, CCCC02/B/44/29.

scholars downstairs. Chamber-based tutorials appear in the payments to Sayer (for tutoring Temple and Braborne), Aldrich (for Gold, Plombe, and Abbys), Swet (for Wood), Thaxter (for Golding and Dix), and Yemes (for Stone). These assignments (except for those of the two Norwich fellows) were not based on the fact that the scholar came from the same town, but that he was downstairs.

At the same time, matching that was *not* chamber-based often took place based on other conditions: a fellow's long absence; the room that he inhabited (such as a chamber over the buttery); and/or an earnest request from a patron, parents, or the scholar himself. For instance, Henry Yemes, a fellow from Norfolk, was paid for teaching William Lawse, a Canterbury scholar resident in another unit, as well as for teaching a scholar downstairs. This was probably due to a personal link between them. It is possible, therefore, to explain the match made between Thexton and Austen according to any of these common practices. Thexton obtained his fellowship in 1581 from Yemes, which means that he inherited the first floor of Chamber 8 and took over responsibility for the scholars downstairs: that is, the Canterbury scholars grouped in a cluster. Austen may have been one of the residents of this chamber. There is another possibility, however: since Austen succeeded to William Lawse's scholarship in 1580, the personal affinity between Yemes and Lawse may have been handed over to the following generation, namely Thexton and Austen.

Thexton's closeness to the scholars from Canterbury probably explains why he trusted Beadle to act as his proxy in the courts. The mutual confidence and interdependence between the two can also be confirmed by the chamber swap that enabled Beadle to take up his residence at the storehouse. Although Thexton was not in any sense Marlowe's roommate, it is possible, given his close relationships with both Beadle and Austen, that he had intimate channels of communication with the circle of Canterbury students, including Marlowe himself. Moreover, there is certainly evidence that Thexton and his Aylsham associates shared Marlowe's enthusiasm for drama, because it was at a stage production that Thexton was injured.[42] Robert Norgate, the college master from Aylsham and brother of Thexton's roommate, was similarly well disposed to dramatic entertainments. During his mastership from 1573 to 1587, the expenses for staging plays were recorded once every two years on average; this frequency of staging theatrical entertainments is the highest among the succession of masters.

Whether Beadle himself was interested in stage plays is a matter of conjecture, but an interesting fact is worth noting here. Though his trail cannot be traced after he obtained an MA in 1584, Beadle may have been

---

[42] See above, pp. 69–70.

living in or around Cambridge or Canterbury, seeking employment. The next occasion when we come across him is at an assembly in Boston in Lincolnshire on 6 January 1589, when the mayor, aldermen, and common council members agreed that 'Mr Samuell Beadlee Mr. of Arte late of Bennett Colledge is chosen by the Comon Consent of this house to be schollmaster' of Boston Grammar School.[43] There is no way of knowing how Beadle came to the attention of the magnates of Boston, but it may have been through a local connection with his immediate predecessor in the post, Peter Lyly, the younger brother of the playwright John Lyly, who was born in 1563 to a famous family in Canterbury. Peter's attendance record at King's School can be found in the chapter accounts from Christmas 1572 to March 1575, along with mention of his seniors Christopher Pashley, Robert Stone, Richard Manwaring, and William Lawse.[44] Although Peter's name disappears from the accounts after 1575, this does not necessarily mean his absence from King's School, for, as Urry points out, 'we have for the most part only the names of Scholars, or members of the Foundation, at this early date, as opposed to Commoners of the school'.[45] It is likely that Lyly continued to attend as a commoner until 1579 and became acquainted with Beadle (and possibly with Marlowe) at King's School.

Having obtained his BA in 1583, Lyly was elected schoolmaster at the assembly of Boston on 13 October 1585. However, he found this profession and/or the social climate of Boston rather uncongenial, and in 1587, following his dismissal, he proceeded to work towards his MA.[46] The assembly agreed on 10 October 1588 that 'Mr Lylley the scollemaster shalbe allowed iij^{li} for his quarters wages althoughe he hathe bene absent & done noe service for the same & to be discharged of the Scholemaster-shipp because he dothe not attend upon the teachinge of the schollers'.[47] Three months after Lyly's dismissal, Beadle came to Boston to make up for his friend's mismanagement. He served devotedly as a schoolmaster for a full ten years, and, when he left Boston School in late 1597, the assembly

---

[43] The minutes of the Boston council are transcribed in John F. Bailey, *Transcription of Minutes of the Corporation of Boston, Vol. 1 1545–1607* (Boston, Lincs, 1980), 261 A (378).

[44] CCAL, DCc TA 7 and DCc MA 40, fol. 432v.

[45] Urry, 'John Lyly and Canterbury', p. 24. A similar case to that of John and Peter Lyly is the abovementioned Abraham Tilman, 'Queenes scholler in Canterburye' (i.e. a commoner at the school), whose name also cannot be found in the chapter accounts of Canterbury.

[46] After having obtained his MA, Peter Lyly was appointed to the chaplaincy of the Savoy Hospital: see Robert Somerville, *The Savoy: Manor, Hospital, Chapel* (London, 1960), pp. 243–4.

[47] Bailey, *Transcription of Minutes*, 259 B (375).

ordered that 'there shallbe given to Mr Beadle xl^s in consideracon of his paynes heretofore taken in this towne & Mr Maior is requested to paye the same which he is to be alowed againe upon his accompte'.[48]

The Canterbury social network, as can be discerned in the case of Beadle, seems to have maintained its interdependence, involving other congenial members from adjacent chambers; it also stretched out to reach other colleges and municipal corporations – and even further, to the royal court. It was through this communication network that local information was rapidly circulated, and by means of it a scholar could seek a way to advance his career. Recent biographers of Marlowe have pointed out the importance of such local networks and consider Nicholas Faunt, in particular, to have been a recruiter who offered Marlowe an opportunity to perform scholarly service for state officials.[49] Although there is no historical evidence to justify this assumption, it does seem to be valid when we consider the fact that Faunt came from King's School and was the immediate predecessor of Beadle in receiving the Canterbury scholarship.

Moreover, on the first floor of Chamber 4 we can find further (although circumstantial) evidence for supporting the assumption. Bacon's plan of 1577 shows that the new Parker scholars of the storehouse were assembled under the aegis of Richard Willoughbye, a fellow from Wiggenshall in Norfolk. The 'Ninth' fellowship, which Willoughbye held, had been founded by Parker out of the college revenue of 1569; according to the college statute, the fellowship had to be granted at all times, if possible, to 'Norfolk men'.[50] It is possible to trace the sequence of succession to this fellowship through the 1570s and 1580s. In 1579, Willoughbye relinquished the post and his chamber to Thomas Harris, who also came from Norfolk, and who had been Willoughbye's foremost pupil.[51] Harris was succeeded by Edward Elwin, again of Norfolk, in 1586.

Admittedly, this does not necessarily mean that Harris and Elwin were Marlowe's tutors while he was living downstairs, as the chamber-based tutorial system cannot be applied to all cases. In fact, according to the list of tutorial payments to fellows, Willoughbye had a number of other

---

[48] *Ibid.*, 41 B (561).
[49] Charles Nicholl, *The Reckoning: The Murder of Christopher Marlowe* (London, 1992), p. 119; Constance Brown Kuriyama, *Christopher Marlowe: A Renaissance Life* (Ithaca, 2002), pp. 71–2; David Riggs, *The World of Christopher Marlowe* (London, 2004), p. 67; and Park Honan, *Christopher Marlowe: Poet and Spy* (Oxford, 2005), p. 120.
[50] John Lamb, *Masters' History of the College of Corpus Christi* (London, 1831), pp. 99 and 426.
[51] John Venn describes Harris as being from Kent, but the list of college membership in NRO, NRS 23372, Z99 attests to his Norfolk origin.

students to look after from 1576 to 1577.[52] Nevertheless, since no reference to the new Parker scholars living in the storehouse survives in the list, the possibility that Harris and Elwin took charge of Marlowe downstairs cannot be entirely ruled out. Rather, the residential propinquity may naturally have brought about deeply enmeshed relations between Marlowe and these fellows in financial, disciplinary, and academic aspects. David Mateer has discovered in the court record of the King's Bench a document which suggests Marlowe's financial dependence upon Elwin.[53] Considering the fact that a college tutor usually supervised (and often exploited) the finances of his pupils, this document about the case between Marlowe and Elwin may similarly be regarded as showing traces of such a tutorial relationship.

What is of greater interest here, however, is the fact that Marlowe had spent five years with Thomas Harris in the same unit, Chamber 4. It is extremely likely that Harris was one of those who had been well acquainted with Marlowe's character, behaviour, and talent. This assumption may be supported by the fact that the supplicat from the college for the conferring of Marlowe's BA degree has the autograph of Harris as a praelector (figure 4).[54] Harris confirmed with this signature that the candidate had satisfactorily performed the public exercises which were required for obtaining the degree. This close relationship between Marlowe and Harris may give us a clue to understanding how Marlowe could find the opportunity to perform service for the Privy Council.

To take this investigation further, we must turn our attention to Parker's plan of 1575, where we find that Faunt and Harris were sharing accommodation in the room below the dial (Chamber 6). These two were also coupled in the list of tutorial payments as the pupils of Richard Willoughbye. The combined evidence suggests that they fostered chamber-mate camaraderie throughout their collegiate lives, and that their college ties were maintained even after Faunt's departure from the college. If Faunt, as a secretary to Walsingham, was looking around in 1585 for talented scholars to enter the diplomatic service, Harris may have recommended Marlowe to his ex-roommate, giving him a full report of Marlowe's abilities. It was this

[52] CCCA, CCCC02/B/44/29. Willoughbye's pupils were Thomas Harris, Nicholas Faunt, John Temple, and Stephen Snat. The reason why there is no reference to the Parker scholars in the list is unknown. It is possible that their tutor had not yet been formally assigned.

[53] David Mateer, 'New Sightings of Christopher Marlowe in London', *Early Theatre*, 11:2 (2008), 13–38. We can often find fellows who engaged in money-lending enterprises. Elwin seems to have been one of those fellows and to have had a number of lawsuits against citizens. See CUA, Buckle Book, p. 623* (13 December 1588).

[54] CUA, Supplicats, 1583–84, no. 199.

social network of the chamber-based community that could have given Marlowe an excellent opportunity to take up scholarly service with the Privy Councillors.

NICHOLAS FAUNT AS LOCAL ROLE MODEL

What career path seemed ideal and attainable to Marlowe? Obviously, a career as an ordinary poet to a theatrical company, such as that followed by Shakespeare, was not attractive enough either for him or for the university wits to pursue. In fact, Marlowe identified himself when examined by Robert Sidney, the governor of Vlissingen, in 1592, as 'by his profession a scholar': that is, one who, having studied at the university, was earning his living by literary work and, at the same time, still seeking more fixed employment. Let us remember that his close friend Thomas Watson, having written for the Queen's Men, was employed as a tutor by Sir William Cornwallis, and that Samuel Daniel worked for Sir Edward Dymock after having officiated as a messenger for Walsingham. John Lyly complains in his letter to Robert Cecil dated 9 September 1598 that 'so as one of the Queen's patients, who have nothing applied these ten years to my wants but promises, I humbly end, hoping that, seeing her Majesty is pleased that your Honour and Mr. Grevil may be her remembrancers, I shall find a speedy repair of my ruined expectation'.[55] Admittedly, following his literary career Lyly tried to secure advancement in court, though it proved to be 'a miserable example of misfortune'.[56]

Similarly, for Marlowe, who tried to carve out a career by utilizing humanist cultural capital, the playwriting profession may have seemed to be a staging-post for the next phase of his career. Robert Baldock in *Edward II*, asked by King Edward about his family background, says 'my gentry / I fetched from Oxford, not from heraldry'.[57] While the historical Baldock was indeed a cleric and held a doctorate from Oxford, Marlowe deviated from his dramatic source in putting emphasis upon Baldock's former career as a private tutor or household secretary for Lady Margaret. 'Then hope I by her means to be preferred, / Having read unto her since she was a child';[58] what the playwright indicates here is one of the high roads to a prosperous career that he was eager to follow at that time.

---

[55] R. A. Roberts *et al.* (eds), *Calendar of the Manuscripts of the Most Hon. the Marquis of Salisbury* (24 vols, London, 1883–1976), vol. 8, p. 340.
[56] Feuillerat, *John Lyly*, p. 555.
[57] Christopher Marlowe, *Edward the Second*, ed. Charles R. Forker, The Revels Plays (Manchester, 1994), II.ii.242–3.
[58] *Ibid.*, II.i.29–30.

When the socioeconomic status of scholarship students limited their choice of employment, a local role model who had the same social background as their own and who had taken the lead in achieving his goals may have made a strong impression on them, and particularly upon ambitious scholars, in making their career choices. In this respect, the career path of Nicholas Faunt, Marlowe's senior at both King's School, Canterbury and Corpus Christi College, provided Marlowe not only with a role model but also with an opportunity to ally himself with Faunt's political network.

Nicholas was the son of John Faunt, 'mediocris fortunae' ('of middling fortune'). The stipendary book of the Treasurer of the Cathedral shows that he received a quarterly allowance of £1 as a King's scholar from Midsummer 1568 to Michaelmas 1569.[59] An entry such as 'To Gressop. pd to fant –– xx^{s}' suggests that the schoolmaster in charge of Faunt was John Gresshop, the devoted Protestant headmaster of the school from 1566 to 1580, under whose guidance Marlowe may also have spent his King's School days.[60] It is worth mentioning that the name of Stephen Gosson, the later anti-theatrical polemist, appears almost simultaneously with that of Faunt. Since Gosson was also supervised by Gresshop and admitted to Corpus Christi College, Oxford in 1572, when he was eighteen years old, Faunt and Gosson belonged to the same generation and learned in the same school under the same schoolmaster.[61]

Faunt was admitted to Gonville and Caius College on 29 January 1572 and was probably the only Canterbury student at this college, as we can find no other scholar coming from that city – at least from 1559, when the admission register of the college became detailed, up until 1571.[62] This singularity derives from the features of the scholarship Faunt obtained. On 20 January 1572, Matthew Parker donated to the college the total sum of £60 13s. 4d., with which the college was to endow a scholar, paying him annually £3 0s. 8d.[63] This scholarship was unique at that time, as it was intended for a student of medicine. The student had to be a native of Canterbury and

---

[59] On his first appearance, see CCAL, DCc MA 40, fol. 354v, which records the payment to Faunt on the Feast of St John the Baptist (24 June) in 1568. On the social status of Faunt's father, see John Venn, *Biographical History of Gonville and Caius College 1349–1897* (3 vols, Cambridge, 1897), vol. 1, 69.

[60] Urry, *Marlowe and Canterbury*, Appendix II, pp. 108–22, transcribes the inventory of Gresshop, which shows that he had a mass of polemical reformation literature in his study.

[61] Gosson's name first appears in Michaelmas 1567 (CCAL, DCc TA 5, fol. 62r).

[62] Venn, *Biographical History*, vol. 1, p. 69. For information on Faunt's life, see Sutherland's account in P. W. Hasler (ed.), *The House of Commons, 1558–1603* (3 vols, London, 1981), vol. 2, pp. 109–10.

[63] On the Parker scholarship at Gonville and Caius College, see Venn, *Biographical History*, vol. 3, p. 228.

a graduate of a school in the city; he also had to be nominated by Parker himself. The nomination of a scholar was not just an honorary office, but rather a prerogative that enabled a nominator to choose a nominee at his own discretion and even to patronize him. The relationship between the two was, therefore, closer than we might suppose. There were just nine days between Parker's donation and the admittance of the first Parker scholar. The timing is such that we cannot but suspect that Parker had Faunt in mind before founding the scholarship.

After about one year's residence, however, Faunt resigned his scholarship and migrated to Corpus Christi. There is no known reason for this move, but it was supposedly due to his disappointment in medical science. Besides, as he had a leaning towards radical Protestantism, which can be detected in his letters, the Catholic tendency of the college may have discouraged him.[64] Or was it because he had no friend from the same city? Whatever the reason, Faunt came to Corpus at the beginning of March in 1573 and was dropped into Chamber 6 as a Canterbury scholar of the Westminster foundation.[65] He was again lucky enough to win this scholarship with ease. It is possible that Parker, having chosen Faunt as the first scholar of medicine and appreciating his talent, responded to his appeal with good intentions and intervened in the nomination of a new Canterbury scholar. Parker could easily prevail upon the college authorities, and the dean and chapter of Canterbury, by exploiting his position as archbishop and the founder of the scholarship.

Though we cannot minutely trace his movements after obtaining his BA in 1576, Faunt seems to have succeeded in securing a position, considering that he was employed by Sir Francis Walsingham as a foreign agent around 1578, when he was sent on a mission, possibly to William Davidson in the Netherlands, together with Baptista Spinola.[66] By 1580 Faunt was already active as Walsingham's confidential secretary. What linked Faunt to Walsingham? There is no evidence that they were related. Moreover, in May 1575, Faunt had lost his influential benefactor Parker, who could have recommended him to Walsingham or his political clientele. The most plausible explanation, it seems, is that Roger Manwood, the Member of

---

[64] On Faunt's religious stance, see Thomas Birch, *Memoirs of the Reign of Queen Elizabeth, from the Year 1581 till Her Death* (2 vols, London, 1754), vol. 1, pp. 41–2, 47.

[65] In the Buttery Book of Corpus Christi College, his name appears in 3a quadragesima (that is, the third week of the Lent term) without a record of his expenses. This seems to suggest that Faunt was not yet resident in Corpus. We find, however, that he spent 2 pence at the buttery by the entry 'Faunte -- ii^d' in the following week, which began on 1 March. I believe this is the exact date of his appearance at Corpus.

[66] *APC*, vol. 10, p. 323.

Parliament for Sandwich, and Parker's intimate friend, introduced Faunt to Walsingham.

It is worth noting here that both Parker and Manwood were actively involved in local educational administration. In 1563, the mayor and representatives of Sandwich agreed to raise money for founding a grammar school and entrusted Manwood entirely with the project. He was a person fit for the post, not only being the town's recorder and a man with many contacts but also having a keen interest in education. In order to endow the school with sufficient lands to provide the necessary income, he asked for the assistance of his comrade Parker, who became his trusted collaborator.[67] Manwood shared Parker's Reformist enthusiasm and industriousness for founding educational facilities and college scholarships for the poor. Their professional intimacy in the cause of education is well attested by the fact that Parker left a bequest of £6 13s. 4d. to Manwood on his death in 1575.[68]

Not only did they work together closely in founding Sandwich School, but they also exchanged information on talented persons who sought employment. As a director of the school, Manwood had to recruit a headmaster more than once. He asked his close friends – among them Thomas Wotton, a country gentleman of Boughton Malherbe in Kent, and Parker – to find a person fit for the post.[69] When a new headmaster was required in 1570, Parker recommended William Absalon, whom we have encountered in the case of Stephen Church. In a letter to the mayor and the representatives of Sandwich dated 5 September of that year, Manwood wrote:

> This bearer mr Abselon borne here at canterburye, to me especially comendyd by my lords grace of Canterbury his letters to be skole master of my gramer skole with you [...]. And as I am assertayned by my lords grace that ffor his conversyon (conversacyon) in Relygyon and skylfulnes in teaching, he ys such a meet man as for that purpose hardly the lyke ys to be had.[70]

Manwood was also, like Parker, instrumental in establishing scholarships at Gonville and Caius College. In 1563, Joan Trapps, widow of a London goldsmith, left money for the purchase of land to establish four scholarships at the college. Manwood, who had been in contact with the college as a legal adviser, was the executor of her will. Though probate was granted in that year, Manwood was slow in carrying out the provisions (for unknown

---

[67] William Boys, *Collections for a History of Sandwich* (Canterbury, 1792), p. 199.
[68] John Strype, *The Life and Acts of Matthew Parker* (3 vols, Oxford, 1821), vol. 3, p. 337.
[69] George Eland (ed.), *Thomas Wotton's Letter-Book 1574–1586* (London, 1960), pp. 1–2.
[70] Boys, *Collections*, p. 483. See also John Cavell and Brian Kennett, *A History of Sir Roger Manwood's School Sandwich, 1563–1963, with a Life of the Founder* (London, 1963), pp. 30–2.

reasons), and it was not until 1568 that he outwardly executed her will and founded the scholarships. I say 'outwardly' because, according to the allegation of the college, 'Mr Manwood hath kept from the college the money which she appointed'. Moreover, presumably in contradiction of the will, he availed himself of this good opportunity to reserve two scholarships for the benefit of students from Sandwich School. The college complained that he had 'diverted to Kent only what she meant for all England'.[71]

Manwood may have been a dishonest legal adviser to the college, but he was always a beneficent and faithful patron to poor boys in Kent. On 3 February 1569, the first two Trapps scholars from Sandwich, Thomas Waferer and Villers Aldye, were admitted to Gonville and Caius as pensioners; both had been educated at Manwood's school for five years.[72] Manwood doubtless knew them well and took good care of them. His great interest in the scholars is indicated by an article of the indenture: 'The said scholars to be nominated by Sir Roger during his life, and afterwards by the governours of the said free school, and by the said master or custos, &c. alternately.'[73]

Considering the fact that Parker and Manwood were generous in giving assistance to their scholars, it is possible that Faunt, a native of Canterbury and ex-scholar of Gonville and Caius, was well known to Manwood. No evidence can be found for this, but there is a curious coincidence. Around 1578, when Faunt came into Walsingham's service, Manwood was on intimate terms with Walsingham. His friendship was promoted partly by political necessity, for at that time he was in need of Walsingham's assistance to obtain the position of Chief Baron of Exchequer. Walsingham wrote to Christopher Hatton on 27 June 1578:

> I may not forget to acquaint you with the honourable entertainment the Lord Cobham and I have received at Mr. Justice Manwood's house in his absence; the same being performed not only very bountifully, but also most orderly. The man is greatly loved and esteemed here, for his uprightness and integrity, of the best sort of the gentlemen of this shire; which is a most apparent argument of his good and just dealings amongst them: and therefore it were great pity that the malice of some few for their particulars should blemish the credit of a man of his sufficiency for her Majesty's service, and so well able for living to bear the countenance of a place of credit.[74]

---

[71] On these complaints, see Venn, *Biographical History*, vol. 3, pp. 227–8.
[72] *Ibid.*, vol. 1, p. 64.
[73] Boys, *Collections*, pp. 202–3.
[74] Harris Nicolas, *Memoirs of the Life and Times of Sir Christopher Hatton* (London, 1847), pp. 67–8.

Manwood's 'bountiful' entertainment and the terms of high commendation of his local associates moved Walsingham to vindicate 'his sufficiency for her Majesty's service'. In another (undated) letter to Hatton, Walsingham straightforwardly wrote 'to recommend unto you Mr. Manwood, to be by your good means furthered to the Chief Baronry'.[75] In November of that year Manwood was elected to the position.

As Peter Clark demonstrates, Manwood was 'extremely active manipulating posts and places on behalf of his followers and clients'.[76] Richard Boyle, another native of Canterbury, who was admitted to Corpus Christi College in 1583, was one of Manwood's henchmen and served as one of his clerks.[77] It is no wonder, therefore, that Faunt's close relationship with Parker would draw him into Manwood's extensive network; and it is difficult to imagine anyone else who could have offered Faunt such an opportunity to work for Walsingham around this time. Faunt's career is one of the fortunate cases of a poor scholar who sought advancement through his talents and local connections, climbing the ladder of success up to attaining a seat in Parliament for Boroughbridge in 1584 and then the Clerkship of the Signet in 1595.

MARLOWE AND THE EPITAPH ON ROGER MANWOOD

Marlowe was not so fortunate in obtaining lucrative employment as Faunt had been, and consequently had to find other means to earn a living, notably through writing for the public playing companies. At the same time, he seems to have been active in exploiting his seniors' Kentish network to his own economic advantage. One of these men was none other than Manwood. No doubt Marlowe was personally acquainted with him, for he wrote a Latin epitaph on Manwood's death in December 1592, the only known poem eulogizing a local contemporary figure.

The epitaph has not survived directly in print but was copied in a commonplace book of Henry Oxinden, a Kentish country gentleman from Barnham near Canterbury. Mark Eccles has established the authenticity of the lines, and has drawn our attention to the fact that Marlowe and Manwood met once in a court of justice.[78] This was on the occasion when Marlowe and the poet Thomas Watson were detained on suspicion

---

[75] *Ibid.*, p. 94.
[76] Peter Clark, *English Provincial Society from the Reformation to the Revolution: Religion, Politics and Society in Kent 1500–1640* (Hassocks, 1977), p. 278.
[77] Thomas Birch (ed.), *The Works of the Honourable Robert Boyle* (6 vols, London, 1772), vol. 1, p. vii.
[78] Mark Eccles, 'Marlowe in Kentish Tradition', *N&Q*, CLXIX (1935), 58–61.

of the murder of William Bradley, an innkeeper's son, in 1589.[79] As part of the legal proceedings, on 3 December Marlowe appeared at the Old Bailey before a bench of judges, among whom sat Roger Manwood. Marlowe's plea of self-defence was accepted, and, after thirteen days' detention, he was released on recognizance of £40. Some scholars imagine that Manwood's lenient sentence might have prompted Marlowe to write the flattering epitaph later on.

However, this conjecture does not explain the reason why Marlowe chose Manwood in particular, for on the bench sat four great judges of the Crown, four city officials, and other Middlesex justices. It is more reasonable to assume that his local connection with the cultivated circles of Kent, including the Walsingham family at Chislehurst, motivated Marlowe to write the eulogy. David Riggs considers it to be a 'sycophantic epitaph' and 'another indication that the poet was actively seeking patronage and protection, and hoped to find it in Kent if not elsewhere'.[80]

Although it does suggest that Marlowe sought patronage from his Kentish associates, the eulogy also shows his personal intimacy with Manwood and his activities; it was not just a trifling 'sycophantic' piece of work.[81] Marlowe obviously well knew, or may have even seen, Manwood's elaborate monument erected before his death in the parish church of St Stephen, Canterbury. He mentions in the poem the cinerary urn of Manwood with the line phrase *Urna subtegitur* ('he lies in this urn'), and concludes the poem with reference to the monument: *sic cum te nuntia Ditis / Vulneret exsanguis, feliciter ossa quiescant, / Famaque marmorei superet monumenta sepulchri* ('so, though the pale messenger of Dis assails you, may your bones rest peacefully, and your fame outlast the monuments of your marble sepulchre').[82] The monument still survives in the church, and in the central niche sits a marble bust in the costume of the Chief Baron of the Exchequer, beneath which Manwood's family kneels and his life-sized skeleton lies (figure 11). The bust is flanked by two black marble tablets, whose Latin inscriptions encourage the viewer 'to reject the very materiality of the monument itself' and provide 'a didactic reading of his life', proclaiming: *Transit lux, ubi lex ubi laus, mea fama silescunt* ('Light goes away and where there is law,

---

[79] Mark Eccles, *Christopher Marlowe in London* (Cambridge, MA, 1934), pp. 9–22.
[80] Riggs, *World of Marlowe*, pp. 304–5.
[81] Dympna Callaghan points out that: 'in the lines of *In Obitum*, we have evidence in Marlowe's own words of a firm ideological allegiance with Sir Roger Manwood'. See 'Marlowe's Last Poem: Elegiac Aesthetics and the Epitaph on Sir Roger Manwood', in Sarah K. Scott and M. L. Stapleton (eds), *Christopher Marlowe the Craftsman: Lives, Stage and Page* (Farnham, 2010), pp. 159–76, at p. 170.
[82] Translated by Stephen Orgel in *Christopher Marlowe: The Complete Poems and Translations* (New York, 1971), p. 217.

praise and my fame, all come to silence').[83] The imagery and moral of the monument seem to be interlinked with Marlowe's lamentation that *fori lumen, venerandae gloria legis occidit* ('the light of government, the glory of reverend law, has set') and his consciousness of the monument's material evanescence. It seems likely that his contact with Manwood had begun much earlier than the court session at the Old Bailey and provided the poet with the opportunity to make better use of his humanist capabilities.

For aspiring literary young men recently down from the universities, an official post such as secretary in the central government would have been regarded as a good start to their career. It enabled them to manage and invest effectively their cultural capital accumulated through their training in the humanities. As H. R. Woudhuysen points out, 'Very often the only necessary qualification for holding one of these offices was an ability to write'.[84] This humanist skill, which university-trained intellectuals would have been able to perform with expertise, was vital and profitable when they were required to process textual information for the local magnates or the government they served. Nicholas Faunt wrote to Anthony Bacon recommending a 'Student and Fellow of a colledge in Cambridge' as a secretary:

> I do pr[e]sume that his want of forreine language shalbe no hindra[u]nce for yo[u] after yo[u] shalbe entred in that countrey where the Latin is most vsed; so that therby aswell in wryting (wherof I knowe yo[u] shall there have great vse for the coppying out of many thinges w[hi]ch yo[u] shall meet w[i]thall worthy the keeping) as in speeche he shalbe able to do yo[u] s[er]uice having besydes a good fayre hande to wryte, acquainted him selfe w[i]th a ready style to indyte well as I heare and wherof I shall more p[ar]ticularly infourme yo[u] shortly.[85]

---

[83] Claire Bartram shows Manwood's ability 'to manipulate the visual vocabulary of the monument' in her article '"Some Tomb for a Remembraunce": Representation of Piety in Post-Reformation Gentry Funeral Monuments', in Robert Lutton and Elisabeth Salter (eds), *Pieties in Transition: Religious Practices and Experiences, c. 1400–1640* (Aldershot, 2007), pp. 138–43. I have quoted the Latin inscriptions of the monument from her article, which uses the transcription and translation by Marten Rogers in his *Sir Roger Manwood: St Stephens, Hackington 1525–1592* (privately published, 1999).

[84] H. R. Woudhuysen, *Sir Philip Sidney and the Circulation of Manuscripts 1558–1640* (Oxford, 1996), p. 76. For a scholar's use of university attainments as a means to obtain patronage, as well as politicians' recruitment of students, see Paul E. J. Hammer, 'The Uses of Scholarship: The Secretariat of Robert Devereux, Second Earl of Essex, c. 1585–1601', *EHR*, 109:430 (1994), 26–51; and Paul E. J. Hammer, 'The Earl of Essex, Fulke Greville, and the Employment of Scholars', *Studies in Philology*, 91:2 (1994), 167–80.

[85] Letter from Nicholas Faunt to Anthony Bacon, 26 April 1584, LPL, MS 647, fol. 185r. On the friendship between Faunt and Bacon, see Will Tosh, *Male Friendship and*

Lisa Jardine and William Sherman categorize these kinds of scholarly activities as 'knowledge transactions' and illustrate their variety by investigating Henry Wotton's service to Lord Edward la Zouche: 'the providing of local knowledge; detail of the availability of scholarly books [...]; the obtaining and organising of detailed textual material relevant to statecraft, including transcription, abridgement, compilation; the processing of written material on secret matters of diplomatic or political interest.'[86] This cultural capital, derived from the humanities, could therefore be applied to both literary and secretarial work for profit. In fact, the official and social role of a playwright bears close resemblance to that of a confidential secretary, who would act as a transcriber, compiler, translator, and intelligencer. A playwright could obtain knowledge and information from books, plays, and intelligence, and then transcribe, compile, and occasionally translate this information into textual materials, which, with the aid of his imagination, would be carefully processed into a play script appropriate for both statecraft and stagecraft.

Playwriting does not seem to have prevented Marlowe from pursuing newsgathering activities, or from operating as a messenger for government officials. In fact, he could combine playwriting concurrently with other tasks and even coordinate the two. *Massacre at Paris*, dated to late 1592 or early 1593, partially reflects Marlowe's knowledge about political circumstances that he may have acquired by information-gathering from books, manuscripts, or, on occasion, oral sources. Julia Briggs points out that the events of the second half 'had occurred within five years of the play's composition', and that 'In these years Marlowe travelled abroad and was associated with government agents working for Mr Secretary Walsingham, on whose desk the foreign dispatches arrived.'[87] Whatever his service to the Privy Council may have been, Marlowe's livelihood completely depended on this humanist skill, which provided him with an opportunity for survival and, potentially, social advancement.

Testimonies of Love in Shakespeare's England (London, 2016), pp. 21–57.

[86] Lisa Jardine and William Sherman, 'Pragmatic Readers: Knowledge Transactions and Scholarly Services in Late Elizabethan England', in Anthony Fletcher and Peter Roberts (eds), *Religion, Culture and Society in Early Modern Britain: Essays in Honour of Patrick Collinson* (Cambridge, 1994), pp. 102–24, at p. 105.

[87] Julia Briggs, 'Marlowe's *Massacre at Paris*: A Reconsideration', *RES*, NS, 34:135 (1983), 257–78, at p. 261.

Chapter 3

THE ORIGIN OF THE RUMOUR AGAINST MARLOWE

Soon after the time of William Austen's financial trouble with Richard Gee, a rumour about Marlowe spread through Corpus Christi College. Because of this rumour, it was proposed that Marlowe be denied his Master's degree. In June, however, he obtained full support from the Privy Council. The certificate is not extant, but there is a summary in the Privy Council Register on 29 June 1587, in which the members of the council addressed the authorities of Cambridge University, stating that

> Whereas it was reported that Christopher Morley was determined to haue gone beyond the seas to Reames and there to remaine, Their L[ordship]s thought good to certefie that he had no such intent, but that in all his acc[i]ons he had behaued him selfe orderlie and discreetelie wherebie he had done her Ma[jes]tie good service, and deserued to be rewarded for his faithfull dealinge: Their L[ordship]s request was that the *rumor* thereof should be allaied by all possible meanes, and that he should be furthered in the degree he was to take this next Commencem[en]t. Because it was not her Ma[jes]tes pleasure that anie one emploied as he had been in matt[e]rs touching the benefitt of his Countrie should be *defamed* by those that are ignorant in th'affaires he went about.[1]

There is nothing to be gained here from discussing the credibility of 'the rumor' itself. The source is also of little importance, for it is almost impossible to identify the originator of a rumour or an urban legend even in modern times. Rather, as the sociologist Jean-Noël Kapferer points out, 'What must be explained in the genesis of a rumor process is the group's adherence and mobilization. Even if there is an initial speaker, it is the other people who found the rumor for, having heard it, they *pass it on*'.[2] What is

---

[1] TNA, PC 2/14, fol. 381v, emphasis added.
[2] Jean-Noël Kapferer, *Rumors: Uses, Interpretations, and Images*, trans. Bruce Fink (New Brunswick and London, 1990), p. 20, emphasis in original.

of greatest significance about the Privy Council certificate is, therefore, not whether the rumour was true or who started it, but who tended to believe it and to pass it on. In this case, the certificate implies the involvement of a hostile person or group in approving and circulating the report which 'defamed' Marlowe and identified him as a convert to Catholicism.

It is not unusual to come across defamation cases in the records of the vice-chancellor's court at Cambridge. The desire to preserve one's reputation was a shared concern among people at every level of society during this period. This was because the expansion of the economy from the 1520s had necessarily been based on credit and trust, despite the growth of consumption and exchange, due to the limited amount of gold and silver. In this situation, credit became a type of currency, and even 'a sort of knowledge which could be communicated through chains of friends and business associates, and became the basis of deciding who could then be added to structural chains of obligation'.[3] It was by such means that a poor scholar could raise money or obtain the support of a patron. Hence, for a scholar whose livelihood was based on his reputation for faithful dealing, defamation and slander would have deprived him of his capital.[4] The threat of defamation was so serious as to cause a poor scholar to turn to the law or to a local potentate. It was not only because of his desire to obtain a degree, then, but also because of his urgent need to recover his own reputation as a form of currency, that Marlowe requested intervention by the Privy Council.

The seeds of this kind of slander and rumour directed against him had been sown in many places throughout the university as part of widespread anti-Catholic sentiment at that time. The enclosed society of Corpus Christi, which consisted of about a hundred students at the most, fostered intimate contacts and friendships among its members, but could at the same time become a hotbed of suspicion and slander. The mobilization of the group in the genesis of a rumour about Marlowe largely resulted from the sense of solidarity or factionalism existing among the college members with whom he was deeply involved. It is necessary, therefore, to consider how the rumour was shaped in this tight-knit community.

---

[3] Craig Muldrew, *The Economy of Obligation: The Culture of Credit and Social Relations in Early Modern England* (Basingstoke, 1998), p. 152.

[4] *Ibid.*, pp. 148–57. See also R. H. Helmholz, *Select Cases on Defamation to 1600* (London, 1985), pp. lxxxviii–xcii; J. A. Sharpe, *Defamation and Sexual Slander in Early Modern England: The Church Courts at York* (York, 1980); and Martin Ingram, *Church Courts, Sex and Marriage in England, 1570–1640* (Cambridge, 1987), pp. 292–319.

'HEARD HEARTED CLYME' AND THE FORMATION OF THE RUMOUR

What the band of poor but ambitious scholars shared was discontent with their deteriorating socioeconomic circumstances. Marlowe himself demonstrated such deep sympathy for them that he inserted in *Hero and Leander* an Ovidian etiological myth about the poverty of poets and scholars. In it he self-mockingly explains poverty as a punishment that originates in the Fates' hatred for Mercury, the patron of learning:

> Yet as a punishment they added this,
> That he and Poverty should always kiss.
> And to this day is every scholar poor;
> Gross gold from them runs headlong to the boor.
> Likewise the angry Sisters, thus deluded,
> To venge themselves on Hermes, have concluded
> That Midas' brood shall sit in Honour's chair,
> To which the Muses' sons are only heir:
> And fruitful wits that inaspiring are
> Shall discontent run into regions far.[5]

This myth obviously had something that appealed to the sensibilities of university students, because the St John's amateur playwright of *The Pilgrimage to Parnassus* borrowed several lines from the passage for a father's advice to his sons, Studioso and Philomusus:

> Though I foreknewe that gold runns to the boore,
> Ile be a scholler though I liue but poore.
> [...]
> Let schollers be as thriftie as they maye,
> They will be poore ere theire last dyinge daye.
> Learninge and pouertie will euer kiss:
> Each carter caries fortune by his side,
> But fortune will with schollers nere abide.[6]

Moreover, at the end of *The First Part of the Return from Parnassus*, these poor scholars express their great disappointment about the low recognition given by society to their university education, and seek employment outside England. The playwright of *The First Part* expands Marlowe's couplet 'And fruitful wits that inaspiring are / Shall discontent run into regions far' into a dialogue:

---

[5] Christopher Marlowe, *Hero and Leander*, in Millar MacLure (ed.), *The Poems*, The Revels Plays (London, 1968), I. lines 469–78.

[6] *The Pilgrimage to Parnassus*, in J. B. Leishman (ed.), *The Three Parnassus Plays (1598–1601)* (London, 1949), lines 63–4, 76–8.

Studioso.	To Rome or Rhems Ile hye, led on by fate,
	Where I will ende my dayes, or mend my state.
Philomusus.	And soe will I; heard hearted clyme farewell,
	In regions farr Ile thy vnkindness tell.[7]

In the imagination of university students, poor scholars were readily associated with Catholic seminaries. The St John's playwright (or playwrights) who drew on Marlowe's myth about poor scholars and linked the politico-religious issue to the difficulty of finding employment warned that even the dangerous alternative of going over to Rheims could sound attractive to poor scholars seeking to satisfy their pride and lead a better life. A similar sort of bitter complaint is expressed by a Catholic polemicist who, in *Leicester's Commonwealth* (1584), sarcastically asks, 'have they not either gone beyond the seas, or left their places for discontentment in religion, or else become servingmen, or followed the bare name of law or physic, without profiting greatly therein or furthering the service of God's Church or their commonwealth?'.[8]

In fact, numerous scholars travelled to the continent, either to seek their fortunes or out of discontent with the established Church; and the university authorities were on the lookout for seminary priests who were lurking around Cambridge to entice discontented scholars into going to Catholic seminaries on the continent. Robert Persons, a Jesuit missionary in hiding, reported in a letter written in October 1581 to Claudio Aquaviva, Superior General of Society of Jesus, that, although Cambridge was one of the regions into which priests had not penetrated, 'after many remedies had been sought in vain, at length by the help of God I introduced into the University itself a certain priest, nominally as a scholar or gentlemen desirous of study'. Persons triumphantly continues:

> I arranged for him to have some persons to help him not far away from the city. And God gave the enterprise such success that within a few months he gained a harvest of seven young men of very great promise and talent, and now they are on the point of being sent to the Seminary at Rheims. This I learn to-day from one of them who has already arrived here; and a larger harvest is expected there every day.[9]

William Allen, the founder of the English College at Douay and Rheims, similarly wrote to Alfonso Agazario, Rector of the English College at Rome,

---

[7] *The First Part of the Return from Parnassus*, in *ibid.*, lines 1560–3.
[8] Dwight C. Peck (ed.), *Leicester's Commonwealth: The Copy of a Letter Written by a Master of Art of Cambridge (1584) and Related Documents* (Athens, OH, 1985), p. 115.
[9] Leo Hicks (ed.), *Letters and Memorials of Father Robert Persons, S.J.*, vol. 1 (London, 1942), p. 108.

on 5 November 1582: 'We are wonderfully hard put to by the number of new-comers. Within a fortnight, besides those you sent, there have come to us at least twenty students: such is the way in which this persecution puts Catholics to flight from the English universities.'[10]

The movement that stirred university scholars to travel to the continent was indebted partly to Allen's success in administrating the English College and partly to Persons's enthusiasm for 'calling Catholics to a more bracing morality, from intellectual and moral laziness' at the early stage of his missions.[11] At the same time, the Catholic local community within and around the university, in concert with missionaries and exiles, provided further encouragement and logistical support to those students seeking a career overseas.[12] This is well illustrated by the activities of Thomas Legge, the master of Gonville and Caius College (1573–1607), who provided religious asylum for scholars with Catholic tendencies. The Catholic cluster that flocked around Legge had often provoked fierce conflict with the precisian members of the college,[13] and, based on their complaints and the master's pleadings to the university authorities, largely consisted of affluent fellow-commoners, mainly from Catholic families in Yorkshire and Essex.[14]

---

[10] J. H. Pollen *et al.*, *Miscellanea IV* (London, 1907), p. 73.

[11] For Persons's spiritual and political activities in the early 1580s, see Victor Houliston, *Catholic Resistance in Elizabethan England: Robert Persons's Jesuit Polemic, 1580–1610* (Aldershot, 2007), p. 30.

[12] The clandestine activities that conveyed young Catholic students overseas can also be found at Oxford University. William Sterrell was involved in such activities in his early twenties. See Patrick H. Martin and John Finnis, 'Thomas Thorpe, "W.S.", and the Catholic Intelligencers', *ELR*, 33:1 (2003), 3–43, at p. 21.

[13] For the conflict within the college, see James Heywood and Thomas Wrights (eds), *Cambridge University Transactions during the Puritan Controversies of the 16th and 17th Centuries* (2 vols, London, 1854), vol. 1, pp. 314–69. Austin K. Gray first turns our attention to the Catholic cluster in Gonville and Caius College in 'Some Observations on Christopher Marlowe, Government Agent', *PMLA*, 43:3 (1928), 682–700, at pp. 687–9.

[14] These fellow-commoners were, for instance, Henry Cholmeley (Yorkshire), Ralph Babthorpe, Legge's 'bed-fellow' (Yorkshire), Richard Stapilton (Yorkshire), John Huddilston (Essex), Rodolph Creswell (Yorkshire), Edward Dakyns (Yorkshire), Thomas Paulet (Essex), John Aske (Yorkshire), William Vavasoure (Yorkshire), and Richard Stapleton (Yorkshire). There was no scholarship connected with any Yorkshire school, and Venn ascribes this to the local sympathies of Legge and Swale, who 'gave the college a distinctly marked ecclesiastical character'. See John Venn, *Biographical History of Gonville and Caius College 1349–1897* (3 vols, Cambridge, 1897), vol. 1, p. xiv. For the strong recusant traditions in Yorkshire, see D. M. Palliser, *Tudor York* (Oxford, 1979), pp. 254–9; and J. C. H. Aveling, *Catholic Recusancy in the City of York 1558–1791* (London, 1970), pp. 1–76. For information on seminary

Legge showed remarkable dexterity in protecting the fraternal relationships among recusant students and forming strong social ties with them in partnership with fellows of Catholic bent, such as Richard Swale, another Yorkshireman, and Edward Burton. Moreover, his policy of toleration (and possible financial support through the Catholic local network) opened the way for conspicuous numbers of poor scholars to seek advancement by moving to the continent in the late 1570s and throughout the 1580s. John Fingley (admitted to the English College, Douay on 13 February 1579) was a sizar who earned his living by working as a butler. William Flacke was also a sizar; he entered Douay with his senior Robert Seare, a pensioner minor, on 22 February 1582. John Ballard (Douay, 27 November 1579), Edward Osburne (ordained priest from Douay College, 1581), William Deane (Rheims, 9 July 1581), John Robertes (Douay, 28 March 1583), and Reginald Eaton (Rheims, 11 May 1586) were all registered as pensioners or 'pensioners minor'. Robert Humberston (Douay, 15 October 1587) and Francis Mondeforde (Rome, 10 July 1590) were 'admitted to the scholars' table', which possibly means that they were admitted to be on commons, although there were no scholarships vacant.[15] Thus, all these exiled students belonged to the same socioeconomic class. A rare case is Edward Dakyns (Rheims, 4 November 1581), who obtained his MA from Trinity Hall and was admitted to Gonville and Caius as a fellow-commoner in 1578.

Legge's policy of tolerance and the abrupt departures of his resident pupils naturally led to the spread of rumours about those who were thought to be leaving or to have already left for the continent. 'Certeyne disorders for education of youthe since the tyme D. Legge hathe beene master of oure Colledge', composed by the anti-Legge faction in 1581, voices the strong suspicion that Robert Seare 'had used to gather together papisticall bookes, and to convey them secreatly into the country' in cooperation with his senior John Fingley, now returning from Rheims as a seminary priest. Besides this, hearsay about Seare was circulating within the college around the same time, about 'the presidentes puple [i.e. Seare] (now reported to be fled beyond the seas for religion)'. The departures of the scholars tended to be attributed to freedom of conscience and the desire to seek opportunity for advancement.

---

students, see also Godfrey Anstruther, *The Seminary Priests: A Dictionary of the Secular Clergy of England and Wales 1558–1850* (4 vols, Ware, 1969).

[15] We can find several destitute scholars from other colleges who went overseas. James Welche, a former scholar of Magdalene College, Cambridge, went to Douay around 1579 in company with another scholar. Out of his dire poverty, however, Welche turned to the teaching profession in the Norwich diocese. See TNA, SP, 12/170, fol. 66r. John Blackfan of St John's, who arrived at Rheims on 13 February 1588, was also a sizar: see Edwin Henson (ed.), *Registers of the English College at Valladolid 1589–1826* (London, 1930), p. 5, n.†.

Even Legge was considered by his enemies to be the kind of person who would voluntarily go into exile. Richard Stapilton, the master's pupil who 'had many papisticall bookes lyenge openly in the masters bed-chamber', was reported saying that 'he wondred that the master, his tutor, beinge a notable and lerned catholick, would lyve here contrary to his conscience, whereas beyond the seas he might enjoy the liberty of the same, and be sure of greate preferment'.[16]

Such rumours and hearsay – about Catholic scholars in exile, potential converts to Rome, and underground operatives lurking in and around Cambridge – naturally engendered suspicions and anxieties among members of university society; these suspicions and anxieties in turn nourished new slanderous rumours about dissimulating Catholics in their midst. In fact, on 8 January 1587, Hugh Gray, a fellow of Trinity College with puritan extremist tendencies, preached a sermon in Great St Mary's, insinuating that 'it is thought that there be sume amonge us who send ov[e]r newes to Rome and Rheimes and do designate ad cede[m] unumquem-q[ue] nostr[u]m'.[17] As all members of the university were required to attend both the morning and afternoon sermons in Great St Mary's, and the pulpit could have a huge impact upon the university intellectuals,[18] the authorities regarded this accusatory sermon as liable to disquiet the members of the university, and so ordered Gray to appear before the vice-chancellor's court. His public explanation shows that he did not know the details of the rumour but 'spake only upon probable suspicion':

> I said, it is thought that there be some amongst us w[hi]ch are not of us, w[hic]h lurke here to espye out what is done that they may give notice to Rome, & they do lye amongst us, that they may poynt out and set forth as it were w[i]th the finger w[hi]ch of us should first go to the fire, when the dayes of mourning for Jacob should come; where I wold desyre that my meaning may be thus interpr[e]ted, that I did not note particulars, but spake only upon probable suspicion, to stir us up to be diligent in searching if there be any Papistes amongst us, w[hi]ch are the Lordes & hir majestyes enemyes.[19]

Gray's explanation demonstrates that anxiety and suspicion over 'Papists amongst us' had permeated the university, fostering an atmosphere of distrust and slander that tended to aggravate divisions within the college

---

[16] Heywood and Wright (eds), *Cambridge University Transactions*, vol. 1, pp. 318–19.
[17] CCCA, CCCC02/M/19/2.
[18] H. C. Porter, *Reformation and Reaction in Tudor Cambridge* (Cambridge, 1958), p. 260.
[19] CCCA, CCCC02/M/19/2; transcribed in CUA, Mm. I. 41 (Baker MS, vol. 30), fols 294–5.

communities. The incident of his scandalous sermon may have been reported and discussed by the master and fellows of Corpus Christi College. They could not ignore the problem of those 'who send ov[e]r newes to Rome and Rheimes', because one of the fellows at the college had been reported crossing the sea to become a seminary priest. Robert Masters cites a report informing the Privy Councillors about the papists and recusants in Norfolk (unfortunately without date or source):

> [Richard Willoughbye,] A. M. and sometime Fellowe of *Bennet* Colledge in *Cambridge*, then as it seemed a Favourer of true Religion, but by travelinge to *Paris* in Fraunce is become a verie Papist, and supposed nowe to be a Seminarie Prieste, ffor whereas his Father before would repayre to Churche, now he utterly refuseth soe to do, goinge manye times into *Darbishiere*, wheare he lyeth sometymes half a yeare together.[20]

Willoughbye, after relinquishing his fellowship on 28 April 1579 to Thomas Harris, had the canonry of Canterbury.[21] However, the position seems to have been uncongenial to him, and he left England around 1580 for Paris. In 1584, possibly a few years after settling down at Padua, a cosy refuge for English students in exile, he was elected an English *consiliarius* who 'represented the nation to the university and also formed collectively the university's executive council under the rector'.[22] It is not certain whether he was 'a Seminarie Priest', for his name cannot be found in the register of the seminaries in Rome and Rheims, but he clearly belonged to the English Catholic community in exile at Padua. His later responsibilities and known associates at Padua University, including Galileo Galilei, suggest that he successfully advanced in life by going overseas.

Changing religion was a matter not only of faith but also of career path and financial gain. Anthony Tyrrell, a former seminary priest, confessed in retrospect that he had fallen into the company of the seminary in Rome 'partly by perswasion, and partly by flatterie, partlye by fayre promises, & partly by intreaty'.[23] John Grosse, MA of Corpus Christi, told the authori-

---

[20] Robert Masters, *The History of the College of Corpus Christi* (Cambridge, 1753–55), Part 2, pp. 414–15.

[21] CCCA, CCCC01/C/1, Chapter Book 1 (Liber Actorum in Collegio Corporis Christi), p. 84. Willoughbye matriculated as pensioner in October 1564 at Christ's College. See John Peile, *Biographical Register of Christ's College, 1505–1905* (Cambridge, 1910), p. 86. For his canonry of Canterbury, see John Le Neve, *Fasti Ecclesiae Anglicanae* (3 vols, Oxford, 1854), vol. 1, p. 51.

[22] Jonathan Woolfson, *Padua and the Tudors: English Students in Italy, 1485–1603* (Cambridge, 1998), p. 11. For a biographical account of Richard Willoughbye in Padua, see *ibid.*, pp. 283–4.

[23] William Tedder, *The Recantations As They Were Seuerallie Pronounced by Wylliam Tedder and Anthony Tyrrell* (London, 1588), sig. D4r.

ties of the seminary at Rome that by '[k]eeping his conversion secret from his family, he returned to Cambridge and was there disappointed of the fellowship which he expected at Corpus Christi', as a result of which he left Cambridge to go to Rome.[24] As Michael Questier shows in his well-documented reconstruction of the experience of changing religion, 'Protestants certainly thought that Catholic proselytisers deliberately exploited English clerics' career difficulties to attract them to Rome, and adequately maintained them when they converted' and that 'it is certainly true that exterior considerations of career and patronage were always present in decisions to change religion'.[25] Richard Willoughbye was possibly one of those who considered that the ministry in his country was not particularly attractive as a means of earning his living. It would be a mistake simply to assume that all fellows and scholars felt so discontented with the 'heard hearted clyme' of England as to depart for Rheims, or that they might have shared certain antisocial attitudes or antagonism to the English Church. But it is not so difficult to imagine that ambitious fellows and scholars had ideas in common and were more or less discouraged at the thought of entering holy orders as a choice of career.

AN UNPRECEDENTED PARKER SCHOLAR

The social role of the universities was in transition at this time, though they were still expected to serve the nation as institutions 'founded principally for the study of divinity, and [the] encrease of the number of learned preachers and ministers' to meet the spiritual needs of the people.[26] Since there were many parish churches without pastors, vicars, or curates, the demand for clergymen remained considerable. It was primarily for this reason that Matthew Parker and Nicholas Bacon, generous benefactors and graduates of Corpus Christi, provided funds to poor scholars. The qualifications established in some of the foundations, such as the requirement that scholars 'are to enjoy their Exhibitions [i.e. scholarships] for six years, if they should be disposed to enter into Holy Orders, otherwise no longer than three', show a general tendency to regard scholarship principally as

---

[24] Anthony Kenny (ed.), *The Responsa Scholarum of the English College, Rome Part One: 1598-1621* (London, 1962), p. 133. For the complete translation of Gross's autobiographical account, see Henry Foley (ed.), *Records of the English Province of the Society of Jesus* (7 vols in 12, London, 1877-83), vol. 1, pp. 619-22.

[25] Michael C. Questier, *Conversion, Politics and Religion in England, 1580-1625* (Cambridge, 1996), pp. 43-4.

[26] John Strype, *Annals of the Reformation* (4 vols, Oxford, 1824), vol. 3, part 2, Appendix ('The Bishop's answer to the petitions digested into 34 articles offered the last sessions of parliament 1584-1585'), p. 304.

a means of providing candidates for the Church.[27] However, it was those members of the clergy who enjoyed powerful patronage who were able to hold lucrative benefices, and more than one at a time, making it almost impossible for a student without a high-powered career or good connections to secure a profitable benefice.

In spite of the strong demand, therefore, entering holy orders was not a tempting form of employment because students knew well that most of the benefices in the country were far too meagre to enable them to sustain a decent way of life. William Harrison thought that a minimum of £30 a year was necessary to 'mainteine a meane scholar, much lesse a learned man'.[28] However, 'Of the benefices of England almost 90 per cent were assessed at less than £26 yearly income and 75 per cent were worth less than £20 per annum'.[29] Henry Smith, in his sermon 'The True Trial of the Spirits', deplored the state of holy orders, saying that 'they which would study divinity above all, when they look upon our contempt, and beggary, and vexation, turn to law, to physic, to trades, or anything, rather than they will enter this contemptible calling'.[30] Nevertheless, as Ian Green points out, 'the prospect of better things to come could act as an inducement to enter the ministry'.[31]

At this point, it is helpful to note the career choices of the scholarship students at Corpus Christi College. In the Audit Book from 1573, when the register first began to mention each scholar's name, up to 1587, the year of Marlowe's MA commencement, there are 107 scholars to whom payments of a college stipend are recorded, ninety-five of whom took BA degrees (and above). Although in most cases the scarcity of recorded evidence prevents us from knowing what employment these ninety-five scholars obtained, it can be confirmed that seventy of them (in other words, about 73 per cent of the graduates) entered the ministry or a teaching profession licensed by the Church during their residence or after leaving college. Overall, making career choices outside the Church seems not to have been so unusual among

---

[27] Masters, *History of Corpus Christi*, p. 201.
[28] Frederick J. Furnivall (ed.), *Harrison's Description of England in Shakspere's Youth*, part 1 (London, 1877), p. 22.
[29] Rosemary O'Day, *The English Clergy: The Emergence and Consolidation of a Profession 1558–1642* (Leicester, 1979), p. 173. For the clerical standards of living, see also Christopher Hill, *Economic Problems of the Church: From Archbishop Whitgift to the Long Parliament* (Oxford, 1956), pp. 199–223.
[30] Henry Smith, 'The True Trial of the Spirits', in *The Works of Henry Smith*, ed. Thomas Smith, with an introduction by Randall J. Pederson (2 vols, 1867; repr. Stoke-on-Trent, 2002), vol. 1, p. 138. For details of the scholars' frustration in the pursuit of their careers, see also Mark H. Curtis, 'The Alienated Intellectuals of Early Stuart England', *Past & Present*, 23 (1962), 25–43.
[31] Ian Green, 'Career Prospects and Clerical Conformity in the Early Stuart Church', *Past & Present*, 90 (1981), 71–115, at p. 88.

their peers. It is interesting, however, to consider these ninety-five scholars according to the category of the scholarships they held. The breakdown is as follows, with the number in square brackets indicating those scholars who were known to have entered holy orders or become schoolmasters:

> Bible clerks: 16 [9]
> Scholars of the College Foundation: 23 [16]
> John Mere's scholars: 4 [2]
> Norwich scholars (Parker): 16 [14]
> Canterbury scholars of the Westminster Foundation (Parker): 9 [6]
> Scholars of the Eastbridge Foundation (Parker): 8 [7]
> John Parker's scholars (Parker): 7 [6]
> Nicholas Bacon's scholars: 12 [10].[32]

What is most conspicuous is that the proportion of graduates seeking a career in the Church is surprisingly high among those who held scholarships founded by Matthew Parker and Nicholas Bacon. Of the scholarships founded in 1577 by Nicholas Bacon, ten out of the twelve recipients whose scholarships had been funded until they acquired their BA or MA became clergymen. The exceptions were John Burman, who continued his studies in law at Cambridge and later became the commissary and official to the Bishop of Norwich, and John Clarke, who relinquished his scholarship after obtaining his BA and who possibly pursued his career somewhere other than in the Church.

The situation of the scholars supported by Parker's four foundations is rather more complicated. There were forty Parker scholars, of whom thirty-three sought a career in the Church. The seven scholars who did not enter holy orders were Ralph Joyner (Norwich), Francis Sadler (Norwich), Abraham Tilman (Canterbury), Nicholas Faunt (Canterbury), Henry Brownrigge (Canterbury), William Austen (Eastbridge), and Christopher Marlowe (John Parker). Of these, however, Abraham Tilman should be discounted, as he died at the college in 1589, while Ralph Joyner, a son of a cooper in Norwich, made his last will and testament on 8 January 1582, with probate granted on 16 August 1585.[33] Among Parker's forty scholars, therefore, only five (less than 15 per cent of the total, and with four coming from Canterbury) followed a life outside the Church.

The fact that the majority of scholars holding stipends established by Parker and Bacon took holy orders seems to have stemmed partly from the

---

[32] For details of the scholars, see Appendix 4, 'Foundation Scholars of Corpus Christi College, 1573–87'.
[33] TNA, PROB 11/68/492.

principles of the foundation administrators, including the heirs of Parker and of Bacon, the mayor and aldermen of Norwich, and the dean and chapter of Canterbury, whose memory of the founders and their personal religious zeal must still have been fresh. John Parker, the heir of Matthew Parker, showed great enthusiasm for making the general requirements for his scholarships still more specific, and 'claimed the right to make the appointments himself during his lifetime, after which the college authorities were to do so'.[34] The Buttery Book shows his occasional presence at the high table, which may have tacitly yet constantly reminded the scholars of their benefactor's sentiments and wishes.[35] Moreover, fellows of Corpus Christi College frequently had to visit Sir Nicholas Bacon in Gorhambury and his heir in Redgrave concerning matters to do with the foundation and other college business.[36] The administrators' serious concerns about the scholars and their close relationship with the college authorities seem to indicate that they selected scholars with great care, supervised their conduct, and sometimes gave advice on their careers, in addition to finding employment for them.

Another possibility is that most of these scholars were held by a bond of obligation to, and respect for, those benefactors who had provided them with learning opportunities, and who had also played a major role in the development of the English Church. In 1583, Robert Dallington, a graduate of Corpus Christi, compiled and published *A Booke of Epitaphes Made vpon the Death of the Right Worshipfull Sir William Bvttes*, to which at least three fellows and seven scholars of the college contributed eulogies of Butts, an active MP for Norfolk, who in turn had a close acquaintance with Nicholas Bacon and his heirs.[37] These members of the college no doubt felt indebted to Butts and Bacon and seem to have been more or less united in the esteem and affection they had for their patrons and their political circles. Five of the contributors were or had been Norwich scholars; Thomas Corbold, 'Baconum alumnus' of Redgrave School, who had held a Nicholas Bacon

---

[34] John Bakeless, *The Tragicall History of Christopher Marlowe* (2 vols, Cambridge, MA, 1942), vol. 1, p. 64.

[35] See, for instance, CCCA, CCCC02/S/33, Buttery Book 1582–86, septimana post annuntiationis 3a 1585, septimana paschalis.

[36] For example, see CCCA, CCCC02/B/4, Audit Book 1550–80, fol. 7v of 1577; CCCC02/B/5, Audit Book 1578–90, fol. 8r of 1581, fols 8r and 8v of 1585, etc.

[37] Robert Dallington, *A Booke of Epitaphes Made vpon the Death of the Right Worshipfull Sir William Bvttes* (London, 1583), sigs A7v–A8r, B1r–B3v, B4v–B5r, C7r–D1v. For the close regional relationship between William Butts and the Bacons, see A. Hassell Smith, *County and Court: Government and Politics in Norfolk 1558–1603* (Oxford, 1974), pp. 33, 207–8; Robert Tittler, *Nicholas Bacon: The Making of a Tudor Statesman* (Athens, OH, 1976), pp. 148–67.

scholarship at Corpus, joined them.[38] Thus, the high number of scholars holding a Parker or Bacon foundation scholarship and seeking a career in the Church can be explained by their sense of shared aspiration, as well as the close relationship that persisted between the foundation administrators and the scholars.

Providing a remarkable contrast to the religious enthusiasm of the Norwich scholars, an orientation towards a secular career seems to have been shared specifically among the four scholars from Canterbury. Although the later careers of William Austen and Henry Brownrigg cannot be traced, we know that Nicholas Faunt obtained the secretaryship to Sir Francis Walsingham. All these scholars, including Francis Sadler of the Norwich foundation, relinquished their scholarships either without or before obtaining an MA. This was due to the rule that those who had held a scholarship for more than three years must enter the ministry, a requirement that we also find in the qualifications for a stipend drawn from Parker's other foundations. In other words, a scholar could often excuse himself from entering holy orders by giving up his scholarship before obtaining his MA. Admittedly, apart from Christopher Marlowe, we can find at least three MA scholars who had been fully funded for six years but who apparently did not work for the Church: two Bible clerks, Daniel Godfrey and his successor, Robert Smyth;[39] and Christopher Tucke, the scholar of the College Foundation who became a fellow after obtaining his MA. However, these three scholars were outside the powerful sphere of influence of the Parker or Bacon foundation administrators and may have been allowed, at least to some degree, to evade their binding power.

In these circumstances, the general feeling that a funded scholar should enter holy orders to repay his moral obligation to his benefactor may have been easily encouraged, particularly among those scholars who had benefited from Matthew Parker munificence. It would have been difficult, and even regarded as scandalous, for a scholar to seek a secular career after having obtained an MA with the long-term support of a benefactor. In this respect, Marlowe's case is unprecedented, for he had received Parker's full exhibition for six years to finish his MA and then, of all things, gave up his ecclesiastical career in order to write plays. This extraordinary career choice would very likely have made a negative impression on his contemporaries at Corpus Christi, and this could have been sufficient reason for those

---

[38] The three fellows were John Dix, Christopher Abbys, and Sophonius Smith; the seven scholars were Henry Mihel (or Mihill), John Weld, Ralph Joyner, Robert Parker, Andrew Style, Phillip Walker (or Watker), and Thomas Corbold 'Baconum alumnus'. Dix, Abbys, Mihel, Weld, and Joyner all held Norwich scholarships.

[39] Robert Smyth was probably the scholar who became a surety of William Austen. See Chapter 2, p. 73.

zealous administrators and college members to become hostile enough to bend their ears to a defamatory rumour about the ungrateful scholar, and then to pass it on.

It was thus the economically and politically intricate relationships of college society that provided the basis for representing Marlowe as an ambitious traitor leaving Cambridge for Rheims. His supposed two-facedness, being both 'kind Kit' and a turncoat, arose from the fact that most poor scholars had to depend on the closeness/closedness of the collegiate community. It was their dependence upon a beneficent patron and their intricate friendships with each other that enabled them to survive their difficult lives. No wonder this nurtured a tight-knit network of friendship and solidarity among the members of the community, a typical case of which we have observed in Marlowe's compassion for Austen in his time of need. In the same way, it is possible that this closeness and closedness would have readily aroused hostility towards a renegade element that threatened their religious unity and ideals. Considering the zeal of a community united in reverence for its great benefactors, it is not difficult to imagine the nature of the friction that led to the circulation of the defamatory rumour about Marlowe.

ENTER ANTHONY HICKMAN

When the mutual confidence of the members was eroded, the close-knit society of Corpus Christi became a hotbed of violence and slander. We often come across displays of two-facedness – firm camaraderie on one side and violent hostility on the other – within the college community. An act of violence that occurred on 13 October 1595 between Ralph Dawson, BD, a fellow of the college, and Thomas Field, MA, also from Corpus, seems a typical case that originated in pecuniary and fiduciary troubles that arose between a fellow and his pupil.[40]

Field, after having obtained his MA in 1591, stayed on at the college for four years to pursue the next stage of his studies. He was possibly provided with academic and financial assistance by Dawson, his former tutor: in fact, Field was able to obtain a sizeable loan from Dawson 'by the space of one yere [...] vntill aboute the xvth or xvjth day of October' 1595, and

---

[40] The following description of the incident is based on the depositions of the litigants and those who were involved in the *Field v. Dawson* lawsuit: see CUA, V. C. Ct. II. 1. Depositions (9 July 1593–2 April 1597), Ralph Dawson (fols 198r, 202v–203r, 204r–v), Nicholas Martin (fols 198v–200v), John Fletcher (fols 200v–201v), Thomas Field (fol. 203r–v), Thomas Brookes (fols 206r–208r), and John Smith (fols 205r–206r). As for the details of this incident, see Arata Ide, 'John Fletcher of Corpus Christi College: New Records of His Early Years', *Early Theatre*, 13:2 (2010), 63–77.

was allowed to use a study in 'Dawson's upper chamber': that is, a room in the roof space above Dawson's first-floor room, Chamber 7 on the north side.[41] In October 1595, Field secured the vicarage of Babraham, a village six miles from Cambridge, and there took up his residence. Field's difficulty in repaying Dawson, however, seems to have put an end to Dawson's personal favour and their fraternal relationship. On the afternoon of 13 October, with the due date for the repayment of the loan impending, Field stopped by the college for some reason (probably to contrive a way to raise money or to pack up for removal), and spent his time, not in the study of Dawson's upper chamber, but in the first-floor room of Nicholas Martin, another fellow of Corpus Christi and Field's close friend.[42]

Meanwhile, Dawson, who was then walking in the courtyard of the college, sent for Nicholas Martin and said, 'Mr martin, I vnderstande that Mr Feilde is in your Chameber, whoe is indebted vnto me, and hathe greatlie Iniuried me besides, I woulde be lothe to come vppe into your Chamber w[i]thoute your consente'. Martin, who was elected fellow, tersely replied, 'The dore is open and you (speakeinge to the said Mr Dawson) maye goe vppe if you will', whereupon Dawson sent for the beadle, then called Thomas Brookes, an executive officer under the vice-chancellor's mandate, and, with the beadle, went up to Martin's room in order to take Field 'awaye from thence vnto or before Mr Vicechauncellar to answere the sayd Mr Dawson in a cause of debte'.[43]

Resisting these coercive measures, Field locked himself in Martin's chamber. After struggling for a while to break into the room, Dawson called for a blacksmith's apprentice to have him wrench the door open. Martin, who was present at the scene, forbade the boy from doing it; nevertheless, according to Martin's deposition, 'then & there the sayd Mr Dawson takeinge the tooles from the sayd Smithe boye; sayd that he (*predictus* Dawson) would open the same studye doare him selfe'. Martin remonstrated with his colleague, saying: 'Mr Dawson I thincke you cannot neither may you lawfully doe yt, and I wishe you to doe noe more then lawfully you may doe.'[44] This admonition, however, fell on deaf ears. Martin continued in his testimony:

> And not w[i]thstandinge all this; the sayd Mr Dawson did then & there w[i]th a chisell & a ham[m]er vnnayle the hingells of the sayd studye

---

[41] CUA, V. C. Ct. II. 1, fols 202v–203r. Dawson was elected and admitted as fellow on 5 August 1586 in place of Moses Fowler, who was resident in Chamber 7 of Bacon's plan in 1577.
[42] CUA, V. C. Ct. II. 1, fols 198v, 200r.
[43] Ibid., fol. 199r–v.
[44] Ibid.

doare, & soe opened the same, and then seeinge the sayd Mr Fyeld there in the sayd studye and sayd to Mr Brookes the Bedell (whoe was then & there all this while) thus: or the like in effecte: viz: nowe I haue opened the doare, and there is the p[ar]tye (meaninge the sayd Mr Fyeld) doe what you haue to doe.[45]

As soon as he was dragged out of the room, Field was taken to the parlour of John Duport, the vice-chancellor and master of Jesus College, to make apology for the debt.

Dawson's extreme method of coercion, hauling his former pupil out of the chamber, seems to have been modelled on an incident that had happened seven years earlier, in 1588, when Anthony Hickman, a fellow of the college, was also violently dragged out of his chamber on the instruction of John Copcot, the new college master and successor to Robert Norgate. Dawson, a fresh college fellow at that time, happened to be resident immediately above Hickman's ground-floor room in Chamber 7, and was thus in a good position to witness the incident close up.[46] The high-handedness of the college authorities in this matter may have made an ineradicable impression upon him and later encouraged him to treat his unpleasant pupil in a similar way. The contentious case between Hickman and Copcot was, however, more serious than that between Dawson and Field and had in fact been running for several years, revealing the political divisions and factionalism within the college. To get the whole picture, we must go back to the point when Norgate secured a fellowship for Hickman in 1583.

It was often difficult for an outsider from a dissimilar local background to establish his place in a locally defined and very intimate social group. A fellow who spent almost all his academic career outside Corpus Christi might well be obliged to establish himself in a social environment that he found uncongenial. Hickman's case is typical. The fourth son of Anthony Hickman of Woodford Hall, Essex, a merchant from London, Anthony junior was educated under William Malym at St Paul's School, and matriculated as a pensioner at St John's College in the Michaelmas term of 1575.[47] Robert Greene came to St John's in the same term, so they might have had an opportunity to become acquainted with each other. Hickman subsequently transferred to Peterhouse to obtain his BA in 1579–80 and then his MA in 1583; though he had had no connection with Corpus Christi up to then, he was elected as a fellow of that college in 1583. Hickman's

---

[45] *Ibid.*, fol. 199v. As for Dawson's coercive measures, see also Thomas Brookes' deposition: *ibid.*, fol. 207r.

[46] Hickman occupied the ground floor of Chamber 7 in 1583 when Philip Nichols relinquished the fellowship to him. See Chapter 1, pp. 35–6.

[47] Michael McDonnell, *The Annals of St Paul's School* (Cambridge, 1959), p. 99.

extraordinary promotion was made following a mandate from the queen, who requested that he be exempted from the college statutes that would normally disqualify him. This election of an outsider through cronyism naturally created much dissatisfaction among the college fellows at Corpus, one of whom took the lead in expelling Hickman five years afterwards with the assistance of John Copcot, the new college master.

Robert Norgate was a man of political astuteness, a quality that often led him to employ manipulative tactics in personal affairs and to resist political pressure at the election of a college fellow. Hickman's appointment was not the first time that he had come under such pressure. In September 1577, Norgate had written to Burghley:

> Whereas vpon information made vnto your Honour that a roome of a Felloweshipe in o[u]r Colledg of Corpus Christi in Cambridg ys voyd, yo[u]r Lordshipe did write yo[u]r letters vnto me for the pr[e]ferment of one S[i]r Booth, borne in Rutlandshire vnto that Felloweshipe.[48]

Norgate successfully rejected the proposal on the pretext that the candidate was unqualified according to college regulations and because of his refusal to take the examination.[49] The university authorities naturally regarded preferment by private letters as a serious problem, because it entailed circumventing the college statutes that gave them the power to elect fellows and scholars free from any external interference. As a consequence, in March 1579 the vice-chancellor and the masters of certain colleges asked Burghley 'to diminish the frequency of the queen's mandates for elections to fellowships and scholarships, as a result of which university men were now looking to courtiers as the means of preferment, rather than diligently concentrating on becoming good scholars'.[50] Notwithstanding this official request, Norgate was forced to become entangled in Hickman's promotion case by royal mandate five years later. This time, for some reason he accepted the proposal. Under the heading '26 die Aprilis Anno Domini 1583' in the college's Chapter Book, we find the entry: 'et eodem die et Anno ex Mandato Dominae Reginae Anthonius Hickman electus est socius in idem sodalicium prae consensis Magistri et sociorum'.[51]

Was Norgate a victim of the oppressive administration of the Court? Probably not. Rather, he seems to have made use of external pressure to

---

[48] TNA, SP, 12/115, fol. 59r (13 September 1577).
[49] Ibid., fol. 97r (27 September 1577).
[50] Victor Morgan, with a contribution by Christopher Brooke, *A History of the University of Cambridge, Volume II, 1546–1750* (Cambridge, 2004), p. 391.
[51] 'On the same day and year, by the mandate of the queen, Anthony Hickman is elected fellow of the same college with the consent of the Master and associates.' CCCA, CCCC01/C/1, Chapter Book 1, p. 86.

secure his own political stability within the college. The ringleader of the anti-Norgate faction was Philip Nichols, who had brought a suit against the master in 1580 for his mismanagement of the college finances and for nepotism in electing a fellow.[52] Norgate protested to John Hatcher, the vice-chancellor, that the college master should not make his appearance by 'the complaynt of one onely fellowe', but agreed that, 'yf by due proofe such a sufficient numb[e]r of the Fellowes shall ioyne w[i]th him in this complaynt', he would submit himself to be judged in public.[53] Although Nichols insisted that several fellows had supported his claim, Norgate seems to have succeeded in suppressing internal opposition: Nichols's suit eventually fizzled out. After a few years of negotiating this tense relationship within the college, Nichols's relinquishment of his fellowship on account of his marriage in April 1583 gave Norgate a good opportunity to consolidate his mastership by appointing a new fellow, Hickman, who was supportive of his position. The factional infighting naturally stimulated Norgate and his allies to adopt a measured strategy for selecting a candidate for the fellowship.

The royal letter recommending Hickman as successor to Nichols was so well timed that it was as if Norgate had worked in tandem with the Court in this process. Norgate certainly never gave the slightest indication of his reluctance to accept the royal mandate. Rather, he seems to have been painstakingly prepared, and even well disposed, to elect Hickman. In fact, so as to prevent college disputes about the validity of Hickman's appointment by the queen, 'the Master took the Opinions of some Civilians in the University who adjudged the Dispensation valid, and thereupon with the consent of the major part of the Society, he made a Decree in favour of *Hickman*'.[54]

While Norgate's interests coincided with those of the candidate on the matter of the appointment, this provoked retaliation from the anti-Norgate faction immediately after the master's death in November 1587. Christopher Abbys, the senior fellow and first president under the new mastership of John Copcot, set out with his allies to deprive Hickman of the fellowship in concert with Copcot. The letter of the master and fellows to Lord Burghley dated 7 May 1588 (in Abbys's own italic handwriting) shows the five fellows who supported the expulsion of Hickman: Christopher Abbys, Henry Rewse, John Brome, Matthew Sethell, and Edward Elwin, of whom only Abbys had been involved as a fellow in the process of Hickman's

---

[52] For Nichols's suit against Norgate, see Chapter 1, pp. 55–7.
[53] TNA, SP, 12/143, fol. 112.
[54] Masters, *History of Corpus Christi*, p. 120.

election in April 1583.[55] Abbys had been cultivated along with John Dix to pursue a policy of religious conformity and stability within the college in the 1570s, and so may have tended to champion the policy of the new master, who had flourished under the aegis of John Whitgift, Archbishop of Canterbury.[56] Copcot and these five fellows explained that Hickman had stirred up a dispute on the matter of 'seniority' (or priority) in fellowship and was expelled 'for disobedience, by vertewe of a statute'.[57] However, a hint of political contrivance cannot be overlooked, for Hickman's testimony demonstrates that 'there were but the Mr. & five felloes onely (w[hi]ch cannot be the major pars of xij) consenting to my pretended deprivation'.[58] Moreover, 'the question of seniority was decided by Dr. Norgat then mr., & the greater part of the society, according to the statute of the colledge'.[59]

Despite Hickman's urgent appeal to the vice-chancellor's court to reverse its decision, Copcot proceeded to elect Henry Mihil, the Norwich scholar and pupil of Abbys, in place of Hickman, and resorted to force in the end:

> After the sentence of expulsion mr. Hykman[n] appealed, & exhibited his appeale to Dr. Legge then vicechanceller, who p[re]sently sent his inhibition, by one of the Beadles: w[hi]ch inhibition notw[i]thstanding, Dr. Copcot proceeded to the choise of an other, into mr. Hykman[n]s place: And mr. Hykman[n] was by extraordinary force, caried out of his chamber, & kept out of the colledge.[60]

Hickman sought immediate redress from Burghley 'agaynst this violent oppression, so notoriously known & noted in the vniv[e]rsitye whose testimony I have vnder there severall handes, for the justifying of my behauiour agaynst there opprobrious slanders'.[61] A small disagreement on a matter of seniority gave rise to a scandal that made a great stir in the university.

Robert Masters says that Copcot was 'thought to be somewhat prejudiced against [Hickman] for not readily joining with his Friends in his Election, and because of [Hickman's] being well affected towards the Puritans'.[62] Admittedly, it is well known that Copcot became the target of Martin Marprelate and was reviled as a malicious Episcopalian: 'The treader was Cankered Malice, his eyes were fiery, his face thin and withered, pined away

---

[55] BL, Lansdowne MS 57 (86), fol. 200r. Rewse was elected fellow on 22 June 1583, Brome on 28 June 1583, Sethell on 7 December 1585, and Elwin on 3 December 1586.
[56] See Chapter 1, pp. 51–2, 53–4.
[57] BL, Lansdowne MS 57 (94), fol. 222v.
[58] BL, Lansdowne MS 57 (95), fol. 224r.
[59] BL, Lansdowne MS 68 (29), fol. 65r.
[60] Ibid.
[61] BL, Lansdowne MS 57 (95), fol. 224r.
[62] Masters, History of Corpus Christi, p. 120.

with melancholy, and this was Doctor Copcot.'[63] No evidence survives, however, of Hickman's radical tendency in religion except for the fact that his parents were committed Protestants in exile under the Marian regime.[64] It is hard, therefore, to understand why Copcot, even though he was prejudiced against puritanism, resorted to such forcible and outrageous means against Hickman without assuming there was some political infighting behind the scenes. What seems obvious is that Abbys insinuated himself into Copcot's confidence and incited his hostility and prejudice against Hickman, for Abbys was the only person who had been well informed about the former dispute regarding Hickman's seniority and could thus make a report of Hickman's reluctance to elect Copcot as the new master.

WAR BY PROXY: WALSINGHAM VS WHITGIFT

What we *can* see may just be the tip of the iceberg; nevertheless, troubles and disputes in the university suggest that intense religio-political factionalism in the college community was often grafted onto such problems at Court and aggravated divisions. In fact, Copcot's strong measures dragged Court magnates into the political rivalries within the college owing to Hickman's close connection with Sir Francis Walsingham, who may have helped Hickman to gain access to the queen's mandate. Copcot had to explain their situation to Burghley, stating that 'according vnto oure statutes, [Hickman] was depriued of his place, which was not done w[i]t[h]out Mr Secretarye Walsingham his h[onour]s privitye, for that in sume sorte he belonged unto him'. Moreover, the master emphasized that he had made every possible effort to persuade Walsingham of his cause: 'Sins that tyme, Mr. Secretarye being informed, that his behavior was not suche as he was charged with, I and the fellowes confirmed the matters exhibited against him with our voluntarye oathes before youre lordships vicechancellour.'[65]

Copcot and his confederates wrote to Walsingham directly as well:

> We did not deale agaynst Mr. Hickman w[i]t[h]out yo[u]r H. privitye, and were enformed that yo[u]r H. woulde not mainteyne him, if such matter were true, as we pr[e]ferred against him. Eleven articles & one halfe he confesseth, we haue by o[u]r oathes confirmed them all for yo[u]r

---

[63] *Hay Any Work for Cooper*, in Joseph L. Black (ed.), *The Martin Marprelate Tracts: A Modernized and Annotated Edition* (Cambridge, 2008), p. 138.

[64] See Maria Dowling and Joy Shakespeare, 'Religion and Politics in Mid-Tudor England through the Eyes of an English Protestant Woman: The Recollections of Rose Hickman', *Bulletin of the Institute of Historical Research*, 55:131 (1982), 94–102. For Hickman's family and Rose's memoir, see Adam Stark, *The History and Antiquities of Gainsburgh* (London, 1817), pp. 124–39.

[65] BL, Lansdowne MS 57 (91), fol. 210r.

H. satisfaction, according to yo[u]r H. desier, & therfore thincke that in lawe we should not be troubled any further about him. After it pleased yo[u]r H. as we take it, vpon importunitye of suite to com[m]ende the matter vnto certayne in this vniu[er]sity, who haue dealt so favourably w[i]t[h] the offendor in respect of affinity betwene him & one principall partye amonge them able to leade the rest & so iniuriouslye for some private respectes in regarde of vs, as in certifyinge that w[hi]ch they little knewe, & lesse considered haue not well vsed yo[u]r H. Vpon whose certificate as we heare yo[u]r H. hath requested the L. Archbishoppe of Canterbury his grace to ende ye matter.[66]

Copcot and his henchmen, apprehensive of and keen to avoid Walsingham's displeasure, were trying to impress upon him their urgency to take up 'legal' proceedings against the 'offendor'. At the same time, Copcot here gives a mild hint, delivered behind the shield of John Whitgift, that the matter was none of Walsingham's business. This suggests, in other words, that Abbys, along with his confederates, now had a hold over college affairs by being closely affiliated with Copcot and Whitgift and had turned the solidarity of the Norwich–Parker cluster into a power base from which to strike back against an opponent or social group that had been under the aegis of the former master, Norgate, and of Walsingham. Thus, we can see the dispute between Copcot/Abbys and Norgate/Hickman developing into a war by proxy between Whitgift and Walsingham. Notwithstanding Hickman's reasonable appeal, supported by several prominent civil lawyers and college heads, Whitgift's obstinacy prevented Hickman from being restored until 1591, when John Jegon held the tenure as master, following Copcot's death.[67] Hickman's downfall under Copcot's mastership suggests the deep-seated antagonism towards Norgate among one particular cluster within the college community; and conversely reveals the close political alliance between Hickman, Norgate, and Walsingham.

The Norgate–Walsingham alliance, because of the common interests it expressed, may also have been the target of Tobias Bland's notorious libel. Bland migrated to Corpus Christi in 1581 after having completed his BA at Pembroke Hall. It was in 1582, just before Hickman's disputed appointment to a fellowship, that Bland published a libel against Norgate. Although no detailed records of an incident survive, 'Articles against Tobias Blande' give us a glimpse of its outline: 'Tobias Blande did make & publish about two yeres since in Bennet College one infamous lible, blasphemous to the

---

[66] TNA, SP, 12/216, fol. 40r.
[67] On 30 April, Robert Some, the master of Peterhouse and vice-chancellor, wrote to Lord Burghley about Hickman's case, insisting that he was wrongfully expelled. See BL, Lansdowne MS 68 (30), fol. 66r.

dishonoure of god, directed manifestlye against Mr Doctor Norgate, Mr of that College & now Vicechancellor of the university.'[68] Norgate and the other fellows, having discovered that Bland was the author of the libel, made him confess his guilt before all the members of the college; they put him 'to shame of sytting in the stockes', and then expelled him from the college. To make doubly sure of his banishment, Norgate, installed as the vice-chancellor in 1584, sent an official request to every master of a college 'lest any of them ignorantlye might receave him into their Colleges'.

The blasphemous libel was titled 'A necessary Cathechisme to be red every sunday morninge' and began with the line: 'In the name of the father, the sonn & the old wife'. What most concerned Norgate and the university authorities, however, was not only Bland's slander against the master but also a strong suspicion that 'in the saide Libell an honorable personage was touched'. We can easily determine who this 'honorable personage' was by looking at the following sanction against Bland:

> The sayde Tobias Bland, com[m]ing to request favor in his sute, was advised by Mr vicechancellor, who had before throughly examined his libell, & was not ignorant of any thing therin conteined, to go up to S[i]r Francis Walsingham, to confesse his faulte, to request his favor, & obteine his letters for his degree; otherwise he shoulde never be admitted Mr of Art by him. [...] In the sayde libell this name S[i]r Francis was suspiciouslye brought in.[69]

No document survives to explain why Bland slandered Norgate and Walsingham, but it seems to have been another case of war by proxy within the college. After he was expelled from the college, Bland joined the anti-Marprelate campaign organized by John Whitgift and Richard Bancroft with his *A Baite for Momus* (1589). Martin Marprelate junior satirized Bland as 'Sir Tom Blan. o' Bedford', who must carry 'a looking glass for [John Bridges, dean of Sarum], to see whether his catercap doth every way reach over his ears, and so stand according to his calling'.[70]

The banishment of Bland throws an oblique light on the nature of the factional struggle within Corpus Christi during the 1580s. A strained atmosphere obviously pervaded the college, generated by small-community animosities that involved some influential figures behind the scenes. This marked tendency towards factionalism and polarization manifested itself particularly in the long dispute over Hickman's fellowship. If we assume that Marlowe was initiated into the social network of Walsingham during his student days and consequently pursued his career outside the Church,

[68] BL, Lansdowne MS 45 (65), fol. 138r.
[69] *Ibid.*
[70] Black (ed.), *Martin Marprelate Tracts*, p. 181.

then understanding the social context of this college community would be profitable in helping us to see why the defamatory rumour against Marlowe began to be circulated in and around the college. Marlowe, like Hickman, was a victim of this factional struggle.

A document in the possession of Corpus Christi College Archive, which, until now, had been overlooked, could support the assumption that there was a close alliance between Hickman, Norgate, and Marlowe. This is Norgate's memorandum for the college accounts with the caption 'Reckoned with Mr Chever 22 February 1582 [1583]', in which we find the notes recording sums received from and paid to Robert Chever, the fellow acting as steward or bursar, with other jottings relating to 1583 and 1586.[71] The document suggests that Norgate had several accounts to settle on 26 April 1583 – the day when Hickman was formally elected a fellow 'ex Mandato Dominae Reginae'. That morning, Norgate called Chever into his study and delivered to him the sum of twenty pounds for payment to Thomas Hodiloe, a brewer, and duly noted the expense in his memorandum: 'I payd him 26 of Aprill 1583 in my studye of ye Colledg w[hi]ch was then payd to mr Hodelo in ye forenoone before 8 of ye clocke -- xx^{li}.' Having finished his dinner, Norgate once again called Chever into his great chamber and paid him the sum of five pounds for an unknown purpose. At that time, two guests were in the chamber with Norgate: 'It[e]m I payd him yt day aft[e]r diner in my great chamb[e]r in gold in p[re]senc of Sr Hickman & marlin -- v^{li}.' Obviously, 'Sr Hickman' is the fellow who officially obtained the fellowship on that day. It would have been natural for the college master, precise about noting the members' degrees, to refer to Hickman as 'Sr', not 'Mr', as Hickman would only receive his MA in the coming commencement ceremony at the beginning of June. There was no 'Sr Hickman' in Cambridge other than this newly appointed fellow.

But who was 'Marlin'? We should remember that Norgate's small handwritten letter 't' often looks like a small letter 'l' with its loop collapsed, so this could be read as 'Martin', not 'Marlin'. It could follow, then, that this man might have been John Martin, a mason who was involved in the building work of the new chapel and who often appears in the accounts as one of the payees. Martin might have been present because some of the money was due to him. However, why did Martin the mason have to be present before Norgate and the new fellow, Hickman, when the master handed five pounds in gold to the college steward? This scenario seems unlikely; it is more likely that it was our undergraduate, Christopher Marlowe of Corpus Christi.

It is important to consider what purpose these two men, Hickman and Marlowe, had for being in the great chamber of the college master. The

---

[71] CCCA, CCCC02/B/44/42.

situation is not hard to imagine. Norgate, in handing over gold coins to the value of five pounds to Chever, would have been naturally compelled to ask for someone to be present as a witness in order to avoid any litigation over damages of the kind that the master himself had often been involved in at the vice-chancellor's court.[72] As Craig Muldrew points out, 'Witnesses, rather than account books, were the most important form of security for debts and other agreements, throughout all levels of society'.[73] The college master chose his possible attendees from the residents of Corpus Christi, and later put the names of the witnesses down scrupulously in his memorandum. We cannot be certain whether Norgate invited them to dinner to celebrate Hickman's inauguration. What this document suggests, however, is that, under the strain of administering the college in crisis, he considered them to be a reliable pair of witnesses, and was not only familiar enough with them to ask for assistance but also considered them worthy enough to place in them his full trust and confidence as college members. Thus it seems unlikely that this 'Marlin' could be the mason 'Martin'.

When Hickman came to Corpus Christi as a fellow, Marlowe was at the last stage before completing his BA degree. The Chapter Book in the college archives has a list of fellows appointed to lecture on each subject for 1583–84. There we can find Thomas Harris, the praelector in philosophy and Nicholas Faunt's roommate, who appended his signature to Marlowe's supplicat to certify that the candidate had satisfactorily performed his public exercises. Hickman, who was elected 'in lectorem Rhetor[ices]', provided academic training along with the praelector to develop Marlowe's skill at disputation.[74] He was therefore one of the fellows, along with Harris, who could report on Marlowe's talent to Walsingham and to his secretary, Nicholas Faunt.

It is also interesting to note that, in 1585–86, Hickman helped Sophonius Smith, his Corpus Christi colleague and the senior proctor for the academic year, to examine the university 'questionists' for their degrees.[75] At this time, Hickman happened to examine Thomas Nashe of St John's College, among a number of other candidates, and so Nashe's supplicat, obviously in Nashe's own handwriting, bears the signature 'Anth:

---

[72] CUA, Collect. Admin. 6a [Caryl B. 24], Buckle Book, pp. 129, 142, and 152.
[73] Muldrew, *Economy of Obligation*, p. 63.
[74] CCCA, CCCC01/C/1, Chapter Book 1, p. 86.
[75] J. R. Tanner, *The Historical Register of the University of Cambridge* (1917; repr. Cambridge, 1984), p. 389. Elisabeth Leedham-Green informed me in private correspondence that proctors nearly always chose examiners from their own college and Hickman was probably better qualified than any other fellow, which would certainly have made him unpopular.

Hykman[n]' (figure 1).[76] Hickman is a unique figure in having an academic acquaintance with both Marlowe and Nashe. If these future dramatists, as some critics suppose, came to know each other at Cambridge, Hickman could have acted as an intermediary between them. Although we will never know what Hickman's penchant for dramatic entertainments was – if he had any – he seems to have had none of the anti-theatre prejudice. Henry Hickman, his brother and a senior fellow of St John's, was well known across the university as an actor who had played Richmond in Thomas Legge's *Richardus Tertius* and Erophilus in *Hymenaeus*.[77] The puritan tendency of Henry's family was clearly no serious impediment to his enthusiasm for the stage. And there is evidence that the brothers' friendship remained firm until the death of Anthony in 1597, when he bequeathed Henry 'his bookes and willed him to dispose of his apparell as he thought good'.[78]

Both Anthony Hickman and Marlowe seem to have had something provocative enough about them to make them victims of 'opprobrious slander' within the college. What they shared may not just have been their keen interest in rhetoric; they also had common enemies within the college, headed by Christopher Abbys, who had been ill-disposed toward Norgate and his henchmen under the patronage of Walsingham and had experienced a sense of crisis that the unity and conformity of the college community would be threatened by those fellows and scholars. In other words, the strong connection with Walsingham allowed Hickman and possibly Marlowe to protect their interests and credit under the mastership of Norgate. With the master's declining health and eventual death in 1587, the anti-Norgate/Walsingham faction set out to rally themselves by gaining the political support of Whitgift and Copcot. Placing the malicious rumour about Marlowe in the context of this political struggle within the college community gives us a probable explanation of its genesis: that it formed part of an anti-Norgate, anti-Walsingham campaign throughout the 1580s. It is impossible, and so futile, to attempt to identify the originator of the rumour about Marlowe, but it seems highly likely that Christopher Abbys, with his college faction, would have found it to be a convenient instrument for harassing the Norgate/Walsingham faction, and thus to have been its chief disseminator and propagator.

---

[76] CUA, Supplicats, 1585–6, no. 83. See also Introduction, pp. 8–9.
[77] Martin Wiggins, *British Drama 1533–1642: A Catalogue* (Oxford, 2012), vol. 2, p. 240.
[78] Guildhall Library, MS 9171/18, fol. 452v.

Chapter 4

MARLOWE AND THE PRIVY COUNCIL

WHAT THE PRIVY COUNCIL'S CERTIFICATE SUGGESTS

The details of Marlowe's 'good service' to Elizabeth I (mentioned in the previous chapter) are unknown. A. L. Rowse and A. D. Wraight attach too much importance to the rumour that he went to Rheims, concluding that Francis Walsingham sent Marlowe to report on the goings-on at the seminary: almost all the other biographers are sceptical about this assumption.[1] Marlowe's name appears nowhere in the diary of the English College. He may have taken an alias, but this would have been almost impossible to do and would have been dangerous, as scholars from Cambridge, including Samuel Kennet, Marlowe's former classmate at King's School in Canterbury, lived there at that time.[2] Moreover, the president and staff of the seminary, who had learnt a lesson from the activities of Richard Baines and other dubious seminarians, were on the lookout for English spies.[3]

In place of Walsingham, one of the leading candidates for Marlowe's patron has been Sir James Croft. According to the summary of the Privy Council minutes, the Councillors present on 29 June 1587 were Lord Burghley the Treasurer, John Whitgift the Archbishop of Canterbury, Christopher Hatton the Lord Chancellor, Henry Carey the Lord Chamberlain, and James Croft the Controller of the Household, all of whom urged the Cambridge University authorities to restore Marlowe's reputation. Austin K. Gray points out that these four of the five were pursuing a strategy that ran counter to Walsingham's belligerent foreign policy. Croft, who had

---

[1] A. L. Rowse, *Christopher Marlowe: A Biography* (London, 1964), p. 30; A. D. Wraight and Virginia F. Stern, *In Search of Christopher Marlowe: A Pictorial Biography* (Chichester, 1993), p. 90.

[2] For Samuel Kennet's interesting career, see William Urry, *Christopher Marlowe and Canterbury*, ed. with an introduction by Andrew Butcher (London, 1988), p. 49.

[3] Henry Foley (ed.), *Records of the English Province of the Society of Jesus* (7 vols in 12, London, 1877–83), vol. 6, p. 7.

concluded the peace with Alexander Farnese, Duke of Parma, was 'the moving spirit behind it', was steadfastly pro-Spanish, and was known to be in the pay of Philip II of Spain. Gray assumes that, 'Inasmuch as Crofts and three of his colleagues in this policy endorse Marlowe's claim for an M.A., it is possible that he was employed on the peace-manoeuvres with Parma and went to the Netherlands'. Walsingham, who remained critical of the policy, 'did not endorse the Privy Council document'.[4]

This assumption sounds reasonable, but it contains several flaws. For one thing, it is doubtful whether Burghley, Whitgift, and Hatton aligned themselves with Croft's peace negotiations or coalesced into a single body against Walsingham. Burghley seems to have placed less confidence in the septuagenarian Croft than Elizabeth did.[5] Croft had taken the lead in the peace manoeuvres at their initial stages, but, according to Conyers Read, 'no doubt at the Queen's bidding, Burghley himself took over' and 'kept Walsingham in touch with every step in the proceedings'.[6] Moreover, Walsingham was improving his relations with Burghley around that time, as Burghley had appealed to the queen for redress of Walsingham's debt and had supported him in his attempt to win the chancellorship of the Duchy of Lancaster, vacated following Sir Ralph Sadler's death on 30 May 1587. Whitgift owed his appointment as Privy Councillor to Burghley's influence, which had the effect of consolidating Burleigh's power on the Privy Council, but his own attitude towards Croft's policy is hazy. Hatton, who, according to a kinsman of Croft, was in favour of peace, was well known as one of Leicester's staunchest allies. Read concludes that 'It does not appear that [Hatton] took any active part in the negotiations'.[7]

What is more, the absence of other councillors does not necessarily suggest their indifference to the agenda for the meeting, still less that they were avoiding the need to endorse it. William Brooke, Lord Cobham, who joined Croft and the Earl of Derby on the peace mission to Parma in 1588, was also absent from the meeting, for an unknown reason. Walsingham's rate of attendance was very high; thus, given his office as the principal secretary, his failure to attend the meeting seems unusual. However, his infirmities often prevented him performing the duties of his office in the

---

[4] Austin K. Gray, 'Some Observations on Christopher Marlowe, Government Agent', *PMLA*, 43:3 (1928), 682–700, at pp. 692–3. Brooke and Riggs agree with Gray in this. See C. F. Tucker Brooke, *The Life of Marlowe and 'The Tragedy of Dido Queen of Carthage'* (1930; repr. New York, 1966), pp. 34–6; David Riggs, *The World of Christopher Marlowe* (London, 2004), pp. 180–1.

[5] Steven G. Ellis, 'Sir James Croft (c. 1518–1590)', in *ODNB*.

[6] Conyers Read, *Lord Burghley and Queen Elizabeth* (London, 1960), pp. 397–8.

[7] Conyers Read, *Mr. Secretary Walsingham and the Policy of Queen Elizabeth* (3 vols, 1925; repr. New York, 1978), vol. 3, p. 146.

spring of 1587. In fact, he had a sudden seizure during his stay in London in June.[8] On 27 June, two days before the meeting, Walsingham wrote to Edward Stafford, the ambassador in France: 'I haue ben of late and am yet constrayned to keepe my bed as this bearer can tell you by reason of a fever that I am fallen into.'[9]

A Privy Council letter authorized at a meeting would be drawn up by a clerk with the date left blank to be filled in later on. A day or so afterwards, the letter would be submitted by either the principal secretary or a clerk to the councillors – at least six of them – for their signatures. Usually, as Michael Barraclough Pulman notes, 'there were enough of them available to subscribe sufficient names, even if some of them had not been at the original meeting, and in most cases the signatures all appear to have been added at the same time'. Sometimes, however, 'the letter had to be carried around the Court from councillor to councillor until enough had been approached for the letter to be dispatched'.[10] If the purported council letter in defence of Marlowe was sent to the university authorities through this routine procedure, Walsingham, responsible for conducting and controlling the Council, would naturally have been well informed about the matter, and would not have shirked his responsibility to endorse the document.

Whether Walsingham was present or not at the meeting, Burghley seems to have been the right chairperson to propose the item, not because of the nature of Marlowe's employment but because of his status as a student at Cambridge. In theory, Burghley, as the chancellor of the university, had official authority over all its acts, so that masters, fellows, and even humble scholars often made direct appeals to him in the last resort. Marlowe, faced with the threat of losing his credit as well as his MA degree, was no exception, and possibly took the same measures to restore his reputation. Burghley was extremely influential – enough to persuade the university authorities to grant an MA to a scholar whom he considered worthy 'to be rewarded for his faithfull dealinge'. In this respect, as Peter Roberts suggests, the certificate for Marlowe can be regarded as 'a substitute for the landlord/parson certificate' that a non-resident student who qualified for an MA had to present to the vice-chancellor to show that he had 'lived soberly and studiously the course of a scholar's life' during his absence.[11]

---

[8] *Ibid.*, pp. 446–7.
[9] TNA, SP, 78/17, fol. 200r.
[10] Michael Barraclough Pulman, *The Elizabethan Privy Council in the Fifteen-Seventies* (Berkeley, 1971), p. 162. For the function and administration of the Privy Council, see also Penry Williams, *The Later Tudors: England 1547–1603* (Oxford, 1995), p. 143.
[11] Peter Roberts, '"The Studious Artizan": Christopher Marlowe, Canterbury and Cambridge', in Darryll Grantley and Peter Roberts (eds), *Christopher Marlowe and English Renaissance Culture* (Aldershot, 1996), pp. 17–37, at p. 25. David Masson

What should not be overlooked, however, is the crucial fact that Marlowe's conduct was guaranteed by the mandate of the Privy Council itself; that is, Burghley responded to Marlowe's appeal not as an internal issue within the university but as one of the matters that must be brought before, and shared among, the council. This may have been due to the great importance of the certificates issued by the council, and the fact that they came into immediate effect. An extant certificate, drawn up by Burghley with the signatures of several councillors on 9 October 1590, demonstrates its extraordinary protective power. John Edge, 'a gentleman in the horse band of Sir John Pooly', offered the council his services as a spy in the Spanish camp of the Duke of Parma 'to discover some things in the said duke's army profitable for her [Majesty's] service', and asked the council 'to preserve his credit against such as might maliciously, or ignorantly, and for lack of knowledge of his good intent to do such good service to her majesty, condemn or reprove him'. The council, finding in his favour, duly provided him with the certificate to declare 'his good intent', and gave its perpetual guarantee:

> And if he shall [...] discover any thing worthy of knowledge, and shall perform any action laudable, and profitable for her majesty at any time, within the space of [blank] here after the date hereof, we will acquit him against any that shall accuse or reprove him for his absence from his place of service at Berghen, and for his familiarity and conversation with any of his countrymen, serving under the duke of Parma.[12]

This prompt action to protect Edge's credit sheds some light on the nature of any certificate that may have been issued to Marlowe. Rowse is possibly right in noting that 'it needed the direct, and very exceptional, intervention of the Privy Council itself to force the university authorities to grant it'.[13] Moreover, the matter was urgent. On Thursday, 29 June, the council approved the decision that Marlowe 'should be furthered in the degree he was to take this next Commencement', scheduled for the following Tuesday, 4 July. Burghley would have been unable to validate the emergency motion without the mutual understanding or express intention of any of the other prominent councillors, including Walsingham, who were absent from the meeting. However, he brought the matter before the board and effected his purpose without difficulty.

---

points out the existence of this kind of certificate in his *The Life of John Milton* (7 vols, Cambridge, 1859), vol. 1, pp. 120–1.

[12] John Strype, *Annals of the Reformation* (4 vols, Oxford, 1824), vol. 4, pp. 52–3 (no. xxx). We can find Burghley's draft of the certificate in BL, Lansdowne MS 104 (28), fol. 64r.

[13] Rowse, *Christopher Marlowe*, p. 27.

What we can detect here are not divisions, but the collaborative workings of the Privy Council as a consultative body. Inevitably, there were differences in the degree of enthusiasm over the peace negotiations within the council itself, arising from personal rivalries, policy disagreements, or religious differences. But, as Pulman points out, 'There is no evidence that bouts of huffiness interfered with the smooth running of the machinery of state'. Rather, a fundamental harmony can be detected among 'an extremely adult, unemotional, business-like group of people, going about their common concerns without undue fuss and without making more scenes than were strictly necessary, yet letting their ill feeling show without restraint where it existed'.[14] This system of alliances, which continued throughout the 1570s and 1580s, may be due to what Simon Adams calls 'the existence of a stable inner ring' composed of Leicester, Burghley, Walsingham, Hatton, and the Earl of Sussex.[15] It also seems to have been at work in Marlowe's case.

What seems equally important is that in granting Marlowe his certificate the Privy Council found that he 'deserved to be rewarded for his faithfull dealinge'. It was against the council's, as well as 'her Majesties', will that 'anie one employed as he had been in matters touching the benefitt of his countrie should be defamed'. The phrasing implies the councillors' adherence to the socio-political values of a hierarchical society, in which 'faithfulness' to lords and friends was widely approved of. A reputation for faithful dealing was the solid foundation of honour, and it secured a livelihood for a servant. George Whitehead, the receiver and deputy-captain of Tynemouth, declared his commitment to these traditional values when writing to his master, Henry Percy, the 9th Earl of Northumberland, that: 'my care shall be only to deal faithfully with your lordship, as I may answere before God as a true Christiane, and before the world as a faithful steward and true servant.'[16] John Guilpine likewise attached great importance to a servant's religious faithfulness, writing a recommendation to William Davidson, secretary to the queen, concerning an MA student of Cambridge: 'I have had good triall of his honestie and my Mr. knowes yt. […] he is zelous in godes trewe Religion and desirous to spend his yowth in your S[e]rvice for the good report that eche honest man geves yow.'[17]

Marlowe thus had to gain credibility in his patron's eyes through an impressive performance of his duty so that he would be recognized as a 'true servant'. If he had, indeed, been recruited by Nicholas Faunt, Walsingham's

---

[14] Pulman, *Elizabethan Privy Council*, p. 50.

[15] Simon Adams, *Leicester and the Court: Essays on Elizabethan Politics* (Manchester, 2002), p. 18.

[16] Cited in Mervyn James, *Society, Politics and Culture: Studies in Early Modern England* (Cambridge, 1986), p. 53.

[17] TNA, SP, 12/194, fol. 84r.

secretary, such faithfulness would have been even more necessary. In his *Discourse Touching the Office of Principal Secretary of Estate* (1592), Faunt advocated 'by [his] experience' that

> the multitude of servantes in this kinde is hurtfull [...] for if in a principall servant to the secretarie, secrecie and faithfulnes bee cheifly required what trust canne therebee reposed in manie, and if manie bee imploied in matters of secrecie, whoe shall thinke himself principall in trust in those thinges which are hardly to bee imparted to anie though the most faithfull in the world.[18]

Charles Nicholl suggests that 'The government described Marlowe's service as "faithful dealing", but in the performance of it there must have been much deception.'[19] Yet for Marlowe, a recent graduate seeking a good start to his professional career, it would have been almost impossible to play a double game. Robert Burton, when writing about the misery of a university student, compared the pains he endured to 'please his Patron' with that of an apprentice, saying:

> If he bend his forces to some other studies, with an intent to be *à secretis* to some Nobel man, or in such a place with an Embassador, he shall finde that these persons rise like Prentises one under another, as in so many tradesmens shops, when the master is dead, the fore-man of the shop commonly steps in his place.[20]

In this regard, the certificate delivered to the university authorities was not only a manipulative request for Marlowe to have his MA degree conferred on him but also a demand for an official endorsement of his political conduct. This certificate would have enabled him to achieve credit or symbolic capital, just as it had for John Edge. A letter from the Privy Council on behalf of William Harborne similarly demonstrates ongoing concern about his personal circumstances. In 1593, long after the completion of Harborne's mission to Constantinople as merchant and diplomat in the 1580s, he requested the council's intervention in a quarrel over his inheritance. In response, the council wrote to Harborne's adversary and requested, 'Forsomuch as the gentleman is of good desert and accompt both with her Majestie and our selves, having formerlie bin employed in her

---

[18] Charles Hughes, 'Nicholas Faunt's Discourse Touching the Office of Principal Secretary of Estate, & c. 1592', *EHR*, 20:79 (1905), 499–508, at pp. 500–1.

[19] Charles Nicholl, *The Reckoning: The Murder of Christopher Marlowe* (London, 1992), p. 101.

[20] Robert Burton, *The Anatomy of Melancholy*, ed. Thomas C. Faulkner, Nicolas K. Kiessling, Rhonda L. Blair, J. B. Bamborough, and Martin Dodsworth (6 vols, Oxford, 1989–2000), vol. 1, pp. 308–9.

Highnes' important services, wee have thought good to pray and require you in his behalf not to offer him anie hard measure'.[21]

The protective power granted by Marlowe's certificate seems to have remained effective when he was at work as a playwright – in particular when his lodging, which he shared with Thomas Kyd, was subject to a search following the scandal of xenophobic libels published in May 1593. The seizure of a fragmentary copy of 'vile hereticall conceiptes' led to Kyd's arrest and torture as the suspected author. Marlowe escaped with impunity. He was simply summoned before the Privy Councillors and 'commanded to give his daily attendance' at this meeting, probably as an informer.[22] In employing this privilege of clientelism, Marlowe would entangle himself in an inescapable net of mutual responsibilities and obligations to the members of the council.

This suggests that the council's power may have been exercised over all Marlowe's actions after he left Cambridge, including his literary activities in London. And so, while the playwright gained protection and support from the council, the dynamics of patronage compelled him, to a greater or lesser extent, to uphold, endorse, and promote its ideological stance.

'GOOD SERVICE' TO HER MAJESTY

Can Marlowe's local network shed light on when, where, and for what purpose he had operated during his collegiate days? Admittedly, the lack of evidence prevents us from reaching a conclusion, permitting little more than guesswork about this interesting problem. However, it is not useless, even by way of pure supposition, to make a rough sketch about Marlowe's 'good service' on the basis of his connections. It would provide an alternative to some common assumptions about how he became engaged in the government intelligence service and allow us to reconsider the spy scenario on which the student Marlowe was sent on a mission improbable.

First, we should recognize that Marlowe was still a fledgling scholar when 'emploied [...] in matters touching the benefitt of his countrie'. Considering his youth and lack of expertise, it is likely that he was employed for more respectable and uncomplicated public duties than those that Walsingham imposed upon his wily double agents.[23] The Privy Councillors appointed a large number of men of different backgrounds as messengers or letter

---

[21] APC, vol. 24, p. 44. Gary M. Bell, 'Elizabethan Diplomatic Compensation: Its Nature and Variety', Journal of British Studies, 20:2 (1981), 1–25, at pp. 15–18, points out the queen's continual exercising of influence upon diplomats as compensation for their services.

[22] Constance Brown Kuriyama, Christopher Marlowe: A Renaissance Life (Ithaca, 2002), p. 219.

[23] Ibid., p. 71; Brooke, Life of Marlowe, pp. 36–7.

carriers, and Marlowe could have been one of these employees. We cannot know whether he was employed for overseas or domestic service, but, if he *was* sent abroad, he may have been required to journey in company, as Stephen Powle and others usually did, to avoid the dangers that attended travel. Powle, travelling on the continent as an agent for Walsingham, wrote to his friend Edward Egerton on 26 December 1588:

> I haue performed the moste parte of my iourney: w[hi]ch was boath lesse dangerous, and more compfortable to me by the good companie of Mr Geratt. For whose courtezie I thanke you, as the author: and I repute myself greatly bounde vnto him, for beinge an actor w[i]th me in so dangerous a Tragedie, as this voyage might haue brought vs vnto.[24]

The Corpus Christi authorities seem to have had no concerns about the business that Marlowe was engaged in, until they received the Privy Council's letter. This does not mean, of course, that scholars could go anywhere without permission. The master and fellows kept careful note of the activities of their scholars, and even a fellow had to get the college authorities' grant when going abroad: the Chapter Book of Corpus has an entry for the leave grant given to John Dix, a fellow, on 20 January 1586/7 to travel overseas until 26 March 1588.[25] In Marlowe's case, it is possible that he became engaged in the Privy Council's business while seeking employment after obtaining his BA in 1583/4. It is common to find such 'absentee' BAs who, while keeping their scholarship posts, took to the road to look for work. Marlowe's sporadic absences, conspicuous from 1584 to 1586, suggest that he could have found an opportunity to affiliate himself with those who could offer him employment around that time.

The Privy Council was eager to create and maintain multiple channels of information by establishing connections with English merchants, priests, stationers, and university residents abroad and turning these expatriates into information-gathering satellites to gain insight into the turbulent international situation. It was perhaps for this purpose that Nicholas Faunt was sent 'into the Lowe Cuntries to her Majesties Ambassadours there in the service of her Majestie' together with Baptista Spinola in 1578, two years after he completed his BA, possibly to carry and send back dispatches.[26] In August 1580, Faunt was sent again (obviously as the agent of Walsingham

---

[24] Bodleian Library, Tanner MS 309, fol. 57r. For Stephen Powle's itinerary, see V. F. Stern, *Sir Stephen Powle of Court and Country* (Selinsgrove, PA, 1992), pp. 58–94. Anthony Munday was likewise accompanied by Thomas Nowell, and James Welch by Francis Gybbon. See Anthony Munday, *Anthony Munday: The English Roman Life*, ed. Philip Ayres (Oxford, 1980), p. 6; and TNA, SP, 12/170, fol. 66r.

[25] CCCA, CCCC01/C/1, Chapter Book 1, p. 88.

[26] *APC*, vol. 10, p. 323.

this time) to Paris, where he met Anthony Bacon;[27] and he spent three and a half months in Germany early in 1581. Later that year, he moved on to Italy, staying in Padua for three months.

The reason for Faunt's long stay in Padua cannot be known, but it is possible that while he was there he met a former fellow from Corpus Christi, Richard Willoughbye, who, after relinquishing the fellowship on 28 April 1579 to his successor, Thomas Harris, travelled to Paris and was staying there in 1580. In the intelligence report dated 27 April 1580, we find the name 'Willoughby' among 'The Englishe Protestantes in Paris' with 'Mr [Anthony] Bacon'.[28] Willoughbye went on from there to Padua, where he settled for life. Both Faunt and Harris were closely acquainted with him: the document of tutorial payments to fellows of Corpus Christi College demonstrates that Willoughbye had supervised them in person.[29] Faunt (and possibly Walsingham as well) may have been informed of Willoughbye's movements and regarded him as a prospective intelligence provider. In fact, we find him sending news on the political situation of Rome, France, Germany, and Hungary to Dr Henry Hawkins, a fellow of Peterhouse and Essex's agent, in the 1590s.[30] This clear local association between Willoughbye and Faunt encourages us to search for any trace of Corpus Christi men in Padua.

Padua was one of the popular destinations for English visitors, both Catholic and Protestant, in the sixteenth century. Walsingham himself stayed there as a Marian exile and was elected *consiliarius* and *electionarius* of the English nation in 1555–56. The city's popularity was due to its great renown as a centre of medical, astronomical, and legal studies, but it also had fine traditions of liberty and religious tolerance. Marlowe seems to have well known the free and open atmosphere of Padua, for Bellamia, the courtesan in *The Jew of Malta*, complains: 'From Venice merchants, and from Padua / Were wont to come rare-witted gentlemen, / Scholars I mean, learned and liberal.'[31]

---

[27] Thomas Birch, *Memoirs of the Reign of Queen Elizabeth, from the Year 1581 till Her Death* (2 vols, London, 1754), vol. 1, p. 13.

[28] TNA, SP, 78/4A, fol. 64r.

[29] CCCA, CCCC02/B/44/29. See also Chapter 2, pp. 79–80; and Chapter 3, pp. 96–7.

[30] See BL, MS Harley 288 (125), fol. 242r-v; MS Harley 296 (27), fol. 54r-v; R. A. Roberts *et al.* (eds), *Calendar of the Manuscripts of the Most Hon. the Marquis of Salisbury* (24 vols, London, 1883–1976), vol. 5, pp. 45–6, 189–91. For Henry Hawkins, see Paul E. J. Hammer, 'Essex and Europe: Evidence from Confidential Instructions by the Earl of Essex, 1595–6', *EHR*, 111:441 (1996), 357–81, at pp. 361–4.

[31] Christopher Marlowe, *The Jew of Malta*, ed. N. W. Bawcutt, *The Revels Plays* (Manchester, 1978), III.i.6–8. Subsequent references will be to this edition and will appear parenthetically in the text by act, scene, and line number.

Samuel Foxe, the eldest son of the martyrologist John Foxe, was one of the travellers to Padua, and was unique in leaving his detailed itinerary (figure 12), now in the British Library.[32] He reached Padua on 13 October 1584, after residing in Leipzig for a year and in Basel for a few months; he stayed until May 1586. In his itinerary, Foxe gives an account of Englishmen in the city: 'At my cominge to Padua I found English me[n] ther Mr Griffin[,] Richard Willoby[,] Bruss / Middilton / ther came after Mr J: Wrath[,] Mr W: Cicell & J Cyiel[,] Mr Gorge Talbot & Maneringe[,] Herson[,] Cokk[,] Loke[,] Martin / Vere / Teder a preist[,] Dr Walker.'[33]

This account clearly shows that Foxe met Willoughbye, who had just been elected *consiliarius* of the English Nation at the university. Some of the travellers who came after Foxe are of great interest. 'Mr J: Wrath' is no doubt John Wrothe, who, while studying at Padua, was working as an intelligencer for Walsingham.[34] We also see William Cecil, the grandson of Lord Burghley, and 'J: Cyiel', possibly John Cecil (alias Snowden), a graduate of Trinity College, Oxford and a priest. George Talbot may have been the son of John Talbot of Grafton, educated at Amiens and Rome in his youth, and later the 9th Earl of Shrewsbury.[35] William Tedder, or 'Teder a priest', was possibly on his way back to Italy after his release from imprisonment in London in 1584. Although lack of evidence makes it difficult to identify other visitors, Willoughbye's background might lead us to suppose that 'Maneringe' could be Richard Manwaring, the Canterbury Scholar from King's School at Corpus Christi, who obtained his BA in 1579/80 and his MA in 1583.[36] The two years undocumented until his appointment as

---

[32] BL, Lansdowne MS 679, fols 43r–46r. Samuel Foxe's itinerary was transcribed with some inaccuracies in William Winters, *Biographical Notes on John Foxe the Martyrologist, with an Account of His Family and Friends at Waltham Abbey* (Waltham Abbey, Essex, 1876), pp. 20–3.

[33] BL, Lansdowne MS 679, fol. 44v.

[34] John Wrothe's correspondence with Walsingham can be found in TNA, SP, 99/1, fol. 57r–v. Wrothe wrote to Walsingham, 'my singulare goode Patrone', in March 1588: 'I have retired my self to Padoa wheare withe more quietnesse I may follow my studies' (fol. 57r).

[35] For George Talbot, see B. FitzGibbon, 'George Talbot, Ninth Earl of Shrewsbury', *Biographical Studies*, 2 (1953–4), 96–110. In a 'note of such Papists as are known to be beyond seas, and of their friends here in England', we can find a reference to George Talbot: 'Mr John Talbot of Grafton hathe his eldest sonne George beyond the seas except to be latelie comen over' (TNA, SP, 12/219, fol. 196v).

[36] Jonathan Woolfson thinks that 'Maneringe' may be Richard Manwaring of Corpus Christi, or one of the Manwarings from Cheshire. See his 'The Paduan Sojourns of Samuel and Simeon Foxe', *Quaderni per la storia dell'Università di Padova*, 30 (1997), 111–24, at p. 118, n. 32; and Jonathan Woolfson, *Padua and the Tudors: English Students in Italy, 1485–1603* (Cambridge, 1998), p. 255. For the Manwarings of

vicar of Petham, Kent, on 2 September 1585 make it possible that he came to Padua sometime between the autumn of 1584 and the spring of 1585.

Of most interest here is the person described as 'Martin'. Woolfson thinks that he might be Thomas Martyn, a civil lawyer and Catholic polemicist who enjoyed an active diplomatic career during the reign of Mary, but this is unlikely as he continued to work as a lawyer in England into his sixties.[37] My question is whether this name *is* 'Martin' (figure 13). Although Winters transcribes it as 'Martin' and Woolfson follows his reading, Foxe's handwritten letter 't' often looks like a small letter 'l'.[38] This is well attested in the case of 'Italicis' (figure 14) and 'etiam' (figure 15), where the 'ti' and 'li' are indistinguishable.[39] Moreover, as 'Martini' (figure 16) shows, Foxe often uses an obvious letter 't' when writing 'Marti'.[40]

This does not prove that Foxe wrote 'Marlin', not 'Martin', but his peculiar way of writing the letter 'l' leaves room for the possibility that Christopher 'Marlin' or Marlowe went to Padua, with his senior Richard Manwaring as his trail-mate. They may have been tasked with carrying dispatches to their acquaintance Richard Willoughbye and returning to Faunt and Walsingham with a bundle of news. Marlowe, in describing Faustus's travel to Venice and Padua, deviates from his source, the English Faustus Book, and adds a description about a temple with an 'aspiring' steeple: 'From thence to Venice, Padua, and the rest, / In midst of which a sumptuous temple stands / That threats the stars with her aspiring top' (A-text, III.i.16–18). The passage has been interpreted as a reference to St Mark's in Venice, with the 'aspiring top' indicating that of the campanile, which stands at some distance from the church.[41] However, as Roma Gill and Ros King suggest, it surely 'must refer to the striking silhouette of the Basilica of St Anthony in Padua'.[42] If that is the case, it may have been based on Marlowe's own personal experience.

We know that Marlowe, dwelling in Norton Folgate near to the Curtain and the Theatre, had joined up with Thomas Watson and the Alleyn

---

Cheshire, see Joseph Foster, *Alumni Oxonienses* (4 vols, Oxford, 1891–92), vol. 3, pp. 959–60; and James Croston, *County Families of Lancashire and Cheshire* (London, 1887), pp. 376–9.

[37] Woolfson, *Padua and the Tudors*, p. 256.
[38] Winters, *Biographical Notes on John Foxe*, p. 21.
[39] BL, MS Lansdowne 679, fols 49r and 73v.
[40] *Ibid.*, fols 44r.
[41] See, for instance, Michael Keefer (ed.), *Christopher Marlowe's* Doctor Faustus: *A 1604-Version Edition* (Peterborough, 1991), p. 56.
[42] Christopher Marlowe, Doctor Faustus *Based on the A Text*, ed. Roma Gill and Ros King, revised with a new introduction, The New Mermaids (London, 1989), p. 49, n. for lines 16–18.

brothers at least by September 1589, when he and Watson were detained on suspicion of the murder of William Bradley.[43] Watson, an Oxford student of law who had pursued his studies abroad for over seven years in the 1570s, had been working as an intelligencer for Walsingham since his return to England.[44] Watson seems to have cultivated a friendship with Thomas Walsingham at Paris in the early 1580s; Thomas was Sir Francis's young cousin and later Marlowe's patron, and had worked for the Secretary as a courier from 1580 to 1584. Watson later published *Meliboeus* (1590) with a dedication to Thomas Walsingham and *An Eglogve vpon the Death of the Right Honorable Sir Francis Walsingham* (1590), the English version of *Meliboeus* being dedicated to Frances Sidney (Walsingham's daughter) 'vnder the Patronage of M. Thomas walsingham'. In *An Eglogve*, Watson recalled his friendship with Thomas Walsingham in Paris, where Tityrus (figured as Walsingham) says to Corydon, the poet:

> Thy tunes haue often pleas'd mine eare of yoare,
> when milk-white swans did flocke to heare thee sing,
> Where *Seane* in *Paris* makes a double shoare,
> *Paris* thrise blest if shee obey her King.[45]

Charles Nicholl dates their initial encounter to between the summer of 1581 and the spring of 1583, based on a reference to Watson in *Ulysses upon Ajax* (1596): 'the froath of wittie *Tom Watsons* jests, I heard them in *Paris* 14. yeares agoe: besides, what balductum play is not full of them?'[46] Although we cannot identify the anonymous author or validate whether he is really suggesting that Watson *was* in Paris, it is clearly a possibility.[47] It is more reasonable, however, to date it earlier, considering the evidence for Watson's sporadic presence in Paris. As Albert Chatterley points out, the name 'Watson' (which often appears in government correspondences

---

[43] Mark Eccles, *Christopher Marlowe in London* (Cambridge, MA, 1934), pp. 65–8. For the relationship between Marlowe and Edward Alleyn, see also Roslyn L. Knutson, 'Marlowe, Company Ownership, and the Role of Edward II', in S. P. Cerasano (ed.), *MRDE*, vol. 18 (Madison, 2005), pp. 37–46, at p. 42.

[44] For Watson's confidential service to Walsingham, see Nicholl, *Reckoning*, pp. 177–90.

[45] Thomas Watson, *An Eglogve vpon the Death of the Right Honorable Sir Francis Walsingham* (London, 1590), sig. B3r–v.

[46] Anon., *Ulysses upon Ajax Written by Misodiaboles to His Friend Philaretes* (London, 1596; STC 12783), sig. A8v. See Nicholl, *Reckoning*, pp. 177–90. Dana F. Sutton supports his conjecture in her edition of *The Complete Works of Thomas Watson* (2 vols, Lewiston, 2006), vol. 1, p. xiv.

[47] For its authorship, see Rick Bowers and Paul S. Smith, 'Sir John Harington, Hugh Plat, and Ulysses upon Ajax', *N&Q*, 54:3 (2007), 255–9. Another edition published in the same year (STC 12782) has 'Iohn Watson', which is possibly a misprint or suggests the uncertainty of the author's memory.

to denote a courier) cannot be found in relation to Paris after August 1581, when 'he seems finally to have left for England [...] carrying official letters from the secretary [Walsingham] to William Cecil'.[48]

It is difficult to track Watson's course around 1580, but the intelligence report dated 27 April 1580 that lists 'sondry Englishmen Papistes, p[rese]ntly abyding in Paris' includes two Watsons: one of 'Such Gent. & others, as be accompted for studentes and placed in Colledges, or app[er]tayning thervnto' and the other 'Watson, sonne to the Atturney in London'.[49] Kuriyama argues that: 'In view of Watson's London origins, his keen interest in law, the money required to support his lengthy peripatetic education, and the many hints of Catholic sympathies in his personal history, [the latter Watson] could very well be Thomas Watson the poet.'[50] Thomas Walsingham conveyed dispatches to the Court from France on 13 October 1580 and brought others back on 11 November, so Watson's acquaintance with him may date to that year.[51]

Kuriyama's argument for the date is persuasive because both Nicholas Faunt and Richard Willoughbye, Corpus Christi men who may have later become the key persons connecting Marlowe with the two Walsinghams, were in Paris throughout 1580. It was possibly around that time that the network between Watson, Thomas Walsingham, and Faunt was established under the aegis of Secretary Walsingham; and it was probably these protégés of Sir Francis who embroiled Marlowe in the literary activities of London.

STRUGGLES FOR SURVIVAL

What can we say about Marlowe's life in the capital? Poverty was ubiquitous in Elizabethan London. While the expansion of the market economy afforded opportunities for the 'better sort' to accumulate wealth and to invest it, the labour power of the numerous poor was transacted as a highly marketable commodity and naturally exploited at the expense of their living standards.[52] The urban demographic boost that followed the influx of job-seeking apprentices, discharged soldiers, and immigrants also made it difficult for young adults to achieve an independent living. At the same

---

[48] Albert Chatterley, 'Watson, Thomas (1555/6–1592)', in *ODNB*. See also Albert Chatterley (ed.), *Thomas Watson: Italian Madrigals Englished* (1590; repr. London, 1999), pp. xxix–xxx.

[49] TNA, SP, 78/4A, fols 63v–64r.

[50] Kuriyama, *Christopher Marlowe*, pp. 86–7.

[51] John Bakeless, *The Tragicall History of Christopher Marlowe* (2 vols, Cambridge, 1942), vol. 1, p. 161.

[52] Keith Wrightson, *Earthly Necessities: Economic Lives in Early Modern Britain* (New Haven, 2000), pp. 22–3.

time, as a negative attitude towards unemployment was politically encouraged, poverty constituted a constant threat to those living in the metropolis, as well as to the city authorities.[53] The will to overcome just such a serious financial threat is the initial condition of Marlowe's *The Jew of Malta*:

> What, will you thus oppose me, luckless stars,
> To make me desperate in my poverty?
> And knowing me impatient in distress,
> Think me so mad as I will hang myself,
> That I may vanish o'er the earth in air,
> And leave no memory that e'er I was?
> No, I will live: nor loathe I this my life;
> And since you leave me in the ocean thus
> To sink or swim, and put me to my shifts,
> I'll rouse my senses, and awake myself. (1.ii.260–9)

With all his possessions confiscated by the governor of Malta, Barabas begins a fierce struggle for existence in fear that he will otherwise 'vanish o'er the earth in air / And leave no memory that e'er I was'. This acute desire to live and his insatiable ambition were obviously a matter of concern not only for Barabas but for Marlowe himself, who was likewise swimming in the turbulent 'ocean' of London. In Cambridge, a small exhibition payment enabled Marlowe to survive. However, life in London was impossible without another source of income or patronage: he needed capital for rent, food, books, entertainment, transport, clothing, fuel, and lighting, and occasionally lawsuits. The 'partial heavens' compelled Marlowe just as much as Barabas to resort to drastic measures to keep his head above water: 'in extremity / We ought to make bar of no policy' (1.ii.272–3).

In this context, considering why the four plays Marlowe wrote for the Admiral's Men (i.e. *I and II Tamburlaine*, *The Jew of Malta*, and possibly *Doctor Faustus*) were clustered together between 1587 and 1589, gives us a glimpse of the self-protective measures he took to survive. One possible explanation for this concentration of output is that the success of *I Tamburlaine*, which he may have written partly or wholly during his college days and offered to the playing company, gave further opportunity for material gain.[54] The monetary rewards for playwriting may not have been trivial.

---

[53] A. L. Beier, *Masterless Men: The Vagrancy Problem in England 1560–1640* (London, 1985), pp. 4–7.

[54] Philip Gawdy, a law student at Clifford's Inn, reported in a letter to his father dated 16 November 1587 an accident during a play performed by the Admiral's Men, the circumstances of which some critics, including Wiggins, have suggested closely resemble the execution of the Governor of Babylon in the last act of the second part. We can therefore date the first part to Marlowe's college days in 1587, and the

Philip Henslowe's payment for a play oscillated between £5 and £7 from 1597 to 1603.[55] Thus, the production of three or four plays would have provided Marlowe with an income roughly equivalent to the headmaster of an endowed grammar school (whose annual income was typically £20).[56]

Another reason for this clustering could relate to his faithful dealings with the Alleyns in fulfilling his obligations. By contributing a series of high-quality plays to the Admiral's Men, what benefited Marlowe even more than direct financial remuneration may have been the establishment and maintenance of credit networks of interested persons involved in theatre. In fact, it was this network that furnished him with two sureties when he was detained at Newgate.[57]

This kind of financial interdependency, however, seems to have rarely improved the living standards of playwrights. Henry Chettle's annual earnings can be estimated as ranging from £18 to £25, yet he constantly borrowed money from Henslowe.[58] Harold Jenkins suggests that 'By keeping the poverty-stricken dramatists in debt to him for small sums, Henslowe secured a strong hold over them, so that they could scarcely have taken their plays elsewhere, had they so desired.'[59] George Chapman and Thomas Dekker, frequent borrowers from Henslowe, were also entangled in debt throughout their lives. While each playwright's consumption was affected by his particular disposition, eating habits, and circumstances, what seems common to all is the fact that their economic difficulties were *not* due to unemployment. Rather, it seems that business opportunities for financial gain involved them in complex credit transactions, and that, with low levels of accumulated capital, they had to spend a relatively large fraction of their income on necessary (and often conspicuous) consumption in order to sustain their credit reputation. Sir John Davies, the lawyer and poet, points out this growing economic phenomenon in 'A Preface Dedicatory' to *Le Primer Report* (1615):

---

second part to the autumn of 1587. See Isaac Herbert Jeayes (ed.), *Letters of Philip Gawdy* (London, 1906), p. 23; Martin Wiggins, *British Drama 1533–1642: A Catalogue* (Oxford, 2012), vol. 2, pp. 385–9.

[55] Gerald Eades Bentley, *The Profession of Dramatist in Shakespeare's Time* (Princeton, 1971), pp. 97–104.

[56] David Cressy, 'A Drudgery of Schoolmasters: The Teaching Profession in Elizabethan and Stuart England', in Wilfrid Prest (ed.), *The Professions in Early Modern England* (London, 1987), pp. 129–53, at pp. 144–7.

[57] Eccles, *Christopher Marlowe in London*, p. 86. See also Park Honan, *Christopher Marlowe: Poet and Spy* (Oxford, 2005), pp. 226–7.

[58] Neil Carson, *A Companion to Henslowe's Diary* (Cambridge, 1988), p. 66.

[59] Harold Jenkins, *The Life and Work of Henry Chettle* (London, 1934), p. 22.

the comodities of the earth being more improued, there is more wealth, & consequently there are more contracts reall, & personall, then there were in former ages. Besides there is more luxury & excess in the world, which breedeth vnthryftes, banckruptes, & bad debtors, more couetousnesse & more malice, which begetteth force & fraud, oppression & extortion, breach of the peace, & breach of trust.[60]

Marlowe may have been rewarded for his intelligence activities but this is only conjecture. The income of diplomatic officials was sufficient to ensure a stable livelihood through a regular, though not generous, salary. Gary M. Bell points out that 'no diplomat was ever ruined by an assignment, and very few were even hurt financially'.[61] This is not the case, however, with one 'who operated in the inferior status of an agent or of a chargé d'affaires', because 'pay was as varied as the tasks undertaken, and no generalizations readily emerge. They received what the government felt their services were worth, or, more accurately, what they could cajole from the principal secretary'.[62] Samuel Daniel, who brought a letter from Sir Edward Stafford at Paris to the Court at Windsor, received twenty marks upon a warrant signed by Walsingham in September 1586. The sum is relatively small compared to the £15 or £16 paid to Richard Hakluyt or Henry Constable for similar service.[63]

This practice of remuneration contingent on success caused self-promoting agents, who collected intelligence for sale at home or abroad, much more difficulty when trying to secure funds. Useless or out-of-date information did not bring them any money to balance out their initial investment. William Lewkenore, a former agent of Walsingham, wrote: 'In the life of Sir Thomas [sic] Walsingham, when I was living at Lyons, I was employed to watch Dr. Parry and one Aldred and others, of whose proceedings I gave secret intelligence, not without my great charge, being glad to do her Majesty and my country that service.'[64] Robert Barnard, who gathered intelligence concerning Catholics at home in the 1580s, wrote to Walsingham on one occasion: 'I am indettyd to myne hoste in London in good faythe, above iiij^{li}. who doth threaten to Lay me in pryson for the same, w[hi]ch occasion doth forse me at this presente to troble yo[u]r honoure, not hauynge receuyde anye from you, in iij monthes paste.'[65] Pecuniary

---

[60] Sir John Davies, *Le Primer Report* (Dublin, 1615), sig. *6r.
[61] Bell, 'Elizabethan Diplomatic Compensation', p. 19.
[62] *Ibid.*, pp. 5–6.
[63] Mark Eccles, 'Samuel Daniel in France and Italy', *Studies in Philology*, 34:2 (1937), 148–67.
[64] Roberts *et al.*, *Manuscripts of the Marquis of Salisbury*, vol. 9, p. 157.
[65] Barnard to Walsingham, 1581, TNA, SP, 12/151, fol. 68r. On the pecuniary embarrassment of Walsingham's spies, see Read, *Secretary Walsingham*, vol. 2, pp. 322–39.

embarrassment was so common that we can find spies repeatedly pestering their bosses for money. Even Thomas Walsingham, Marlowe's patron, was heavily in debt to the tune of 200 marks, possibly through his intelligence activities in the 1580s, and was detained in Fleet Prison in early 1590.[66]

The Privy Councillors willingly offered opportunities or protection to their clients but rarely full financial support, let alone monthly salaries. Each had to depend on his own efforts in order to get over credit crunches; and, often with the assistance of financiers, they tried to wriggle their way out. George Chapman's case against John Wolfall provides a good illustration of how a self-promoting servant, notwithstanding his connection with some of the Privy Councillors, could bring financial distress upon himself. According to Chapman's plea, Wolfall, the moneylender who had already swindled Thomas Lodge, 'sought and practised by flatterye and deceytfull speeches to Insinuate himselfe in the good opinion' of Chapman, who was pressed for money in 1585.[67] Wolfall 'offered greate and extraordinarye freindshipp and love', promising that he would not only procure money but would also be bound with Chapman for his good credit, 'allthoughe the Acquaintance were then newlye growne' between them.[68] Wolfall then tempted Chapman into concluding with another London broker a loan of various sums upon forfeiting £100. However, Chapman seems to have failed to keep his promise and was later sued by Wolfall's son for default.

Wolfall junior gave evidence that 'the saide Complainant [Chapman], whoe att the first beinge a man of verry good parts and expectacion, hath sethence verry vnadvisedly spent the most parte of his tyme and his estate in ffrutlesse and vayne Poetry'.[69] Although it is inconceivable that the £100 was spent exclusively on Chapman's literary activities, there is a grain of truth in Wolfall's testimony. Chapman's own explanation supplies some of the remaining details:

> your Orator [Chapman] beecame Acquainted with one John Wollfall Citizen and Broker of London and youre Orator then haveinge occasion to vse a Sum of money to furnish himselfe < [blank] > fitt for his proper vse in Attendance vppon the then Right Honorable Sir Rafe Sadler

---

[66] Kuriyama, *Christopher Marlowe*, p. 99.
[67] Mark Eccles, 'Chapman's Early Years', *Studies in Philology*, 43:2 (1946), 176–93, at p. 182. For the case between Lodge and Wolfall, see N. Burton Paradise, *Thomas Lodge: The History of an Elizabethan* (1931; repr. Hamden, 1970), pp. 25–9. Nicholas Skeres, another moneylender, drew Matthew Roydon the poet into a similar money-lending trap set by John Wolfall. See G. C. Moore Smith, 'Matthew Roydon', *MLR*, 9:1 (1914), 97–8.
[68] Eccles, 'Chapman's Early Years', p. 182.
[69] *Ibid.*, p. 184.

Knighte then Chauncellor of the Dutchye of Lancaster and one of the privye <Council to> the late Queenes Matie of famouse Memorye.[70]

We have corroboration for Chapman's acquaintance with Sadler, because the Inner Temple Library copy of Chapman's translation of *Batrachomyomachia* has his presentation inscription: 'In desire to celebrate and eternise / The Noble Name and House / where his youthe / was initiate / In the now honor'd Owner of the virtues / thereoff, in supplie of the Titles; / The righte virtuouse / and worthie Gent / Raphe Sadler / Esquire.'[71] The Sadler in question was the grandson of the Privy Councillor, and so this inscription indicates that Chapman's youth was spent in the household of Sir Ralph Sadler of Standon Hall around 1585.[72] It is not clear what benefits Chapman received there, but these documents, when pieced together, indicate that his literary activities would have brought him just enough to cover his living expenses, but not enough to invest in efforts to obtain good credit with his patron. In fact, since Sadler was commissioned around that time to act as custodian of Mary, Queen of Scots (detained first at Sheffield, then at Wingfield in Derbyshire, and finally at Tutbury, Staffordshire), Chapman's attendance on him would have necessitated moving from place to place, possibly covering any losses out of his own pocket.

Although a comparison between Marlowe and Chapman cannot be carried too far, it seems that in Marlowe's case, too, the patronage of the Privy Council did little to improve his financial condition. The evidence that most clearly suggests this is the letter of Robert Sidney, the governor of Vlissingen (Flushing), to William Cecil dated 26 January 1592, reporting that Sidney was repatriating 'one named Christofer Marly, by his profession a scholer'.[73] Marlowe was sharing a room in Vlissingen with Richard Baines, Walsingham's former intelligencer, and Gifford Gilbert, a goldsmith. At the time of the letter, the playwright was in custody along with Gilbert on a charge of counterfeiting coins, based on Baines's information. Baines himself seems to have been involved in this forgery, but, 'fearing the succes', he was driven to inform the governor against his roommates. Marlowe admitted the charge under interrogation but vindicated himself by 'protesting that what was done was onely to se the Goldsmiths conning'.

---

[70] *Ibid.*, p. 182.
[71] G. Thorn-Drury first drew our attention to the document in 'George Chapman', *RES*, OS, 1:3 (1925), 350.
[72] See Eccles, 'Chapman's Early Years', pp. 177–81; and Jean Robertson, 'The Early Life of George Chapman', *MLR*, 40:3 (1945), 157–65.
[73] TNA, SP, 84/44, transcribed by R. B. Wernham, 'Christopher Marlowe at Flushing in 1592', *EHR*, 91:359 (1976), 344–5.

There is no knowing why Marlowe was counterfeiting along with his roommates, except for his own monetary gain. Recent biographers tend to consider the incident in relation to the plot of English Catholic exiles to enthrone Ferdinand Stanley, the fifth Earl of Derby, a man Marlowe claimed was 'very wel known' to him. Since the exiles were in financial difficulties, Marlowe and his chamber fellows might have conceived a plan to use their (counterfeit) money to infiltrate the enemy under the guise of sympathizers.[74] This conjecture is intriguing, but the document clearly shows that they lacked the coordination to execute such a delicately concerted operation. Sidney wrote that Baines and Marlowe accused one another of having the intent 'to goe to the Ennemy or to Rome, both as they say of malice one to another'. It seems unlikely that both Marlowe and Baines were so ill-prepared as to suffer such a strategic setback in carrying out the counterfeiting scheme. It is more likely that the prospect of immediate profit was the only principle governing their conduct. Kuriyama argues that, 'While they were in Flushing, a remote English outpost where government oversight was ostensibly weaker than in London, Marlowe [...] proposed to Baines that they experiment with counterfeiting to supplement their chronically insufficient incomes'.[75]

Considering the severe attitude of the authorities towards coining (which was judged high treason), Marlowe's counterfeiting scheme seems to have been regarded as politically subversive. However, it is worth noting how the common people at large regarded coining. Despite its legal definition as treason, their attitudes were complicated and contradictory. In fact, ample evidence suggests that the populace considered coining a relatively easy way to get ready money, and many even claimed to be unaware of its illegality. Malcolm Gaskill argues that coining was seen as a 'social crime': that is, it was among those 'activities which, although technically illegal, were sanctioned by popular notions of legality'.[76] This attitude would have encouraged people to 'coin', or clip, on a small scale, as one of the measures taken to alleviate their destitution.

The case of one Abel Fernam, which Gaskill mentions as typical, shows how commonplace it would have seemed to Marlowe's contemporaries to counterfeit money. Fernam was arrested for coining in 1594, but convinced the alderman Richard Martin, his examiner, that he had been driven to do so 'for want of maintenance in the time of the last great infection, being

---

[74] For the conjecture about Marlowe's involvement with the Stanley conspirators, see, for instance, Nicholl, *Reckoning*, pp. 246–9; and Riggs, *World of Christopher Marlowe*, pp. 275–9.

[75] Kuriyama, *Christopher Marlowe*, p. 110.

[76] Malcolm Gaskill, *Crime and Mentalities in Early Modern England* (Cambridge, 2000), p. 132.

then newly married and not having work to keep himself and his family'.[77] At the same time, the authorities were often lenient towards those who were repentant, able to display superior skill, and willing to uncover other coiners. Martin found Fernam penitent and, 'being a very good workman, young, and able to do Her Majesty good service in graving under Mr. Hillyard, who set him in work'.[78] Cases of this kind are too frequent to enumerate.[79]

In this social atmosphere, people tended to find someone with great coining skill highly useful, would treat him considerately, and would even set him up as a kind of folk hero. Subtle, in Ben Jonson's *Alchemist*, is just such a trickster, who can offer to supply false coins for his customers in need, Tribulation and Ananias, the puritans of Amsterdam, who are investing considerable sums in Subtle's alchemic venture 'to the holy cause'. Later in the play, Subtle draws them into his counterfeiting plot:

> [...] If the holy purse
> Should with this draught fall low, and that the saints
> Do need a present sum, I have a trick
> To melt the pewter you shall buy now, instantly,
> And with a tincture make you as good Dutch dollars
> As any are in Holland.[80]

Tribulation expresses his doubts about the procedure's illegality and asks his partner, 'This act of coining, is it lawful?' Ananias, who denies the authorities' interference in matters of conscience, retorts, 'Lawful? / We know no magistrate, or if we did, / This's foreign coin'. Their response, though somewhat caricatured by Jonson, is a striking example of how the populace viewed counterfeiting. The incentive to commit coining was much commoner and stronger than we have imagined.

What is evident from Sidney's letter is that Marlowe was acquainted with Gilbert and was assessing his skill in counterfeiting a Dutch coin. Marlowe's excuse that 'what was done was onely to se the goldsmith's conning' seems to have been a half-truth. Certainly, the counterfeiting project was a preliminary process, for the matter was revealed 'the day after it was done' and 'a dutch shilling was uttred, and els not any peece: and indeed I do not thinck that they wold have uttred many of them'. The coin was made

---

[77] Ibid., p. 142.
[78] Roberts *et al.*, *Manuscripts of the Marquis of Salisbury*, vol. 4, p. 537.
[79] See further Gaskill, *Crime and Mentalities*, p. 181; and Henry Symonds, 'The Mint of Queen Elizabeth and Those Who Worked There', *Numismatic Chronicle*, 4th ser., 16 (1916), 61–105.
[80] Ben Jonson, *The Alchemist*, ed. Peter Holland and William Sherman, in David Bevington, Martin Butler, and Ian Donaldson (gen. eds), *The Cambridge Edition of the Works of Ben Jonson* (7 vols, Cambridge, 2012), vol. 3, III.ii.140–5.

of 'plain peuter and with half an ey to be discovered'. This was possibly a kind of experiment, then, especially considering Sidney's report that 'The Goldsmith is an eccellent worckman'. Marlowe was perfectly aware of the necessary pretext to free himself from custody: to acknowledge his offence voluntarily, with the caveat that it was done to check the goldsmith's skill, and to accuse Baines of being the instigator.[81] In fact, Marlowe and Baines did 'accuse another to have been the inducers of him, and to have intended to practis yt hereafter'.

Although there is no knowing who incited whom, it is doubtful if either Marlowe or Baines tested their goldsmith's skill as a coiner without intending to practise it. What seems obvious is that both men were able to obtain a possibly lucrative source of funds by ensuring Gilbert could practise the coiner's art. Counterfeiting money was the easiest shortcut to compensate for their financial shortcomings. By balancing the losses and profits, however, Baines chose to be a proactive informant for the governor. The incident seems to have been the outcome of the pursuit of immediate gain, rather than of a concerted operation to undermine the enemy.

Having been sent back to England, Marlowe incurred no serious penalty for his offence. He had already been set at liberty by May 1592, when he was bound to keep the peace towards a constable of Holywell Street in Shoreditch.[82] The reason for the Privy Council's leniency can well be imagined. Marlowe was not a stranger to William Cecil, who was well acquainted with the financial conditions of government spies. At the same time, the pragmatic attitude of Sidney, who stated that he was unwilling to 'stretch my commission to deale in such matters', suggests that the governor of Vlissingen was familiar with the trouble caused by agents' financial difficulties. It is natural, therefore, to assume that Cecil and the Privy Councillors, as well as Sidney, considered Marlowe's attempt to counterfeit as something unpleasant yet necessary to his way of life. They were experienced and sensible enough to regard the playwright not with indignation, but with a tacit understanding of his hardships.

Marlowe's financial difficulties seem not to have improved by the time of his death at Deptford eighteen months after the incident in Vlissingen. There is no need here to enter into a detailed discussion of the circumstances – the well-wrought scenarios of conspiracy and assassination concerning his

---

[81] Peter Evers, a young gentleman of Lincolnshire who is said to have been incited to counterfeit foreign coins in 1574, also voluntarily acknowledged his offence and was later discharged by the Privy Council. See Robert Lemon (ed.), *Calendar of State Papers, Domestic, 1547–1580* (London, 1856), p. 482 (1 July 1574).

[82] Kuriyama, *Christopher Marlowe*, pp. 210–11.

death have stimulated Marlovian scholars to further investigations[83] – but the absence of conclusive evidence naturally leads us to reappraise the coroner's report and its plausibility.[84] Admittedly, coroners – who were no more immune to corruption than other persons in authority – often became involved in behind-the-scenes manoeuvres and accepted bribes to invent verdicts. At the same time, however, 'Early modern murder investigations tended to be far more public affairs in which ordinary people fully engaged themselves, sometimes with alacrity'.[85] What Gaskill terms 'collective responsibility' may prevent us from considering the report on the manner of Marlowe's death and his corpse as an unreliable account hastily fabricated by William Danby, the coroner of the Queen's Household, in a conspiracy with the three witnesses concerned, Ingram Frizer, Nicholas Skeres, and Robert Poley. In fact, the coroner's description of the group's quiet demeanour at Eleanor Bull's lodging house earlier in the day demonstrates that the report also drew on other public witness sources. Kuriyama's point should be taken seriously: 'the coroner's use of the verb "publicaverunt" (they made public) to describe how Marlowe and Frizer spoke their malicious words suggest that the quarrel was audible to others, either in the room or throughout the house.'[86]

What the coroner's report suggests is that Marlowe's accidental death was due to stabbing during the fight over the payment incurred at the lodging house. This explanation, though it may appear disappointingly simple, seems to be most plausible when we consider his disposition and financial straits. This kind of affray was not the first for Marlowe, obviously a man of hot blood. He had a street fight with William Bradley in 1589, possibly over financial matters, and was sued in September 1592 for his attack with a stick and dagger on William Corkine, a tailor and part-time chorister in Canterbury Cathedral.[87] Although the business for which the meeting at

---

[83] See, for instance, Samuel Tannenbaum, *The Assassination of Christopher Marlowe* (New York, 1926); Ethel Seaton, 'Marlowe, Robert Poley, and the Tippings', *RES*, OS, 5:19 (1929), 273–87; Nicholl, *Reckoning*, pp. 324–9; and Riggs, *World of Christopher Marlowe*, pp. 330–5.

[84] Kuriyama, *Christopher Marlowe*, pp. 222–3; and J. A. Downie, 'Marlowe, May 1593, and the "Must-Have" Theory of Biography', *RES*, NS, 58:235 (2007), 245–67.

[85] Gaskill, *Crime and Mentalities*, p. 250.

[86] Kuriyama, *Christopher Marlowe*, p. 138. See also J. A. Downie, 'Marlowe: Facts and Fictions', in J. A. Downie and J. T. Parnell (eds), *Constructing Christopher Marlowe* (Cambridge, 2000), pp. 13–29, at p. 26. Rosalind Barber disagrees with Kuriyama, based on the assumption that 'the only confirmed witnesses are three men who specialized in deception' and that 'Marlowe was not the aggressor'. See her 'Was Marlowe a Violent Man?', in Sarah K. Scott and M. L. Stapleton (eds), *Christopher Marlowe the Craftsman: Lives, Stage and Page* (London, 2010), pp. 47–61, at p. 58.

[87] For Marlowe's violence against Corkine, see Urry, *Marlowe and Canterbury*, pp. 65–8.

Deptford was convened cannot be known, the attendance of both Marlowe, who was financially in a tight spot, and a pair of loan sharks, Frizer and Skeres, working for Thomas Walsingham, suggests a sort of conference in which a request for a loan was discussed. In fact, Frizer was active in arranging loans in collaboration with Skeres around the time of Marlowe's death, for he duped Drew Woodleff, a young indebted gentleman of Peterley, Buckinghamshire, into taking out a series of extortionate loans.[88] Paul Hammer argues that 'In considering this world of sharp operators and debt-ridden gentlemen, it takes no great feat of imagination to construct a scenario that explains Marlowe's death in Deptford', and assumes that Frizer and Skeres 'initiated the meeting in order to discuss money which Marlowe owed them'.[89] Thus, both the direct and circumstantial evidence suggests that Marlowe had been vexed with the continual stringency of poverty and had never been able to achieve financial stability.

Marlowe's faithful duty to the queen assuredly gave him political backing powerful enough to force the university to grant his degree. With the benefit of hindsight, however, it was possibly this personal involvement with a number of Privy Councillors that undermined his financial stability in later life. The profits that playwriting brought him had to cover his living expenses, but they also had to be invested in efforts to satisfy his patrons and obtain good credit with them. The traces Marlowe left behind suggest his intense efforts to maintain good relationships, as well as good credit, with his patrons and their associates. These efforts quite probably afforded him some financial opportunities but also imposed a great strain on his resources.

---

[88] For the case of *Woodleff v. Frizer*, see J. Leslie Hotson, *The Death of Christopher Marlowe* (1925; repr. New York, 1967), pp. 45–9.

[89] Paul E. J. Hammer, 'A Reckoning Reframed: The "Murder" of Christopher Marlowe Revisited', *ELR*, 26:2 (1996), 225–42, at pp. 239–40.

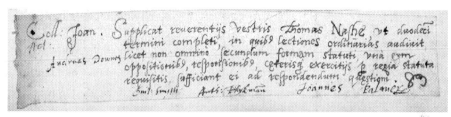

Figure 1 The supplicat of Thomas Nashe: CUA, Supplicats, 1585–86, no. 83.
Reproduced by kind permission of the Syndics of Cambridge University Library.

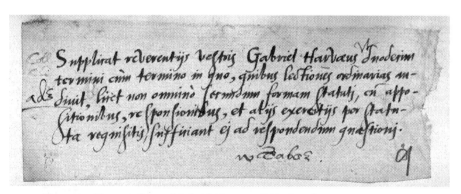

Figure 2 The supplicat of Gabriel Harvey: CUA, Supplicats, 1569–70, no. 9.
Reproduced by kind permission of the Syndics of Cambridge University Library.

109

Colleg: Corp: Christi: Supplicat Reverentijs vestris Nicolaus Fauntus ut duodecim terminis completis, in quibus ordinarias lectiones audivit, licet non omnino secundum formam statuti, una cum omnibus oppositionibus et responsionibus caeterisque exercitijs p statuta regia requisitis sufficiat ei ad respondendum quaestioni.

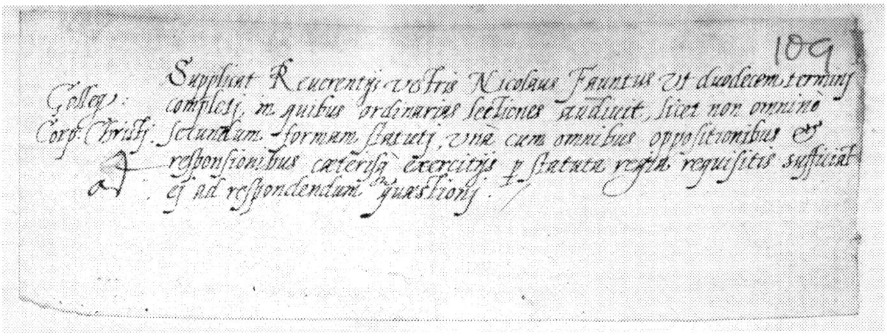

Figure 3 The supplicat of Nicholas Faunt: CUA, Supplicats, 1575–76, no. 109.
Reproduced by kind permission of the Syndics of Cambridge University Library.

Coll. Supplicat reverentijs vestris Christopherus Marlin, ut a
termini completi, in quibus ordinarias lectiones audivit (lice
Corp. secundum formam statuti) una cum omnibus oppositionibus, r
caeterisque exercitijs, per statuta regia requisitis, sufficiant ei
Christi dendum quaestioni.

199

Thomas Harris: pr

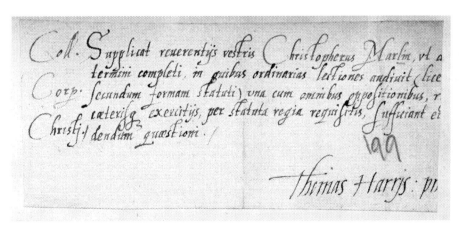

Figure 4 The supplicat of Christopher Marlowe: CUA, Supplicats, 1583–84, no. 199.
Reproduced by kind permission of the Syndics of Cambridge University Library.

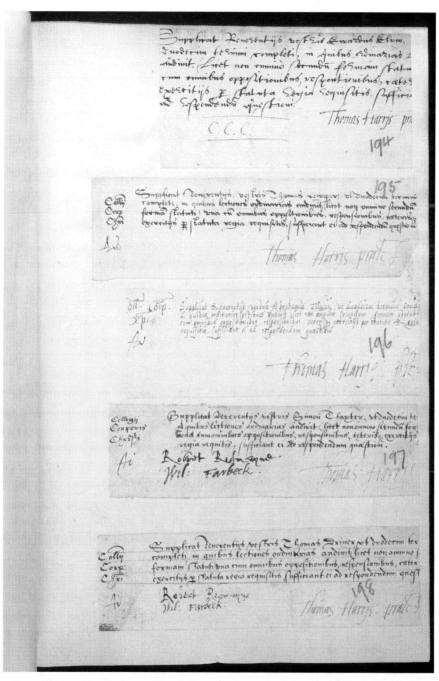

Figure 5   The supplicats of the scholars at Corpus Christi College: CUA, Supplicats, 1583–84, no. 194 (Edward Elwin), no. 195 (Thomas Lewgar), no. 196 (Abraham Tilman), no. 197 (Simon Thaxter), and no. 198 (Thomas Driver). Reproduced by kind permission of the Syndics of Cambridge University Library.

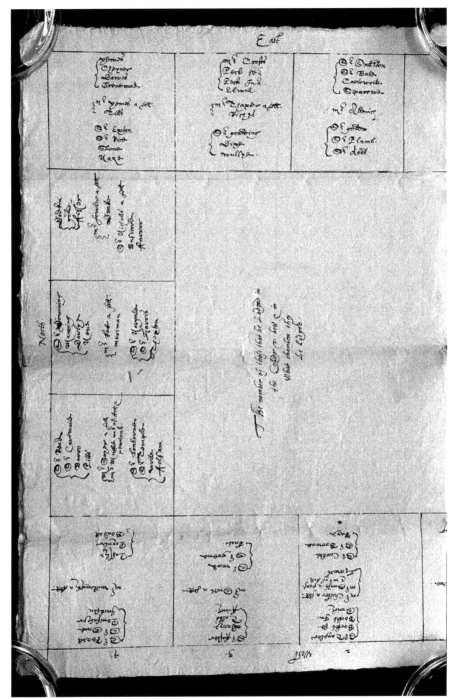

Figure 6 Nicholas Bacon's Plan of Corpus Christi College, 1577, 'The number of those that be Lodged in the Colleg & how & in what chambers they be lodged', left half. NRO, NRS 23372, Z99. Reproduced by kind permission of Norfolk Record Office.

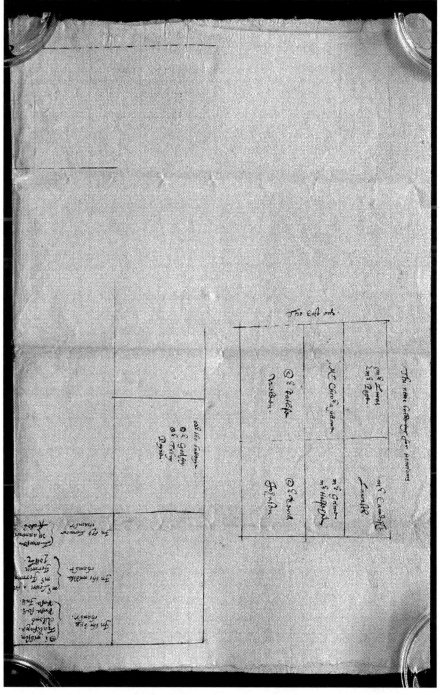

Figure 7   Bacon's plan, right half. NRO, NRS 23372, Z99. Reproduced by kind permission of Norfolk Record Office.

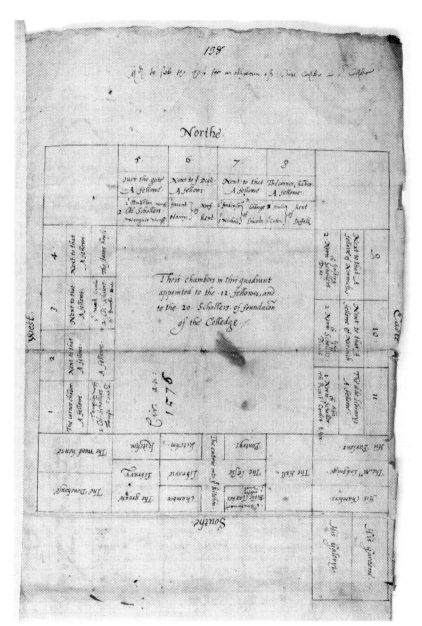

Figure 8 Matthew Parker's Plan of Corpus Christi College, 1574–75. CCCA, CCCC08/28, recto. Reproduced by kind permission of The Parker Library, Corpus Christi College, Cambridge.

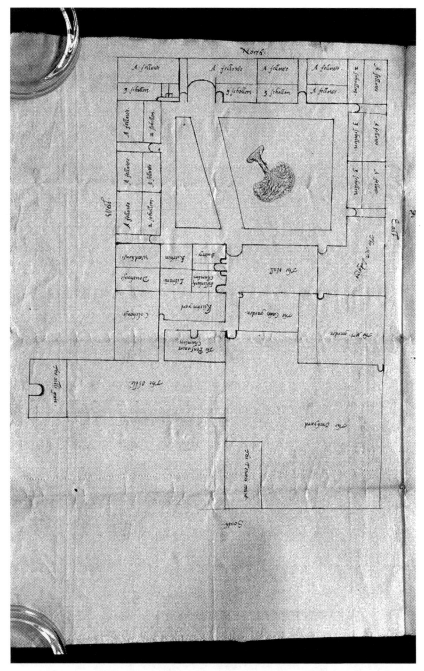

Figure 9　Corpus Christi College, plan of the college site, 1576, first verso of the document endorsed as 'The annuall revenuewes and exspences of Benet Colledge in Cambridge'. NRO, NRS 23372, Z99. Reproduced by kind permission of Norfolk Record Office.

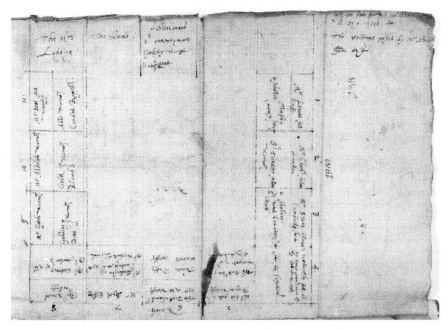

Figure 10   Parker's plan, verso. Reproduced by kind permission of The Parker Library, Corpus Christi College, Cambridge.

Figure 11   Manwood's monument in the parish church of St Stephen, Canterbury.
© Arata Ide.

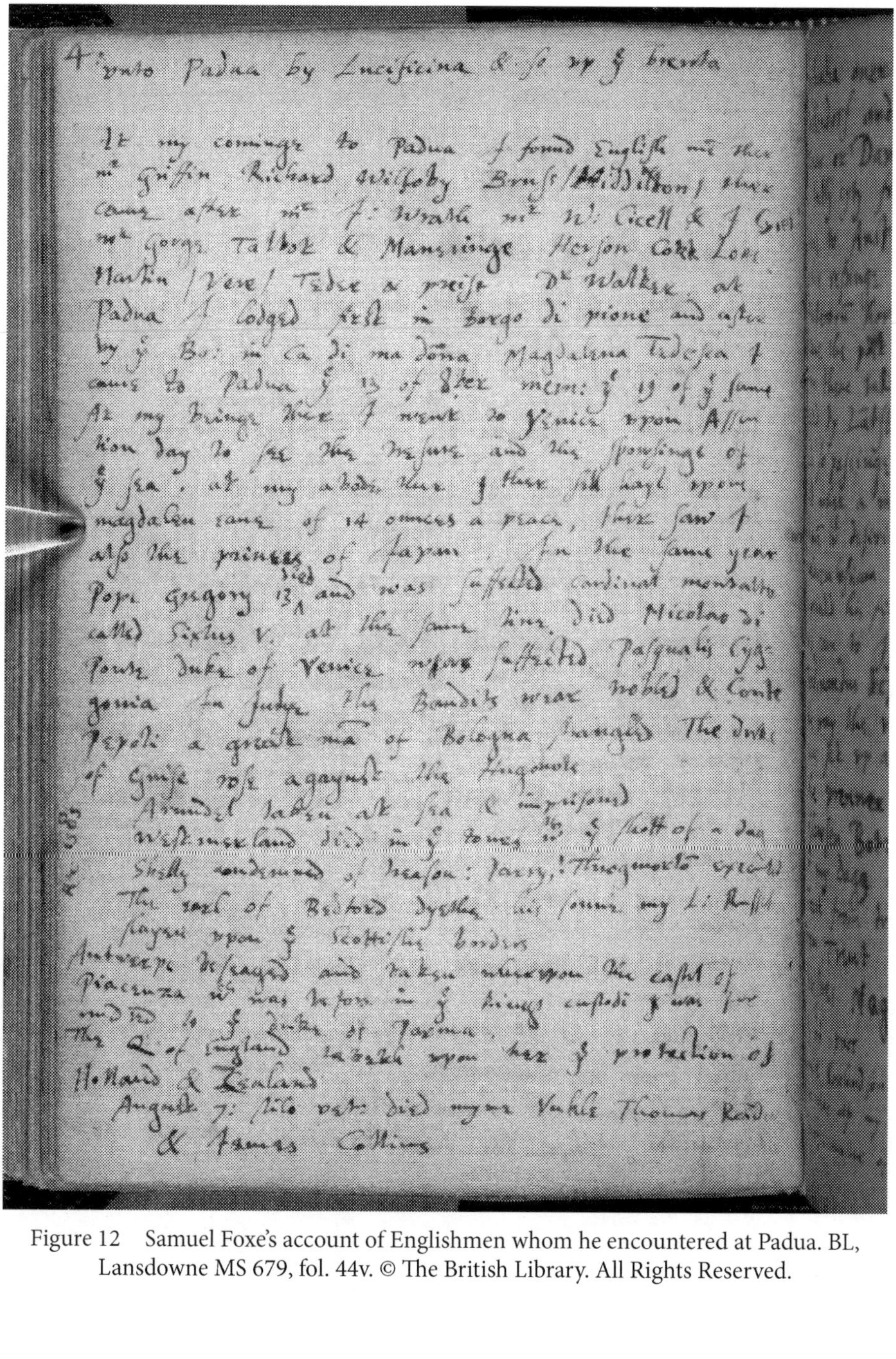

vnto Padua by Lucificina & so by y brenta

At my cominge to Padua I found English mē ther
mr Griffin Richard Wilfoby Bruff/Widdrinton/ ther
came after mē fr Wrath mr N: Cicell & J Gil
mr Georg: Talbot & Mansringe Herson Cock Low
Martin /Vere/ Tedier a preist Dr Walker, at
Padua I lodged first in Borgo di pione and after
by y Br: in Ca di ma dona Magdalena Tedesca I
came to Padua y 13 of 8ter mens: y 19 of y same
At my beinge ther I went to Venice vpon Assen-
tion day to see the Inesure and the spowsinge of
y sea. at my aboide ther I ther sild hay vpon
magdalen sane of 14 ounces a peace, ther saw I
also the princes of Parma. In the same year
Pope Gregory 13, died and was succeeded cardinal mentalto
called Sixtus V. at the same time died Nicolao di
Ponte Duke of Venice who succeded Pasquali Cyg-
gonia to Judge the Bandits wear nobles & Conte
Pepoli a great ma of Bologna strangled The Duke
of Guise rose agaynst the Hugonots
Arundel taken at sea & imprisoned
Westmereland died in y towne w'in y space of a day
Shirly condemned of treason: Parry! Throgmorton executed
The earl of Bedford dyethe his sonne my L: Russll
stayen vpon y Scottishe borders
Antwerpe betrayed and taken wherevpon the castel of
Piacenza w was before in y kinges custodi y was ser-
rendred to y Duke of Parma,
The Q: of England taketh vpon her y protection of
Holland & Zealand
August 7: stilo vet: died my vnkle Thomas Reid
& James Collins

Figure 12 Samuel Foxe's account of Englishmen whom he encountered at Padua. BL, Lansdowne MS 679, fol. 44v. © The British Library. All Rights Reserved.

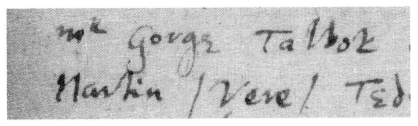

Figure 13   Foxe's handwritten 'Martin'. BL, Lansdowne MS 679, fol. 44v (detail).
© The British Library. All Rights Reserved.

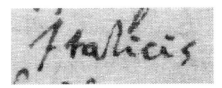

Figure 14   Foxe's handwritten 'Italicis'. BL, Lansdowne MS 679, fol. 49r (detail).
© The British Library. All Rights Reserved.

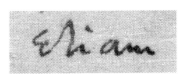

Figure 15   Foxe's handwritten 'etiam'. BL, Lansdowne MS 679, fol. 73v (detail).
© The British Library. All Rights Reserved.

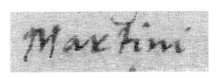

Figure 16   Foxe's handwritten 'Martini'. BL, Lansdowne MS 679, fol. 44r (detail).
© The British Library. All Rights Reserved.

Part II

PLAYS

Chapter 5

DIDO, ELIZABETH I, AND THE UNIVERSITY PLAYWRIGHTS

The heyday of Cambridge University drama lay between the 1540s and 1560s, during which time more than a third of all known performances occurred.[1] This was primarily due to the strong influence of humanists and Reformers, who regarded acting in classical plays as a good way to train the youth in schools and universities, but it went hand in hand with the reorganization of the traditional pedagogy of the liberal arts. It is no coincidence that St John's College established a statute in 1545 requiring students to act in a play at the same time that John Seton, a fellow at the college, published the first edition of *Dialectica*, a humanist textbook on dialectics.[2]

Yet the university authorities seem to have realized the potential political threat of religious drama as early as 1545, when *Pammachius* was acted at Christ's College.[3] This anti-papal polemical play was written in 1538 by Thomas Kirchmayer of Sulza in Thüringen, 'possibly for a production for school-boys'.[4] It tells of Pammachius, an imaginary Roman bishop and

---

[1] Alan Nelson (ed.), *Cambridge*, REED (2 vols, Toronto, 1989), vol. 2, p. 712 and appendix 8.

[2] *Ibid.*, p. 1113. See also Alan Nelson, 'Contexts for Early English Drama: The Universities', in Marianne G. Briscoe and John C. Coldewey (eds), *Contexts for Early English Drama* (Bloomington, 1989), pp. 138–50, at p. 141. For the humanist aspects of *Dialectica*, see Chapter 8, pp. 238–9.

[3] For the influence of Thomas Kirchmayer upon England and the plot of the play, see Charles E. Herford, *Studies in the Literary Relations of England and Germany in the Sixteenth Century* (1886; repr. Abingdon, 1966), pp. 119–32. C. C. Love's English translation of *Pammachius* is available on the REED website: <https://ccltlp.artsci.utoronto.ca/pammach.html> [accessed 21 November 2022].

[4] Paul Whitfield White, 'The Pammachius Affair at Christ's College, Cambridge in 1545', in Peter Happé and Wim Hüsken (eds), *Interlude and Early Modern Society: Studies in Gender, Power and Theatricality* (Amsterdam, 2007), pp. 261–90, at p. 264. For its political context, see also Alec Ryrie, *The Gospel and Henry VIII: Evangelicals in the Early English Reformation* (Cambridge, 2003), pp. 179–83.

anti-Christ who has grown weary of the gospel and now wants to team up with Satan to gain worldly power and pleasures. According to the report of Matthew Parker, the vice-chancellor at that time, the two fellows at Christ's who produced the play omitted 'all such mattyer wherby offense might Iustly haue rysen', as there was 'inspersed thorough out the tragedie both slanderous, cavillatious & suspitious sentence'.[5] However, a fellow of the college, possibly with Catholic sympathies, submitted a complaint to Stephen Gardiner, the chancellor of the university and defender of orthodoxy. Having perused 'the boke of the Tragedie', Gardner himself found 'moch matier not stryken out' and that 'vntruth is soo maliciously weved / with truth as making the bishop of Rome with certain his abuses [...] soo many abhominable and detestable lyes be added and mingled with the othir truth as noo christen eares shuld paciently heare'.[6] This controversy demonstrates that dramatic productions could often become politically combustible through entanglements in local and religious struggles, and it is no wonder that the authorities, by taking a cautious stance towards the performance of drama, tended to put a dampener on its growth.

The rise of religious radicals openly expressing grave doubts about the benefits of humanist practice was not the only cause of the change in both the cultural climate and the social role of college drama. Ironically, it was the university authorities, as well as a college amateur playwright, which transformed the social role of academic drama from a humanist medium of learning to a political medium for the purposes of commemoration, panegyric, persuasion, and satire. The major turning point seems to have come in 1558 with the ascension of Queen Elizabeth, 'with a hereditary passion for theatrical entertainments', which gave stimulus to 'forms of dramatic activity' and also encouraged amateur playwrights' political inventiveness to make the most of the oblique allusions and analogies in their plays.[7] The revitalization of drama as a political medium, readily detected in the revels both at Court and at the Inns of Court, also had immediate repercussions for the university stage.

A conspicuous case concerns the dramatic entertainments performed in August 1564, when the queen made a royal progress to Cambridge. The university authorities coordinated closely with the members of several colleges to stage plays for the sovereign and the prominent personages accompanying her. On 7 August, the third day of her visit, 'a tragic poem of Dido and Aeneas' was brought before the queen, with William Cecil and Robert Dudley as guests. The memorandum of Nicholas Robinson at

---

[5] Nelson, *Cambridge*, vol. 1, p. 134.
[6] *Ibid.*, pp. 138–9.
[7] Frederick F. Boas, *University Drama in the Tudor Age* (Oxford, 1914), p. 89.

Queen's College referring to her sojourn shows that the play was 'a new work' compiled by Edward Halliwell, a former fellow of King's College, who composed it 'in large part of verses from Virgil' and 'worked out the successive events of the story into the form of a tragedy in a not infelicitous way'.[8] Although we have no details of the play, the performance may have addressed the issue of royal marriage – as did the premiere of *Gorboduc* at Christmas 1561/2 at the Inner Temple and the Gray's Inn entertainment given at Whitehall on 5 March 1564/5[9] – in order to give the queen tacit warning against choosing a foreign prince as her consort.[10]

On the following evening (8 August), Nicholas Udall's *Ezechias*, a lost play possibly dated around 1545, was performed, expressing a different political message.[11] According to the detailed description of the play in Abraham Hartwell's *Regina Literata* (London, 1564), *Ezechias* contained the biblical episode of the religious reform by King Hezekiah, who shattered the brazen image of the serpent on account of idolatrous worship (2 Kings 18). The queen would have been encouraged to identify herself with Hezekiah, with the play's message urging her to root out Catholic idolatry from the Church of England (and possibly also, in an oblique way, from her private chapel, which still had a crucifix hanging in it).[12]

As Jonathan Walker points out, since 'the academy resided within the purview of the state and the church, whose ideological and economic interests it served by regularly producing suitably educated young men to fill governmental, diplomatic, and clerical posts, among other esteemed occupations', academic drama tended to 'dramatize a variety of religious,

---

[8] Nelson, *Cambridge*, vol. 2, p. 1137.
[9] See Norman Jones and Paul Whitfield White, '*Gorboduc* and Royal Marriage Politics: An Elizabethan Playgoer's Report of the Premiere Performance', *ELR*, 26:1 (1996), 3–16; and Michael A. Winkelman, *Marriage Relationships in Tudor Political Drama* (Aldershot, 2005), pp. 115–19. For the Gray's Inn entertainment (the lost play of Juno and Diana), see Marie Axton, *The Queen's Two Bodies: Drama and the Elizabethan Succession* (London, 1977), pp. 49–50; and Susan Doran, 'Juno versus Diana: The Treatment of Elizabeth I's Marriage in Plays and Entertainments, 1561–1581', *Historical Journal*, 38:2 (1995), 257–74, at pp. 264–5.
[10] Siobhan Keenan, 'Spectator and Spectacle: Royal Entertainments at the Universities in the 1560s', in Jayne Elisabeth Archer, Elizabeth Goldring, and Sarah Knight (eds), *The Progresses, Pageants, and Entertainments of Queen Elizabeth I* (Oxford, 2007), pp. 86–103, at p. 92, points out this possibility.
[11] William L. Edgerton, *Nicholas Udall* (New York, 1965), p. 82, notes that Udall referred to Ezechias in the preface to *The Paraphrase of Erasmus* (London, 1548), and dates the play to 1545 as 'a reasonable conjecture'.
[12] On contemporary criticisms of Elizabeth's keeping a crucifix in her private chapel, see Margaret Aston, *The King's Bedpost: Reformation and Iconography in a Tudor Group Portrait* (New York, 1993), p. 123.

political, and economic problems, sometimes deliberately and directly, sometimes implicitly'.[13] With Elizabeth's visit providing impetus, both the university authorities and government officials often took the lead in politicizing academic drama and employing it as a sugar-coated pill hiding more unpalatable truths designed to affect her policy-making processes. In fact, the Court continued to request that universities entertain domestic and foreign dignitaries throughout the 1570s and 1580s and for academic drama to be actively involved in urgent religious and political issues at Court.[14] This way of dramatic entertainment to address the queen and her officials naturally prompted university amateur playwrights to turn themselves into something like literary secretaries working for the motives of their local patrons at Court.

ELISA AFRICA ET ANGLIA

Very little external evidence survives to pin down the date of *Dido, Queen of Carthage* except the 1594 title page of the play, stating that it was 'played by the Children of her Maiesties Chappell' and 'written by Christopher Marlowe, and Thomas Nash'. Scholars have been cautious about the credibility of this claim, for no trace of any London performance by the Children of the Chapel can be found between 1584, when the troupe lost their lease of the Blackfriars theatre, and their appearance at Court in 1600/1. David Riggs and Park Honan speculate that Marlowe might have prepared the play for the troupe about 1584 or 1585, at a time when John Lyly's career 'had a magnetic effect on those who cared for theatrical success'.[15]

There are two reasons why biographers date *Dido* as early as 1584: the possible local connection of Marlowe with John Lyly and Thomas Nashe, and the almost unanimous assumption that *Dido* was Marlowe's dramatic effort in his early career while he was still in Cambridge. It is possible to push the date towards 1587 on the ground that, until its appearance at Court, the troupe continued acting outside London when not serving in the Queen's Chapel.[16] In fact, the traces of their appearance in Norwich

---

[13] Jonathan Walker, 'Learning to Play', in Jonathan Walker and Paul D. Streufert (eds), *Early Modern Academic Drama* (Farnham, 2008), pp. 1–18, at pp. 4–5.

[14] Linda Shenk points to 'the political relationship between crown and gown' in her article 'Gown before Crown: Scholarly Abjection and Academic Entertainment under Queen Elizabeth I', in Walker and Streufert (eds), *Early Modern Academic Drama*, pp. 19–44. For the court's requests for entertainments, see in particular pp. 26–7.

[15] Park Honan, *Christopher Marlowe: Poet and Spy* (Oxford, 2005), pp. 98–9; and David Riggs, *The World of Christopher Marlowe* (London, 2004), p. 113.

[16] Michael Shapiro, *Children of the Revels: The Boy Companies of Shakespeare's Time and Their Plays* (New York, 1977), p. 17. The payment to the Children of the Chapel

and Ipswich in the summer of 1587 have encouraged several scholars to assume that Marlowe, in collaboration with Nashe, may have prepared the play for the troupe to perform near to Cambridge.[17] If this was the case, we can assume that Nashe's share was small because it was early in his career, as compared to Marlowe, who had by now shot to pre-eminence on the London public stage. Nashe may simply have done 'something to prepare the tragedy for publication' after Marlowe's death.[18]

Some scholars speculate that Marlowe wrote *Dido* for academic performance at Cambridge. At the time of his election as a Parker scholar, he had to 'be so entred into the skill of song as that [he] shall at the first sight solf and sing plaine song' and to be 'such as can make a verse'.[19] Moreover, Robert Norgate was obviously so well disposed to dramatic entertainments that the college paid the expenses for staging one every two years on average during his mastership between 1573 and 1587. Both English and Latin plays may have been performed at Corpus Christi, as were 'both the english plaies' at Trinity in 1559–60.[20] Latin was the main language of academic drama; and John Still, the vice-chancellor, ill-disposed to Lord Burghley's urgent commission of English comedies for the queen's entertainment in 1592, wrote that they had 'no practize in this Englishe vaine' and found 'our principale Actors (whome wee haue of purpose called before vs) very vnwillinge to playe in Englishe'.[21] However, the college academic plays, unlike prestigious productions for the queen that were coordinated closely with talented members of several colleges, were produced at the expense of each college and with limited resources of personnel.[22] The vice-chancellor's solemn excuse cannot exclude the possibility of an English

---

Royal is registered in the Chamberlains' Accounts 1586–87 of Ipswich on 14 July. See John Webb (ed.), *The Town Finances of Elizabethan Ipswich: Select Treasurers' and Chamberlains' Accounts* (Woodbridge, 1996), p. 125.

[17] See C. F. Tucker Brooke, *The Life of Marlowe and 'The Tragedy of Dido Queen of Carthage'* (1930; repr. New York, 1966), p. 116, n. 1; Frederick S. Boas, *Christopher Marlowe: A Biographical and Critical Study* (Oxford, 1940), p. 49; Irving Ribner (ed.), *The Complete Plays of Christopher Marlowe* (New York, 1963), p. xx; and Roslyn L. Knutson, 'Marlowe, Company Ownership, and the Role of Edward II', in S. P. Cerasano (ed.), *MRDE*, vol. 18 (Madison, 2005), pp. 37–46, at pp. 38–9.

[18] G. R. Hibbard, *Thomas Nashe: A Critical Introduction* (Cambridge, MA, 1962), p. 87. See also Charles Nicholl, *A Cup of News: The Life of Thomas Nashe* (London, 1984), p. 29. More recently, however, Thomas Merriam has argued for their collaboration in his 'Marlowe and Nashe in Dido Queen of Carthage', *N&Q*, 47:4 (2000), 425–8.

[19] John Bakeless, *The Tragicall History of Christopher Marlowe* (2 vols, Cambridge, 1942) vol. 1, p. 64.

[20] Nelson, *Cambridge*, vol. 1, p. 208.

[21] *Ibid.*, p. 347.

[22] Boas, *University Drama*, p. 89. Nelson, *Cambridge*, vol. 2, p. 721.

performance at college. Moreover, the desire for 'publicke showes and commen plaies' among the young students can readily be detected in the university authorities' ban on such entertainments and the students' violations of that ban.[23] Even some vice-chancellors were lenient towards professional companies, as Paul Whitfield White discusses concerning the Queen's Men's visit to Cambridge: 'it was largely up to the particular vice-chancellor in office whether the university rigorously enforced the 1575 prohibition, or conversely, welcomed the Queen's Men and other players'.[24]

Considering these cultural circumstances, the point that Peter Roberts makes regarding college drama at Corpus Christi seems reasonable: 'Most of these college performances were probably of Latin rather than English plays, but at Corpus both seem to have been encouraged and not merely tolerated by the Master and Fellows.'[25] The highly supportive atmosphere of Corpus Christi, as well as of King's School at Canterbury, has prompted some Marlowe scholars to associate his creative adaptation of Vergil with the pedagogical praxis of disputations and dramatic activities at those institutions. Kuriyama considers it likely that his early exposure to the *Aeneid* at King's School 'led him to conceive his play of Dido as a quasi-didactic work suitable for performance by boys' and to revise it later, making it 'a considerably more sophisticated work dramatically, while still retaining the original concept of a play intended for performance by schoolboys'.[26]

On the other hand, Martin Wiggins takes the title-page statement at face value and, by mobilizing the best available evidence from theatrical and bibliographical sources and finding that the play 'has affinities with the repertory of the London boy companies in the 1580s', argues against the 'myth' of *Dido* as Marlowe's juvenilia. He hypothesizes that the Children of

---

[23] See, for example, Nelson, *Cambridge*, vol. 1, pp. 365, 378, and vol. 2, p. 727. Notwithstanding the vice-chancellor's discouragements and the suppression of public plays, the city authorities seem to have often neglected the order. For instance, the mayor of Cambridge commanded touring players to perform plays at his own house in 1587. See Nelson, *Cambridge*, vol. 1, p. 322.

[24] Paul Whitfield White, 'The Queen's Men in Elizabethan Cambridge', in Helen Ostovich, Holger Schott Syme, and Andrew Griffin (eds), *Locating the Queen's Men: Material Practices and Conditions of Playing* (Farnham, 2009), pp. 41–49, at p. 45. See also Scott McMillin and Sally-Beth MacLean, *The Queen's Men and Their Plays* (Cambridge, 1998), p. 77.

[25] Peter Roberts, '"The Studious Artizan": Christopher Marlowe, Canterbury and Cambridge', in Darryll Grantley and Peter Roberts (eds), *Christopher Marlowe and English Renaissance Culture* (Aldershot, 1996), pp. 17–37, at p. 24.

[26] Constance Brown Kuriyama, *Christopher Marlowe: A Renaissance Life* (Ithaca, 2002), p. 25. See also Riggs, *World of Marlowe*, pp. 113–14; and Donald Stump, 'Marlowe's Travesty of Virgil: *Dido* and Elizabethan Dreams of Empire', *Comparative Drama*, 34:1 (2000), 79–107.

the Chapel, more commercially vulnerable than the London-based Children of Paul's under the patronage of the Court, attempted to gain access to 'a theatre, well-equipped by the standards of the time and presumably London', commissioned Marlowe to script a play in order 'to compete with their adult rivals, and climbed onto the *Tamburlaine* bandwagon' around 1588.[27] Wiggins' argument encourages us to regard *Dido* as one of Marlowe's post-*Tamburlaine* undertakings for the private stage.

Whether the play was written for the boys' company or for college performance, the fact that its date oscillates between 1584 and 1588 seems to be little obstacle to considering that *Dido* emerged out of the dramatic traditions and political interests shared among university members in the 1580s. The cultural interactions between the academic stage and private productions in London around that time are well attested by such examples as William Gager in Oxford requesting George Peele, his college friend who had already gained some experience of productions for Court and the London private stage by associating himself with John Lyly, to come from London and act as one of the technical directors of academic productions at Christ Church in 1583.[28]

What gives additional weight to the argument that *Dido* was composed within the cultural orbit of university drama is Marlowe's choice of subject. Admittedly, the selection of this famous story from the *Aeneid* is not so extraordinary considering the fact that Marlowe and his contemporaries would have been familiar with the account from reading Vergil at grammar school and university. However, the myth came to assume a special meaning in Elizabeth's reign, particularly after royal progresses to the universities had made leading courtiers and university intellectuals aware of the political availability of theatrical entertainments as a means to address the issue of royal marriage negotiations, as Halliwell in Cambridge and Gager in Oxford did.[29] This dramatic tradition obviously sparked another Dido, which Marlowe created in *Dido, Queen of Carthage* for college performance and/or the London private stage: the Dido that naturally gave the play political overtones, as in the former Dido plays. It may have been almost impossible for Marlowe to be immune to political sentiments circulating in the 1580s or the ingenious ways of representing the queen that his contemporaries

---

[27] Martin Wiggins, 'When Did Marlowe Write Dido, Queen of Carthage?', *RES*, NS, 59:241 (2008), 521–41, at pp. 540–1.

[28] John R. Elliott Jr, Alan H. Nelson, Alexander F. Johnston, and Diana Wyatt (eds), *Oxford*, REED (2 vols, Toronto, 2004), vol. 1, pp. 183, 187–8; and David H. Horne, *The Life and Minor Works of George Peele* (New Haven, 1952), pp. 57–64.

[29] On the use of the story of Dido to address the marriage issue, see Keenan, 'Spectator and Spectacle', p. 92; Deanne Williams, 'Dido, Queen of England', *ELH*, 72:1 (2006), 31–59, at pp. 38–9.

had employed to good end. It is likely, as Donald Stump points out, that 'when Marlowe finished his own Tragedy of Dido in the 1580s, then, the connection between his protagonist and the Queen of England was already well established'.[30]

The tragic history of Dido, which was widely known at that time, begins with the murder of Acerbas (Sychaeus in Vergil's story), her husband and a Tyrian priest. Pygmalion, her avaricious brother and the tyrant of Tyre, kills him in hopes of obtaining Acerbas's considerable wealth through his sister. Dido flees from Tyre to the coast of Libya, where she purchases a site by making a bargain with the native king, Hiarbas (Iarbas in Vergil), and founds the new city of Carthage. When the city becomes prosperous, Hiarbas threatens Dido with war and demands her for his wife. Dido then falls in love with Aeneas, in exile from the battlefield at Troy. The gossip that circulates about their love affair, which Dido calls a marriage, greatly provokes Hiarbas, who complains to Jupiter, his father, about her decision to spurn him. Jupiter instructs Aeneas to keep on sailing in search of the promised Italian land, which compels the 'pious' Aeneas to depart for Italy. The grief-stricken Dido, deserted and guilty of falling away from her loyalty to Sychaeus, kills herself with the sword that Aeneas has given her. Her death brings Carthage into national crisis and causes long-lasting enmity against the descendants of Troy, foreshadowing the Punic Wars.

What inspired the political analogy between Dido and Queen Elizabeth was not merely their single status. They also shared a name, since Dido was known as 'Elissa', or 'Elisa' in some sources. More significant is the fact that the story of Dido or Elisa existed in another form, lacking the account of her love for Aeneas. Elizabethan intellectuals, while familiar with Vergil's Augustan myth that tended to blacken Dido's reputation, were very familiar with another tradition that presented a portrait of the queen as the pattern of female honour.[31] Lodowick Lloyd, a learned courtier with wide classical knowledge and an 'old servant' to Christopher Hatton, pointed out the fictionality of Vergil's narrative on the authority of Flavius Josephus: 'This *Carthage* was builded at such time as *Hiarbas* reigned in *Libya*, by a lady named *Elissa*, otherwayes named *Dido*, king *Pigmalio[n]s* sister of *Tyre*, borne in *Phoenicia*, after who[m] *Tirians* long inhabited: a hundred thirtie fiue yeeres before the building of *Rome* was *Carthage* builded.'[32]

[30] Stump, 'Marlowe's Travesty of Virgil', p. 84.
[31] For the intertextuality of the myth, see John Watkins, *The Specter of Dido: Spenser and Virgilian Epic* (New Haven, 1995), pp. 30–61; and Agnès Lafont, 'Multi-Layered Conversations in Marlowe's *Dido, Queen of Carthage*', in Janice Valls-Russell, Agnès Lafont, and Charlotte Coffin (eds), *Interweaving Myths in Shakespeare and His Contemporaries* (Manchester, 2017), pp. 195–215.
[32] Lodowick Lloyd, *The Consent of Time Disciphering the Errors of the Grecians in Their Olympiads* (London, 1590), sig. Ff3r. Lloyd describes himself to Hatton as 'Your

Dido, Elizabeth I, and the University Playwrights

Menaced by Hiarbas, the constant Dido kills herself with Acerbas' sword in order to defend the Carthaginian state and preserve her faithfulness to her husband. This Dido, a symbolic figure of chastity, had developed via Petrarch and Boccaccio as an antithesis to the character who appears in Vergil, and had no less strong an impact upon the imagination of intellectuals, so that 'a student of Cambridge' placed Dido in the literary lineage of faithful wives in his anthology *A Poore Knight His Pallace of Priuate Pleasures Gallantly Garnished* published in 1579:

> For Poets say, shee loued, *Aeneas* Knight of *Troy*,
> And when hee priuily fled from thence, her selfe shee did distroy.
> But tatling Poets lye, *Aeneas* was vnknowne,
> And *Troyan* seede in *Carthage* towne, by him was neuer sowne.
> *Iarbas* griped with loue, and could not her attayne,
> (For once shee made a faithfull vow, that chast shee would remayne)
> Laide seege vnto the towne, Dame *Dido* to mollest,
> But shee to saue her plighted othe, to die did thinke it best.
> And with a glittering blade, shee banisht breathing life,
> This was the constant ende of her, which was *Sicheus* wife.[33]

Accordingly, it was unsurprising for a poet to associate Elizabeth with Dido when praising her as the model of self-sacrifice and fidelity, as James Aske did in his *Elizabetha Triumphans* (1588), which celebrated the victory against the Armada. Aske lauds Elizabeth as the 'most Dido-like' sovereign, 'whose stately heart doth so abound with loue', without giving the slightest reference to Aeneas.[34]

In a similar way, Samuel Walsall, scholar and fellow of Corpus Christi, brought out the analogy between Dido and Elizabeth in the eulogy he contributed to *Threno-Thriambeuticon* (1603), an anthology of elegiac verses by the members of Cambridge University on the death of the queen. In order to idealize the self-sacrifice and fidelity of the Virgin Queen, however, Walsall made a sharp contrast between Elisa Africa, 'stained by Trojan love', and Elisa Anglia by utilizing Vergil's misogynistic adaptation of the Dido myth, praising Elizabeth as the virgin queen who, by avoiding marriage, had protected her people against foreign powers:

> There is both an African and English Eliza.
> We know that both are renowned

---

honors old seruant during life' in the second edition of *The Pilgrimage of Princes* (London, 1586), sig. ¶4r; and also in *The First Part of the Diall of Daies* (London, 1590), sig. A3r.

[33] *A Poore Knight His Pallace of Priuate Pleasures Gallantly Garnished* (London, 1579), sig. C1v.

[34] James Aske, *Elizabetha Triumphans* (London, 1588), p. 25.

In eternal praise, both were female
And both were queen. But the African is famed
In Maro's verses, the English by her own powers.
But the African is stained by Trojan love,
While the English virgin is celibate.[35]

Thus, Dido is a symbolic figure both of chastity – choosing to die for the nation rather than contemplate a royal intermarriage – and of female vulnerability, a ruling queen liable to destabilize the nation. This equivocal and contested character provided courtiers and poets with a favourite tool to give voice to their discontent and anxiety about Elizabeth's diplomatic policy, even while loudly panegyrizing her virtue. As Diane Purkiss notes, for those who feared that Elizabeth would never marry, as well as those who thought she would, 'The figure of Dido offered a superb way to express both kinds of anxiety while hedging one's bets and avoiding offence'.[36] In representing Dido as a counterpart of the queen, poets reworked the Vergilian and anti-Vergilian traditions in various ways to respond to the demands of each occasion and political situation.

WILLIAM GAGER'S *DIDO* AND THE MILITARIST FACTION

With all the attention paid to the figure of Dido in the university dramatic tradition, that of Aeneas is often forgotten. The roles of Aeneas and Dido took on very different complexions before and after the emergence of the Virgin Queen cult in the late 1570s.[37] Edward Halliwell's *Dido* was performed before Elizabeth, Robert Dudley, and William Cecil at King's College and seems to have celebrated marriage itself as a preferable state to celibacy, for Hartwell's *Regina Literata* shows that the play highlighted not

---

[35] *Threno-Thriambeuticon* (Cambridge, 1603), p. 7, as translated by Martin Brooke and Dana Sutton in Elizabeth Goldring, Faith Eales, Elizabeth Clarke, and Jayne Elisabeth Archer (eds), *John Nichols's The Progresses and Public Processions of Queen Elizabeth: A New Edition of the Early Modern Sources* (5 vols, Oxford, 2014), vol. 4, p. 322.

[36] Diane Purkiss, 'Marlowe's *Dido, Queen of Carthage* and the Representation of Elizabeth I', in Michael Burden (ed.), *A Woman Scorn'd: Responses to the Dido Myth* (London, 1998), pp. 151–67, at p. 152.

[37] In 'Juno versus Diana', Susan Doran considers the Norwich entertainments of August 1578 as the first recorded public occasion where the appearance of the Virgin Queen cult can be found. Roy Strong, *Gloriana: The Portraits of Queen Elizabeth I* (London, 1987), pp. 95–108, also finds 'a new departure in Elizabeth's portraiture' in Sieve portraits that cast Elizabeth as Tuccia, the Roman Vestal Virgin, produced c. 1579. For the marriage negotiation with the Duke of Anjou as the turning point, see also Helen Hacket, *Virgin Mother, Maiden Queen: Elizabeth I and the Cult of the Virgin Mary* (Basingstoke, 1995), pp. 94–127.

only the 'marriage rite' of Dido and Aeneas in the cave but also Juno, who 'as *pronuba* lit their sacred wedding torches', impressing upon the audience the legitimacy of Dido's marriage.[38] At the same time, Aeneas was presented as a 'great' and 'pious' personage compelled to launch his fleet by heavenly command. This portrayal of Aeneas, which faithfully follows Vergil's account, may have been influenced by the Habsburg marriage negotiation that Cecil and Elizabeth actively pursued in 1564.[39] Considering Charles, Archduke of Austria as a serious suitor was ample reason for Halliwell to shape the foreign consort of Dido into a 'pious' magnate so as to avoid offending the main guests, while implementing the pro-Dudley 'lesson' of the play in order to offer an oblique warning against wedlock with a foreign monarch.

The problem of the queen's marriage, which would dictate the destiny of the nation, was of great concern not only to government officials but also to the fellows and scholars who were or would be under their patronage, and this would have fostered an atmosphere unsettled enough to motivate a student to turn the logic class into a site of political agitation. On 28 April 1581, John Morden, BA of Peterhouse, made an oration or invective against the Duke of Anjou in the style of Cicero's orations *contra Verrem et Catelinam*, which was 'wickedly withowte all discrecion applied agaynst Monsire'; he was immediately thrown into prison for his 'lewde & slaunderous oracion made agaynst such a noble prince'.[40] Morden was banished from the college by Andrew Perne, the vice-chancellor, on 22 May, but he seems to have had more than a few backers among the authorities, because he obtained his MA as normal the following year.[41]

What needs to be stressed here is that, even after the marriage negotiation with the Duke of Anjou, the political expediency of the Dido–Aeneas myth continued to encourage university playwrights to rework it. In fact, on 12 June 1583, William Gager, a fellow of Christ Church, Oxford, produced his *Dido* for the entertainment of Albertus Alasco (or Olbracht Laski), palatine of Sieradż, who came to England as an ambassador from the King of Poland and was accompanied to Oxford by the Earl of Leicester

---

[38] Abraham Hartwell, *Regina Literata* (London, 1565), sig. D1v–2r, cited from the translation in Nelson, *Cambridge*, vol. 2, pp. 1139–40.

[39] That Halliwell followed Vergil's portrayal of Aeneas can be inferred from Nicholas Robinson's testimony that the play was 'made up in large part of verses from Virgil' (Nelson, *Cambridge*, vol. 2, p. 1137). For details on the matrimonial project with Charles the Archduke of Austria, see Susan Doran, *Monarchy and Matrimony: The Courtships of Elizabeth I* (London, 1996), pp. 73–98.

[40] Charles Henry Cooper, *Annals of Cambridge* (5 vols, Cambridge, 1842–53), vol. 2, p. 386.

[41] CUA, Collect. Admin. 6a [Caryl B. 24], Buckle Book, p. 144.

and Philip Sidney.[42] Holinshed describes the spectacular aspect of the play, 'all strange, maruellous, and abundant', along with its ingenuity in staging the banqueting scene in Dido's palace, its hunting scene, its use of rare mechanical devices, and its hails of small comfits, rains of rosewater, and artificial snow.[43]

The surviving text of the play leaves some traces of its political design. At the welcoming feast in the first book of the *Aeneid*, Iopas with his golden lyre sings of the creation of the world through the toils of sun and moon and basks in the applause from the audience. Gager remakes Iopas' song into his own paean to the main guest and the hostess:

> Hail, glory of heroes, famous light of your nation, of your ancient line.
> No ship has ever attained our shores more welcome than yours.
>
> But though you are so great and overwhelm my heart's understanding,
> Elisa is yet greater, oh guest so fortunate to have Elisa as hostess.[44]

This song functions as a pointer to the whole scheme of the play. The banquet given in Aeneas' honour under the direction of Elisa is ingeniously superimposed on the entertainment held on the occasion of welcoming Alasco. The dramatic device that makes Aeneas the counterpart of the archduke seems to have urged Gager to prepare a dialogue between the Trojan hero and Illioneus in Act IV. Against Illioneus, who blames him for breaking his faith (referring to Paris' betrayal of Oenone), Aeneas argues that: '[Paris] is called guilty who does wrong of his own will. I am leaving unwillingly. I have made up my mind to obey Jupiter's command. Our departure will not be obstructed by any argument' (913–14). Through this dialogue, Gager allows Aeneas to defend himself by elucidating the unusual situation that compels him to leave Carthage, thus moderating Aeneas' negative image.

The epilogue addressed to Dido reveals the play's political aim in a more straightforward manner:

> But, Dido, one woman surpasses you by far: our virgin queen. In her piety, how many reversals has she endured! What kingdoms has she

---

[42] For Leicester and Sidney's attendance on Alasco's journey, see Elliott *et al.* (eds), *Oxford*, vol. 1, p. 185. J. W. Binns, 'William Gager's Dido', *Humanistica Lovaniensia*, 20 (1971), 167–254, at p. 170, calls our attention to the presence of Philip Sidney at Oxford.

[43] Raphael Holinshed, *Holinshed's Chronicles of England, Scotland, and Ireland*, with a new introduction by Vernon F. Snow (6 vols, 1807–08; repr. New York, 1976), vol. 4, p. 508.

[44] Dana F. Sutton (ed.), *William Gager: The Complete Works* (4 vols, New York, 1994), vol. 1, pp. 282–3, lines 333–40. Subsequent references to and translations of Gager's works will be to Sutton's edition and will appear parenthetically in the text by line number.

founded! To what foreigners has she plighted her trust! But she has not condescended to marry any Sychaeus, and may no Aeneas sway her affections! But behold, here is a guest greater than Aeneas. To this man, Dido, your words would better apply: 'What new guest has come to our home? How handsome his face! How brave with his deep chest, distinguished in battle! I believe he is descended from the gods, and this is no empty belief.' (1241–51)

The flattery is mainly directed towards Alasco as the 'guest greater than Aeneas', whose good looks may well attract Elisa so irresistibly that, if Elisa Africa had been the hostess to the archduke, she might have made the same mistake. Gager uses this negative aspect of Elisa Africa to bring out the marked contrast between her and Elisa Anglia, who, with her patient and unruffled self-control over the marriage negotiations and her restraint in adversity, will play a pivotal role in the stability of her nation-state. At the time when Gager's *Dido* was being performed, the prospect of Elizabeth's marriage to Anjou had completely collapsed; as a consequence, the emphasis of the play seems to have been placed on upholding and celebrating the *de facto* status of the queen as *regina virgo* rather than on either warning against or supporting the marriage. At the same time, however, the Virgin Queen still often stirred discontent among her courtly subjects by demanding power, which they believed might deprive them of the basis of their martial identity and, furthermore, bring disaster upon the nation. A ruling queen eager to dominate her subjects, just as much as one who would dote on a foreign suitor, could be a grave menace to the stability of the nation.

In *Meleager*, Gager seems to have given voice to the discontent and anxiety of the warlike courtiers. This play was originally performed at Christ Church in February 1582 and staged again on 12 January 1585 (about a year and half after the performance of *Dido*), when the Earl of Leicester, Henry Herbert, the second Earl of Pembroke, and Sir Philip Sidney came to Oxford. Gager obviously bore in mind the fact that this audience comprised militarists who were related by marriage and who shared an imperialist vision of a Protestant league under the leadership of England. As a result, as suggested in the epilogue specifically written for Leicester and Pembroke, he presents Oeneus, King of Aetolia, who does not offer incense to Diana, as an *exemplum domi* (1925) – a lesson to their household. Oeneus is portrayed as a Tamburlaine-like profane character whose disdain for Diana's power incurs her displeasure and brings trouble on his whole family. Diana sends a Calydonian boar to devastate his ancestral territory. Meleager, Oeneus' son and a heroic warrior, leads a hunting party that Atalanta, the virgin huntress of Diana's cult and princess of Arcadia, joins as his partner. Meleager kills the boar and, with high-minded generosity, gives her the spoils of its head and hide as an emblem of high virtue (909). This extraordinary gift arouses the jealousy of his misogynistic uncles and impels Meleager to kill them, ultimately leading to his own tragic end at the hands of Althaea, his mother, seeking vengeance.

What concerns us here is Gager's panegyric to Elizabeth by investing Atalanta with the characteristics of the queen. As in *Dido*, he points to a 'better Atalanta' in England at the end of the play: 'To her Arcadian Atalanta has yielded place, just as Arcadia herself has yielded to famous England. How harsh our Atalanta has always been to her Meleagers! Ah so harsh, more than her suitors would have wished!' (1891–4). The allusion to the English Atalanta's stern and cruel attitude towards her admirers could be a subtle form of flattery extolling the virtue of Elizabeth as 'a marvellous virgin whether waging harsh battles or plying the arts of peace' (1903–4). This flattery, however, seems to have been inherently unsettling, for Gager and the audience members well knew that among the suitors whom she had treated coldheartedly was the Earl of Leicester, one of the main guests. This situation naturally urged Gager to express his strong sympathy with Leicester by likening him to Meleager, an unrewarded warrior, even while praising the unrelenting sternness of the Virgin Queen. Moreover, Gager pays special tribute to Sidney in the epilogue and, curiously enough, celebrates him as *spes nostra* and *Meleager ipse noster*, making an ill-omened joke in addition: 'let there be no sad omen in my words, and I trust Meleager's regrettable end will not be his destiny' (1923–5). This reference to Sidney allows us to see Meleager as a symbol of an unsuccessful suitor to the queen; yet he is also shown to be a high-minded and chivalrous servant whose self-sacrificing devotion to his mistress under the influence of her strong power is rewarded only with cold contempt, and which even invites disaster on his household. The play's allusion to these discontented Meleagers allows us to see Oeneus' unreasonable animosity against Diana as the negative equivalent of Meleager's devotion to Atalanta. Gager intentionally aggrandizes Oeneus' hubris and admirable fortitude against Diana, as he states in the preface, in order to present the king as a useful 'lesson' to Leicester's household. At the same time, he gives voice to the smouldering discontent among the Protestant militarists under the guise of Oeneus' bombastic and provocative words against Diana.

In fact, there was a perceptible gap between the cult of Elizabeth as a self-controlled queen of chastity and the misogyny felt among martial courtiers frustrated by her ambivalent attitude towards foreign military affairs throughout the 1580s. The ambitions of Leicester and his faction for military intervention in the Netherlands had often been checked by Elizabeth, a situation that continued until August 1585 when she finally agreed to send expeditionary forces there; even then, she felt inclined to give Leicester, the commander in chief, little freedom of action. Before leaving England on 3 December 1585, Leicester complained about the limited scope of his authority, which Elizabeth had reduced through her vacillating instructions.[45] It is likely that the queen's equivocal support, 'which she routinely undercut by inadequate funding, erratic diplomacy, and quarrels with her commander', deepened the frustration and misogyny felt by her pro-war courtiers and civilians.[46] Sidney himself grumbles in his letter to Walsingham about her parsimoniousness in paying her soldiers for the expedition and 'how apt the queen is, to interpret euery thing to my disaduantage'.[47] Even after the triumph over the Armada, Elizabeth 'never spent a penny cheerfully and her wars were waged in the same cheese-paring spirit that had characterized her days of peace'.[48] Oeneus' blasphemy against Diana seems to have echoed their complaint against Elizabeth, who had been 'so harsh, more than her suitors would have wished' (1894).

Clearly, the militarist faction – mainly composed of Leicester, Walsingham, and Sidney – was an emerging political powerhouse whose influence over Court politics could strongly motivate aspiring university intellectuals to align themselves with their policy. Their political leverage at that time turned a number of ambitious scholars into 'good heliotropes', to use Ben Jonson's phrase in *Sejanus His Fall*: those who always look towards the sun for warm favour.[49] As Gager praises in the prologue of *Meleager*, Leicester and his faction were 'our Muse, our Minerva, our father Phoebus' (66).

Marlowe, likewise, cannot have been immune to the ambition to win the attention of these noteworthy militarists, for he happened to be closely associated with Walsingham and his clients during his collegiate years. He had to pay attention to his own intellectual, political, and religious identity in that atmosphere, while conducting his collegiate life in obedience to the university authorities and seeking patronage at Court by using local connections. In this respect, his playwriting at college was a highly politicized act.

Discussing the influence of Gager upon Marlowe's *Dido*, Frederick S. Boas claims that 'there is not the slightest internal evidence of connexion

---

[45] See Conyers Read, *Mr. Secretary Walsingham and the Policy of Queen Elizabeth* (3 vols, 1925; repr. New York, 1978), vol. 3, pp. 124–5; R. B. Wernham, *Before the Armada: The Growth of English Foreign Policy 1485–1588* (London, 1966), p. 376; Wallace T. MacCaffrey, *Queen Elizabeth and the Making of Policy, 1572–1588* (Princeton, 1981), p. 359.
[46] Richard C. McCoy, *The Rites of Knighthood: The Literature and Politics of Elizabethan Chivalry* (Berkeley, 1989), p. 49.
[47] Roger Kuin (ed.), *The Correspondence of Sir Philip Sidney* (2 vols, Oxford, 2012), vol. 2, pp. 1213–1214.
[48] Read, *Secretary Walsingham*, vol. 3, p. 334.
[49] Ben Jonson, *Sejanus His Fall*, ed. Tom Cain, in David Bevington, Martin Butler, and Ian Donaldson (gen. eds), *The Cambridge Edition of the Works of Ben Jonson* (7 vols, Cambridge, 2012), vol. 2, iv.i.426.

between the two works'.[50] Recently, however, Dana F. Sutton has noted a feature they have in common, that 'At the end of both plays Anna [Dido's sister] commits suicide, a development not indebted to Vergil'.[51] Moreover, as H. R. Woudhuysen points out, the fact that there are numerous extant copies of academic plays suggests that they had wide circulation in manuscript form and enjoyed literary exchange among various academic institutions.[52] For instance, two copies of Legge's *Richardus Tertius* survive in Oxford libraries; and there is adequate internal evidence that Gager read and even borrowed from it.[53] These traces of circulation do not necessarily provide evidence that Marlowe read Gager's *Dido*, but what seems obvious is that Marlowe, in scripting the play with a degree of political circumspection, had to attend not only to the deliberate association between Elisa Africa and Elisa Anglia but also to the dexterous ways of representing the queen that his university predecessors such as Halliwell and Gager had employed, scrupulously meeting the demands of their patrons. Moreover, Marlowe was well aware of the Gagerian method of combined panegyrizing and complaining about the queen's stern attitude towards her admirers. In Marlowe's play, Iarbas, making a sacrifice to Jupiter, grumbles about the scornful ways and fickleness of 'the woman that thou will'd us entertain', abruptly using Dido's given name: 'Hear, hear, O hear Iarbas' plaining prayers, / Whose hideous echoes make the welkin howl, / And all the woods "Eliza" to resound!'[54] Thus, Marlowe takes advantage of the analogy to turn the 'plaining prayers' of Iarbas into a sort of descant or counterpoint which he interweaves with militarist overtones – a disturbing tune of frustrated anxiety about an arbitrary queen who gets her own way by forcing martial men under her control.

WARLIKE SOLDIERS IN CAPTIVITY

By embroidering Anna's reference to Dido's rejection of the suitors in the *Aeneid*,[55] Marlowe invented a scene where Dido comments on the pictures of rejected suitors hanging on the wall. None of these 'most urgent

---

[50] Boas, *University Drama*, p. 189.
[51] Sutton, *William Gager*, vol. 1, p. 250.
[52] H. R. Woudhuysen, *Sir Philip Sidney and the Circulation of Manuscripts 1558–1640* (Oxford, 1996), pp. 143–4.
[53] Dana F. Sutton (ed.), *Thomas Legge: The Complete Plays* (2 vols, New York, 1993), vol. 1, pp. xxi and xxix.
[54] Christopher Marlowe, *Dido Queen of Carthage and The Massacre at Paris*, ed. H. J. Oliver, *The Revels Plays* (London, 1968), iv.ii.8–10. Subsequent references will be to this edition and will appear parenthetically in the text by act, scene, and line number.
[55] Publius Maro Vergilius, *Vergil I: Eclogues, Georgics, Aeneid I–VI*, ed. H. Rushton Fairclough and trans. G. P. Goold (1999; repr. Cambridge, MA, 2006), vi.35–8.

suitors for my love', she says, could obtain her, and now 'I am free from all' (III.i.150–2). Here, Marlowe seems to have taken the dramatic tradition of panegyrizing the Virgin Queen into account and, interestingly enough, has included among the portraits a figure of Meleager's son. Dido explains it: 'This, Meleager's son, a *warlike* prince, / But weapons gree not with my tender years' (III.i.162–3, italics added). As Meleager is not known to have had a son, this 'warlike prince' is entirely Marlowe's own invention. Considering the popularity of Gager's play *Meleager*, this might have been an implicit reference to Sidney or to his household.

What is more important is that, while Aeneas in Vergil's *Aeneid* is frequently described as 'pious', Marlowe applies to him the epithet 'warlike' with a tinge of irony. Aeneas is introduced to Dido by Illioneus, a Trojan soldier, as 'our General: / Warlike Aeneas', to which Dido teasingly responds, 'Warlike Aeneas, and in these base robes?' (II.i.77–9). Moreover, just before the discovery of Aeneas and Dido 'sporting in this darksome cave', Cupid, in the disguise of Aeneas' son Ascanius, is looking for Aeneas: 'where is my warlike father, can you tell?' (IV.i.15). Marlowe seems to have intended to present Aeneas as an essentially admirable soldier, as Iarbas describes Trojan refugees at his first encounter as 'brave men-at-arms' (I.ii.32). In fact, at the beginning of the play, Aeneas makes fire with the (anachronistic) tinderbox to make them warm and 'roast our new-found victuals on this shore' (I.i.168). Roma Gill remarks that Marlowe's Aeneas looks 'like the man-in-the-street, who was never meant for noble action' and 'From first to last he is the practical man, organizing food and fire for his companions'.[56] This point is crucial because what the audience saw on stage was a foreign coast near the woods and an expedition of English men-at-arms, far from the legendary founders of Rome. This scene thus localizes, rather than demystifies, the 'pious' and 'golden-tongued' hero of Vergil, transforming him into a 'warlike' soldier of Elizabethan England.

Aeneas' long narrative in Act II (more than 150 lines) can be regarded as another device for localizing Vergil's hero. It is Dido who first urges him to play a heroic orator: 'What, faints Aeneas to remember Troy, / In whose defence he fought so valiantly? / Look up and speak' (II.i.118–20). She demands that Aeneas show his well-balanced combination of soldier's and rhetorician's attributes by speaking, as well as by fighting, 'so valiantly', so as to represent himself as an embodiment of the republican ideal of the citizen militia. His narrative picks up momentum when he describes the bloody massacre at Troy:

---

[56] Roma Gill, 'Marlowe's Virgil: Dido Queene of Carthage', *RES*, NS, 28:110 (1977), 141–55, at pp. 150–1.

> By this, the camp was come unto the walls
> And through the breach did march into the streets,
> Where, meeting with the rest, 'Kill, kill!' they cried.
> Frighted with this confused noise, I rose,
> And looking from a turret might behold
> Young infants swimming in their parents' blood,
> Headless carcases piled up in heaps,
> Virgins half-dead dragg'd by their golden hair
> And with main force flung on a ring of pikes,
> Old men with swords thrust through their aged sides,
> Kneeling for mercy to a Greekish lad,
> Who with steel pole-axes dash'd out their brains. (II.i.188–99)

This passage has no counterpart in Vergil. Marlowe seems to have associated the appalling landscape of Troy with that of Paris, by putting into the mouths of the Greek soldiers the dreadful outcry of the Guisians against the Protestants in *The Massacre at Paris*. To borrow Susan Harlan's phrase, his representation of violence in nostalgic form is treated 'as a feature not only of war narratives, but also of the relationship between the past and the present'.[57] The infantry with its 'ring of pikes' may have reminded the audience of the popular military disposition or arrangement of troops on which Thomas Styward gives a commentary in his companion to the art of war (figure 17).[58] 'Steel pole-axes' were also common infantry weapons, often employed for onstage fights and frequently in formal entrances.[59]

Significantly, Aeneas' rhetoric sounds like that of a Tamburlainean militarist, expressed with admirable composure, having complete mastery over the language of violence in which the public theatre took pleasure with feverish excitement. The emphasis on such martial qualities seems to have been encouraged by an upsurge of jingoistic sentiment in the 1580s and, in this respect, was in alignment with William Webbe's understanding of Aeneas. In *A Discourse of English Poetrie* (1586), Webbe, finding in the *Aeneid* a mine of 'the braue warlike phrase and bygge sounding kynd of thundring speeche, in the hotte skyrmyshes of battels', proclaims that Vergil represents Aeneas as the ideal military man: 'Vnder the person of *Æneas* he expresseth the valoure of a worthy Captaine and valiaunt Gouernour, together with the perrilous aduentures of warre, and polliticke deuises at all assayes.'[60]

---

[57] Susan Harlan, *Memories of War in Early Modern England: Armor and Militant Nostalgia in Marlowe, Sidney, and Shakespeare* (New York, 2016), p. 94.
[58] Thomas Styward, *The Pathwaie to Martiall Discipline* (London, 1581), p. 68.
[59] Alan C. Dessen and Leslie Thomson, *A Dictionary of Stage Directions in English Drama, 1580–1642* (Cambridge, 1999), p. 168.
[60] William Webbe, *A Discourse of English Poetrie*, in G. Gregory Smith (ed.), *Elizabethan Critical Essays* (2 vols, Oxford, 1904), vol. 1, pp. 237, 260.

Dido, Elizabeth I, and the University Playwrights

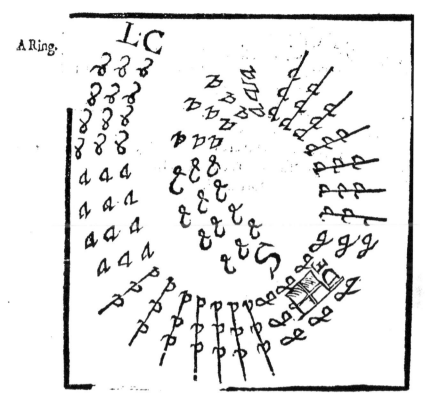

Figure 17 'Ring of Pikes' in Thomas Styward, *The Pathwaie to Martiall Discipline* (London, 1581), p. 68. RB 14636, The Huntington Library, San Marino, California.

At the same time, however, Marlowe's Aeneas, as if assigned by the master of his grammar school to practise *ethopoeia*, rouses himself to speak 'with Achilles' tongue' to 'Myrmidons' harsh ears' (II.i.121, 123); that is, he 'casts himself in the role of his city's most powerful enemy, and casts his audience as Achilles' followers'.[61] His use of the narrative persona, though he succeeds in arousing the 'melting ruth' of the audience, entails artificiality and theatricality, giving us a faint impression that he is making a strenuous effort to be a Vergilian 'warlike' hero at the imperial court of Carthage. Marlowe, while following the dramatic traditions of the universities to panegyrize

---

[61] For the drama-based pedagogy of *ethopoeia* (a technique of rhetoric to create a pathetic speech by imitating another's style) at grammar schools and Marlowe's adaptation of its technique to Aeneas' speech, see Kathryn Rebecca Van Winkle, '"Then Speak, Aeneas, with Achilles' Tongue": Ethopoeia and Elizabethan Boyhood in Marlowe's *Dido Queen of Carthage*', in David S. Thompson (ed.), *Theatre Symposium: A Publication of the Southeastern Theatre Conference, Vol. 23, Theatre and Youth* (Tuscaloosa, 2015), pp. 42–51, at p. 45.

Elizabeth through Dido, localizes the character of Aeneas, shifting his focus from the political issue of her marriage negotiations to the military power and force of rhetoric under her control.

The most clearly distinguishing feature of *Dido, Queen of Carthage* is the way in which 'warlike' Aeneas loses his heroic and martial traits as the play progresses and is disempowered under Dido's patronage. His masculine epic is not welcomed at her court, and she concludes his tale of Troy's fall: 'Come, let us think upon some pleasing sport, / To rid me from these melancholy thoughts' (II.i.302–3).[62] The rhetoric that dominates the Carthaginian court is that of Renaissance love poetry, as we can detect in Dido's offer to renovate the damaged fleet of Troy, a poetic discourse embroidered by Marlowe's mastery of what C. S. Lewis termed 'the material imagination', which bears close resemblance to that in *Hero and Leander*:[63]

> I'll give thee tackling made of rivell'd gold
> Wound on the barks of odoriferous trees;
> Oars of massy ivory, full of holes,
> Through which the water shall delight to play;
> Thy anchors shall be hew'd from crystal rocks,
> Which if thou lose shall shine above the waves;
> The masts whereon thy swelling sails shall hang,
> Hollow pyramides of silver plate;
> The sails of folded lawn, where shall be wrought
> The wars of Troy, but not Troy's overthrow. (III.i.115–24)

Dido transforms 'twice twelve Phrygian ships', bravely ploughing the waves, into a fleet of treasure ships gaudily decorated, and 'sails all rent in sunder with the wind' into a tapestry beautified with a picture of the Trojan War. In the empire where the sovereign mistress rules, the rhetoric demanded by the courtier is that of the lover in service to her complimenting her beauty, sublimity, and hospitality.

Dido first tells Aeneas to 'Remember who thou art: speak like thyself' (II.i.100), but later urges him to 'speak like my Aeneas, like my love' (v.i.112). The heroic oratory of Vergilian epic is totally incongruous at her court. Their relationship is exquisitely suggested in the symbolic scene where Dido, taking shelter from the sudden storm, bumps into Aeneas in the cave:

---

[62] Aeneas' epic narrative may also have been unwelcome in the court of Elizabeth, for Thomas Churchyard, recollecting the career of his literary works thus far in *Churchyards Challenge* (London, 1593), refers to 'Aeneas tale to Dydo, largely and truely translated out of Virgill, which I once shewed the Qu. Ma. and had it againe' (sig. **r).

[63] C. S. Lewis, *English Literature in the Sixteenth Century Excluding Drama* (Oxford, 1954), p. 486.

Dido.	Aeneas!
Aen.	Dido!
Dido.	Tell me, dear love, how found you out this cave?
Aen.	By chance, sweet Queen, as Mars and Venus met.
Dido.	Why, that was in a net, where we are loose;
	And yet I am not free – O would I were! (III.iv.1–5)

Marlowe superimposes Aeneas upon Mars, and Dido upon Venus, associating their love affair with the Homeric fable of Venus and Mars caught *in flagrante delicto* in Vulcan's net.[64] Dido and Aeneas are entangled in the invisible meshes of their own circumstances: Dido, as the sovereign queen of Carthage, is bound to her country, while Aeneas is bound by his oath to establish the new Troy in Italy. Marlowe perfectly represents the lovers' inescapable entanglement by invoking Vulcan's net.[65] At the same time, he seems to recall the Renaissance allegorizing of the fable that his contemporaries had often exploited. In the traditions of Renaissance iconography, the union of Venus and Mars represents the harmonious concordance of the two ruling passions, love (Venus) and the martial spirit (Mars); even more importantly for our purposes here, it symbolizes the subjugation of Mars, or the emasculation of the martial spirit, to the power of love.[66]

Barnabe Riche, a poet-soldier who joined the expedition to Ireland in the 1570s, used this symbolic dynamic of Venus and Mars to complain about the decline of the military profession.[67] In his *A Right Exelent and Pleasaunt Dialogue, betwene Mercvry and an English Souldier* (1574), dedicated to Ambrose Dudley, the military Earl of Warwick, the soldier narrator, in order to hand to Mars a petition from discarded soldiers, visits Venus' court, where the god of war is sojourning, and finds him, to his surprise, 'layed in *Venus* Lap'. The soldier's petition leads Mars, 'not ignoraunt' about the deplorable state of the soldiers 'obedient to the lawes of loue', to complain of '*Hermaphroditus* halfe men, halfe women, such as willy rowling in a Ladies lap kissing her hands, feeding hyr eares with

---

[64] Homer, *The Odyssey*, trans. A. T. Murray (2 vols, 1919; repr. Cambridge, MA, 1984), vol. 1, VIII.266–342.

[65] For Marlowe's use of the fable and its allegory in the cave scene and his parody of Lyly's *Sapho and Phao*, see Yuzo Yamada, *Writing under Influences: A Study of Christopher Marlowe* (Tokyo, 1999), pp. 55–8.

[66] Edgar Wind, *Pagan Mysteries in the Renaissance* (1958; enlarged and repr. New York, 1968), pp. 86–96.

[67] For Riche's military and literary career, see Juliet Fleming, 'The Ladies' Man and the Age of Elizabeth', in James Grantham Turner (ed.), *Sexuality and Gender in Early Modern Europe: Institutions, Texts, Images* (Cambridge, 1993), pp. 158–81; Rory Rapple, *Martial Power and Elizabethan Political Culture: Military Men in England and Ireland, 1558–1594* (Cambridge, 2009), p. 126.

philed flattering talke'; but he contradicts himself by falling into such a state under the influence of Venus' dominant power.[68] Similarly, Marlowe employs the literary device to suggest, as W. L. Godshalk notes, that 'Dido-Venus attempts to emasculate her Aeneas-Mars, to force him into the ways of love not martial conquest'.[69] Thus, Marlowe's Aeneas, bound up in Carthage with Dido, loses his epic identity as a warlike commander, while Dido assumes power and dignity sufficient to enclose her lover within her own private sphere:

> Stout love, in mine arms make thy Italy,
> Whose crown and kingdom rests at thy command;
> Sichaeus, not Aeneas, be thou call'd;
> The King of Carthage, not Anchises' son. (III.iv.56–9)

The Italy that Aeneas would establish in Dido's arms is not the military regime of the new Troy but the Carthaginian regime of love where the queen, stripping Aeneas of his patriarchal heritage, rewrites his identity as the second Sychaeus. Dido's power is so dominant that Aeneas cannot get away from Carthage even after Hermes in a dream reminds him of 'fruitful Italy' and his vital mission; instead he resigns himself to Dido's eager desire to put the imperial crown on his head and give him the Punic sceptre. What Marlowe highlights is Aeneas' loss of martial identity under the irresistible aegis of Dido:

> How vain am I to wear this diadem
> And bear this golden sceptre in my hand!
> A burgonet of steel and not a crown,
> A sword and not a sceptre fits Aeneas. (IV.iv.40–3)

In order to depart for Italy and regain his warlike identity, Aeneas has no alternative but to escape from Carthage by making impromptu excuses and telling half-truths.[70] Opposing his cowardly measures, Dido resorts to force, blocking his flight by taking away the oars, tackling, and sails of his fleet. Thus, she makes Aeneas a captive rather than becoming his captive: 'Not all the world can take thee from mine arms' (IV.iv.61).

---

[68] Barnabe Riche, *A Right Exelent and Pleasaunt Dialogue, betwene Mercvry and an English Souldier* (London, 1574), sigs M1v and M3v.

[69] William Leigh Godshalk, 'Marlowe's Dido, Queen of Carthage', *ELH*, 38:1 (1971), 1–18, at pp. 10–11.

[70] In characterizing Aeneas as a cowardly traitor, Marlowe was possibly influenced by anti-Vergilian traditions such as we can find in Thomas Fenne's *Fenne's Fruits* (London, 1590), sig. Bb1v. Emma Buckley, '"Live False Aeneas!" Marlowe's *Dido, Queen of Carthage* and the Limits of Translation', *Classical Receptions Journal*, 3:2 (2011), 129–47, understands the play from this perspective.

Dido seems to gain a warlike masculinity and even heroic dignity in inverse proportion to Aeneas' loss of martial identity. Marlowe may be hinting at the iconographical correspondence between Dido and *Venus armata*, a variant of the bellicose Venus;[71] and what the audience hears is a Tamburlainean rhetoric of violence and an eloquent iconoclastic speech that would have sounded bravely in their ears. As Irving Singer points out, 'By the end of the play she has turned into a raging Tamburlaine, an embodiment of the aggressive male in Western society'.[72] A typical example is Dido ordering her sister, Anna, to proclaim publicly that Aeneas is to be her husband:

> Those that dislike what Dido gives in charge
> Command my guard to slay for their offence.
> Small vulgar peasants storm at what I do?
> The ground is mine that gives them sustenance,
> The air wherein they breathe, the water, fire,
> All that they have, their lands, their goods, their lives;
> And I, the goddess of all these, command
> Aeneas ride as Carthaginian King. (IV.iv.71–8)

These lines, which have no source in Vergil, shape Dido as 'a goddess' ruling over the four elements with divine authority, making one a king and killing another with ease. It is not those opportunistic gods that goad Aeneas on to depart from Carthage who can liberate him from the power of Dido's patronage; rather 'It is Aeneas calls Aeneas hence' (v.i.132). The heart of the Hyrcanian tiger longing for Italy can make him free and revive his martial spirit, as Dido says to Aeneas: 'though thou hast the heart to say farewell, / I have not power to stay thee' (v.i.182–3).

Thus, Marlowe manipulates the Vergilian material to render Dido masculine and eloquent and to deprive Aeneas of his heroic and martial traits. Some have hypothesized that Marlowe's reworking of the characters of Aeneas and Dido is based on his awareness of the satirical conventions of the children's stage, and that his playfulness just 'stops short of outright burlesque of the pathetic-heroine tradition, and functions rather as a foil for Dido's magnificent last scene'.[73] However, we should not overlook the fact that the feminization of Aeneas, as well as the masculinization of Dido, is closely interlocked with the gnawing anxiety shared among Aeneas' Trojan peers, who give voice to their discontent with the dominating and seductive queen. When Aeneas makes up his mind to depart from Carthage

---

[71] For *Venus armata*, see Wind, *Pagan Mysteries*, pp. 91–3.
[72] Irving Singer, 'Erotic Transformations in the Legend of Dido and Aeneas', *Modern Language Notes*, 90:6 (1975), 767–83, at p. 781.
[73] Shapiro, *Children of the Revels*, pp. 166–7.

and tells his men to make ready the fleet, Vergil only says that Mnestheus and Sergestus 'gladly obey his command and do his bidding'.[74] Marlowe, in contrast, has Archates, Cloanthus, and Illioneus unanimously declare their support for Aeneas' decision. Archates criticizes Dido in plain terms:

> Banish that ticing dame from forth your mouth,
> And follow your foreseeing stars in all;
> This is no life for men-at-arms to live,
> Where dalliance doth consume a soldier's strength,
> And wanton motions of alluring eyes
> Effeminate our minds inur'd to war. (IV.iii.31–6)

Illioneus is inflamed with the desire to construct the new Troy and gain freedom from servile subjection to Dido: 'Why, let us build a city of our own / And not stand lingering here for amorous looks' (IV.iii.37–8). Responding to their anxiety at the potential feminization of their Trojan martial spirit, Aeneas articulates his misogynistic discontent with the queen: 'I may not dure this female drudgery: / To sea, Aeneas, find out Italy!' (IV.iii.55–6). The Italy that Aeneas and his peers are longing for seems to be a strong, masculine, military nation, governed by a 'warlike' commander and rhetorician, not by an 'amorous' queen.

This anxiety about feminization and discontent with 'female drudgery' is important because it seems to have been shared by the advocates of militarist solutions to the aggressive Catholic Spanish campaigns in the Low Countries and against England itself.[75] Stephen Gosson, bolstering the reader's vigilance against idle pleasures that 'effeminate the minde', complains in *The Schoole of Abuse* (1579) that 'banqueting playing, pipyng, and dauncing, and all suche delightes' have turned 'our wreastling at armes' into 'wallowying in Ladies laps'. His anti-theatrical discourse primarily aspires to make the English, like the Spartans and the Scythians, 'all steele, fashioned out of tougher mettall', who tend 'to the maintenance of Martiall disciplyne'; above all, he calls upon them to make 'the word and the sword be knit together'.[76] Behind his rallying cry lay the militarist policy of Walsingham and Sidney, whose patronage Gosson had been seeking. John Stubbs, the radical polemicist who lost his right hand for criticizing the queen's policy on marriage negotiations, similarly aligned himself with Walsingham and Leicester, and

---

[74] H. Rushton Fairclough (ed.), and G. P. Goold (trans.), *Vergil I: Eclogues, Georgics, Aeneid I–VI* (1999; repr. Cambridge, MA, 2006), p. 443.

[75] Jonathan Goldberg, *Sodometries: Renaissance Texts, Modern Sexualities* (Stanford, 1992), pp. 133–5, points out the relationship between Aeneas' misogyny and Gosson's anti-theatrical charge that the stage effeminates the martial spirit.

[76] Stephen Gosson, *The Schoole of Abuse* (London, 1579), sigs B3r, B8v, D6v–D7r, and E3v.

was an unequivocal war advocate who attacked pro-French courtiers and officials in *The Discovery of a Gaping Gulf* (1579): 'in times past the noble Englishmen delighted rather to be seen in France in bright armor than in gay clothes and masking attire; they did choose rather to win and hold by manly force than by such effeminate means.'[77]

It would be naïve to consider the Trojans' critical opinions of Dido as a reflection of Marlowe's own about Dido/Elizabeth. But Marlowe gives voice to the anxiety and discontent among the Protestant militarists, putting these feelings into Trojans' mouths. This ventriloquism, which naturally operates to connect the past to the present, Elisa Africa to Elisa Anglia, encourages us to see *Dido, Queen of Carthage* as a political medium. We have already examined the ingenious ways in which playwrights represented Elizabeth on the academic stage and the upsurge of misogynistic sentiments against her and her 'effeminate' policies, especially among the aspiring intellectuals circling around Leicester, Walsingham, and Sidney in the 1580s. Moreover, it is highly likely that Marlowe gained strong protection and support from the members of the Privy Council, specifically from the Secretary, Walsingham, whose patronage compelled him to uphold, endorse, and promote Walsingham's ideological stance.

Contextualizing *Dido, Queen of Carthage* in this way allows us to consider that the play functioned as a medium not only for rendering homage to Elizabeth, but also for giving vent to the pent-up frustrations and anxieties of the militarist factions. Even while panegyrizing Elizabeth as a heroic and masculine queen, Marlowe shows Aeneas to be Dido's feeble captive, confronting the audience with the emasculation of his martial spirit and with the ontological insecurity of his state subjugated by the dominance of the queen's gaze and desire. Alan Shepherd avers that 'Marlowe puckishly manipulates the Trojan material [...] to create an anti-war burlesque', but there is nothing in the play to deny the possibility that Marlowe was creating a *pro-war* burlesque by ingeniously rewriting the Dido–Aeneas myth.[78] The play invites the audience to perceive his double-edged rewriting of the myth and to share the frustration and disappointment of the militarist faction, whose fervent aspiration to realize the British Protestant imperialist vision and resuscitate the Vergilian masculine epic had been continually thwarted by the vacillating policies of the queen.

The outbreak of war with Spain, as well as the marriage negotiations with the Duke of Anjou, caused university playwrights to become highly

---

[77] Lloyd E. Berry (ed.), *John Stubbs's 'Gaping Gulf' with Letters and Other Relevant Documents* (Charlottesville, VA, 1968), p. 57. See also Barnabe Riche, *Farewell to Militarie Profession* (London, 1581), p. 8.

[78] Alan Shepherd, *Marlowe's Soldiers: Rhetorics of Masculinity in the Age of the Armada* (Aldershot, 2002), p. 57.

sensitive to the political value of the rhetoric of masculine epic. So William Fulbecke, a student at Gray's Inn and one of the co-authors of *The Misfortune of Arthur*, wrote: 'the harpe of *Achilles* sounded with grauity, and was a kinde of motiue to the warlike courage: but on the effeminate harpe of Paris, nothing was played but amatorious sonnets, and ridiculous Iigges.'[79] Marlowe seems to have been well acquainted with the value of Vergilian epic, which could raise the national morale, as well as with the declamatory and parodic acting styles of the boy's companies which could make the hero appear ridiculous and diminish his martial traits.[80]

However, the burlesque emasculation of the men-at-arms in the play does not necessarily mean that Marlowe derided the political values and ideals of Vergilian epic, or that his representation of the anxiety of the men-at-arms constituted a serious obstacle to realizing the militaristic demands of his patron(s). In fact, the literary motif of a hero's humiliating subjection to a dominating queen, or the disempowering of a warlike soldier, would have strongly motivated pro-war polemicists and poets such as William Gager and Edmund Spenser.[81] As Juliet Fleming points out in her analysis of Barnabie Rich's *Farewell to Militarie Profession*, 'the production of fiction is often represented as an enforced service to women, and therefore becomes a point at which the poet both fears and can express his fear of emasculation.'[82] It was these discursive trends towards misogyny and militarism that Marlowe developed in rewriting the Dido myth.

'To sea, Aeneas, find out Italy!' The urgent challenge that Marlowe, like Aeneas, now had to undertake was to build an 'Italy' where a warlike commander could energetically dominate and use his overwhelming oratory to reign over all aspects of – and even constitute – the world. Leaving Cambridge in the summer of 1587, Marlowe was bound for London, to establish in the public theatre his Italy, where, to borrow Gosson's phrase, the Scythian Tamburlaine would perfectly knit 'the word and the sword' together and create a strong military empire by employing his 'high astounding terms'.

---

[79] William Fulbecke, *A Booke of Christian Ethicks or Moral Philosophie* (London, 1587), sig. A8r.

[80] For the acting styles of the boy's companies, see Shapiro, *Children of the Revels*, pp. 116–27.

[81] Patricia Parker, *Literary Fat Ladies: Rhetoric, Gender, Property* (London, 1987), pp. 54–66, detects Spenser's discontent with Elizabeth who, as a ruling queen, dominates her subjects in *The Faerie Queene*.

[82] Fleming, 'The Ladies' Man', p. 177.

Chapter 6

TAMBURLAINE'S PROPHETIC ORATORY AND THE ENGLISH HOLY WAR

The cultural shockwaves that ran through London in the 1580s seem to have emanated from the public theatre by way of *Tamburlaine the Great*. The extent of its impact can be gauged from an assessment of the abundant evidence suggesting that Tamburlaine 'rauishes the gazing Scaffolders'.[1] It is remarkable that a play of this period left so many contemporary references and was imitated so incessantly. What most interests us, however, is how the play's protagonist was perceived by contemporary audiences. Today, we may be embarrassed by Tamburlaine's two-facedness: one aspect a divine hero who leads his army and a brave soldier famous for his military skill; the other a demonic tyrant who exterminates his enemies and boldly justifies his heinous deeds in the name of God. Yet, far from making a negative impression upon the Elizabethan audience, Tamburlaine was lauded as a perfect heroic figure. In fact, none of the numerous contemporary references contain 'any suggestion that Tamburlaine's triumphs were hollow, or that he failed in any way, or suffered any kind of defeat or punishment'.[2]

One of the reasons for *Tamburlaine*'s popularity and the admiration for the protagonist seems to have originated from the chivalric romance framework of the play: his miraculous victories and conquests over the 'Islamites'; his 'discipline of arms and chivalry' and divine talent as a military leader,[3] which gains him the respect of his comrades and even of his enemies; the difficulty he experiences in obtaining the love of the fair Zenocrate, the daughter of the Sultan of Egypt; and the happy ending he enjoys in marriage.

---

[1] Joseph Hall, *Virgidemiarum* (London, 1597), p. 7.
[2] Richard Levin, 'The Contemporary Perception of Marlowe's *Tamburlaine*', in J. Leeds Barroll (ed.), *MRDE, Vol. 1* (New York, 1984), pp. 51–70, at p. 57.
[3] Christopher Marlowe, *Tamburlaine the Great*, ed. J. S. Cunningham, *The Revels Plays* (Manchester, 1981), *One*, v.i.175. Subsequent references to *Tamburlaine* will be to this edition and will appear parenthetically in the text by part, act, scene, and line number.

Clyomon and Clamydes, an anonymous play performed in the public playhouse around 1580, gives us a glimpse of similar elements then in favour with audiences: chivalric knights, adventures, deadly enemies, combat, and the love of a beautiful princess.[4] Moreover, several obvious borrowings from Edmund Spenser's *The Faerie Queene* show that Marlowe had a Protestant chivalric romance in mind when composing *Tamburlaine*.[5]

Considering the play in this literary context, it is important to recognize that Tamburlaine himself is shaped as a 'Scythian shepherd' – like David, the King of Israel. He claims to be chosen by God and makes heroic conquests of the neighbouring nations, thus rendering him akin to an Israelite hero:

> Nor am I made arch-monarch of the world,
> Crowned and invested by the hand of Jove,
> For deeds of bounty or nobility:
> But since I exercise a greater name,
> The scourge of God and terror of the world,
> I must apply myself to fit those terms,
> In war, in blood, in death, in cruelty,
> And plague such peasants as resist in me
> The power of heaven's eternal majesty. (*Two*, IV.i.150–8)

Marlowe represents the historical pagan soldier as God's scourge – crucially, someone not of noble lineage but of base stock – by following his dramatic sources. This cross-class hero presented a challenge to the traditional premises of chivalry, and broke new ground by setting up the civic ideal of achieving social promotion by one's own bravery and fortitude. With triumphant conviction, Tamburlaine boasts that 'I am a lord, for so my deeds shall prove, / And yet a shepherd by my parentage' (*One*, I.ii.34–5). Victor Skretkowicz gets straight to the point when he says:

> Tamburlaine's entire being presents a challenge to the two corner-stones of chivalric authenticity, noble birth and virtuous behaviour. While exposing the inadequacies of noble lineage in effeminate rulers such as Mycetes, Marlowe creates in Tamburlaine a figure who possesses the

---

[4] Holger Schott Syme points out the continued popularity and importance of the play in 'Marlowe in His Moment', in Emily C. Bartels and Emma Smith (eds), *Christopher Marlowe in Context* (Cambridge, 2013), pp. 275–84, at pp. 279–80.

[5] On the romance framework of *Tamburlaine*, see, for instance, Richard A. Martin, 'Marlowe's Tamburlaine and the Language of Romance', *PMLA*, 93:2 (1978), 248–64; and Arthur B. Ferguson, *The Chivalric Tradition in Renaissance England* (Washington, DC, 1986), pp. 98–101. For Marlowe's borrowings from *The Faerie Queene*, see John Bakeless, *The Tragicall History of Christopher Marlowe* (2 vols, Cambridge, 1942) vol. 1, pp. 205–9; and Vivien Thomas and William Tydeman, *Christopher Marlowe: The Plays and Their Sources* (London, 1994), p. 81.

innate ability to attract popular support, admiration, and even love from fighting men from a full range of social standing.[6]

This chapter first considers Tamburlaine's chivalric novelty from a slightly different perspective, namely in the context of the civic culture of London, where the achievements of chivalric heroes were daily commemorated and used to strengthen the audience's allegiance to the community, the state, and/or the divine. I then turn to the concept of God's scourge, which was prominent among advocates of Protestant chivalric militarism in the 1580s.

ISRAELIZING CHIVALRIC KNIGHTS

On 16 February 1587, Philip Sidney's coffin was followed by a stately procession of the nobility, the Lord Mayor, the 'Aldermen Knights', and 'Other Cittizins called the Company of Grocers in theyr livery to the number of 120'. After these mourners came 'Capitaneus, Mr Tho: Smyth', who led 'certayne younge men of the Cittye' 'practised in Armes', 'marching by three and three, in blac Cassokins with their Shott, Pikes, Halberds, and Ensigne trayling on the grounde, to the number of 300' (figure 18).[7] The pageantry, which Francis Walsingham personally organized on the scale of a state funeral and for which he 'spared not any coste', seems to have been successful in commemorating the deceased as a Protestant chivalric hero and in arousing shared feelings of national identity, if we believe the testimony of Thomas Lant, a servant in Walsingham's household, that 'streets all along were so thronged with people, that the mourners had scarcely rome to pass. the houses likewise weare as full as they might be of which great multitude ther wear few or none that shed not some tears as the corps passed by them'.[8] The extravagant expenditure and painstaking preparations suggest Walsingham's keen awareness of the need to cultivate the citizens' sympathy for the nation's political cause – war against Spain – as well as his affection for his son-in-law.

In the midst of the national crisis, belligerent courtiers such as Sidney, Walsingham, and Robert Dudley were struggling to rework the medieval

---

[6] Victor Skretkowicz, 'Chivalry in Sidney's Arcadia', in Sydney Anglo (ed.), *Chivalry in the Renaissance* (Woodbridge, 1990), pp. 161–74, at p. 164.

[7] Sander Bos, Marianne Lange-Meyers, and Jeanine Six, 'Sidney's Funeral Portrayed', in Jan van Dorsten, Dominic Baker-Smith, and Arthur F. Kinney (eds), *Sir Philip Sidney: 1586 and the Creation of a Legend* (Leiden, 1986), pp. 38–61, at p. 58; and Thomas Lant, *Sequitur Celebritas & Pompa Funeris* (London, 1588), plate 24.

[8] Bos, Lange-Meyers, and Six, 'Sidney's Funeral Portrayed', p. 58. For a discussion of the active role of the citizens in Sidney's funeral, see Ronald Strickland, 'Pageantry and Poetry as Discourse: The Production of Subjectivity in Sir Philip Sidney's Funeral', *ELH*, 57:1 (1990), 19–36.

Figure 18 Captain Thomas Smith and young citizens in the funeral procession of Sir Philip Sidney, depicted in Thomas Lant, *Sequitur Celebritas & Pompa Funeris* (London, 1588), fol. 24. BL, General Reference Collection 74/C.20.f.12. © The British Library. All rights Reserved.

ideals of virtue and to align notions of aristocratic chivalry with their pro-Protestant, jingoistic militarism. They reinforced their aggressive foreign policy by activating a 'nostalgia for an idealised chivalric order', as Henry VIII had done at the time of the conflict with France and Scotland.[9] This gave them an opportunity to fashion themselves into Protestant chivalric heroes who, under the pretext of demonstrating self-sacrificing loyalty to the queen, conducted the military expeditions that they had been longing for. The funeral procession organized by Walsingham was one of the cultural devices employed for this purpose.

What seems to have been essential in this critical situation was not only reinforcing the sinews of war and drilling soldiers but also uplifting the nation's morale and recruiting men for the military. As a consequence, symbolic forms of chivalry began to permeate the fabric of civil society, and 'the rites of knighthood' ceased to be exclusive to the aristocracy. Rites, sermons, civic organizations, and dramatic entertainments invoked the names of chivalric heroes from the richest sources of English medieval history and employed them as exemplars to mobilize citizens for war.

One such development led to the organization of the Society of Prince Arthur, consisting of 300 prosperous citizens who were ardent advocates of archery training. Although few records of the society have survived, Richard Robinson's panegyric in the dedicatory epistle of *A Learned and True Assertion of the Original, Life, Actes, and Death of the most Noble, Valiant, and Renoumed Prince Arthure* (1582) sheds some light upon the organization and its background. This book is a translation of John Leland's *Assertio Inclytissimi Arturii* (1544), which aimed to establish the historicity of Arthur, though Leland's nationalist ideology was evidently motivated by an enthusiasm perfectly aligned with that of his royal benefactor, Henry VIII.[10]

---

[9] Simon Barker, *War and Nation in the Theatre of Shakespeare and His Contemporaries* (Edinburgh, 2007), p. 89. For discussions of the chivalric revival among the bellicose courtiers, see Roger B. Manning, *An Apprenticeship in Arms: The Origins of the British Army 1585–1702* (Oxford, 2006), pp. 27–9; Susan Frye, *Elizabeth I: The Competition for Representation* (New York, 1993), pp. 78–86; Alex Davis, *Chivalry and Romance in the English Renaissance* (Cambridge, 2003), pp. 80–1; Richard C. McCoy, *The Rites of Knighthood: The Literature and Politics of Elizabethan Chivalry* (Berkeley, 1989), pp. 17–19.

[10] James Carley, 'Polydore Virgil and John Leland on King Arthur: The Battle of Books', in Edward Donald Kennedy (ed.), *King Arthur: A Casebook* (New York, 1996), pp. 185–204. See also Roberta Florence Brinkley, *Arthurian Legend in the Seventeenth Century* (London, 1932; repr. 1967), pp. 87–8. Robinson was a keen sympathizer with Protestant chivalric militarism; three years beforehand, he had dedicated his English translation of Philip Melanchthon's Latin prayers to Philip Sidney and his father, acknowledging their repeated support for him. See BL, Royal MS 18 A. LXVI,

In the dedicatory epistle of the *Assertio* translation, Robinson explains the value of reading 'in the deuine histories from time to time how and by what ordenarie meanes of power, force, and defence, he reached vnto his feeble flocke his mightie arme to the discomforture of the enemie'. Just as history had biblical and Christian worthies such as Judas Maccabeus and Godfrey of Bullion acting 'as the scourge' of their enemies, 'so in like manner there were neuer Brittaines wanting of excellent learning and exquisite knowledge to leaue with carefull diligence and credible commendation, the progenie, life, prowesse prosperitie, and triumphant victories of our said auncient Arthure worthely published vnto the worlde'.[11] Here, Robinson inspires his readers to recollect the history of the elect nation through Arthur, whom he deems to be a figure just as 'historical' as the Israelite military leaders.[12]

Robinson's celebration of Arthur was clearly motivated by his own leanings, but he was also influenced by the political attitude cultivated among those to whom his translation was dedicated. These were the Protestant military allies Arthur Grey, the Lord Deputy of Ireland; Henry Sidney, the Lord President of Wales; Thomas Smith, a wealthy London merchant who financed Leicester's expedition to the Low Countries; and, last but not least, 'the Worshipfull Societie of Archers, in London Yearely celebrating the renoumed memorie of the Magnificent Prince ARTHVRE & his Knightly Order of the Round Table'. Robinson seems to have been Smith's protégé at that time, for he dedicated his next work, *The Avncient Order, Societie, and Vnitie Laudable, of Prince Arthure* (1583) to Smith and the society, describing himself as 'Your worthy good worships most humble and dutiful Orator'.[13] He was rewarded for his pains with a gift of five shillings.[14]

---

fol. 5v. For more information on Robinson's manuscript, see George McGill Vogt, 'Richard Robinson's *Eupolemia* (1603)', *Studies in Philology*, 21:4 (1924), 629–48. On his literary activities, see William Hamilton Bryson, 'A Note on Robinson's Brief Collection of ... Courts of Records', *TCBS*, 6:3 (1974), 181–7. Robinson's enthusiasm for civic militarism can be detected in BL, Royal MS 18 A. LXVI, fols 14r–29v.

[11] John Leland, *A Learned and True Assertion of the Original, Life, Actes, and Death of the Most Noble, Valiant, and Renoumed Prince Arthure, King of Great Brittaine*, trans. Richard Robinson, in William Edward Mead (ed.), *The Famous Historie of Chinon of England by Christopher Middleton to Which Is Added The Assertion of King Arthur*, Early English Text Society, OS, 165 (London, 1925), pp. 4, 7.

[12] For Robinson's support of imperialist Protestant ideology, see Andrew King, *The Faerie Queene and Middle English Romance: The Matter of Just Memory* (Oxford, 2000), pp. 163–4, 177–8.

[13] Richard Robinson, *The Avncient Order, Societie, and Vnitie Laudable, of Prince Arthure* (London, 1583), sig. ˙*˙3r.

[14] BL, MS Royal 18 A. LXVI, fol. 7r (transcribed in Vogt, 'Richard Robinson's Eupolemia (1603)', p. 636.

Robinson describes the origin of the society and its activities in the dedication of *A Learned and True Assertion*:

> Hereupon by patent of his [Henry VIII] princely prerogatiue ordayned, graunted, and confirmed hee vnto this honorable Citie of London, free election of a Chieftaine and of Citizens representing the memory of that magnificent King Arthure, and the Knightes of the same order, which should for the mayntenance of shooting onely, meete together once a yeare, with solemne and friendly celebration therof. So much in his noble minde preuayled all prouident care of princely prowesse, valiancie, cheualrie, and actiuitie, that he not onely herein imitated the examplers of godly K. Dauid for his Israelites as before, and of that noble Emperour Leo in ouerthrowing idolatrie, and exalting archerie maugre the mallice of that Romane Antichrist, and all his members.[15]

Since the patent is not extant, it is impossible to be sure of the authenticity of this account of the society's foundation. As for its activities, however, Richard Mulcaster gives sufficient evidence in his *Positions* (1581) to support Robinson's sketch. He recommends archery practice for the maintenance of the health of the young, and highly values the activities of the Society of Prince Arthur.[16] The names and heraldic bearings of the Knights of the Round Table were given to the 'chieftain' and to the elected citizen executives of the society. It was Thomas Smith who held the post of Prince Arthur around that time – the same 'Capitaneus, Mr Tho: Smyth' who was at the head of the procession of young Londoners attending Philip Sidney's funeral rites.

Hugh Offley, a rich citizen of a leather-seller company, held the post of Sir Lancelot, and it is reported that around 1587 he 'set forth, at his own expence, a costly show of Prince Arthur, with his Knights of the Round Table'. In this show, 300 archers in black satin doublets and black velvet hose marched 'in goodly and orderly array' from the Merchant Taylors' Hall to Mile End Green. The queen happened to pass by and was amazed at the military ritual, saying 'that in her life she never saw a more stately company of archers'.[17] The annual stately show was certainly designed to commemorate the military conquests of the historical Arthur, but it also demonstrated the outstanding capacity of civic labourers to present themselves as valiant

---

[15] Leland, *Learned and True Assertion*, p. 8.
[16] Richard Mulcaster, *Positions Concerning the Training Up of Children*, ed. William Barker (Toronto, 1994), pp. 108–9.
[17] Elizabeth Goldring, Faith Eales, Elizabeth Clarke, and Jayne Elisabeth Archer (eds), *John Nichols's The Progresses and Public Processions of Queen Elizabeth: A New Edition of the Early Modern Sources* (5 vols, Oxford, 2014), vol. 3, p. 394.

soldiers and orient the populace towards an orchestrated response to the national crisis.

Robinson's translation of the *Assertio* and the activities of the Arthur Society under the patronage of municipal magnates shared a desire to celebrate Arthurian history while employing its cultural symbolism for the militarization of civil society. Similarly, Robinson's dedicatory epistle of his *Avncient Order* contains a strange and far-fetched argument about David's vision of fraternal unity in Psalm 133. Robinson interprets the biblical phrase 'brethren to dwell euen together' (Psalm 133.1) to mean the happy congregation of the 'Round Table of cheefest Cheualry ordained by the Lord of Lords', and entreats Smith and the society to follow King David, who purportedly always held his elite troops at hand 'for maintenance of princely chiualry and knighthood'.[18] For Robinson, the Society of Prince Arthur was the embodiment of the 'chivalric' ideal which had been handed down from God to his own generation through the kings of Israel. This identification of English history with the biblical model of the Israelites indicates the propensity to construct the meaning of warfare during the 1580s crisis by 'Israelizing' the chivalric tradition and projecting history as providential drama.[19]

The same tendency to equate Old Testament leaders and chivalric heroes is manifest in the portrayal of the Israelite military leaders in *A Briefe Discourse of* [...] *the Nine Worthies* (1584) by Richard Lloyd, another nationalist, who attested to the historical achievements of Guy of Warwick. In this case, we find not the Israelization of chivalric knights but the 'chivalrization' of Old Testament charismatics. In the section headed 'The historie of the conquests of the noble and vertuous Duke Iosva', the conqueror himself relates the story of his achievements, to which is added the engraved portrait of 'Duke' Joshua accoutred like a medieval knight (figure 19). Enumerating the kings and cities that he has subjugated, Joshua brags that 'I put ech woman, man, and child, therein vnto the sword: / As I had in commandement by Gods most holie word. [...] For God appointed me his scourge, to accomplish his iust ire'.[20] The legitimization of genocide is likewise voiced directly by Lloyd in the dedicatory epistle to Thomas Bromley, Lord Chancellor:

---

[18] Robinson, *Avncient Order*, sig. ⁎2r.

[19] I have borrowed the word 'Israelize' from Cyril Tourneur, *The Transformed Metamorphosis* (London, 1600), sig. B4r, who prays to the God of the Bible to make his eloquence equal to God's: 'Ioue, Israellize my tongue, and let my voyce Preuayle with thee'.

[20] Richard Lloyd, *A Briefe Discourse of the Most Renowned Actes and Right Valiant Conquests of Those Puisant Princes, Called the Nine Worthies* (London, 1584), sigs B1v–B2r.

Figure 19 'Duke' Joshua portrayed in Richard Lloyd, *A Briefe Discourse of the Most Renowned Actes and Right Valiant Conquests of Those Puisant Princes, Called the Nine Worthies* (London, 1584), sig. B1r. Bodleian Library, Mal. 649 (1). By permission of The Bodleian Libraries, University of Oxford.

> How God exalted them [the nine worthies] on hie, to earthly dignitie,
> And gaue them Kings and kingdomes by tryumphant victorie:
> Appointing them to be his scourge, the wicked to confound,
> And their vnrighteous seede vnroote, with sword from of the ground.
> How God remained to the end, with them that godly weare,
> And prospered all their attempts, which him did loue and feare.[21]

Here, the stories of King Arthur and Guy of Warwick, whom Lloyd mentions as English worthies, are tightly interwoven with those of Israelite leaders as instruments of God. Although they have moral flaws peculiar to the medieval era, these can be selectively forgotten in consideration of their 'contrite hart'.[22] Moreover, the heroes' flaws are trivialized by turning them into a scourge modelled on Old Testament figures, elected and appointed by God to accomplish their brilliant 'historical' achievements. Here we find the emergence of a civic chivalry in which godly warlike heroes can easily fall into the grip of crusader logic.

The idea of 'the scourge of God' was not necessarily monolithic. Roy W. Battenhouse, citing various Renaissance writers, defines the concept by stating that 'it serves to explain historical calamities by showing that they are chastisements of sin permitted by God; and it assures tyrants that God is not helpless before their power but that He will, when He has used them, destroy them utterly'. However, the phrase did not always suggest evil tyrants whose progress towards world conquest 'is to be admired as the judgment of God – a judgment which will be complete when the Scourge himself is cast into the fire.'[23] As we have seen, Joshua, the prophetic leader of Israel, is portrayed as God's scourge, used to castigate the gentiles, but suffering no destruction in his own life. Rather, he wages a holy war and wins God's favour through committing genocide against 'idolatrous' people. Even Francis Walsingham, who 'hated all Idolatours and popish Traytors', was eulogized by a ballad-writer in this manner: 'Gone is the cheefe of worthie Knights in whom did wisedome flowe, / Gone is Sir *Frauncis Walsingham* the scourge of Englands foe.'[24]

These seemingly antinomic perspectives of God's scourge derive from its semantic polysemy, which the German humanist Johan Ferrarius illustrates:

---

[21] *Ibid.*, sig. A2v.
[22] *Ibid.*, sig. G2r.
[23] See Roy W. Battenhouse, 'Tamburlaine, the "Scourge of God"', *PMLA*, 56:2 (1941), 337–48, at p. 342; and R. W. Battenhouse, *Marlowe's* Tamburlaine: *A Study in Renaissance Moral Philosophy* (1941; repr. Nashville, 1964), p. 149.
[24] Thomas Nelson, *A Memorable Epitaph […] for the Death of the Right Honorable Sir Frauncis Walsingham Knight* (London, 1590), lines 19–20.

Nether is it so that God alwaie stirreth vp cruell men and tirantes to reuenge mans wickednes, that one mischief shulde be expelled with another: but somtimes therein he vseth his owne au[n]gels, somtimes he worketh by men of sincere liuing, sometimes he sendeth floudes & aboundance of waters, as we doe reade in the scripture: so likewise for the malice of man he plagueth vs with famine, pestilence, and warre.[25]

Not only evil tyrants but also disasters, angels, and 'men of sincere liuing' can be the scourge of God. As Andrew Hadfield writes: 'the "scourge of God" could be an ambiguous figure, celebrated by those who benefited from his actions but condemned by those who suffered from them.'[26] Naturally, in the midst of a nationalist upsurge, any heroic leader or dramatic character who chastised Spain and Rome, the enemies of England, could be represented as God's scourge without hurting his public image. For the advocates of civic chivalry, therefore, this multivalent and convenient notion was a good morale booster as military confrontation intensified in the 1580s.

TAMBURLAINE'S 'PROPHETIC' ORATORY

What makes a king a king? *Tamburlaine* gives a relatively definite answer to this question. At the beginning of the play, we are presented with a regal misfit, Mycetes, who lacks the eloquence demanded of his position. Cosroe, his brother, having 'a better wit', deplores the miserable state of Persia. One of the reasons he will not acknowledge Mycetes as king is that Mycetes cannot produce the kind of 'great and thundering speech' that can captivate his subjects: wit and eloquence are gifts that confer the true title and authority of a king. Mycetes thus naturally endangers the state of Persia, bringing unhappiness. When raising his army against Cosroe, Mycetes arranges for Meander to make a proclamation speech; on another occasion he chooses Theridamas as his substitute: 'Go, stout Theridamas, thy words are swords, / And with thy looks thou conquerest all thy foes' (*One*, I.i.74–5). In contrast to the king, his subjects are such skilful orators that we can take Cosroe's rebellion or Theridamas' betrayal for granted.

Indeed, in valuing wit and eloquence so highly, all the kings in *Tamburlaine* seem obsessed with the humanistic lauding of the virtues of wit and articulate oratory.[27] In this respect, Tamburlaine, despite being a Scythian

[25] Johannes Ferrarius, *A Worke of Ioannes Ferrarius Montanus, Touchynge the Good Orderynge of a Common Weale* (London, 1559), sig. Yy2v.

[26] Andrew Hadfield, 'Tamburlaine as the "Scourge of God" and The First English Life of King Henry the Fifth', *N&Q*, 50:4 (2003), 399–400. See also Mark Hutchings, 'Marlowe's Scourge of God', *N&Q*, 51:3 (2004), 244–7.

[27] On humanistic eloquence and wit, see G. K. Hunter, *John Lyly: The Humanist as Courtier* (London, 1962), pp. 10–11; and Neil Rhodes, *The Power of Eloquence and*

shepherd, is also a prospective king. His entitlement to the kingship is confirmed by Theridamas, when, on their first meeting, Theridamas is struck by Tamburlaine's majestic appearance, and is persuaded by his eloquence to become his ally: 'Not Hermes, prolocutor to the gods, / Could use persuasions more pathetical' (*One*, I.ii.209–10). Tamburlaine is a match for the Persian lords in oratory, as well as in looks and bravery. What, then, is it that makes Tamburlaine cut such a conspicuous figure among the other candidates? What gives him the authority that makes Theridamas submit to him?

It is worth noting that Tamburlaine alone regards his words as oracles or prophecies and 'is absolutely convinced of [their] *prophetic* efficacy'.[28] Just before his encounter with Bajazeth, he encourages his comrades: 'Fight all courageously and be you kings: / I speak it, and my words are oracles' (*One*, III.iii.101–2). He never doubts his supremacy, for he is assured of his election by God. What Tamburlaine has put into words reflects God's will, so he sees his eventual act of conquest as propelled by God's word. Meander reproaches him for hoping, 'misled by dreaming prophecies, / To reign in Asia, and with barbarous arms / To make himself the monarch of the East' (*One*, I.i.41–3). The energy of Tamburlaine's 'working words' originates not from his acquired faculty of speech or humanistic rhetorical art but from the fact that his words are divine 'prophecies'. Tamburlaine represents himself not only as a warrior and a monarch but as a prophet in the Old Testament sense: 'I wil raise the[m] vp a Prophet from amo[n]g their brethren like vnto thee, and wil put my wordes in his mouth, and he shal speake vnto them all that I shal commande him' (Deuteronomy 18.18).

These aspects – Tamburlaine's role as God's agent who receives the word of God, delivers its substance to the people, and at times carries out the message himself – are more or less characteristic of all Old Testament prophets: David, for instance, receives God's messages directly, proclaims them, and sometimes puts them into action according to God's will, and so can be regarded as a prophet in this sense, as Peter declares in Acts 2.30. Tamburlaine likewise claims that, by receiving the divine oracle directly from God, he obtains absolute licence to fulfil it, and that, by accomplishing his mission, he gives his – or God's – vision substance. Hence, 'Will and Shall best fitteth Tamburlaine' (*One*, III.iii.41). Neil Rhodes has pointed out that 'the oracular power of which he speaks comprises not only the supremely persuasive eloquence of the Humanist orator, but also the destructive fury

---

English Renaissance Literature (Hemel Hempstead, 1992), pp. 69–101.

[28] Johannes H. Birringer, *Marlowe's 'Doctor Faustus' and 'Tamburlaine'* (Frankfurt am Main, 1984), p. 108, emphasis in original. See also Regina Balla Reed, 'Rebellion, Prophecy and Power in Four Works of the English Renaissance' (unpublished PhD dissertation, State University of New York, Buffalo, 1970), pp. 62–101.

of the divine Word itself'.[29] The singularity of Tamburlaine's oratory lies in his divinely inspired words. Paul says in Ephesians 6.17 that his words work as 'the sworde of the Spirit, which is the worde of God' and have a substantive reality. So too Tamburlaine asserts: 'Nor are Apollo's oracles more true / Than thou shalt find my vaunts substantial' (*One*, I.ii.211–12); his words have a great potential for destructive power.[30]

If Tamburlaine's *word* is both literally and homophonically his *sword*, his divine word corresponds to his divine sword. As the prologue's outline of the play indicates, his marvellous language is linked to his heroic conquests. Here we are informed that Tamburlaine threatens neighbouring countries with both word and sword: 'Where you shall hear the Scythian Tamburlaine / Threat'ning the world with high astounding terms / And scourging kingdoms with his conquering sword' (*One*, Prologue, 4–6). The last two lines are close parallels in meaning; they also define Tamburlaine's divine role as 'the scourge of God' in order to gain supremacy over other nations. His divine word is in line with his holy war against his enemies; he describes the nature of his conquests in relation to God's authorization of his prophetic status: 'For fates and oracles of heaven have sworn / To royalise the deeds of Tamburlaine / And make them blest that share in his attempts' (*One*, II.iii.7–9).

When Tamburlaine and Bajazeth meet face to face just before the military encounter, each vows that he will be victorious. Bajazeth swears by his religious authority: Muhammad's sepulchre and the Qur'an. Tamburlaine swears by his sword. This is not because he puts his faith in strength of arms alone and denies all religious authority: quite the opposite. It shows that he regards his word/sword as the absolute truth revealed by God himself. Immediately after, Tamburlaine defeats Bajazeth 'with a wondrous ease', proving his word's infallibility and demonstrating that he is invested with the full authority of God's power. His confidence, almost indistinguishable from zeal, makes him profess that 'the chiefest God [...] / Will sooner burn the glorious frame of heaven / Than it should so conspire my overthrow' (*One*, IV.ii.8–11). Una Ellis-Fermor comments that 'his tone recalls less the boasting of some Scandinavian thane than the fervour of religious

---

[29] Rhodes, *Power of Eloquence*, p. 91. For the function of prophet and prophecies, see Howard Dobin, *Merlin's Disciples: Prophecy, Poetry, and Power in Renaissance England* (Stanford, 1990), pp. 19–60; and Keith Thomas, *Religion and the Decline of Magic* (London, 1971), pp. 389–432.

[30] I have discussed Tamburlaine's prophetic eloquence in my article 'Tamburlaine's Prophetic Oratory and Protestant Militarism in the 1580s', in Yasunari Takahashi and Yasuo Tamaizumi (eds), *Essays on Shakespeare and His Contemporaries* (New York, 2000), pp. 215–36.

fanaticism'.[31] His standard of judgement on warfare transcends human experience, but he challenges his followers to judge him by this standard, just as he ironically challenges Theridamas to 'Judge by thyself, Theridamas, not me' (*One*, II.v.93), and to share his privileged point of view.

Tamburlaine's repeated slaughters and atrocities appear repellent to modern audiences and make his self-confidence seem like megalomaniacal self-justification. Yet a number of contemporary references survive which show that audiences at the time had a positive attitude towards the character. George Wither reveals that some were astonished by his oratory: 'Great *Tamberlaine* upon his Throne, / [Was] utt'ring a majesticall Oration, / To strike his hearers dead with admiration.'[32] These 'hearers' were also Tamburlaine's followers, who, admiring his prophecies and transcendental power, had fallen into his way of thinking. But why did Elizabethan audiences admire Tamburlaine in spite of his moral flaws?

It is possible that some sort of dramatic mechanism was at work to justify his cruelties. The play's framework – pagan setting and civic chivalric romance, both of which place Tamburlaine outside the Christian world of divine retribution – may have functioned as a device to emphasize his heroic aspect. Moreover, his characterization as a pagan chivalric defender of Christian Europe against Islam may have been a factor.[33] At the same time, the play's ingenious way of justifying Tamburlaine's slaughters by Israelizing him, or by superimposing him on Israelite prophets in the socio-religious milieu fostered by the dominant Protestant ideology of holy war, may have encouraged the audience to approve his religious justifications for military action.

Robert Greene was the earliest critic to perceive the dangerous potential of Tamburlaine. His criticism, however, was not levelled against the protagonist's barbarism or atrocities but against his magniloquent blasphemy, and the fact that 'this character was *not* condemned by the play'.[34] In the preface to *Perimedes the Blacksmith* (1588), Greene showed his contempt for the stage poets who won sweeping popularity with such bombastic language as 'daring God out of heauen with that Atheist *Tamburlan*, or blaspheming with the mad preest of the soone'; and who 'haue propheticall spirits, as bred of *Merlins* race'.[35] Here Greene implicitly accused the protagonist, as well as the playwright, of abusing the divine power and authority of prophetic

---

[31] U. M. Ellis-Fermor, *Christopher Marlowe* (London, 1927), p. 27.
[32] George Wither, *Britain's Remembrancer* (London, 1628), sig. S2r.
[33] Irving Ribner, 'The Idea of History in Marlowe's *Tamburlaine*', *ELH*, 20 (1953), 251–66, at p. 257.
[34] Levin, 'Contemporary Perception', p. 52, emphasis in original.
[35] Alexander B. Grosart, ed., *The Life and Complete Works in Prose and Verse of Robert Greene* (15 vols, 1881–86; repr. New York, 1964), vol. 7, p. 8.

language without scruples. In his *Menaphon* (1589), he makes a similarly disparaging remark about Marlowe/Tamburlaine as a 'propheticall full mouth'.[36] C. L. Barber finds in this remark 'affinities between Tamburlaine's sense of election and the energy and commitment of radical reformers' who drove forward the practice and doctrine of 'prophesying', expounding biblical truth as an expression of divine inspiration.[37] Greene's attack was no doubt aimed at Tamburlaine's, as well as Marlowe's, heaven-daring arrogance to pose as a prophet expounding God's will and purporting to exercise his power and authority.

Several critics have brought out the affinities between the prophetic confidence and militancy of Tamburlaine and those of Protestant radicals. Regina B. Reed comments:

> The play never associates Tamburlaine specifically with a Biblical figure: it is the history of a Tartar warrior, as the story came down from the past. But Marlowe's presentation, especially his use of prophetic method to enhance and justify the figure of the protagonist, though laced with classical allusion, is, both in the manner and the matter of the presentation, close to the extreme beliefs of the Reformers.[38]

Admittedly, the radicals, needing both to defend the legitimacy of their Presbyterian cause and to obtain the freedom of exegesis or prophecy without being censored by the ecclesiastical authorities, tended to regard themselves as an elected Israel that the superstitious customs and ceremonies of the English Church had forced into an exodus. The sole authority they relied on was the divinely inspired prophecy that might justify their outspoken defiance of 'superstitious' authorities. G. K. Hunter terms this 'energetic individualism', and Barber describes Tamburlaine's character as closely paralleling their way of thinking: 'Though he is not acting on behalf of a religious sect, he is a one-man sect, his own "Scourge of God" sect.'[39] In fact, I. F., usually identified as John Field, the leader of the Presbyterian movement, used the character 'as a displaced image of violent agency' to increase the energy driving radical reform.[40] At the same time, however,

---

[36] Ibid., vol. 6, p. 86.
[37] C. L. Barber, *Creating Elizabethan Tragedy: The Theater of Marlowe and Kyd*, ed. with an introduction by Richard P. Wheeler (Chicago, 1988), p. 82. For the practice and doctrine of prophesying, see Patrick Collinson, *The Elizabethan Puritan Movement* (1967; repr. Oxford, 1990), pp. 168–76; and Leo F. Solt, *Church and State in Early Modern England 1509–1640* (New York, 1990), pp. 93–9.
[38] Reed, 'Rebellion, Prophecy and Power', p. 78.
[39] G. K. Hunter, 'The Beginnings of Elizabethan Drama: Revolution and Continuity', *Renaissance Drama*, NS, 17 (1986), 29–53, at pp. 38–9; Barber, *Creating Elizabethan Tragedy*, p. 80.
[40] David Riggs, *The World of Christopher Marlowe* (London, 2004), p. 229.

the English Church, despite having every reason to attack the radicals for identifying themselves as an elected Israel, and desiring to suppress such prophecies and prophesyings, did not deny the validity of prophecy itself, as prophetic language was recognized as indispensable for the consolidation of its own authority. The Church needed 'true' prophets of the English Israel to stand against opposition not only from foreign Catholic powers but also from radicals lurking within.

It is important to understand, therefore, that Tamburlaine's resemblance to the religious radicals lies not in his use of the prophetic mode itself but in his absolute confidence in God's (and his own) prophetic powers. In this respect, he could well have been a compelling source of inspiration for the religious radicals to accelerate their demands for drastic reform. His oratorical power and confidence in his singularity had a strong mimetic effect upon the radicals, firing their zeal and driving their movement forward. At the same time, Tamburlaine was one of the literary sources that the established Church used to invent and reinvent a character type to slander and demonize the radical faction, with its subversive tendencies, in the 1590s. His prophetic oratory gave the ecclesiastical authorities an important perspective from which to construct the satirical prototype of a 'Puritan'. But we will leave further consideration of this Tamburlaine effect to Chapter 8.

The prophetic mode of Tamburlaine against which Greene sounds his warning gives us an important clue when considering the dramatic device justifying military action. Kocher describes the nature of God in the play: 'Desire for power, unchecked by morality, is characteristic of the deity. God is a God of Force.'[41] By the oracles of God, Tamburlaine's extermination policy is legitimized and any code of ethics is cancelled. Kocher comments that Tamburlaine 'speaks like a prior incarnation of Nietzsche', but it is unnecessary to look for such a God of force outside the Elizabethan world. Marlowe was able to find that God in the Old Testament. The God whom Tamburlaine serves has absolute authority to exterminate the enemy, just as Jehovah commands King Saul to 'destroye ye all that perteineth vnto them, and haue no co[m]passion on them, but slay bothe man and woman, bothe infant and suckeling, bothe oxe, and shepe, bothe camel, and asse' (I Samuel 15.3). The Old Testament is littered with episodes of genocide at Jehovah's command. When Israel laid siege to cities or fought against neighbouring enemies, its leaders were given oracles by prophets and sometimes even functioned as prophets themselves. God gave them sanction to commit wholesale destruction, specifically of the idolatrous people within the

---

[41] Paul H. Kocher, *Christopher Marlowe: A Study of His Thought, Learning, and Character* (1946; repr. New York, 1974), p. 71.

boundaries of the Land of Israel (Deuteronomy 20.16–18).[42] God declared the enemy to be *cherem* (Hebrew חרם, *ḥērem*): that is, of accursed status, damned to destruction. Henoch Clapham, the lapsed separatist, expounds on the word *cherem* 'or deuoting of things to destruction, so termed in *Ioshuah* 7.1. and elsewhere'.[43] Roger Gostwick, the minister of Sampford Courtenay, goes further, arguing that the notion of *cherem* is applicable not only to things but to nations: 'this [*cherem*] we finde in Moses, where God speaking of the cursed nations, whom his people were to exterminate, and possess their places.'[44] In this way, Israel, the scourge of God, was permitted to exterminate any enemy that God considered an abomination as an act of devotion or profession of faith. Jehovah pours blessings upon the Israelite leaders, whom he commands to wipe out the accursed enemy, consume their possessions with fire, and seize their land. Thus, consecration through destruction was uncompromising and thorough, for '*cherem* simply signified not killing, but with horror and detestation: as of a thing accursed'.[45]

In *Tamburlaine*, this vision of Israel's holy wars is described by a Christian character, Frederick, the lord of Buda, when he goads Sigismond, King of Hungary, to make war against the Turks:

> Assure your grace, 'tis superstition
> To stand so strictly on dispensive faith:
> And should we lose the opportunity
> That God hath given to venge our Christians' death
> And scourge their foul blasphemous paganism?
> As fell to Saul, to Balaam and the rest
> That would not kill and curse at God's command,
> So surely will the vengeance of the Highest,
> And jealous anger of His fearful arm,
> Be poured with rigour on our sinful heads
> If we neglect this offered victory. (*Two*, II.i.49–59)

Here Frederick refers to Saul, who was the King of Israel but a defective 'scourge', failing to complete God's command to exterminate the Amalekites by sparing 'Agag, & the better shepe, and the oxen, and the fat beastes, and the lambes, and all that was good'. He was, consequently, replaced by David

---

[42] See also Reuven Firestone, *Holy War in Judaism: The Fall and Rise of a Controversial Idea* (Oxford, 2012), p. 23.

[43] Henoch Clapham, *Three Partes of Salomon His Song of Songs* (London, 1603), sig. P2v.

[44] Roger Gostwick, *The Anatomie of Ananias* (Cambridge, 1616), sig. D3r. See also Cecil Roth *et al.* (eds), *Encyclopaedia Judaica* (16 vols, Jerusalem, 1972), vol. 8, s.v. 'ḥērem'.

[45] Andrew Willet, *Hexapla, That Is, A Six-fold Commentarie vpon the Most Diuine Epistle of the Holy Apostle S. Paul to the Romanes* (Cambridge, 1611), p. 407.

because he had 'cast away the worde of the Lord' (I Samuel 15.9, 26). Frederick mentions Balaam as well, reminding Sigismond about the prophet who, blinded by his self-interest, hesitates to give his blessing to Israel and to prophesy their role in stamping out other nations (Numbers 22–23).

Una Ellis-Fermor, bearing in mind the outcome that Balaam eventually curses the Moabites and the Amalekites at God's behest (Numbers 24), comments that 'Marlowe's scriptural knowledge is not so sound as his knowledge of Ovid, for Balaam's position is the converse of Sigismund's'.[46] However, the point Frederick makes does not concern Balaam's eventual (but unsatisfactory) accomplishment of his duty to curse the Israelites' enemies but his unwillingness to obey God's command because of his covetousness. Marlowe's understanding of Balaam's flawed character perfectly corresponds with that of New Testament writers, who take the harsh view that Balaam 'put a stumbling blocke before the children of Israel' (Revelation 2.14) and 'loued the wages of vnrighteousnes' (II Peter 2.15). William Fulke, chaplain to the Earl of Leicester, comments on the passage in Revelation that Balaam was 'the olde false Prophete' who 'for rewardes sake, taught and instructed Balac [King of Moab], withe what engines the helth and safegard of the Israelites might be ouerthrowen'.[47] Thus, Frederick invokes the lesson of Saul and Balaam, who fell out of God's favour because of their disobedience, in order to encourage Sigismond to complete his task of stamping out the 'foul blasphemous paganism'. The scene seems to be convincing proof that Marlowe not only had accurate biblical knowledge but also was acquainted with the Old Testament concept of uncompromising destruction as a devotional act.

The dramatic sources that Marlowe may have consulted in writing the play depict Tamburlaine as one of the most evil tyrants in history. For instance, Thomas Fortescue's *The Forest or Collection of Historyes* (1571), the English adaptation of Pedro Mexia's *Silva de Varia Lecion*, describes Tamburlaine's end as rightful retribution, an expression of God's wrath, for 'all sutche cruell and incarnate Deuils, are instruments wherewith God chastiseth sinne, as also, with the same approueth, and trieth the iuste: and

---

[46] Christopher Marlowe, *Tamburlaine the Great*, ed. Una M. Ellis-Fermor (1930; repr. New York, 1966), p. 207, n. 54. David Fuller follows Ellis-Fermor in saying that the example of Balaam 'does not illustrate Fredericke's argument as he implies'. See Christopher Marlowe, *Tamburlaine the Great*, ed. David Fuller, in David Fuller and Edward J. Esche (eds), *The Complete Works of Christopher Marlowe Vol. 5* (Oxford, 1998), p. 242.

[47] William Fulke, *Praelections vpon the Sacred and Holy Reuelation of S. Iohn* (London, 1573), sig. C3r. This view of Balaam was widely accepted. We can find in the Geneva Bible a short note in the margin of the account that Balaam was 'Moued rather with couetousnes, the[n] to obey God'. See Numbers 22.22, n. k (sig. S4r).

yet they notwithstandinge are not hence helde for iuste, ne shall they escape the heauy iudgement of God'.[48] However, Fortescue does openly extol Tamburlaine's achievements. George Whetstone suggests in *The English Mirrour* (1586), another source of the play, that Tamburlaine, though acknowledging himself to be 'no other then the ire of God', dies in the end 'without disgrace of fortune, after su[n]dry great victories, by the course of nature'.[49] These sources do not place Tamburlaine's military career within the conventional narrative of God's judgement upon his scourge. Rather, as Troni Y. Grande suggests, 'even in the sources, Tamburlaine threatens to become a moral anomaly, a law unto himself'.[50]

Marlowe seems to have been well aware of this 'moral anomaly' and to have followed the sources in foregrounding some heroic aspects of the historical Tamburlaine – for instance, in attributing Tamburlaine's cause of death to 'distemper', which resulted from his violent passions in circumventing the Christian framework of divine retribution for his cruelties.[51] What differentiates *Tamburlaine* from its sources, however, is Marlowe's unique reworking of this morally anomalous Tamburlaine into a prophetic military leader after the fashion of God's scourge, modelled on figures of the Old Testament such as Moses and Joshua. In Marlowe's protagonist we find no conscience-stricken hesitation nor timidity,[52] but only absolute (or rather fanatical) self-assurance. Tamburlaine maintains that heaven's majesty should be displayed in war, blood, death, and cruelty, as if 'he implies that his divine role requires him to be more vicious than he might'.[53] The tone of his speech is, however, not ironic but devotional. His theocentric justification seems to show the traits of the Old Testament scourge who receives blessing by exterminating God's – and by extension the nation's – enemies. The concept of *cherem*, exterminating the enemy as an act of consecration, makes up the unprecedented prophetic heroism of Marlowe's Tamburlaine.

---

[48] Thomas Fortescue, *The Forest or Collection of Historyes* (London, 1571), sig. L3r. For the influence of *The Forest* upon *Tamburlaine*, see Leslie Spence, 'The Influence of Marlowe's Sources on *Tamburlaine I*', *Modern Philology*, 24:2 (1926), 181–99; and Marlowe, *Tamburlaine the Great*, ed. Fuller, pp. xx–xxii, and 204–5.

[49] George Whetstone, *The English Myrror* (London, 1586), sig. F1v.

[50] Troni Y. Grande, *Marlovian Tragedy: The Play of Dilation* (Lewisburg, PA, 1999), p. 59.

[51] Many critics point out Tamburlaine's natural death. See, for instance, Ribner, 'Idea of History', pp. 257–8; and Johnstone Parr, *Tamburlaine's Malady and Other Essays on Astrology in Elizabethan Drama* (Tuscaloosa, 1953), pp. 3–23.

[52] Robert Rentoul Reed, *Crime and God's Judgment in Shakespeare* (Lexington, 1984), adumbrates the features of the conscience syndrome of evil tyrants, especially in the chapters on *Richard III* and *Macbeth*.

[53] Alan Sinfield, *Literature in Protestant England 1560–1660* (London, 1983), p. 111.

THE HOLY WAR OF THE ENGLISH ISRAEL

No doubt this Israelization of Tamburlaine, as well as of English monarchs and chivalric knights, was culturally aligned with and relied upon the analogical way of thinking that the pulpit and the print media frequently employed in national crises by identifying England with the warlike Israel of the Old Testament. The earliest Protestant polemic for a holy war came from the Swiss reformer Heinrich Bullinger, whose great influence upon the English Church can be seen in the fact that Archbishop Whitgift and other bishops ordered all inferior clergy in 1586 to provide 'a Bible, and Bullinger's Decads in Latin or English' and 'read over one sermon in the said Decads' every week.[54] In the sermon 'Of War', included in *Fiftie Godlie and Learned Sermons Diuided into Fiue Decades* (1577), Bullinger encourages his audience to think that 'the magistrate of duetie is compelled to make warre vppon men which are incurable, whom the verie iudgemente of the Lord condemneth and biddeth to kill without pittie or mercie. Such were the warres as Moses had with the Madianites, and Josue with the Amalechites'; and he justifies 'the warres that are taken in hand for the defence of true religio[n] against idolatrers and enimies of the true and Catholique faith'.[55] Here we can find Bullinger's bent towards a radical doctrine of warfare, identified as holy war. As James Turner Johnson notes, his argument was innovative in its 'introduction of a concept of "commanded" war, replacing war that is only "permitted"; and almost exclusive reliance on the Old Testament in place of the just war doctrine's heavy reliance on New Testament teachings'. What seems particularly important is the point that 'the Old Testament model is essential to the developing English theory of holy war'.[56]

Bullinger's modification, endorsed by ecclesiastical authority, allowed holy war proponents threatened by Spanish and Roman power to elaborate on doctrine based on the Old Testament model, and to make use of such arguments to boost public morale. Anthony Anderson, a vicar of Stepney who dedicated his sermon to Walsingham, spurred on his audience:

---

[54] John Strype, *The Life and Acts of John Whitgift* (3 vols, Oxford, 1822), vol. 3, p. 194. For the establishment outlook of Bullinger's theology, see Peter White, *Predestination, Policy and Polemic: Conflict and Consensus in the English Church from the Reformation to the Civil War* (Cambridge, 1992), pp. 74–81.

[55] Heinrich Bullinger, *Fiftie Godlie and Learned Sermons Diuided into Fiue Decades*, trans. H. I. (London, 1577), sig. O2r.

[56] James Turner Johnson, *Ideology, Reason, and the Limitation of War: Religious and Secular Concepts 1200–1740* (Princeton, 1975), pp. 113, 129. For the medieval Christian theory of just war from Augustine to Aquinas, see Frederick H. Russell, *The Just War in the Middle Ages* (Cambridge, 1975).

Wherefore our true English hartes, doe not feare at all your Romaine force. Goe to then *Abner* thou *Abington*, and all the broode of Sathan, for our God for his Dauid *Elizabeth*, is encamped against thee, & watcheth for the further protection, of our English *Israell*, whose holy name be blessed for euer, and euer *Amen*.[57]

Here, Anderson attempts to legitimize the anti-Spanish war from a theological perspective. His discourse is founded on biblical analogy that makes equivalences between Elizabeth and David or England and Israel possible.[58] The same analogical idea can be seen in William Gravet's sermon, in which he refers to several champions for justice in the Old Testament and compares England's situation to the miraculous episode in which 'Gedeon accompanied with three hundred men onely fought against Madian, and Amalec, and the east people which were gathered togither like a multitude of locusts, and ouercame them'.[59] The preference for Gideon in sermons addressed to a civic audience may have come not only from the miraculous victory but also from his status as a labourer: Abraham Gibson stirred up his audience of the Artillery Company by saying '[Gideon] was not trained vp in *feates* of *armes*, or *facts* of *chiualrie*; more skilfull in tilling the *ground* then pitching a *feild*; in handling a *flaile* then tossing a *pike*: yet when God had made him their *Prince*, appointed him their *Captaine*'.[60]

At the height of the crisis, during the Armada years, preachers were keen to build morale in exactly this way by justifying the holy war of the 'English *Israell*' through a strong emphasis on the inhuman abominations of their Catholic enemies. Spain and the pope not only became the direct target of denunciation as enemies of the true faith but were identified as the Antichrist and the Babylonian strumpet. This sort of eschatological identification was not, of course, uncommon, and became more conspicuous with England's worsening diplomatic relations with Catholic countries; as Richard Bauckham argues: 'The older view that only the Gospel itself was

---

[57] Anthony Anderson, *A Sermon Profitably Preached in the Church within Her Maiesties Honourable Tower, neere the Citie of London* (London, 1586), sig. F1r.

[58] Richard Robinson considered England's victory in 1588 as the triumph of 'English Israel' over 'Spanish Amalek and the Romish Kenite': see BL, MS Royal 18 A. LXVI, fols 19v–20r. See also Patrick Collinson, *The Birthpangs of Protestant England: Religious and Cultural Change in the Sixteenth and Seventeenth Centuries* (London, 1988), pp. 17–20.

[59] William Gravet, *A Sermon Preached at Pavles Cross on the XXV Day of June Ann. Dom. 1587* (London, 1587), p. 73. On propaganda through the pulpit before the coming of the Armada, see Millar MacLure, *The Paul's Cross Sermons 1534-1642* (Toronto, 1958), pp. 70–2; and Lindsay Boynton, *The Elizabethan Militia 1558-1638* (London, 1967), pp. 151–2.

[60] Abraham Gibson, *Christiana-Polemica* (London, 1618), p. 19, emphasis in original.

an effective weapon against Antichrist gave way to an increasing stress on the role of the temporal power, the Protestant prince and the Protestant army.'[61] The anti-Catholic fervour encouraged pro-war polemicists, who were particularly prone to present the fulfilment of Revelation's prophecies in the contemporary politico-religious situation of Europe, to bring apocalyptic visions into their argument, and to reinforce the framework of holy war by branding their enemies as embodying the rising power of the Antichrist. This eschatological approach formed the core of Protestant ideology in backing up the national cause during the critical stages of war. George Gifford, the influential godly minister who had served as chaplain to the Earl of Leicester's troops in 1586, declared:

> This pure word doth not only slay Antichrist with spirituall death, but also manifesteth and discloseth their abominations, and so weakeneth their multitude, and layeth them open to the materiall sword of princes. For in this last battaile of Christ against the beast, there shall be not onely a spirituall slaughter, but also a killing of their bodies here vpon earth with the sword in warres.[62]

The Old Testament model spurring the development of the holy war theory naturally encouraged preachers and the press to associate familiar chivalric heroes with God's scourges of Israel in the biblical narratives. Anthony Marten, the Queen's steward, who had a strong nationalist and apocalyptic fervour directed against 'that horrible beast, who hath receiued power from the Dragon [and a]gainst the princes of the Nations, which haue entred into League with the whore of Babylon', imagined England as an Israel beleaguered by a new Sennacherib – as preachers often did.[63] He exhorted his readers to 'follow the noble and worthie acts of our owne Progenitors in sundrie warres and battailes, fought for the

---

[61] Richard Bauckham, *Tudor Apocalypse* (Oxford, 1978), p. 174. See also Philippe Buc, *Holy War, Martyrdom, and Terror: Christianity, Violence, and the West, ca. 70 C.E. to the Iraq War* (Philadelphia, 2015), p. 101.

[62] George Gifford, *Sermons upon the Whole Booke of the Revelation* (London, 1596), p. 380. For his 'optimistic' stance towards apocalyptic exegesis, see Bauckham, *Tudor Apocalypse*, pp. 173–6. For the practical application of the apocalyptic vision in inspiring the morale of the soldiers and sailors engaged in actual warfare, see Simon Harward, *The Solace for the Souldier and Saylour* (London, 1592), sigs A3r and C1v–C2r; and Paul A. Jorgensen's 'Moral Guidance and Religious Encouragement for the Elizabethan Soldier', *HLQ*, 13:2 (1950), 241–59.

[63] Anthony Marten, *An Exhortation, to Stirre vp the Mindes of All Her Maiesties Faithfull Subiects, to Defend Their Countrey in This Dangerous Time, from the Inuasion of Enemies* (London, 1588), sig. A2v. For this identification of England as an Israel beleaguered by a new Sennacherib, see, for example, Isaac Colfe, 1588. *A Sermon Preached on the Queenes Day* (London, 1588), sig. B4r; Edward Harris, *A Sermon*

defence of this kingdome, and for the perpetual honor and renowne of themselues' by recalling the hero of medieval chivalric romances: 'What enterprises did famous king *Arthur* attempt, both at home against the Saxons and abroade with other Nations? What Cities and people did hee conquer? What battailes fought hee? What victories obteyned he? Whereby he was reputed of all wryters, for one of the nine Woorthies of the world.'[64] In stirring up the minds of the public by taking advantage of King Arthur's memorable military exploits, Marten was well acquainted with the tactics of public relations.

Stephen Gosson, who had encountered chivalric romance as a playwright and later became one of the pro-holy war divines, was another who well knew the effectiveness of juxtaposing chivalric heroes with Israelite ones. He drew an analogy between the victory over the Armada and that of Gideon over the Midianites, and encouraged the congregation at St Paul's Cross:

> As in publike Theaters, when any notable shew passeth ouer the stage, the people arise vp out of their seates, & stand vpright with delight and eagernesse to view it well. [...] Assure your selues therefore that in these inuasions and wrongs of the enemie still attempted against our countrey, the God of *S Stephen*, the God of *S George*, the God of her maiestie, the God of vs all stands in the confines of heauen and earth, to see & marke, who sendes his strokes nearest to the face of the enemy.[65]

Gosson seems to have been unable to fully abandon the worldly imagination of the theatre, even after he turned over a new leaf, and he remained skilled in boosting the morale of his audience. In this sermon, by making a comparison between God and the audience in public theatres eager to watch a stately spectacle, Gosson linked St George, the popular chivalric hero, with Gideon, Stephen the proto-martyr, the queen, and the nation, all rallied against the power of the Antichristian enemy. In so doing, he aroused the audience's religious sentiments in the same way that the public theatre and cheap print media did, through recourse to the symbolic system of Protestant civic chivalry.

Preached at Brocket Hall (London, 1588), sig. C6r; and Robert Humpston, *A Sermon Preached at Reyfham in the Countie of Norff* (London, 1589), sig. D2r.

[64] Marten, *Exhortation*, sig. E2r-v.

[65] Stephen Gosson, *The Trumpet of Warre: A Sermon Preached at Paules Crosse the Seuenth of Maie 1598* (London, 1598), sigs C7v-C8r. For Gosson's attitude towards holy war, see Johnson, *Ideology, Reason, and the Limitation of War*, pp. 96–104. Useful information on the sermons which recalled the Israelite scourges is given by J. R. Hale, *Renaissance War Studies* (London, 1983), pp. 496–7.

Thus, biblical analogy enabled pro-war polemics to validate the application of the traditional concept of holy war in the Old Testament to the case of the 'English Israel', sanctioning the chivalric crusade against their enemies. The enthusiastic orators of the pulpit and the print media encouraged their audience to follow their lead and copy the Israelized heroes in fighting an Antichristian enemy. By employing such high-sounding and evocative words of poets, prophets, and polemics, England was rushing to arm itself with the lawful authority of the sword.

TAMBURLAINE AS APOCALYPTIC AGENT

The presentation of Tamburlaine as a prophetic scourge typologically associates him with another scourge of God's wrath, one found in the New Testament. Tamburlaine defeats the invincible Turkish army in spite of his inferior strength, and immediately afterwards, at the beginning of Act IV, he brings Bajazeth in a cage and takes him out to be his footstool. The scene is the climax of the first part, when Tamburlaine is at the zenith of his powers. There he declares:

> Now clear the triple region of the air
> And let the majesty of heaven behold
> Their scourge and terror tread on emperors.
> [...]
> So shall our swords, our lances and our shot
> Fill all the air with fiery meteors;
> Then, when the sky shall wax as red as blood,
> It shall be said I made it red myself,
> To make me think of naught but blood and war. (*One*, IV.ii.30–2, 51–5)

Note how his acts of war overlap with the Last Judgement in terms of apocalyptic images. Making Bajazeth his footstool recalls Psalm 110.1, 'I make thine enemies thy fotestole', David's prophetic song about the Messiah who 'shal wounde Kings in the daie of his wrath' and 'shal fil *all* with dead bodies, *and* smite the head ouer great countreis' (Psalm 110.5–6). Tamburlaine's phrase 'blood and war' also reminds us of the sort of eschatological terror described in Joel: 'I wil shewe wonders in the heauens and in the earth: blood and fyre, and pillers of smoke. The sunne shalbe turned into darkenes, & the moone into blood, before the great and terrible daie of the Lord come' (Joel 2.30–1). We may reasonably suppose that Marlowe deliberately employs these biblical allusions in *Tamburlaine* to mould Tamburlaine's character based on his knowledge of their context.[66]

---

[66] For Marlowe's effective use of biblical allusions, see James H. Sims, *Dramatic Uses of Biblical Allusions in Marlowe and Shakespeare* (Gainesville, 1966), chap. 2. The most

If we consider Tamburlaine, as Fortescue and Battenhouse do, to be a tyrant upon whom heaven inflicts vengeance in the end, eschatological allusions should naturally correspond to his Antichrist-like character.[67] A close examination of the biblical allusions in the play, however, makes it clear that Tamburlaine is far from a representation of the Antichrist. Lynette and Eveline Feasey conclude:

> the Biblical passages on which Marlowe draws are not only those where a cruel enemy is sent by God to plague His people for their sins; he draws equally from passages where the people of God are themselves the avengers. Sometimes Tamburlaine appears to be not so much the Wrath of God, as the God of Wrath himself, who at the head of the armies of heaven shall 'smite the nations' with his conquering sword. Sometimes, indeed, he appears to stand for the God of the Final Judgment.[68]

Their conclusion can be more or less supported by historical and literary evidence. Marlowe obviously found in Whetstone's *The English Mirrour* Tamburlaine's ritual for siege warfare, employing a sequence of white, red, and black tents, and seems to have embellished it with touches of apocalyptic imagery drawn from Revelation 6, where the coming of 'the great day of his wrath' (6.17) is heralded by the symbolic white, red, black, and pale horses, their riders leading the world to death and destruction.[69] In fact, Marlowe adds Tamburlaine's black horse as well as his black military equipment when describing his customary method:

> Black are his colours, black pavilion,
> His spear, his shield, his horse, his armour, plumes,
> And jetty feathers menace death and hell –
> Without respect of sex, degree, or age,
> He razeth all his foes with fire and sword. (*One*, IV.i.59–63)

The coordination of these black elements is followed by the war of extermination, 'death and hell', which may have reminded the audience not only

---

important study on Marlowe's use of biblical allusions in *Tamburlaine* is Lynette Feasey and Eveline Feasey, 'Marlowe and the Prophetic Dooms', *N&Q*, CXCV (1950), 356–9, 404–7, 419–21.

[67] This kind of argument can be seen, for instance, in Battenhouse, *Marlowe's Tamburlaine*, pp. 171–7; J. P. Cutts, *The Left Hand of God: A Critical Interpretation of the Plays of Christopher Marlowe* (Haddonfield, 1973), pp. 54–5, 100–7; and John N. King, *English Reformation Literature: The Tudor Origins of the Protestant Tradition* (Princeton, 1982), p. 196.

[68] Feasey and Feasey, 'Marlowe and the Prophetic Dooms', p. 420.

[69] For the apocalyptic connotations in Tamburlaine's ritual, see also Riggs, *World of Christopher Marlowe*, pp. 209–11; and Brian Chalk, *Monuments and Literary Posterity in Early Modern Drama* (Cambridge, 2015), pp. 53–4.

of the popular representation of death but also of the sequence in Revelation where hell comes after death (6.8).[70] Tamburlaine is therefore represented as a Messianic agent appointed as a representative of God's wrath, and may have been associated through God's prophetic 'working words' with Christ of the second coming – the apocalyptic warrior

> clothed with a garment dipte in blood, and his name is called, THE WORDE OF GOD. And the warriers which were in heaue[n], folowed him vpon white horses, clothed with fine linen white and pure. And out of his mouth went out a sharpe sworde, that with it he shulde smite the heathen. (Revelation 19.13–15)

This juxtaposition of Christ and Tamburlaine seems to have left a vivid impression upon Thomas Nashe, who employed the motif from *Tamburlaine* in describing Christ's coming upon the terrible destruction of the proud city of Jerusalem in his *Christs Teares over Iervsalem* (1593):

> When neither the White-flag or the Red which *Tamburlaine* aduaunced at the siedge of any Citty, would be accepted of, the Blacke-flag was sette vp, which signified there was no mercy to be looked for; and that the miserie marching towardes them was so great, that their enemy himselfe (which was to execute it) mournd for it. Christ, hauing offered the Iewes the White-flagge of forgiuenesse and remission, and the Red-flag of shedding his Blood for them, when these two might not take effect nor work any yeelding remorse in them, the Black-flagge of confusion and desolation was to succeede for the obiect of their obduration.[71]

If Tamburlaine had been regarded by contemporary audiences as an undesirable apocalyptic figure, Nashe's comparison would have been irrelevant and even controversial. But it is highly likely that Marlowe's ingenious way of shaping his protagonist to fit the model of Old Testament prophets, and typologically superimposing him on the figure of the apocalyptic agent of God's word/sword, inspired Nashe to make this comparison, and also encouraged the audience to regard Tamburlaine as a chivalric commander of God's army against the Antichrist.

Tamburlaine's acts of warfare seem to have brought to mind the final war at Armageddon, at a time when the apocalyptic vision had taken on growing importance in society, and when the prophecy that 'an vtter, and finall ouerthrowe, and destruction of the whole world' would be fulfilled in

---

[70] Michael Neill makes this point in his *Issues of Death: Mortality and Identity in English Renaissance Tragedy* (Oxford, 1997), p. 93.

[71] Ronald B. McKerrow (ed.), *The Works of Thomas Nashe*, 2nd edn, rev. F. P. Wilson (5 vols, Oxford, 1958), vol. 2, p. 20.

1588 was 'so rife in euery mans mouth'.[72] In fact, Arthur Dent, a popular writer and godly minister, looked back upon the defeat of the Spanish Armada as a partial fulfilment of the prophecy of Armageddon when kings who were seduced by the spirits of devils 'shall be destroyed, and that with such horrible slaughter'. Dent furthermore gave a political exegesis of Revelation 16 and historicized the triumph over the Armada in a biblical context by referring to the concept of *cherem*:

> the kings of the earth, and their armies which shall fight against the Church, at the instigation of the Iesuits, shall come to a place, where they shall haue a notable ouerthrow. This word *Armageddon* may fitly bee deriued of two Hebrue words, that is to say, *Cherem*, which signifieth destruction, and *Gedudh*, which signifieth an armie; that is, the destruction of an army.[73]

'To Babylon, my lords, to Babylon!' At the end of Act IV in the second part, Tamburlaine raises the morale of the troops. It is noteworthy that Marlowe inserted the siege of Babylon into the last act, for the play's historical sources mention Babylon as merely one of the cities conquered by Tamburlaine, and it is not vital that the climax occurs there. The citizens, terrified at the apocalyptic spectacle of 'vermilion tents, / Which threatened more than if the region / Next underneath the element of fire / Were full of comets and of blazing stars / Whose flaming trains should reach down to the earth' (*Two*, v.i.86–90), appeal to the governor to begin peace negotiations with Tamburlaine. The governor's misgovernment and stubbornness, however, lead the city to destruction, just like the tragic case of Damascus in the first part. Tamburlaine orders Techelles to 'drown them all, man, woman, and child; / Leave not a Babylonian in the town' (*Two*, v.i.169–70).

Here we see that the representation of Tamburlaine as an apocalyptic agent associates Babylon closely with 'the great whore' of Revelation, the symbol of the Antichrist, the pope, and Rome. At the symbolic and typological level, Tamburlaine completes his task as a soldier prophet by eradicating Babylon, the seat of the Beast. '[W]here's the Turkish Alcaron / And all the heaps of superstitious books?' he asks in the climactic scene. His hostility

---

[72] Richard Harvey, *An Astrological Discourse* (London, 1583), sig. C6v. See also Anthony Marten, *The Second Sound, or Warning of the Trumpet vnto Judgement* (London, 1589), sig. G2r.

[73] Arthur Dent, *The Ruine of Rome: or An Exposition vpon the Whole Reuelation* (London, 1603), sig. Gg1v. The etymology of the word 'Armageddon' has long been disputed and there are several interpretations. One of the popular ones is 'hill of lacerating' (הר *har*, meaning mountain or hill; מגדי *Megiddo*, lacerating or invading). Dent's interpretation of the etymology seems to have been influenced by the politico-religious circumstances at that time.

is levelled at all the 'superstitious books', as well as at the Qur'an. As the word 'superstitious' was frequently used by preachers to attack the Roman Catholic Church, it can readily be imagined that Tamburlaine's burning of superstitious books in the city of the Antichrist made a favourable impression upon the audience.

> In vain, I see, men worship Mahomet:
> My sword hath sent millions of Turks to hell,
> Slew all his priests, his kinsmen, and his friends,
> And yet I live untouched by Mahomet.
> There is a God full of revenging wrath,
> From whom the thunder and the lightning breaks,
> Whose scourge I am, and him will I obey.
> So Casane, fling them in the fire. (*Two*, v.i.178–85)

This speech has often been taken as Tamburlaine's defiance not only of Muhammad but also of the God of moral law, including the Christian deity, and has consequently been employed to support the claim that Marlowe held monstrous opinions. However, Tamburlaine here intends to exalt 'the chiefest God' as an antithesis to Muhammad, who can never touch God's scourge and prophet, and to deride 'superstitious' religious authority in a deliberately provocative way.

Tamburlaine's battles and sieges assume the aspect of the wars of extermination in the Old Testament, while the eschatological analogies reinforce the power of the prophet's self-sanctioning and work to justify his cruelties. This was highly relevant in the midst of the anxiety and euphoria of the Armada years, when the usual moral code began to be modified and even nullified. When the concept of holy war set up a different code which encouraged the public to uncompromisingly destroy the Catholic/Antichristian enemies as *cherem*, it is no wonder that Tamburlaine, the apocalyptic agent of God's word, was scarcely considered by audiences to be blameworthy for his many cruelties, his hubris, and his self-justifications. Equally, it is no wonder that Marlowe did not present the protagonist as embodying a moral lesson about God's punishment of a tyrant.

'POLICY HATH FRAMED RELIGION'

It has often been argued that Marlowe wrote the two parts of *Tamburlaine* to constitute a single performative action.[74] This promotes a belief in his ingenuity, in giving the play organic unity, but there is no proof that, when

---

[74] See, for instance, Helen Gardner, 'The Second Part of *Tamburlaine the Great*', *MLR*, 37:1 (1942), 18–24; and E. M. Waith, *The Herculean Hero in Marlowe, Chapman, Shakespeare and Dryden* (London, 1962), pp. 60–87. William Tydeman and Vivien

he wrote the first part, he intended a continuation up to Tamburlaine's death. In fact, there are grounds for believing that he had no intention to write a second part at all. Marlowe used up all of his historical sources in the first part. Moreover, the prologue to the second part says, 'The general welcomes Tamburlaine received / When he arrived last upon our stage / Hath made our poet pen his second part' (*Two*, Prologue, 1–3), and there is no reason to doubt the authenticity of this speech. We should therefore consider not one but two Tamburlaine plays.[75] When we take this separate design into account and consider the way in which 'holy' war is justified in each play, it becomes obvious that there is a crucial difference in how Marlowe handles the subject in the two parts. In the first part, his efforts are focused on, and find success in, shaping Tamburlaine into a chivalric hero through his majestic and prophetic oratory, so that the audience scarcely perceive the 'just war' logic and its ingenious working in the play. In the latter part, however, Marlowe seems to call our attention to the function and legitimacy of the logic itself.

The second part has many more scenes in which characters swear by their religious authorities, and this tendency is so conspicuous that it looks as if swearing and swaggering are the main themes of the play. In fact, almost all the political manoeuvres and military actions are legitimized by the names of Christ or Muhammad. The most palpable case is when Orcanes, the Turkish leader, enters into the peace treaty with Sigismond of Hungary, the representative of the European Christians:

Orcanes.	But, Sigismond, confirm it with an oath,
	And swear in sight of heaven and by thy Christ.
Sigismond.	By him that made the world and saved my soul,
	Thy son of God and issue of a maid,
	Sweet Jesus Christ, I solemnly protest
	And vow to keep this peace inviolable.
Orcanes.	By sacred Mahomet, the friend of God,
	Whose holy Alcaron remains with us,
	Whose glorious body, when he left the world
	Closed in a coffin, mounted up the air
	And hung on stately Mecca's temple roof,
	I swear to keep this truce inviolable. (*Two*, I.i.131–42)

Thomas succinctly sort out the points for discussion, in 'One Play or Two?', in their *Christopher Marlowe: A Guide through the Critical Maze* (Bristol, 1989), pp. 17–20.

[75] G. I. Duthie argues that the first part of Tamburlaine has its own unity and theme. See 'The Dramatic Structure of Marlowe's *Tamburlaine the Great, Parts One and Two*', *English Studies*, NS, 1 (1948), 101–26.

Shortly after, when this oath of truce is nullified by Sigismond's betrayal, the name of Christ is again employed to justify his breach of faith. His followers, Frederick and Baldwin, remind him of the Turk's 'cruel slaughter of our Christian blood' and assert that the holy laws of Christendom cannot impose restrictions on them since their enemies are infidels 'In whom no faith nor true religion rests' (*Two*, II.i.34). Using the Old Testament concept of holy wars, Frederick urges Sigismond to destroy the pagan troops lest they draw down divine wrath upon themselves, as Saul or Balaam did.

These Christians appear to us like Machiavellian plotters employing religion for their political aims. In this respect, Orcanes is akin to them. After the battle, he comments on the triumph over Sigismond, declaring: 'Now lie the Christians bathing in their bloods, / And Christ or Mahomet hath been my friend' (*Two*, II.iii.10–11). As far as he is concerned, Christ and Muhammad are interchangeable. It is, however, noteworthy that, although the actions of these characters are certainly grounded in Machiavellian principles, they do not realize that they are employing religion for their own convenience. They are too blind to realize that their 'policy hath fram'd religion', as Guise clearly does in *The Massacre at Paris*.[76] Sigismond asks his followers 'What motion is it that inflames your thoughts / And stirs your valours to such sudden arms?' Frederick's answer is that of the belligerent opportunist: 'It resteth now, then, that your majesty / Take all advantages of time and power, / And work revenge upon these infidels' (*Two*, II.i.2–3, 11–13). Moreover, he demonstrates that they should not miss the opportunity God has given them to '*scourge* their foul blasphemous paganism' (emphasis added). What drives them to war is not so much their political craftiness as their fervent warring spirit, which is in line with Tamburlaine's zealous devotion as 'the scourge of God'.

Even Tamburlaine, who regards his sword as religious authority when he meets Bajazeth face to face, no longer swears by it in the second part, but turns to Muhammad instead and repeatedly makes an oath by the Prophet. It seems strange for the protagonist to swear by Muhammad's name, for, though the historical Timur was a devout Muslim, this kind of oath is not found in the first part. Moreover, in that play, Muhammad is ridiculed when Tamburlaine, along with his comrades, torments Bajazeth at the banquet scene (*One*, IV.iv.53–5). This seems to link not to Marlowe's opportunism but to his tacit intent to connect the swearing by Muhammad to Tamburlaine's burning of the Qur'an. In the name of Muhammad, Tamburlaine makes war against the Turks and kills his effeminate son Calyphas; then, unexpectedly, at the end of the play he pulls down Muhammad from the seat of religious

---

[76] Christopher Marlowe, *Dido Queen of Carthage and The Massacre at Paris*, ed. H. J. Oliver, *The Revels Plays* (London, 1968), ii. 62.

authority. This defiance of Muhammad seems to impress upon the audience the protagonist's zealous faith in 'the God that sits in heaven', while obliquely tarnishing his lustre by aligning Tamburlaine with the characters who deploy the name of God for their own political expediency.

The historical battle of Varna was fought in 1444, some forty years after Timur's death, between Amurath II and King Vladislaus of Poland and Hungary. Sigismond, a contemporary of Tamburlaine, was king of the Romans and of Hungary, whom Bajazeth completely defeated in the Battle of Nicopolis in 1396. Marlowe transfers the battle of Varna to the age of Tamburlaine by changing the name Vladislaus to Sigismond. This transposition of episodes may have been influenced by John Foxe, who had associated Vladislaus' treachery before the Varna war with Sigismond's breach of faith with John Huss and Jerome of Prague at the Council of Constance as a thematically parallel episode of perjury.[77] It seems, however, that Marlowe's handling of the sources works together with his design of the second part: using the account of Varna, he focuses on Christian characters who readily abuse the concept of holy war.

There is little possibility that the treacherous behaviour of these Christian characters was regarded as subversive by the authorities, for Sigismond and his comrades were Catholics of the fifteenth century who had no direct relation to Elizabethan England. Rather, their method of justifying their war bears close resemblance to that of Tamburlaine and, furthermore, of pulpit oratory in England. By displaying their religiously motivated military actions on the stage, Marlowe spotlights the mechanism of the divine legitimation of war, which is scarcely mentioned in the first part. He obliquely stains Tamburlaine with a fault common to the Christians in the play, who with religious enthusiasm appropriate God's name for their military actions, and suggests that Tamburlaine might be 'a second (non-Christian) Sigismond, setting himself up in God's name as an avenger'.[78]

Marlowe seems not to have been as interested in censuring and blackening the hero as he was in displaying the workings of the self-justifying logic of holy war, which was central to the contemporary religious discourse of the English Church. His manner of handling prophetic discourse reminds us of William Fulbecke, who spent his university career at Oxford in the 1580s and had an intense interest as a playwright in Lucan's *Bellum Ciuile*, as did Marlowe.[79] In arguing 'some causes of making warre, which wee

---

[77] For the influence of John Foxe upon Marlowe's transposing of these episodes, see Thomas and Tydeman, *Marlowe: The Plays and Their Sources*, p. 78.
[78] Marlowe, *Tamburlaine the Great*, ed. Cunningham, p. 77.
[79] William Fulbecke, later a historian and lawyer, was a close associate of Francis Bacon at Gray's Inn in the 1580s and wrote two speeches in *The Misfortune of Arthur* performed at Greenwich on 28 February 1588. Edward Paleit, *War, Liberty,*

referre to God, as commaunding warre; as when the *Iewes* did referre to God the cause of the warre mooued against the *Cananites*', Fulbecke aligns the Jewish holy wars with the Ethiopians' wars in the name of Jupiter, with those of the Turks, who 'doe alwaies pretende this cause of their warre, that it is the commaundement of *Mahomet*', and with those of the Spanish king, who 'did pretende this defence of his warres (as some testifie) that they were against Infidels, and Heretikes', to highlight the self-justifying logic that they share. He then warns his readers: 'in grounding warre vpon diuine causes, it is good to be certaine of God his will, and not to credit the æquiuocall prophecies and fantasies of men light-headed and possest of fierie spirits, fit to kindle tumults and vprores'.[80]

In *Tamburlaine*, Marlowe does not contend or dispute in a loud voice, but, like Fulbecke, observes, analyses, and elucidates (and obliquely relativizes) the self-justifying logic of contemporary discourses of holy war. In the latter half of the 1580s, when English chauvinism was given a boost and moral religious sensibility had become strongly biased, Marlowe seems to have gained an unaffected insight into these processes, allowing him to expose how the dominant ideology underlay the discourse of holy war. Thus, the former Parker scholar intent on taking holy orders developed a perfect understanding not only of the function of religious discourses on holy war but of the delicate social dynamics that connected the authorities, the public, and the playwright. Here we can discern a spark of the 'excellent wit' that aroused Robert Greene's deep envy and jealousy.[81]

---

and Caesar: Responses to Lucan's 'Bellum Ciuile', ca. 1580–1650 (Oxford, 2013), pp. 133–40, notes Fulbecke's interest in Lucan, which can be detected in the play.
[80] William Fulbeck, *The Pandectes of the Law of Nations* (London, 1602), fol. 40r–v.
[81] Grosart, ed., *Works of Greene*, vol. 12, p. 142.

Chapter 7

THE JEW OF MALTA AND THE DIABOLIC POWER OF THEATRICS

The beginning of *The Jew of Malta* highlights Barabas' demonic ambition and thirst for monetary power. Unreasonably forced to forfeit his property, Barabas goes into a frenzy of rage against Christians. His Jewish fellows add fuel to the fire, acting like Job's comforters. After a while, however, the audience realizes that Barabas is not a sufferer like Job, but only pretends to be. After his friends have left the stage, he says with admirable composure:

> See the simplicity of these base slaves,
> Who for the villains have no wit themselves
> Think me to be a senseless lump of clay
> That will with every water wash to dirt!
> No, Barabas is born to better chance
> And framed of finer mould than common men,
> That measure naught but by the present time.
> A reaching thought will search his deepest wits,
> And cast with cunning for the time to come,
> For evils are apt to happen every day.[1]

Here Barabas defines his new personality. According to him, humanity can be divided into two types: 'base slaves' who 'have no wit themselves', and those 'framed of finer mould than common men'. His admiration for the 'finer mould' brings us back to his famous soliloquy at the beginning of the play. Barabas feels disgusted with the 'silverings', or Jewish silver coins called shekels, and it is on the 'metal of the purest mould' from the New World that he sets a higher value (I.i.6, 20). As Sandra K. Fischer comments, Barabas 'throws off his heritage and becomes representative of the modern

---

[1] Christopher Marlowe, *The Jew of Malta*, ed. N. W. Bawcutt, *The Revels Plays* (Manchester, 1978), I.ii.216–25. Subsequent references will be to this edition and will appear parenthetically in the text by act, scene, and line number.

mercantilist'.[2] In the same way, he rejects the simplicity of the Jewish 'earth-mettled villains', turning himself into a representative of emergent villains having metal/mettle of finer mould (I.ii.79). What makes him so distinctively modern is the wit with which he casts schemes 'with cunning for the time to come', referring not only to the ability to plan ahead, as will be evident throughout the play, but also to his talent for devising fictions with tricks and disguises that 'shall be cunningly performed' (II.iii.369). His strategy to survive thus consists of his wit to 'cast' a variety of plots and 'like a cunning spirit feign some lie' (II.iii.384). I will term this strategy 'theatrics', with a connotation of *theatrical tricks* or *theatricks*.

Barabas uses the word 'simplicity' again when criticizing hypocritical Christians: 'Ay, policy, that's their profession, / And not simplicity as they suggest' (I.ii.161–2). Here he may have in mind the passage from II Corinthians 11.3: 'I feare lest as the serpent beguiled Eue through his subtiltie, so your mindes shulde be corrupte from the simplicitie that is in Christ.'[3] Profession should be entirely consistent with practice. Stephen Gosson puts it another way: 'such is the integritie, uniformitie, and simplicitie of trueth that it is euer like it selfe, it neuer carrieth two faces in one hoode' and 'euery man must show him selfe outwardly to be such as in deed he is'.[4] Simplicity is the complete opposite of the subtle deceits of the Devil; for Barabas, however, simplicity carries the negative connotation of a lack of theatrical power.

If Jewish silver coins have 'earth-mettled' simplicity, what kind of currency represents the mettle/metal of Barabas, who possesses exceptional powers of counterfeiting and impersonating? Despite his preference for New World gold, the mettle/metal of which he is made may have reminded the audience of the cliché that a liar resembles a counterfeit coin. William Gouge says that 'the faithfull haue a single, simple, honest, vpright, perfect heart', while many hypocrites 'doe more resemble the faithfull, then counterfeit coine doth current money: for herein the Diuell helpeth mans wit'.[5] Thomas Lupton accused the Jesuits, who had become synonymous with religious hypocrisy in the 1580s, by using similar metaphors: 'you haue slaundred our ministers and preachers without any proofe or any argument but this your owne bare wordes, thinking belike that you Iesuites shoulde be of such credite, that your bare sayinges shoulde bee taken forsooth, and

---

[2] Sandra K. Fischer, *Econolingua: A Glossary of Coins and Economic Language in Renaissance Drama* (Newark, DE, 1985), p. 121.

[3] Similar phrases, such as 'singlenes of heart' (Colossians 3.22), can be seen in other Pauline epistles: see, for instance, Ephesians 6.5 and Romans 12.8.

[4] Stephen Gosson, *Playes Confuted in Five Actions* (London, [1582]), sigs E4r, E5r.

[5] William Gouge, *The Whole-Armor of God* (London, 1619), pp. 236–7. See also Anthony Copley, *Wits Fittes and Fancies* (London, 1595), sig. B3v.

your counterfaite coyne should goe for currant'.[6] Like a counterfeit coin that 'sheweth more goodly then the good', Barabas' mettle/metal has a fine outward appearance, is easy to stamp using whatever impress and seal he chooses, usurps Maltese authority, and threatens the political and economic stability of society.[7]

BARABAS AND THE 'COUNTERFEIT PROFESSION'

Barabas asks his daughter, Abigail, to play a proselyte for Christianity in order to trick the abbess and the friars into allowing her access to the treasures hidden in Barabas' house, now a nunnery. He gives her this advice: 'As good dissemble that thou never mean'st / As first mean truth, and then dissemble it; / A counterfeit profession is better / Than unseen hypocrisy' (1.ii.290–3). The primary meaning of 'a counterfeit profession' is, as N. W. Bawcutt puts it, 'the insincere vows as a nun which Abigail is about to take'.[8] At the same time, the phrase evokes contemporary denunciations of religious dissimulation and disguised religiosity. Robert Bolton, a godly preacher and casuist, pronounces God's judgement upon dissembling hypocrites who 'make profession of Religion hypocritically'. According to Bolton, some of these hypocrites 'can well enough sound and fathome with the crooked line of their owne deceitfull hearts, the inuisible depths of their Machiuellian proiects and plots and knauery', while others are wont to 'conforme to the outward formes of Religion, and liue reseruedly vnder the Canopie of a counterfeite profession'. Their purpose is pure self-interest, and so 'The Play being done, they are Rogues again'.[9]

William Burton, another godly polemic, associated such dishonesty more closely with the impersonations performed by players, because 'the nature and practise of players doth most fitly serue to set foorth the nature & practise of such as do but counterfeit and dissemble in the profession and practise of religion, when they would be thought to be in good earnest'. He describes the characteristics of religious hypocrites:

> But here are enough and too many, to act a play that shall please the world, the flesh and the Diuell. Now what is the religion of all theses I pray you? or (to speake the truth) of most men now adaies, but hypocrisie? that is to say, a very play, which euery one studieth to act as artificially as he can, vpon the tickle Stage of this vaine world, to winne thereby credite and

---

[6] Thomas Lupton, *The Christian against the Iesuite* (London, 1582), sig. E1r.
[7] George Pettie, *A Petite Pallace of Pettie His Pleasure* (London, 1576), sig. Dd2r.
[8] Marlowe, *Jew of Malta*, ed. Bawcutt, p. 92, n. 292.
[9] Robert Bolton, *Some Generall Directions for a Comfortable Walking with God* (London, 1626), pp. 44, 47.

commoditie amongst men, being before God nothing lesse, then that which they seem to be vnto men. Now all these hypocrites or players may be deuided into two sorts or companies. First, such as make a counterfeit profession of religion. Secondly, such as make a counterfeit practise of that which they professe.[10]

The player's impersonating strategy becomes alike in nature and practice to that of a dangerous hypocrite who fakes his or her religious profession. It seems natural, therefore, that Barabas' counterfeiting in the play is meta-theatrically taken to resemble the impersonations performed by actors. For Barabas, the only sure way to survive in a difficult world is this theatrical power: to mean the truth, yet to be counterfeit. As a consequence, his remarkable dexterity as a player of roles transforms him from a Jewish merchant into a superhuman villain.

Many critics have regarded the striking theatricality of Barabas as an obstacle to full acceptance of the play. For instance, J. B. Steane complains that 'the dignity involved in tragedy gives way before the absurdity involved in farce'.[11] We should remember, however, that it is in keeping with Marlovian dramaturgy that frivolous shows dominate the plays and suspend 'moral' endings, as in *Doctor Faustus*. What has troubled the critics is, it seems, one of the most ingenious contrivances of *The Jew of Malta*. Sara Munson Deats and Lisa S. Starks, who read *The Jew of Malta* as a meta-drama, identify the structurally essential role of Barabas who, 'functioning simultaneously as playwright, actor, and audience of his own theatrics, both creates fictions and is created by them'.[12] In fact, he variously appears as a Job-like sufferer, an obstinate Jewish father, a Christian proselyte, a French musician, or a dead person, presenting to the audience elaborate shows 'so neatly plotted, and so well performed' (III.iii.2), while other characters are repeatedly manipulated through his theatrics. Thus, over the course of the play, Barabas becomes a protean monster who possesses exceptional powers of impersonation and manipulates others by means of theatrical fictions. Through the repetition of his character's successful theatrical enterprises, Marlowe seems to draw the attention of the audience to Barabas'

---

[10] William Burton, *Ten Sermons vpon the First, Second, Third and Fourth Verses of the Sixt of Matthew* (London, 1602), sigs D3r, D4r.

[11] J. B. Steane, *Marlowe: A Critical Study* (Cambridge, 1964), p. 203.

[12] Sara Munson Deats and Lisa S. Starks, '"So Neatly Plotted, and So Well Perform'd": Villain as Playwright in Marlowe's *The Jew of Malta*', *Theatre Journal*, 44:3 (1992), 375–89, at p. 388. See also Roger Sales, 'The Jew of Malta', in *Christopher Marlowe, English Dramatists* (Basingstoke, 1991), pp. 84–110. I fully discussed Barabas' theatrics in Arata Ide, '*The Jew of Malta* and the Diabolic Power of Theatrics in the 1580s', *SEL*, 46:2 (2006), 257–79.

monstrosity: that is, to the diabolic power of theatrics that threatens the well-being of Maltese society.

The power of theatrics was not only an ingenious dramatic device but a critical component of society. The intensity of the anti-theatrical movement after the mid-sixteenth century shows that Elizabethan society felt a serious unease with *impersonations* made by Machiavellian politicians, shape-shifting actors, and deceitful merchants.[13] The 'artificial persons' of emergent capitalism could be subversive of the established order.[14] And, although these cultural dynamics can be observed taking place over a long period, they had a particularly strong impact within a briefer span: in the 1580s, the power of theatrics was a grave menace to the Protestant government. This was a time when the nation was facing the crisis of Spanish invasion and was increasing the domestic surveillance of Catholics.[15] Moreover, following the arrival of the two Jesuit missionaries Edmund Campion and Robert Persons, the government was increasingly haunted by fears of plots by seminary priests travelling incognito. The question of impersonating either a Protestant or a Catholic thus had political significance; and undoubtedly the government had to be alert to the threat posed by the theatrics of subversive recusants.[16]

At the same time, this sensitivity to or anxiety about the power of theatrics meant that it was a part of daily life, and an especially useful tool for an ambitious or malcontent intellectual, as well as for recusants and nonconformists. Religious deceit and dissimulation often gave such people the opportunity to survive in troubled times. In fact, the 1580s saw the

---

[13] N. W. Bawcutt gives a full account of the anxiety aroused by pro- and anti-Machiavellian discourses in Elizabethan England in 'Machiavelli and Marlowe's *The Jew of Malta*', *Renaissance Drama*, NS, 3 (1970), 3–49. On the association between Machiavellianism and theatricality, see Jonas Barish, *The Anti-Theatrical Prejudice* (Berkeley, 1981), pp. 96–8; Phyllis Rackin, *Stages of History: Shakespeare's English Chronicles* (Ithaca, 1990), pp. 72–5; and Vickie Sullivan, 'Princes to Act: Henry V as the Machiavellian Prince of Appearance', in Joseph Alulis and Vickie Sullivan (eds), *Shakespeare's Political Pageant: Essays in Politics and Literature* (Lanham, 1996), pp. 125–52.

[14] See Jean-Christophe Agnew, 'Artificial Persons', in *Worlds Apart: The Market and the Theater in Anglo-American Thought, 1550–1750* (New York, 1986), pp. 101–48.

[15] Governmental surveillance at this period is well documented in Curtis C. Breight, *Surveillance, Militarism and Drama in the Elizabethan Era* (Basingstoke, 1996), pp. 45–91.

[16] The phenomenon of religious dissimulation and the range of controversies surrounding it are discussed in Perez Zagorin, *Ways of Lying: Dissimulation, Persecution, and Conformity in Early Modern Europe* (Cambridge, MA, 1990), pp. 131–52; and Peter Holmes, *Resistance and Compromise: The Political Thought of the Elizabethan Catholics* (Cambridge, 1982), pp. 117–25.

emergence of acquisitive, self-made intelligencers who exploited the power of theatrics to pursue business leads and referrals.

A typical case is that of Anthony Munday, who went to Rome, 'was allowed the Popes Scholler, and liued there in the Seminarie among them' under the alias of Antonius Auleus.[17] Soon afterwards, he returned to England to work as an intelligencer for the government and published news pamphlets about Catholic missionaries. Munday was well aware of the trend that 'Apostate seminarists suddenly became of considerable use to the authorities'.[18] A Catholic priest, impatient of Munday's 'macheuillian' counterfeiting of his professed faith and his 'rayling a[n]d rauing at uertuous and good men deseassed', tried to ruin Munday's credibility testimony by exposing his career as a player and playwright: '[M]unday, who first was a stage player (no do[u]bt a calling of some creditt) after an aprentise which tyme he wel feined with deceauing of his master then wandring towardes Italy, by his owne report became a coosener in his iourney.'[19] This polemic intended to disgrace Munday not only by publicizing his humble calling but also by suggesting that he possessed practical expertise in all theatrical tricks, thereby undermining the authenticity of his discourses.

At the same time, this personal attack reveals that Munday had considerable clout in the way he represented Catholic missionaries. The theatrics of impersonating Catholics in the Roman seminary provided him with a range of materials and information for writing *The English Roman Life* (1582) and other news reports about seminary priests, and secured him the patronage of several members of the Privy Council.[20] As 'a stage player', Munday may have been well acquainted with the power of theatrics and with the way an intelligencer could make use of it, as Thomas Nashe contemptuously describes: 'To bee an Intelligencer is to haue oathes at will,

---

[17] Anthony Munday, *A Discouerie of Edmund Campion, and His Confederates* (London, 1582), sig. D1v. For Munday's alias, see Anthony Kenny, 'Anthony Munday in Rome', *Recusant History*, 6 (1962), 158–62. On Munday's leaning towards Catholicism, see Celeste Turner, *Anthony Munday: An Elizabethan Man of Letters* (Berkeley, 1928), pp. 16–23; Tracey Hill, *Anthony Munday and Civic Culture: Theatre, History and Power in Early Modern London 1580-1633* (Manchester, 2004), pp. 84–6; and Donna B. Hamilton, *Anthony Munday and the Catholics, 1560-1633* (Aldershot, 2005), pp. 31–52.

[18] Michael C. Questier, 'English Clerical Converts to Protestantism, 1580-1596', *Recusant History*, 20:4 (1991), 455–77, at p. 455.

[19] Thomas Alfield, *A True Reporte of the Death & Martyrdome of M. Campion Iesuite and Preiste, & M. Sherwin, & M. Bryan Preistes, at Tiborne the First of December 1581* ([London], [1582]), sigs D4v-E1r.

[20] *Anthony Munday: The English Roman Life*, ed. Philip J. Ayres (Oxford, 1980), p. xvi.

and thinke God nere regards them; to frame his religion and alleageance to his Prince according to euerie companie he comes in.'[21]

Richard Baines, Marlowe's enemy and sometime roommate during his stay in Vlissingen around 1592, was another of those who had the dexterity to make money out of his theatrics. He sought advancement by going to the English seminary in Rheims in the late 1570s, and had been living at the seminary for three years when he was imprisoned in May 1582 for seeking to poison its well.[22] In April 1583, he was transferred from the prison to his chamber, and his confession was made there on 13 May in the presence of William Allen and the seminary authorities. Immediately afterwards, Allen published 'The confession of Richard Baines priest and late stvdent of the colledge of Rhemes, made after he was remoued out of the common gaile to his chamber'. Baines revealed that 'the holy writers of my Christian profession and priesthood, began daily to waxe more and more tedious and lothsome'; he then proceeded further in wickedness and 'began to mocke at the lesser points of religion, which is the high way to Heresie, Infidelitie & Athisme'. Consequently, he secretly drew a colleague to Protestantism and declared to him his intention 'to goe into England, there to preach heresie: and to annoye the common cause of Christs Church, and specially this Seminary, the President and superiors thereof, as much as I could possibly'.[23]

What most offended the authorities of the seminary were Baines's subversive theatrics or 'the abhominable periurie dissimulation & fiction', employed when he read mass daily, and when he asked permission to return home 'to encrease by preaching and al endeuours the Catholick cause, and toke an oth vpon the Euangelists that I beleeued al points of the Catholick faith, and had no other purpose of going into England but for the aduancement of the same'.[24] The summary of the confession related in prison clearly shows the monetary motivation of his theatrical dissimulation:

> In the midst of such conversations on religion, there grew dissatisfaction with my present state and desire for a better fortune, which I thought myself certain of obtaining by setting off for England, especially as I claimed to know the secret intentions of Alanus, our President, his counsellors and the whole seminary against the Queen and her government.

---

[21] Ronald B. McKerrow (ed.), *The Works of Thomas Nashe*, 2nd edn, rev. F. P. Wilson (5 vols, Oxford, 1958), vol. 3, p. 106.

[22] Fathers of the Congregation of the London Oratory (eds), *The First and Second Diaries of the English College, Douay*, with intro. by Thomas Francis Knox (London, 1878), p. 154.

[23] William Allen, *A Trve Report of the Late Apprehension and Imprisonnement of Iohn Nichols* (Rheims, 1583), sigs D6v–D8r.

[24] Ibid., sig. D8v.

I was unwilling to divulge this information before reaching London. At this time I told a friend, whom I was keen to have as a companion on the journey, that the Queen's Secretary would give us 3,000 crowns for revealing what goes on here.[25]

Thus, the power of theatrics enabled not only Barabas but also intellectual opportunists such as Munday and Baines to fight for their lives in the fear that otherwise they would 'vanish o'er the earth in air / And leave no memory that e'er I was' (1.ii.262–3). The need to survive and the allure of insatiable ambition in the turbulent world of fierce religious conflicts made them resort to the counterfeit profession of faith, clipping of coins, and fake gestures, evidence, news, and friendships. What Barabas' theatrics stirred among the audience of *The Jew of Malta* seems to have been a sense of the religiously divided society of England, filled with anxiety about the national crisis and the emergence of persons with a mastery of artificial identities in their midst.

A PHANTOM MENACE WITHIN THE BELEAGUERED ISLE

In representing the rise and fall of the shape-shifting Barabas, Marlowe chose Christian Malta in a state of national crisis as a backdrop. He may have come across an account of the Turkish siege of Malta in 1565 in contemporary historical and geographical writings when gathering materials for *Tamburlaine*. However, the play makes no claim to the historical veracity of the siege. Marlowe cannot have been ignorant of the Christian victory over Islam, when Malta repelled the disease-ridden enemy troops whose morale had failed. Why, then, did he choose this setting? In adapting the historical siege of Malta to fit his play, Marlowe may have been influenced by Joseph Mendez-Nassi, a Portuguese Marrano in Constantinople.[26] Nassi's financial power and influence with the Sultanate made him a confidential adviser to Selim II. After taking possession of Naxos in 1566, Selim II deposed the Christian duke and made Nassi the Duke of Naxos. In 1570, according to François de Belleforest (1575), Nassi affirmed

> how important for him the isle of Cyprus was, and how greatly it dishonoured his name that the Venetians should retain such a handsome possession right in the heart of his empire. This incited the tyrant to demand

---

[25] Cited in Roy Kendall, 'Richard Baines and Christopher Marlowe's Milieu', *ELR*, 24:3 (1994), 507–52, at p. 547.

[26] Leon Kellner first drew attention to Joseph Mendez-Nassi, or Juan Miques, in 'Die Quelle von Marlowe's *Jew of Malta*', *Englische Studien*, 10 (1887), 80–111. On Marlowe's knowledge of Nassi, see Ethel Seaton, 'Fresh Sources for Marlowe', *RES*, OS, 5:20 (1929), 385–401.

it back, and to declare war on the citizens of St Mark if they refused to abandon the island.[27]

These episodes more or less suggest that at Nassi's instigation the Turks gained mastery of Naxos and Cyprus. As for Jewish political intrigue, there was a contemporary rumour that Jewish bankers had helped to finance the Turkish siege of Malta.[28]

What did Marlowe find in these episodes? Nassi may have been a real-life prototype for the figure of Barabas, but Marlowe seems to have been more interested in the framework of a little Christian island occupied by enemy troops because of the assistance of a Jew. He must have thought this setting adaptable to a play in which an island kingdom is betrayed by a subversive alien stranger, exposing it to invasion and military threat. For Marlowe, it was this critical situation that mattered, whether the island was Malta, Naxos, or Cyprus. The beginning of the play informs the audience that 'A fleet of warlike galleys [...] / Are come from Turkey' and that 'their coming will afflict us all' (1.i.145–6, 155). Bellamira reinforces the sense of growing popular anxiety, even though strictly speaking the siege has not yet begun: 'Since this town was besieged, my gain grows cold' (III.i.1). The coming of the Turkish power exposes the weakness of 'this paltry land' (IV.ii.94), provoking unease in Maltese minds. Into this crisis, Marlowe introduces Barabas, a theatrical Machiavellian stranger. Like one of those anti-theatrical controversialists who issued warnings against the diabolic power of players, Marlowe directs the audience's attention to Barabas' dangerous theatrics with their potential to undermine the foundations of Maltese society.

Before the conspiracy of Roderigo Lopez, physician-in-chief to the Queen, in 1594, and notwithstanding the fact that there was a Portuguese Marrano community in London, Elizabethans had not yet come to see Jews as dangerous aliens. Their society 'was capable of accommodating alternative portrayals' of honest and admirable Jews, such as Gerontus in *The Three Ladies of London*, as well as stereotypical villainous Jews.[29] However,

---

[27] François de Belleforest, 'La Cosmographie Universelle de tout le Monde [...] Beaucoup plus Augmentée, Ornée, et Enrichie', in Vivien Thomas and William Tydeman, *Christopher Marlowe: The Plays and Their Sources* (London, 1994), pp. 306–8, at p. 308.

[28] Cecil Roth, 'The Jews of Malta', *Transactions of the Jewish Historical Society of England*, 12 (1928–31), 187–251, at p. 216.

[29] Charles Edelman, 'Which Is the Jew that Shakespeare Knew? Shylock on the Elizabethan Stage', *Shakespeare Survey*, 52 (1999), 99–106, at p. 101. Anti-Jewish stereotypes in the medieval era and the Renaissance are well documented in Frank Felsenstein's 'Jews and Devils: Anti-Semitic Stereotypes of Late Medieval and Renaissance England', *Journal of Literature and Theology*, 4:1 (1990), 15–28. See also G. K. Hunter,

the negative stereotypes were used as a weapon against troublesome minorities. For instance, during the upsurge of xenophobic sentiment in 1593, a libel was pasted to the wall of the Dutch churchyard identifying London merchants with Jews: 'like the Jewes, you eate us vp as bread.'[30] The libeller was well acquainted with the practical utility of anti-Jewish prejudice in attacking Dutch and French neighbours. This incident suggests that, in a certain social context, a monstrous Jewish figure on stage could represent a concrete living person or group which posed a real threat to the peace of society. It is possible, therefore, that an acquisitive Jew such as Barabas could have been a cue for the audience to recognize threatening aliens in their community. It is even possible that the play itself could have assumed a social role in provoking hostility against them.[31] The enthusiastic revival of *The Jew of Malta* in 1594–95 clearly shows that Barabas could have been perceived as a dramatic representation of a living person. In this case, since Roderigo Lopez happened to be Jewish, Barabas was readily associated with the physician charged with treason, and the crisis situation of the play with that of England.

It is no wonder, then, that in the 1580s Jewish stereotypes were often equated with seminary priests and conspirators. Thomas Lupton, in the dedication of *The Christian against the Iesuite* (1582) to Sir Francis Walsingham, gives a warning against the seed sowed by the Devil and highlights a recent 'seditious sect of Satanical sowers' that replaces the gospel of Christ with the doctrine of the Devil: 'these are they that call themselues Iesuites, but they rather deserue to be called Iudaites: for they follow Iudas in betraying, not Iesus in sauing.'[32] Jesuits were commonly identified with notorious biblical models, such as Judas Iscariot and Cain, in terms of treacherousness and deceitfulness.[33]

Similarly, the facial features of a stereotyped Jew were often associated with those of Catholic conspirators. On 10 August 1586, when the Babington

---

'The Theology of Marlowe's *The Jew of Malta*', *Journal of the Warburg and Courtauld Institutes*, 27 (1964), 211–40. For the Portuguese Marrano community in London, see Lucien Wolf, 'Jews in Elizabethan England', *Transactions of the Jewish Historical Society of England*, 11 (1924–27), 1–91; and David S. Katz, *The Jews in the History of England 1485–1850* (Oxford, 1994), pp. 15–106.

[30] For this libel, see further in Chapter 8, pp. 262–3. Arthur Freeman provides a detailed account of the libel, along with its text, in 'Marlowe, Kyd, and the Dutch Church Libel', *ELR*, 3:1 (1973), 44–52, at p. 50.

[31] See James Shapiro, *Shakespeare and the Jews* (New York, 1996), pp. 184–5. This possibility has also been suggested by James R. Siemon in 'Appendix: The Dutch Church Libel', in Christopher Marlowe, *The Jew of Malta*, ed. James R. Siemon, *The New Mermaids*, 2nd edn (London, 1994), pp. 115–17.

[32] Lupton, *The Christian against the Iesuite*, sig. ¶2r-v.

[33] See John Norden, *A Mirror for the Multitude* (London, 1586), sig. F3r-v.

plot had thrown England in turmoil, William Cecil, Lord Burghley came to Enfield by coach on his way to London. He noticed a number of watchmen standing by the roadside, supposedly searching for the missing conspirators. According to Burghley's letter to Francis Walsingham, he stopped and

> asked them wherto they stood there, and one of them answered, to take 3 yong men: and demandyng how they should know the persons, one answered with these wordes 'Mary my Lord, by intelligence of there favor.' 'What meane you by that', quod I; 'Marry' sayd they 'one of the partyes hath a hooked nose': 'and have you', quoth I, 'no other mark?' 'no', sayth they.[34]

These watchmen unanimously assumed that one of the Catholic conspirators would display stereotypical Jewish characteristics. They may have seen the portraits of the Babington plotters, which were 'in open places of the city of London published, and shall also be dispersed to sundry other places of the realm'.[35] Although the hooked nose was a sign of demonic evil, not just of Jewishness,[36] this episode suggests that the 'bottle-nosed' Barabas (III. iii.10) reminded the audience of dissembling Catholic conspirators, who were commonly imagined to have physiognomic characteristics similar to Jews and devils, and that subversive Catholics were readily associated with Jews on stage.

Machevil in the Prologue, openly sanctioning the extreme wickedness of his disciples, briefly sketches his career in relation to Catholicism. He says that anyone wishing to 'attain / To Peter's chair' (Prologue, 11–12) will eagerly read his books, and that, before coming to England, his soul had transmigrated to the Duke of Guise. As Bawcutt points out, it is difficult to find 'contemporary accusations that [the Duke of Guise] was a disciple or reincarnation of Machiavelli'.[37] So, it seems possible that Marlowe himself could have taken the idea of 'Pythagoras' *metempsychosis*' and demonstrated that this charismatic Catholic leader, like Barabas, 'favours' or resembles Machevil (Prologue, 35).[38] The Duke of Guise whom Marlowe has in mind

---

[34] Letter from Lord Burghley to Francis Walsingham, 10 August 1586, quoted in William Durrant Cooper, 'Notices of Anthony Babington, of Dethick, and of the Conspiracy of 1586', *Reliquary*, 2 (1861–62), 177–99, at p. 178.

[35] Elizabeth I, Proclamation 683, Westminster, 2 August 1586, in Paul L. Hughes and James F. Larkin (eds), *Tudor Royal Proclamations* (3 vols, New Haven, 1969), vol. 2, p. 526.

[36] See Robert Copland, *The Shepardes Kalender* (London, 1570), sig. L7r; T. W. Craik, *The Tudor Interlude: Stage, Costume, and Acting* (1958; repr. Leicester, 1967), p. 51.

[37] Marlowe, *Jew of Malta*, ed. Bawcutt, p. 62, n. 3.

[38] For 'Pythagoras' *metempsychosis*', see Christopher Marlowe, *Doctor Faustus*, ed. David Bevington and Eric Rasmussen, *The Revels Plays* (Manchester, 1992), A-text, v.ii.107, and p. 196, n. 107.

is just such a Machiavellian, as depicted in *The Massacre at Paris*. Before the assassinated body of Guise, Henry IV briefly sums up the popular view of Guise held by Elizabethans:

> Did he not draw a sort of English priests
> From Douai to the seminary at Rheims
> To hatch forth treason 'gainst their natural Queen?
> Did he not cause the King of Spain's huge fleet
> To threaten England and to menace me?[39]

Guise and Barabas are dedicated disciples of Machevil, the mastermind of Catholic treason and invasive wars. Moreover, Machevil has come to England to 'frolic with his friends' (Prologue, 4), a statement with political connotations when we consider that Marlowe repeatedly uses the term 'frolic' to suggest sexual and political transgression.[40] These 'friends' with whom Machevil intends to revel/rebel are thus superimposed upon Catholic conspirators in England, and Barabas comes to be associated with those devising wily tactics to endanger the welfare of the nation.[41]

The clandestine arrival of the seminary priests in 1580, headed by Campion and Persons, undoubtedly increased political anxiety about the national situation. The government was eager to collect information about the missionary priests and to declare that they had been smuggled into England as spies and traitors to overthrow the nation. The overestimation of papal power and the haunting fear of Catholics, however, often led the Privy Council to misjudge the actual state of things, and information about the incognito priests caused them neurotic anxiety, undermining the emotional security that would have been provided by having a firm grip on the situation.[42] In fact, most of the priests came to England not to plot against the government but to nurture the faithful and win back the lapsed. Yet excessive concern drove the government to step up the surveillance of

---

[39] Christopher Marlowe, *Dido Queen of Carthage and The Massacre at Paris*, ed. H. J. Oliver, *The Revels Plays* (London, 1968), xxi.101–5.

[40] See Christopher Marlowe, *Edward the Second*, ed. Charles R. Forker, *The Revels Plays* (Manchester, 1994), I.ii.67, I.iv.73, II.ii.62. Jonathan Gil Harris draws our attention to Marlowe's usage of the term 'frolic' in his *Foreign Bodies and the Body Politic: Discourses of Social Pathology in Early Modern England* (Cambridge, 1998), p. 87.

[41] The linkage of Barabas and Catholics is also pointed out by Eric Rothstein in 'Structure as Meaning in *The Jew of Malta*', *JEGP*, 65:2 (1966), 260–73, at pp. 267–8.

[42] For the government's anxiety about seminary priests, see Frederic A. Youngs Jr, 'Definitions of Treason in an Elizabethan Proclamation', *Historical Journal*, 14:4 (1971), 675–91. On the English Protestants' overestimation of papal power and their misunderstanding of national politics, see Carol Z. Wiener, 'The Beleaguered Isle: A Study of Elizabethan and Early Jacobean Anti-Catholicism', *Past & Present*, 51:1 (1971), 27–62.

The Jew of Malta *and the Diabolic Power of Theatrics*

the priests' activities and to use every means available to stamp out Catholic conspirators.[43] *An Aduertisement and Defence for Trueth against Her Backbiters* (1581) openly denounced the seminary priests as having been sent

> to moue the people by their secret perswasions to change their professions in the matter of Religion [...] and to be reconciled to the obedience of the Pope, and withdrawen from their naturall allegiance due to the Queenes Maiestie, and by these meanes to be readie in their heartes and mindes and otherwise prouided, to ioyne their forces [...] to depriue her Maiestie of her life, crowne and dignitie.[44]

Burghley makes similar complaints against seminary priests and counters criticisms of the harshness of their persecution in *The Execution of Justice in England* (1583).[45]

The fear of missionary priests seems to have been no less intense at a popular level. Active priests were few and scattered, but prejudice could conjure up images of these infamous Jesuit monsters lurking in every neighbourhood. This growing unease is documented by a reference in Robert Persons' letter from London addressed to the Jesuit General Claudio Acquaviva on 16 June 1581:

> the talk here is about the Jesuits. About them there are more fables than used to be told about monsters – about their origin, their manner of life, their institute, their teaching – things various and at variance with each other and manifestly false are spread about not only in private conversation and in addresses but also in printed books.[46]

William Elderton, a ballad-writer, was no doubt one of those who promoted the dissemination of such prejudices against seminary priests:

---

[43] The purpose of their mission is thoroughly discussed in Robert M. Kingdon (ed.), *The Execution of Justice in England by William Cecil and A True, Sincere, and Modest Defense of English Catholics by William Allen* (Ithaca and New York, 1965), pp. xxxi–xxxvii; and Thomas M. McCoog, '"Playing the Champion": The Role of Disputation in the Jesuit Mission', in Thomas M. McCoog (ed.), *The Reckoned Expense: Edmund Campion and the Early English Jesuits* (Woodbridge, 1996), pp. 119–39. Michael L. Carrafiello has discussed Robert Persons' political mission in 'English Catholicism and the Jesuit Mission of 1580–1581', *Historical Journal*, 37:4 (1994), 761–74. See also Francis Edwards, *Robert Persons: The Biography of an Elizabethan Jesuit 1546–1610* (St Louis, 1995), pp. 55–121.

[44] Anon. *An Aduertisement and Defence for Trueth against Her Backbiters* (London, 1581), sig. A2r.

[45] See, for instance, Kingdon (ed.), *Execution of Justice*, pp. 17–19.

[46] Letter from Robert Persons to Claudio Acquaviva, 16 June 1581, quoted in Thomas M. McCoog, *The Society of Jesus in Ireland, Scotland, and England, 1541–1588: 'Our Way of Proceeding?'* (Leiden, 1996), p. 149, n. 67.

> Theyle make you beleue that white is fayre blacke,
> Except by strong fayth ye put them quite backe;
> Th' effecte is playne treason against God and our Queene,
> As by these late Traytours well tryed hath beene.[47]

According to Thomas Dekker, a Jesuit had 'A *Mandrakes* voice, whose tunes are cries, / So peircing, that the *Hearer* dies'.[48] In light of this anti-Catholic propaganda, Jesuits were regarded unquestionably as the root of all social evils. Robert Southwell, in his *Humble Supplication to Her Maiestie*, presumably written in 1591, complains:

> If any displeasing accident fall out, wherof the Authors are either vnknowne or ashamed, Catholiques are made common Fathers of such infamous Orphanes, as though none were so fitt sluces as they, to let out of euery mans sinke these vnsavoury reproaches. Not so much but the Casuall Fiers that somtimes happen in *London*; The late vprores betwene the gentlemen and the Apprentices were layd to our Charge, though th'occasioners of both were so well knowne.[49]

If the ebb and flow of popular fear coincided, as Robin Clifton argues, with that of political crisis, it is reasonable to think that the crises of the 1580s would have repeatedly aroused anxiety.[50] By 1590 England had already experienced several Catholic conspiracies; above all, that unprecedented national crisis, the coming of the Armada, must have confirmed that popular anxiety was well-founded.

Although the diabolic theatrical power of seminary priests can now be classified as legend or urban myth, at the time it was seen to pose a real menace to a nation facing attack from within and without. In a proclamation titled *A Declaration of Great Troubles Pretended against the Realme by a Number of Seminarie Priests and Jesuists* (1591), the government proclaimed that the Jesuits would 'be ready to continue their reconciled people in their lewd constancy to serve their purpose both with their forces and with other traitorous enterprises when the Spanish power shall be ready to land' and issued a warning against Jesuits' shape-shifting tricks:

---

[47] William Elderton, *A Triumph for True Subiects*, in Hyder E. Rollins (ed.), *Old English Ballads 1553–1625: Chiefly from Manuscripts* (Cambridge, 1920), pp. 62–9, at p. 67, stanza 10, lines 5–8.

[48] Thomas Dekker, 'The Pictvre of a Iesuite', in *The Double PP* (London, 1606), in Alexander B. Grosart (ed.), *The Non-Dramatic Works of Thomas Dekker* (5 vols, London and Aylesbury, 1885), vol. 2, pp. 155–91, at p. 162.

[49] Robert Southwell, *An Humble Supplication to Her Maiestie*, ed. R. C. Bald (Cambridge, 1953), p. 41.

[50] Robin Clifton, 'The Popular Fear of Catholics during the English Revolution', *Past & Present*, 52:1 (1971), 23–55.

And furthermore, because it is certainly known and proved by common experience, upon the apprehension of sundry of the said traitorous persons sent into the realm, that they do come into the same by secret creeks and landing places disguised both in their names and persons; some in apparel as soldiers, mariners, or merchants pretending that they have been heretofore taken prisoners and put into galleys and delivered; some come in as gentlemen with contrary tales in comely apparel as though they had travailed into foreign countries for knowledge; and generally all, or the best part, as soon as they are crept in are clothed like gentlemen in apparel, and many as gallants, yea, in all colors and rich feathers and such like disguising themselves, and many of them in their behavior as ruffians, far off to be thought or suspected to be friars, priests, Jesuits, or popish scholars.[51]

The government thus described Jesuit strategy as highly theatrical. William Lightfoote comments on 'The practises of Iesuites & Seminarie priests': 'so come ye disguised in your habite marching on like Maskers, hauing in stead of visors shameles foreheads, and fronts vntaught to blush'.[52] These Catholic strangers, exercising their powers of impersonation for subversive purposes, could evade the regime of strict surveillance and wander

in the realme secretly, & in a disguised maner [...] with fethers and all ornaments of light couloured apparel, like to the fashion of Courtiers, and do vse many meanes to entice all people, with whom they dare aduenture to speake, not onely to be reconciled to the Pope, & Church of Rome, but to induce them by vowes and othes to renounce their obedience to the Queene.[53]

John Hull, a Protestant polemicist, claimed that Jesuit doctrine was 'turning the truth of God into a lye, and religion into superstition: perswading men to all vngodlinesse, and yet ouershadowing all with the shew of religion', and they are 'well practised in Machieuel, turning religion into policie'.[54]

Considering the exaggeration of the missionaries' skill and cunning, it is no wonder that English Protestants made an unrealistic appraisal of their talents at dissembling. George Whetstone portrays them thus: 'these *Iesuits* in disguised habits [...] transformed themselues at pleasure like

---

[51] Elizabeth I, Proclamation 738, Richmond, 18 October 1591, in Hughes and Larkin (eds), *Tudor Royal Proclamations*, vol. 3, pp. 86–93, at pp. 89, 91.
[52] William Lightfoote, *The Complaint of England* (London, 1587), sig. C2r-v.
[53] Richard Leigh, *The Copie of a Letter Sent ovt of England to Don Bernardin Mendoza Ambassadovr in France for the King of Spaine* [by William Cecil] (London, 1588), sig. B2v.
[54] John Hull, *The Vnmasking of the Pollitique Atheist* (London, 1602), sig. A4r-v.

vnto *Protew*'.[55] William Averell similarly declares that: 'These counterfaite sheepe, these papisticall Iesuites, or rather apisticall Iebusites, are dispenst with by the Pope to weare sundrie habites, you cannot knowe them by their Priestly garmentes, for sometimes they iet in Lions skins, but you may discry them by their asses eares, peeping out from vnder their hoodes.'[56] Dekker's portrayal of a Jesuit may accurately indicate the perceived menace of their protean power: 'Hee's *Brown*, hee's *Gray*, hee's *Black*, hee's *white*, / Hee's Any thing. A *Iesuite*.'[57] Thus, the missionary priests were represented and recognized as theatrical Machiavellian strangers in the beleaguered isle of England.

The Jew of Malta seems to share this sentiment. The play juxtaposes the critical situation of England with that of Malta, where the dissembling Machiavellian Barabas transgresses the social code of 'simplicity' and cooperates with the Turkish invasion of the 'paltry' island. This contemporary connection may have resonated powerfully with an audience seized with a kind of collective paranoia. The play itself assumes the power to provoke dramatic excitement by living out the nightmare envisaged by Francis Hastings, a Puritan parliamentarian, of rebellious plots and 'an inuasion vpon this little Island of *England*'.[58]

THE TACTICS OF THEATRICS TO CONSOLIDATE POWER

Every arrest and execution of a seminary priest gave hack writers in Grub Street an opportunity to make money by denouncing them as traitors and then penning panegyrics for the government. The influence of their news pamphlets cannot be overestimated, for they were a close counterpart of modern journalism and played an important role in moulding public opinion.[59] This is why William Allen expresses his loathing for 'many pretty pa[m]phlets':

> by practise and pollicie of certain crafty co[n]scie[n]celes men, by falshood & forgerie, altering in the sight of the simple the causes of their [priests'] death & punishment, & making their liues & actio[n]s odious to the

---

[55] George Whetstone, *The Censure of a Loyall Subiect* (London, 1586), sig. D2r.
[56] William Averell, *A Meruailous Combat of Contrarieties* (London, 1588), sig. E1r.
[57] Dekker, *Double PP*, p. 164.
[58] Francis Hastings, *A Watchword to All Religious, and True Hearted English-Men* (London, 1598), p. 53.
[59] For the importance of news pamphlets that influenced public opinion, see Richard Cust, 'News and Politics in Early Seventeenth-Century England', *Past & Present*, 112:1 (1986), 60–90, at pp. 67–9; Alexandra Walsham, *Providence in Early Modern England* (Oxford, 1999), pp. 8–64; and Adam Fox, *Oral and Literate Culture in England 1500–1700* (Oxford, 2000), pp. 335–405.

world. Whereby they disadua[n]taged in deede the Catholike part much more then by any plaine viole[n]ce or prete[n]ded iustice whatsoeuer.[60]

Defending against these obnoxious publications, Catholic polemicists were eager to discover how 'shamfull fiction' was fabricated with the 'falshood & forgerie' of ambitious intelligencers.[61] This was why Allen published the confessional letters of ex-Protestant intelligencers, in one of which John Nicols admits that 'I was the writer in deede, but (God knoweth) other men were the Authors'.[62] The intended target of Allen's attack was a government in league with fraudulent pamphleteers, playwrights, and spies, responsible for the wide diffusion of fictions suggesting that seminary priests and Spanish forces endangered England, God's sacred nation.[63] It was important for Catholics to make the public aware of Protestant theatrical fraud because, by revealing the enemy's discourse to be a variety of fictions, they could lay bare the political strategy of the Establishment itself.

Marlowe, as a playwright, must have been highly aware that fiction-making was a powerful tool for the government to construct an ideology of English nationhood. It is interesting to consider, therefore, how he treats the Maltese government's involvement in theatrics against Barabas' diabolic power. At the climax of the play, Barabas, 'with a hammer above', devises a plot to blow up all the Turkish soldiers in a monastery and make Calymath and his consorts fall into a cauldron (stage direction, v.v). He is no longer the acquisitive merchant of the play's beginning but a dangerous conspirator who has become powerful enough to pursue his malign purpose and gain ascendancy over Maltese society. As a playwright, actor, and director, Barabas devises a variety of fictions suitable to his undertakings and transforms himself into a more highly theatrical villain in order to gain control of a critical situation. However, just as his success lies in 'his deepest wits', his downfall is brought about by a person who has the wit to 'cast with

---

[60] Allen, *Imprisonnement of Iohn Nicols*, sigs A2v–A3r.
[61] Ibid., sig. A4r.
[62] Ibid., sig. C1v.
[63] Fiction-making by Elizabeth's government has frequently been discussed. See Leo Hicks, *An Elizabethan Problem: Some Aspects of the Careers of Two Exile Adventurers* (New York, 1964), pp. 30–57; and Conyers Read, 'William Cecil and Elizabethan Public Relations', in S. T. Bindoff, J. Hurstfield, and C. H. Williams (eds), *Elizabethan Government and Society: Essays Presented to Sir John Neale* (London, 1961), pp. 21–55. For the conflicts between Catholic and anti-Catholic discourses, see Arthur F. Marotti, 'Alienating Catholics in Early Modern England: Recusant Women, Jesuits and Ideological Fantasies', in Arthur F. Marotti (ed.), *Catholicism and Anti-Catholicism in Early Modern English Texts* (London, 1999), pp. 1–34; and Alison Shell, *Catholicism, Controversy and the English Literary Imagination, 1558–1660* (Cambridge, 1999), pp. 107–40.

cunning for the time to come'. The big flaw in Barabas' elaborate design consists in his confiding his stratagem to Ferneze, the governor:

> And thus we cast it: to a solemn feast
> I will invite young Selim-Calymath,
> Where be thou present only to perform
> One stratagem that I'll impart to thee,
> Wherein no danger shall betide thy life,
> And I will warrant Malta free for ever. (v.ii.96–101)

Ferneze is invited to participate as an actor in the theatrical entertainment of destroying the Turks that Barabas cunningly devises. Yet at the same time, unknown to both the audience and Barabas until the denouement of the play, a deeper plot is concocted by the governor. Barabas assumes that he himself has taken the initiative in presenting the show of mass murder, but does not realize that Ferneze is planning to take advantage of his devices and exploit Barabas as an actor who is carrying out a yet more sinister plot. Barabas informs the governor of his 'policy' to exterminate the Turkish army and brags: 'say, will not this be brave?' (v.v.41). He completely forgets his first maxim: 'policy' or duplicity is '[Christians'] profession, / And not simplicity as they suggest' (I.ii.161–2).

Ferneze pretends to admire him: 'O, excellent! Here, hold thee, Barabas; / I trust thy word, take what I promised thee' (v.v.42–3), and cunningly impersonates an 'earth-mettled villain' before the protean Barabas. It is Ferneze's power of theatrics that debases Barabas to the level of 'a senseless lump of clay' and brings destruction upon him. In other words, the governor appropriates the theatrical stratagem of Barabas, an unruly stranger on the margins, to restore and maintain the order of Christian society.[64] Unlike Barabas, however, he does not refer to or proudly display his own talent for impersonation, but instead covers up the design of his spectacular plan by giving the official dictum: 'let due praise be given / Neither to fate nor fortune, but to heaven' (v.v.122–3).

Ferneze's tendency to attribute every piece of good fortune and misfortune to divine providence is so conspicuous throughout the play that the governor comes near to being represented as an Elizabethan Protestant moralist, and his providentialism seems to lead to an orthodox moral ending. However, the audience would have been left with a palpable sense of unease. This is because Ferneze's way of ascribing miraculous occurrences

---

[64] For Ferneze's Machiavellian stratagem to outwit Barabas, see Douglas Cole, *Suffering and Evil in the Plays of Christopher Marlowe* (Princeton, 1962), p. 143; and Catherine Minshull, 'Marlowe's "Sound Machevill"', *Renaissance Drama*, NS, 13 (1982), 35–53, at p. 41. Roger Sales has pointed out the importance of the governor's Machiavellian theatrics: see Sales, *Christopher Marlowe*, pp. 84–96.

to heaven works to expose the hypocrisy of the Maltese government that behind the scenes uses the same theatrical strategy as Barabas. By displaying the governor's crafty manoeuvring to regain control of the nation, Marlowe ingeniously focuses an oblique spotlight on the Elizabethan regime itself. While making a pretence of innocence or 'simplicity' and praising God's providence at work in defeating the enemy, Elizabeth's government actually appropriated Machiavellian tactics to consolidate its power.

Marlowe himself, while feigning providentialism, applies the same Machiavellian tactics in the play to expose the hypocrisy of the government. He may have recognized the risk of self-contradiction in creating a villain with exceptional theatrical power on the stage. Barabas, functioning as actor and playwright, devises fictions to manipulate simple-minded people, and comes to resemble the playwright himself, as well as a seminary priest. Judging from the cunningly schemed metadramatic structure of the play, Marlowe seems to have accepted this subtle resemblance. By highlighting the diabolic power of theatrics that had aroused popular anxiety, and by outwardly endorsing divine retribution against the protean Barabas, he seems to be casting doubt on the legitimacy of the English Protestant state by disclosing that the very same power was being appropriated to forge an image of a divinely sanctioned regime in league with fraudulent pamphleteers, playwrights, and spies.

In suggesting that the nation was fabricated and maintained by theatrics or fictions, Marlowe is in line with some of the Catholic polemics. *The Copy of a Letter, Lately Written by a Spanishe Gentleman, to His Freind in England* (1589) denounces the Elizabethan regime:

> This intolerable feare is more manifested in your Englishe Gouernment, then in any state els in the whole world: the great impression thereof enforcing them, to all their spyings abroad, and inquisitions at home: searchings of houses more at midnighte then at noone dayes, apprehensions, examinations, and such daily exercise, and practise of the racke, as neuer the like was hard of [...] norwithstanding all which, the remedies remaining (rather to patch vp the state of a body so far infected, then to cure an incurable disease) are principally grounded, vpon extreme tyranny, and deepe dissimulation. [...] Touching their dissimulation, being the grounde and substance of their gouernment, and conteyning the infynite nombers of deceatfull practises, false fictions, and slaunderous lies, which aswell in the world abroade, as also at home, they haue artificially exercysed, in euery action, is suche a laborinthe to looke into, that it would rather require a whole volume, then a brief relation.[65]

---

[65] I. B., *The Copy of a Letter, Lately Written by a Spanishe Gentleman, to His Freind in England* (Antwerp, 1589), sig. A3r–v. Richard Verstegan was probably the principal

What this polemic criticizes is the fiction-making strategy of the English government in the late 1580s. The government, obsessed with 'intolerable feare', steps up strict surveillance on Catholics at home and abroad and exercises 'infynite numbers of deceatfull practises, false fictions, and slaunderous lies' to maintain the Protestant regime.

We should, of course, be cautious about the politico-religious bias displayed in this pamphlet, but it does give us an insight into the political meaning of theatrics in this period. We may infer from the pamphlet's argument that the escalating conflict between England and the Roman/Spanish powers intensified consciousness about theatrics on both sides, and that the Protestant government, seriously threatened by Catholic subversives, employed equally sophisticated strategies to invent Protestant nationhood. The pamphlet was intended to dispel the ideology of the imagined community of the Protestant nation. Likewise, Marlowe seems to show real understanding of the issues raised by those Catholics who launched attacks on the 'extreme tyranny and deepe dissimulation' of the English regime. He analyses the diabolic power of theatrics operating in the political struggle for ascendancy and exposes the workings. He even seems to jeer at the 'simplicity' of those who are deluded by government theatrics as well as by the subversives. What we find in *The Jew of Malta* is Marlowe's analytical mind at work as a social critic.

I am not arguing that Marlowe was a Catholic or had sympathy with the Catholic cause. There is little hint in *The Jew of Malta* of religious enthusiasm or resolution; rather, what impresses us is the cold, sardonic tone of the play, which compels us to consider it as a farce with 'savage comic humour'.[66] This may be partly due to Marlowe's deliberate repetition of a commonplace dictum about providence where mysterious occurrences are in fact produced by tricky theatrics. As Bawcutt notes: 'though an equivalent [of God], "Heaven", does occur sixteen times, Ferneze's attempts to assert that divine providence is at work seem weak and unconvincing.' This is largely because 'we have been shown only too clearly that the events of the play have occurred not by chance or divine intervention but through human machinations'.[67]

In the scene where Abigail deceives the abbess and friars to ensure access to the treasures, what is most interesting is the friars' ridiculous explanation for Abigail's conversion; they excitedly take turns with their puritanical

---

author of this pamphlet: see A. F. Allison and D. M. Rogers, *The Contemporary Printed Literature of the English Counter-Reformation between 1558 and 1640* (2 vols, Aldershot, 1994), vol. 2, p. 150, no. 758.

[66] T. S. Eliot, 'Christopher Marlowe', in *Selected Essays* (London, 1951), pp. 118–25, at p. 123.

[67] Marlowe, *Jew of Malta*, ed. Bawcutt, p. 29.

comments: 'No doubt, brother, but this proceedeth of the spirit' and 'Ay, and of a moving spirit too' (1.ii. 326–7). To them, her conversion seems to have been the work of the Holy Spirit, but this only shows their gullibility, since the audience knows that she is practising theatrical fraud. Similar comic devices can be observed throughout the play. At the beginning of Act v, Barabas gets into a scrape when Bellamira charges him with murder; he then takes sleep-inducing drugs to impersonate a dead man. The Vice Admiral of Spain, seeing Barabas' body carried by the officers onto the stage, comments on his 'strange' death; Ferneze replies, 'Wonder not at it, sir, the heavens are just' (v.i.54–5). Barabas' timely impersonation, however, makes Ferneze's providentialism seem superficial or even absurd; the next moment, having been thrown down outside the walls, Barabas suddenly stands up, saying 'Well fare, sleepy drink!' (v.i.61). Ferneze gives a providential interpretation for events that are in fact enabled by theatrics, and the audience's laughter is provoked by the dramatic device undermining religious explanations.

This device works most effectively in the denouement: although the governor's victory over Barabas is covered up by the concluding panegyric on divine providence, in reality it has been brought about by his greater skill. Presumably, the audience recognizes that the political stability of Maltese society is maintained by the governor's application of a Machiavellian theatrical strategy under the cloak of religiosity, since the ridiculousness of a providential explanation is fixed firmly in their minds by the reiteration of these theatrical devices. Pretending to be protected by divine providence at times becomes a laughing matter.

In a note addressed to Sir John Puckering, Thomas Kyd reports Marlowe as saying, 'things esteemed to be donn by devine power might have aswell been don by observation of men'.[68] Since Kyd had undergone severe tortures when writing this note, its authenticity cannot be fully confirmed. However, *The Jew of Malta* and this 'monstrous' opinion have a similar intellectual orientation: things that seem to happen by divine power can be created by the power of theatrics. This is not an aggressive stance against Christian dogma or a Jesuitical enthusiasm for counter-reformation, but rather the sort of empirical and experimental spirit that can be discerned in Reginald Scot's *The Discouerie of Witchcraft* (1584), in which the miraculous performances of magicians are empirically analysed and castigated as 'iuggling knacks' to delude simple onlookers, and that their amazing spectacles and miracles can be explained simply in terms of theatrical dexterity.[69]

---

[68] Quoted in Constance Brown Kuriyama, *Christopher Marlowe: A Renaissance Life* (Ithaca, 2002), p. 231.

[69] Reginald Scot, *The Discouerie of Witchcraft* (London, 1584), p. 351.

Like Marlowe's play, *The Discouerie of Witchcraft* was the product of the Kentish intellectual milieu and an anti-Catholic campaign inflamed by the Jesuit missions and the growing threat of a Spanish military invasion in the early 1580s, as we can detect in its dedications.[70] The first is addressed to Roger Manwood, with whom Scot shared a Kentish philanthropic enthusiasm to promote social welfare programmes, such as can be discerned in his *A Perfite Platforme of a Hoppe Garden*, published in order 'to satisfie the necessitie of my Countrie' and for the benefit of 'the Countrie people [...] placed in the frontiers of pouertie'.[71] Scot highly praises Manwood's intellectual attitude: 'I know you to be perspicuous, and able to see downe into the depth and bottome of causes, and are not to be carried awaie with the vaine persuasion or superstition either of man, custome, time, or multitude, but mooued with the authoritie of truth onlie.'[72] Manwood's attitude underlies the approach taken by Scot himself, who gives advice to another dedicatee, his cousin Sir Thomas Scot of Scot's Hall in Smeeth, Kent: 'See first whether the euidence be not friuolous, & whether the proofs brought against them be not incredible, consisting of ghesses, presumptions, & impossibilities contrarie to reason, scripture, and nature', because 'we are commanded by Christ himselfe to search for knowledge: for it is the kings honour (as Salomon saith) to search out a thing.'[73] Scot's way of examining so-called witches and impostors was therefore to focus his attention on their mechanical and discursive devices of theatrics, as he explains to the other dedicatees, John Coldwell, Dean of Rochester, and William Redman, Archdeacon of Canterbury: 'My question is not (as manie fondlie suppose) whether there be witches or naie: but whether they can doo such miraculous works as are imputed vnto them.'[74]

It should be remembered that Scot's agenda was backed by an anti-Catholic desire to 'demonstrate, through equating Catholicism with conjuring practices, that both were mere juggling and deceit, not any kind of "real" magic'.[75] He draws an obvious analogy between Jesuits and 'witch-

---

[70] For this point, see also Pierre Kapitaniak, 'From Grindal to Whitgift: The Political Commitment of Reginald Scot', *Études Épistémè*, 29 (2016), <http://episteme.revues.org/1263> [accessed 23 November 2022].

[71] Reginald Scot, *A Perfite Platforme of a Hoppe Garden* (London, 1574), sigs A4r and B2r–v. For Scot's sympathy with Manwood in terms of Kentish philanthropy, see Claire Bartram '"Melancholic Imaginations": Witchcraft and the Politics of Melancholia in Elizabethan Kent', *Journal of European Studies*, 33:3 (2003), 203–11.

[72] Scot, *Discouerie of Witchcraft*, sig. A5r.

[73] *Ibid.*, sigs A6r and A7r.

[74] *Ibid.*, sig. A8v.

[75] Pierre Kapitaniak, 'Reginald Scot and the Circles of Power: Witchcraft, Anti-Catholicism and Faction Politics', in Marcus Harmes and Victoria Bladen (eds), *Supernatural and Secular Power in Early Modern England* (Farnham, 2015), pp. 41–66, at p.

mongers' in the dedication to Coldwell and Redman: 'The papist hath some colour of scripture to mainteine his idoll of bread, but no Iesuiticall distinction can couer the witchmongers idolatrie in this behalfe.'[76] Thus, Scot's empirical and anti-Catholic attitude aligns with that of *The Jew of Malta* in its intellectual probing into the power and workings of diabolic theatrics. This throws up the question of how and to what extent Marlowe had access to the intellectual assets of the Kentish gentry networks.

MARLOWE AND THE KENTISH INTELLECTUAL MILIEU

On Hellespont, guilty of true love's blood,
In view and opposite two cities stood,
Sea-borderers, disjoin'd by Neptune's might. (*Hero and Leander*, 1.1–3)

There is no evidence that Marlowe had ever seen the Dardanelles strait. What he recollects at the beginning of *Hero and Leander* may have been the strait of Dover. The town, within a half-day's walk from Canterbury, commands a fine view of Calais, as Thomas Nashe describes: 'a man standing vpon *Callis* Sands may see men walking on *Douer Clyffes*'.[77] There were several opportunities for Marlowe to visit Dover, as his mother, Katherine, came from the Arthur family of Dover and her relatives were closely associated with the St James area, near to the harbour front under the castle cliffs.[78]

The harbour, according to Sir Amias Paulet, was in September 1576 'in such utter ruin as the passage thereby is utterly decayed', though the benefit of building it had been recognized ever since the public works were launched by Henry VIII in 1535. Paulet wrote to Lord Burghley that 'Dover should be provided with a better harbour'.[79] As Thomas Digges claims in 'A Discourse of Sea-Ports; principally of the Port and Haven of *Dover*', rebuilding would help reinforce the national defences and revitalize local marine transportation and foreign trade.[80] The greatest difficulty standing in the way of the harbour's reconstruction was a large sandbar that had

---

53. For Scot's anti-Catholic fervour, see also Annabel Patterson, *Reading Holinshed's Chronicles* (Chicago, 1994), p. 226.
[76] Scot, *Discouerie of Witchcraft*, sig. B1r.
[77] McKerrow and Wilson (eds), *Works of Thomas Nashe*, vol. 1, p. 219.
[78] William Urry, *Christopher Marlowe and Canterbury*, ed. with an introduction by Andrew Butcher (London, 1988), pp. 13–14.
[79] Mary Anne Everett Green (ed.), *Calendar of State Papers Domestic, Addenda 1566–1579* (1871; repr. Nendeln, 1967), p. 504.
[80] Thomas Digges, 'A Discourse of Sea-Ports: Principally of the Port and Haven of Dover', in William Oldys (ed.), *The Harleian Miscellany* (8 vols, London, 1744–46), vol. 4, pp. 292–6.

accumulated not only in the entrance but also along the entire length of Dover bay. Low tide uncovered a shallow lagoon into which the River Dour poured its waters and mud, while the flood tide carried with it large quantities of sand, silt, pebbles, and shingle that prevented large vessels from accessing the haven. The monopoly licence for the export of grain granted by the Queen to Dover in 1580 gave impetus to rebuilding the harbour under the initiative of the committee, composed of Privy Councillors and Kentish magnates including Sir Thomas Scot, Thomas Wotton, and Thomas Digges. The local network attracted civil engineers, navigators, fortifiers, and workmen, making the project the largest cash-heavy public enterprise in the 1580s. Reginald Scot, in his 'note' inserted into the second edition of Holinshed's *Chronicles* (1587), exults over the success of the enterprise, 'a perfect and an absolute worke, to the perpetuall maintenance of a hauen in that place, being such a monument as is hardlie to be found written in anie record'.[81]

The basic principle shared among all the approved plans of April 1582 was turning the lagoon into what was called a 'pent' or reservoir by building seawalls on the shingle to dam up the river water (figure 20). The pent would be supplied by the Dour and filled to the top with water. A sluice gate in the cross wall would regulate the water flow and be opened at low tide to release the water stored in the reservoir. The flood of water from the sluice would gush out through the harbour entrance, scouring out the sand and shingle that had accumulated there.

The daunting challenge was how to construct walls that would be able to hold such a large quantity of water. Scot explains the pivotal point of the work: 'the life of the hauen consisteth in the pent, and consequentlie in the long wall and crosse wall, without the which no pent could be made, so as wals must be erected.'[82] It was especially difficult to build the cross wall of 40 rods (about 200 metres) in length, because it would be nearer to the sea than the long wall of 120 rods and would have to cross the channel (figure 21). Moreover, it needed to be made deeper and higher, broader and wider (90 feet (27 metres) broad at the base), because 'the weight of the pent water was to lie altogither vpon this wall'.[83] In March 1583, Thomas Scot

---

[81] Raphael Holinshed, *Holinshed's Chronicles of England, Scotland, and Ireland*, with a new introduction by Vernon F. Snow (6 vols, 1807–08; repr. New York, 1976), vol. 4, p. 845. For the rebuilding of Dover harbour, see also Martin H. Biddle and John Summerson, 'Dover Harbour', in H. M. Colvin (ed.), *The History of the King's Works, Vol. 4, Part 2* (London, 1982), pp. 729–68; and Eric H. Ash, *Power, Knowledge, and Expertise in Elizabethan England* (Baltimore, 2004), pp. 55–86. The 1595 plan of Dover Harbour is in BL, Cotton MS Augustus, I.i.46.

[82] *Holinshed's Chronicles*, vol. 4, p. 852.

[83] Ibid., p. 861.

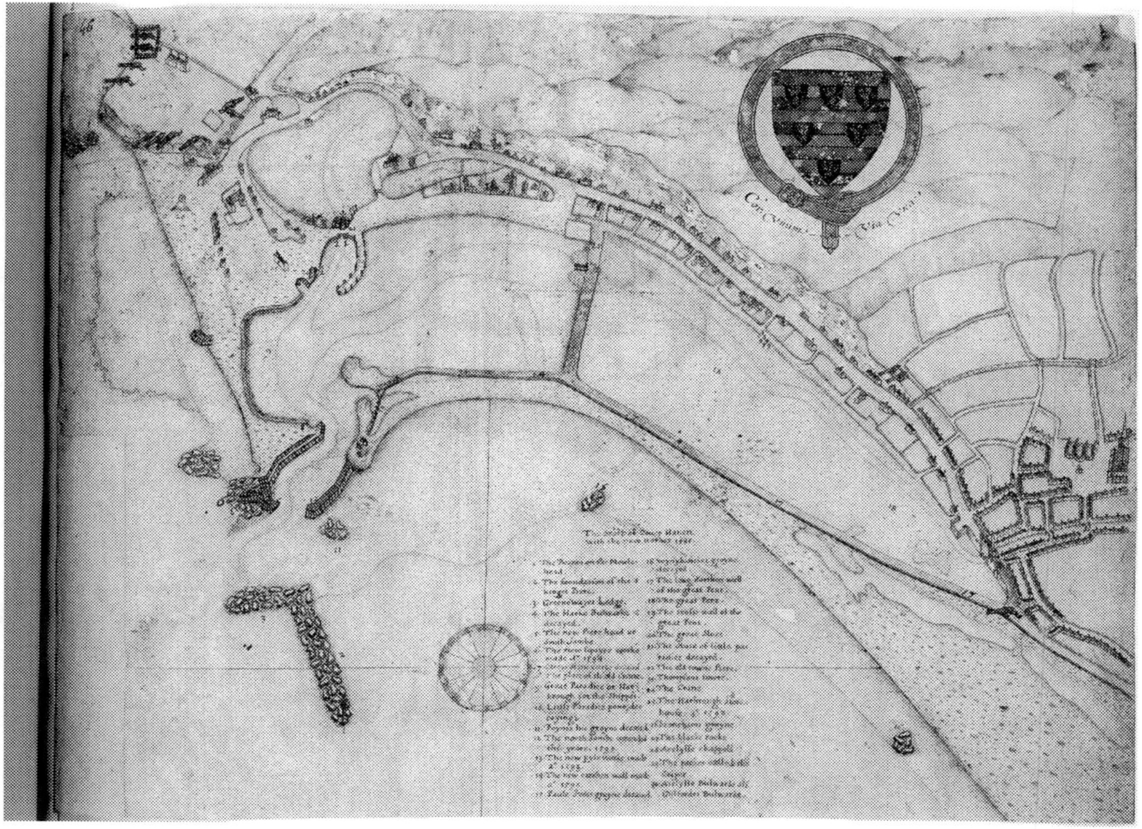

Figure 20 Plan of Dover Harbour, perhaps drawn by John Hill in 1595. BL, Cotton MS Augustus, I.i.46. © The British Library. All Rights Reserved.

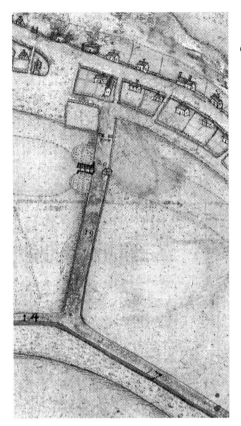

Figure 21 The 'cross wall' of the great pent in Dover Harbour. BL, Cotton MS Augustus, I.i.46 (detail). © The British Library. All Rights Reserved.

(Reginald's cousin and the head overseer) suggested to Walsingham, now 'the chiefe director and furtherer of Douer hauen', a technique employed in the reclaimed area of Romney marsh. Walsingham sent for Reginald, 'who had beene deputed a surueior of Romneie marsh by the space of foure yeares togither',[84] and his colleague, to confer with them. The Secretary was satisfied with their proposal to construct waterproofed walls similar to the ones that the Romney workers had built using a mixture of earth and chalk.

Surprisingly enough, Thomas Scot triumphantly wrote to Walsingham on 21 July 1583, informing him that everything 'is accomplyshed in lytle more than two monethes', although the project had been expected to take two years and at greater expense.[85] The core of Reginald's account in Holinshed's *Chronicles* emphasizes the 'impossibility' of their miraculous work: 'I am to make description of the things performed, and of the manner of the execution thereof, in which thing consisted the difficultie,

[84] *Ibid.*, p. 855.
[85] TNA, SP, 12/161 fol. 103r.

and (as some thought) the impossibilitie of this enterprise.'[86] Although it did seem unattainable, the enterprise was accomplished through collective wisdom and egalitarian solidarity. Reginald praises the industry of the marshmen and takes pride in the fact that 'in all those busines not one person slaine'.[87] He gives unstinting praise in particular to his cousin: 'had not the other commissioners beene comforted herein by sir Thomas Scot, the impossibilitie presupposed would haue discouraged and ouerthrowne the whole enterprise.'[88]

What had percolated among the network of Kentish intellectuals was a sense of the empirical and experimental technological marvels that allowed them to explain and exploit the mechanisms that had made the incredible possible. In *The Discouerie of Witchcraft*, Scot uses his knowledge of civil engineering, employing empirical insights as weapons to expose impostors, asserting that the power of mechanical and theatrical devices, not the power of witchcraft, had made 'the impossibilitie presupposed' possible. For him, the dexterous manipulations of natural phenomena such as Pharaoh's magicians were trained in should be explained by experience and industrious study, and then applied for the benefit of the local community.

This empirical attitude, banishing every sort of magic from the realm of human affairs, was often branded as 'Sadduceeism', and can be observed in the vehement attacks on Scot by his enemies, including godly clerics such as Henry Holland and William Perkins.[89] It was so called because it cast doubt on the authenticity of heavenly miracles mentioned in the scriptures, as well as those of magicians.[90] Sadduceeism saw not only the miraculous exorcisms of puritan divines but even the mighty works of

---

[86] *Holinshed's Chronicles*, vol. 4, p. 857.
[87] Ibid., p. 865.
[88] Ibid., p. 861.
[89] Henry Holland, *A Treatise against Witchcraft* (London, 1590), sig. A3r; and William Perkins, *Discovrse of the Damned Art of Witchcraft* (London, 1608), sig. ¶6r and p. 188. For the reception of Scot's *Discouerie of Witchcraft*, see S. F. Davies, 'The Reception of Reginald Scot's *Discovery of Witchcraft*: Witchcraft, Magic, and Radical Religion', *Journal of the History of Ideas*, 74:3 (2013), 381–401.
[90] Sydney Anglo, 'Reginald Scot's *Discoverie of Witchcraft*: Scepticism and Sadduceeism', in Sydney Anglo (ed.), *The Damned Art: Essays in the Literature of Witchcraft* (London, 1977), pp. 106–39, argues that Scot's position cannot be distinguished from the Sadducean argument. James Sharpe, *Instruments of Darkness: Witchcraft in England, 1550–1750* (London, 1996), p. 55, supports this view. By contrast, Leland Estes, 'Reginald Scot and his *Discoverie of Witchcraft*: Religion and Science in the Opposition to the European Witch Craze', *Church History*, 52:4 (1983), 444–56, attempts to identify Scot's rationalism as 'Erasmian'; and David Wootton, 'Reginald Scot / Abraham Fleming / The Family of Love', in Stuart Clark (ed.), *Languages of Witchcraft: Narrative, Ideology and Meaning in Early Modern Culture* (Basingstoke,

Hebrew religious leaders as the manipulation of natural phenomena and theatrical tricks, not the workings of divine power. To borrow Richard Baines's shocking phrase, it could be summarised as: 'Moyses was but a Jugler, & that one Heriotes being Sir W Raleighs man can do more then he.'[91] Though this is a mere fragment of Baines's slanderous report about Marlowe, it gives us good grounds for seeking in *The Jew of Malta* the 'Sadducean' or empirical mindset that Marlowe may have shared with Scot and his associates.

Whether Marlowe was acquainted with Reginald Scot remains a matter of speculation. There is no evidence for it, except for the fact that both had connections with Roger Manwood and Sir Francis Walsingham, suggesting Marlowe's affinity with the intellectual milieu of Kentish magnates. In addition, John Coldwell, one of the dedicatees of *The Discouerie of Witchcraft*, may have been involved with the Marlowe family. Born in Faversham, and having obtained his MA from St John's College, Cambridge in 1558, Coldwell became the lessee of the ancient hospital of the Maison Dieu in the village of Ospringe near Faversham in 1560.[92] Marlowe's father was born in Ospringe and grew up around Faversham before his enrolment as an apprentice in Canterbury in 1559. Coldwell became chaplain and personal physician to Archbishop Parker in 1569; Thomas Coldwell, whom Marlowe knew well as his junior at King's School and at Corpus Christi College, was probably his son.[93]

What seems more important than these speculations is the possibility that Marlowe learned about or even saw the rebuilding of Dover harbour when returning to Canterbury. He was away from Cambridge from April to June 1583, and again from July to December 1584, and came back home in August 1585 to help his friend John Benchkin secure his inheritance by signing the will of Benchkin's mother. Marlowe's signature appears next to that of Thomas Arthur, his uncle, who was born and grew up in Dover, and the news of the large enterprise and the influx of workmen into Dover was possibly circulating around Canterbury at that time.

Marlowe showed great interest in civil engineering and fortification technology. Tamburlaine tells his sons about the importance of technical expertise in military earthworks:

2001), pp. 119–38, finds 'striking similarities between the beliefs of the Family of Love and those of Scot'.

[91] Quoted in Kuriyama, *Christopher Marlowe*, p. 221.
[92] For biographical information on John Coldwell, see Penelope Rundle, 'Coldwell, John', *ODNB*; and C. H. Drake, 'The Hospital of St Mary of Ospringe, Commonly Called Maison Dieu', *AC*, 30 (1914), 35–78.
[93] Urry, *Marlowe and Canterbury*, p. 102.

> I'll teach you how to make the water mount,
> That you may dry-foot march through lakes and pools,
> Deep rivers, havens creeks, and little seas,
> And make a fortress in the raging waves,
> Fenced with the concave of a monstrous rock,
> Invincible by nature of the place. (*Two*, III.ii.85–90)

In composing this speech on the 'rudiments of war', Marlowe draws directly on Paul Ive's manual of military practices, *The Practise of Fortification* (1589), which was dedicated to Walsingham and William Brooke, Lord Cobham, the directors of the Dover harbour reconstruction. Unless he added the passage when *Tamburlaine* was published in 1590, Marlowe had possibly read Ive's work in manuscript form.[94] The hints that he had read *The Practise of Fortification* – in showing a keen interest in bulwarks and 'how to make the water mount' – allows us to assume that he had a vibrant curiosity in harmony with those Kentish technologically minded supervisors and craftsmen who worked on the harbour project.

It seems no mere coincidence that in 1584, the year following the successful construction of the pent, Walsingham sent Paul Ive to Dover, a man who had developed his expertise while constructing fortifications in the Low Countries, and put him in charge of building new groynes on the shingle bank to check erosion and drifting. The period of Ive's involvement in the project was comparatively short, for, in December 1585, Walsingham sent him back to the Low Countries to work as an intelligencer and surveyor.[95] However, we find Ive again in Kent, supervising work on the canal scheme in Canterbury, in September 1592, when Marlowe was at home to avoid the plague in London and when he became involved in the quarrel with William Corkine.[96] Although there is no evidence for Marlowe's association with Ive, it is highly possible that, given his technological bent for civil and military engineering, the playwright paid close attention to the workmanship of the Dover harbour project and gained a rapport with the empiricism of the minds behind it.

In August 1583, one month after the pent had been completed, John Whitgift was appointed as Archbishop of Canterbury and immediately launched a harsh crackdown on nonconformist clergy. Nicholas Faunt wrote dismally to Anthony Bacon on 20 November: 'The choice of that man

---

[94] Christopher Marlowe, *Tamburlaine the Great*, ed. Una M. Ellis-Fermor (1930; repr. New York: Gordian, 1966), pp. 8–10.

[95] For the life of Paul Ive, see Mark Eccles, 'Brief Lives: Tudor and Stuart Authors', *Studies in Philology*, 79:4 (1982), 1–135, at pp. 73–7. Ive's discharge is in TNA, SP, 12/175 fol. 81r.

[96] See Chapter 4, p. 135. Urry, *Marlowe and Canterbury*, p. 68.

at this time to be archbishop maketh me to think, that the Lord is determined to scourge his church for their unthankfulness.'[97] Faunt's premonition became a horrible reality to the godly ministers following Whitgift's demand for subscription to the Prayer Book. In January 1584, the ministers of Kent were called to subscribe, and seventeen non-subscribers were suspended. On 8 May, a delegation of twenty-five Kentish gentlemen led by Sir Thomas Scot descended upon Whitgift at Lambeth in order to protest on behalf of the deprived ministers and demand the lifting of the ban. This interview ended in disaster, and all departed angry except for Scot, 'who was impressed with the strength of the archbishop's case'.[98]

Recent scholarship has turned our attention to Reginald Scot's authorship of the report 'upon which Whitgift based his case against the Kentish ministers' in referring to the Privy Council, and argues for a similar switch of allegiance among his associates (i.e. Thomas Scot, Roger Manwood, and William Redman) to this Whitgiftian reaction.[99] We can therefore assume that Reginald, fashioning himself as the archbishop's watchdog over the extreme radicals who had supposedly incurred 'deadly hatred and bitter division' within the local communities,[100] was now setting his sights on them in order to expose their diabolical theatrics, just as Samuel Harsnet, a protégé of Richard Bancroft, did to puritan exorcists such as John Darrell.[101]

In focusing on Marlowe's intellectual sympathy with Scot and his Kentish associates, we should remember that, in *The Jew of Malta*, the playwright turned his perspicacious eye in a direction that Reginald Scot scarcely did in his later career, either as a defender of the Whitgiftian episcopal government or as the author of *The Discouerie of Witchcraft*. What was most extraordinary about Marlowe, compared to those Kentish Sadducean intellectuals who displayed their allegiance to Whitgift, was that he analysed the fiction-making strategies not only of political subversives such as Jews and Jesuits but also of the government itself, exposing its appropriation of theatrical strategies to delude a gullible public. As represented in

---

[97] Thomas Birch, *Memoirs of the Reign of Queen Elizabeth, from the Year 1581 till Her Death* (2 vols, London, 1754), vol. 1, p. 42.

[98] Patrick Collinson, *The Elizabethan Puritan Movement* (1967; repr. Oxford, 1990), p. 259.

[99] Peter Elmer, *Witchcraft, Witch-Hunting, and Politics in Early Modern England* (Oxford, 2016), pp. 18–19. A puritan supporter of the suspended ministers denounced Reginald Scot's report as 'a false and sclaunderous libell'. The contents of the report, which does not survive, can be reconstructed from the charges against Scot brought by his adversary. See Albert Peel (ed.), *The Seconde Parte of a Register, Being a Calendar of Manuscripts under that Title Intended for Publication by the Puritans about 1593* (2 vols, 1915; repr. Cambridge, 2010), vol. 1, pp. 230–41.

[100] Peel (ed.), *Seconde Parte of a Register*, vol. 1, p. 238.

[101] Paul H. Kocher, *Science and Religion in Elizabethan England* (San Marino, 1953), p. 132.

the theatrics of the governor of Malta, a political regime could apply the same tactics as those of playwrights and subversives, manipulating public opinion with ingenious fictions to consolidate its power. By ostensibly upholding the justice of providential retribution against a protean monster, Marlowe tacitly exposed the hypocrisy of the Maltese/English government and hinted at the fictitiousness of the ideas of nation and national identity. Thus, the military and ideological conflicts of the 1580s acquainted him with the power of theatrics in all its aspects, especially through his roles as a dramatist and an intelligencer, undertaken under serious financial pressure. Moreover, his orientation towards an empirical frame of mind encouraged a demystification of politico-religious discourse in terms of fiction-making, an attitude that naturally proved troublesome to the Church and to the political authorities.

Chapter 8

RAMISM, THOMAS NASHE, AND THE 'NEW SECTS OF SINGULARITIE'

Robert Norgate's memorandum titled 'The exercises of Learning in Corpus Christi Colledg in Cambridg every daye in the weke from the beginning of the terme until the ending thereof', found among the documents collected under NRS 23372, Z99, shows the college syllabus of a week at Corpus Christi.[1] At six in the morning, after morning prayers (and after the exegetical sermons on Wednesdays and Fridays), the students read Aristotle's *Natural Philosophy* and *Organon* and John Seton's *Dialectica* in the hall for an hour. At noon, they attended Greek lectures in construction and grammar based on the writings of Homer, Demosthenes, Hesiod, and Isocrates. At three o'clock they listened to Tully's lectures on rhetoric, and at four they began the practice of logic and rhetorical disputation. The core of the programme was thus founded on the *trivium* and markedly preserved the vestiges of the medieval scholastic system of education.[2]

Some scholars assume that, as a consequence of this kind of traditional and theologically oriented curriculum, disillusionment and boredom had been fermenting among the students; the university showed 'an almost total lack of anything to stimulate the imagination or encourage original thought', and the students were cramped 'by the Reformation and so much of Calvin, the boring Reformers, the excruciating tedium of theology, stuffed with logic-chopping and syllogisms and dialectic'.[3] Documents detailing disorder in the colleges and recording the repeated issuing of statutes are often considered as good evidence of this, as well as of the

---

[1] NRO, NRS 23373, Z99.
[2] On the traces of the medieval scholastic system in early modern Cambridge, see William T. Costello, *The Scholastic Curriculum at Early Seventeenth-Century Cambridge* (Cambridge, MA, 1958), pp. 7–35.
[3] Philip Henderson, *And Morning in His Eyes: A Book About Christopher Marlowe* (1937; repr. New York, 1972), p. 32; A. L. Rowse, *Christopher Marlowe: A Biography* (London, 1964), p. 35.

reluctance by the university administration to meet the supposed needs of an influx of students who were not necessarily headed for careers in the Church.[4] Superimposing the famous passage in *Doctor Faustus*, 'What doctrine call you this, *Che serà, serà*, / What will be, shall be? Divinity, adieu!',[5] on this theology-ridden atmosphere makes Faustus appear like a hero who stands in open rebellion confronting the crusty establishment of the university.

However, this interpretation of a heroic Faustus is a romantic illusion. The protagonist does not actually ponder what concerns him most as a research project. In terms of his academic interests, Aristotle's *Analytics* is stimulating enough, as he is happy to 'live and die in Aristotle's works. Sweet *Analytics*, 'tis thou hast ravished me!' (A-text: 1.i.5–6). Rather than demonstrating an idealistic stand, then, Faustus is making a materialistic enquiry, with a foregone conclusion, about what form of art might be most effective in helping him to obtain 'a world of profit and delight, / Of power, of honour, of omnipotence' (A-text: 1.i.55–6). The familiar curriculum was not at issue. Moreover, an arts course in the sixteenth century was not necessarily an outdated educational model, as the new paradigm of humanism was brought into the old one of medieval scholasticism.[6] As Lisa Jardine points out, as a direct response to the needs of the new type of student, 'the focus of the arts course shifted squarely on to the "art of discourse", as the universal, indispensable basis for training in all professional fields, including teaching'.[7] John Seton's popular textbook *Dialectica*, first printed in 1545, was one of the specimens for reorganizing the traditional method of teaching dialectics and was intended to provide a humanist praxis for analysing all kinds of discourse.

---

[4] For the reluctance to accept new ideas and to assimilate them into the curriculum, see Kenneth Charlton, *Education in Renaissance England* (London, 1965), pp. 151–3; and Christopher Hill, *Intellectual Origins of the English Revolution* (Oxford, 1965), appendix.

[5] Christopher Marlowe, *Doctor Faustus*, ed. David Bevington and Eric Rasmussen, *The Revels Plays* (Manchester, 1992), A-text: 1.i.49–50. Subsequent references to *Doctor Faustus* will be to this edition and will appear parenthetically in the text by version, act, scene, and line number.

[6] Lawrence Stone, 'The Educational Revolution in England, 1560–1640', *Past & Present*, 28:1 (1964), 41–80, at p. 76.

[7] Lisa Jardine, 'The Place of Dialectic Teaching in Sixteenth-Century Cambridge', *Studies in the Renaissance*, 21 (1974), 31–62, at p. 60. See also her 'Humanism and the Sixteenth Century Cambridge Arts Course', *History of Education*, 4:1 (1975), 16–31; and Margo Todd, *Christian Humanism and the Puritan Social Order* (Cambridge, 1987), pp. 61–3.

FEVERISH DISPUTE AND 'FACTIONS IN ART'

In fact, a lecture room debating Aristotle's dialectics or Cicero's rhetoric, though admittedly far from satisfying all kinds of audience, could be an arena for heated discussions, and often infused youthful minds with intellectual excitement. The young had a particularly acute sensitivity to new approaches to dialectics and rhetoric such as those proposed by Peter Ramus, the Regius Professor at the Collège de France and master of the college of Presles, who criticized the complex methodology of Aristotle and turned it into a practical technique of discoursing well.[8] There is every reason to believe Gabriel Harvey's testimony about his own jam-packed commencement address in 1574, his first year as Praelector of Rhetoric, introducing the latest Ramist praxis that may have strongly appealed to young novelty-lovers in Cambridge:

> Last year, to be sure, I expected (why should I pretend?) a crowded and well attended meeting of all the Colleges and Inns, and my expectations did not deceive me. All the benches were full, a full lecture. Scholars of all ranks and ages were present. We saw a ring around us, as in the Roman election places; we saw a great crowd as in the forum; we saw excited spectators and listeners as in a public theatre. And no wonder! Novelty itself procured an audience for me.[9]

The extraordinary publication of Harvey's lectures, *Rhetor* (1577) and *Ciceronianus* (1577), by Henry Bynneman, the prestigious stationer of London, demonstrates his popularity and the air of excitement that would have attended them in the lecture hall. For Harvey, Ramus was 'a man of the keenest sort both in native talent and in judgment', who had successfully worked towards the practical use of rhetoric and who had enlightened him on 'how dangerous it is for one enslaved to prejudiced opinions to take shelter in the authority of this or that group of men'.[10] Hence, while avoiding traditional Aristotelian terms such as 'topics' and 'loci', Harvey introduced Ramus' 'method' into his pedagogy to achieve mastery of Ciceronian eloquence and methods of argument with logical preciseness, employing the 'analysis' of logical and rhetorical elements in discourse and the 'genesis'

---

[8] For Ramus' zeal to reform the liberal arts, see James Veazie Skalnik, *Ramus and Reform: University and Church at the End of Renaissance* (Kirksville, MO, 2002), pp. 41–62.

[9] Gabriel Harvey, *Gabrielis Harueij Rhetor* (London, 1577), sigs A1r–A2r. Cited from Robert M. Chandler's translation in 'Gabriel Harvey's *Rhetor*: A Translation and Critical Edition' (unpublished PhD dissertation, University of Missouri-Columbia, 1978), p. 26.

[10] *Gabriel Harvey's Ciceronianus*, intro. Harold S. Wilson and trans. Clarence A. Forbes (Lincoln, NE, 1945), p. 71.

(or composition) of discourse by reassembling those elements in his own configurations.[11]

The enthusiasm for Ramist logic and rhetoric was shared by his contemporaries. For instance, Lawrence Chaderton of Christ's College, where Harvey had spent his undergraduate days, also read logic in the public schools in the 1570s and, 'lecturing on the *Ars logica* of Peter Ramus, roused a great interest in that study through the University'.[12] Abraham Tilman, fellow of Corpus Christi and Marlowe's close acquaintance, had in his library not only Aristotle's and Cicero's *Rhetoric* but also Ramus' *Dialecticae libri duo*, Johannes Piscator's edition of Ramus' *Dialecticae libri duo*, and *Rhetorica, una cum* [...] *commentationibus per Claudium Minoem* by Audomarus Taleus, Ramus' close ally.[13] Harvey seems to have ingeniously caught the prevailing intellectual wind blowing in the university.

What the spread of Ramus' methodology effected was not a total reinvention of the arts course curriculum or a dramatic revolution in forms of communication but rather the sharply divided reactions that aroused strong rivalries and gave impetus to the drive for factional solidarity among the collegiate communities. John Case, a fellow of Oxford, describes in his *Speculum moralium qvaestionum* (1585) the general atmosphere at the university, where violent arguments broke out over Ramism: 'Still I cannot but acknowledge that the youthful ardor of mind in both universities has of late been fighting it out to determine whether in the mastering of the arts the great acuteness of Aristotle is of more worth than the flowing genius of Ramus.'[14] This 'youthful ardor of mind' often sparked emotional, political, and religious conflicts between communities; and the wildfires in the arena of rhetoric eventually engulfed politics, theology, and even the university administration. As Mordechai Feingold points out, Ramism was 'turned

---

[11] For Ramist 'analysis' and 'genesis', see Walter J. Ong, *Ramus, Method, and the Decay of Dialogue* (Cambridge, 1958), pp. 263–7; Harold S. Wilson, 'Introduction', in Harvey, *Ciceronianus*, pp. 28–9.

[12] Richard Farmer, *Laurence Chaderton, D.D. Translated from a Latin Memoir of Dr. Dillingham with Notes and Illustrations* (Cambridge, 1884), p. 5. For the spread of Ramist rhetoric in Cambridge, see Wilbur Samuel Howell, *Logic and Rhetoric in England, 1500–1700* (New York, 1961), pp. 247–81; and John Charles Adams, 'Gabriel Harvey's *Ciceronianus* and the Place of Peter Ramus' *Dialecticae Libri Duo* in the Curriculum', *Renaissance Quarterly*, 43:3 (1990), 551–69.

[13] For Abraham Tilman's library, see Elisabeth S. Leedham-Green, *Books in Cambridge Inventories: Book-Lists from Vice-Chancellor's Court Probate Inventories in the Tudor and Stuart Periods* (2 vols, Cambridge, 1986), vol. 1, pp. 481–3.

[14] John Case, *Speculum Moralium Quaestionum* (Oxford, 1585), sig. ¶4r–v. The translation is from Howell, *Logic and Rhetoric*, p. 190.

into a wanton vehicle for fomenting disputes' and, provoking the authorities' hostility, 'served as an extension of religious militancy'.[15]

The hostility towards Ramism was one of the reasons why Harvey suffered hardship in 1573, a year before he was elected praelector, when some of his peers at Pembroke Hall declared against him receiving his MA degree. Harvey may have been isolated within the college as an outsider, having been elected to the fellowship at Pembroke through the influence of Sir Thomas Smyth, principal secretary to the queen, who, like him, came from Saffron Walden. The ringleader of the anti-Harvey camp was Thomas Neville, the fellow who had supported John Marley of Canterbury in the vice-chancellor's court in the dispute over William Austen's cloak.[16] In a letter dated 21 March 1573 appealing to John Young, the master of Pembroke, for support, Harvey claims that Neville had declared him to be 'A great and continual patron of paradoxis, and A main defender of straung opinions, and that communly against Aristotle too'. At the same time, Harvey believed that his 'arroganci and disdainfulnes' (though he says he is 'falsly chargid') gave impetus to his peers' antipathy towards him.[17] He later reminisced about the incident: 'I was then yong in yeares, fresh in courage, greene in experience, and as the manner is, somewhat ouerweening in conceit.'[18] Thus, the emotional conflict within the tight-knit community, fuelled by the wider conflict concerning the new trend of Ramism, developed into administrative sanctions against Harvey that led to the suspension of his MA degree.

This competitive, disputatious atmosphere concerning Ramism extended to the core of religious confrontation within the university, the intensely heated controversy provoked by Protestant radicals in the 1570s. For a university fellow or scholar, theology – which Faustus considered to be the 'best' means to obtain his end – was not deskbound discussion but something more closely involved with his intellectual attitude, accruing of comrades, and future career. His theological and ecclesiological stance substantially affected not only his choice of friends and patrons but also his involvement with society, the Church, and the state. In this sense, as Mark H. Curtis argues, the vast majority of university members 'possessed lively interests in religious matters and an immense appetite for lengthy religious discourses. They

---

[15] Mordechai Feingold, 'English Ramism: A Reinterpretation', in Mordechai Feingold, Joseph S. Freedman, and Wolfgang Rother (eds), *The Influence of Peter Ramus: Studies in Sixteenth and Seventeenth Century Philosophy and Sciences* (Basel, 2001), pp. 127–76, at pp. 146–7.
[16] See Chapter 2, pp. 67–8, and Appendix 3.
[17] BL, Sloane MS 93, fols 4r, 6r.
[18] Gabriel Harvey, *Four Letters, and Certaine Sonnets*, in Alexander B. Grosart (ed.), *The Works of Gabriel Harvey* (3 vols, 1884; repr. New York, 1966), vol. 1, p. 178.

enthusiastically attended the sermons and lectures of popular preachers and professors'.[19] In fact, we can find in a letter of Archbishop Grindal a report complaining about the popularity of Thomas Cartwright, fellow of Trinity College and reader of the Lady Margaret's Lecture:

> who, as I am very credibly informed, maketh in his Lectures daily invections against the extern policy and distinction of states, in the ecclesiastical government of this realm. [...] The youth of the University, which is at this time very toward in learning, doth frequent his Lectures in great numbers; and therefore in danger to be poisoned by him with love of contention and liking of novelties; and so become hereafter, not only unprofitable, but also hurtful to the Church.[20]

Enthusiasm for 'novelties' turned the lecture room, the pulpit at Great St Mary, and the chapel where college fellows delivered morning sermons, into places of agitation and dispute. The Act Books of the vice-chancellor's court contain numerous records of fellows and scholars who openly criticized the authorities in their sermons and debates without fearing punishment. Owing to intense fears about the new threats Ramism posed to established ways of thinking, it was frequently associated with religious radicalism, and was regarded as inciting the tumultuous heat and excitement of debate.[21] This disputatious atmosphere could transform an ambitious youth, whether conservative or radical, into a contentious polemicist or, to borrow Marlowe's phrase, 'a bold sharp sophister' (*Hero and Leander*, I.197).

Gabriel Harvey was not the only man who had 'floted in a sea of encountring waues; and deuoured many famous confutations, with an eager, and insatiable appetite'.[22] Thomas Nashe was similarly caught up in the feverish mood at Cambridge, and transplanted its turmoil into the print culture in London by launching invectives against 'absurditie' in the arts and Martin Marprelate's libels. The authorities were not able to identify Martin, the bold anonymous radical, but it is interesting that most of those who came under suspicion in the initial investigation were radicals with Cambridge backgrounds who were notorious for their controversial opinions and

---

[19] Mark H. Curtis, *Oxford and Cambridge in Transition 1558–1642* (Oxford, 1959), p. 186. See also Stone, 'Educational Revolution in England', p. 80.

[20] John Strype, *The History of the Life and Acts of the Most Reverend Father in God, Edmund Grindal* (Oxford, 1821), pp. 240–1.

[21] For intellectual similarities between puritanism and Ramism, see Frances A. Yates, *The Art of Memory* (London, 1966), pp. 273–84; Donald K. McKim, *Ramism in William Perkins' Theology* (New York, 1987), pp. 43–50; and Feingold, 'English Ramism', pp. 146–7.

[22] Grosart (ed.), *Works of Gabriel Harvey*, vol. 2, p. 45.

publications by that time.[23] In *An Almond for a Parrat* (1590), Nashe, employed by Richard Bancroft as an anti-Martinist, slanders John Penry, widely taken to be the author of Marprelate pamphlets:

> For whiles hee was yet a fresh man in Peterhouse, and had scarce tasted, as we say, of *Setons modalibus*, he began to affect factions in art, & shew himselfe openly a studious disgracer of antiquitie. Who then such an vnnatural enemie to *Aristotle*, or such a new-fa[n]gled friend vnto *Ramus*? This one thing I am sure of, hee neuer went for other then an asse amongst his companions and equalles, yet such a mutinous block-head was he alwaies accounted that through town and Colledge he was co[m]monly called the seditious dunce.[24]

Nashe equates Penry's puritanism with Ramism for its 'new-fangled', 'mutinous', and 'seditious' nature, and associates the differences in rhetorical pedagogy between Aristotle and Ramus with the religio-political opposition between the defenders of the established ideas of 'antiquitie' and those fundamental radicals who raised an outcry against them. What seems unique here is that Nashe himself shared their intense enthusiasm for affecting 'factions in art', shown by the fact that his penchant for university gossip, his fierce reaction to Ramism, and his religio-political belligerence against puritanism were all merged into an angry torrent of sarcastic criticism directed against his enemies. His vocal attacks on Martinists, and his harsh criticisms of Gabriel Harvey, were in this regard an extension of practices that had become normalized in the communities of the university.

MARLOWE AND RELIGIOUS RADICALISM AT CORPUS CHRISTI COLLEGE

What Marlowe depicted in the murder of Ramus in *The Massacre at Paris*, then, was this flammable milieu where rhetorical, religious, and political views were too explosive to air. Nothing has survived documenting the incident except for very brief accounts in some possible sourcebooks such as *Mémoires de l'état de France sous Charles neuvième* (1576), and *Le Tocsin contre les Massacreurs* (1579), and so the comparatively long scene dramatizing Ramus' death suggests Marlowe's own interest in the eminent liberal arts scholar. The location that the playwright chose for the murder scene

---

[23] Those are Giles Wigginton (Trinity College: BA 1568–89, MA 1572, Fellow 1571); Henry Barrow (Clare Hall: BA 1569–70); Francis Marbury (Christ's College: matric. 1571); John Penry (Peterhouse: BA 1583–84); and John Udall (Christ's College: BA from Trinity 1580–81, MA 1584).
[24] Ronald B. McKerrow (ed.), *The Works of Thomas Nashe*, 2nd edn, rev. F. P. Wilson (5 vols, Oxford, 1958), vol. 3, pp. 367–8.

was Ramus' study, presumably at the college of Presles, as the *Mémoires* specifies, where Ramus had been in hiding. Audomarus Taleus, with whom Ramus shares his room and bed like a pensioner at Cambridge, warns him against the Guisians, who are 'hard at thy door and mean to murder us',[25] and leaps out of the window, though the presence of Taleus in the play is anachronistic because he had died ten years before the massacre.[26] Ramus remains in his study to confront the Duke of Guise, who bursts into the room accompanying his allies. Ramus asks him 'wherein hath Ramus been so offensious?'. Guise presses him hard, demanding that he surrender his life, as if wishing to silence his opponent's argument in a public disputation by ironically using the terminology of logic:

> Was it not thou that scoff'dst the *Organon*
> And said it was a heap of vanities?
> He that will be a flat dichotomist
> And seen in nothing but epitomes
> Is in your judgment thought a learned man;
> And he, forsooth, must go and preach in Germany,
> Excepting against doctors' actions
> And *ipse dixi* with this quiddity:
> *Argumentum testimonii est inartificiale.*
> To contradict which, I say: Ramus shall die.
> How answer you that? Your *nego argumentum*
> Cannot serve, sirrah. – Kill him. (IX.26–37)

Guise's menacing speech suggests that Marlowe had a thorough knowledge of the nature and vehemence of the Ramist controversies, and some scholars have even detected anti-Ramist and anti-puritan attitudes in its derisive tone as reflecting Marlowe's own beliefs. For instance, Feingold declares that 'Marlowe, I believe, was deliberate when he made the Guise denounce the poverty of Ramus' logic and his corrupting influence on learning. At the same time, Marlowe also targeted the Puritans who stand accused of similar crimes'.[27] However, there is no way of knowing based on this scene whether Marlowe's attitude was actually similar to that of Nashe, an explicitly anti-Ramist Aristotelian, for the poet gives Ramus the

---

[25] Christopher Marlowe, *Dido Queen of Carthage and The Massacre at Paris*, ed. H. J. Oliver, The Revels Plays (London, 1968), ix.8. Subsequent references to *The Massacre at Paris* will be to this edition and will appear parenthetically in the text by scene and line number.

[26] Marlowe may well have known that Taleus was dead when Ramus was killed. See John Roland Glenn, 'The Martyrdom of Ramus in Marlowe's *The Massacre at Paris*', Papers on Language and Literature, 9:4 (1973), 365–79, at pp. 371–2.

[27] Feingold, 'English Ramism', p. 166, n. 79.

opportunity to make a counterargument against Guise, and explains the crucial role that Ramus played in the scholarly realm of Aristotelian logic:

> I knew the *Organon* to be confus'd
> And I reduc'd it into better form;
> And this for Aristotle will I say,
> That he that despiseth him can ne'er
> Be good in logic or philosophy:
> And that's because the blockish Sorbonnists
> Attribute as much unto their works
> As to the service of the eternal God. (ix.45–52)

Moreover, while both the *Mémoires* and *Le Tocsin* give a brief account of the fact that Ramus in vain paid the assassins a large sum of money to spare his life, the play obviously makes Ramus more 'courageous and dignified' by representing him as a poor pensioner who has no money to give: 'Alas, I am a scholar, how should I have gold? / All that I have is but my stipend from the King, / Which is no sooner receiv'd but it is spent' (ix.17–19).[28]

This scene thus shows not Marlowe's intellectual attitude towards dialectics, but his own peculiar way of representing the religious war as an extension and intensification of university disputes on logic, rhetoric, and divinity. He transforms the ordinary experiences in the college communities – where furious outbursts of emotion, spurred on by the enthusiasm of the 'factions' in art, politics, and religion, often spilled over into violence in word and deed – into a grotesque experience of violence in the religious war represented on the stage.[29] It is therefore wrong to assume that a theologically oriented arts course lacked anything that could stimulate Marlowe's imagination and intellectual curiosity. Rather, it seems that Marlowe was inspired by the radical ideas of dialectics and ecclesiology, as well as by the literary works of ancient Greece and Rome. At the same time, his representation of Ramus' murder in the massacre suggests that he considered the conflicts between the factions in the university as a religious war in miniature. He may have understood the nature of these controversies as a matter of politico-religious factionalism, as well as of belief or thought, that would sway the destiny of a poor scholar.

Several incidents that occurred at Corpus Christi in the 1580s (such as those involving Robert Thexton, struck on the head and injured while attending a stage production at Pembroke Hall; Tobias Bland, banished for

---

[28] Vivien Thomas and William Tydeman, *Christopher Marlowe: The Plays and Their Sources* (London, 1994), p. 255.

[29] G. M. Pinciss, 'Marlowe's Cambridge Years and the Writing of *Doctor Faustus*', *SEL*, 33:2 (1993), 249–64, highlights the influence of the disputatious atmosphere of Cambridge upon Marlowe's plays.

his libel against the college master and Walsingham; Anthony Hickman, violently dragged out of his room and expelled from the college, etc.) suggest that Marlowe had daily experienced such religious wars in miniature. Moreover, religious radicalism was very close to him, not simply as a prevailing ideology but as experienced in his relationships with friends, who were either hostile or committed to it. Although the enthusiasm of Corpus's radical generation under the mastership of Thomas Aldrich had receded into the background by the 1580s, this does not necessarily mean that intellectual defiance of the ecclesiastical authorities had been totally stamped out in and around the college.

A good illustration of this is John Greenwood, one of the followers of the extreme radical wing of puritanism (here termed 'separatist', according to a scholarly tradition of ecclesiastical history). Greenwood emerged from the cultural and social environment of the radical Norwich clusters in the college and fully embodied its martyrdom mentality, as Nathaniel Woodes delineates in *The Conflict of Conscience*.[30] His origin cannot be identified, but he might have been related to one 'Mr Grenewood', the schoolmaster of Aylsham, who counted Robert Harrison among 'his dearest freindes' in the town.[31] It is also unclear when Greenwood became a follower of separatism. As Patrick Collinson points out, however, 'the tendency of the Church to divide into puritan and anti-puritan factions equally had its beginnings in the universities'.[32] Nor can we ignore the influence of Robert Browne, who had been preaching since 1579 in Cambridge and at St Bene't's church adjoining Corpus Christi College (that is, during Greenwood's residence as an undergraduate student), witnessing 'that wofull state of Cambridge, whereinto those wicked prelats and doctors of diuinitie haue brought it'. According to Browne's reminiscences, his sermon impressed the parishioners of St Bene't's so much that 'they gathered him a stipend, & woulde haue had hime take charge'.[33] That his influence lingered among the college community long after he left for Norwich is demonstrated by the fact that in April 1583 the university vice-chancellor commanded one Richard Taylor, the vicar of Thorney in Nottinghamshire and bachelor of Corpus Christi, to appear before him to provide information about where Browne could be found and arrested.[34]

---

[30] See Chapter 1, pp. 47–50.
[31] R. A. Houlbrooke (ed.), *The Letter Book of John Parkhurst, Bishop of Norwich* (Norwich, 1974), p. 196.
[32] Patrick Collinson, *The Elizabethan Puritan Movement* (1967; repr. Oxford, 1990), p. 129.
[33] Albert Peel and Leland H. Carlson (eds), *The Writings of Robert Harrison and Robert Browne* (London, 1953), p. 404.
[34] CUA, Collect. Admin. 6a [Caryl B. 24], Buckle Book, p. 234.

Admittedly, Greenwood's testimony that he owed no doctrinal debt to Browne or to his writings prevents us from reaching rash conclusions as to the strength of their bond of faith and friendship.[35] It needs to be stressed, however, that Greenwood, while abhorring Browne for making peace with Archbishop Whitgift in 1586, on the occasion of his appointment as schoolmaster at St Olave's School, Southwark based on the condition that he submit to the Church, obviously shared a fundamental notion of ecclesiology with him.[36] Stephen Bredwell, in his confutation against Brownism, explained the reason for their differences:

> In doctrine I knowe they differ, but diuersitie of practise was cause thereof. *Barow* and *Greenewood* nakedly discouered their profession, and are prisoners. *Browne* cunningly counterfeiteth conformitie, & dissembleth with his owne soule, for libertie. They fullie beleeuing, the Church of England to be no Church of God [...] made conscience to separate themselues at all poynts, accordingly.[37]

Greenwood, like Browne, insisted on the authority of scripture, regarding the Apostolic Church described in the New Testament 'as the golden norm by which all later church structures and constitutions must be tested'.[38] The zeal to obey God's words at a fundamental level and to reconstruct the 'true Church' based on the literal reading of scripture allowed these separatists to be bold enough to deviate from the orthodox reading which the established Church had preached from the pulpit. The one who guided them to the right way of reading was neither a prelate nor a preacher; instead, it was their prophetic spirit directed from within by the Holy Spirit.

During his residence at Corpus Christi, Greenwood obviously became acquainted with Marlowe. Around 1581, Greenwood is likely to have suffered financial embarrassment, for he was a sizar without the aid of any college scholarship and, after obtaining his BA, must have been busy – as were other students in similar conditions – seeking congenial employment. The college's Buttery Book shows that Greenwood remained at Corpus through the vacation term of 1581.[39] In rare cases, students who received a scholar's stipend might give up their share of the provisions to which

---

[35] Leland H. Carlson (ed.), *The Writings of John Greenwood 1587–1590* (London, 1962), pp. 58–9.

[36] B. R. White, *The English Separatist Tradition: From the Marian Martyrs to the Pilgrim Fathers* (Oxford, 1971), pp. 67–90.

[37] Stephen Bredwell, *The Rasing of the Foundations of Brownisme* (London, 1588), sig. A1r.

[38] White, *English Separatist Tradition*, p. 53.

[39] He paid 8d. in 9a post John Baptist 1581: see CCCA, CCCC02/S/29, Buttery Book 1579–82.

they were entitled to destitute fellow students as a favour, and it was during his absence that term that Marlowe the freshman yielded his place in the commons to Greenwood. The Buttery Book registers the charge of 16 pence to Marlowe's account with the note: 'for putting Sr Grenewood in com[m]ons'.[40] Constance Kuriyama assumes that Marlowe 'offered this impressive person access to the inexpensive fare of his old college as a means of learning more about him'.[41] There is no knowing what Marlowe learned, but it is reasonable to think that the college community was acting as a politico-religious catalyst by giving its members these sorts of opportunities for stimulating personal contact and encouraging young ambitious wits to cultivate radical insights into the discourses of the ecclesiastical authorities.

The well-trodden route of the Corpus–Norwich connection opened for Greenwood a similar career path to that of his radical seniors. After leaving Cambridge, he took the decision, as Harrison and Browne had done, to stay in the vicinity of Norwich, serving as a curate in Norfolk, possibly in Rackheath, six miles from the city, until about September 1585. This career path seems to have been natural for a religious radical to take because at that time there were still several powerful aldermen who were well disposed towards radical remnants in Norwich. What distinguishes Greenwood from other separatists is that, after holding the curacy for several years, he travelled to London to secure his foothold, and there made the presence of separatism known among the citizens by professing his faith in public.[42] It is unlikely that Greenwood came to London to cultivate new devotees of separatism on his own account, for there are traces of a separatist congregation there early in 1559.[43] John Field, the organizer of London conventicles in the 1570s, is reported to have said that 'in beating this new reformation into the heads of the common people [...] seeing we cannot compasse these things, by suite nor dispute: it is the multitude and people, that must bring them to passe'.[44] This evidence suggests that there was potential demand among the urban flock for an enthusiastic and highly educated mentor at the time of Greenwood's arrival.

Greenwood came to the fore as a spiritual leader of the London conventicle as a result of his arrest along with his followers on 8 October 1587 in the

---

[40] *Ibid.*, 4a post John Baptist 1581. Marlowe also 'left peetres in co[m]mons being absent' in 1a post John Baptist 1581.
[41] Constance Brown Kuriyama, *Christopher Marlowe: A Renaissance Life* (Ithaca, 2002), pp. 57–8.
[42] Bredwell, *Rasing of the Foundations*, sig. A1r.
[43] R. Tudur Jones with Arthur Long and Rosemary Moore (eds), *Protestant Nonconformist Texts Volume 1: 1550–1700* (2007; repr. Eugene, OR, 2015), pp. 19–20.
[44] Richard Bancroft, *Dangerous Positions and Proceedings* (London, 1593), book 4, chap. 2, p. 135.

midst of the Tamburlaine craze. Henry Barrow, his Cambridge (and possibly Corpus Christi) associate,[45] was also arrested, about a month later, when he went up to London from Norfolk to visit Greenwood and his followers in the Clink in Southwark. Even though they were imprisoned for years, the writings of Barrow and Greenwood were clandestinely published and possibly circulated among their followers to articulate discontent with the established Church among the populace. Their defiant attitude towards the ecclesiastical authorities in a series of interrogations and examinations, the transcripts of which were produced by Barrow and Greenwood themselves and posthumously published, ultimately led to their execution.[46] It is worth noting that among their followers confined in Bridewell around 1590 we find Richard Umberfield and John Cranford, who bore the names of former apprentices of Marlowe's father, the shoemaker in Canterbury.[47] On 6 April 1593, two weeks before Marlowe's arrest at Scadbury, Greenwood and Barrow were hanged at Tyburn. The conjunction of events, though merely coincidental, does seem worthy of our attention when we gauge the intellectual and empirical distance between Marlowe and religious radicalism.

What is most important here is the fact that Greenwood, along with his separatist followers, cast himself as a Foxeian martyr and directed his censure towards the 'popish' bishops of the established Church. Richard Verstegan, a militant Catholic in Antwerp, reported with detachment in his letter addressed to Father Robert Persons on the executions of Greenwood and Barrow: 'they came againe early to place using lyke long protestation of prayers, and thirsting after drinck, which presently was in a redynesse for them, they died obstinately. Their followers canonizing them for more then martirs, do enveighe privately against the bishopes as the princiapll procurers thereof.'[48] Admittedly, it is a stretch to argue that Greenwood's orientation towards Foxeian martyrdom in order to confront episcopal tyranny was cultivated in his collegiate years, as there is no evidence to support this assumption. However, the driving energy cultivated among the

---

[45] Robert Masters, *The History of the College of Corpus Christi* (Cambridge, 1753–55), pp. 227–9, suggests Barrow's residence at Corpus Christi.

[46] For the transcripts, see Henry Barrow, *The Examinations of Henry Barrowe Iohn Grenewood and Iohn Penrie, before the High Commissioners, and Lordes of the Counsel* (n.p., 1596).

[47] Carlson (ed.), *Writings of John Greenwood*, pp. 119, 322, 323–5, 330, 331. Umberfield was accused in 1570 of making a local woman pregnant and later left Canterbury. John Cranford was married to Marlowe's sister, Anne, in June 1593. See William Urry, *Christopher Marlowe and Canterbury*, ed. with an introduction by Andrew Butcher (London, 1988), p. 23.

[48] Anthony G. Petti (ed.), *The Letters and Despatches of Richard Verstegan* (London, 1959), p. 151.

radicals linking Corpus Christi with the municipal corporation of Norwich seems to have permeated Nathaniel Woodes's Foxeian martyrological rhetoric for spurring martyr-like resolution, and likewise Greenwood's self-representation as a martyr-saint persecuted under the 'false Church'. The origin of such anti-episcopal sentiments shared by Woodes and Greenwood can be traced back to the radical faction of Thomas Aldrich, the Norwich-oriented fellows and scholars influenced by Thomas Cartwright in the early 1570s. Even after Aldrich's resignation, the residual discourse of contesting episcopal tyranny seems to have been primed for activation throughout the decade and to have formed a part of the cultural experiences and meanings within the college community. And it was this driving energy of fervent religious radicalism that Marlowe ingeniously employed to create Tamburlaine, the militant leader of prophetic oratory.

CONSTRUCTING THE 'NEW SECTS OF SINGULARITIE'

Patrick Collinson calls the 1590s an 'ugly decade' that launched the Martin Marprelate controversies, full of mockery and satirical barbs, and ended with the bishops' ban forbidding the printing of satires and epigrams. The 'torrent of fictions' helped audiences and readers to identify, scoff at, and demonize the putative politico-religious enemy in their midst; eventually, the paradigms that those fictions employed in order to construct and manipulate reality 'became part of the reality they structured and used'.[49] What made the nineties 'ugly' was precisely the poisonous discourses that originated from the flammable and disputatious atmosphere in Cambridge and that led to the invention of a variety of heretical monsters on stage and in print.

The government's increasingly vigorous repression of godly radicals in the 1590s was obviously triggered by the series of libels published by Martin Marprelate in 1588–89 and the 'conspiracy' of William Hacket, a religious fanatic who claimed to be the Messiah, in 1591. In *The Plea of the Innocent* (1602), the godly divine Josias Nichols complains that 'three most greeuous accidentes' that did 'verie much darken the righteousnes of our cause' were Martin Marprelate, the Brownists, and Hacket.[50] The frightening threat that the separatists posed to the authorities was obviously serious, judging from the fact that, on the heels of the publication of the Marprelate libels, the High Commissioners, who operated under the leadership of Richard

---

[49] Patrick Collinson, 'Ecclesiastical Vitriol: Religious Satire in the 1590s and the Invention of Puritanism', in John Guy (ed.), *The Reign of Elizabeth I: Court and Culture in the Last Decade* (Cambridge, 1995), pp. 150–70, at p. 169.

[50] Josias Nichols, *The Plea of the Innocent Wherein Is Auerred* (London, 1602), sigs D5r–D6v.

Bancroft, delivered to every parish in the Diocese of London an injunction forbidding the reception of irregular preachers in March 1589 and, in the following year, set out to imprison the leading Presbyterian ministers including Thomas Cartwright.[51]

What seemed dangerous to the Church about these religious radicals was, according to Bancroft, their alliance with 'the laie factious'.[52] In fact, the separatists of London do seem to have had a relatively strong connection with the citizens. Verstegan, in his report of the execution of Barrow and Greenwood, wrote:

> It seemeth that the officers durst not execute them by reason of the great multytude of Puritanes there present, as also flocking together in the City of London, who began openly to murmur and to give oute threatning speeches, insomuch that a presente commotion was feared, and what may yet follow is doubtfull, considering the heate of those purified spirites.[53]

The worst fears of the authorities – that these dangerous radicals would become closely allied in an uprising with the vast mass of the populace – were realized in the incident involving William Hacket.[54] On 16 July 1591, Edmund Coppinger and Henry Arthington, 'two prophets', came into Cheapside, and from a cart gave a frantic cry for repentance that attracted a 'mightie concourse of the common multitude'. They proclaimed that Hacket, an illiterate maltmaker, 'represented *Christ*, by partaking a part of his glorious body: by his principall spirit' and made a prophecy of judgement against London that 'men should (there) kill and massacre one another (as Butchers do kill swyne) all the day long, and no man shoulde take compassion of them'.[55] Moreover, they declared themselves messengers bringing a new reformation of the city and cursed Archbishop Whitgift and the chancellor, Christopher Hatton, condemning them 'to the pit of hell,

---

[51] Collinson, *Elizabethan Puritan Movement*, pp. 404–5. See also Peter Lake, *Anglicans and Puritans? Presbyterianism and English Conformist Thought* (London, 1988), pp. 111–13. For the role the High Commissioners played, see Roland G. Usher, *The Rise and Fall of the High Commission*, with intro. by Philip Tyler (Oxford, 1968), pp. xxix and 71.

[52] Richard Bancroft, *A Sermon Preached at Paules Crosse the 9. of Februarie* (London, 1588), p. 24.

[53] Petti (ed.), *Letters and Despatches of Richard Verstegan*, p. 131.

[54] For a full account of this incident, see Alexandra Walsham, '"Frantick Hacket": Prophecy, Sorcery, Insanity, and the Elizabethan Puritan Movement', *Historical Journal*, 41:1 (1998), 27–66.

[55] Richard Cosin, *Conspiracy for Pretended Reformation: viz. Presbyterial Discipline* (London, 1592), pp. 56–7.

as Opposers of the sincere Religion.'[56] The suppression and arrest of these fanatics by armed soldiers made the commotion fizzle out in a few hours.

George Paule, the comptroller of Whitgift's household, was extremely careful to represent these religious radicals as conspirators acting under the pretence of reforming the Church, and associated them with those 'promoters of this reformation' currently in prison, 'Amongst whom there were very forward to the like presumption *Henry Barrow*, Gentleman, and *Iohn Greenwood*, Clearke'.[57] Thomas Rogers, chaplain to Sir Christopher Hatton and Richard Bancroft, took the same line of argument: 'Without the prince, the people may reforme the Church and must not tarrie for the magistrate: so thought Barrow, Greenewood, and Wigginton. Hence Hackets, Coppingers, and Arthingtons insurrection at London, an. 1591.'[58] Thus, a pressing issue for the establishment authorities was to prevent the infection of the schismatic 'heresy' from spreading, which they achieved by oppressing the separatists, alerting the populace to the virulence of the heresy, and inventing the monstrosity of these 'conspirators' by mobilizing propaganda, rather than by investigating their opinions closely through a carefully managed legal process.

What is noteworthy here is the cultural process of inventing and reinventing a character type through multi-layered discourses in order to slander and demonize a person or faction, accusing either of religiously subversive tendencies. The most well-documented and investigated case is that of the stage puritan, a figure that can be traced back to the Martin Marprelate controversy.[59] Kristen Poole points out the cultural significance of this incident: 'the Marprelate controversy spawned a new mode of representing religious zeal. In both textual and theatrical representations, religious nonconformity was now portrayed primarily through the images and language of the grotesque.'[60]

In this process of constructing puritanism, the role that Richard Bancroft played cannot be overlooked. He initiated the determined campaign of the anti-Martinists to smear Marprelate in a similar manner to Martin's own ribald writing, and abundantly demonstrated his journalistic capacity to

---

[56] William Camden, *The Historie of the Most Renowned and Victorious Princesse Elizabeth* (London, 1630), book 4, p. 29 (sig. Ddd3r).

[57] George Paule, *The Life of the Most Reuerend and Religious Prelate Iohn Whitgift* (London, 1612), sig. G2r.

[58] Thomas Rogers, *The Faith, Doctrine, and Religion* (London, 1607), pp. 208–9.

[59] Patrick Collinson, 'The Theatre Constructs Puritanism' in David L. Smith, Richard Strier, and David Bevington (eds), *The Theatrical City: Culture, Theatre and Politics in London, 1576–1649* (Cambridge, 1995), pp. 157–69, at pp. 164–7.

[60] Kristen Poole, *Radical Religion from Shakespeare to Milton: Figures of Nonconformity in Early Modern England* (Cambridge, 2000), p. 32.

collect gossip, libels, letters, and writings of and about religious radicals and to write so as to 'abate the edge of the Factious'. In a testimonial that summed up Bancroft's activities, Whitgift highly esteemed not only his talent as a diligent detector but also his capability to organize the literary counterattack against Marprelate: 'By his advice, that Course was taken, w[hi]ch did principally stop Martin & his Fellow's mouths viz: to have them answered after their own vein in writing'.[61] Francis Bacon, who had an entirely negative view of this strategy, turns our attention to Bancroft's inclination to adopt this 'vein in writing':

> And therefore as much do I dislike the invention of him who (as it seemeth) pleased himself in it as in no mean policy, that these men are to be dealt withal at their own weapons, and pledged in their own cup. This seemed to him as profound a device. [...] But these things will not excuse the imitation of evil in another.[62]

Bancroft's tendency can be detected early, in his sermon at Paul's Cross, printed at the direction of Hatton and Lord Burghley in 1589. John Davidson, a Scottish Presbyterian minister, witnessed Bancroft's cleverness in his ability to make 'the whol drift of his speach, to serue his intended turne, for a bitter inuection against the godlie brethren of Englande', and criticized his 'rashnes in rayling'.[63]

One of Bancroft's strategies in slandering radicals was to mould their characters based on the religious discourses of the early and middle Church Fathers against heresies. These discourses consequently offered to the anti-Martinists a basic policy for representing those radical enemies. The specific characteristic that Bancroft chose to target was the radicals' boldness in displaying wilful disobedience to authority. Following St Augustine's appropriation of St Cyprian in the anti-Donatist and anti-Pelagian campaign, Bancroft argued that 'The beginning of heretikes (saith [Cyprian]) and the first springing up and enterprise of schismatikes

---

[61] Albert Peel (ed.), *Tracts Ascribed to Richard Bancroft* (Cambridge, 1953), pp. xviii–xix. During his residence at Cambridge, Bancroft had already earned a reputation for his extreme diligence as a detector. See also Owen Chadwick, 'Richard Bancroft's Submission', *Journal of Ecclesiastical History*, 3:1 (1952), 58–73, at pp. 71–2.

[62] Francis Bacon, *An Advertisement Touching the Controversies of the Church of England*, in Brian Vickers (ed.), *Francis Bacon* (Oxford, 1996), pp. 1–19, at p. 4. Both Vickers and Collinson believe that Bacon meant Bancroft by 'him'. See Vickers (ed.), *Francis Bacon*, p. 503; and Patrick Collinson, *Richard Bancroft and Elizabethan Anti-Puritanism* (Cambridge, 2013), p. 80.

[63] John Davidson, *D. Bancrofts Rashnes in Rayling against the Church of Scotland* (Edinburgh, 1590), sig. 2r. For the context of Davison's criticism of Bancroft, see Gordon Donaldson, 'The Attitude of Whitgift and Bancroft to the Scottish Church', *Transactions of the Royal Historical Society*, 4th ser., 24 (1942), 95–115.

thinking amisse, & c. groweth of this, that being puffed up with pride they contemne their governors.'[64] If pride is the initiator of heresy, self-love is its promoter. Augustine gave self-love as the reason why the number of false prophets had been increasing, and now Bancroft set out Augustine's argument with a Bernardian twist: 'Selfe-love saith [Augustine], did build the city of the divel. For heerin is their cheefe vaunt and glorie (as *Bernard* saith) *Captare laudem de singularitate scientiæ*: to hunt after co[m]mendation by singularitie of knowledge.'[65] In the heated polemical atmosphere of the controversy, Bancroft drew on the patristic representation of a heretic as someone swollen with the pride of singularity employed to invent or reinvent the character of English separatists.

Admittedly, this kind of characterization is in no way peculiar to Bancroft. George Gifford, for instance, drawing on just such an image of a proud heretic, complained about Brownists, who, 'vnder a perswasion of zeale against all falsehood and wickednes [...] are lifted vp with swelling', and drew a thumbnail sketch of Greenwood's character: 'Master *Greenwood* doth so raginglie take on, and strike he knowes not whom, such furie is not fit for disputation in the Church.'[66] Bancroft's speciality, however, lay in his ability to collect gossip and construct a profane blasphemer out of it. Having been well acquainted with Barrow's former dissolute career, he shows verbal dexterity in manipulating those materials to frame Barrow and his followers as a mob of atheists:

> And will sacrilegious persons become *Barrowists*? I easilie belieue it. Like will to like. When *Barrow* by roisting and gaming had wasted himselfe, and was runne so far into manie a mans debt, that he durst not shew his head abroad: he bent his wits another waie to mischiefe, and is now become a *Iulianist*, deuising by all the meanes he can possiblie imagine, his hypocrisie, railing, lying, and all manner of falshood, euen as *Iulian* the Apostata did: how all the preferments, which yet remaine for learning,

---

[64] Bancroft, *Sermon Preached at Paules Crosse*, p. 15. For the appropriation of Cyprian by Augustine in his anti-Pelagian campaigns, see Matthew Alan Gaumer, *Augustine's Cyprian: Authority in Roman Africa* (Leiden, 2016), chap. 7. A similar pattern of quoting Augustine alongside Cyprian can be detected in the Marian heresy campaign. See Kenneth Carleton, *Bishops and Reform in the English Church 1520–1559* (Woodbridge, 2001), pp. 148–9.

[65] Bancroft, *Sermon Preached at Paules Crosse*, p. 21. Bernard warns against vainglory in *Sermo* LXV: 'Omnibus una intentio haereticis semper fuit, captare gloriam de singularitate scientiae' ('In all it has ever been the intent of heretics to seek the glory of singular knowledge'). See Jean Leclercq, Charles H. Talbot, and Henri M. Rochais (eds), *Sancti Bernardi Opera* (8 vols, Rome, 1957–77), vol. 2, p. 173, lines 2–3.

[66] George Gifford, *A Plaine Declaration that Our Brownists be Full Donatists* (London, 1590), sig. A2r–v, and p. 117.

Benefices, Tithes, Glebela[n]d, Cathedrall Churches, Bishops liuings, Colledges, Vniuersities and all, might be vtterlie spoiled and made a pray for Bancrouts, Cormorants & such like Atheists.[67]

Thomas Nashe, while carefully following Bancroft's method of representation, was eager to develop what he saw as the chief traits of separatists in his own manner. In *Pierce Penilesse His Svpplication to the Divell* (1592), he attacks the pride of those who 'haue good parts, and beare the name of deepe scholers', namely the Cambridge separatists Barrow and Greenwood. He believed that higher education in the universities, which could give men a good opportunity to serve the 'Ecclesiasticall State' by making full use of their talents, also tended to cultivate, much to his regret, 'their selfe-loue to studie to inuent new sects of singularitie.[68] Nashe clearly made his claim with Bancroft's argument in mind, attributing the rise of these 'false' prophets to their self-love.[69] However, what made him uneasy was more specific: the proud singularity of those university religious radicals who entirely distanced themselves from the Church of England. Elsewhere, he bears witness, under the alias Cutbert Curryknave, not just to 'these new fangled positions' that 'entred the tables of young students' of Cambridge, but also to their grievous consequences when 'Singularity, the eldest childe of heresy, consulted with male-conted mela[n]choly how to bring this misbegotte[n] scisme to a monarchy'. This new sect, 'pufte vppe with the pride of singularity, seekes to peruerte the name and methode of magistracy'.[70]

What lay behind this religious inclination, according to Nashe's sarcastic estimation, was the sort of ambition whereby 'they will get a name to their vaineglory [...] thinking to liue when they are dead, by having theyr sects called after their names, as *Donatists* of *Donatus*, *Arrians* of *Arrius*'. Thus, those who 'cannot be content to participate one faith with all Christendome' divide Christ's flawless garment, or 'vesture of saluation', into small pieces, sharing it between them, and some of them make of it 'gally-gascoines or a shipmans hose, like the Anabaptists and adulterous Familists; others, with the Martinists, a hood with two faces, to hide their hypocrisie: &, to conclude, some, like the Barrowists and Greenwoodians, a garment full of the plague, which is not to be worne before it be new washt'.[71] The grotesque image of a garment infected by the plague shows how Nashe reinforces the existing stereotype in his own manner.

---

[67] Richard Bancroft, *A Suruay of the Pretended Holy Discipline* (London, 1593), p. 249.
[68] McKerrow and Wilson (eds), *Works of Thomas Nashe*, vol. 1, pp. 171–2.
[69] Bancroft, *Sermon Preached at Paules Crosse*, pp. 21, 23, and 33.
[70] McKerrow and Wilson (eds), *Works of Thomas Nashe*, vol. 3, pp. 358–9.
[71] *Ibid.*, vol. 1, pp. 171–2.

The representation of a separatist as a fanatic found its way into the character of the stage puritan in later years. Shakespeare seems to have been reminded of it when creating Malvolio as 'a kind of puritan'.[72] Malvolio, being 'sick of self-love' (I.v.85), enthusiastically puts himself 'into the trick of singularity' (II.v.142) and talks as if possessed by a 'hyperbolical fiend' (IV.ii.26). Similarly, Ben Jonson knew well how to construct puritan figures in his plays and put slanderous discourse – 'drawn from the very centre of the establishment puritan project' – into the mouths of his comical puritan characters.[73] Zeal-of-the-Land Busy in *Bartholomew Fair* is depicted as a 'prophet' who is 'ever in seditious motion, and reproving for vainglory; of a most lunatic conscience and spleen, and affects the violence of singularity in all he does'.[74] This characterization obviously derives from Bancroftian and anti-Martinist representations of separatism, which Jonson appropriated and reworked to make Busy a proud and hypocritical puritan. Having drunk copiously and eaten large quantities of pork in Ursula's booth, Busy blames the fairgoers for their pride, though his accusations come back to roost: 'bottle-ale is a drink of Satan's, a diet-drink of Satan's, devised to puff us up, and make us swell in this latter age of vanity'.[75]

AFTEREFFECTS OF TAMBURLAINE

The word 'singularity' was often used in ambiguous ways. 'To be singular' in sixteenth-century terms, as Stephen S. Hilliard points out, 'was to be different and original, estimable characteristics in literature and on the streets of London to the point that they threatened to become disruptive to the traditional social order'.[76] At the same time, humanists and churchmen were apprehensive that singularity would goad people to be ambitious, or, worse, seditious, by dividing themselves 'from the common fashions and

---

[72] William Shakespeare, *Twelfth Night*, ed. Roger Warren and Stanley Wells, The Oxford Shakespeare (Oxford, 1994), II.iii.130. Subsequent references to *Twelfth Night* will be to this edition and will appear parenthetically in the text by act, scene, and line number.

[73] Peter Lake and Michael Questier, *The Anti-Christ's Lewd Hat: Protestants, Papists and Players in Post-Reformation England* (New Haven, 2002), p. 620. See also John Creaser, 'Jonson's *Bartholomew Fair* and Bancroft's *Dangerous Positions*', RES, NS, 57:229 (2006), 176–84, at p. 184.

[74] Ben Jonson, *Bartholomew Fair*, ed. John Creaser, in David Bevington, Martin Butler, and Ian Donaldson (gen. eds), *The Cambridge Edition of the Works of Ben Jonson* (7 vols, Cambridge, 2012), vol. 4, pp. 253–428 at I.iii.107–9.

[75] Ibid., III.vi.24–5.

[76] Stephen S. Hilliard, *The Singularity of Thomas Nashe* (Lincoln, NE, 1986), p. 3.

Localizing Christopher Marlowe

customes of the world'.[77] Roger Ascham considered it dangerous to dissent 'from the best mens iudgementes', particularly among university students: 'I knew one student in Cambrige, who for a singularitie, began, first to dissent, in the scholes, from *Aristotle*, and soone after became a peruerse *Arian*, against Christ and all true Religion.'[78] In other words, to be singular was to deviate with conviction and ambitious zeal from orthodox doctrine, and from the exegeses that the Church of England had enforced on the nation.

From Nashe's perspective, the new sectarians' claim to hermeneutical or prophetic freedom in the light of the Holy Spirit, such as St Paul proposes (II Corinthians 3.17–18), should be dismissed as abuse of scriptural authority and considered within the context of the spread of atheism, for it allowed 'atheists', as well as Arians and separatists, to interpret the scriptures in a singular or revisionary way rather than in terms of traditional apologetics: 'Hence Atheists triumph and reioyce, and talke as prophanely of the Bible, as of Beuis of Hampton. I heare say there be Mathematitions abroad that will prooue men before *Adam*; and they are harboured in high places, who will maintaine it to the death, that there are no diuels.'[79] It is difficult to identify what Nashe means by 'mathematicians abroad', but he is obviously picking up on the methods that Christian polemicists such as John Rogers had used to attack heretical sects, and aligns heretics with atheists who threaten the Church with their radical and 'singular' redefinitions of traditional exegesis on the Old Testament.[80]

Despite his attack on the pride of heretics, however, Nashe himself was not immune to the sort of zeal for singularity that the intellectual atmosphere of Cambridge engendered in those religious dissenters. In fact, he was characterized by his enemies as a literary radical who shared traits with separatists. In *Pierces Supererogation*, Gabriel Harvey criticizes Nashe for being 'puffed vp with winde, and bumbasted with vanitye' and for his villainy 'in regard of [...] outragious singularity'. It was supposedly because of his pride that Nashe 'with a confidence preasseth into the rowte of that humorous rake, that affecteth the reputation of supreme Singularity'.[81] Harvey's censure implied that Nashe flaunted his extraordinary rhetoric, motifs, and ideas, which seems to have denoted, as Hilliard points out, 'the arrival of new writers who can use a singular style to promote orthodox

---

[77] Robert Bolton, *A Discourse about the State of True Happinesse Deliuered in Certaine Sermons in Oxford, and at Pauls Crosse* (London, 1611), p. 45.
[78] Roger Ascham, *The Scholemaster* (London, 1571), sig. L2r.
[79] McKerrow and Wilson (eds), *Works of Thomas Nashe*, vol. 1, p. 172.
[80] John Rogers, *The Displaying of an Horrible Secte* (London, 1578), sig. K2r. On the prevalence of pre-Adamist discourses, see Philip C. Almond, *Adam and Eve in Seventeenth-Century Thought* (Cambridge, 1999), pp. 49–51.
[81] Grosart (ed.), *Works of Gabriel Harvey*, vol. 2, pp. 61 and 277.

Ramism, Thomas Nashe, and the 'New Sects of Singularitie'

values'.[82] Those writers, who created an innovative cultural movement with their intellectual and emotional energy, were considered a serious threat to society, along with the religious radicals they vehemently attacked. Harvey, scathing about their ambition, named their new doctrine after them: 'no Art, but Euphuisme; no witt, but Tarletonisme; no honesty, but pure Scogginisme; no Religion, but precise Marlowisme; no consideration, but meere Nashery.'[83]

The rise of these popular writers encouraged religious polemicists to employ their innovative and powerful rhetoric, motifs, and ideas on the stage and in print when inventing either the positive or negative image of the religious radicals. In particular, the mighty rhetoric and singular pride of the stage character Tamburlaine may well have been one of the most powerful creations for representing the religious zeal of a prophetic sectarian such as Robert Browne, who, Thomas Fuller reported, 'was of an imperious nature, offended if what he affirmed but in common discourse were not instantly received as an oracle'.[84]

In fact, there is evidence to suggest that the threatening power of Tamburlaine, the prophetic agent of God's fury, could be conjoined with that of the religious radicals in the popular imagination. In the preface of Edward Dering's *Two Godly Sermons*, secretly printed in Middelburg, a certain 'I. F.', usually identified with the leader and polemicist of the London Presbyterian movement John Field, urges the advancement of the godly religion 'againste this time especially, because that a Parliament is instant and at hande'.[85] I. F. is possibly making reference to the Parliament of February 1589, when Whitgift suppressed 'certain motions' made by puritans about the administration of ecclesiastical laws,[86] and warns the reader by alluding to the popular protagonist on the public stage, stating that the world cannot escape unpunished if 'Gods Spirite speakinge in his Prophetes' is neglected:

> Tamerlan, Gods vengeance, when his blacke tentes are once vppe, though wee come out neuer so humbly with Laurell in our handes becladde in white garmentes, yet will hee not bee intreated, but by the selfe same sinnes whereby we haue offended, with the same wee shall bee punished.[87]

---

[82] Hilliard, *Singularity of Nashe*, p. 24.
[83] Grosart (ed.), *Works of Gabriel Harvey*, vol. 2, p. 234.
[84] Thomas Fuller, *The Church History of Britain*, ed. John Sherren Brewer (6 vols, Oxford, 1845), vol. 5, p. 68.
[85] Edward Dering, *Two Godly Sermons the First Preached before the Queenes Maiestie, the 25. of Februarie, 1569* (Middelburg, 1590?), sig. ¶3r.
[86] On the Parliament of February 1589, see T. E. Hartley (ed.), *Proceedings in the Parliaments of Elizabeth I* (3 vols, London, 1995), vol. 2, pp. 403–10 and 439–69.
[87] Dering, *Two Godly Sermons*, sig. ¶3r–v.

For I. F., Tamburlaine signifies the terrifying vengeance that will befall them if Parliament takes little account of God's zeal to drive radical reform. David Riggs points out that I. F. 'apparently refers to a live performance of *Tamburlaine*', because the detail of the laurel is unique to Marlowe's *Tamburlaine*.[88] In the play, the supplicants of Damascus bring 'branches of laurel in their hands' to make peace with Tamburlaine,[89] while in the standard sources for this scene they bring olive branches.

It is noteworthy that I. F. chose Tamburlaine on stage as 'a displaced image of violent agency' to achieve what the militant Presbyterian saw in his mind's eye.[90] It seems no mere coincidence, therefore, that William Hacket fashioned himself (or Richard Cosin, the press officer, fashioned Hacket) into a Tamburlainean prophet. Convinced that 'hee was reserued of God for some great and excellent worke, being blowen forward by the shew of zeale', Hacket was reported to have grown 'to such a dexteritie in conceiuing of extemporall prayers, with bumbasted and thundering wordes' and have been marvelled at 'as a man of a singular spirit, albeit vtterly vnlearned of the booke'.[91] Cosin set down Hacket's last prayer at the scaffold:

> O God of heauen, mightie Iehouah, *Alpha* and *Omega*, Lord of Lordes, King of Kings, and God euerlasting, that knowest me to be that true Iehouah, whome thou hast sent: send some miracle out of a cloude to conuert these Infidels, and deliuer me from these mine enemies: If not, I will fire the heauens, and teare thee from thy throne with my handes.[92]

This blasphemous speech, so powerful that William Camden did 'tremble to repeat it', held a tone reminiscent of Tamburlaine, who proclaims that 'The chiefest God [...] / Will sooner burn the glorious frame of heaven / Than it should so conspire my overthrow' (*One*, IV.ii.8–11).[93] Richard Bauckham argues that such a display is characteristic of Hacket and Tamburlaine; Stephen Greenblatt takes a similar view by attributes to these two rebels 'an act of radical freedom'.[94] Thus, for I. F., and possibly also for Hacket,

---

[88] David Riggs, *The World of Christopher Marlowe* (London, 2004), p. 229.
[89] Christopher Marlowe, *Tamburlaine the Great*, ed. J. S. Cunningham, The Revels Plays (Manchester, 1981), *One*, v.i.0. Subsequent references to *Tamburlaine* will be to this edition and will appear parenthetically in the text by part, act, scene, and line number.
[90] Riggs, *World of Christopher Marlowe*, p. 229.
[91] Cosin, *Conspiracy for Pretended Reformation*, pp. 7–8 and 24.
[92] *Ibid.*, pp. 71–2.
[93] Camden, *Historie of Princesse Elizabeth*, book 4, p. 30 (sig. Ddd3v).
[94] See Richard Bauckham, *Tudor Apocalypse* (Oxford, 1978), p. 202; and Stephen Greenblatt, *Renaissance Self-Fashioning from More to Shakespeare* (Chicago, 1980), p. 212.

Tamburlaine may have been a powerful source of inspiration in helping them to advocate, and provoking the populace to enact, drastic reform.

While Tamburlaine inspired those radicals to pursue godly reform, at the same time the character was crucial to the Church polemicists' invention (or reinvention) of puritans as possessing 'hyperbolical' or overreaching pride. The representation of false prophets 'pufte vppe with the pride of singularity' often took this element of Tamburlaine's character and was employed by several professional mouthpieces for the English Church to impress upon the public how heretics combined excessive and injurious pride. In *Hell's Broke Loose* (1605), a little pamphlet in verse on the life of John of Leiden, the prophet and leader of the Münster Anabaptist rebellion, Samuel Rowlands presents the similarities between Hacket and John, just as Cosin and other polemicists did, specifically in relation to their proud prophetic zeal.[95] He also seems to have been well aware of these radicals' inclination toward Tamburlaine and, by depicting John as his devotee, merges Tamburlaine's destructive agency with that of the Anabaptist. John bolstered the morale of the soldiers by declaring 'where you finde a Vsurer, be bold / To cut his throat, and take away his gold', continuing: 'Haue you not heard that *Scythian Tamberlaine* / Was earst a Sheepheard ere he play'd the King?'[96]

Nashe, another polemicist for the Church, links Tamburlainean pride with that of John Penry, a Cambridge separatist scholar whom Nashe considered to be proud enough to usurp the place of 'The great commaunder of the world': 'Thou hast railed vpon the Iudges, and spoken euill of the Rulers of thy people: thou hast ascended aboue the clowdes and made thy selfe like to the most High.'[97] Nashe likewise lampoons his deadly enemy Gabriel Harvey by imagining him swaggering around the stage 'like *Tamberlaine* drawne in a Chariot by foure Kings' and playing a bombastic orator intent on advertising himself. In his imagination, Harvey's Tamburlainean pride is closely aligned with that of separatists: '*the puffing and swelling Satiricall spirit* came vpon [Harvey], as it came on *Coppinger* and *Arthington*, when they mounted into the pease-cart in Cheape-side and preacht.'[98] This representation of religious radicals that emerged in the 1580s was carried over to some extent into that of stage puritans at the beginning of the seventeenth century when the bombast of Tamburlaine came to be the target of parody.[99]

---

[95] Samuel Rowlands, *Hell's Broke Loose* (London, 1605), sig. A2r; and Cosin, *Conspiracy for Pretended Reformation*, p. 97.
[96] Rowlands, *Hell's Broke Loose*, sig. D3r–v.
[97] McKerrow and Wilson (eds), *Works of Thomas Nashe*, vol. 1, p. 115.
[98] *Ibid.*, vol. 1, pp. 293–5, emphasis in original.
[99] See Poole, *Radical Religion*, pp. 34–44; Hamel Hamlin, *The Bible in Shakespeare* (Oxford, 2013), pp. 231–70; and Mary Jo Kietzman, *The Biblical Covenant in*

The power of Tamburlaine's oratory was also infectious to an anonymous agitator who pasted up a libel of fifty-three lines on the wall of the Dutch Church cemetery in Austin Friars on the evening of 5 May 1593. He seems to have been especially enthused by Tamburlaine's prophetic eloquence, giving vent to the citizens' anger against immigrant merchants:

> Your Machiavellian Marchant spoyles the state,
> Your vsery doth leave vs all for deade
> Your Artifex, & craftesman works our fate,
> And like the Iewes, you eate us vp as bread
> [...]
> Weele cutt your throtes, in your temples praying
> Not paris massacre so much blood did spill
> As we will doe iust vengeance on you all
> In counterfeitinge religion for your flight.[100]

The libeller subscribed his name as 'per. Tamberlaine', menacing foreigners with the threat of an uprising of apprentices and extreme violence to follow. The document draws a terrifying comparison between the force of London mobs and the violence of Tamburlaine. The libeller's threats can be summed up as follows: acquisitive immigrants are nothing but traitors who scheme to overthrow our nation; we sacrifice our own interests in order to support their lives of idleness; and so we fight a just war against these enemies who invade our country under the cover of religion.

The libeller, who specifically emphasizes the Machiavellian acquisitiveness and covert treacherousness of alien strangers like Barabas, seems to have been a skilled provocateur and to have well understood the government's anxiety about the influx of religious immigrants. In fact, criticisms raised in Parliament were levelled against merchants who immigrated to England purely for economic reasons, and Elizabeth herself, as well as her Privy Councillors, kept her eye on rebellious heretics and spies.[101] The libeller establishes his position not as a discontented rebel against the authorities but as a defender of his country against subversive invaders. Admittedly, his pseudonym, 'Tamberlaine', and his references to motifs in *The Jew of Malta* and *The Massacre at Paris*, suggests that he was (or pretended to be) a Marlowe aficionado fired up by what he had seen on the stage or read in print. What seems more important, however, is that he identified himself

---

Shakespeare (London, 2018), pp. 163–200.

[100] For the text and the background of the Dutch Church libel, see Arthur Freeman, 'Marlowe, Kyd, and the Dutch Church Libel', *ELR*, 3:1 (1973), 44–52, at pp. 50–1.

[101] For the anti-alien movement, see in particular Irene Scouloudi, *Returns of Strangers in the Metropolis 1593, 1627, 1635, 1639: A Study of an Active Minority* (London, 1985), pp. 57–93.

with Tamburlaine and posed as a fighter for justice against Machiavellian strangers. Tamburlaine's oratorical power and confidence in his prophetic agency appear to have exercised a strong mimetic effect on the libeller, as they did on religious radicals, and he availed himself of Tamburlaine's self-justifying logic in declaring violence against his enemies.

We do not know whether the libeller's xenophobic agitation was successful, but we do know that his Tamburlainean call for uprising irritated and provoked the authorities to make a thorough investigation into the matter. The allusion to Marlowe's plays was obviously one of the reasons why the authorities made a search of the room that Marlowe had shared with Thomas Kyd. The testimony of Kyd, arrested and tortured on suspicion of being the author of the libel and other heretical writings, led the Privy Council to apprehend Marlowe, who happened to be at Scadbury with Thomas Walsingham at that time, bring him before the court, and afterwards command him 'to give his daily attendaunce on their Lordships'.[102]

In hindsight, we might suppose that the libeller was someone ambitious enough to hope that Marlowe's arrest would take place by launching the smear campaign, but it is difficult for us – as it was for the authorities – to determine his identity, and far more difficult to figure out his ulterior motive.[103] His pseudonym and reference to Marlowe's plays may have been, as Kuriyama assumes, 'less an attack on Marlowe than a crude attempt to tap the same emotions aroused by his plays and channel them into political unrest'.[104] However, more important is the fact that, in this social and political context, the fanatical enthusiasm for Tamburlainean singularity worked as a morale boost for disaffected citizens, as it did for religious radicals, propelling their momentum and helping them express their bold contention. As a result, the incident provided a timely impetus for moulding the sort of negative opinion about Marlowe that Robert Greene had already created in late 1592 with the publication of his repentance pamphlets, giving several moralists and enemies of Marlowe convenient opportunities to jump on the bandwagon and demonize him as a demagogue of religious and political subversives.

---

[102] *APC*, vol. 24, p. 244.

[103] Charles Nicholl, *The Reckoning: The Murder of Christopher Marlowe* (London, 1992), pp. 284–9, attempts to identify the libeller as Richard Cholmeley and looks for an ulterior purpose cunningly concealed in the libel. For the counterargument, see Paul E. J. Hammer, 'A Reckoning Reframed: The "Murder" of Christopher Marlowe Revisited', *ELR*, 26:2 (1996), 225–42.

[104] Kuriyama, *Christopher Marlowe*, p. 131.

Part III

MYTHS

Chapter 9

ROBERT GREENE ON MARLOWE'S ATHEISM

'THE ATHEIST TAMBURLAN'

The considerable impact of *Tamburlaine*, which astonished audiences in the 1580s, is well attested by the abundant contemporary references to the play. Its success earned Marlowe both rivals and admirers in the stage business. Robert Greene may have been one of those envious of Marlowe's success. Greene appears to have initially been favourably inclined towards Tamburlaine as a historical figure. In *Mamillia*, published in 1580 – that is, before hearing Tamburlaine's verses ringing upon the public stage – Greene had recognized him as 'Prince *Tamberlane*, the most bloody butcher in the world, [who] neuer shed blood, where there was submission'.[1] In the preface written to the readers of *Perimedes the Blacksmith* (1588), however, Tamburlaine, and the manner in which he was portrayed on the stage, seems to have become a cause of intense irritation to him. Responding to the 'two Gentlemen Poets' who collaborated in a play to mock Greene's skill at writing tragic verse, Greene expressed his contempt for using a bombastic style: 'I could not make my verses iet vpon the stage in tragicall buskins, euerie worde filling the mouth like the faburden of Bo-Bell, daring God out of heauen with that Atheist *Tamburlan*, or blaspheming with the mad preest of the sonne' (vol. 7, pp. 7–8).

Here we see that Greene nurtured a grudge against a peer group of playwrights who emulated such 'intollerable poetrie: such mad and scoffing poets, that haue propheticall spirits, as bred of *Merlins* race'. The failure of his own play, *Alphonsus* (*c.*1587), a blank-verse imitation of *Tamburlaine*, was possibly one of the causes of his frustration and the butt of the 'gentlemen' poets' ridicule. This disgrace seems to have been so humiliating

---

[1] Alexander B. Grosart (ed.), *The Life and Complete Works in Prose and Verse of Robert Greene* (15 vols, 1881–6; repr. New York, 1964), vol. 2, pp. 81–2. Subsequent references to Greene's prose works will be to this edition and will appear parenthetically in the text.

that Greene took to slandering not just the tremendously popular play but the author of *Tamburlaine* himself. His innuendo about 'Merlin' clearly identifies Marlowe as author and prime mover of the innovation in heroic tragedy and sets him as his ultimate target.[2] Although it is up for debate whether 'the mad preest of the sonne', Tamburlaine's equal in blasphemy, can be identified as a real person or as a character of the lost play, undoubtedly Greene aligns the 'atheist' Tamburlaine with his creator to suggest that Marlowe shares the protagonist's blasphemous attitude towards God.[3]

The unusual reference to Marlowe naturally drives us to question why Greene employed such a peculiar phrase as 'that Atheist *Tamburlan*'. This condemnation is all the more marked when considered in the light of the Tamburlaine craze at that time in London, with the popularity of the play at its height in the midst of the Armada crisis. As I have demonstrated in Chapter 6, Tamburlaine was regarded as a Christ-like apocalyptic hero whose prophetic oration of 'mighty lines' was welcomed with enthusiastic applause. Greene was the first and only person to point out the negative aspects; he was, as Kuriyama notes, 'the first person we know of to accuse Marlowe of atheism in print, albeit indirectly'.[4]

This is the reason why Marlovian scholars have tended to consider the possibility that Marlowe had been 'infected' with 'atheism' or outright heterodoxy as early as his college days.[5] If this were the case, his religious heterodoxy might have been well known among his Cambridge acquaintances by the time Greene picked it up in *Perimedes*. Paul H. Kocher, based on Greene's denunciation of Marlowe for his 'atheism' in *Greene's Groatsworth of Wit* (1592), considers the reference in *Perimedes* as direct evidence of Marlowe's 'personal irreligion' and concludes that 'The comment has special value as coming from one who probably knew Marlowe personally'.[6] David Farley-Hills supposes that 'Marlowe's "atheism" became legendary in

---

[2] We can find the earliest attribution of the play to Marlowe in Robert Henderson's *The Arraignment of the Whole Creature* (1631), which has two episodes from *Tamburlaine* with the marginal gloss '*Marlow* in his Poem', at p. 240. See Hallett Smith, 'Tamburlaine and the Renaissance', in E. J. West (ed.), *Elizabethan Studies and Other Essays in Honor of George F. Reynolds* (Boulder, CO, 1945), pp. 126–31, at pp. 130–1.

[3] Tom Rutter, 'Marlowe, the "Mad Priest of the Sun", and Heliogabalus', *Early Theatre*, 13:1 (2010), 109–19.

[4] Constance Brown Kuriyama, *Christopher Marlowe: A Renaissance Life* (Ithaca, 2002), p. 114.

[5] For instance, see Austin K. Gray, 'Some Observations on Christopher Marlowe, Government Agent', *PMLA*, 43:3 (1928), 682–700, at p. 686; John Bakeless, *Christopher Marlowe* (London, 1938), p. 50; and Kuriyama, *Christopher Marlowe*, p. 58.

[6] Paul H. Kocher, *Christopher Marlowe: A Study of His Thought, Learning, and Character* (1946; repr. New York, 1974), p. 23.

his lifetime and the evidence that he was a man of extreme unorthodoxy by Elizabethan standards is too strong to allow of much doubt'.[7]

Certainly, it might be possible to assume that Greene had perceived Marlowe's 'Diabolicall Atheisme' by 29 March 1588, when the Stationers' Register recorded the entry for *Perimedes*, well before his condemnation in the *Groatsworth of Wit*. However, except for the reference to the 'atheist' Tamburlaine, no historical evidence survives to suggest that Marlowe's own 'atheism' or unorthodoxy was a popular topic at Corpus Christi or in London before 1592. In fact, it was only after the publication of the *Groatsworth of Wit*, registered on 20 September 1592, that Marlowe first became a gossip-column favourite in London. Moreover, there is too little evidence to suggest a close friendship between Marlowe and Greene, though new archival findings about Greene's godly associates in Norwich indicate that he could have gleaned gossip from his Norwich links at Corpus Christi.

More clear-cut, however, is Greene's *ex parte* verbal abuse of Marlowe. In *Menaphon* (1589), mocking a rustic love passage which he called 'a Canterbury tale', Greene makes its narrator out to be 'some propheticall full mouth that as he were a Coblers eldest sonne, would by the laste tell where anothers shooe wrings' (vol. 6, p. 86) and casts aspersions on Marlowe's humble origin. In *Francesco's Fortunes* (1590), he turns on Edward Alleyn as 'Roscius', who had acted the leading roles of Marlowe's plays, and asks: 'why Roscius, art thou proud with *Esops* Crow, being pranct with the glorie of others feathers? of thy selfe thou canst say nothing, and if the Cobler hath taught thee to say *Aue Cæsar*, disdain not thy tutor, because thou pratest in a Kings chamber' (vol. 8, p. 132). Greene's relentless animosity towards Marlowe precludes the assumption that they had personal contact sufficient to help them develop mutual understanding. It is therefore likely that his source of information was not first-hand knowledge obtained through personal acquaintance, and that his slander against Tamburlaine was due largely to his jealousy of and prejudice towards the successful younger playwright newly arrived from Cambridge.

It is understandable, therefore, that several scholars have read the passage in *Perimedes* as an allusion to the shocking scene in *Tamburlaine, Part 2* where the protagonist throws the Alcoran and other religious works of the Muslims into the fire at his camp before Babylon. To understand Greene's peculiar phrase, they focus their attention on Marlowe's provocative method of characterizing Tamburlaine.[8] Greene sniffed out, in Tambur-

---

[7] David Farley-Hills, 'Tamburlaine and the Mad Priest of the Sun', *Journal of Anglo-Italian Studies*, 2 (1992), 36–49, at p. 38.

[8] For instance, see Christopher Marlowe, *Tamburlaine the Great*, ed. Una M. Ellis-Fermor (1930; repr. New York: Gordian, 1966), pp. 6–8; Charles Nicholl, *The*

laine's audacious contempt for religious authorities, a hint of the attitude that transgressed the accepted principles of morality, and so attempted (or pretended) to sound the alarm concerning the pernicious influence of the play. This method of denunciation was quite familiar to him: in his *Greene's Vision* (1592) he complained about *The Cobler of Canterbury* published by 'some madde fellow': 'At this booke the grauer and greater sorte repine, as thinking it not so pleasant to some, as preiudiciall to many, crossing it with such bitter inuectiues, that they condemne the Author almost for an Atheist' (vol. 12, p. 213). The provocativeness of some of the scenes in the play may account for Greene's peculiar wording, suggesting that his invective does not necessarily point to the possibility that Marlowe had become infected with atheism in his college days. It would be unprofitable, therefore, to consider the phrase in *Perimedes* as a valid witness to Marlowe's atheism, or to seek in its accusation evidence for Marlowe's own opinions.

What we *can* say is that it was Greene alone who launched invectives at the earliest stage of Marlowe's playwright career, who first incited the smear campaign against the 'atheist' Marlowe in 1592, and who continued to disrespect Marlowe throughout his life.[9] Moreover, as David Riggs notes, Marlowe himself was 'an irretrievably textual being, the protagonist in a series of overlapping narratives that commences about six months before his death and persists on into its immediate aftermath'.[10] If Greene was the first author or mythmaker who built up and widely disseminated the literary representation of 'the atheist' Marlowe, the right questions to ask would be: what cultivated Greene's critical attitude towards Tamburlaine/Marlowe as an 'atheist' at the time of publication of *Perimedes*? What led him to denounce Marlowe's literary works as typically atheist in his pamphlets? And why did Greene and his followers represent Marlowe in this way?

To answer these questions, it is necessary to locate Greene's remarks on *Tamburlaine* and Marlowe within a specific set of cultural and social circumstances, and to examine what literary context fomented the earliest and extraordinary criticisms made by Greene, in *Perimedes*. Frederick S. Boas was the first scholar who gave much attention to Greene's slander, devoting a section to it titled 'First Charges of Atheism'. While rejecting the possibility that Marlowe had come under suspicion of being an atheist during his residence at Corpus, Boas highlights the social impact of the

---

Reckoning: The Murder of Christopher Marlowe (London, 1992), p. 204; and David Riggs, *The World of Christopher Marlowe* (London, 2004), p. 89.

[9] For Greene's persistent attacks against Marlowe, see Park Honan, *Christopher Marlowe: Poet and Spy* (Oxford, 2005), p. 185.

[10] David Riggs, 'Marlowe's Quarrel with God', in Paul Whitfield White (ed.), *Marlowe, History, and Sexuality: New Critical Essays on Christopher Marlowe* (New York, 1998), pp. 15–37, at p. 19.

communal, as well as theatrical, sensation that Marlowe had been creating in both Cambridge and London:

> Yet the violation by the Archbishop's scholar of the understood obligation to take holy orders and his sensational début immediately afterwards as a London playwright must have caused no little scandal. And it was natural that some of the most challenging tirades of his first tragic hero should be interpreted by unfriendly hearers as the utterances of the dramatist himself.[11]

Boas does not closely examine in what circumstances such an attitude towards Marlowe could have been locally cultivated, nor pursue why this social impact had turned Greene into the ringleader of 'unfriendly hearers' who identified the utterances of Tamburlaine with those of the dramatist himself, but his line of thinking is worth reconsidering and developing.

What channels gave Greene access to the rumours and gossip about Marlowe? The first person we encounter is Thomas Nashe. As I pointed out in Chapter 3, Anthony Hickman, the Senior Proctor of 1585/6 and Marlowe's close associate at Corpus Christi, became acquainted with Nashe through the *viva voce* for his bachelor's degree and affixed his signature to Nashe's own handwritten supplicat in 1586. Moreover, at that time Nashe was likely to have become interested in his Canterbury literary associates because of his familiarity with Stephen Gosson's *Ephemerides of Phialo* and through his admiration for John Lyly's *Euphues*: '*Euphues* I readd when I was a little ape in Cambridge, and then I thought it was *Ipse ille*.'[12] This evidence supports the argument that Nashe was associated with Marlowe. Thus, when contributing the preface to Greene's *Menaphon*, Nashe could well have been the primary source of information on Marlowe.

It is doubtful, however, whether Greene would have been able to access to Nashe's repository of gossip before his arrival in London. Nashe says that he 'tooke vp my inne' at St John's 'for seuen yere together lacking a quarter'.[13] If, as Charles Nicholl suggests, by 'a quarter' he means one term, it is likely that 'a career running from late 1581 to summer 1588 would lack just the Michaelmas Term to make up seven years', and so his move to London can be dated to around the summer of 1588.[14] It is unlikely, therefore, that Greene was provided with much defamatory information by Nashe prior to

---

[11] Frederick S. Boas, *Christopher Marlowe: A Biographical and Critical Study* (Oxford, 1940), pp. 110–11.
[12] Ronald B. McKerrow (ed.), *The Works of Thomas Nashe*, 2nd edn, rev. F. P. Wilson (5 vols, Oxford, 1958), vol. 1, p. 319. For Nashe's close reading of Gosson's *Ephemerides of Phialo*, see ibid., vol. 5, p. 119.
[13] Ibid., vol. 3, p. 181.
[14] Charles Nicholl, *A Cup of News: The Life of Thomas Nashe* (London, 1984), p. 38.

the publication of *Perimedes*, which was entered in the Stationers' Register on 29 March that year.

The more likely source for Greene's information about Corpus Christi is the local network of Norwich old boys. It was 'no little scandal' that a student whose violation of the foundation statutes requiring him to take holy orders had goaded some of the fellows and scholars to cast a sceptical eye on his religious opinions, had made his sensational appearance on the London literary scene. As noted in Chapter 3, Christopher Abbys and his Norwich-based faction were likely to have been among the principal originators of the rumour about Marlowe. Their channels of information could have provided Greene, eager to find fault with his threatening new rival, with a source of college gossip. The partial and biased information coming out of the Norwich cluster may have turned Greene into one of the 'unfriendly hearers' among the audience, and led him to make the earliest ill-disposed reference to *Tamburlaine*.

Admittedly, it is a matter of speculation whether Greene's connection with the Norwich-based faction at Corpus Christi played an important role in shaping his attitude towards Marlowe. What seems obvious, however, is that both Greene's religious mindset and his local network were cultivated during his formative years in Norwich, and that his new project, a conversion narrative in which condemnation of sin and celebration of sincere repentance are repeatedly expressed, employed the religious communal identity of Norwich in order to position himself as a godly writer against his literary rivals – particularly Marlowe. To understand Greene's negative approach in *Perimedes*, we must therefore reappraise his 'moralist' project: *A Looking-Glass for London and England* (c.1588), *The Repentance of Robert Greene* (1592), and *Greene's Groatsworth of Wit* (1592). This analysis will reveal how the urban legend of Marlowe the atheist may have started, and how it developed later on.

GREENE'S NEW PROJECT: *A LOOKING-GLASS FOR LONDON AND ENGLAND*

Jean E. Howard aptly terms the anti-theatrical tracts 'a genre of anxiety'. These tracts, which should be regarded 'as ideological productions designed to master or to mask contradictions in the social and economic life of the culture in which they were produced', function as an index to 'the level of barely suppressed anger, fear, and intolerance that characterize their depictions of the practices and the social groups they attack'.[15] The first peak

---

[15] Jean Howard, *The Stage and Social Struggle in Early Modern England* (London, 1994), p. 22.

of anxiety came from 1577 to 1583, when the city waged a fierce war on the public playhouses with the ideological support of religious polemicists such as John Northbrooke, Stephen Gosson, and Philip Stubbes. After this upsurge of anti-theatricalism, the orders of regulation issued by the Privy Council became relatively sporadic, and this might suggest that there was a partial cessation between 1584 and 1592.[16] Admittedly, the city authorities and the Privy Councillors seem to have worked out a political compromise that narrowly averted another intense conflict. However, an undercurrent of anxiety and discontent seems to have remained among the citizens, who felt uneasy about the moral issues of the public stage, as well as among the city authorities and anti-stage campaigners. In fact, anti-theatrical tracts were still selling well in 1587. Gosson's *Ephemerides of Phialo* (1579) was reprinted in 1586 and *The Schoole of Abuse* (1579) in 1587. Stubbes's *The Anatomie of Abuses* (1583) went through several impressions in 1584 and 1585, while *The Second Part of the Anatomie of Abuses* was published in late 1583. The popularity of these tracts must have acted as a trigger for William Rankins, another overnight polemicist for the godly, to publish his attack on playhouses and players, *A Mirrour of Monsters*, in 1587. The increasing sales of these tracts clearly reflect the social unrest permeating through the populace at that time.

One of the most deep-seated causes of anxiety was the Sabbath-breaking committed by a multitude of playgoers, which the godly thought would surely provoke the fierce wrath of God. The disaster at Paris Garden on 13 January 1583, which took eight lives, brought about the desire to stir up in the London populace a sense of impending crisis. John Field, the parish lecturer at St Mary Aldermary in London, urged the people to observe the Sabbath and explained the necessity for this in his *A Godly Exhortation, by Occasion of the Late Iudgement of God, Shewed at Parris-Garden* (1583), dedicated to the Lord Mayor and William Fleetwood, the recorder of the City: 'many are brought vnto, by frequenting the *Theater*, the *Curtin* and such like, [and] one day those places wyl likewise bee cast downe by God himself.'[17]

Despite the admonitions of God and his ministers, the hoped-for agreement not to perform on Sundays often seems to have been disregarded, for the Lord Mayor wrote to the Privy Council on 3 July, half a year after the disaster, that 'in great contempt of god the scaffoldes ar new builded, and the multitudes on the Saboath daie called together in most excessiue number'.[18]

---

[16] Virginia Crocheron Gildersleeve, *Government Regulation of the Elizabethan Drama* (New York, 1908), p. 175.

[17] John Field, *A Godly Exhortation, by Occasion of the Late Iudgement of God, Shewed at Parris-Garden* (London, 1583), sig. C5v.

[18] E. K. Chambers, *The Elizabethan Stage* (4 vols, 1923; repr. Oxford, 1974), vol. 4, p. 295.

What this report suggests is not only the authorities' exasperation over the impenitence of the pleasure-seeking public but also the increasing sense of real anxiety among the godly. In a letter dated 25 January 1586 (i.e. 1587) to Sir Francis Walsingham, an army officer and spy expresses his fear of divine retribution: 'The profaning of the Sabbath is redressed; but as bad a custom entertained, and yet still our long-suffering God forbeareth to punish. [...] I write not hypocritically, but from the very sorrow of my soul.'[19] It is no coincidence that around that time the doctrine of the Sabbath became a major controversial issue both in Parliament and in print, and that the godly launched a collective struggle to bring about the application of their regulative principle.[20] The public fear of disaster, plague, and famine gave a boost to their enthusiasm for removing any evil cause of God's fury.

The popularity of prognostications about approaching divine retribution also suggests the infiltration of a sense of impending crisis among the godly magistrates and citizens and the lower strata of society. Richard Harvey's *An Astrological Discourse vpon the Great and Notable Coniunction of the Two Superiour Planets, Saturne & Iupiter* (1583), together with the several astrological books of his brother John, created a sensation by affirming an old common prophecy about an unprecedented discord within the state that would be provoked in 1588.[21] According to Raphael Holinshed, its impact would be far-reaching and enhancing: 'the common sort of people [...] were in no small imaginations, supposing that no lesse would haue beene effectuated, than by the said discourse was prophesied.'[22]

Straunge Newes out of Calabria (1587), a cheap pamphlet with a striking woodcut, similarly reported the prediction of John Doleta, 'a learned astronomer' of Calabria, about the danger of a flood, a great alteration in religion, an earthquake, etc. In its preface, the anonymous writer fits this vague prediction into the current social context to frighten the reader 'with the feare of Gods heauy displeasure' and to bring about their repentance.[23] Intellectuals were cautious yet tolerant of such kinds of prognostication.

---

[19] BL, Harley MS 286, fol. 102, cited from Glynne Wickham, Herbert Berry, and William Ingram (eds), *English Professional Theatre 1530–1660* (Cambridge, 2000), pp. 90–1.

[20] For the intensification of the campaign for Sabbath observance, see James T. Dennison, *The Market Day of the Soul: The Puritan Doctrine of the Sabbath in England, 1532–1700* (Lanham, 1983), p. 30.

[21] Thomas Tymme gives us a summary of this common prophesy in *A Preparation against the Prognosticated Dangers of This Yeare, 1588* (London, 1588), sig. A6r.

[22] Raphael Holinshed, *Holinshed's Chronicles of England, Scotland, and Ireland*, with a new introduction by Vernon F. Snow (6 vols, 1807–08; repr. New York, 1976), vol. 4, p. 510.

[23] *Straunge Newes out of Calabria Prognosticated in the Yere 1586, vpon the Yere 87* (London, 1586), sig. A2v.

T. R., the author of *A Confutation of the Tenne Great Plagues, Prognosticated by Iohn Doleta*, while deriding the pamphlet as 'the late iest of *Doleta*', encourages the reader to learn from the 'manifest tokens of Gods heauy displeasure euen at hand which partly we feele by this bitter dearth without neede, through out all the land'. Referring to the biblical example of Jonah and Nineveh, he employs the same narrative strategy as his opponent: 'A fatherly scourge surely for our iniquities, especially for neglecting our dutie to God and our Soueraign, whose health is our safty. Therfore it is high time that we fall to hearty repentaunce, the onely salue against sinne, after the example of the greate citie Niniuie.'[24]

These calls for repentance were frequently employed to explain immediate misfortune and to give a strong impetus for further social solidarity. And they were far from restricted to the godly; indeed, they were eagerly aroused in all layers of society, and shared and endorsed as ways to propitiate God. As Alexandra Walsham points out, at critical junctures when the people were undergoing social stresses, 'the moral exhortations of preachers and pamphleteers and the penitential instincts of their hearers and readers had a tendency to coalesce. Social, cultural, and ideological differences in outlook and opinion faded as communities united against adversity and pulled together to stamp out vice and appease God's wrath.'[25]

The coalescing of the people against dangerous elements within society through this sort of campaign naturally aroused public wariness towards and anxiety about the London playhouses, where the audiences had been offered sufficient inducement to break the Sabbath and, as a logical consequence, to risk divine retribution in the form of plagues and famines. The public at large may have shared Anthony Munday's opinion that 'common plaies [...] bring both the Gospel into slander; the Sabboth into contempt; mens soules into danger; and finalie the whole Commonweale into disorder.'[26] It is natural, therefore, that the disaster at Paris Garden served as a kind of cultural memory of God's judgement upon the playgoers, which was reiterated and shared among the public. Stubbes evokes memories of that judgement at Paris Garden in *The Anatomie of Abuses*, as did Henry Cave in his lost 'Narration of the fall of Paris Garden' in 1588.[27] This catastrophe

---

[24] T. R., *A Confutation of the Tenne Great Plagues, Prognosticated by Iohn Doleta from the Country of Calabria* (London, [1587]), p. 16.

[25] Alexandra Walsham, *Providence in Early Modern England* (Oxford, 1999), p. 166.

[26] Anthony Munday, *A Second and Third Blast of Retrait from Plaies and Theaters* (London, 1580), pp. 43–4.

[27] Philip Stubbes, *Philip Stubbes*, The Anatomie of Abuses, ed. Margaret Jane Kidnie (Tempe, AZ, 2002), pp. 245–6. For the lost account by Henry Cave, see William Prynne, *Histrio-Mastix: The Player's Scourge, or Actor's Tragedy*, with an introduction by Peter Davison (2 vols, New York, 1972), vol. 1, fol. 556v, in the margin.

seems to have been still 'famous and memorable' to Thomas Beard, who exploited it to mould the religious mindset of the public in 1597.[28]

Stakeholders in the theatre seem to have taken concerted measures against the social pressures brought to bear on the stage in the 1580s. The managers of playhouses came to an agreement with the authorities to prohibit performances on Sundays, at least on an *ad hoc* basis, and did not openly oppose orders forbidding plays in order to avoid infection from the plague. Moreover, playwrights such as Robert Wilson and Robert Greene, who offered plays to the Queen's Men in the early phases of their London careers, astutely spotted the political function of this company 'for bringing the theatre back into the service of a Protestant ideology' and supported 'a campaign to give legitimacy to a Protestant drive for substantial truth and plain speech'.[29] Greene, in particular, seems to have made an important contribution to the company by offering his *Friar Bacon and Friar Bungay* and possibly *Selimus*.[30] It is also likely that, as his *James IV*, *Alphonsus*, and *A Looking-Glass for London and England* were printed by Thomas Creed, who in the early 1590s acquired the plays of the failing Queen's Men, Greene came 'as close as anyone to being the company's signature playwright' and wrote plays oriented towards the political concerns of the company and its patron.[31]

To understand Greene's social and literary environment in 1588, when he wrote *Perimedes the Blacksmith*, we need to consider his *A Looking-Glass for London and England*, written around the same time. Wiggins dates this play to 1589 based on Henslowe's entry of its revival performance in 1592, while Clugston and Gayley both place it earlier, to late 1587, just after *Tamburlaine*, based on the strange absence of any reference to the Armada.[32] Though the date is difficult to pin down, neither option would be a serious

---

[28] Thomas Beard, *The Theatre of Gods Iudgements* (London, 1597), sig. N6r.
[29] Scott McMillin and Sally-Beth MacLean, *The Queen's Men and Their Plays* (Cambridge, 1998), p. 33.
[30] For recent discussions on Greene's authorship of Selimus, see Daniel J. Vitkus (ed.), *Three Turk Plays from Early Modern England: Selimus, A Christian Turned Turk, The Renegado* (New York, 2000), p. 17.
[31] Helen Ostovich, Holger Schott Syme, and Andrew Griffin (eds), *Locating the Queen's Men: Material Practices and Conditions of Playing* (Farnham, 2009), p. 4. See also G. M. Pinciss, 'Thomas Creede and the Repertory of the Queen's Men 1583–1592', *Modern Philology*, 67:4 (1970), 321–30.
[32] Martin Wiggins, *British Drama 1533–1642: A Catalogue* (Oxford, 2012), vol. 2, p. 470; George Alan Clugston (ed.), *Thomas Lodge and Robert Greene, 'A Looking Glasse for London and England'* (New York, 1980), pp. 71–3; Charles Mills Gayley, *Representative English Comedies* (2 vols, New York, 1912), vol. 1, pp. 405–8. For those preferring the earlier date, see N. Burton Paradise, *Thomas Lodge: The History of an Elizabethan* (1931; repr. Hamden, 1970), pp. 151–2.

obstacle to considering the play as one of the cultural products yielded by the ideological struggle between the City and the stage at that time. In fact, *Looking-Glass*, aligned with the authorities' campaign for moral reform, earnestly exhorts Nineveh/London to make sincere repentance based on the pattern of the Book of Jonah, and shares the format of the repentance narrative which proliferated in society.

In a time of social crisis and anxiety, the account of Jonah was an effective cultural implement for a would-be moralist. In 1593, when the plague was rampant, the astrologer and playgoer Simon Forman joined in the campaign to eradicate social evils with a warning: 'O England, England take Example by Nyniue, w[hi]ch repented at the p[rea]chinge of Ionas, Repent thou Alsoe, that the Lord may haue mercie on thee as he had on Nenive.'[33] In Greene's play also, the prophet Oseas, acting as chorus, anachronistically works in harmony with the pulpit of London, cautioning: 'Sin raignes in thee, O London, euery houre. / Repent and tempt not thus the heauenly power.'[34]

The preaching of Jonas proves to be successful in reforming the King of Nineveh and his subjects, while the stage clown who has broken the public injunction to fast and pray (functionally equivalent to Sabbath-keeping) is sent to the gallows. Moreover, as Beatrice Groves points out, the play borrows divine portents from Josephus's *Jewish War* to respond to 'the eschatological fervour which ran high in the 1580s and 1590s'.[35] Thus, Greene fashioned himself as a moralistic playwright, as he says in the epistle of *Greene's Mourning Garment* (1590): 'hauing my selfe ouerweaned with them of *Niniuie* in publishing sundry wanton Pamphlets [...] and hearing with the eares of my heart *Ionas* crying, *Except thou repent*, as I haue changed the inward affectes of my minde, so I haue turned my wanton workes to effectuall labours' (vol. 9, pp. 119–20). The play's message and its timely connection with the growing campaign to stamp out social evils suggest that *Looking-Glass* was possibly one of Greene's early attempts to gain a foothold in the literary market, which he made by launching a public appeal for understanding and recognition to be given to the moral effectiveness of the public theatre and, thereby, to his own good moral standing as a playwright.

---

[33] Bodleian Library, Oxford, Ashmole MS 208, fol. 130v.
[34] John Churton Collins (ed.), *The Plays and Poems of Robert Greene* (2 vols, Oxford, 1905), vol. 1, p. 157 (1.iii.404–5).
[35] Beatrice Groves, '"They repented at the preachyng of Ionas: and beholde, a greater then Ionas is here": *A Looking Glass for London and England*, Hosea and the Destruction of Jerusalem', in Adrian Streete (ed.), *Early Modern Drama and the Bible: Contexts and Readings, 1570–1625* (Basingstoke, 2012), pp. 139–55, at p. 148.

Greene's collaboration with Thomas Lodge in writing *Looking-Glass* possibly contributed to enhancing the moral positioning of the play. According to Stephen Gosson's testimony, Lodge was employed by some of his associate players to write a defence of the stage (probably titled *Honest Excuses* and published in 1580), and he became embroiled in the theatrical controversy.[36] In this pamphlet, while he agrees with Gosson that 'I cannot allow the prophaning of the Sabaoth, I praise your reprehension in that', Lodge brings up the need to reform the traditional vulgar stage and align it with the new medium of moral education, and turns Gosson's attention to the religious potential of drama: 'The Germanes when the vse of preaching was forbidden them, what helpe had they I pray you? forsoth the learned were fayne couertly in comodies to declare abuses, and by playing to incite the people to vertues, whe[n] they might heare no preaching.'[37]

There is no knowing what encouraged Greene and Lodge's collaboration, though their intimate friendship is revealed by Lodge's eulogistic French sonnet for Greene's *Spanish Masquerado* (1589), in which Lodge calls Greene 'Mon doux ami' and states that 'Tu de morteles compagnon de Dieux' ('you of mortals are the companion of the gods') (vol. 5, p. 240). It is also worth noting that both men had been working under the strong influence of *Tamburlaine*. Greene, who had been accustomed to 'pen / The praise of loue and *Cupids* peerles power', turned his hand 'to treat of bloudie Mars, / Of doughtie deeds and valiant victories' and hastily responded to *Tamburlaine* with his *Alphonsus* in 1587.[38] Lodge's career as a playwright began with *The Wound of Civil War* (c.1588), in which he imitated *Tamburlaine* by staging a scene of a chariot carrying a triumphant conqueror drawn by captive kings.[39] It seems no coincidence, therefore, that in *Looking-Glass* these two playwrights produced another character in the mould of Tamburlaine – Rasni, the King of Assyria – and highlighted Rasni's blasphemous attitude strongly enough for the audience to recognize the connection.

---

[36] John Dover Wilson, 'The Missing Title of Thomas Lodge's Reply to Gosson's *School of Abuse*', *MLR*, 3:2 (1908), 166–8.

[37] Thomas Lodge, 'A Reply to Stephen Gosson's *Schoole of Abuse*', in Edmund W. Gosse (ed.), *The Complete Works of Thomas Lodge* (4 vols, 1883; repr. New York, 1963), vol. 1, p. 42.

[38] Collins (ed.), vol. 1, p. 80 (Prologue, 37–40).

[39] Houppert and Paradise both assume that in this scene Lodge owed nothing to *Tamburlaine* but instead drew on Gascoigne's *Jocasta*, and date *The Wounds of Civil War* earlier than 1587. See Thomas Lodge, *Wounds of the Civil War*, ed. Joseph W. Houppert, Regents Renaissance Drama (Lincoln, NE, 1969), pp. xviii–xx; and Paradise, *Thomas Lodge*, pp. 134–6. *Contra*, see William A. Armstrong, '*Tamburlaine* and *The Wounds of Civil War*', *N&Q*, 203 (1958), 381–3; and Wiggins, *British Drama*, vol. 2, pp. 408–9.

From the beginning of the play, Rasni's hubris comes to the fore, and the diction and aspiring character of Tamburlaine is shown in his speech:

> This Citie is the footestoole of your King;
> A hundredth Lords do honour at my feete;
> My scepter straineth both the poralels;
> And now to enlarge the highnesse of my power
> I haue made Iudeas Monarch flee the field,
> And beat proud Ieroboam from his holds,
> Winning from Cades to Samaria.
> Great Iewries God, that foilde stout Benhadad
> Could not rebate the strength that Rasni brought,
> For be he God in heauen, yet, Viceroyes, know,
> Rasni is God on earth and none but he.[40]

Having participated in the cultural struggle between the stage and the anti-theatricals, Greene and Lodge were probably aware of 'the implicit dialogue' between Marlowe and William Rankins, a law student and anti-theatrical polemicist, at Clifford's Inn.[41] In *A Mirrour of Monsters* (1587), Rankins explores the dangers of social and cultural apostasy in the monstrousness of Tamburlainean self-magnification:

> For as the Maiestie of God is impacient of any aspiring mind to be partaker of his deitie, so dooth hee with a sharpe whippe scourge those blasphemers, that attribute anie dignitie belonging to heauen his head, or the earth his footstoole to any other but himselfe, his honor will not be defaced, his maiestie mangled, and his holie name blasphemed. [...] Of which sort of men in the chiefe place, may be placed Players, when they take vpon them the persons of Heathen men, imagining themselues (to vaineglory in the wrath of God) to be the men whose persons they present, wherein, by calling on *Mahomet*, by swearing by the Temples of Idolatry dedicate to Idols, by calling on *Iupiter, Mars, Venus* & other such petty Gods, they doo most wickedly robbe God of his honour, and blaspheme the vertue of his heauenly power.[42]

What motivated Rankins to see the playhouse as culturally problematic was not the Muslim conquerors strutting and swaggering about the stage but rather their blasphemous arrogance, which he thought the players shared. It was difficult for Greene and Lodge to escape censure, given that they had turned their hands to such abuses in their plays. In *Looking-Glass*,

---

[40] Collins (ed.), vol. 1, p. 146 (I.i.17–27).
[41] For this 'implicit dialogue' between Marlowe and Rankins, see Jonathan V. Crewe, 'The Theatre of the Idols: Theatrical and Anti-Theatrical Discourse', *Theatre Journal*, 36:3 (1984), 321–44.
[42] William Rankins, *A Mirrour of Monsters* (London, 1587), sigs F4v and G1v.

however, they align themselves with critics such as Rankins, who caution the audience against the blasphemy of 'any aspiring mind to be partaker of his deitie'.[43] They meticulously counteract the socio-religious threat of Rasni's self-magnification by employing the framework of the repentance narrative, and in so doing aim to vindicate the cause of the players and themselves.

The point which most distinguishes this play from *Tamburlaine* is that Rasni's sacrilegious practices are in all cases checked or corrected by the intervention of the Judaeo-Christian God, to such an extent that Rasni loses all his Tamburlainean attributes. His pride, which propels him towards the incestuous marriage with his sister, brings the punishment of a thunder strike down on her; a flame of subterranean fire swallows Radagon, the wily vicegerent, whose flattery misleads the king into misgovernment; and a hand with a burning sword emerging from a cloud gives Rasni a warning of destruction. Thus, Greene and Lodge integrate the Tamburlainean Rasni into the biblical repentance framework to give the audience an antidote to blasphemy, making a counterattack on Tamburlaine and on Marlowe himself.

Detoxifying Tamburlaine in this way naturally provided Greene with the opportunity to pose as an ardent theatrical advocate of the popular repentance movement, both in order to dodge the attack of the anti-theatrical polemicists and to shift the direction of the attack towards Marlowe, the originator of Tamburlainean profanity, by magnifying and proclaiming the play's moral danger. Greene's criticism of *Tamburlaine* may have originated in the failure of *Alphonsus* and his envy of the upcoming playwright, but ultimately it seems to have been one of his manoeuvring strategies to define himself as a didactic, edifying playwright.

The accident that happened during a performance by the Admiral's Men may have given Greene, who had mainly offered his plays to the Queen's Men, another opportunity to set himself against Marlowe. On 16 November 1587, Philip Gawdy, a law student at Clifford's Inn, wrote to his father in Norfolk with news about an incident that had caused a stir in London. According to Gawdy, in a scene where a player was tied to a post and shot dead, a child and a pregnant woman in the audience were accidentally killed by a blank shot.[44] There is wide consensus among Marlowe scholars that Gawdy's reference was to the shooting of the Governor of Babylon in *Tamburlaine, Part 2*. Gawdy's comment on the accident reveals the same

---

[43] *Ibid.*, sig. F4v.
[44] Charles Edelman, '"Shoot at Him All at Once": Gunfire at the Playhouse, 1587', *Theatre Notebook*, 57:2 (2003), 78–81, reconstructs the circumstances of the accident.

mindset as those who had attempted to construe each accident and disaster as a message of divine origin:

> How [the players] will answere it I do not study vnlesse their profession were better, but in chrystyanity I am very sorry for the chaunce but God his iudgementes ar not to be sear[ched] nor enquired of at mannes handes. And yet I fynde by this an old proverbe veryfyed ther never comes more hurte then commes of fooling.[45]

Casualties often led the public to apply this kind of framing or mental filter and access the accumulated cultural memory of God's judgements, construing the meaning of disasters from a providential perspective. The non-appearance of the Admiral's Men at Court in the Christmas season of 1587/8 may have been due to the aftereffects of the incident, which required the company to demonstrate its compunctions publicly.[46] The accident was scandalous enough to exacerbate the unrest that was already brewing and to encourage Greene to stigmatize the play as a potential source of God's wrath.

When undertaking a smear campaign against the 'mad and scoffing poets' in *Perimedes*, Greene naturally needed to fashion himself as a counter to those 'bred of Merlins race'; consequently, he had to adopt a similar stance to the anti-theatrical polemicists in demonstrating the moral unwholesomeness of certain playwrights. Representing his discourses as 'full of diuerse precepts interlaced with delightfull histories', Greene aimed to differentiate himself from those 'blaspheming' poets who produced 'impious instances of intolerable poetrie' and publicly reject ostentation. This political manoeuvre, embedded in the preliminary remarks of *Perimedes*, corresponds with the conciliatory gesture that can be detected in *Looking-Glass*. In order to secure his status as a playwright loyal both to God and to the authorities, it was necessary for Greene, with the assistance of Lodge, to stand aloof from the new theatrical trend, and to point out the flaws in its symbolic figure, Tamburlaine. In doing so, Greene would be seen to be in sync with the anti-theatrical discourses, gaining a moral advantage over his rivals (with Marlowe at their head). Thus, his defamatory innuendo in *Perimedes* should be considered a cue prompting him to rework Tamburlaine's blasphemous speech into Rasni's repentance narrative set against the backdrop of the anti-theatrical upsurge in the 1580s.

---

[45] Isaac Herbert Jeayes (ed.), *Letters of Philip Gawdy of West Harling, Norfolk, and of London to Various Members of His Family 1579–1616* (London, 1906), p. 23.

[46] Andrew Gurr, *The Shakespearian Playing Companies* (Oxford, 1996), p. 232.

SELF-FASHIONING AS A GODLY MORALIST: *THE REPENTANCE OF ROBERT GREENE*

In the process of fashioning himself as a didactic, edifying playwright and writer, Greene identified the baseness of his life itself as worthy to be published for the greater good of society, and decided to write the conversion narrative that made his 'real-life' experience so important: 'When thus I had considerately thought on the wretchednes of my life, and therewithall looked into the vncertainty of death, I thought good to write a short discourse of my [life]' (vol. 12, p. 170). The money he made from his writing may not have been enough to improve his financial situation; far more important was the opportunity to further his personal credit or cultural capital. By making public his financial and moral bankruptcy, he was refashioning himself into an ex-prodigal and godly author through his repentance pamphlets, struggling to restore his impaired reputation and even trying to retain the moral high ground through warning the reader against licentiousness and atheism. Reed Barbour has identified the 'two tricks' of Greene's dramatic conversion: 'to elevate his own life as a model for the repentance of the errant prodigal, and to remove his discoveries from their troublesome social contexts by baptizing them in the rites of spiritual justification.'[47] Moreover, as Alexandra Halasz points out, Greene's autobiography placed him in the strategic position of a godly author who 'constructs himself as a figure of authority by acknowledging himself as the begetter of "offspring" which he must repudiate in order to claim the position of authority.'[48]

Considering these literary tactics, it would be naïve to assume that *The Repentance of Robert Greene* comprises an unvarnished and unmediated factual account of his own conversion. Rather, while it includes descriptions of his personal relationships, experiences, and feelings – of varying degrees of accuracy – *Repentance*, like other repentance pamphlets, seems to have been fashioned as a multi-layered narrative serving to construct Greene's persona. By way of illustration, let us recall that Greene offers a thumbnail sketch of his conversion at St Andrew's. As we saw in Chapter 1, his connection with the puritan factions at that church probably motivated him to record a tribute to the minister, John More, which may have been intended as a modest eulogy. At the same time, Greene's reference to St Andrew's defines the narrative identity in *Repentance* and strengthens his new social role as a godly moralist.

The essential features of English conversion narratives as outlined by Bruce Hindmarsh are helpful when we consider *Repentance*: the conversion

---

[47] Reid Barbour, *Deciphering Elizabethan Fiction* (Newark, DE, 1993), p. 60.
[48] Alexandra Halasz, *The Marketplace of Print: Pamphlets and the Public Sphere in Early Modern England* (Cambridge, 1997), p. 36.

narrative 'is something of a hybrid or transitional genre: part self-examination and confession, part biblical exposition, part sermonic exhortation, and part factual narrative'.[49] Hindmarsh traces their origin back to William Perkins's cases of conscience, but concludes with Judith Pollmann that 'there is no genre of sixteenth-century Reformation conversion narrative'.[50] Certainly, the output is relatively slight, but Hindmarsh and Pollmann have overlooked *Repentance*, which was an important precursor of the genre because for the first time in print it gave an autobiographical account of a man's conversion from atheism, acknowledging his spiritual affinity with or indebtedness to his local puritan congregation. It is therefore vital to examine not the supposed historical 'accuracy' of Greene's account but how the narrative refashions him into a godly author by association with the particular religious locality of Norwich: in other words, what 'reality' it was designed to create, and what social repercussions it entailed.

Exploring the features of Greene's works of repentance and prodigality, Richard Helgerson argues that 'in explaining his own repentances Greene does move toward radical Protestantism'.[51] In fact, the real explanation lies a little deeper: Greene moves towards the Norwich puritanism of St Andrew's in narrating his life and repentance and deliberately attracts the reader's attention to his religious locality. Why is he so specific about the church and the preacher at whose exhortation he was seized with the inward compunction to repent his former sins? This kind of specificity might well have been unnecessary and even awkward if Greene had been entertaining his usual readership. In trying to understand his approach, it is helpful to remember Eckhard Auberlen's point that Greene had to 'claim a secure place within the ranks of society' as a repentant prodigal. There is 'a far more radical break with the tone of his earlier writings' in *Repentance*:

> Like Bunyan in *Grace Abounding*, he now speaks as a member of the Protestant congregation who, no matter how low his social rank, would be attentively listened to when relating his religious experiences: his struggle against sin was of great importance for all members of the congregation to strengthen their faith.[52]

---

[49] D. Bruce Hindmarsh, *The Evangelical Conversion Narrative: Spiritual Autobiography in Early Modern England* (Oxford, 2005), p. 39.

[50] *Ibid.*, p. 26. See also Judith Pollmann, 'A Different Road to God: The Protestant Experience of Conversion in the Sixteenth Century', in Peter van der Veer (ed.), *Conversion to Modernities: The Globalization of Christianity* (New York, 1996), pp. 47–64, at pp. 47–8.

[51] Richard Helgerson, *The Elizabethan Prodigals* (San Marino, 1976), p. 102.

[52] Eckhard Auberlen, *The Commonwealth of Wit: The Writer's Image and His Strategies of Self-Representation in Elizabethan Literature* (Tübingen, 1984), p. 162.

In fact, Greene himself makes the purpose of his conversion narrative clear in *Greene's Vision*: praying to God for his gracious favour so that 'I may for euer keepe my soule an vndefiled member of thy church, and in faith, loue, feare, humblenessse of heart, praier, and dutifull obedience, shew my selfe regenerate, and a reformed man from my former follies' (vol. 12, p. 208). Just as in the seventeenth century, a puritan conversion narrative became the requirement for candidates to be admitted to the Church, Greene's account was, or at least purported to be, his testimony that 'Gods grace did so fauorablie worke in me' (vol. 12, p. 160), allowing him to regain, in a sense, the lowest seat available as the member of a godly congregation.[53] His reference to the puritan community of Norwich provided a guarantee of his moral stance, simultaneously offering him a new narrative identity. In this way, whenever facing a moral crisis of his own, or identifying the moral failings of society, Greene could assume a puritan self that had been cultivated and constructed by the radical religious milieu of Norwich in the 1570s.

Greene's literary project allowed him to exhort his readers to live with honesty and uprightness. At the same time, it enabled him to attack those who were recognizably at the opposite end of the moral spectrum, positioning them as a social hazard. Recasting the mode of his literary production in this way was not unique, for we can find similar cases in the careers of other anti-theatrical polemicists such as Munday, Gosson, and Rankins who earned their living by writing *for* the stage and, as occasion demanded, *against* it.[54] One of the most conspicuous and unusual traits in *Repentance*, however, is the fact that the author's harsh criticism is directed mainly at himself. He denounces his own prodigal way of life in order to give warnings against love pamphlets and 'blasphemous' plays that have been wreaking havoc with the morals of youth. Inviting the reader to focus on his own ungodliness, Greene follows his accustomed manner of writing: 'in seeking to salue priuate wants, I haue made my selfe a publique laughing stock. Hee that commeth in Print, setteth himselfe vp as a common marke for euery one to shoote at' (vol. 12, p. 195). As the born-again godly writer, he sets his old self up as the primary target for public criticism.

How, then, does Greene represent his old self as an object of attack? A good place to start is the passage where he meets with his wicked companions after having received the 'inward motion' by hearing the sermon at St

---

[53] For the origins of autobiographical testimony about one's own religious experience in order to obtain church membership, see Patricia Caldwell, *The Puritan Conversion Narrative: The Beginnings of American Expression* (New York, 1983), pp. 45–80.

[54] On the anti-theatrical polemicist's pose as a godly moralist, see Tracey Hill, '"He hath changed his coppy": Anti-Theatrical Writing and the Turncoat Player', *Critical Survey*, 9:3 (1997), 59–77.

Andrew's church: 'in ieasting manner' they called him 'Puritane and Presizian' and 'wished [he] might haue a Pulpit, with such other scoffing tearmes' (vol. 12, p. 176). Here Greene is clearly describing behaviour that is the opposite of the godly: those who mock the preacher's (or God's) words – through which they might have faith – and 'by their foolish perswasion' wipe out his 'wholesome lesson' from remembrance. In a sense, they represent the author's former self. At the beginning of *Repentance*, Greene sums up what he was like:

> I seemed as one of no religion, but rather as a meere Atheist, contemning the holy precepts vttered by any learned preacher: I would smile at such as would frequent the Church, or such place of godly exercise, & would scoffe at any that would checke mee with any wholesome or good admonition. (vol. 12, pp. 161–2)

His narrative strategy seems well defined in this passage: he invites the reader to see his former self as a typical representation of a 'meere', or unadulterated, atheist.

This is not atheist in our modern sense, meaning a rational and freethinking philosopher, but one who is fully alienated from God's grace. Greene evidently recognized the defamatory power of the term, which was frequently employed because of both its power and its usefulness as a slur, as a literary tool in polemics and apologetics against religio-political opponents. What enhanced the term's aggressiveness and venom was the upsurge of anti-atheist literature that had repeatedly proclaimed and disseminated the mythical monstrosity of the atheist.[55] Aspiring literary writers who aimed to affect a pose of anti-atheism as an intellectual accomplishment and wished to embroider their narratives with morals, were closely acquainted with these polemicists' ways of confuting atheists. Sir Philip Sidney, possibly stimulated by de Mornay's apologetics, inserted in *The Countess Pembroke's Arcadia* a dialogue between Pamela and Cecropia, an atheist.[56] The apologetics against atheism also encouraged Thomas Nashe to pose as an intellectual moralist: in his *Christs Teares over Iervsalem*, he

---

[55] George T. Buckley, *Atheism in the English Renaissance* (1932; repr. New York, 1965), pp. 61–120, outlines the major trends of anti-atheism literature in early modern England. See also Don Cameron Allen, *Doubt's Boundless Sea: Skepticism and Faith in the Renaissance* (Baltimore, 1964), pp. 1–27; Sara Warneke, *Images of the Educational Traveller in Early Modern England* (Leiden, 1995), esp. chap. 5; and Kenneth Sheppard, *Anti-Atheism in Early Modern England 1580–1720: The Atheist Answered and His Error Confuted* (Leiden, 2015), chap. 2.

[56] On the sources of the dialogue, see Roger Kuin, 'Life, Death, and the Daughter of Time: Philip and Mary Sidney's Translation of Duplessis-Morney', in Catherine Gimelli Martin and Hassan Melehy (eds), *French Connections in the English Renaissance* (Aldershot, 2013), pp. 143–60. See also D. P. Walker, 'Ways of Dealing with

urges 'all able pennes to Arme themselues against thyne Atheisticall maledictours' and aligns himself with the polemists in portraying the peculiarities of atheists.[57]

These portraits of atheists show that Robert Greene modelled the narrative of his internal conflict on the standard mode of representing an atheist and amplified it by giving more personal details of how and when an atheist would feel the 'threatninges by the holy Ghost' and the terror of God's judgement in his conscience. For instance, Greene's godly friends in *Repentance*, persuading him to leave his bad course of life in vain, change their approach and admonish him: 'If you feare not death in this world, nor the paines of the body in this life, yet doubt the second death, & the losse of your soule, which without hearty repentance must rest in hell fire for euer and euer.'[58] Greene pretends to be tough by making light of God's judgement, responding: 'Hell (quoth I) what talk you of hell to me? I know if I once come there, I shal haue the company of better men than my selfe.' However, 'beeing departed thence vnto my lodging, and now grown to the full, I was checked by the mightie hand of God'. What frightens him most is the necessary consequence of his beliefs that the reader expects: death and hell. 'Sicknes (the messenger of death) attached me, and tolde me my time was but short, and that I had not long to liue' (vol. 12, pp. 163–4).[59] Here, Greene, in concert with the polemicists, clearly attempts to shape himself into a cowardly atheist.

This unique literary attempt at fashioning himself as a former atheist turned godly moralist and narrating his dramatic conversion may have helped Greene to ensure that *Repentance* had a degree of compatibility with anti-atheism apologetics. This argument is supported by Thomas Bowes's preface to the reader in *The Second Part of French Academie* (1594), de la Primaudaye's sequel to *French Academie*, which belongs to the main branch of Christian apologetics in terms of natural theology, and is directed against atheism. Bowes, in his dedication to Sir John Puckering, exhibits a sense of impending crisis, as if the whole world 'were plunged irrecouerably in this bottomlesse gulfe of Atheisme', and presents several moral exempla of God's judgements on atheists, one of which is the reference to *Repentance* with

---

Atheists: A Background to Pamela's Refutation of Cecropia', *Bibliothèque d'Humanisme et Renaissance*, 17:2 (1955), 252–77.

[57] McKerrow and Wilson (eds), *Works of Nashe*, vol. 2, p. 117.

[58] A similar technique can be seen in John Bate, *The Portraiture of Hypocrisie* (London, 1589), p. 111, where a Christian attempts to silence his atheist opponent with 'threatninges by the holy Ghost'.

[59] On the representation of atheists as uneasy about the next world, see Henry Smith, *Gods Arrowe against Atheists* (London, 1593), sig. B4r; and George Gifford, *A Briefe Discourse of Certaine Points of the Religion* (London, 1582), sigs E1v–E2r.

the above-mentioned quotation from Greene's blasphemous words to his friends.[60] Bowes saw this part of Greene's narrative as a good illustration of '[t]he voyce of a meere Atheist', as Greene himself declares: 'I seemed as one of no religion, but rather as a meere Atheist.' Moreover, Bowes followed Greene in warning the reader against the contagiousness of his works, saying that the minds of the young are 'no lesse possessed with the toyes of his irreligious braine, then their chambers and studies were pestered with his lewde and wanton bookes'.[61]

Even though he levels harsh criticism against the popular pamphleteers, Bowes does seem to have recognized the intrinsic value of Greene's conversion narrative, which 'so afterwardes hee pronounced of himselfe when hee was checked in conscience by the mightie hand of GOD',[62] considering it to be a useful and familiar supplement to his own anti-atheism discourse. This offers eloquent proof that the conversion narrative of *Repentance* not only worked to represent Greene as a repentant atheist but also helped him to assume the posture of a moralist by affiliating himself with the anti-atheism campaign.

'BLASPHEMOUS RHETORICKE' AND AUTOBIOGRAPHICAL HERMENEUTICS

What stuck firmly in Greene's mind, or could not be ignored when recasting the mode of his literary representation and making his gesture of repentance, seems to have been the 'blasphemous Rhetoricke' scattered throughout his literary output. Greene is deeply concerned about his 'detestable vice of swearing, taking a felicitie in blaspeming & prophaning the name of God' (vol. 12, p. 162). The chief crime of blasphemy does not just refer to the casual and perjurious oaths frequently used among the populace, such as by braggart soldiers and young gallants, which gave serious offence to the godly.[63] The meaning of blasphemy was so broad in scope at that time as to have become synonymous with both libertinism and heresy, and suggested open defiance of the supremacy of God. Thomas Bowes was fully aware of the seriousness of the vice and highlighted, in presenting atheists' 'horrible blasphemies against pure religion',[64] Greene's contemptuous atti-

---

[60] Pierre de la Primaudaye, *The Second Part of the French Academie*, trans. Thomas Bowes (London, 1594), sig. a4r.
[61] *Ibid.*, sig. b4r–v.
[62] *Ibid.*, sig. b4r.
[63] See Edmond Bicknoll, *A Swoord agaynst Swearyng* (London, 1579), sig. D1v; and Frances A. Shirley, *Swearing and Perjury in Shakespeare's Plays* (London, 1979), pp. 44–71.
[64] De la Primaudaye, *Second Part of the French Academie*, sig. b3v.

tude towards God by quoting the profane speeches that made his friends shudder directly from *Repentance*. Greene frequently gave his mind over to his own acts of blasphemy, which he says aroused his guilt: 'Oh knowe (good Countrymen) that the horrible sins and intollerable blasphemie I haue vsed against the Maiestie of God, is a blocke in my conscience' (vol. 12, p. 174).

Greene's religious sensitivity to blasphemy was not limited to the private spheres of his life but should be understood in the wider context of his actions in the public sphere, specifically as a playwright. In fact, he juxtaposes his vicious practice of blasphemy with playwriting:

> After I had wholy betaken me to the penning of plaies (which was my continuall exercise) I was so far from calling vpon God, that I sildome thought on God, but tooke such delight in swearing and blaspheming the name of God, that none could think otherwise of mee, than that I was the child of perdition. (vol. 12, pp. 177–8)

Greene may have duly recognized that the playhouses, saturated with scoffing and jesting at things sacred, had incurred the charge of blasphemy, and that anti-theatrical polemicists had vigorously campaigned against the theatre by claiming: 'intermingle not his blessed word with such prophane vanities.'[65]

These social and religious circumstances naturally urged him, when writing for or against the theatre, to be conscious of, and even scrupulous about, his own blasphemy on stage. In the preface to *Greene's Farewell to Folly*, addressed to the students of both universities, Greene expresses his deep concern about the 'blasphemous Rhetoricke' that a rival playwright employed by appropriating scriptural passages for his own use:

> As for example two louers on the stage arguing one an other of vnkind-nesse, his Mistris runnes ouer him with this canonicall sentence, A mans conscience is a thousand witnesses, and hir knight againe excuseth him selfe with that saying of the Apostle, Loue couereth the multitude of sinnes. I thinke this was but simple abusing of the Scripture. In charitie be it spoken I am perswaded the sexten of Saint Giles without Creeplegate, would haue beene ashamed of such blasphemous Rhetoricke. (vol. 9, p. 233)

What Greene targets here is his rival's clumsy piece of writing, 'to bring Scripture to proue any thing he sayes, and kill it dead with the text in a

---

[65] Stubbes, *Anatomie of Abuses*, p. 199. For the blasphemousness of playhouses, see Indira Ghose, 'Laughter and Blasphemy in the Shakespearean Theater', in John Pitcher (ed.), *MRDE, Vol. 16* (Madison, 2003), pp. 228–39; and Hugh Gazzard, 'An Act to Restrain Abuses of Players (1606)', *RES*, NS, 61:251 (2010), 495–528.

trifling subiect of loue'. This critical stance allows him to affect a pose of godliness as a moralist pamphleteer, his voice resonating with those of the anti-theatrical polemicists who complained bitterly about the use of biblical material and allusions in plays. Anthony Munday, too, attacks the uneasy hybrid of the sacred and the profane on stage, exhibiting deep concern for 'holie things to be handled by men so prophane, and defiled by interpositio[n] of dissolute words':

> The reuerend word of God, & histories of the Bible set forth on the stage by these blasphemous plaiers, are so corrupted with their gestures of scurrilitie, and so interlaced with vncleane, and whorish speeches, that it is not possible to drawe anie profite out of the doctrine of their spiritual moralities.[66]

As a playwright, however, Greene himself could not have been immune to this kind of anti-theatrical accusation, nor could he have ignored his own criticism of blasphemous rhetoric, because launching a literary endeavour to imitate Tamburlainean hubris, as well as affecting a godly pose as a didactic playwright, entailed extreme risks of using, misusing, and abusing the sacred in his plays.

Even in *A Looking-Glass for London and England*, which highlights God's vengeance upon the sin of hubris and foregrounds the urgent necessity for social repentance, Greene would have been unable to escape the charge of blasphemy in the anti-theatricalist way of thinking. Appropriating the biblical material in the play enabled him to create Rasni, King of Nineveh, as a repentant sinner, but its Old Testament setting naturally compelled him to juxtapose the God of Judaism against Rasni the blasphemer. The moral purpose of the play as a whole does not seem to have been frustrated by Rasni's attributing God's dignity to himself, partly because the rigid framework of repentance confirms the play's moral legitimacy, but mainly because Rasni brings about his salvation by lamenting his own sin at the end. Rasni's blasphemous speech in itself, however, obviously did risk incurring the anger of those who thought the playhouses would surely bring down the weight of God's wrath, and who therefore imposed on them the sort of high moral standards that Greene did on his rival.

William Rankins, emphasizing the speedy and sure judgement of God on blasphemers, censured the stage under the guise of a moral lesson in his *Mirrour of Monsters*: 'Oh men in worse condition then brutish beasts, yet can they couer theyr deformitie in thys poynt with the Masker blasphemy, in shrouding themselues vnder the visarde of godly learning.' His target was not only the hypocrisy of playwrights and players, but also their

---

[66] Munday, *Second and Third Blast of Retrait*, sig. H2r–v.

impiety in representing 'the persons of Heathen men' who strutted upon the stage calling upon the sacred entities with 'termes of pompous pryde'.[67] For him, the blasphemy of the players who imagined themselves 'to be the men whose persons they present' could not be overlooked as fictitious, but should be understood as a projection of their own deformity and ungodliness by acting as arrogant characters. Munday shared Rankins's fundamentalist literalism, assuming a straightforward correspondence between the character and the player/playwright: 'And if [the writers of our time] write of histories that are known, as the life of *Pompeie*; the martial affaires of *Cæsar*, and other worthies, they giue them a newe face, and turne them out like counterfeites to showe themselues on the stage.'[68] This superimposition of the impious activities of a blasphemous character onto the player or even onto the writer himself, a practice that Greene and the godly polemicists shared, seems to have been one of the tactics that they used to turn audiences against the stage.

It was natural, therefore, for Greene to demonstrate his acute consciousness that the profanity of the protagonists could also be identified with that of the author himself. According to this line of thought, whoever willingly creates profane characters to delight the audience also commits, and even delights in, the sin of blasphemy: this fundamentalist, literalistic mindset seems to have motivated Greene to confess repeatedly to his 'taking a felicitie in blaspeming & prophaning the name of God'. In fitting his own life into the conversion narrative of his repentance pamphlets, he had to atone for blasphemy both in his playwriting and in his ordinary life, thereby expiating his guilt, earning forgiveness from society, and gaining the opportunity for rehabilitation as a godly author. As the printer of *Repentance* indicates, readers were familiar with the fact that '[Greene's] pen in his lifetime pleased you as well on the Stage, as in the Stationers shops' (vol. 12, p. 155); so Greene, when fashioning himself into a moralist, was compelled either to attack others or to vindicate himself as a playwright. This sense of guilt about his own blasphemous literary output, as well as his new venture as a moralist, naturally makes the narrative of his repentance pamphlets highly autobiographical. Richard Helgerson, citing Paul Goodman's famous remark that 'the guilty do not pay attention to the object but only to themselves', gives an astute analysis of Greene's state of mind: 'As his guilt increased, so did his attention to himself, until, in one of the most remarkable passages in sixteenth-century fiction, he breaks off his *Groatsworth of Wit* to confess that he and his protagonist are one.'[69]

---

[67] Rankins, *Mirrour of Monsters*, sigs. G1v–G2r.
[68] Munday, *Second and Third Blast of Retrait*, sig. H3r.
[69] Helgerson, *Elizabethan Prodigals*, p. 80.

This intense consciousness of the correspondence between the author and his fictionalized characters is Greene's distinguishing feature, in creating not only the atheist self in *Repentance* but also the characters in his other pamphlets. He explains to the reader how he represents his narrative self when identifying himself with Roberto in *Greene's Groatsworth of Wit*: 'Heereafter suppose me the said *Roberto*, and I will goe on with that hee promised' (vol. 12, p. 137). To paraphrase Stephen Greenblatt on Marlowe, all his characters are not Greene, but Greene is 'deeply implicated' in all of them.[70] Patrick Cheney, defining John Keats's famous notion of the 'negative capability' of Shakespeare as 'an author's ability to inhabit characters other than his own', applies the notion to explain Marlowe's 'positive capability', which makes the author's biography of his character emerge 'as a biographical representation of the author himself'.[71] What Cheney and Greenblatt say about Marlowe actually lends itself most clearly to Greene's habit of inventing characters that reflect parts of his own personality.

The 'positive capability' might have encouraged Greene, when writing his plays, to project his own mental attitude on characters such as Alphonsus, Rasni, and Selimus (assuming Greene's authorship of the play). However, though it may be tempting to consider his stage characters in this way, there have been few critics who argue for this possibility, and it is not my intention to insist on such a naïve correspondence. Nevertheless, we should not overlook the fact that it was Greene, as well as the anti-theatrical polemicists, who first set out the interpretive framework of autobiographical representations and encouraged the public to look at characters in fiction in that way.

The reason why Greene first became an overnight moralist possibly arose from his failure to capitalize on the popularity of *Tamburlaine*, which had prompted 'two Gentlemen Poets' to cast ridicule upon him. Against their criticism, Greene, posing as a humane Horatian moralist writer, declares in the preface addressed to the reader of *Perimedes the Blacksmith* that 'I keepe my old course [...] vsing mine old poesie still, *Omne tulit punctum*', and says that he will refrain from exhibiting 'such impious instances of intollerable poetrie: such mad and scoffing poets, that haue propheticall spirits, as bred of *Merlins* race' (vol. 7, pp. 7–8). Thus, while contriving to exploit Tamburlainean blasphemy in his plays, he tries to superimpose the atheist and blaspheming protagonist onto Marlowe, his literary rival, just as the godly polemicists employed this tactic against the stage and Greene himself appropriated it to fashion himself as an ex-atheist moralist later on.

---

[70] Stephen Greenblatt, *Renaissance Self-Fashioning from More to Shakespeare* (Chicago, 1980), p. 220.
[71] Patrick Cheney, 'Biographical Representations: Marlowe's Life of the Author', in Takashi Kozuka and J. R. Mulryne (eds), *Shakespeare, Marlowe, Jonson: New Directions in Biography* (Aldershot, 2006), pp. 183–204, at pp. 184–5.

This autobiographical hermeneutics of character on both page and stage allowed Greene to take control of his self-fashioning as a moralist, develop his godly selfhood, and secure the privilege of urging moral reform upon the reader. He is therefore not just 'deeply implicated' in all his fictionalized characters, but confesses to the reader how he is also implicated in their offences against God. This position as the godly polemicist, who was once an atheist and playwright, permits Greene to assume a temporary space that is immune to his former vice of playwriting and enables him to exhort Marlowe, his 'quondam acquaintance' in rivalry, and other playwrights in *Greene's Groatsworth of Wit*.

GREENE THE MYTHMAKER

According to Henry Chettle's preface in *Kind-Harts Dreame* (1592), Greene's posthumous manuscripts were left 'in sundry Booke sellers hands', and Chettle happened to procure the manuscript of *Groatsworth*.[72] Around that time, he was intending to 'write the remembrance of sundry of my deceased frends' and to deliver 'his dreame; with euery Apparition simply as it was vttered' in *Kind-Harts Dreame*,[73] where the apparition of Greene complains of Gabriel Harvey's malicious slander against his life and works, and asks his friend Nashe to avenge him. Kind-Hart's gesture to plead for the deceased author perfectly coincides with Chettle's interest in the manuscript of *Groatsworth* as a literary executor. It is likely, as Harold Jenkins points out, that Chettle became involved in its publication 'out of a friendship for Greene'.[74] In fact, Chettle praised Greene as 'a man of indifferent yeares, of face amible, of body well proportioned, [...] of singuler pleasaunce the verye supporter',[75] and dared to be the first defender of Greene against numerous slanders, in particular from Harvey and his brothers. To make a fair copy of *Groatsworth* and transmit it to William Wright, a London bookseller, Chettle transcribed the autograph manuscript faithfully, but deleted what he thought Greene had 'in some displeasure writ' in a letter addressed 'to diuers play-makers'. Apart from this deletion, he claims to have put 'in the whole booke not a worde in, for I protest it was all *Greenes*'.[76]

Naturally, this excuse has led several scholars to challenge the authenticity of *Groatsworth*'s attribution to Greene; moreover, circumstantial

---

[72] Henry Chettle, *Kind-Harts Dreame*, in G. B. Harrison (ed.), *Elizabethan and Jacobean Quartos* (1923; repr. New York, 1966), pp. 5–6.
[73] *Ibid.*, pp. 9–10.
[74] Harold Jenkins, *The Life and Work of Henry Chettle* (London, 1934), p. 8. See also pp. 39–40.
[75] Chettle, *Kind-Harts Dreame*, p. 13.
[76] *Ibid.*, pp. 6–7.

and stylistic evidence has convinced them that it is a hoax by Chettle.[77] However, as David Bevington points out, Chettle's role in *Groatsworth* remains a matter of speculation, and it is unlikely that the whole work was his elaborately concocted forgery.[78] The part that particularly argues against his authorship is Greene's libellous epistolary exhortation to several playwrights, which was 'offensiuely by one or two of them taken'. Chettle recognizes these offended playwrights as highly respected 'schollers' who raised themselves to the gentry by obtaining their degrees from the university,[79] yet he says he does not know them personally: 'with neither of them that take offence was I acquainted.'[80] If Chettle wrote this famous exhortation, it is difficult to understand why he, under the guise of Greene, could have written such libellous words against playwrights with whom he had no personal stake or contact, or what could have motivated him to undermine the credit of these 'gentlemen' whose social prestige he would have held in esteem.[81] Moreover, apparently scenting trouble, Wright did not forget to clarify who was responsible for the resulting publication when he entered *Groatsworth* in the Stationers' Register on 20 September 'vppon the perill of Henrye Chettle',[82] and it is reasonable to assume that the stationer's concern was shared by Chettle himself. There is little room to doubt Chettle's claim: 'How I haue all the time of my conuersing in printing hindred the bitter inueying against schollers, it hath been very well knowne, and how in that I dealt I can sufficiently prooue.'[83]

---

[77] See John Jowett, 'Johannes Factotum: Henry Chettle and *Greene's Groatsworth of Wit*', *Papers of the Bibliographical Society of America*, 87:4 (1993), 453–86; and Robert Greene, *Greene's Groatsworth of Wit Bought with a Million of Repentance (1592)*, ed. D. Allen Carroll (New York, 1994), pp. 1–22.

[78] David Bevington, *Shakespeare and Biography* (Oxford, 2010), p. 16. See also Richard Westley, 'Computing Error: Reassessing Austin's Study of *Groatsworth of Wit*', *Literary and Linguistic Computing*, 21:3 (2006), 363–78; and Brian Vickers, '"Upstart Crow"? The Myth of Shakespeare's Plagiarism', *RES*, NS, 68:284 (2017), 244–67, at pp. 247–9.

[79] For the significance of the term 'scholar', see Lukas Erne, 'Biography and Mythography: Rereading Chettle's Alleged Apology to Shakespeare', *English Studies*, 79:5 (1998), 430–40, at pp. 433–4.

[80] Chettle, *Kind-Harts Dreame*, p. 6.

[81] This point was also suggested by Harold Jenkins, 'On the Authenticity of *Greene's Groatsworth of Wit* and *The Repentance of Robert Greene*', *RES*, OS, 11:41 (1935), 28–41, at p. 33; and Hanspeter Born, 'Why Greene Was Angry at Shakespeare', in S. P. Cerasano (ed.), *MRDE, Vol. 25* (Madison, 2012), pp. 133–73, at p. 135.

[82] Edward Arber, *A Transcript of the Registers of the Company of Stationers of London 1554–1640* (5 vols, London, 1875), vol. 2, p. 620.

[83] Chettle, *Kind-Harts Dreame*, p. 6.

What Chettle reveals in the preface to *Kind-Harts Dreame* is Greene's (not Chettle's) ingrained prejudice against Marlowe. There is general agreement that one of the offended gentleman playwrights was Marlowe, who had publicly suffered from Greene's exhortation dissuading him from atheism. Chettle details the circumstances that compelled him to delete some of the passages on Marlowe, 'whose learning I reuerence, and at the perusing of *Greenes* Booke, stroke out what then in conscience I thought he in some displeasure writ: or had it beene true, yet to publish it, was intollerable'.[84] The 'intollerable' passage deleted by Chettle may have been, as some scholars believe, a reference to Marlowe's homosexuality, but this remains a matter of speculation. It may also have been related to the sort of 'blasphemous' speech that Greene criticized as 'impious instances of intollerable poetry'.

What seems certain is that Chettle's way of addressing the problematic passage bears testimony to Greene's prejudice against Marlowe. Chettle, who was unacquainted with Marlowe and did not care 'if I neuer be', may have shared that prejudice to a greater or lesser extent; at the least, he had obviously recognized Greene's personal 'displeasure' found in the epistolary exhortation. At the same time, by adding 'had it beene true', Chettle expresses cautiousness about the reliability of the passage, which ran the risk of defamation, and seems to have felt dubious about trusting all of Greene's statements on Marlowe. This is partly because Chettle had to admit his ignorance of Marlowe's own beliefs, and partly because, to borrow Una Ellis-Fermor's words, Greene's exhortation 'does not sound like the writing of a man who knew what were Marlowe's deepest interests or understood his most representative thought'.[85]

In the exhortation, the conversion narrative allows Greene to assume a moralist position and address Marlowe, his former companion in atheism. This conventional address, the sort that was frequently employed in the confutations of anti-atheist polemicists, fittingly constitutes the beginning of Greene's epistolary satire on Marlowe. He refers to *inscrutabilia Dei iudicia* ('the inscrutable judgements of God') on monstrous atheists such as Cain, Judas, Julian the apostate, and Machiavelli, just as Thomas Bowes and Philippe de Mornay did in their apologetics, and then threatens Marlowe and the reader with fearful pictures of God's vengeance (vol. 12, pp. 142–3). Greene feels (or pretends to feel) guilty about having used his wit in vain in rivalry with Marlowe, working on 'blaspheming' with his own Tamburlainean characters on stage in the same way that Marlowe did with his 'Atheist *Tamburlan*'. Citing Psalm 14.1, he calls both Marlowe and

---

[84] *Ibid.*, p. 6
[85] U. M. Ellis-Fermor, *Christopher Marlowe* (London, 1927), p. 162.

himself fools: 'Greene, who hath said with thee like the foole in his heart, There is no God, should now giue glorie vnto his greatnesse' (vol. 12, p. 142). Straining their wits to make 'profane' plays has caused them to abuse God's gifts and engage in the evil practices of foolish atheists. Thus, while obliquely admitting Marlowe's powerful hold over him, Greene assumes the role of a former atheist playwright turned godly moralist.

This was the first overt charge that took the form of a literary libel against Marlowe, which may well have had a strong impact on society and created a public image of him that was possibly more contagious than even Marlowe himself could have imagined. No evidence has yet appeared to support the idea that, before late 1592, Marlowe's reputation as an atheist had become widespread, except for the fact that a defamatory rumour about him had spread among the hostile members of Corpus Christi, and that Greene himself, having had close connections with these college members and having been well known as 'a meere Atheist' in his later career, had attempted to acquire a godly narrative identity through his repentance pamphlets. All we can say, cautiously, using this circumstantial evidence is that it was Greene who first laid down the moralist principle or prejudice that introduced not only his contemporaries but also the critics of his and our time to the governing idea of the 'atheist' Marlowe and his self-projecting dramatic representations.

Malcolm Kelsall, criticizing the assumption of John Bakeless that 'All his characters are Marlowe', points out that the argument shows 'no advance upon the opinions of Greene's *Groatsworth of Wit*' and says: 'Since the plays contain blasphemous protagonists and demonstrate, in Greene's words, "pestilent Machivilian policy", their writer was all too likely to be interpreted by ill-informed or malicious critics as holding the views expressed by his characters. This may merely betray the naivety of the critic, however.'[86] Kelsall's caution urges us to reconsider how the literary criticism of Marlowe first emerged and to what extent Greene can be trusted as an impartial critic. Rather than following Greene's suit and reinforcing his line of thought, we ought to consider the alternative, and perhaps more plausible, possibility that he was the originator of this 'ill-informed or malicious' criticism. In that case, we cannot overlook those cultural and literary conditions – among them Greene's origins in Norwich, the two playwrights' rivalry in the theatrical business, and Greene's self-fashioning of his puritan narrative identity – which led him to pose as a moralist critic and then to create the public image, or rather the myth, of Marlowe. What is needed is not just an assessment of Greene's autobiographical hermeneutics but a thorough reappraisal of Greene as the mythmaker of Marlowe.

---

[86] Malcolm Kelsall, *Christopher Marlowe* (Leiden, 1981), p. 5.

Chapter 10

THE GENESIS OF THE MARLOWE MYTH

RALEIGH'S SCHOOL OF ATHEISM

The proclamation dated 18 October 1591 and titled *A Declaration of Great Troubles Pretended against the Realme by a Number of Seminarie Priests and Jesuists* expresses open hostility towards English seminaries financially supported by Philip II, the King of Spain, and deep concern about 'a multitude of dissolute young men' who had gathered together to 'become fugitives, rebels, and traitors'.[1] This proclamation is presumed to have been drawn up by William Cecil, who uses harsh and sardonic words throughout the text. One of the passages in which we can detect his bitterness is where he condemns the seminaries as a hotbed of sedition:

> there are in Rome and Spain and other places certain receptacles made to live in and there to be instructed in *school points of sedition*, and from thence to be secretly and by stealth conveyed into our dominions with ample authority from Rome to move, stir up, and persuade as many of our subjects as they dare deal withal to renounce their natural allegiance due to us and our crown.[2]

Cecil is particularly furious with 'the heads of these dens and receptacles', whom he assumes have recently motivated Philip to renew his war against England by assuring him that a multitude of young Catholics would be ready to assist his invasion. Cecil specifies two of the ringleaders, with heavy sarcasm: 'a schoolman named Parsons, arrogating to himself the name of the King Catholic's Councilor' and 'another scholar called Allen, now for his treasons honored with a cardinal's hat'.[3] While his malicious

---

[1] Elizabeth I, Proclamation 738, Richmond, 18 October 1591, in Paul L. Hughes and James F. Larkin (eds), *Tudor Royal Proclamations* (3 vols, New Haven, 1969), vol. 3, pp. 86–93, at p. 88. The title of the proclamation is quoted from *STC* 8208, sig. A2r.
[2] Hughes and Larkin (eds), *Tudor Royal Proclamations*, vol. 3, p. 88, emphasis added.
[3] *Ibid.*, p. 89.

wording may seem peculiar, it shows how wary he was of these institutions. He imagined discontented students debating the key issues for sedition under the guidance of a headmaster who was well versed in the methods and teachings supporting treason.

Although we do not know why Cecil coined the phrase 'school points of sedition', he might have picked up the expression from Martin Marprelate. In 1589, Martin published the broadsheet *Certain Mineral and Metaphysical Schoolpoints*, which he possibly designed on the model of the Cambridge 'act verses': the set of briefly propounded theses that were circulated by those taking part in public disputations as acts for degrees, to offer a mock academic debate.[4] However, it is more likely that Cecil was responding to William Allen's defence of English Catholic seminaries on the continent as 'the noblest Schooles in Christendom'. In *An Apologie and True Declaration of the Institution and Endeuours of the Two English Colleges* (1581), Allen mockingly complains of an acute lack of professional learning among the Protestant clergy, in stark contrast to the proper training of seminary students: 'There is not the poorest artificer of al the Anabaptistes in Holland, or of the Puritans, Brethren of loue, and Protestants in England, nor the yongest Grammarian, or Logician in the Vniuersities or *schooles of Sectaries*.'[5]

The 1591 proclamation provoked a swift response from the Catholic side. In August 1592, Richard Verstegan published *An Aduertisement Written to a Secretarie of My L. Treasurers of Ingland* at Philip's suggestion and with his funding.[6] This pamphlet was the abridged English version of Robert Persons's *Elizabethae, Angliae Reginae Haeresim Calvinianam Propugnantis, Saevissimum in Catholicos sui Regni Edictum [...] cum responsione ad singula capita* (1592, usually abbreviated and hereafter cited as *Responsio*), in which Persons the 'schoolman' rebutted Cecil's criticism. Clearly, the phrase 'school points of sedition' stuck in Persons's craw, and he derided it by saying:

---

[4] For 'act verses' as the possible model of *Mineral and Metaphysical Schoolpoints*, see Joseph L. Black (ed.), *The Martin Marprelate Tracts: A Modernized and Annotated Edition* (Cambridge, 2008), p. 90; the usage of these verses at Cambridge is well documented in William T. Costello, *The Scholastic Curriculum at Early Seventeenth-Century Cambridge* (Cambridge, MA, 1958), pp. 12–34.

[5] William Allen, *An Apologie and True Declaration of the Institution and Endeuours of the Two English Colleges* ([Rheims?], 1581), sigs I3v and G5r, emphasis added.

[6] For the date of its publication and authorship, and Philip II's assistance, see Albert J. Loomie, 'The Authorship of "An Advertisement Written to a Secretarie of M. L. Treasurer of England"', *Renaissance News*, 15:3 (1962), 201–7; and 'Philip II and the Printing of "Andreas Philopater"', *Library*, 5th ser., 24:2 (1969), 143–5.

M. Cecil in this proclamation by a new fonde, phantastical phrase tearmeth [matters of judgment and learning] *Schoole points of sedition*, as for example, to teach that a man muste confesse his synnes to a prieste, that he muste make restitution of such things as he hath taken wrongefully from others, that he muste heare masse, that he muste acknowledge the Bisshop of Rome to be superame [*sic*] heade of the Church next vnder Christe, and the like which were poyntes of schoole, and accompted both currant and Catholique doctrine in Ingland for a thousand yeares before Cecil was borne.[7]

From Persons's standpoint, Cecil's criticism was a long way off the mark, for the 'poyntes of schoole' in which Cecil imagined Catholic youth being instructed at the seminaries were not those of a political or martial nature, but of traditional Catholic doctrine intended to cultivate their virtue.[8]

It was not just Cecil's sarcastic use of 'schoolpoints' that irritated Persons: 'By which occasion of the wordes *Scholler and Schoolman, and the like fond tearmes* impertinently thruste in, this defender discourseth vpon M. Cecils wit and discretio[n] in vsing these and like woordes, and phrases so much out of order, sense, propriety and methode in this proclamation.'[9] The ridicule employed in the official proclamation provoked Persons to counterattack by using similar terms in a withering retort.[10] He acidly remarked that Cecil was eager to appeal for the need to keep the people steadfast in the Protestant faith partly because of a marked deterioration in the quality of the clergy and partly because of 'their division, wrangling, and dissension among themselues'; and he attributed the ecclesiastical decline of the English Church, again with a tinge of sarcasm, to the 'lacke of study, and learning (those few apostatas being dead that at the beginning made some flourishe with theire skill gotten in the Catholique *schooles*)'.[11]

[7] Richard Verstegan, *An Aduertisement Written to a Secretarie of My L. Treasurers of Ingland* ([Antwerp], 1592), p. 43, emphasis in original. In Robert Persons, *Elizabethae, Angliae Reginae Haeresim Calvinianam Propugnantis, Saevissimum in Catholicos sui Regni Edictum* [...] *cum responsione ad singula capita* ([Antwerp], 1592), p. 151, we have 'quid sibi volunt, *seditiones scholasticae*? vel puncta quaedam scholastica, de seditione*, vt Anglicè habetur?' ('what do "schools of sedition or some schoolpoints of sedition" mean when considered in English?').

[8] Robert Southwell was similarly offended by the phrase in his, *An Humble Supplication to Her Maiestie*, ed. R. C. Bald (Cambridge, 1953), p. 13.

[9] Verstegan, *Aduertisement*, p. 53, emphasis in original.

[10] Victor Houliston, 'The Lord Treasurer and the Jesuit: Robert Persons's Satirical *Responsio* to the 1591 Proclamation', *Sixteenth Century Journal*, 32:2 (2001), 383–401, examines Persons's skill as a satirical polemicist. He specifically focuses on Persons's mock-heroic caricature of Cecil rather than on the school metaphor that I have discussed here.

[11] Verstegan, *Aduertisement*, p. 58, emphasis added.

The belief that sectarian division was a cause of the decline was shared by other Catholic polemicists in exile and used to attack the Elizabethan regime and Church, and had often been associated with the rise of atheism in England.[12] These Catholic writers were unanimous in their opinion (and played a major role in disseminating that opinion) that the natural consequence of Protestant sectarianism was 'coldnes & doubtfulnesse in Religion, and at length also plaine atheisme and contempt'.[13] Allen declared that 'Atheisme is the end of al these vnhappy reuolts from the vnitie of Gods people'.[14] It is not difficult, therefore, to understand why Persons attacked Cecil as 'the old atheiste' and blamed the chancellors of universities for having 'laide open the way to dissolution, Ruffianry, and Atheisme'.[15]

Furthermore, Persons rebutted Cecil's invective against the English seminaries as schools of sedition when turning his attention to Sir Walter Raleigh, an opportune target. Persons warned against Raleigh's well-attended 'school of atheism', where young gentlemen learned to mock holy precepts under the direction of a certain conjurer, and expressed his deep concern that, if this school of atheism were to take root too deeply and if Raleigh were appointed a Privy Councillor, the English people might shortly receive from that conjurer – Raleigh's epicurean instructor (*à Mago illo atque Epicureo Raulaeo praeceptore*) – an edict in the name of the queen that would flatly deny all divinity and the immortality of the soul.[16] Verstegan in *An Advertisement* sums up Persons's point:

> Of Sir Walter Rauleys schoole of Atheisme by the waye, and of the Coniurer that is M[aster]. thereof, and of the dilige[n]ce vsed to get young gentleme[n] to this schoole, where in both Moyses, and our Sauior; the olde, and new Testamente are iested at, and the schollers taught amonge other thinges, to spell God backwarde.[17]

The phrase 'the schollers taught amonge other thinges, to spell God backwarde' has no equivalent in the same section of *Responsio*, and so Verstegan seems to have inserted his own invented thumbnail sketch of the atheist school.

---

[12] On this point, see Thomas H. Clancy, *Papist Pamphleteers: The Allen–Persons Party and the Political Thought of the Counter-Reformation in England, 1572–1615* (Chicago, 1964), pp. 173–4.

[13] Robert Persons, *A Relation of the Triall Made before the King of France* ([Saint-Omer], 1604), p. 45; see also Robert Persons, *A Treatise of Three Conuersions of England from Paganisme to Christian Religion* (3 vols, [Saint-Omer], 1603), vol. 1, pp. 622–3 (sig. Rr1v).

[14] Allen, *Apologie and True Declaration*, sig. H2r.

[15] Verstegan, *Aduertisement*, pp. 44, 46.

[16] Persons, *Responsio*, pp. 28–9.

[17] Verstegan, *Aduertisement*, p. 18 (sig. B1v).

It is not clear why Persons chose to accuse Raleigh, not yet a member of the Privy Councillors, as an accomplice atheist. However, his antagonism makes more sense if we accept that he recognized Raleigh as one of 'these new vpstarts' who were dominating England and who were highly influential in the queen's decisions on religious and political matters.[18] Raleigh was an outspoken advocate of nationalist policy against Spain and maintained an impressive yet threatening presence against Catholics. Moreover, as Ernest A. Strathmann points out, Raleigh showed favouritism towards the Protestant radicals in early 1591.[19] It is possible, therefore, that he was considered by the Catholic exiles as a promoter of sectarian division and atheism who deserved his share of personal criticism.

We have only limited information to help explain Persons's attack on Raleigh himself, but we can identify two reasons why the attack was directed at the 'schoole of Atheisme'. The first was the exiles' unhappiness about the political situation in England, where recusant gentlemen and university students were compelled to seek opportunities to learn abroad, and their strong concerns about the religious soundness of the younger generation at Elizabeth's court. Verstegan's letter to Persons dated 5 March 1592 – that is, around the time when Persons was hard at work on *Responsio*[20] – expresses these sentiments in similar wording, though the man suspected of atheism is not Raleigh but William Cecil's grandson:

> The yonge youth is as pretely instructed in athisme as the Lady Arbella is in puresy, for he will not stick openly to scof at the Byble, and will folkes to spell the name of God backward. I cannot thinck that there was half so great iniquitie in Sodoma as is now in England, besydes the shedding of innocent bloud, which daily crieth for vengeance and may give us most hope of our countrie's recoverie.[21]

Second, and more importantly, Persons was eager to counter Cecil's criticism that the seminary youth had been instructed in the 'school points of sedition', and seems to have appropriated the school metaphor to draw a marked contrast between the religious discipline of the English seminaries and that of the English Court, as represented by Raleigh's school of

---

[18] *Ibid.*, p. 18 (sig. B1v).
[19] Ernest A. Strathmann, *Sir Walter Ralegh: A Study in Elizabethan Skepticism* (1951; repr. New York, 1973), pp. 34–40. See also T. E. Hartley (ed.), *Proceedings in the Parliaments of Elizabeth I* (3 vols, London, 1995), vol. 3, p. 162.
[20] In his letter to Aquaviva dated 12 August 1592, Persons writes that Philip II was showing a deep interest in his handwritten *Responsio* and intended to subsidize its printing. See Loomie, 'Authorship of "An Advertisement"', p. 204.
[21] Anthony G. Petti (ed.), *The Letters and Despatches of Richard Verstegan* (London, 1959), p. 40.

atheism.[22] The argument went that, unlike the seminaries, where students were encouraged in their divinity studies under the guidance of Cardinal Allen, with the financial support of the King of Spain, the sectarian division in England produced only the school of atheism, where young gentlemen were seduced to study blasphemy under the supervision of the schoolmaster of necromancy, the 'conjurer' of the devil, with the support of Raleigh, the upstart privateering courtier.

The contrasting images of the two schools, with their respective spiritual schoolmasters, may appear to us rather ridiculous now, but the contrast may have been crucial to Persons's argument. He seems to have employed and highlighted the underlying Augustinian metaphor about an ecclesiastical community, *schola Christi* ('the school of Christ'), which had been prevalent in the Latin Christian tradition.[23] John Calvin often considered a Christian as a 'schoolefelow in the schoole of Christ' and gave warning against the 'cursed seede' that was 'so rooted in all men, as there is none of vs all but hee may keepe a schoole of superstition, without hauing any schoolemaster to teach him'.[24] The minister John Baker declared his firm belief in the immortality of soul and body, saying that 'we that are Christians and trayned vp in the schole of Christ our master, must beleeue this point'.[25] Thus, by weaving a metaphor that was widespread at that time into the incidental gossip concerning Raleigh, Persons seems to have invented the 'schoole of Atheisme', or sectarianism, as the antithesis of 'the noblest Schooles in Christendom', as a way to retaliate against Cecil's jibes.

It is natural, therefore, to consider the 'schoole of Atheisme' as the product of imagination and derision, not a genuine intellectual coterie or circle of freethinkers. The publication of Person's *Responsio* in eight editions and four languages within two years may have greatly contributed to the wide circulation of printed and oral information about the 'school', which necessarily decontextualized Persons's meaning and the purpose of his narrative and helped the gossip to take on its own momentum and develop into a myth. This cast a long shadow not only over the investigation of Raleigh

---

[22] For Persons's emphasis on this contrast, see also his *A Relation of the King of Spaines Receiuing in Valliodolid* [sic] (Antwerp, 1592), pp. 13–14 and 22–3.

[23] For the metaphor of 'the school of Christ', see Raymond A. Blacketer, *The School of God: Pedagogy and Rhetoric in Calvin's Interpretation of Deuteronomy* (Dordrecht, 2006), pp. 37–40.

[24] John Calvin, *A Harmonie vpon the Three Euangelists* (London, 1584), sig. C2r; *The Sermons of M. Iohn Caluin vpon the Fifth Booke of Moses* (London, 1583), p. 310.

[25] John Baker, *Lectures of I. B. vpon the xii. Articles of Our Christian Faith* (London, 1581), sig. X7r. See also Edwin Sandys, *Sermons* (London, 1585), p. 98; Pierre Viret, *The Worlde Possessed with Deuils* (London, 1583), sig. D5v.

at Cerne Abbas in 1594 but even over his trial in 1603; and it enjoyed a remarkable longevity until the twentieth century as 'the School of Night'.[26]

What concerns us here, however, is the conjurer schoolmaster, whose name Persons does not mention. It is generally agreed that he meant the astronomer and mathematician Thomas Harriot, who lived and worked under Raleigh's aegis, but we should not overlook the fact that, by preserving the conjurer's anonymity, Persons allowed speculation about his identity and activities. Apparently, Harriot certainly did consider that 'the conjurer' referred to him. On the back of the final folio of his manuscript work 'The Doctrine of Nauticall Triangles Compedious', he compiled a brief list of references that had been made to him in printed works. The list includes 'Item a libellum intituled An advertisement &c. 1592' (i.e. Verstegan's translation), as well as Persons's Latin version: 'Item a boke in Latin 1593 contra edictum Elizabethe'.[27]

However, Harriot was not the only one who considered himself to be 'the conjurer'. John Dee, upon whom Persons's gossip had a strong and troublesome impact, later drew up a petition to James I for removing his lifelong social stigma as a necromancer and clearing the 'most grieuous and dammageable Sclaunder' that 'he is, or hath bin a Coniurer, or Caller, or Invocator of diuels'. Dee assigned the origin of the stigma to a printed libel:

> some impudent and malicious forraine enemie, or English traytor to the florishing State and Honor of this Kingdome, hath in Print (*Anno* 1592. 7. *Ianuarij*) affirmed your Maiesties said Supplicant, to be the *Coniurer* belonging to the most Honorable Priuie Counsell, of your Maiesties most famous last Predecessor, (*Queene Elizabeth*).[28]

No edition of *Responsio* survives with the precise date of 7 January 1592, and the two earliest extant editions are from October 1592, though there is reason to believe that neither is the first edition. If we take the date '*Anno* 1592. 7. *Ianuarij*', as Strathmann does, as that of the publication, it would therefore be difficult to identify it with *Responsio*.[29] Nor can we find any foreign or exiled 'English traytor' who denounced John Dee as 'a Coniurer'

---

[26] On the myth of the School of Night, see Lindsay Ann Reid, 'The Spectre of the School of Night: Former Scholarly Fictions and the Stuff of Academic Fiction', *Early Modern Literary Studies*, special issue 23 (2014), 1–31.

[27] David B. Quinn and John W. Shirley, 'A Contemporary List of Hariot References', *Renaissance Quarterly*, 22:1 (1969), 9–26, at p. 26; E. G. R. Taylor, 'The "Doctrine of Nauticall Triangles Compendious" I: Thomas Hariot's Manuscript', *Journal of the Institute of Navigation*, 6 (1953), 131–40.

[28] John Dee, *To the Kings Most Excellent Maiestie* (London, 1604).

[29] Ernest A. Strathmann, 'John Dee as Ralegh's "Conjurer"', *HLQ*, 10:4 (1947), 365–72, at p. 371.

in print around 1592, apart from Persons in *Responsio* and Verstegan in *Advertisement*. Glyn Parry has argued that Dee was alluding not to a printed book but to the slanderous rumour mentioned in Allen's letter to Persons of that date, printed in Persons's *A Briefe Apologie, or Defence of the Catholike Ecclesiastical Hierarchie, & Subordination in England* (1601), which reveals that 'D. Dee their coniurer or Astrologer is said to haue put them in more doubt, for that he hath told the Counsel by his calculation, that the Realme indeed shalbe conquered this Somer, beleeue him who wil'.[30] This suggests that the identification of Dee as the conjurer at Elizabeth's court was shared widely among Catholic exiles, including Verstegan, by 1592. If that is so, Verstegan and Persons may have picked up the rumour and deliberately mixed up Dee with the conjurer of Raleigh's school of atheism; and Dee may have been another who thought Persons's (or Verstegan's) allusion to be a libellous and malicious swipe at him. In any case, it was difficult for readers to identify precisely who the conjurer master of the school was.

The evidence supporting the impact of *Responsio* indicates that the gossip would have aroused widespread speculation about the identity of the conjurer and could also have been employed as powerful ammunition for slandering Persons's political enemies. In this respect, it was the principal component in the social process whereby the legend concerning the school of atheism was created in the latter half of 1592.

CHOLMELEY, BAINES, AND THE CONJURER LAUREATE

An undated document concerning the government agent Richard Cholmeley's rebellious views, while only a small part of the overall information about recusants, separatists, and dissenters, is a useful snippet that enables us to see how the myth of Marlowe was created and how it rapidly developed over the course of a few months. It cannot be dated, but presumably preceded a warrant for Cholmeley's arrest on 19 March 1593.[31] Cholmeley was under suspicion of organizing a group of atheists for a treasonable conspiracy. The document consists of two reports. The first (BL Harley MS 6848, fol. 190), which endorses 'Remembraunces of wordes & matter againste Ric Cholmeley', is a list of allegations and hearsay statements

---

[30] Glyn Parry, *The Arch-Conjuror of England: John Dee* (New Haven, 2011), pp. 225–31. Robert Persons, *A Briefe Apologie, or Defence of the Catholike Ecclesiastical Hierarchie, & Subordination in England* (Antwerp, 1601), sig. F3r–v. William H. Sherman, *John Dee: The Politics of Reading and Writing in the English Renaissance* (Amherst, 1995), p. 85, points out that Dee's concern with the conditions under which a text was produced meant paying attention to its date.

[31] For the nature and date of the document, see Constance Brown Kuriyama, *Christopher Marlowe: A Renaissance Life* (Ithaca, 2002), p. 214.

drawn up by an unknown informant for some of the Privy Councillors. The second (BL Harley MS 6848, fol. 191), written in the same hand, is a fair copy of a letter that provides hearsay information concerning Cholmeley's religious opinions and his slanderous speech against Privy Councillors. The two reports were presumably produced by the same informant, who was eloquent in representing Cholmeley as a libellous atheist. According to the informant, Cholmeley 'speaketh in generall all evill of the Counsell: sayenge that they are all Atheistes & Machiavillians', mentioning by name Burghley, Lord Hunsdon, Charles Howard, and Robert Cecil, who, he says, 'have profounde wittes, bee sounde Athiestes & their lives & deedes showe that they thinke their soules doe ende vanishe & perishe with their bodies'.[32] Thus, Cholmeley is represented as if he were a Catholic sympathetic to Allen, Persons, and Verstegan in his attack on the Privy Councillors as a set of atheists whose monstrous doctrine permeated the queen's administration.

In representing the contagion of these 'sounde atheists', Cholmeley (and/or the informant) closely follows the methods of the anti-atheist polemicists such as Thomas Nashe, who, in *Christs Teares over Iervsalem* (1593), cautions the reader: 'These Atheists (with whom you are to encounter) are speciall men of witte. The Romish Seminaries haue not allured vnto them so many good wits as Atheisme. It is the superaboundance of witte that makes Atheists.'[33] This contemporary stereotype of the highly intellectual atheist obviously encouraged Cholmeley to consider himself to have abundant wit. In fact, the informant reports that Cholmeley 'so highly esteemeth his owne witt & judgement that hee saieth that noman are sooner deceyved & abused then the Counsell themselves'. This document is valuable for understanding Cholmeley's (and/or the informant's) invention of an atheist, as well as a heretic, in the context of the heated atmosphere of the heresy-hunting craze of the early 1590s and the print warfare over the proclamation against English seminaries.

We can detect Persons's influence in the way that Cholmeley scoffed at scripture. Persons claims that, in Raleigh's school of atheism, 'both Moses and Christ; the old and new Testament are jested at'. The informant of 'Remembraunces' closely follows and enlarges on these two points by declaring that Cholmeley stated that

> Jhesus Christe was a bastarde St Mary a whore & the Anngell Gabriell a Bawde to the holy ghoste & that Christe was justly persecuted by the Jewes for his owne foolishnes. That Moyses was a Jugler & Aaron

---

[32] BL, Harley MS 6848, fols 190–1, transcribed in Kuriyama, *Christopher Marlowe*, pp. 214, 216.
[33] Ronald B. McKerrow (ed.), *The Works of Thomas Nashe*, 2nd edn, rev. F. P. Wilson (5 vols, Oxford, 1958), vol. 2, p. 124.

a Cosoner the one for his miracles to Pharao to prove there was a god, & the other for taking the Eareringes of the children of Israell to make a golden calfe with many other blasphemous speeches of the devine essence of god which I feare to rehearse.[34]

These abusive words were derived from readily available sources. Regarding Christ's illegitimacy, the informant (or Cholmeley) was obviously appropriating a particular Jewish tradition that Philippe de Mornay mentions: 'The Prophets haue told us that [Christ] should be borne of a Uirgin. The Gospell affirmeth Mary his mother to haue bin such a one; and yet the *Iewes* which haue come afterward, haue written that she was taken in adulterie.'[35]

At the popular level, the Reformed authorities condemned the 'popish' drama for questioning and even mocking the doctrine of the incarnation. Christopher Goodman notes that 'the absurdities' in the Chester Cycle plays reveal a trace of widespread popular disbelief: 'Ioseph chargeth his wife with open words, contrary to the Scriptures.' Although the angel Gabriel is not represented as a panderer, Goodman finds blasphemy, as the informant on Cholmeley did, in the impersonation or farcical personification of the Holy Ghost.[36] This disposition to question the virgin birth was readily employed in abusive attacks on a person's character or reputation. For instance, the Earl of Oxford was accused of atheism in 1581 by his former friend Charles Arundel, who witnessed Oxford saying 'that Christ was a simple man / that Iosephe was bothe a cuckckold and a wittold / that nothinge was so defensible by the scripture as bawderie.'[37]

The latter half of the blasphemous statement, concerning Moses' miracles in the Old Testament, is another piece of popular belief about what constituted 'atheism' at that time. Doubt about Moses' divine potency, like the argument about Christ's illegitimacy, can be found in Christian

---

[34] BL, Harley MS 6848, fol. 191, transcribed in Kuriyama, *Christopher Marlowe*, p. 216.

[35] Philippe de Mornay, *A Woorke concerning the Trewnesse of the Christian Religion*, trans. Philip Sidney and Arthur Golding, intro. F. J. Sypher (1587; repr. New York, 1976), p. 543. See also Calvin, *Harmonie*, p. 60; and Thomas Lodge, *Wits Miserie, and the Worlds Madnesse* (London, 1596), in Gosse (ed.), *Works of Thomas Lodge*, vol. 4, pp. 10–11.

[36] For Christopher Goodman's 'Notes of the absurdities & c in the Chester plays', see Elizabeth Baldwin, Lawrence M. Clopper, and David Mills (eds), *Cheshire including Chester*, REED (2 vols, Toronto, 2007), vol. 1, pp. 147–8. Erin E. Kelly makes a critical comparison between Baines's and Goodman's notes in 'Doubt and Religious Drama across Sixteenth-Century England, or Did the Middle Ages Believe in Their Plays?', in Jessica Dell, David Klausner, and Helen Ostovich (eds), *The Chester Cycle in Context, 1555–1575: Religion, Drama, and the Impact of Change* (Farnham, 2012), pp. 47–63, at pp. 62–3.

[37] TNA, SP, 12/151/46, fols 103–4, transcribed in Alan H. Nelson, *Monstrous Adversary: The Life of Edward de Vere, 17th Earl of Oxford* (Liverpool, 2003), pp. 209–10.

apologetics against heathen authors. Reginald Scot was well aware of this sort of conventional argument: '*Apollonius Molon, Possidonius, Lisimachus,* and *Appian* terme *Moses* both a magician and a coniuror: whom *Eusebius* confuteth with manie notable arguments.'[38] The criticism levelled against Aaron for cozening the Israelites to steal their earrings is difficult to trace. It may have originated in the anti-Catholic typology employed by the Protestant polemicists who promoted the interpretation of Aaron as a false high priest.[39] Aaron, who proposed that the Israelites should deliver their earrings to make a golden calf, was readily associated with the 'false preachers' who had defrauded the commonality by soliciting donations.[40]

What we see, therefore, in this document is a significant aspect of the mythmaking process: that the various fragments of information picked up from contemporary religious discourses were reworked into a sensationalist account converging on the two points of Christ and Moses that Persons presented as the schoolpoints of Raleigh's atheism. At the same time, the informant attempts to shed light on who indoctrinated Cholmeley with these atheistic beliefs by affiliating him with Marlowe: 'That [Cholmeley] saieth & verely beleveth that one Marlowe is able to shewe more sounde reasons for Atheisme then any devine in Englande is able to geve to prove devinitie & that Marloe tolde him that hee hath read the Atheist lecture to Sir Walter Raliegh & others.'[41] This was the second allegation (albeit private in this instance) made against Marlowe during his lifetime, following the first, public one made in *Greene's Groatsworth of Wit.*

The informant represents Cholmeley as an enthusiastic devotee of Marlowe, whom the informant (or Cholmeley) considered to be an intellectual atheist under the aegis of Raleigh. Naturally, Marlowe *had* to be able to show 'sounde reasons for Atheisme' because anti-atheist polemicists were wont to consider an atheist as highly contagious and to be superabundant in wit. The two-line insertion into the note Richard Baines produced for the Privy Council that Cholmeley 'hath confesst that he was perswaded by Marloes reasons to become an Atheist' may have been reworked on the basis

---

[38] Reginald Scot, *The Discouerie of Witchcraft* (London, 1584), pp. 451–2. See also John Rogers, *The Displaying of an Horrible Secte* (London, 1578), sig. C5r; McKerrow and Wilson (eds), *Works of Thomas Nashe*, vol. 2, p. 116; and John Calvin, *Institution of Christian Religion* (London, 1561), sig. C1v.

[39] See, for instance, William Tyndale, *The Whole Workes of W. Tyndall, Iohn Frith, and Doct. Barnes, Three Worthy Martyrs* (London, 1573), pp. 114 and 125. Alexander Nowell employed a similar typological contrast in his attack on Thomas Dorman in *A Reproufe* (London, 1565), fol. 60r–v.

[40] See John King, *Lectures vpon Ionas Deliuered at Yorke in the Yeare of Our Lorde 1594* (London, 1597), pp. 389 and 463.

[41] BL, Harley MS 6848, fol. 190, transcribed in Kuriyama, *Christopher Marlowe*, p. 215.

of the informant's allegations.[42] This turned the playwright and scholar into a great atheist philosopher who engaged in reading lectures to famous audiences, and the sort of stereotyped figure that the common people would have imagined a philosopher to be: 'the common sort suppose [...] that to be a Philosopher, is nothing els, but to discourse and dispute in the schooles at certeine times of philosophicall points aloft in a chaire, and reade lecture at their houres out of their books.'[43]

An important point about 'Remembraunces' is that it suggests for the first time Marlowe's relationship with Raleigh. However, the passage is the only surviving concrete evidence for this relationship and the document's greater interest lies in being one of the responses produced as a result of the profound impact of both Persons's *Responsio* and Verstegan's *Advertisment*, which not only allowed the reader to imagine the identity of 'the Coniurer that is M[aster]. thereof' but also provided the crucial element in the informant's report on Marlowe's atheist lecture. In other words, the statement suggests that the informant (or Cholmeley) intended to identify Marlowe as the conjurer at Raleigh's school of atheism, just as Dee and Harriot identified themselves. Thus, Cholmeley's statement on Marlowe seems to have had its origin in Persons's anti-Cecilian propaganda.

What, then, encouraged the informant (or Cholmeley) to choose Marlowe as such a symbolic figure? It seems that behind the report lay a pure coincidence of time and circumstance. The preface of Verstegan's *Advertisement* is dated 'this first of August. 1592', so it was smuggled into England possibly immediately after. The evidence for its circulation can be found in the letter of Edward Jones, the secretary to Sir John Puckering. He sent Anthony Bacon a copy of the *Advertisement* from Hertford on 8 November, calling it '*a seditious vile book*, which he desired might be kept from any but such as were affected, and knew how to use such things.'[44] It is highly possible, therefore, that the *Advertisement* had been in circulation before early November 1592. It is a strange coincidence that, around the same time, Marlowe was framed as an arch-atheist by Robert Greene. The

---

[42] J. A. Downie, 'Reviewing What We Think We Know about Christopher Marlowe, Again', in Sarah K. Scott and M. L. Stapleton (eds), *Christopher Marlowe the Craftsman: Lives, Stage, and Page* (Farnham, 2010), pp. 33–46, at p. 44, argues that the contemporary references to Marlowe's atheistic opinions have their origins in this paragraph.

[43] Plutarch, *The Philosophie, Commonlie Called, the Morals*, trans. Philemon Holland (London, 1603), p. 399.

[44] LPL, MS 648, fol. 305, cited in Thomas Birch, *Memoirs of the Reign of Queen Elizabeth, from the Year 1581 till Her Death* (2 vols, London, 1754), vol. 1, p. 90. Houliston, 'The Lord Treasurer and the Jesuit', p. 389, n. 19, identifies 'a seditious vile book' as the *Advertisement*.

famous passage in *Greene's Groatsworth of Wit* (entered in the Stationers' Register on 20 September) gave rise to the literary scandal which offended Marlowe, according to Henry Chettle's testimony in his *Kind-Harts Dreame* (8 December). It is worth noting that these two divisive pieces of gossip, published by different authors for different purposes from different countries, circulated among the public at the same time, in October and November 1592. This coincidence possibly cultivated a close link between Marlowe the 'atheist' playwright and the unknown conjurer at Raleigh's school of atheism, which opened up the way not only for the informant (or Cholmeley) to invent Marlowe as a lecturer of atheism but also for other subsequent reports of hearsay to construct Marlowe, as well as Raleigh, as an atheist icon.

We do not need to enter into a detailed discussion of how Richard Baines's note was crafted in the light of 'Remembraunces against Cholmeley' and amplified with materials of theological discourses; the matter is treated adequately by Kocher and others.[45] As Curtis C. Breight points out, 'the Baines Note is really evidence for a frame-up of Marlowe when read in relation to other documents such as Remembrances'.[46] Naturally, those who had known or had been associated to some degree with Marlowe were eager to protect their own interests, particularly after his death, as Thomas Kyd did 'to cleere my self of being thought an Atheist', and therefore set out to demonize Marlowe by employing discursive materials of atheism within their reach.[47]

It is more important here to examine the purpose behind the production of a scribal copy of an original undated document, usually called the Baines Note (BL, Harley MS 6848, fols 185–6), which seems to have been hastily prepared, and has a heading with several deletions: 'A note containing the opinion of on[e] Christopher Marly concerning his damnable ~~opini~~ Judgment of Regligion, and scorn of Godes word.' This scribal copy (BL, Harley MS 6853, fols 307–8) bears the revised heading, 'A note deliv[er]ed on Whitsun eve last of the most horrible blasphemes and damnable opinions uttered by Xpofer Marly who w[i]thin iii dyes after came to a soden &

---

[45] Paul H. Kocher, 'Backgrounds for Marlowe's Atheist Lecture', in Baldwin Maxwell, W. D. Briggs, Francis R. Johnson, and E. N. S. Thompson (eds), *Renaissance Studies in Honor of Hardin Craig* (Stanford, 1941), pp. 112–32; Roy Kendall, 'Richard Baines and Christopher Marlowe's Milieu', *ELR*, 24:3 (1994), 507–52; Curtis C. Breight, *Surveillance, Militarism and Drama in the Elizabethan Era* (Basingstoke, 1996), pp. 157–65; and Nicholas Davidson, 'Christopher Marlowe and Atheism', in Darryll Grantley and Peter Roberts (eds), *Christopher Marlowe and English Renaissance Culture* (Aldershot, 1996), pp. 129–47.

[46] Breight, *Surveillance*, p. 160.

[47] Kuriyama, *Christopher Marlowe*, p. 229.

The Genesis of the Marlowe Myth

Figure 22   The scribal copy of the Baines Note. BL, Harley MS 6853, fol. 307r (detail). © The British Library. All Rights Reserved.

fearfull end of his life' (figure 22). The day in question was 2 June; accordingly, if the copyist meant that the original document had been delivered on that day, he may have been entirely ignorant of the exact date of Marlowe's death on 30 May. However, several Marlowe scholars tend to assume that the copyist mistook the date of delivery (Saturday 26 May) for Whitsunday eve: he intended to show in the headline that the original document was submitted on Saturday 26 May and was closely followed by Marlowe's death a few days later.

The circumstances surrounding Marlowe at that time make this line of thought persuasive. The Privy Council issued the warrant for his arrest on 18 May with the intention of interrogating him, possibly about a copy of a fragment on the Arian heresy (actually copied from John Proctor's *The Fall of the Late Arian* published in 1549) that was found among the papers of Thomas Kyd, his roommate; and on 20 May Marlowe appeared before the Privy Councillors to be 'commanded to give his daily attendaunce on their Lordships'.[48] Obviously, they were searching for information about and from Marlowe at that time, and Baines's promise to produce more 'good & honest' witnesses against the poet suggests that the note was hurriedly produced as one of the reference documents to be used in the process of the interrogation. Yet in the scribal copy of the Baines Note produced after Marlowe's death we can detect slight differences in tone and purpose. The anonymous scribe crossed out those allegations not strictly relevant to Marlowe's purported religious views: the counterfeiting scheme he worked on with Poole while a prisoner in Newgate; his penchant for tobacco and boys; and the whole passage of Baines's conclusion promising to produce more witnesses.[49] The scribe also seems to have censored himself in order

---

[48] *APC*, vol. 24, p. 244.

[49] This manuscript was written in a hand different from that of the Baines Note. The whole copy, including revised additions, is in the same hand except the endorsement 'Copye of Marloes blasphemes / As sent to her H.' and the notation that Cholmeley is 'layd for'.

to avoid impairing Raleigh reputation, to the extent that he deleted the wording 'being Sir W Raleighs man' from the original passage: 'Moyses was but a Jugler, & that one Heriotes being Sir W Raleighs man can do more then he.' Consequently, this scribal copy appears like an official news report on Marlowe's atheist manifesto.

Such remodelling of the original Baines Note may have been in line with the purpose of the scribal copy, which was drawn up and revised after Marlowe's death in order to be 'sent to her H[ighness]', as the endorsement of the copy suggests.[50] But why should the official report about 'the most horrible blasphemes and damnable opinions' of a dead man have been of any interest to the queen? Constance Kuriyama assumes that 'Apparently someone was trying to convince Elizabeth that an atheist threat existed, and that vigilance and timely action on the part of the government were necessary to contain it'.[51] Anti-atheist polemicists trumpeted at every opportunity any urgent countermeasure that could be launched against the threat of atheism, and so it is no wonder that an officious person among the queen's councillors sounded a warning against treasonable atheists.

What seems more important, however, is the fact that the revising scribe brought a journalistic aspect to the official report by communicating to the queen, who tended to look for evidence of the workings of divine providence in her own life and experiences,[52] details of the monstrosity of Marlowe's atheism, expressing a palpable fear of God's judgement upon the blasphemous playwright. The copyist initially transcribed the original heading of the Baines Note and then started a new line about Marlowe's death (indicated in italics): 'A note contayninge the opinion of one Christofer Marlye concernynge his damnable opinions of and Judgment of Relygion and scorne of Godes worde. [/] *Who since Whitsundy dyed a soden & vyolent deathe.*' He then revised the heading and added more information about Marlowe's death and monstrousness (additions indicated in italics): 'A note deliv[er]ed on Whitsun eve last of *the most horrible blasphemes* and damnable opinions uttered by Xpofer Marly who *w[i]thin iii dyes after came to a soden & fearfull end of his life.*'[53] What the scribe/corrector intended by revising the headline was to remind the queen of the time sequence – that Marlowe's sudden death came immediately after the delivery of the Baines Note – and to emphasize its scandalous nature by inserting 'horrible blasphemes' into it. Kuriyama points out that, 'Although the author fussed

---

[50] BL, Harley MS 6853, fol. 308v.
[51] Kuriyama, *Christopher Marlowe*, p. 226.
[52] Susan Doran, 'Elizabeth I's Religion: The Evidence of Her Letters', *Journal of Ecclesiastical History*, 51:4 (2000), 699–720, at pp. 715–16.
[53] BL, Harley MS 6853, fol. 307r. The original and revised headings are transcribed in Kuriyama, *Christopher Marlowe*, p. 227.

over his exact wording, his basic meaning is clear: Marlowe's end [...] was a direct result of his horrible blasphemies and damnable opinions'.[54] Moreover, he made the remarkable change to the last passage, from Marlowe 'dyed a soden & vyolent deathe' into the declaration that he 'came to a soden & fearfull end of his life'. Charles Nicholl supposes that '[t]he purpose seems to be to soften the event' because the queen was fretful and would have wanted to be informed.[55] But the phrase 'a soden & fearfull end of his life' sounds as if the document was a news report, and it seems that the correction was journalistically motivated by the shocking death of the atheist playwright. It happened exactly at the time when the Privy Councillors commanded him in connection with the arrest of Thomas Kyd to give daily attendance at court, and when they had secured the Baines Note that testified to Marlowe's 'monstrous' opinions.

We should not underestimate what 'sudden death' meant at that time. As Houlbrooke argues, 'The appropriateness of the cause or time of sudden deaths often underlined their providential character'.[56] In fact, Archbishop Grindal considered a sudden death to be the sign of God's judgement: 'sudden destruction lighteth upon such as in the midst of worldly prosperity have not God before their eyes, but cast him clean out of their remembrance.'[57] At the same time, Greene's advice to Marlowe on his deathbed proved scarily prophetic: 'I knowe the least of my demerits merit this miserable death, but wilfull striving against knowne truth, exceedeth all the terrors of my soule. Defer not (with me) till this last point of extremitie; for litle knowst thou how in the end thou shalt be visited.'[58] In other words, Marlowe proved himself to be an atheist precisely *by his death*. The 'fact' of his atheism had no existence before it appeared as an element of his tragic end. The incident was a matter of wonder and terror, as well as threat,

---

[54] Kuriyama, *Christopher Marlowe*, p. 143.

[55] Charles Nicholl, *The Reckoning: The Murder of Christopher Marlowe* (London, 1992), p. 313.

[56] Ralph Houlbrooke, *Death, Religion and the Family in England 1480–1750* (Oxford, 1998), p. 208; See also Alexandra Walsham, *Providence in Early Modern England* (Oxford, 1999), pp. 99–104; Keith Thomas, *Religion and the Decline of Magic* (London, 1971), pp. 78–89.

[57] William Nicholson (ed.), *The Remains of Edmund Grindal* (1843; repr. New York, 1968), p. 9.

[58] Alexander B. Grosart (ed.), *The Life and Complete Works in Prose and Verse of Robert Greene* (15 vols, 1881–6; repr. New York, 1964), vol. 12, p. 143. Robert W. Maslen, 'Marlowe's Ghost: The Second Report of Doctor John Faustus', in Karin E. Olsen and Jan R. Veenstra (eds), *Airy Nothings: Imagining the Otherworld of Faerie from the Middle Ages to the Age of Reason: Essays in Honour of Alasdair A. MacDonald* (Leiden, 2014), pp. 1–23, at p. 4, points out the impact on any reader who recalled the passage.

worth sharing as a tragic moral exemplum. It was exactly at this point that the contemporary legend of Marlowe began to take shape.

THE URBAN LEGEND OF MARLOWE/FAUSTUS

The public and political concerns over atheists which began in earnest with Persons's controversial discourse concerning Raleigh's school of atheism seem to have grown rapidly after Greene's attack on Marlowe's atheism and ensuing tragic death, and may well have spurred the authorities, agents, and polemicists to appropriate 'blasphemous' literary discourses to help invent 'real' atheists. Naturally, in the midst of the heresy-hunting furore, in which hyperbolic rhetoric was escalating as the reputations of those suspected of being atheists were smeared, the stage became an extraordinary power-house of ideas abundant in literary materials used for constructing 'real' atheists, for it had already resorted to radical ideas current in the culture when creating monstrous villains and their profane opinions.

A typical example of this cultural process of constructing 'reality' through theatrical discourse can be found in the document prepared by one of Raleigh's enemies with the intention of discrediting his reputation on the eve of his trial in 1603. It is a manuscript poem of fifty-nine lines, beginning with the title 'Certaine hellish verses devysed by that Atheist and traitor Rawley as yt is said'.[59] One passage that may have sounded shocking to his contemporaries runs:

> Then som sage man amonge the vulgarr
> knowing that lawes could not in quiet dwell
> unles the[y] were observed did first devyse
> *the name of god*, religion, heaven and hell
> and gaine of paines and faire rewardes to tell
> paines for theis that did neglecte the lawe
> rewardes for him that lived in quiet awe
> whereas in deid they were mere fictions
> and if they were not *yet (I thinke) they were*
> and those religious observationes
> onely bugberes to keepe the worlde in feare
> and make them quietly the yoke to bere
> so that religion of itself a fable
> was onely found to make that peaceable.

---

[59] C. Dyfnallt Owen (ed.), *Calendar of the Manuscripts of the Marquis of Bath Preserved at Longleat* (5 vols, London, 1904), vol. 2, pp. 52–3, emphasis added. Another copy of Raleigh's 'hellish verses' identical with this Longleat copy survives: BL, Add. MS 32092, fol. 201.

These 'hellish' words remind us of those of the Baines Note concerning Marlowe's 'horrible blasphemes and damnable opinions'.

More important here, however, is the authorship of the poem. Jean Jacquot first brought our attention to the poem's close resemblance to the soliloquy of Selimus in *The First Part of the Tragicall Raigne of Selimus* (published in 1594) and concluded that they were identical except for a few variants and corruptions.[60] The comparison enables us to understand the malicious intent of the anonymous informant, who was, it seems, intimately acquainted with the play's script in print. He attempts to aggravate Raleigh's offence of blasphemy by rewriting 'the names of gods' (*Selimus*, line 98), moving from the plural to the singular form, 'the name of god'. Moreover, he eliminates the identity of the speaker who declares that the gods, religion, heaven, and hell are mere fictions and attributes these words to Raleigh by altering 'Selim thinks they were' (*Selimus*, line 103) into 'yet (I thinke) they were'. In this way we learn how blasphemous discourses on the stage were appropriated to invent a 'real' atheist: the informant picks up the passage in *Selimus* and presents it as Raleigh's authentic opinion, which could have been submitted to the treason trial in order to frame up 'that Atheist and traitor Rawley'. What we see in this case is one of the phases in the process of creating a contemporary legend of Raleigh by manipulating literary and theatrical discourse.

This method of constructing 'reality' suggests how Marlowe's scandalous death would have empowered godly polemicists, intelligencers, playwrights, and the theatre-going public to set Marlowe up as an atheist cultural icon by resorting to shocking motifs and ideas voiced on stage. These pieces of information were reinforced with additional snippets, including those appropriated from Marlowe's plays, to constitute new items of gossip or contemporary legends, whose circulation helped to invent the moral meaning of Marlowe's tragic death. The mythmaking process also supported the quasi-autobiographical readings of his sensational plays encouraged by Greene, intended to reveal Marlowe's fictionalized characters as self-portraits.

The gossip about Marlowe told by Simon Aldrich, a Cambridge graduate and son of a Canterbury registrar of the Church courts, demonstrates that Marlowe's 'providential' death could have induced contemporaries to apply the Greeneian perspective on Marlowe in understanding his characters, specifically Doctor Faustus, as a projection of Marlowe's 'atheist' self.

---

[60] Jean Jacquot, 'Ralegh's "Hellish Verses" and *The Tragicall Raigne of Selimus*', MLR, 48:1 (1953), 1–9. See *Selimus, Emperor of the Turks*, ii.95–108. The citation, the scene and the line numbers given in the text are from Daniel J. Vitkus (ed.), *Three Turk Plays from Early Modern England*: Selimus, A Christian Turned Turk, and The Renegado (New York, 2000).

Henry Oxinden, a literary connoisseur and early collector of printed plays who had a particular interest in Marlowe, derived his information from Aldrich, who happened to be enjoying his retirement in the neighbourhood of Oxinden in Barham, Kent. What makes Aldrich's account unique is the sketchy rumour about one Fineaux, whom he says Marlowe converted into an atheist:

> one Fin[eau]x of Dover was an Atheist, & that hee would go out at midnight into a wood, & fall down uppon his knees & pray heartily that the Devill would come that he might see him: for he did not beleive there was a Devil: Mr Alderich said he was a verie good scholer but would never have above one booke at a time, & when he was perfect in it he would sell it away & buy another. he learned all Marlo by heart & divers other bookes: Marlo made him an Atheist. This Fin[eau]x was faine to make a speech uppon the foole hath said in his heart there is noe god, to gett his degree.[61]

Mark Eccles and William Urry have tried to identify this 'Mr Fin[eau]x' as Thomas Fineaux, who matriculated at Corpus Christi in the Easter term of 1587 and was possibly the eldest son of Thomas Fineaux of Hougham.[62] However, there is some difficulty in supposing that Marlowe, under the threat that his MA degree would be withheld, became acquainted with this freshman from Dover and made him an atheist. Moreover, as far as we know, Thomas Fineaux left Corpus without obtaining his degree. Kuriyama instead proposes that this Fineaux was John Fineaux, the younger brother of Thomas, who matriculated at Trinity College, Cambridge, in 1593.[63] There, John was a college classmate of Simon Aldrich, and both of them obtained their BA degrees in 1597 and their MAs in 1600. John Fineaux may have received information about Marlowe from Aldrich (whose father was closely associated with Marlowe's family) and become a devotee of his works.

No matter which Fineaux was 'Mr Fin[eau]x of Dover', the gossip about him shows traces of a developing urban legend promoting moral and cultural values, as suggested by the punchline: that Fineaux the atheist, in obtaining his degree, was obliged to make a speech on a biblical passage (Psalm 14.1: 'The foole hathe said in his heart, *There is* no God'), and

---

[61] BL, MS Add. 28012, fols 514v–515r.
[62] Mark Eccles, 'Marlowe in Kentish Tradition', *N&Q*, 169 (1935), 58–61; and William Urry, *Christopher Marlowe and Canterbury*, ed. with an introduction by Andrew Butcher (London, 1988), pp. 60–1.
[63] See Kuriyama, *Christopher Marlowe*, p. 160. Kuriyama says that 'a John Fineaux was a scholar at the King's School in Canterbury in 1590', but does not give a reference to the source.

proved himself to have been just such a fool. J. P. Collier's transcript of the inscription about Fineaux (in Colonel W. F. Prideaux's lost copy of *Hero and Leander*) reads: 'so that hee was faine to make a recantation uppon this Text' and implies that there was a moral ending to the story.[64] The reference to Fineaux's recantation can also be found in the catalogue of the sale of Richard Heber's books: '[Marlowe] had a friend at Dover, whom he made an Atheist, but who was obliged to recant, &c.'[65] As is typically the case with portrayals of atheists in this period, Fineaux is represented as an excellent scholar and, more tellingly, a talented man with a good memory and a habit of memorizing a whole book, like an actor, until 'hee was perfect in it'.

Fineaux was such an enthusiastic follower of Marlowe that he 'learned all Marlo by heart'. The way in which he was imagined to have become an atheist was not by direct contact with Marlowe but by immersing himself in the playwright's literary output, and this naturally suggests that the ideas, motifs, and gestures inspired by *Doctor Faustus* were utilized in constructing the 'monstrous' atheist of Dover. His behavioural pattern of 'going out at midnight into a wood' to 'pray heartily that the Devill would come' seems to be modelled on that of Faustus, who asks his friends, 'Come, show me some demonstrations magical, / That I may conjure in some lusty grove / And have these joys in full possession'.[66] This representation of Fineaux, whose behaviour has features similar to fandom activities in learning his lines by heart, re-enacting the conjuring scene of the play, and impersonating a Faustian magician, demonstrates that the shocking motifs, ideas, and gestures of the play had infiltrated popular conceptions of what constituted a profane atheist.

At the same time, we should not overlook a moral lesson intrinsic to the urban legend concerning the atheist who poses a threat to society by invoking the devil for his own interests. Fineaux attempted to conjure the devil in order to satisfy his intellectual curiosities, 'for hee did not beleive that there was a Devil'. We do not know the result of his conjuring – missing along with the rest of the story – but the moral orientation of the narrative encourages us to imagine a surprise twist, with the devil appearing before him and bringing about his 'recantation' of atheism at the end. This moral perspective obliquely points to the contagious power of Fineaux's guru,

---

[64] J. P. Collier, *A Bibliographical and Critical Account of the Rarest Books in the English Language* (2 vols, London, 1865), vol. 1, p. 522.

[65] *Bibliotheca Heberiana: Catalogue of the Library of the Late Richard Heber* (13 vols, London, 1834–7), vol. 4, p. 183.

[66] Christopher Marlowe, *Doctor Faustus*, ed. David Bevington and Eric Rasmussen, The Revels Plays (Manchester, 1992), A-text: i.i.152–4. Subsequent references to *Doctor Faustus* will be to this edition and will appear parenthetically in the text by version, act, scene, and line number.

Marlowe the 'atheist' playwright, who was considered a real threat by calling the devil on stage for his own pecuniary interests. Marlowe's providential death allowed people to suppose that the atheistic mindset had made him bold or curious enough to summon the devil as a spectacle, and also encouraged them to consider that this conjuring act, and *Doctor Faustus* as a whole, brought not only upon Faustus but also upon Marlowe divine retribution. Eventually, similar judgement would fall upon the profane players and the audience.

It was this threatening moral framework that gave rise to another urban legend, regarding the devil's appearance in a performance of *Doctor Faustus*, several versions of which survive. They share a stereotyped outline: that a real devil appeared during the performance and threw the audience and the players into consternation. For instance, William Prynne, an anti-theatrical polemicist, presents a peculiar anecdote about

> the visible apparition of the Devill on the stage at the Belsavage Play-house, in Queen Elizabeths dayes (to the great amazement both of the Actors and Spectators) whiles they were there prophanely playing the *History of Faustus (the truth of which I have heard from many now alive, who well remember it)* there being some distracted with that fearful sight.[67]

This may have been a performance at Belsavage Playhouse in the late 1580s,[68] but it is difficult to accept the account at face value, and more difficult to pin down when the legend took shape. However, the narrative suggests that the legend had already come into being after the popularity of the play had been affirmed in 'Queen Elizabeths dayes'. Moreover, since the storyteller can be identified, we can understand the nuances of the legend concerning the devil's appearance. Prynne presents an anecdote that had already circulated among the public, and exploits the devil's appearance to justify and strengthen his denunciation of the stage.

Another legend survives, in which a critical attitude similar to Prynne's can be observed

> Certaine Players at Exeter acting *upon* the stage the tragical storie of Dr. Faustus the Conjurer; as a certain number of Devels kept everie one his circle there, and as Faustus was busie in his magicall invocations, on a *sudden* they wer all *dasht*, every one harkning other in the eare, for they were all perswaded there was one devell too many amongst them; and so after a little pause desired the people to pardon them, they could

---

[67] William Prynne, *Histrio-Mastix: The Player's Scourge, or Actor's Tragedy*, with an introduction by Peter Davison (2 vols, New York, 1972), vol. 1, fol. 556r.
[68] Martin Wiggins, *British Drama 1533–1642: A Catalogue* (Oxford, 2012), vol. 2, pp. 425–6.

go no further *with this* matter: the people also understanding the thing as it was, every man hastened to be first out of dores. The players (as I heard it) contrarye to their custome spending the night in reading and in prayer got them out of the towne the next morning.[69]

The man behind this interesting anecdote cannot be identified. The account itself is cited in the *Gentleman's Magazine* by one J. G. R., who copied the text of a manuscript note 'on the last page of a book in my possession, printed by Vautrollier in 1585'. The anonymous reporter, judging from his snide remarks upon the players' rapid departure, is, like Prynne, inviting the reader to draw a lesson from it about God's judgement.

Devils could appear not only in the theatre but also in the church, as we find in the case of *The Wonders of This Windie Winter* (1613). During Sunday evening prayers at a church in Great Chart, near Canterbury, there 'broake into the Church a most vgly shape out of the ayer like vnto a broad eyd bul, [...] whereupon the whole audience so fearefully pressed one vpon another to get forth that many were hurt and almost bruzed to death'. The reason the devil was able to make his appearance even inside a church is made clear:

> the parishioners haue an euil custome among them, for continually, be it either in seruice or sermon time, they wil stand in troupes of foure or fiue in a company in diuers parts of the Church, conferring & talking of worldly affaiers, not regarding at al the words of the Minister, but rather behaue themselues as it were in a faier or market.[70]

This moral explains that the devil necessarily appears wherever the profane flock together, and God inflicts a terrifying punishment upon them.

These stories of unusual and horrible events show the characteristics of an urban legend combined with awareness of contemporary social issues, variations of which are told in diverse places and times as something that either did happen or may have happened; they also have moral implications for the reader.[71] The devil's appearance during the performance of *Doctor Faustus* played an important social and religious role at the time, particularly for anti-theatrical polemicists such as William Prynne, who used it to advocate their own political and moral positions. The devil was considered to be God's 'instrument', executing God's punishment against reprobates, so it is no wonder that he appeared in places that were morally degenerate

---

[69] Reproduced in *Gentleman's Magazine*, 2nd ser., 34 (1850), 234.
[70] *The Wonders of This Windie Winter* (London, 1613), sig. C2v.
[71] Nicholas DiFonzo and Prashant Bordia, *Rumor Psychology: Social and Organizational Approaches* (Washington, DC, 2007), p. 23.

and attracted impious people.[72] For the anti-theatrical polemicists eager to wage a spiritual battle with 'irreligious' people or the social institutions they opposed, the devil could be an indispensable instrument for attacking and rejecting others as social pariahs. By inventing and reinventing stories of God's judgement, those polemicists could construe and make sense of disasters, pandemics, and accidents while promoting their own moral and cultural values.[73]

It would be futile to attempt to determine the credibility or historicity of the urban legend. Rather, what should be recalled here is the insight afforded by Jody Enders into the social function of theatre, which 'takes its audiences to a moment in real time during which belief is created, developed, reaffirmed, suspended, denied, or even destroyed'. Whether it is medieval or early modern, 'theater captures both the construction of belief and the reality of the emotional experiences attendant upon that construction'.[74] This social function leads us to ask why the devil had to appear during a performance of this particular play. The devil in *Doctor Faustus* was far from being a new object of terror or criticism. Indeed, the way in which the devil was represented seems to have been quite conventional; John Melton wrote that a man who went to see *Doctor Faustus* might 'behold shagge-hayr'd Deuills runne roaring ouer the Stage with Squibs in their mouthes, while Drummers make Thunder in the Tyring-house, and the twelue-penny Hirelings make artificiall Lightning in their Heauens'.[75] Melton's description reminds us of Titivillus or Satan in morality plays, and this kind of character was readily familiar to Elizabethan audiences.

What, then, prompted these contemporary legends to spring up *specifically* around the play *Doctor Faustus*, not other plays that featured the devil? Certainly, a necromancer who conjures up a spirit and makes a contract with the devil had never been staged before Faustus.[76] Considering the novelty of the stage sorcerer, it may be possible to discern the audience's

---

[72] George Gifford, *Discourse of the Subtill Practises of Devilles* (London, 1587), sig. I2r. See also Thomas, *Religion and the Decline of Magic*, pp. 472–3.

[73] Thomas, *Religion and the Decline of Magic*, pp. 469–77; Stuart Clark, 'King James's *Daemonology*: Witchcraft and Kingship', in Sydney Anglo (ed.), *The Damned Art: Essays in the Literature of Witchcraft* (London, 1977), pp. 156–77, at p. 175.

[74] Jody Enders, *Death by Drama and Other Medieval Urban Legends* (Chicago, 2002), p. 6; see also chap. 7, 'The Devil Who Wasn't There', where she makes a critical analysis of these kinds of urban legend. I have discussed the urban legend of *Doctor Faustus* in Arata Ide, 'Doctor Faustus and the Appearance of the Devil', in Yoshiko Kawachi (ed.), *Japanese Studies in Shakespeare and His Contemporaries* (Newark, DE, 1998), pp. 11–24.

[75] John Melton, *The Astrologaster, or, the Figure-caster* (London, 1620), p. 31.

[76] Robert R. Reed Jr, *The Occult on the Tudor and Stuart Stage* (Boston, 1965), pp. 87–9, points out the novelty of the stage sorcerer. John D. Cox argues at length about

shock at the play's realism. In particular, the invocation scene, and the Latin words used in the spell, may have had such verisimilitude and have been so impressive that they stimulated and worked on the audience's, as well as the players', imagination.[77] Yet it is unlikely that the urban legend was created merely from the dramatic effects of a conjuring scene that is some twenty lines long, given that any urban legend is generated, as we can see today, from a variety of culturally and socially intertwined factors. Rather, we must consider the legend within the context of the construction of Marlowe as an atheist in a short space of time around 1593, the religious fervour of the godly to propel the repentance movement, and the social role that the devil had played in the pandemic crisis. The legend instead turns out to be an important means to understand *Doctor Faustus* as part of the creative tension between the theatre and its social context, to show how the 'fearfull end' of Marlowe could be superimposed on that of Faustus, and to illuminate what momentum *Doctor Faustus* provided for the further demonization of Marlowe and his plays.

DOCTOR FAUSTUS AND THE PLAGUE IN 1592–93

London in 1593 was indeed a hell on earth. Early in September 1592, the plague had greatly increased within the city and would be rampant until the end of the following year. The plague burials registered in the city and liberties of London totalled 10,775 in 1593.[78] England had not experienced such a large-scale and prolonged disaster since the virulent bubonic plague outbreak in 1563. In a letter that Richard Verstegan dispatched to Robert Persons in September 1593 he reported that 'The lyke plague as is now in England hathe not bene sene in our age so long continuing and so vehement'.[79] Thomas Dekker illustrated the misery of the plague with a journalistic touch: 'Surely the loud grones of rauing sicke men; the strugling panges of soules departing: In euery house griefe striking vp an Allarum: Seruants

---

Marlowe's borrowing and deconstructing traditional stage devils in *The Devil and the Sacred in English Drama, 1350–1642* (Cambridge, 2000), pp. 107–26.

[77] See, for instance, K. M. Briggs, *Pale Hecate's Team: An Examination of the Beliefs on Witchcraft and Magic among Shakespeare's Contemporaries and His Immediate Successors* (London, 1962), p. 127.

[78] John Stow, *Annales, or, a Generall Chronicle of England*, augmented by Edmund Howes (1607; repr. London, 1631), p. 766. On Stow's mistaken calculation, see Samuel Schoenbaum, *William Shakespeare: A Compact Documentary Life* (1978; repr. Oxford, 1987), p. 168. On annual burials and other information about the plague in 1592–93, see also J. F. D. Shrewsbury, *A History of Bubonic Plague in the British Isles* (1970; repr. Cambridge, 1971), pp. 226–30; and Paul Slack, *The Impact of Plague in Tudor and Stuart England* (London, 1985), pp. 144–72.

[79] Petti (ed.), *Letters and Despatches of Richard Verstegan*, p. 185.

crying out for maisters: wiues for husbands, parents for children, children for their mothers.'[80]

Thomas Lodge noted the plague's principal symptoms: a high fever, rigidity of the body, mental derangement, and 'blewnesse and blacknesse appearing about the sores and carbuncles'.[81] Not until the nineteenth century was it known that the bacterium *Pasteurella pestis* caused these symptoms. Physicians in the Elizabethan age tried in vain to discover efficacious treatments for the disease, and medical charlatans drove a prosperous trade by taking advantage of people's fears. Dekker railed against physicians for their incompetence: 'their Drugs turned to Durt, their simples were simple things, *Galen* could do no more good, than *Sir Giles Goosecap: Hipocrates, Auicen, Paraselsus, Rasis, Fernelius*, with all their succeeding rabble of Doctors and Water-casters, were at their wits end.'[82]

Although Elizabethans could not cure the disease, they thought they knew its major cause. They had only to look in the Bible and take note of Jehovah's plague on the children of Israel. Simon Forman, in 'A Discourse of the Plague', classifies the cause of the pestilence into three categories: 'the firste and leaste plague is the plague of nature by influence of the heave[n]s. The second is the plagues of the diuells. the Laste and greateste is the plague of God which is to be feared aboue all the reste', elucidating at length by quoting the scriptures.[83] His attitude to the disease suggests that he despaired of all human remedies, believing that divine sovereignty would punish sinners and heal them of the disease through God's miraculous grace. Forman associated the plague of 1592 with the earthquake of 1576, the famines of 1585 and 1589, and the coming of the Armada in 1588, declaring 'thes I say are the messengers And forwarnors of the wrath of God to calle vs to Repentaunce'.[84] The unprecedented prevalence of the plague, especially in urban areas, made intellectuals suspect a divine cause and drove them to look for scapegoats.[85]

---

[80] Thomas Dekker, *The Wonderfull Yeare*, in Alexander B. Grosart (ed.), *The Non-Dramatic Works of Thomas Dekker* (5 vols, London and Aylesbury, 1885), vol. 1, p. 105.

[81] Thomas Lodge, *A Treatise of the Plague*, in Edmund W. Gosse (ed.), *The Complete Works of Thomas Lodge* (4 vols, 1883; repr. New York, 1963), vol. 4, sig. C3r.

[82] Dekker, *Wonderfull Yeare*, pp. 116–17.

[83] Simon Forman, 'A Discourse of the Plague', Bodleian Library, Ashmole MS 208, fols 110–34 (quotation from fol. 111r). The moral tone of medical literature concerning the plague did not essentially change throughout the seventeenth century. See Lucinda McCray Beier, *Sufferers and Healers: The Experience of Illness in Seventeenth-Century England* (London, 1987), pp. 154–63.

[84] Forman, 'Discourse', fol. 127r.

[85] See, for instance, Anthony Anderson, *An Approved Medicine against the Deserued Plague* (London, 1593), sig. A3v.

For the populace, it mattered little whether the ultimate cause was natural or supernatural. To be freed from anxiety and horror must have been paramount. The swift publishing of books of medical instruction, such as *Present Remedies against the Plague* (1592) by an anonymous 'learned phisition', or Simon Kellwaye's *A Defensatiue against the Plague* (1593), shows how urgent was the public need for relief. Unfortunately, there were few physicians who could give the people any medical consolation. The total number of physicians, surgeons, apothecaries, and practitioners in London at that time, either licensed or unlicensed, is estimated to have been only around 500. Since the city and liberties of London had a population of approximately 150,000 in 1593, that meant there was at most one practitioner for every 300 individuals.[86] Even if a patient was lucky enough to be able to consult a licensed doctor, he or she could not have relied on a guaranteed promise of recovery. People knew only that they could not be saved without the miraculous intervention of a supernatural being, and that if the black spots commonly called 'Gods markes or Tokens' were seen 'on one that hath the blacke plague then he dyeth w[ith]out Remedie'.[87]

Even so, people did not have to look far for consolation. There is no doubt that it was not only taverns and recreational facilities that gave them relief; the Church, the authority in matters of the supernatural, played an important role in offering them spiritual solace. The Church was able to explain the tragic situation, and it alone could assemble the people under licence, while other meetings were regulated because of infection.[88] The Church saw the plague as a scourge of God, to punish stubborn people, and promised relief through repentance and prayer. It may readily be imagined that, at the time of the plague, the people's devotion to a supernatural power was temporarily revived and that they would have gathered in churches to seek a remedy. James Bamford says in the preface of *A Short Dialogve Concerning the Plagves Infection* (1603):

> Ye frequent Friday Lecture as diligently (euer since the Plague was kindled) as in winter nights: wheras many in & about Londo[n] are winter hearers, attending the word when they haue nothing else to do: and ye fill Gods house vpo[n] the daies of humiliation, & holy rest,

---

[86] Roger Finlay, *Population and the Metropolis: The Demography of London 1580–1650* (Cambridge, 1981), pp. 51–69 and appendix 1; Margaret Pelling and Charles Webster, 'Medical Practitioners', in Charles Webster (ed.), *Health, Medicine and Mortality in the Sixteenth Century* (Cambridge, 1979), pp. 165–235, at p. 188.

[87] Forman, 'Discourse', fol. 113r.

[88] E. K. Chambers, *The Elizabethan Stage* (4 vols, 1923; repr. Oxford, 1974), vol. 4, p. 313. For the Church's attitude toward the notion of contagion, see Leeds Barroll, *Politics, Plague, and Shakespeare's Theatre: the Stuart Years* (Ithaca, 1991), p. 96.

notwithstanding there haue died in our parish from the 7. of May to this day 2640.[89]

Dekker had good reason to say 'This was a rare worlde for the Church'.[90]

Yet the plague also gave 'superstitious idolaters', who had already resorted to popular magic, opportunities to seek moral support from sorcerers or witches, who they thought were able to offer magical relief, rather than from the Church, even though the Church was trying to 'eliminate the protective ecclesiastical magic which had kept the threat of sorcery under control'.[91] They could turn to the devil as a last resort, as he had been not only an executor of God's judgement but also a heroic figure who ruled the world and granted all requests in exchange for souls. At the sight of the Clown in dire poverty in *Doctor Faustus*, Wagner says, 'Alas, poor slave, see how poverty jesteth in his nakedness! The villain is bare and out of service, and so hungry that I know he would give his soul to the devil for a shoulder of mutton, though it were blood raw'.[92]

Undoubtedly, the Clown was not the only one who craved the devil's help when an inescapable hell unfolded before his eyes, for the plague deprived the populace of all means of living, as reported in a letter dated 23 November 1593: 'Many Londoners tasting want in the sicknes tyme, and now wanting the terme, do fall to plaine begging, yet must a double subsidy be payed presently, thoughe not so soon as nede requires.'[93] It is not hard to imagine, as Robert Burton did in *The Anatomy of Melancholy*, that there were many who thought: 'if I be troubled with such a malady, what care I whether the divell himselfe, or any of his ministers by Gods permission redeeme me?'[94] In *Spirituall Preseruatiues against the Pestilence* (1593), Henry Holland, an anti-theatrical godly clergyman, censures the people who ask the devil for help when tested by God: 'the wicked run to any of the creatures, rather then to God, yea sometimes to Sathan himselfe,

---

[89] James Bamford, *A Short Dialogve concerning the Plagves Infection* (London, 1603), sig. A4r.

[90] Dekker, *Wonderfull Yeare*, p. 113.

[91] Thomas, *Religion and the Decline of Magic*, p. 498. See also Michael MacDonald, 'Religion, Social Change, and Psychological Healing in England, 1600–1800', in W. J. Sheils (ed.), *The Church and Healing* (Oxford, 1982), pp. 101–25.

[92] Christopher Marlowe, *Doctor Faustus*, ed. David Bevington and Eric Rasmussen, *The Revels Plays* (Manchester, 1992), A-text: I.iv.7–10. Subsequent references to *Doctor Faustus* will be to this edition and will appear parenthetically in the text by version, act, scene, and line number.

[93] Petti (ed.), *Letters and Despatches of Richard Verstegan*, p. 193.

[94] Robert Burton, *The Anatomy of Melancholy*, ed. Thomas C. Faulkner, Nicolas K. Kiessling, Rhonda L. Blair, J. B. Bamborough, and Martin Dodsworth (6 vols, Oxford, 1989–2000), vol. 2, pp. 3–4.

before they seeke any refuge or comfort in the Almighty'.[95] William Cupper was likewise well aware of human frailty, and preached that

> we are willing to vse any Phisition so that he hath skill, although he haue other faults, yea we will seek to those that are prophane, yea to a Turke or a Iew, yea to Sathan him selfe, as we do when we seeke to witches and sorcerers and all to procure our bodily health, or to recouer some worldly losse.[96]

Puritans took advantage of the disaster to denounce their enemies as the chief causes of the plague. It was inevitable that the theatre became the first victim of their attack. The plague inflicted such a great loss of lives by God's permission that the theatre was readily characterized as a hotbed of disease and vice. The basic attitude of the Corporation of London towards it was that 'To play in plagetime is to encreasce the plage by infection: to play out of plagetime is to draw the plage by offendinges of God vpon occasion of such playes'.[97] Holland praised the Lord Mayor for his efforts to 'cast downe the deuillish theaters, the nurceries of whoredome and vncleannesse' and asked him to exterminate 'the spiritual causes' as well as 'the naturall causes' of the plague, for playhouses are

> *Cupids* and *Venus* temples, they are Bacchus and Sathans pallaces, they corrupt the youth of your citie intollerablie: all eies can see, and all chast eares can witnes & some of the masters of these euils are driuen to confesse (when the Lord hath humbled them by some great terrors) in extreame passions and pangs of death.[98]

The theatre had no persuasive counterargument and, naturally, could not prove its innocence against their attacks. Hence, venues were more susceptible to being smeared as 'deuillish theatres' or 'Sathans pallaces' than normal.

On 23 June 1592, all plays were forbidden in and around London until 28 September, but the prohibition was not lifted until late December owing to the prevalence of plague. On 28 January 1593, the severity of the plague compelled the Privy Council to order the prohibition of 'all manner of concourse and publique meetinges of the people at playes, beare-baitinges, bowlinges and other like assemblyes for sportes [...] (preacheing and Devyne service at churches excepted)'. In the following winter, the plague

---

[95] Henry Holland, *Spirituall Preseruatiues against the Pestilence* (London, 1593), sig. B5r.
[96] William Cupper, *Certaine Sermons concerning Gods Late Visitation in the Citie of London* (London, 1592), pp. 43–4.
[97] Chambers, *Elizabethan Stage*, vol. 4, p. 301.
[98] Holland, *Spirituall Preseruatiues*, sigs A5v–A6r.

abated, allowing a short-term revival of performances, but on 3 February 1594, the Privy Council cautiously ordered restraint on the ground that 'the dangerous infection of the plague, by Gods great mercy and goodnes well slaked, may again very dangerously encrease and break foorth'. Although theatres were open in April and May, the authorities kept constant vigilance over them until October, for 'infected people, after theire longe keepinge in, and before they be clerd of theire disease and infection, beinge desirous of recreacion, vse to resort to suche assemblies, where throughe heate and thronge, they infecte manie sound personnes'.[99]

Doctor Faustus reopened at the Rose Theatre on 30 September, and six more performances were recorded before the end of 1594. The audience enthusiastically welcomed the play just at a time when they were still haunted by the plague, and when the theatre was still closely associated with the devil on an imaginary level.[100] As if intending to offend Puritan susceptibilities, the Admiral's Men staged a play in which the devil took an active part; and the people, for their part, willingly went to the 'deuillish' theatre to see the devil and 'seeke to Sathan and his artes' for a remedy to the overwhelming emotional and psychological trauma they had suffered.[101] So what exactly did *Doctor Faustus* offer to audiences 'desirous of recreacion'?[102]

MATERIALIST FANTASY IN THE 'DEVILISH' THEATRE

The Clown, who is completely stunned by the appearance of two devils and 'runs up and down crying' on the stage, is motivated to conjure them up for himself when learning that the devil can offer him magical power to fulfil his desire. He asks Wagner for guidance: 'would you teach me to raise up Banios and Belcheos?' (A-text: I.iv.59–60). What prompts the Clown, who 'would give his soul to the devil for a shoulder of mutton', to this action is his desire for vulgar entertainment:

> O, this is admirable! Here I ha' stol'n one of Doctor Faustus' conjuring books, and, i'faith, I mean to search some circles for my own use. Now will I make all the maidens in our parish dance at my pleasure stark naked before me, and so by that means I shall see more then e're I felt or saw yet. (A-text: II.ii.1–6)

The same desire to enjoy a pleasurable pastime may well have been shared by the audience, who had undergone the disastrous experiences of disease,

---

[99] Chambers, *Elizabethan Stage*, vol. 4, pp. 313–15.
[100] For the influence of the plague upon *Doctor Faustus*, see Christopher Ricks, '*Doctor Faustus* and Hell on Earth', *Essays in Criticism*, 35:2 (1985), 101–20.
[101] Holland, *Spirituall Preseruatiues*, sig. B5r.
[102] Chambers, *Elizabethan Stage*, vol. 4, p. 315.

poverty, and starvation, and who were still under great stress 'after theire longe keeping in'. Although the audience members would not have given their souls to the devil either for temporary pleasures or 'for a shoulder of mutton', within the imaginary space of the theatre they were obviously eager and able to obtain through the devil's assistance what they could not get in reality. That public, escapist realm of necromantic entertainment could offer them a fascinating, imaginary experience that interacted with reality closely enough for them to pretend for a time that it was, indeed, real. The devil had such a great hold over both worlds, of imagination and reality – just as virtual reality, artificial intelligence and deepfake technology does now – that he could blur the boundaries between them and so create the illusion of reality and the reality of illusion. The social and dramatic role that the devil filled unexpectedly made the play a morally dangerous, highly thrilling entertainment that could attract the thousands of victims of the traumatic experience of the plague; but the consequence might be the wrath of God being brought upon the players and the audience.

Commanded to appear by the Clown, who has stolen one of the conjuring books of Faustus, Mephistopheles complains, 'How am I vexed with these villains' charms! / From Constantinople am I hither come / Only for pleasure of these damned slaves' (A-text: III.ii.32–4). There is clearly cause for this complaint, given that Mephistopheles has to appear for the mere pleasure of the Clown and his friend Rafe. But, in fact, Faustus is an accomplice of 'these damned slaves' who employ the devil for pleasure's sake. Immediately after the decision to discard his theological study and deliver his lofty manifesto to become a demi-god in power, honour, and omnipotence, Faustus substitutes his intellectual willpower with intense material appetite:

> I'll have them fly to India for gold,
> Ransack the ocean for orient pearl,
> And search all corners of the new-found world
> For pleasant fruits and princely delicates. (A-text: I.i.84–7)

Here, Faustus is dominated by the same materialism as the Clown.[103] He cannot free himself from an ardent desire for delights and gives himself up to materialist fantasy. The only difference between Faustus and the Clown is that Faustus is privileged to taste what the devil offers as much as he likes.

The source of the play, *The Historie of the Damnable Life, and Deserued Death of Doctor Iohn Faustus*, has many comic tales of Faustus as a trickster, which may have appealed greatly to the public. What most differentiates

---

[103] On Faustus's materialism, see Michael Hattaway, 'The Theology of Marlowe's *Doctor Faustus*', *Renaissance Drama*, NS, 3 (1970), 51–78, at p. 60.

the source from the play, however, is that almost all of the comic pleasures in Marlowe's *Doctor Faustus* are offered in the form of a spectacle or show. The play is interspersed with entertainments, such as the dance of the devils and the pageant of the Seven Deadly Sins, helping Faustus to evade momentarily his powerful awareness of the time limit of his life and the hell to come as the reward for his pleasure. The devil is the director of these entertainments and entices Faustus to indulge himself in worldly delight. Lucifer tells Faustus why he has appeared: 'Faustus, we are come from hell to show thee some pastime. Sit down, and thou shalt see all the Seven Deadly Sins appear in their proper shapes' (A-text: II.iii.100–2). Faustus welcomes his offer and becomes addicted to these narcotic pleasures, which the audience shares with him alongside the spectators of the play-within-the-play. Consequently, Marlowe's Faustus seems more self-deluded and more mundane than the Faustus in *The Historie of the Damnable Life*.

The distinctive character of Faustus is demonstrated in the way he becomes involved with these theatrical entertainments. Travelling around the world with Mephistopheles, he comes to Rome to see St Peter's feast. Faustus cannot be satisfied with his role as a spectator, as Mephistopheles detects: 'I know you'd fain see the Pope / And take some part of holy Peter's feast'. Faustus is willing to participate in the feast: 'Well, I am content to compass then some sport, / And by their folly make us merriment' (A-text: III.i.50–1, 54–5). His request to Mephistopheles in the B-text appropriately sums up his dramatic role in this scene: 'There did we view the kingdoms of the world, / And what might please mine eye I there beheld. / Then in this show let me an actor be' (B-text: III.i.73–5).[104] In order to get more pleasure out of the devil's entertainment, Faustus himself participates in it as an actor.[105]

Later in the play, however, Faustus transforms himself into an entertainer who acts as an intermediary between the devil and the audience, and regales the audience with his magical entertainment. Here, Faustus acquires the position not of a profane conjurer but of an entertaining hero whose devoted performance will make the audience feel a stronger affinity to him. The Duke of Vanholt, who is one of the spectators at Faustus's shows, voices the audience's feeling toward Faustus: 'Believe me, Master Doctor, this merriment hath much pleased me' (A-text: IV.ii.1–2). The B-text further explains why Faustus should be bountifully rewarded: 'His artful sport

---

[104] I have focused upon the A-text as the text with primary authority, but I have quoted some passages from the B-text to understand the mood of the earlier play. For the textual problems of *Doctor Faustus*, see Eric Rasmussen, *A Textual Companion to Doctor Faustus* (Manchester, 1993).

[105] Judith Weil, *Christopher Marlowe: Merlin's Prophet* (Cambridge, 1977), pp. 64–5, notes this tendency of Faustus.

drives all sad thoughts away' (B-text: IV.vi.125). The spectators who watched these magical entertainments cannot have chosen to condemn him from a theological or ethical viewpoint, for in the play they have been urged to take part in the devil's performance, with Faustus as the entertainer, and to enjoy the show under his direction.

While sharing the pleasurable wonders and adventures generously with the audience as an entertainer, Faustus is often seized with religious fear and forced to face reality, where all his pleasure is turned to melancholy. For instance, in the scene of the contract with Lucifer, the joyful intoxication that follows his hope of omnipotence suddenly turns to horror:

Consummatum est. This bill is ended,
And Faustus hath bequeathed his soul to Lucifer.
But what is this inscription on mine arm?
'*Homo fuge!*' Whither should I fly?
If unto God, he'll throw thee down to hell. —
My senses are deceived; here's nothing writ. —
I see it plain. Here in this place is writ
'*Homo fuge!*' Yet shall not Faustus fly. (A-text: II.i.74–81)

As James H. Sims points out, here Faustus 'becomes a kind of perverted Christ' by associating himself with Christ on the cross.[106] In the biblical context, *Consummatum est* is Christ's proclamation of complete victory over death and hell, uttered in committing his soul to God; in *Doctor Faustus* it is used as a symbolic speech that suggests Faustus's proclamation of temporary victory over death and hell in committing his soul to Lucifer. The desire for momentary escape naturally entails sporadic and final outbursts of panic about death and hell. The line '"*Homo fuge!*" Whither should I fly?', which echoes Psalm 139.7 praising God's omnipresence, ironically suggests the omnipresence of hell. In fact, Faustus's conviction that 'he confounds hell in Elysium' (A-text: I.iii.61) is suddenly shattered by the inscriptions on his arms.

Faustus and the audience find themselves surrounded by hell: the inner hell that Faustus occasionally feels in his conscience, and which Mephistopheles explains to him so that he knows 'this is hell, nor am I out of it' (A-text: I.iii.78); and the hell on earth, where the plague has been rampant and is still vivid in the audience's memory. They cannot evade the pangs of hell when the 'inscription' from God or 'gods markes' appear on their arms and bodies. Each time Faustus becomes disillusioned, the audience is forced to feel the sense of the impermanence of this escapist realm. However, neither Faustus nor the audience is ever compelled to face up

---

[106] James H. Sims, *Dramatic Uses of Biblical Allusions in Marlowe and Shakespeare* (Gainesville, 1966), p. 17.

to hell at length, for the devil suspends these pangs until the last moment by presenting delightful spectacles: 'I'll fetch him somewhat to delight his mind' (A-text: II.i.82). Thus, the juxtaposition of imaginative space, providing escape, with the disastrous realities awaiting Faustus as well as the audience has a reciprocal effect: a striking contrast between entertainment and tragedy. The dynamism of *Doctor Faustus* depends on this exquisite balance and lively tension.

At the end of the play, however, Faustus, who has been a good entertainer, becomes enslaved by his illusion and hopes for its realization so earnestly that he begins to confuse illusion with reality. He seriously wishes 'That I might have unto my paramour / That heavenly Helen which I saw of late' (A-text: v.i.84–5). He is well aware that characters in the spectacle 'are but shadows, not substantiall' (B-text: vI.i.104). In the A-text, moreover, he explains the nature of the devil's spectacle to the Emperor of Germany, who longs to see Alexander and his beautiful paramour:

> it is not in my ability to present before your eyes the true substantial bodies of those two deceased princes, which long since are consumed to dust. [...] But such spirits as can lively resemble Alexander and his paramour shall appear before your Grace in that manner that they best lived in. (A-text: IV.i.47–50, 53–5)

Ironically, however, Faustus blindly seeks his heaven and immortality in what is not substantial:

> Sweet Helen, make me immortal with a kiss.
> Her lips sucks forth my soul. See where it flies!
> Come, Helen, come, give me my soul again.
> Here will I dwell, for heaven be in these lips,
> And all is dross that is not Helena. (A-text: v.i.93–7)

Although he knows that Helen is but a shadow for entertaining the spectators, he fanatically convinces himself that she *is* substantial and that her 'sweet embracings may extinguish clean / These thoughts that do dissuade me from my vow' (A-text: v.i.86–7). The audience, who have enjoyed participating in the spectacles of the play-within-the-play with Faustus and may have become so ravished that they, like the Emperor, might think 'these are no spirits, but the true substantial bodies of those two deceased princes' (A-text: IV.i.72–3), now see that the heroic entertainer has himself become caught up in the self-made illusion of reality. It would have been difficult for them to dismiss Faustus's behaviour as absurd with the same detachment as the Old Man, for the trinitarian bonds that bind Faustus, the devil, and the audience together as a theatrical community are too tight for the audience and their imagination to escape the intense desire to turn illusion into reality, shadow into substance. The voltage coursing between the polarities in *Doctor Faustus* – the heavenly bliss found in Helen's beauty and the frightfulness of hell encircling it; the vehement desire for the escapist realm and the acute cognition of its fictitiousness – reaches its peak in the scene with Helen. Then, Faustus suddenly confuses illusion with reality and the well-balanced tension between entertainment and tragedy is finally lost. What remains after the culmination of pleasure is the harsh reality: Faustus 'must live still to be plagued in hell' (A-text: v.ii.112), and the audience in hell on earth. It was deep despair of the future and the desire to indulge in the confused sense of reality in the audience that allowed the 'real' devil to make his appearance on stage.

When *Doctor Faustus* gained public favour just after the populace's decimation by the plague, the anti-theatrical polemicists made the most of the devil's appearance as an instrument to smear the theatre as the hotbed of moral degeneration, stirring up the prejudice that the 'Play-house is the Devils Chappell'. Marlowe's 'providential' death gave these polemicists momentum to envisage the possibility that the play could bring about divine retribution upon the players and the audience, just as the practice of being 'a Poet, and a filthy Play-maker' had brought upon Marlowe.[107] It was not only the polemicists who fervently welcomed the devil's real appearance, however, but the audience as well. In the midst of the upsurge of anti-theatrical sentiment caused by the social crisis of the plague, the stage took advantage of these anti-theatrical attacks, and, by invoking the devil in 'the deuillish theatre', gave the audience an opportunity to emancipate themselves from the plague restrictions, relieve their repressed emotions, and, at least partly, fulfil their materialist fantasies with Faustus's assistance. The theatre, where the devil, the object of worship under extreme conditions, came on stage alongside the conjurer as an entertainer, became a highly entertaining public institution for venting the deep frustrations of the public.

Thus, the legend of *Doctor Faustus* seems to have been formed by internal and external agencies converging on the theatre: the audience's desire to turn illusion into reality and the social and political pressures of anti-theatricalism on the stage. These two agencies both within and outside the theatre, with the contemporary social crisis of the plague as a backdrop, created a social phenomenon that recognized the appearance of the 'real' devil as something desirable. What the *Doctor Faustus* legend essentially suggests is the audience's latent desires in the extraordinary circumstances of the early 1590s.

---

[107] Edmund Rudierde uses these epithets in *The Thunderbolt of Gods Wrath against Hard-hearted and Stiffe-necked Sinnes* (London, 1618), sig. E3r.

THE THUNDEROUS COLLAPSE OF THE OLD THEATRE

In concluding this chapter, I would like to examine briefly *The Second Report of Doctor Iohn Faustus*, published in the midst of the revival of Marlowe's play (it was entered in the Stationers' Register on 16 November 1593), as one of the most important documents for understanding how powerfully the untimely death of Marlowe captured the popular imagination and set a hermeneutical framework for envisaging the play *Doctor Faustus* as a social threat that would bring divine retribution down upon society.[108] The beginning of this work aims to invite readers to connect the play's performance with the sequel on the printed page. Kit Wagner, left alone in his master's library, falls into 'a deepe considering of his former meriments, sports and delights', and, when 'comming into the same Hall wherein his Maisters latest Tragedy was perfourmed' and remembering that 'after his death he should be a spirite in nature and essence as others were', decides to conjure up Faustus.[109] The 'merry Enterlude' of Faustus's triumphal entry with the devils is then presented before him and encourages Kit to follow his master as a conjuring entertainer who offers the reader pleasant diversions:

> *Wagner*, albeit he was newly reuiued from a feare, and scarcely throughly wakened from this his great terrours, yet with this comicall iest his decayed spirites began to recouer their olde strength and power, turning these great braueries of Diuels into a meriment, and his conceiued fear into a meere fansie.[110]

Robert W. Maslen argues that *The Second Report* can be classified as one of the ghost narratives of the 1590s, alongside *Tarlton's News Out of Purgatory* and *Chettle's Kind-Harts Dreame*, in which 'boundaries between truth and fiction, the theatre and the written page became blurred'. In *The Second Report*, as a consequence,

> the most famous creation of the notorious 'atheist' Marlowe (as Greene called him) returns from the dead to lend his services to the Doctor's former houseboy, Wagner; […] the houseboy Wagner (whose nickname here is the same as Marlowe's, Kit – in the *Famous History* he is always

---

[108] *The Second Report* is not a translation of the so-called German *Wagnerbuch*, the sequel of the story of Christopher Wagner, Faustus's apprentice, after his master's death, but an independent prose fiction on his adventures purportedly written by an 'English Gentleman student in Wittenberg'. On the difference between the two, see Harold Jantz, 'An Elizabethan Statement on the Origin of the German Faust Book', *JEGP*, 15:2 (1952), 137–53.

[109] *The Second Report of Doctor Iohn Faustus: Containing His Apparances, and the Deeds of Wagner* (London, 1594; *STC* 10715), sig. B2r-v.

[110] Ibid., sig. B3r.

Christopher), takes on his master's mantle not just as conjurer but playwright: it is he who stages the production of Faustus's trial in the sky above Wittenberg.[111]

The first part of *The Second Report* culminates in the performance of 'The Tragedy of Doctor Faustus' that Wagner necromantically produces at the 'excellent faire Theator erected' in the air in the presence of a thousand people in Wittenberg.[112] Although the visionary tragedy itself has nothing in common with *Doctor Faustus*, the role of Wagner in the narrative as a conjuring entertainer and playwright is clearly superimposed on that of Faustus and Marlowe, the late conjuring masters who offered the audience in the playhouse a thrilling theatrical entertainment of devils.

What is more interesting about the performance of Faustus in *The Second Report* is its dramatic ending, with the collapse of the stage into the River Elbe, and the legendary allusion that seems to have partly originated from the following passage:

> When *Faustus* having long raged, of a soddaine howling lowde, and tearing his haire, laide both his armes vppon his necke, and leapt down headlong of the stage, the whole company immediately vanishing, but the stage with a most monstrous thundering crack followed *Faustus* hastely, the people verily thinking that they would haue fallen vppon them ran all away, and he was happiest that had the swiftest foote, some leapte into the Riuer and swam away, and all of them with greate affright ranne into the Citty and clapt the Citty gates together, streight, and to encrease this feare they thought they hard a thing fall into the riuer as if a thousand houses had fallen downe from the toppe of Heauen into it.[113]

This thunderous collapse was in no way seen as God's judgement upon the town by spectators of the demonic entertainment, but a mere illusion created by Wagner, as it was described that 'afterwards this was knowne to bee *Wagners* knauery', intended to show off his magical skills to a Viennese imperial messenger. Furthermore, there are no moral overtones in *The Second Report* to blame Wagner for frightening the townsmen with a hallucinatory ending that they might have mistaken for reality. Nevertheless, evidence survives that this stage collapse during the illusionary performance was later connected to a 'providential' disaster, such as happened at Paris Garden in 1583. A reference to *Doctor Faustus* in Thomas Middleton's *The Black Book* (1604) shows a vestige of the airy tragedy of Faustus: 'He had a head of hair like one of my devils in *Doctor Faustus* when the old

---

[111] Maslen, 'Marlowe's Ghost', p. 12.
[112] *Second Report of Doctor Iohn Faustus*, sig. E2v.
[113] *Second Report of Doctor Iohn Faustus*, sig. F1r.

Theatre cracked and frighted the audience.'[114] Several theatre historians consider this to be a reference to the play's early performance and the real (but unrecorded) disaster at the Theatre in Shoreditch. However, it is hard to imagine that such a disaster occurred and left no circumstantial evidence; it is more likely, as Eric Rasmussen has argued, that the allusion is linked to the collapse of the envisioned stage in *The Second Report*.[115]

It is therefore more pertinent to ask what made Middleton or, more generally, the public, mistake the fictional collapse in *The Second Report* for the one that putatively happened during the performance of Marlowe's *Doctor Faustus*. It may have been a simple misconception. However, we cannot overlook the underlying moral trend of anti-theatrical opinion that construed any such incident as a sign of divine displeasure. Moreover, the 'providential' death of Marlowe, who had been rumoured to be the master conjurer of Raleigh's school of atheism, may have allowed those who viewed *Doctor Faustus* from a providential and quasi-biographical perspective to consider its performance as a cultural trigger for incurring such divine penalties. Constant anxiety about the potential recurrence of the plague was also still strong enough to accelerate the trend of such an opinion. For these reasons, it is highly likely that *Doctor Faustus* was seen as a dangerous drama in which the master conjurer offered a profane but absorbing entertainment involving devils, and that under such social circumstances the illusionary collapse of the stage in *The Second Report* was taken for a real incident that happened during the performance of *Doctor Faustus*.

Admittedly, it would be difficult to trace the origin and causes of the urban legend of *Doctor Faustus* in any detail, or the trajectory of its development. However, every surviving document on the legend seems to point unerringly to the unique impact of the play, and that it promoted the emergence of the social and cultural phenomena that bolstered society's collective perception of the feared providential retribution upon its audiences, fans, and players. This implies that the best, or perhaps only, way to understand the meaning of the legend would be to localize it within the context of the 'ugly decade' in the 1590s. This conviction has led us thus far to consider the formation of the legend as being due not only to the realistic and mass-entertaining power of the play itself, with Faustus the conjurer as its hero, but also to the social psyche within which the fear and anxiety propagated by the plague epidemic of 1592–93 remained entrenched long after it died out. Moreover, the localization of the legend encourages us to

---

[114] Thomas Middleton, *The Black Book*, ed. G. B. Shand, in Gary Taylor and John Lavagnino (eds), *Thomas Middleton: The Collected Works* (Oxford, 2007), pp. 204–18, at p. 209.

[115] Eric Rasmussen, '*The Black Book* and the Date of *Doctor Faustus*', *N&Q*, 37:2 (1990), pp. 168–70.

consider its formation within a larger picture and as part of the cultural drive to construct and demonize Marlowe as an atheist icon: the drive that Greene's scandalous criticism in his repentance pamphlets triggered, activating the quasi-biographical hermeneutics of Marlowe's plays, and which had been enhanced by the accidental (though seemingly providential) death of Marlowe immediately following the distribution of the rumour about Raleigh's atheist school.

Identifying how citizens actually perceived the thunderous collapse of the sumptuous theatre could be one of the prime objects for new Marlovian biographical scholarship if we are to understand the fragmentary documents concerning him, as well as his plays, in their locally and temporally specific contexts. Localizing the Marlovian mythos as a posthumous phenomenon would afford us a new understanding of the social and cultural function of literary discourses of/about Marlowe that constructed reality from fiction, fiction from reality, in the 1590s.

CONCLUSION

Localizing Christopher Marlowe has been intended as a humble resistance against the strong cultural impetus to mystify or demonize Marlowe based on the anti-atheist narrative that was first set out by Robert Greene and subsequently consolidated by a succession of unreliable informers and godly moralists. This defensive bulwark is rooted in the historical and literary scholarship to which I have been profoundly indebted in writing this book. It can also be traced back to some of the voices of Marlowe's associates that have appeared in print, and so narrowly escaped from being buried in obscurity.

As several scholars reasonably assume, *Dido, Queen of Carthage* (1594), *Edward II* (1594), and the *Massacre at Paris* (c.1594–96), all displaying Marlowe's name on their title pages, were published as a result of his shocking death, and stirred up the contemporary trend to make 'Marlowe something of a phenomenon within the book trade'.[1] These printed plays, which may have achieved a wide readership, obviously added fuel to the spreading flames of the hostile discourses demonizing Marlowe as an atheist playwright. The upsurge of the anti-Marlowe campaign seems to have come at the turn of the sixteenth century. Thomas Beard describes Marlowe's death as God's punishment for his 'atheisme and impiety' in *The Theatre of Gods Judgements* (1597). Francis Meres, a divinity scholar from Pembroke Hall, Cambridge, followed this line, and in *Palladis Tamia, Wits Treasury* (1598) he reiterates what Beard had already approved, even embellishing it with crude gossip, saying that '*Marlow* was stabd to death by a bawdy Seruingman, a riuall of his in his lewde loue'.[2] William Vaughan, in *The Golden-Groue, Moralized in Three Bookes* (1600), similarly sees 'the

---

[1] András Kiséry, 'An Author and a Bookshop: Publishing Marlowe's Remains at the Black Bear', *Philological Quarterly*, 91:3 (2012), 361–92, at p. 365. See also Adam G. Hooks, 'Making Marlowe', in Kirk Melnikoff and Roslyn L. Knutson (eds), *Christopher Marlowe, Theatrical Commerce, and the Book Trade* (Cambridge, 2018), pp. 97–114, at p. 101. The title page of *The Massacre at Paris* has no date, but see Fredson Bowers (ed.), *The Complete Works of Christopher Marlowe*, 2nd edn (2 vols, Cambridge, 1981), vol. 1, p. 357.

[2] Francis Meres, *Palladis Tamia, Wits Treasury* (London, 1598), sigs. Oo6v–Oo7r.

effects of Gods iustice' in Marlowe's tragic death.[3] The book market was thus invigorated by the incident and so tended to reinforce the providential framework that would come to define the event in due course. Who would have dared to struggle against this impetus and fight a losing battle except for Marlowe's few friends?

It was, in fact, over the course of this anti-Marlowe campaign that Edward Blount published *Hero and Leander* in 1598 as an 'executor to the unhappily deceased author of this poem'. At the time of Marlowe's death, Blount was yet a fledgling stationer who had been apprenticed for ten years (longer than the usual period of seven years) to William Ponsonby from 24 June 1578, and was finally admitted to the freedom of the Stationers' Company on 25 June 1588.[4] His obvious taste for literary works and his adventurous investments seem to have been cultivated through his long apprenticeship to Ponsonby, who had become associated with the literary circle of Mary Herbert by 1586 and published the works of Sir Philip Sidney, Edmund Spenser, and Abraham Fraunce in the following years.[5]

In the dedication of *Hero and Leander* to Sir Thomas Walsingham, Blount discloses his intention to publish 'this unfinished tragedy' and inscribe it to Walsingham:

> Sir, we think not ourselves discharged of the duty we owe to our friend, when we have brought the breathless body to the earth: for albeit the eye there taketh his ever farewell of that beloved object, yet the impression of the man, that hath been dear unto us, living an after life in our memory, there putteth us in mind of farther obsequies due unto the deceased. And namely of the performance of whatsoever we may judge shall make to his living credit, and to the effecting of his determinations prevented by the stroke of death.[6]

---

[3] William Vaughan, *The Golden-Groue, Moralized in Three Bookes* (London, 1600), sig. C4v.

[4] For the life of Edward Blount, see Gary Taylor, 'Blount, Edward', *ODNB*. Leona Rostenberg, *Literary, Political, Scientific, Religious and Legal Publishing, Printing and Bookselling in England, 1551–1700: Twelve Studies* (2 vols, New York, 1965), vol. 1, pp. 50–1, depicts Blount as 'a man of literary instinct and appreciation'.

[5] See Michael Brennan, 'William Ponsonby: Elizabethan Stationer', *Analytical and Enumerative Bibliography*, 7 (1983), 91–110; Jean R. Brink, 'William Ponsonby's Rival Publisher', *Analytical and Enumerative Bibliography*, 12:3–4 (2001), 185–205; and Stacy Erickson, '"I do more confidently presume to publish it in his absence": William Ponsonby's Print Network', in John Hinks and Victoria Gardener (eds), *The Book Trade in Early Modern England: Practices, Perceptions, Connections* (New Castle, DE, 2014), pp. 45–60.

[6] Christopher Marlowe, *The Poems*, ed. Millar MacLure, *The Revels Plays* (London, 1968), p. 3.

Conclusion

A. L. Rowse finds in this dedication Blount's 'very personal' feelings towards the deceased author and his patron.[7] In contrast, Constance Kuriyama takes it to be 'an elaborate conceit' and 'no more than a figure of speech, since there is nothing in the dedication to indicate that Blunt had direct knowledge of Marlowe', and concludes: 'Blunt wanted to collect some of the reward Marlowe might have received by dedicating his finished poem to Walsingham.'[8] Admittedly, it would be easy to see Blount as an acquisitive and cheating stationer who, as Henry Chettle and other stationers did after the death of Robert Greene, attempted to exploit the legacy of the author and his unfortunate death to his own advantage. However, without reappraising his dedication within a specific local and historical context, we will not be able to know for sure whether 'the duty' Blount owed to Marlowe was truly of the utmost significance.

All the surviving evidence that points to Marlowe's business and friendly contacts with stationers in St Paul's Churchyard is circumstantial, though it is strong enough to indicate a personal relationship between Blount and Marlowe. Immediately after Marlowe's death, Gabriel Harvey gloated over his downfall: 'Weepe Powles, thy *Tamberlaine* voutsafes to dye.'[9] He tells us that the public space crammed with bookshops was well known as one of Marlowe's favourite haunts and a place to hang out with friends. This happens to correspond with Thomas Kyd's hearsay testimony to Sir John Puckering that, among 'such as [Marlowe] conversd withall', there were 'some stationers in Paules churchyard'.[10] Moreover, in the autumn of 1592 Marlowe brought the manuscript of a poem by the late Thomas Watson to William Ponsonby, Blount's former master, who entered it in the Stationers' Register as 'A booke entituled *Amint[a]e gaudia*' on 10 November and published it with Marlowe's dedication to Mary Herbert. These circumstances may well have afforded Marlowe and Blount with further regular opportunities to get acquainted with each other at St Paul's Churchyard.

What should be more closely examined is Blount's way of presenting the publication 'as a memorial to Marlowe, as an elegiac gesture which will gather his friends in shared activities of commemoration and celebration'.[11]

---

[7] A. L. Rowse, *Christopher Marlowe: A Biography* (London, 1964), p. 202. Kiséry, 'An Author and a Bookshop', p. 366, also argues that the dedication has a 'markedly personal tone'.

[8] Constance Brown Kuriyama, *Christopher Marlowe: A Renaissance Life* (Ithaca, 2002), p. 158.

[9] Gabriel Harvey, *A New Letter of Notable Contents*, in Alexander B. Grosart (ed.), *The Works of Gabriel Harvey* (3 vols, 1884; repr. New York, 1966), vol. 1, p. 295.

[10] Quoted in Kuriyama, *Christopher Marlowe*, p. 229.

[11] Georgia E. Brown, 'Gender and Voice in *Hero and Leander*', in J. A. Downie and J. T. Parnell (eds), *Constructing Christopher Marlowe* (Cambridge, 2000), pp. 148–63, at p. 163.

Georgia E. Brown notes the importance of Blount's role in constructing and reflecting a literary community in relation to Marlowe's poem, while András Kiséry has given a good picture of how Blount, with his working mates at the Black Bear, 'attempted to use Marlowe as something like a brand name, and to capitalize on the unpublished Marlovian texts available to them'.[12] Blount certainly seems to have taken the lead in the publication of Marlowe's remaining works, but, as far as the publication of *Hero and Leander* is concerned, its circumstances were more complex than we might imagine.

We can gain some knowledge of Blount's preferred way of working with patrons and authors by studying his dedication to the Earl of Southampton in the English translation of *The Historie of the Vniting of the Kingdom of Portugall to the Crowne of Castill* (1600):

> I do heere offer vp on the altar of my hart, the first fruits of my long-growing endeuors; which (with much constancie and confidence) I haue cherisht, onely waiting this happie opportunitie to make them manifest to your Lordship. [...] I woulde still pursue the happines of my first choice; which hath since beene confirmed to me by my respected friend the translator, a Gentleman most sincerely deuoted to your Honor.[13]

In this dedication, as Sonia Massai points out, 'Blount's investment in textual patronage is [...] highlighted as a primary function of the publication of literary texts'.[14] His 'long-growing endeuors' were possibly made not only to finance the printing costs, but also to negotiate with his 'respected friend' in order to acquire his copy and secure Southampton's patronage by forging a relationship of mutual trust between them.

We find a similar attitude to business in *Hero and Leander*. In the dedication to Thomas Walsingham, we should not overlook Blount's affectionate attitude towards his patron in the use of the plural 'we', and his compelling sense of duty to serve as a working unit and as one of the core members in the small community commemorating Marlowe. It would have been difficult for Blount to begin his dedication in such an intimate and personal way without being closely acquainted with both of those to whom he thought it necessary to fulfil a 'double duty'. Moreover, his physical description of burying 'the breathless body' in the grave and of their eyes seeing 'the beloved object' interred there is so graphic that it has encouraged several

---

[12] Kiséry, 'An Author and a Bookshop', p. 381.
[13] Gerolamo Franchi di Conestaggio, *The Historie of the Vniting of the Kingdom of Portugall to the Crowne of Castill* (London, 1600), sig. A2r.
[14] Sonia Massai, 'Edward Blount, the Herberts, and the First Folio', in Marta Straznicky (ed.), *Shakespeare's Stationers: Studies in Cultural Bibliography* (Philadelphia, 2013), pp. 132–46, at p. 136.

scholars to consider the presence of Blount, as well as of Walsingham, as a mourner at St Nicholas's church, Deptford.[15]

It would be a naïve and inexperienced biographer to suggest that what motivates a person to commemorate and celebrate a well-known author is love or amity rather than political acquisitiveness, self-interest, social ambition, feigned friendship, or whatever sounds pragmatic and objective. We must be cautious in reading into documents what we expect to find there. It cannot be ignored, however, as I have demonstrated in the earlier chapters, that fraternity and friendship based on community, faction loyalty, patronage, and locality were among the essential elements for those seeking employment in order to survive and thrive in response to drastic changes in the social and economic environment. This feeling of comradeship was founded on duty and credit and developed through mutual interests, pleasures, and even hardships. Blount's emphasis on 'duty' and 'credit' in the dedication should be understood within his relationships of patronage and friendship. He intended to share with Walsingham 'the duty we owe to our friend', a duty which urged them to perform 'whatsoever we may judge shall make to [Marlowe's] living credit and to the effecting of his determinations'. The publication of *Hero and Leander* was recognized as one of these efforts to recover the author's (and consequently his friends') credit and to fulfil their duty to execute 'the will of him dead'. This statement should be considered in the light of Blount's investment risks, because the danger of embarking on such a literary enterprise without establishing a trusted relationship with patron and author(s) seems to have been far greater than the profit or the reward that he could have gained by dedicating the work.

Thomas Walsingham was well known among his close acquaintances as a man who did not enjoy being flattered through dedications. George Chapman, in the epistle attached to the edition of his plays *The Conspiracy and Tragedy of Charles Duke of Byron* (1608), excuses his dedication as being due to his patron's 'approbation' of them:

> SIR, though I know, you euer stood little affected to these vnprofitable rites of Dedication; (which disposition in you, hath made me hetherto dispence with your right in my other impressions) yet, least the world may repute it a neglect in me, of so ancient and worthy a friend; (hauing heard your approbation of these in their presentment) I could not but prescribe them with your name.[16]

---

[15] Park Honan, *Christopher Marlowe: Poet and Spy* (Oxford, 2005), p. 355. See also Reavley Gair, 'Walsingham, Thomas', *ODNB*.

[16] George Chapman, *The Plays of George Chapman: The Tragedies with Sir Gyles Goosecappe, A Critical Edition*, ed. Allan Holaday (Cambridge, 1987), p. 277.

Walsingham's reserved or unfriendly 'disposition' towards this literary practice can further be attested to some extent by the scarcity of books that were dedicated to him during his lifetime. As far as we know, there are only three dedicators in four works: Thomas Watson in *Meliboeus* (1590), George Chapman in *All Fools* (1605) and *The Conspiracy and Tragedy of Charles Duke of Byron*, and Blount on behalf of Marlowe in *Hero and Leander*.[17] These writers were all acknowledged by their contemporaries or through their own testimonies as being close friends of Walsingham, and so the dedicated works appear to have been limited to writings by members of the small literary coterie of his household. As a result, Blount would have run the risk of incurring Walsingham's displeasure unless he was closely associated with him and had obtained his approval by publishing *Hero and Leander* under his name, and in addition by claiming to have had a close understanding of Marlowe's personal 'determinations' or fixed purposes that he expressed when he was alive.

There seems to be much truth in Blount's claim to know 'the will of him dead'. He declares that 'whatsoever issue of his brain should chance to come abroad, [...] the first breath it should take might be the gentle air of [Walsingham's] liking'.[18] In fact, we know that Marlowe was staying at Walsingham's house in Scadbury in May 1593 when taking refuge from the plague and supposedly writing his *Hero and Leander*, as the Privy Council described it as being Marlowe's primary residence at that time.[19] This leads us to assume that Walsingham was one of the closest insiders acquainted with Marlowe's intentions: in dedicating his poem to the generous patron and lord of the manor, and so vying with Shakespeare – another insider who had possibly seen Marlowe's poem in manuscript form, and who had been writing *Venus and Adonis* for the Earl of Southampton at that time – for the fame of being a new Ovidian poet of his age by 'creating contrasting variations on the theme of tragic desire'.[20]

Another insider seems to have been George Chapman, who says in the dedication to Audrey Walsingham, Thomas's wife, that he was 'drawn by strange instigation' to compose the sequel to Marlowe's 'unfinished tragedy' *Hero and Leander*. It is possible to understand the word 'strange' as meaning 'alien'; that is, Chapman was requested by others or provoked to write by

---

[17] Franklin B. Williams, *Index of Dedications and Commendatory Verses in English Books before 1641* (London, 1962), p. 193.
[18] Marlowe, *Poems*, ed. MacLure, p. 3.
[19] *APC*, vol. 24, p. 244.
[20] James P. Bednarz, 'Marlowe and the English Literary Scene', in Patrick Cheney (ed.), *The Cambridge Companion to Christopher Marlowe* (Cambridge, 2004), pp. 90–105, at p. 103, suggests the possibility that Shakespeare saw Marlowe's poem in manuscript form and created *Venus and Adonis* 'as a kind of literary diptych'.

some incident or circumstance.[21] In fact, in the third sestiad of *Hero and Leander*, he commands his own poetic inspiration ('most strangely-intellectual fire') to tell Marlowe's 'free soul [...] how much his late desires I tender'.[22] Owing to his hazy rhetoric, it is difficult to understand precisely when and how Chapman was stimulated to write, but the interpretation given by C. S. Lewis seems to be most persuasive: 'Perhaps Chapman poetically feigned, or (quite as probable) actually believed, that he had been strangely instigated by Marlowe since Marlowe's death.'[23]

Chapman's statement about his motives makes us further wonder if he might have been acquainted, directly or indirectly (possibly via Walsingham), with Marlowe and his ambitious literary project well before the playwright's death. This assumption becomes more convincing when we pay attention to Chapman's long-term clientage to Walsingham, whom he described in 1598 as 'my honoured best friend, whose continuance of *ancient* kindness to my still-obscured estate' would 'make my hearty gratitude speak'.[24] A. R. Braunmuller assumes, based on this evidence, that 'the two poet-acquaintances (probably poet-friends) were also joint sharers in the Walsinghams' patronage'.[25]

But how 'ancient' had the continuance of Walsingham's kindness to Chapman been? Chapman dedicated *The Conspiracy and Tragedy of Charles, Duke of Byron* not only to Walsingham himself but also 'to my much loued from his birth, the right toward and worthy Gentleman his sonne Thomas Walsingham, Esquire',[26] suggesting that his 'so ancient and worthy' friendship with the Walsinghams can be traced back at least to the time of the birth of his patron's son. Andrew Thrush has recently shown that the son was born in about 1589, 'for in 1602 his father, offering to compound for his wardship and marriage from the Court of Wards for £50, gave his age as 13'.[27] This new evidence therefore allows us to imagine Chapman sharing the same patronage with Marlowe within the coterie at Scadbury and being one of those insiders who was well versed in Marlowe's aspiring 'determinations' to be a poet.

---

[21] For this interpretive approach, see L. C. Martin (ed.), *Marlowe's Poems* (1931; repr. New York, 1966), p. 67, n. 3.
[22] Marlowe, *Poems*, ed. MacLure, p. 53, line 195.
[23] C. S. Lewis, 'Hero and Leander', in *Selected Literary Essays* (Cambridge, 1969), pp. 58–73, at p. 62.
[24] Marlowe, *Poems*, ed. MacLure, pp. 43–4, lines 37–9, 41–2, emphasis added.
[25] A. R. Braunmuller, *Natural Fictions: George Chapman's Major Tragedies* (Newark, DE, 1992), p. 21.
[26] Chapman, *Plays of Chapman*, ed. Holaday, p. 277.
[27] Andrew Thrush and John P. Ferris (eds), *The House of Commons 1604–1629* (6 vols, Cambridge, 2010), vol. 6, p. 660.

Assuming that this small coterie did exist urges us to consider the possibility that the literary role Blount played in publishing *Hero and Leander* was neither that of an acquisitive stationer working for profit under the guise of friendship with Walsingham nor that of a mastermind inventing the purported literary ambition of the dead Marlowe and constructing this authorial self on the publisher's initiative. Rather, as a 'friend', Blount seems to have intended to reflect the wishes of the patron, whom he knew 'bestowed many kind favours, entertaining the parts of reckoning and worth which [he] found in [Marlowe] with good countenance'. At the same time, Blount seems to have had in mind the wishes of the coterie with whom he himself may have been affiliated, and to have shared their concern for Marlowe's posthumous works. In this sense, he regarded himself as 'executor to the unhappily deceased author of this poem', making sure that the publication was achieved according to the purposes both of the dead and of the patron and dedicatee of his work, and so had to fulfil the 'double duty, the one to [Walsingham], the other to the deceased'. The household support that Blount had obtained from Walsingham possibly helped him to secure the copyright, which John Wolfe first entered in the Stationers' Register on 28 December 1593; publish the first edition of *Hero and Leander*, with his dedication to Walsingham; and, at the same time, secure cooperation from Chapman, the rising poet under the aegis of the Walsinghams, to compose the continuation and the dedication to Audrey Walsingham to accomplish the 'diptych' edition immediately after.[28] The publication was not a project launched and then developed by one stationer, but rather a communal effort by those who cherished and shared the fresh memory of their friend and poet.

In the strong current of the anti-Marlowe campaign that ran through the stark landscape of the heresy-hunting atmosphere of the 1590s, public declaration of friendship with Marlowe, the purported blasphemous atheist, was a very risky matter and could cast his avowed friends in a bad light, as we see in Thomas Kyd's denial of friendship: 'That I should *love or be familiar frend, with one so irreligious*, were verie rare.'[29] This shows what it meant to declare friendship with Marlowe. Accordingly, of course, Blount might have chosen to publish Marlowe's poem without dedication or sequel, as others did in publishing his plays for profit immediately after his death. But for some reason he did not go down that route. Rather, though surrounded by such unfavourable and hostile circumstances, Blount reveals

---

[28] Bowers, *Complete Works of Marlowe*, vol. 2, p. 425, argues for the possibility that Wolfe did not bring out an edition because 'in 1598 when Edward Blount published what appears to be the first, his dedication to Sir Thomas Walsingham could scarcely have been written in such terms if an earlier edition had been marketed'.

[29] Quoted in Kuriyama, *Christopher Marlowe*, p. 229, emphasis added.

his, Chapman's, and the Walsinghams' close alliance and friendship with Marlowe through the paratext of *Hero and Leander*, apparently without any fear of getting them into trouble or of causing great damage to their name. This bold project seems even more surprising when we consider the fact that the fervour of the moralist attacks on atheists and heretics, including Marlowe, was still aglow and posed a serious threat in and around 1598. What encouraged Blount, facing the widespread prejudice against Marlowe, to make their friendship public was probably the favourable turn of fortune that befell Walsingham and Chapman around that time.

On 20 July 1597, the queen was staying at Scadbury.[30] This visit was, no doubt, of a private character, and consequently not documented as one of the celebrated royal progresses. Webb, Miller, and Beckwith note that 'The close proximity of Greenwich would make such a visit easy to accomplish'.[31] Moreover, the visit may have been organized at the request of Audrey Walsingham, the daughter of Sir Ralph Shelton of Shelton, Norfolk, who was closely related to Elizabeth through her mother, Anne Boleyn. The attempt to establish amicable relations with the queen had been made by Audrey well before the visit. The records of the queen's New Year's gift exchanges show that Audrey had presented gifts since 1588, and did so most lavishly from 1597 to 1600.[32]

This closer proximity to the queen had clearly worked successfully enough for the Walsinghams to be honoured: by her departure on the following day, 21 July, Elizabeth had dubbed Thomas a knight. The conferment can be attested by the fact that he was described in the Privy Council Minutes as 'Thomas Walsingham, esquire' on 19 July, but five days later, on 24 July, as 'Sir Thomas' for the first time.[33] This political backing by the queen afforded the Walsinghams firm grounds to enhance their presence on the political and cultural scene, and consequently gave to Blount the confidence to make a tacit protest by giving voice in print to the necessity 'of the performance of whatsoever [Walsingham and Blount] may judge shall make to [Marlowe's] living credit'. Publishing Marlowe's posthumous poem, with Chapman as co-author and Audrey as co-dedicatee, was, as it were, a

---

[30] One of the queen's secretaries (perhaps Robert Cecil) wrote to the Earl of Essex, 'on Wednesday night, I being at Greenwich, and the Queene at Mr. Walsingams'. BL, Lansdowne MS 85 (19), fol. 37r.

[31] E. A. Webb, G. W. Miller, and J. Beckwith, *The History of Chislehurst: Its Church, Manors, and Parish* (London, 1899), pp. 138–9.

[32] Jane A. Lawson (ed.), *The Elizabethan New Year's Gift Exchanges 1559–1603* (Oxford, 2013), p. 731.

[33] *APC*, vol. 27, pp. 298 and 308. This fact was first pointed out by T. A. Bushell in 'Scadbury Manor, Chislehurst', *AC*, 69 (1955), 219–21, at pp. 220–1.

household project given shape by Blount's practical workings in cooperation with Walsingham.

No doubt the substantial participation of Chapman, who had hitherto been forced by 'the unhappiness of [his] life' into 'uncomfortable and painful dumbness', to express his gratitude for Walsingham's long-standing kindness, was also one of the propelling forces of the project, because by 1598 he had succeeded in fashioning himself as an intellectual poet and classicist.[34] His first poem, *The Shadow of Night*, was published by William Ponsonby in 1594 and was followed by the second, *Ovid's Banquet of Senses* (1595), and dramatic works such as *The Blind Beggar of Alexandria* (dated 1596) and *An Humorous Day's Mirth* (1597). The publication thereafter of his *Seaven Bookes of the Iliades of Homere, Prince of Poets* (1598) may well have brought Chapman into the foreground of the literary scene. The queen's backing for Walsingham gave Blount (and Walsingham) full scope to use the resources at their disposal to celebrate the friendship and memory of Marlowe in the face of the cultural impetus to demonize him. At the same time, the literary reputation of Chapman gave authority to Blount to eulogize and represent Marlowe as the English 'divine Musaeus', as did Thomas Nashe immediately after in *Nashes Lenten Stuffe* (1599): 'Leander and Hero, of whome diuine *Musæus* sung, and a diuiner Muse than him, Kit Marlow'.[35]

The publication of *Hero and Leander* undoubtedly renewed Shakespeare's appreciation of Marlowe as a forerunner of drama and of Ovidian narrative poetry, and he inserted a eulogistic quotation from *Hero and Leander* into *As You Like It* (dated 1598–1600): 'Dead shepherd, now I find thy saw of might: / "Who ever loved that loved not at first sight?"'[36] This reference to Marlowe has tempted many critics to identify Shakespeare's response to his death and the publication of the poem.[37] Touchstone's complaint – 'when a man's verses cannot be understood, [...] it strikes a man more dead than a great reckoning in a little room' (III.iii.9–12) – resonates with subtle echoes

---

[34] Marlowe, *The Poems*, ed. MacLure, p. 44, lines 42–3.

[35] *Ibid.*, p. 8, line 52, and p. 42, line 5. For Nashe's description of Marlowe's *Hero and Leander*, see Ronald B. McKerrow (ed.), *The Works of Thomas Nashe*, 2nd edn, rev. F. P. Wilson (5 vols, Oxford, 1958), vol. 3, p. 195. See also Meres, *Palladis Tamia*, sig. Oo2r.

[36] William Shakespeare, *As You Like It*, ed. Alan Brissenden, *The Oxford Shakespeare* (Oxford, 1993), III.v.82–3. Subsequent references to *As You Like It* will be to this edition and will appear parenthetically in the text by act, scene, and line number.

[37] For several interpretations on this scene, see William Shakespeare, *As You Like It*, ed. Richard Knowles, with a survey of criticism by Evelyn Joseph Mattern, *A New Variorum Edition of Shakespeare* (New York, 1977), pp. 188–90. See also James Shapiro, *Rival Playwrights: Marlowe, Jonson, Shakespeare* (New York, 1991), pp. 115–17.

Conclusion

of the 'infinite riches in a little room' at the beginning of Barabas's famous soliloquy, acting as a gentle reminder of the murder over the reckoning in Eleanor Bull's inn room. Moreover, several critics see the parallel between these lines and Sonnet 86, one of the 'Rival Poet sonnets',[38] possibly written between 1598 and 1600, where Shakespeare betrays his anxiety at being in the shadow of his rivals:

> Was it the proud full sail of his great verse,
> Bound for the prize of all-too-precious you,
> That did my ripe thoughts in my brain in-hearse,
> Making their tomb the womb wherein they grew?
> Was it his spirit, by spirits taught to write
> Above a mortal pitch, that struck me dead?
> No, neither he, nor his compeers by night,
> Giving him aid, my verse astonished. (Sonnet 86, lines 1–8)[39]

MacDonald P. Jackson argues that the publication of *Hero and Leander*, which was 'in a manner of speaking, a collaboration between a living poet and a ghost', may have attracted Shakespeare's attention to the artistry and wit of Chapman, as well as of the dead Marlowe. It is reasonable, therefore, that 'we should think in terms not of "either or" but of "both and"' in identifying the main candidate for the chief rival poet.[40] Chapman has long been identified as one of the candidates, but Jackson's suggestion that we should see Marlowe and Chapman as a unit seems to be unique and highly persuasive. Thus, Shakespeare, feeling threatened by his rival's poetic artistry, asks himself: 'Was it his spirit, by spirits taught to write / Above a mortal pitch, that struck me dead?' But he shakes off the thought and tries to emerge from that powerful influence: 'No, neither he, nor his compeers by night, / Giving him aid, my verse astonished.'

Who, then, are the rival's 'compeers by night, giving him aid'? We should be cautious about pursuing the identity of these candidates too far, for the sonnet is not autobiographical. However, we know at least that Blount, who bound and offered the book for sale – 'the proud full sail [proudful sale] of his great verse, / Bound for the prize of all-too-precious you' – was in fact

---

[38] See, for instance, Katherine Duncan-Jones (ed.), *Shakespeare's Sonnets*, The Arden Shakespeare, 3rd ser. (1997; repr. London, 2010), p. 282, n.6.

[39] All quotations and line numbers from Shakespeare's *Sonnets* are from Duncan-Jones (ed.), *Shakespeare's Sonnets*.

[40] MacDonald P. Jackson, 'Francis Meres and the Cultural Contexts of Shakespeare's Rival Poet Sonnets', *RES*, NS, 56:244 (2005), 224–46, at p. 230. For Shakespeare's anxiety about being influenced by Marlowe and Chapman, see also Jonathan Bate, *The Genius of Shakespeare* (London, 1997), pp. 122–32.

one of the 'compeers' helping the Rival Poet to publish it.[41] The sonnet implies Shakespeare's understanding of Blount's publication as a communal project for performing a strikingly personal but concerted duty to restore Marlowe's credit. The comradeship of the coterie, declared in those dedications in *Hero and Leander*, may well have aroused mixed feelings in Shakespeare, as we can detect in the 'Rival Poet sonnets' and *As You Like It*, such as jealousy towards his successful rival, anxiety about his own status, and especially empathy with Marlowe's 'friends', who launched a concerted effort to effect his literary 'determinations'. It was possibly this empathy that motivated Shakespeare to join restrainedly in the project to recuperate Marlowe's reputation. His voice is not loud, but suffices to convince us of its empathic quality. Rosalind's dispassionate response to the death of Leander – 'Men have died from time to time, and worms have eaten them, but not for love' (*As You Like It*, IV.i.97–8) – may have been a gentle reproach of Francis Meres, who attributed Marlowe's death to 'his lewde loue'.[42] We can also read two lines in Sonnet 74 as one of Shakespeare's mild rebukes for the dominant moral discourse disparaging Marlowe's merits: 'The coward conquest of a wretch's knife, / Too base of thee to be remembered' (lines 11–12).[43]

It is these faint but nevertheless recoverable voices of Marlowe's close associates that demand we pay close attention to the local and communal cluster of agents who, sharing his memories and wishes, attempted to shape his literary reputation and withstand the cultural momentum that produced religious deviants and the contemporary legends that surrounded them. Certainly, what we can find here is but a fragment of the author's portrait, constructed by their voices, not the whole or in any way 'true' one. However, the fragment is too personal to be ignored and too communal to be commercial. It is a kind of contemporary community-derived 'biographeme', to use Roland Barthes's term, which relates the literary text to the collective experiences of Marlowe and his associates and even allows us, in spite of the scarcity of biographical documents, to feel 'a piece of' the flesh-and-blood Marlowe.[44]

The documents and memories of a person will eventually be scattered and lost after their death. In some cases this can happen more quickly, in any nation where the falsification and destruction of public documents become a daily occurrence, from fictional realms such as Oceania in

---

[41] Jane Kingsley-Smith, *The Afterlife of Shakespeare's Sonnets* (Cambridge, 2019), p. 83, points out the pun on 'sail'/'sale'.

[42] For this reading of the passage, see Charles Nicholl, *The Reckoning: The Murder of Christopher Marlowe* (London, 1992), p. 73; and Bate, *Genius of Shakespeare*, p. 123.

[43] Jackson, 'Francis Meres and the Cultural Contexts', p. 235, suggests this reading.

[44] Roland Barthes, *Sade Fourier Loyola*, trans. Richard Miller (Berkeley, 1977), p. 9.

Conclusion

George Orwell's *Nineteen Eighty-Four* to, unfortunately, Japan today.[45] What Winston Smith says to Julia in *Nineteen Eighty-Four* pertains to both situations: the only evidence is inside one's own mind, and there is no certainty that any other human being shares one's memories. But, even under the tyranny of Time, holding his scythe and hourglass, I tend to agree with Winston that 'one can imagine little knots of resistance springing up here and there – small groups of people banding themselves together, and gradually growing, and even leaving a few records behind, so that the next generations can carry on where we leave off'.[46] We can perceive and listen to such voices not only from the paratexts and literary rejoinders to *Hero and Leander*, but also from the windows of schools and colleges, from the pits and galleries of playhouses, from the letters to and from Privy Council members, from the garden of Scadbury manor house, and from the small row of bookshops in St Paul's Churchyard – from any locality where Marlowe left his traces. It is these thin, faint, and lingering voices that cast doubt on and urge us to reconsider the dominant narrative in which history is told and appropriated for political and commercial ends.

---

[45] A Finance Ministry official killed himself in 2018 after being ordered to tamper with official documents related to favouritism allegations against then-Prime Minister Shinzo Abe, leaving a handwritten note as his last voice.

[46] George Orwell, *Nineteen Eighty-Four* (London, 1949), part 2, chap. 5.

APPENDIX 1: TRANSCRIPT OF THE PLAN IN NORFOLK RECORD OFFICE, NRS 23372, Z99

East

[8.]

- [Robert] Yemes
- [Robert] Cheyner [or Chawner]
- [?] Dawes
- [Christopher] Grenewood

{ Mr [Henry] Yemes a fell[ow]
{ [Michael] Tills

- Sr [Brian] Exton*
- Sr [John] Rice [or Ruck]*
- [Robert] Stone*
- [William] Naze*

[9.]

- Mr [Thomas] Crofts
- [Thomas] Peck se[nio]r
- [William] Peck Ju[nio]r
- [Thomas] Elwill [or Elwin]

{ Mr [John] Thaxter a fell[ow]
{ [John] Riches

- Sr [Henry] Goulding*
- [John] Dixe*
- [John] Wulsye

[10.]

- Sr [Henry] Sutt[e]rton
- Sr [Nicholas] Bate
- [Miles] Cartewrite
- [Henry] Sparowe

Mr [Henry] Aldrich [a fellow]

- Sr [Henry] Gold*
- Sr [Thomas] Plumb*
- Sr [Christopher] Abbs*

North

[7.]

- [Thomas] Dodkin
- [Robert] Gold
- [Matthew] Fisher

{ Mr [Moses] Fowler a fell[ow]
{ [Roger] Drake

{ Sr [Philip] Nicholls a fell[ow]
{ [Thomas] Bustard
{ [James] Farrar

[6.]

- Sr [George] Downing
- [George] Manning
- [Thomas] Darlye
- [John] Neve

{ Mr [Francis] Kett a fell[ow]
{ [Edward] Meriman

- Sr [William] Norgate*
- Sr [Thomas] Harris*
- [Robert] Thexton*

[5.]

- Sr [William] Read
- Sr [Hamlet] Cartewrite
- [Henry] Barro
- [Jonathan] Pitts

{ Mr [Robert] Sayer a fell[ow]
{ Mr [Thomas] Muffet Mr of Artes & pencion[e]r

- Sr [Richard] Braborne*
- Sr [John] Temple*
- [Samuel] Write
- [Robert] Felsam [or Foulson]

The nomber of those that be Lodged in the Colleg & how & in What chambers they be lodged.

4.

- Sr [Alexander] Revell
- Sr [Stephen] Snat
- [Matthew] Penfather
- [Richard or John] Jackson

Mr [Richard] Willoughby a fell[ow]

- [Christopher] Pashlye*
- [James] Poynter*
- [Samuel] Beadell*

3.

- Sr [Richard] Foster
- [?] Davye
- [?] Talks
- [?] Finch

Mr [Robert] Swet a fell[ow]

- Sr [Edward] Wood*
- Sr [Henry or John] Grene
- [John] Knat*

2.

- Sr [Richard] Tayeler
- [Nicholas] Becket se[nior]
- [William] Becket Ju[nior]
- [John] Smith

{ Mr [Daniel] Chester a fell[ow]
{ Mr [Sophonius] Smith a pens[ioner] & Mr of Artes

- [John] Hawes
- Sr [Thomas] Corbet*
- Sr [John] Browne
- [Robert] Raye

West

348

Appendix 1

The newe building for pencion[e]rs.

The East end.

Mr [Edward] Lucas	Mr [Thomas] Canndishe
Mr [Edward] Page	[Thomas] Lancast[e]r
Mr [Robert] Chev[e]r a fellowe	Mr [George] Grime
	Mr [?] Halfehed
Sr [Edward] Ratife	Sr [Thomas] Tevill [or Tyrrell]
[Thomas] Welden	[Henry or Jeremiah] Johnson

ov[e]r the butterye
Sr [Daniel] Godfry*
Sr [John] Tilny*
[John] Payne

In the Lower chamb[e]r
[William] Lawse*
[Richard] Mannering*
[James] Fokes [or Folkes]

In the middle chamb[e]r
[?] Helsby
[Thomas or John] Jermin
Mr [Thomas or Robert] Jermin
Mr [Henry] Lewes a fell[ow]

In the vpp[er] chamb[e]r
[Simon] Ruse Ju[ni]or
[Henry] Ruse se[ni]o[r]
[Henry] Allens
[Christopher] Halfaxe
Sr [Richard] Gibson

[.1.]

349

APPENDIX 2: TRANSCRIPT OF THE PLAN IN CORPUS CHRISTI COLLEGE ARCHIVES, CCCC08/28

	The Mrs Lodging		The Haule	bible clarkes Sr Hawexworth Godfry Norffi Vacat. Matchet
11	Mr Scot fell[ow] Norffi.	Abbs Norw[i]ch Corbet Regest[e]r		
10	Mr Aldrich Norw[i]ch	Gold Plumb } Norw[i]ch		
9	Mr Gooch Norw[i]ch	Golding Dixe } Norw[i]ch		
	Sr Cotton of Kel[n]t Sr Fowler		Sr Jenkinson of Cambrdg for Mr Meres Sr Nicholls of Lincoln	Faunt Suff Harris Norffi
	Syr Yemes Norffi		Mr Byrd Essex	The Diall chamb[e]r Mr Ket Norffi
	8		7	6 North

Appendix 2

		West		
	1	2	3	4
	Mr Lewes fell[ow] Suff	Mr Chest[e]r fellow London	Mr Swet fellowe Cambridgshire	Mr Willoughby fell[ow] of the newe foundacion of the Colledg Norff
	2 schollers { Temple / Lawse } Norf	Sr Thaxter fellow Norw[i]ch	2 schollers Sr { Wood Cambridgshire / Ruck }	for iij schollers
5				Sr Sutt[e]lrton } Norgate } of the foundacion
				ov[e]r the gate Mr Sayer Norff

351

APPENDIX 3: TRANSCRIPT AND TRANSLATION OF THE JOHN MARLEY VS NEVELL HAYES CASE

JOHN MARLEY VS NEVELL HAYES

5o martij cora*m* d*o*m*i*no d*o*cto*re* perne deputato d*o*m*i*ni p*ro*canc*ellarii*

Jo*hn* marley de Cant*a*brigia gen*e*rosus *versus* nevell hayes cooke

Quib*us* &c / marley allegavit / q*uo*d mutuo dedit cuid*a*m Austen in artib*us* bacch*a*laureo de coll*e*gio corp*or*is *ch*risti pupillo m*a*gist*r*i Taxton toga*m* qua*m* emit de patre d*i*cti Austen in civitate Cantuarie / et in probatio*n*em allegacio*n*is p*ro*ducit que*n*dam sam*uel* beale in artib*u*s bacch*a*laureum qui asseruit q*uo*d m*a*giste*r* Taxton nu*n*c *a*egrotus voluit eundem beale testificari cora*m* d*o*m*i*no p*ro*cancellar*i*o q*uo*d fuit tutor d*i*cti Austen quu*m* d*i*ct*u*s Austen vendidit cu*m* co*n*sensu amicor*um* suoru*m* et d*i*cti Taxton d*i*cto marley / in *pre*sentia d*i*cti hayes confitent*i*s d*i*ctu*m* Austen obligasse d*i*ctam togam sibi et vxori su*a*e pro su*m*ma xiijs iiijd in numerat*is* pecunijs illi mutuo dat*is* / et *p*ro su*m*ma xiijs iiijd in cibarijs illi deliberat*is* vnde d*o*min*u*s decrevit d*i*ctam togam restituenda*m* eidem marley et co*n*de*m*navit eunde*m* haies ad restitutio*n*em eiusdem / et expens*i*s cur*i*ae. Et statim co*m*paruit m*a*giste*r* Nevell / et testificavit q*uo*d cognoscit d*i*ctu*m* Marley esse viru*m* probu*m*, bene fidei / et honeste co*n*versacio*n*is apud vicinos suos /

Translation

5 March, before the lord Doctor [Andrew] Perne, the deputy of the lord vice-chancellor

John Marley of Cambridge, gentleman, against Nevell Hayes, cook

On which etc., Marley alleges that he lent to a certain [William] Austen, Bachelor of Arts of Corpus Christi College and pupil of Master [Robert] Taxton, a cloak bought from Austen's father in the city of Canterbury. For proof of his allegation, Marley produces a certain Samuel Beale, Bachelor of Arts, who asserted that Master Taxton, now being sick, wanted the same Beale to give evidence before the lord vice-chancellor that Taxton had been the tutor of the said Austen when the said Austen sold the cloak with the consent of his friends and the said Taxton to the said Marley's disadvantage. In the presence of the said Hayes, acknowledging that the said Austen had pledged the said cloak to Hayes and his wife for the sum of 13s. 4d. in cash lent to Austen, and for the sum of 13s. 4d. worth of food which was delivered to him. Whereupon the lord deputy decreed the said cloak to be restored to the same Marley and condemned the same Hayes to the restoration of the same and to the costs of the court. And immediately Master [Thomas] Nevell appeared and testified that he recognized the said Marley to be an excellent person of good faith and of decent behavior among his neighbours.

APPENDIX 4: LIST OF FOUNDATION SCHOLARS OF CORPUS CHRISTI COLLEGE, 1573-87

FOUNDATION SCHOLARS OF CORPUS CHRISTI COLLEGE, 1573–1587

The asterisk * indicates scholars taking holy orders and/or entering teaching professions. Academic years in bracket show the period of time when a scholar held his scholarship. No term divisions (1a Michaelmas, 2a Lent, 3a Easter, 4a Trinity) were made in the Audit Book from 1573 to 1575. The Audit records for 1586 and 1588 are missing.

BIBLE CLERKS (FOUR CLERKSHIPS)

Bible Clerk 1

James Hawkesworthe*, of Otley, Yorkshire. Matric. Easter 1571. BA 1573–74; MA 1577. Ord. deacon (London) 21 July 1585, age 34. [? to 1575]

John Tilney* of Norfolk. Adm. 1571. BA 1576–77; MA (Magdalene) 1580. Ord. priest (Norwich) 1581. [1575 to Lent 1579–80]

Robert Pearne*. Matric. (Peterhouse) Easter 1577. BA 1580–81; MA 1584. Ord. deacon and priest (Lincoln) 10 Oct. 1582. [Lent 1579–80 to Trinity 1583]

John Gedney. Matric. Mich. 1583. Left without taking a degree. [Trinity 1583 to Trinity 1584]

Thomas Sayer*, of Norfolk. Matric. 1583. BA 1586–87; MA 1590. Ord. deacon (Worcester) 14 Feb. 1593. [Trinity 1584 to Mich. 1588]

Bible Clerk 2

Daniel Godfrey, of Norwich. Matric. Mich. 1571. BA 1575–76; MA 1579. [12 July 1571 to Lent 1577–78]

Robert Smyth, of Saltfleetby, Lincolnshire. Matric. Lent 1577–78. BA 1581–82; MA 1586. [Lent 1577–78 to Lent 1585]

Appendix 4

Edward Ballard*. Matric. sizar, Mich. 1582. BA 1585–86; MA 1589. Ord. deacon and priest (Peterborough) 23 Oct. 1589. Rector of Badingham, Suffolk 1595. [Easter 1585 to Easter 1587]

Bible Clerk 3 (called 'the senior bible-clerk')

William Matchet*. Matric, sizar. Mich. 1570. BA 1573–74; MA 1579. Ord. deacon and priest (Peterborough) 2 July 1574. [? to 1575]

Thomas Corbet, of Essex. Matric. 1573. BA 1575–76. [15 Nov 1573 to Lent 1578–79]

John Woulsey. Matric. Easter 1577. BA 1580–81. [Easter 1579 to Easter 1582]

Andrew Style. Matric. pens. 1582. Perhaps MA 1584. [Trinity 1582 to Trinity 1584]

Robert Rant. Adm. pens. Lent 1584–85. [Lent 1584–85 to Mich. 1586]

[Vacant Lent 1586–87 to Trinity 1587]

Bible Clerk 4

John Rucke, of Kent. Adm. 1568. BA 1573–74; MA 1577. Transferred from the College Foundation Scholarship 6. [1575 to Mich. 1576]

Stephen Snat*. Matric. Easter 1573. BA 1576–77; MA (Magdalene) 1580. Schoolmaster of Biddenden Free School, 10 Oct. 1584. [Lent 1576–77 to Lent 1578–79]

Richard Jackson. Adm. Easter 1571. Matric. 1575. BA 1578–79. [Lent 1578–79 to Lent 1579–80]

Thomas Tatnall*. Matric. Easter 1579. BA 1582–83; MA 1586. Rector of St Mary Northgate, Canterbury, 1612. [Easter 1580 to Trinity 1583]

William Payne*, of Wye, Kent. Matric. Mich. 1582. BA 1585–86; MA 1589. Ord. priest (Winchester) 1591. [Trinity 1583 to 1588?]

SCHOLARS OF THE COLLEGE FOUNDATION
(SIX SCHOLARSHIPS FOUNDED IN 1548)

College Foundation Scholar 1

Edward Wood*, of Cambridgeshire. Matric. Mich. 1570. BA 1573–74; MA 1577. Ord. deacon and priest (Lincoln) 9 July 1582. [? to Lent 1576–77]

Appendix 4

Robert Yemes. Matric. Mich. 1575. BA 1578–79. [Lent 1576–77 to Lent 1579–80]

Richard Gryme. Matric. Mich. 1580. Left without taking a degree. [Easter 1580 to Mich. 1583]

Thomas Greenwood*. Matric. Mich. 1581. BA 1584–85; MA 1588. Rector of Castor, Norfolk, 1592–1600. [Lent 1583–84 to Easter 1587]

Richard Greenwood, of Norfolk. Matric sizar Mich. 1586. BA 1590–91; MA 1594. Clerk of Playden, Sussex. [Trinity 1587 to 1588?]

College Foundation Scholar 2

William Norgate*, of Norfolk. Adm. 1570; matric. Easter 1572. BA 1575–76; MA 1579. Fellow 1577–83. Ord. deacon and priest (Peterborough) 25 Mar. 1586. [? to Lent 1577–78]

Henry Allen. Matric. Mich. 1575. BA 1578–79. [Lent 1577–78 to Mich. 1579]

Ralph Same*. Matric. Easter 1579. BA 1582–83; MA 1586. Ord. priest (Norwich) 22 Dec. 1587. [Mich. 1579 to Mich. 1583]

Henry Smyth. Matric. Mich. 1582. Left without taking a degree. [Lent 1583–84 to Easter 1587]

College Foundation Scholar 3

Humphrey Travers*, of Nottingham. Matric. sizar from Trinity, Easter 1567. BA (Corpus) 1570–71; MA 1574. Ord. priest (Lincoln) 23 Sept. 1579. [? to 1573]

Thomas Harris, of Norfolk. Matric. Mich. 1573. BA 1576–77; MA 1580. Fellow 1579–86. [1574 to Easter 1579]

Christopher Tucke. Matric. Easter 1579. BA 1582–83; MA 1585. Fellow 1586–88. Possibly succeeded by Nun. [Easter 1579 to Mich. 1586]

Robert Nun*, born Whepstead, Suffolk; school, Bury. Adm. pens. at Caius, 5 June 1584. Migrated to Corpus Christi 1585. BA 1587–88; MA 1591. Ord. priest (Norwich) 28 Oct. 1591. Rector of Ampton, Suffolk, 1591–97. [Mich. 1586 to Trinity 1591]

College Foundation Scholar 4

Henry Sutterton*. Matric. pens. Easter 1571. BA 1573–74; MA 1577. Vicar of West Harptree, Somerset, 1580–1620. [? to Easter 1576]

Richard Braborne*, of Suffolk. Matric. Easter 1573. BA 1576–77; MA 1580; BD 1586–87. Ord. priest (Norwich) 21 Sept. 1586. [Easter 1576 to Lent 1579–80]

Appendix 4

Peter Ritche*, of Calne, Wilts. Matric. Lent 1577–78. BA 1580–81; MA 1584. Ord. deacon (London) 24 Feb. 1586. [Lent 1579–80 to Easter 1584]

Adam Parker. Matric. Easter 1583. Left without taking a degree. Possibly succeeded by Thomas Aldham. [Easter 1584 to 1586?]

Thomas Aldham*, of Norfolk. Matric. pens. Easter 1585. BA 1588–89; MA 1592. Rector of Alphington, Devon, 1638. [Mich. 1586 to Easter 1592]

College Foundation Scholar 5

Henry Yemes, of Norfolk. Matric. sizar. Mich. 1566. BA 1571–72; MA 1575. Fellow 1573–81. [? to 1573]

John Temple*, of Norfolk. Matric. Mich. 1573. BA 1576–77; MA 1580. Schoolmaster of Linton Parish School, 10 Dec. 1582. [3 Dec. 1573 to Lent 1581–82]

Edward Elwin, of Norfolk. Matric. Lent 1579–80. BA 1583–84; MA 1587; MD 1595. Fellow 1586–98. Physician to the royal household. Possibly succeeded by Richard Punder. [Lent 1581–82 to Mich. 1586]

Richard Punder*. Adm. 1583. BA 1587–88. Ord. deacon (Norwich), 24 June 1597. [Mich. 1586 to Trinity 1589]

College Foundation Scholar 6

John Rucke, of Kent. Adm. 1568. BA 1573–74; MA 1577. Transferred to the Bible Clerkship. [? to 1574]

John Knat. Matric. Easter 1575. BA 1578–79. [1575 to Lent 1579–80]

Paul Chapman*. Matric. Easter 1578. BA 1581–82; MA 1585; BD 1600; DD 1613. Ord. deacon and priest (Peterborough) 30 Nov. 1585. [Easter 1580 to Mich. 1584]

Thomas Consant*. Matric pens. Easter 1583. BA 1586–87; MA 1590. Usher at King's School, Canterbury, 1590. [Mich. 1584 to 1587?]

JOHN MERE'S SCHOLARS
(ONE SCHOLARSHIP FOUNDED IN 1569)

John Mere Scholar 1

Robert Jenkinson*, of Cambridgeshire. Matric. pens. Easter 1570. BA 1572–73; MA 1576. Ord. deacon (Peterborough) 10 Apr. 1575. [30 March 1574 to Lent 1575–76]

Appendix 4

William Nase, of Cambridge. Matric. Easter 1576. BA 1578–79; MA 1582. [Easter 1576 to Lent 1581–82]

Robert Jenninges*. Matric. Easter 1578. BA 1582–83; MA 1586. Ord. deacon and priest (Peterborough) 5 Mar. 1586–87. Possibly succeeded by John Crowfoot. [15 August 1582 to 1586]

John Crowfoot, of Cambridgeshire. Matric. pens. Mich. 1586. BA 1590–91; MA 1594. [Mich. 1587 to Lent 1593–94]

NORWICH SCHOLARS (THREE SCHOLARSHIPS FOUNDED IN 1567 AND TWO IN 1569)

Norwich Scholar 1

Paul Goolde*, of Norwich. Matric. pens. Mich. 1569. BA 1572–73; MA (Caius) 1576. Fellow of Caius, 1574–82. Master of Norwich School. [? to 1573]

Christopher Abbys*, of Norwich. Matric. Mich. 1573. BA 1576–77; MA 1580; BD 1588. Fellow 1579–89. Ord. deacon (Lincoln) 30 July 1580. [1574 to Easter 1579]

Ralph Joyner, of Norwich. Matric. Mich. 1579. BA 1582–83. Died August 1585. [Trinity 1579 to Trinity 1585?]

Robert Kent*. Matric. sizar Easter 1586. BA 1589–90; MA 1593; BD 1609. Ord. priest (Norwich) 29 Sept. 1595. [Mich. 1585? to Easter 1593]

Norwich Scholar 2

John Thaxter*, of Norwich. Matric. pens. Mich. 1569. BA 1572–73; MA 1576; BD 1583. Fellow 1576–80. Rector of Bridgham St Mary, Norfolk, 1584–1601. Possibly succeeded by John Dix. [? to 1573]

John Dix*, of Norwich. Adm. 1570. Matric. Easter 1575. BA 1577–78; MA 1581; BD 1588; DD 1598. Ord. deacon (Peterborough) 22 Sept. 1580 and priest 24 Sept. 1580. Fellow 1580–91. [1574 to Mich. 1580]

Thomas Daynes*, nominated by Mayor and Corporation of Norwich. Matric. 1580. BA 1584–85. Ord. priest (Norwich) 7 July 1588. [Mich. 1580 to Easter 1587]

Norwich Scholar 3

Henry Gold*, of Norwich. Adm. 1569; matric. Mich. 1571. BA 1575–76; MA 1579 (Pembroke); BD 1586. Fellow of Pembroke 1578–81. Ord. deacon (Lincoln) 1 Dec. 1582. [1 August 1571 to Mich. 1578]

Appendix 4

Henry Bird*, nominated by Mayor and Corporation of Norwich. Matric. Easter 1578. BA 1581–82; MA 1585. Ord. deacon (Norwich) 4 Apr. 1587. [Mich. 1578 to Lent 1584–85]

Francis Sadler. Matric. pens. 1585. BA 1588–89. [Trinity 1585 to Lent 1591–92]

Norwich Scholar 4

Henry Golding*, nominated by Mayor and Corporation of Norwich. Adm. 1571; matric. Mich. 1572. BA 1575–76; MA 1579. Ord. priest (Norwich) 25 Jan. 1579–80. [? to Lent 1577–78]

William Becket*. Matric. Easter 1577. BA 1580–81. Vicar of Kingston, Surrey, 1613–26. [Easter 1578 to Easter 1582]

Henry Mihil*, of Norwich. Matric. Mich. 1582. BA 1585–86; MA 1589; BD 1596. Fellow 1588–1601. Ord. deacon (Norwich) 23 Sept. 1590 and priest 25 Sept. 1590. [Trinity 1582 to 1588?]

Norwich Scholar 5

Thomas Plombe*, of Norwich. Adm. 1571; matric. Mich. 1572. BA 1575–76; MA 1579. Vicar of St Michael Coslany, Norwich, 1580. [? to Easter 1579]

John Weld*. Matric. Easter 1579. BA 1582–83; MA 1586. Ord. priest (Norwich) 26 Sept. 1588. Possibly succeeded by Edmund Caston. [Trinity 1579 to 1586?]

Edmund Caston*, of Norfolk. Matric pens. Easter 1586. BA 1589–90; MA 1593. Rector of Harrington, Northants, 1606, and vicar of Cold Ashby. [1586? to Easter 1592]

CANTERBURY SCHOLARS OF WESTMINSTER FOUNDATION (THREE SCHOLARSHIPS FOUNDED IN 1569)

Canterbury Scholar 1

Moses Fowler*, of Kent. Matric. pens. Mich. 1569. BA 1572–73; MA 1576; BD 1583. Fellow 1576–86. Vicar of Aylsham, Norfolk, 1584. University preacher, 1585. [? to 1575]

Robert Stone*, of King's School, Canterbury. Matric. Easter 1575. BA 1578–79; MA 1582. Master of Faversham School, Kent. [Mich. 1575 to Trinity 1581]

Abraham Tilman, of King's School, Canterbury. Matric. Mich. 1581. BA 1583–84; MA 1587. Fellow 1586–89. Died 1589. [Mich. 1581 to Lent 1586–87]

Appendix 4

[Vacant Easter and Trinity 1587]

Canterbury Scholar 2

Nicholas Faunt, of King's School, Canterbury. Adm. 29 Jan. 1571–72 (Caius); matric. 1572. BA 1575–76. Secretary to Sir Francis Walsingham, *c.*1578. [? to Lent 1576–77]

Samuel Beadle*, of King's School, Canterbury. Matric. Easter 1577. BA 1580–81; MA 1584. Ord. deacon and priest (Peterborough) 30 Mar. 1594. Master of Boston School, Lincs, 1589–97. [Lent 1576–77 to Easter 1583]

John Boyle*, of King's School, Canterbury. Adm. 9 June 1583. BA 1586–87; MA 1590–91; BD 1598; DD 1614. Rector of Elstree, Herts, *c.*1596–1618. [Easter 1583 to Lent 1589–90]

Canterbury Scholar 3

Philip Nichols*, of Lincolnshire. Matric. pens. Mich. 1569. BA 1573–74; MA 1577. Fellow 1576–83. Ord. deacon and priest (Lincoln), 31 May 1576. [? to Easter 1576]

Richard Manwaring*, of King's School, Canterbury. Matric. Easter 1577. BA 1579–80; MA 1583. Vicar of Petham, Kent, 1585–95. [Trinity 1576 to Mich. 1582]

Henry Brownrigg, of King's School, Canterbury. Matric. Mich. 1582. BA 1585–86. [20 October 1582 to Trinity 1587]

SCHOLARS OF EASTBRIDGE FOUNDATION
(TWO SCHOLARSHIPS FOUNDED IN 1569)

Eastbridge Foundation Scholar 1

Timothy Cotton*, of Canterbury. Matric. pens. Mich. 1568. BA 1571–72; MA 1576. Ord. priest (London) 16 Apr. 1579; 'Age 30; of the Savoy, London.' [? to 1574]

Brian Exton*, possibly of King's School, Canterbury. Adm. 1571; matric. 1572. BA 1575–76; MA 1579. Prebend of Lichfield 1585. Ord. priest (Lincoln) 22 Oct. 1591. [1575 to Easter 1579]

Mark Graceborough*, of King's School, Canterbury. Matric. Easter 1579. BA 1582–83; MA 1586. Vicar of Sibertswold, Kent, 1601–37. [Trinity 1579 to 1586?]

John Boyse*, Born Elmton, in Eythorne, Kent, and of King's School, Canterbury. Adm. pens. Apr. 1586. BA 1589–90; MA 1593; BD (Clare) 1600; DD 1605. Rector of Betshanger, Kent, and Master

Appendix 4

of Eastbridge Hospital, 1597. Fellow of Corpus Christi College 1610. Dean of Canterbury. [1586? to Easter 1593]

Eastbridge Foundation Scholar 2

Thomas Bradley*. Matric. pens. Mich. 1569. BA 1573–74; MA (Caius), 1578. Ord. priest (Norwich) 9 August 1579. [? to 1573]

William Lawse*, of King's School, Canterbury. Adm. 1574. Matric. Easter 1575. BA 1577–78; MA 1581. Ord. deacon and priest (Lincoln) 12 Feb. 1579–80. [1574 to Lent 1579–80]

William Austen, of Canterbury. Matric. Easter 1578. BA 1582–83; MA 1586. [Easter 1580 to Easter 1584]

Benjamin Charier*, of King's School, Canterbury. Adm. 1582; matric. Easter 1583. BA 1586–87; MA 1590; BD 1597; DD 1602. Fellow 1589–1602. Rector of Paddesworth, Kent, 1598–99. Chaplain to Archbishop Whitgift and to James I. [Trinity 1584 to Lent 1589–90]

JOHN PARKER'S SCHOLARS (THREE SCHOLARSHIPS FOUNDED BY MATTHEW PARKER'S WILL IN 1575)

John Parker Scholar 1

Robert Thexton*, of Aylesham, Norfolk. Matric. Easter 1575. BA 1578–79; MA 1582. Fellow 1581–84. Rector of Trunch, Norfolk, 1589–1619. [1575 to Lent 1581–82]

Thomas Monday*. Matric. Lent 1579–80. BA 1583–84. Licensed to teach grammar at Aylsham, Norfolk, 1584. Vicar of Cromer, Norfolk, 1591–1601. [Lent 1581–82 to Easter 1584]

William Cockman*. Matric. Mich. 1582. BA 1585–86; MA 1589. Ord. deacon and priest (Peterborough) 30 Sept. 1589. [Trinity 1584 to Mich. 1588]

John Parker Scholar 2

James Poynter*, of Wymondam School, Norfolk. Matric. Easter 1575. BA 1578–79; MA 1583; BD 1590. Vicar of Blakeney and Glamford, Norfolk, 1584. Ord. priest (Norwich) 13 Jan. 1585–86. [1575 to Lent 1579–80]

Thomas Lewgar*. Matric. Easter 1580. BA 1583–84; MA 1587. Ord. priest (Norwich) 15 Apr. 1590. [Easter 1580 to Lent 1586–87]

[Vacant Easter and Trinity 1587]

Appendix 4

John Parker Scholar 3

Christopher Pashley*, of King's School, Canterbury. Matric. Easter 1575. BA 1578–79; MA 1582. Ord. priest (Ely) 21 Dec. 1580. [1575 to Mich. 1580]

Christopher Marlowe, of King's School, Canterbury. Matric. Lent 1580–81. BA 1583–84; MA 1587. [Mich. 1580 to Lent 1586–87]

[Vacant Easter and Trinity 1587]

NICHOLAS BACON'S SCHOLARS
(SIX SCHOLARSHIPS FOUNDED IN 1577)

Nicholas Bacon Scholar 1

Hamlet Cartwright*. Matric. Mich. 1573. BA 1576–77. Ord. deacon (Ely) 21 Dec. 1578 and priest 21 Dec. 1580. [Mich. 1577 to Lent 1579–80]

John Burman. Matric. Easter 1580. BA 1583–84; MA 1587; LLD (Trinity Hall) 1596. Commissary and official to the Bishop of Norwich. [Easter 1580 to Lent 1586–87]

William Withers*, of Suffolk. Matric. pens. Easter 1587. BA 1590–91; MA 1594. Ord. deacon and priest (Rochester) 21 Sept. 1594. [Easter 1587 to Trinity 1592]

Nicholas Bacon Scholar 2

Thomas Corbold*, of Wortham, Suffolk. Matric. Easter 1573. BA 1577–78; MA 1584. Ord. priest (Peterborough) 13 Aug. 1598. [Mich. 1577 to Trinity 1580]

Thomas Keene. Matric. Mich. 1580. Left without taking a degree. [Mich. 1580 to Easter 1582]

Peter Amies*, of Manningtree, Essex. Matric. Mich. 1582. BA 1585–86; MA 1589. Ord. deacon (London) 6 Apr. 1600. [Trinity 1582 to Lent 1588–89]

Nicholas Bacon Scholar 3

William Lightfoote*, of St Albans, Herts. Matric. Lent 1577–78. BA 1579–80. Ord. deacon (London) 21 Dec. 1583. [Mich. 1577 to Easter 1582]

W. Burre. Matric. Mich. 1582. Left without taking a degree. [Trinity 1582 to 1586?]

Appendix 4

Thomas Wright, son and heir of Thomas of Weeting, Norfolk. Matric. pens. Mich. 1585. Adm. Lincoln's Inn, 7 July 1590; of Norfolk and of Furnival's Inn. Left without taking a degree. [1586? to Easter 1589]

Nicholas Bacon Scholar 4

Thomas Darley*. Matric. 1577. BA 1580–81; MA 1584. Rector of Benacre, Suffolk, 1595–1613. [Mich. 1577 to Easter 1584]

John Fale*. Matric. Easter 1584. BA 1587–88; MA 1591. Rector of Roydon, Essex, 1585–1615. [Easter 1584 to Trinity 1591]

Nicholas Bacon Scholar 5

Robert Gould*. Adm. 1571. Matric. Easter 1577. BA 1579–80; MA 1583. Ord. deacon (Norwich) 26 Sept. 1588 and priest 8 Oct. 1588. [Mich. 1577 to Lent 1582–83]

John Clarke. Matric. Easter 1583. BA 1586–87. [Easter 1583 to Lent 1589–90]

Nicholas Bacon Scholar 6

Henry Rewse*. Matric. Easter 1577. BA 1579–80; MA 1583; BD 1590. Fellow 1583–89. Rector of East Harling, Norfolk, 1595–1631. [Mich. 1577 to Lent 1582–83]

Robert Corbold. Matric. Easter 1583. Left without taking a degree. [Easter 1583 to 1586?]

Robert Seaman*, of Suffolk. Matric. pens. 1586. BA 1589–90; MA 1593. 'Seman Ju[nio]r' appears in Easter 1589 in the Audit Book. This seems to have been William Seaman 'of Norfolk'. Probably Vicar of Carlton Colville, Suffolk, 1596, or Rector of Rame, Cornwall. [1586? to Trinity 1591]

BIBLIOGRAPHY

PRIMARY SOURCES

Manuscript Sources

Bodleian Library
Ashmole MS 208, Simon Forman Manuscript
Tanner MS 309, Stephen Powle's Letters

British Library
Add. MS 28012, Henry Oxinden's Notebook
Add. MS 32092, Raleigh's 'hellish verses' (fol. 201r–v)
Cotton MS Augustus I i 46, Plan of Dover Harbour, perhaps drawn by John Hill
Harley MS 288, Richard Willoughbye's Letter (fol. 242r–v)
Harley MS 296, Richard Willoughbye's Letter (fol. 54r–v)
Harley MS 6848, Baines's Note (fols 185v–186r); 'Remembraunces of wordes and matter againste Richard Cholmeley' (fols 190r–191r)
Harley MS 6853, scribal copy of Baines's Note (fols 307r–308v)
Lansdowne MS 17, Burghley Papers (1573–75)
Lansdowne MS 33, Burghley Papers (1579–81)
Lansdowne MS 36, Burghley Papers (1542–82)
Lansdowne MS 45, Burghley Papers (1563–92)
Lansdowne MS 54, Burghley Papers (1581–87)
Lansdowne MS 57, Burghley Papers (1586–98)
Lansdowne MS 68, Burghley Papers (1590–91)
Lansdowne MS 85, Burghley Papers (1504–97)
Lansdowne MS 104, Burghley Papers (1553–93)
Lansdowne MS 679, Commonplace or Note-book of Samuel Foxe
Royal MS 18 A. LXVI, Richard Robinson's Manuscript
Sloane MS 93, Gabriel Harvey's Letter-Book

Cambridge University Archives
Collect. Admin. 6a, Buckle Book, The Vice-Chancellor's Book (1577–89)
Collect. Admin. 13, *Utinam*, The Vice-Chancellor's Book (1549–78)
Comm. Ct. I. 1, Act Book of Commissary Court (1579–85)
Comm. Ct. II. 1, Depositions (1580–82)
Mm. I. 41 (Baker MS, vol. 30), 'Memoranda collegii Corp. Chri. et B. Marie Cant.'
Supplicats
V. C. Ct. II. 1, Depositions (1593–97)

Bibliography

Canterbury Cathedral Archives and Library
DCc MA 40, Miscellaneous Accounts (1541–76)
DCc MA 41, Miscellaneous Accounts (1576–1643)
DCc TA 5, Treasurers' Accounts (1566–67)
DCc TA 7, Treasurers' Accounts (1572–73)
DCc TA 8, Treasurers' Accounts (1576–77)

Corpus Christi College Archives
CCCC01/C/1, Chapter Book 1 (Liber Actorum in Collegio Corporis Christi)
CCCC02/B/4, Audit Book (1550–80)
CCCC02/B/5, Audit Book (1578–90)
CCCC02/B/44/29, List of Payments to Fellows for Teaching Named Scholars (1576–77)
CCCC02/B/44/42, 'Reckoned with Mr Chever 22 February 1582 [1583]'
CCCC02/M/14/57, Quadripartite indenture concerning nomination of the three Canterbury scholars
CCCC02/M/18/38, Draft of Robert Norgate's protestation (1580)
CCCC02/M/19/2, Records of Proceedings against Hugh Gray
CCCC02/S/29, Buttery Book 1579–82
CCCC02/S/33, Buttery Book 1582–86
CCCC04/S/3/3, Letter to the College Nominating a Scholar (1574)
CCCC06/O/2, 'The Receytes & expenses which I William Norgate ame to account for about the chapel or otherwise howsoever'
CCCC06/O/22, List of Donations to the Funding of the Chapel by the Bachelors Commoners, 1584
CCCC07/18, Parker Register (formerly Small Parker Book 13), 1575–1600
CCCC08/28, Parker's Chamber Plans of Corpus Christi College

Guildhall Library
MS 9171/18, Anthony Hickman's Will (fol. 452v)

Lambeth Palace Library
MS 647–8, Papers of Anthony Bacon

The National Archives of the UK
PC 2/14, Privy Council: Registers, Elizabeth I (19 Feb. 1586–1 Nov. 1587)
PROB 11, Prerogative Court of Canterbury and related Probate Jurisdictions: Will Registers
State Papers
STAC 5/A2/37, Records of the Court of Star Chamber

Norfolk Record Office
DN REG/13/19, Institution Register: Parkhurst (1559–76)
NCC 371 Andrewes, John More's Will, 1591
NCR 16a/9, Mayor's Court Book (13 June 1569–16 June 1576)
NCR 20c/2, 'The Mayor's Booke of the Poore'
NCR 24a/48, God's House Collector and Receiver's Annual Accounts (June 1575–June 1576)
NCR 24a/55, God's House Collector and Receiver's Annual Accounts (June 1582–June 1583)

Bibliography

NRS 23372, Z99, Documents relating to Nicholas Bacon's Foundation for Corpus Christi

RO 44/1, St George Colegate, Baptisms and Marriages, 1538–1653 (microfilm)

Parker Library

Cooper, Thomas, *Thesaurus Linguae Romanae & Britannicae* (London, 1573), shelf-mark L.5.14 (previous shelf-mark N.5.1 / L.3.6), Benjamin Charier's memorial note (sig. Vvvvvv 6v)

Printed Sources

An Aduertisement and Defence for Trueth against Her Backbiters (London, 1581).

Alfield, Thomas, *A True Reporte of the Death & Martyrdome of M. Campion Iesuite and Preiste, & M. Sherwin, & M. Bryan Preistes, at Tiborne the First of December 1581* ([London], [1582]).

Allen, William, *An Apologie and True Declaration of the Institution and Endeuours of the Two English Colleges.* ([Rheims?], 1581).

—— *A Trve Report of the Late Apprehension and Imprisonnement of Iohn Nichols* (Rheims, 1583).

Anderson, Anthony, *An Approved Medicine against the Deserued Plague* (London, 1593).

Arber, Edward, *A Transcript of the Registers of the Company of Stationers of London 1554–1640* (5 vols, London, 1875).

Ascham, Roger, *The Scholemaster* (London, 1571).

Aske, James, *Elizabetha Triumphans* (London, 1588).

Averell, William, *A Meruailous Combat of Contrarieties* (London, 1588).

B., I., *The Copy of a Letter, Lately Written by a Spanishe Gentleman, to His Freind in England* (Antwerp, 1589).

Bacon, Francis, *An Advertisement Touching the Controversies of the Church of England*, in Brian Vickers (ed.), *Francis Bacon* (Oxford, 1996), pp. 1–19.

Bailey, John F., *Transcription of Minutes of the Corporation of Boston, Vol. 1 1545–1607* (Boston, Lincs, 1980).

Baker, John, *Lectures of I. B. vpon the xii. Articles of Our Christian Faith* (London, 1581).

Baldwin, Elizabeth, Lawrence M. Clopper, and David Mills (eds), *Cheshire Including Chester*, REED (2 vols, Toronto, 2007).

Bamford, James, *A Short Dialogve concerning the Plagves Infection* (London, 1603).

Bancroft, Richard, *Dangerous Positions and Proceedings* (London, 1593).

—— *A Sermon Preached at Paules Crosse the 9. of Februarie* (London, 1588).

—— *A Suruay of the Pretended Holy Discipline* (London, 1593).

Barrow, Henry, *The Examinations of Henry Barrowe Iohn Grenewood and Iohn Penrie, before the High Commissioners, and Lordes of the Counsel* (n.p., 1596).

Bate, John, *The Portraiture of Hypocrisie* (London, 1589).

Beard, Thomas, *The Theatre of Gods Iudgements* (London, 1597).

Berry, Lloyd E. (intro.), *The Geneva Bible: A Facsimile of the 1560 Edition* (Madison, 1969).

Bibliotheca Heberiana: Catalogue of the Library of the Late Richard Heber (13 vols, London, 1834–37).

Bicknoll, Edmond, *A Swoord agaynst Swearyng* (London, 1579).

Bibliography

Black, Joseph L. (ed.), *The Martin Marprelate Tracts: A Modernized and Annotated Edition* (Cambridge, 2008).

Bolton, Robert, *A Discourse about the State of True Happinesse Deliuered in Certaine Sermons in Oxford, and at Pauls Crosse* (London, 1611).

—— *Some Generall Directions for a Comfortable Walking with God* (London, 1626).

Boyle, Robert, *The Works of the Honourable Robert Boyle*, ed. Thomas Birch (6 vols, London, 1772).

Boys, William, *Collections for a History of Sandwich* (Canterbury, 1792).

Bredwell, Stephen, *The Rasing of the Foundations of Brownisme* (London, 1588).

Bullinger, Heinrich, *Fiftie Godlie and Learned Sermons Diuided into Fiue Decades*, trans. H. I. (London, 1577).

Burton, Robert, *The Anatomy of Melancholy*, ed. Thomas C. Faulkner, Nicolas K. Kiessling, Rhonda L. Blair, J. B. Bamborough, and Martin Dodsworth (6 vols, Oxford, 1989–2000).

Burton, William, *A Sermon Preached in the Cathedrall Church in Norwich, the xxi. Day of December, 1589* (London, 1590).

—— *Ten Sermons vpon the First, Second, Third and Fourth Verses of the Sixt of Matthew* (London, 1602).

Calvin, John, *A Harmonie vpon the Three Euangelists* (London, 1584).

—— *Institution of Christian Religion*, trans. [Thomas Norton] (London, 1561).

—— *The Sermons of M. Iohn Caluin vpon the Fifth Booke of Moses* (London, 1583).

Camden, William, *The Historie of the Most Renowned and Victorious Princesse Elizabeth* (London, 1630).

Carlson, Leland H. (ed.), *The Writings of John Greenwood 1587–1590* (London, 1962).

Case, John, *Speculum Moralium Quaestionum* (Oxford, 1585).

Chapman, George, *The Plays of George Chapman: The Tragedies with Sir Gyles Goosecappe, A Critical Edition*, ed. Allan Holaday (Cambridge, 1987).

Chettle, Henry, *Kind-Harts Dreame*, in G. B. Harrison (ed.), *Elizabethan and Jacobean Quartos* (1923; repr. New York, 1966).

Churchyard, Thomas, *Churchyards Challenge* (London, 1593).

Clapham, Henoch, *Three Partes of Salomon His Song of Songs* (London, 1603).

Clugston, George Alan (ed.), *Thomas Lodge and Robert Greene, A Looking Glasse for London and England* (New York, 1980).

Coldewey, John C. (ed.), *Early English Drama: An Anthology* (New York and London, 1993).

Colfe, Isaac, *1588. A Sermon Preached on the Queenes Day* (London, 1588).

Conestaggio, Gerolamo Franchi di, *The Historie of the Vniting of the Kingdom of Portugall to the Crowne of Castill* (London, 1600).

Copland, Robert, *The Shepardes Kalender* (London, 1570).

Copley, Anthony, *Wits Fittes and Fancies* (London, 1595).

Cosin, Richard, *Conspiracy for Pretended Reformation: viz. Presbyterial Discipline* (London, 1592).

Cupper, William, *Certaine Sermons concerning Gods Late Visitation in the Citie of London* (London, 1592).

Dallington, Robert, *A Booke of Epitaphes Made vpon the Death of the Right Worshipfull Sir William Bvttes* (London, 1583).

Bibliography

Dasent, John Roche (ed.), *Acts of the Privy Council of England* (32 vols, London, 1890–1907).

Davidson, John, *D. Bancrofts Rashnes in Rayling against the Church of Scotland* (Edinburgh, 1590).

Davies, John, *Le Primer Report* (Dublin, 1615).

A Declaration of Great Troubles Pretended against the Realme by a Number of Seminarie Priests and Jesuists (London, 1591).

Dee, John, *To the Kings Most Excellent Maiestie* (London, 1604).

Dekker, Thomas, *The Double PP*, in Alexander B. Grosart (ed.), *The Non-Dramatic Works of Thomas Dekker* (5 vols, London and Aylesbury, 1885), vol. 2, pp. 155–91.

Dent, Arthur, *The Ruine of Rome: or An Exposition vpon the Whole Reuelation* (London, 1603).

Dering, Edward, *Two Godly Sermons the First Preached before the Queenes Maiestie, the 25. of Februarie, 1569* (Middelburg, 1590?).

Digges, Thomas, 'A Discourse of Sea-Ports: Principally of the Port and Haven of Dover', in William Oldys (ed.), *The Harleian Miscellany* (8 vols, London, 1744–46), vol. 4, pp. 292–6.

Elderton, William, *A Triumph for True Subiects*, in Hyder E. Rollins (ed.), *Old English Ballads 1553–1625: Chiefly from Manuscripts* (Cambridge, 1920), pp. 62–9.

Elliott, John R. Jr, Alan H. Nelson, Alexander F. Johnston, and Diana Wyatt (eds), *Oxford*, REED (2 vols, Toronto, 2004).

Fathers of the Congregation of the London Oratory (eds), *The First and Second Diaries of the English College, Douay*, with intro. by Thomas Francis Knox (London, 1878).

Fenne, Thomas, *Fenne's Fruits* (London, 1590).

Ferrarius, Johannes, *A Worke of Ioannes Ferrarius Montanus, touchynge the Good Orderynge of a Common Weale*, trans. William Bavand (London, 1559).

Field, John, *A Godly Exhortation, by Occasion of the Late Iudgement of God, Shewed at Parris-Garden* (London, 1583).

Foley, Henry (ed.), *Records of the English Province of the Society of Jesus* (7 vols in 12, London, 1877–83).

Fortescue, Thomas, *The Forest or Collection of Historyes* (London, 1571).

Foxe, John, *Actes and Monuments of These Latter and Perillous Dayes* (London, 1563).

Fulbecke, William, *A Booke of Christian Ethicks or Moral Philosophie* (London, 1587).

—— *The Pandectes of the Law of Nations* (London, 1602).

Fulke, William, *Praelections vpon the Sacred and Holy Reuelation of S. Iohn* (London, 1573).

Fuller, Thomas, *The Church History of Britain*, ed. John Sherren Brewer (6 vols, Oxford, 1845).

Furnivall, Frederick J. (ed.), *Harrison's Description of England in Shakspere's Youth*, part 1 (London, 1877).

Gager, William, *William Gager: The Complete Works*, ed. Dana F. Sutton (4 vols, New York, 1994).

Galloway, David (ed.), *Norwich 1540–1642*, REED (Toronto, 1984).

Bibliography

Gawdy, Philip, *Letters of Philip Gawdy of West Harling, Norfolk, and of London to Various Members of His Family 1579–1616*, ed. Isaac Herbert Jeayes (London, 1906).

Gee, Henry, and William John Hardy (eds), *Documents Illustrative of English Church History* (New York, 1896).

Gibson, Abraham, *Christiana-Polemica* (London, 1618).

Gifford, George, *A Briefe Discourse of Certaine Points of the Religion* (London, 1582).

—— *Discourse of the Subtill Practises of Devilles* (London, 1587).

—— *A Plaine Declaration that Our Brownists be full Donatists* (London, 1590).

—— *Sermons upon the Whole Booke of the Revelation* (London, 1596).

Goldring, Elizabeth, Faith Eales, Elizabeth Clarke, and Jayne Elisabeth Archer (eds), *John Nichols's The Progresses and Public Processions of Queen Elizabeth: A New Edition of the Early Modern Sources* (5 vols, Oxford, 2014).

Gosson, Stephen, *Playes Confuted in Five Actions* (London, [1582]).

—— *The Schoole of Abuse* (London, 1579).

—— *The Trumpet of Warre: A Sermon Preached at Paules Crosse the Seuenth of Maie 1598* (London, [1598]).

Gostwick, Roger, *The Anatomie of Ananias* (Cambridge, 1616).

Gouge, William, *The Whole-Armor of God* (London, 1619).

Gravet, William, *A Sermon Preached at Pavles Cross on the XXV Day of June Ann. Dom. 1587* (London, 1587).

Green, Mary Anne Everett (ed.), *Calendar of State Papers Domestic, Addenda 1566–1579* (1871; repr. Nendeln, 1967).

Greene, Robert, *Greene's Groatsworth of Wit Bought with a Million of Repentance* (1592), ed. D. Allen Carroll (New York, 1994).

—— *The Life and Complete Works in Prose and Verse of Robert Greene*, ed. Alexander B. Grosart (15 vols, 1881–86; repr. New York, 1964).

—— *The Plays and Poems of Robert Greene*, ed. John Churton Collins (2 vols, Oxford, 1905).

Hall, Joseph, *Virgidemiarum* (London, 1597).

Harris, Edward, *A Sermon Preached at Brocket Hall* (London, 1588).

Hartley, T. E. (ed.), *Proceedings in the Parliaments of Elizabeth I* (3 vols, London, 1995).

Hartwell, Abraham, *Regina Literata* (London, 1565).

Harvey, Gabriel, *Gabriel Harvey's* Ciceronianus, intro. Harold S. Wilson and trans. Clarence A. Forbes (Lincoln, NE, 1945).

—— 'Gabriel Harvey's *Rhetor*: A Translation and Critical Edition', trans. and ed. Robert M. Chandler (unpublished PhD dissertation, University of Missouri-Columbia, 1978).

—— *Gabrielis Harueij Rhetor* (London, 1577).

—— *The Works of Gabriel Harvey*, ed. Alexander B. Grosart (3 vols, 1884; repr. New York, 1966).

Harvey, Richard, *An Astrological Discourse* (London, 1583).

Harward, Simon, *The Solace for the Souldier and Saylour* (London, 1592).

Hastings, Francis, *A Watchword to All Religious, and True Hearted English-Men* (London, 1598).

Henderson, Robert, *The Arraignment of the Whole Creature* (London, 1631).

Henson, Edwin (ed.), *Registers of the English College at Valladolid 1589–1826* (London, 1930).

Heywood, James and Thomas Wrights (eds), *Cambridge University Transactions during the Puritan Controversies of the 16th and 17th Centuries* (2 vols, London, 1854).

Hicks, Leo (ed.), *Letters and Memorials of Father Robert Persons*, S.J., Vol. 1 (London, 1942).

Holinshed, Raphael, *Holinshed's Chronicles of England, Scotland, and Ireland*, with a new introduction by Vernon F. Snow (6 vols, 1807–08; repr. New York, 1976).

Holland, Henry, *Spirituall Preseruatiues against the Pestilence* (London, 1593).

—— *A Treatise against Witchcraft* (London, 1590).

Homer, *The Odyssey*, trans. A. T. Murray (2 vols, 1919; repr. Cambridge, MA, 1984).

Hughes, Paul L., and James F. Larkin (eds), *Tudor Royal Proclamations* (3 vols, New Haven, 1969).

Hull, John, *The Vnmasking of the Pollitique Atheist* (London, 1602).

Humpston, Robert, *A Sermon Preached at Reyfham in the Countie of Norff.* (London, 1589).

Jones, R. Tudur (ed.), with Arthur Long and Rosemary Moore, *Protestant Noncomformist Texts Volume 1: 1550–1700* (2007; repr. Eugene, OR, 2015).

Jonson, Ben, *The Alchemist*, ed. Peter Holland and William Sherman, in David Bevington, Martin Butler, and Ian Donaldson (gen. eds), *The Cambridge Edition of the Works of Ben Jonson* (7 vols, Cambridge, 2012), vol. 3, pp. 541–710.

—— *Bartholomew Fair*, ed. John Creaser, in David Bevington, Martin Butler, and Ian Donaldson (gen. eds), *The Cambridge Edition of the Works of Ben Jonson* (7 vols, Cambridge, 2012), vol. 4, pp. 253–428.

—— *Sejanus His Fall*, ed. Tom Cain, in David Bevington, Martin Butler, and Ian Donaldson (gen. eds), *The Cambridge Edition of the Works of Ben Jonson* (7 vols, Cambridge, 2012), vol. 2, pp. 195–391.

Josselin, John, *Historiola Collegii Corporis Christi*, ed. John Willis Clark (Cambridge, 1880).

Kenny, Anthony (ed.), *The Responsa Scholarum of the English College, Rome Part One: 1598–1621* (London, 1962).

Kett, Francis, *The Glorious and Beautiful Garland of Mans Glorification* (London, 1585).

King, John, *Lectures vpon Ionas Deliuered at Yorke in the Yeare of Our Lorde 1594* (London, 1597).

Kingdon, Robert M. (ed.), *The Execution of Justice in England by William Cecil and A True, Sincere, and Modest Defense of English Catholics by William Allen* (Ithaca, 1965).

Kirchmayer, Thomas, 'Pammachius (Wittenberg, 1538)', trans. C. C. Love (Toronto, 1992), <https://ccltlp.artsci.utoronto.ca/pammach.html> [accessed 22 November 2022].

La Primaudaye, Pierre de, *The Second Part of the French Academie*, trans. Thomas Bowes (London, 1593).

Lant, Thomas, *Sequitur Celebritas & Pompa Funeris* (London, 1588).

Lawson, Jane A. (ed.), *The Elizabethan New Year's Gift Exchanges 1559–1603* (Oxford, 2013).

Bibliography

Leclercq, Jean, Charles H. Talbot, and Henri M. Rochais (eds), *Sancti Bernardi Opera* (8 vols, Roma, 1957–77).

Legge, Thomas, *Thomas Legge: The Complete Plays*, ed. Dana F. Sutton (2 vols, New York, 1993).

Leigh, Richard, *The Copie of a Letter Sent ovt of England to Don Bernardin Mendoza Ambassadovr in France for the King of Spaine* [by William Cecil] (London, 1588).

Leishman, J. B. (ed.), *The Three Parnassus Plays (1598–1601)* (London, 1949).

Leland, John, *A Learned and True Assertion of the Original, Life, Actes, and Death of the Most Noble, Valiant, and Renoumed Prince Arthure, King of Great Brittaine*, trans. Richard Robinson, in William Edward Mead (ed.), *The Famous Historie of Chinon of England by Christopher Middleton to Which Is Added The Assertion of King Arthur*, Early English Text Society, OS, 165 (London, 1925).

Lemon, Robert (ed.), *Calendar of State Papers, Domestic, 1547–1580* (London, 1856).

The Life off the 70. Archbishopp off Canterbury Presently Sittinge Englished (Zurich, 1574).

Lightfoote, William, *The Complaint of England* (London, 1587).

Lloyd, Lodowick, *The Consent of Time Disciphering the Errors of the Grecians in Their Olympiads* (London, 1590).

—— *The First Part of the Diall of Daies* (London, 1590).

—— *The Pilgrimage of Princes* (London, 1586).

Lloyd, Richard, *A Briefe Discourse of the Most Renowned Actes and Right Valiant Conquests of Those Puisant Princes, Called the Nine Worthies* (London, 1584).

Lodge, Thomas, *The Complete Works of Thomas Lodge*, ed. Edmund W. Gosse (4 vols, 1883; repr. New York, 1963).

—— *Wounds of the Civil War*, ed. Joseph W. Houppert, *Regents Renaissance Drama* (Lincoln, NE, 1969).

Lupton, Thomas, *The Christian against the Iesuite* (London, 1582).

Marlowe, Christopher, *Christopher Marlowe: The Complete Plays*, ed. J. B. Steane (Aylesbury, 1969).

—— *Christopher Marlowe: The Complete Poems and Translations*, ed. Stephen Orgel (New York, 1971).

—— *Christopher Marlowe's Doctor Faustus: A 1604-Version Edition*, ed. Michael Keefer (Peterborough, 1991).

—— *The Complete Plays of Christopher Marlowe*, ed. Irving Ribner (New York, 1963).

—— *The Complete Works of Christopher Marlowe*, ed. Fredson Bowers, 2nd edn (2 vols, Cambridge, 1981).

—— *Dido Queen of Carthage and The Massacre at Paris*, ed. H. J. Oliver, *The Revels Plays* (London, 1968).

—— *Doctor Faustus*, ed. David Bevington and Eric Rasmussen, *The Revels Plays* (Manchester, 1992).

—— *Doctor Faustus Based on the A Text*, ed. Roma Gill and Ros King, rev. with a new intro., *The New Mermaids* (London, 1989).

—— *Edward the Second*, ed. Charles R. Forker, *The Revels Plays* (Manchester, 1994).

—— *Hero and Leander*, in Millar MacLure (ed.), *The Poems, The Revels Plays* (London, 1968).

—— *The Jew of Malta*, ed. N. W. Bawcutt, *The Revels Plays* (Manchester, 1978).

Bibliography

—— *The Jew of Malta*, ed. James R. Siemon, *The New Mermaids*, 2nd edn (London, 1994).

—— *Marlowe's Poems*, ed. L. C. Martin (1931; repr. New York, 1966).

—— *Tamburlaine the Great*, ed. J. S. Cunningham, *The Revels Plays* (Manchester, 1981).

—— *Tamburlaine the Great*, ed. David Fuller, in David Fuller and Edward J. Esche (eds), *The Complete Works of Christopher Marlowe Vol. 5* (Oxford, 1998).

Marten, Anthony, *An Exhortation, to Stirre vp the Mindes of All Her Maiesties Faithfull Subiects, to Defend Their Countrey in This Dangerous Time, from the Inuasion of Enemies* (London, 1588).

—— *The Second Sound, or Warning of the Trumpet vnto Judgement* (London, 1589).

Melton, John, *The Astrologaster, or, the Figure-caster* (London, 1620).

Meres, Francis, *Palladis Tamia, Wits Treasury* (London, 1598).

Middleton, Thomas, *Father Hubburd's Tales*, ed. Adrian Weiss, in Gary Taylor and John Lavagnino (eds), *Thomas Middleton: The Collected Works* (Oxford, 2007), pp. 149–82.

—— *The Black Book*, ed. G. B. Shand, in Gary Taylor and John Lavagnino (eds), *Thomas Middleton: The Collected Works* (Oxford, 2007), pp. 204–18.

Mornay, Philippe de, *A Woorke Concerning the Trewnesse of the Christian Religion*, trans. Philip Sidney and Arthur Golding, intro. F. J. Sypher (1587; repr. New York, 1976).

Mulcaster, Richard, *Positions Concerning the Training Up of Children*, ed. William Barker (Toronto, 1994).

Munday, Anthony, *Anthony Munday: The English Roman Life*, ed. Philip J. Ayres (Oxford, 1980).

—— *A Discouerie of Edmund Campion, and His Confederates* (London, 1582).

—— *A Second and Third Blast of Retrait from Plaies and Theaters* (London, 1580).

Nashe, Thomas, *The Works of Thomas Nashe*, ed. Ronald B. McKerrow, 2nd edn, rev. by F. P. Wilson (5 vols, Oxford, 1958).

Nelson, Alan (ed.), *Cambridge*, REED (2 vols, Toronto, 1989).

Nelson, Thomas, *A Memorable Epitaph [...] for the Death of the Right Honorable Sir Frauncis Walsingham Knight* (London, 1590).

Nichols, Josias, *The Plea of the Innocent Wherein Is Auerred* (London, 1602).

Nicholson, William (ed.), *The Remains of Edmund Grindal* (1843; repr. New York, 1968).

Norden, John, *A Mirror for the Multitude* (London, 1586).

Nowell, Alexander, *A Reproufe* (London, 1565).

Orwell, George, *Nineteen Eighty-Four* (London, 1949).

Owen, C. Dyfnallt (ed.), *Calendar of the Manuscripts of the Marquis of Bath Preserved at Longleat* (5 vols, London, 1904).

Parker, Matthew, *Correspondence of Matthew Parker*, ed. John Bruce and Thomas Thomason Perowne (Cambridge, 1853).

Parkhurst, John, *The Letter Book of John Parkhurst, Bishop of Norwich*, ed. R. A. Houlbrooke (Norwich, 1974).

Paston, Katherine, *The Correspondence of Lady Katherine Paston, 1603–1627*, ed. Ruth Hughey ([Norwich], 1941).

Paule, George, *The Life of the Most Reuerend and Religious Prelate Iohn Whitgift* (London, 1612).

Bibliography

Peck, Dwight C. (ed.), *Leicester's Commonwealth: The Copy of a Letter Written by a Master of Art of Cambridge (1584) and Related Documents* (Athens, OH, 1985).

Peel, Albert (ed.), *The Seconde Parte of a Register, Being a Calendar of Manuscripts under that Title Intended for Publication by the Puritans about 1593* (2 vols, 1915; repr. Cambridge, 2010).

—— (ed.), *Tracts Ascribed to Richard Bancroft* (Cambridge, 1953).

Peel, Albert, and Leland H. Carlson (eds), *The Writings of Robert Harrison and Robert Browne* (London, 1953).

Perkins, William, *Discovrse of the Damned Art of Witchcraft* (London, 1608).

Persons, Robert, *A Briefe Apologie, or Defence of the Catholike Ecclesiastical Hierarchie, & Subordination in England* (Antwerp, 1601).

—— *Elizabethae, Angliae Reginae Haeresim Calvinianam Propugnantis, Saevissimum in Catholicos sui Regni Edictum [...] cum responsione ad singula capita* ([Antwerp], 1592).

—— *A Relation of the King of Spaines Receiuing in Valliodolid [sic]* (Antwerp, 1592).

—— *A Relation of the Triall Made before the King of France* ([Saint-Omer], 1604).

—— *A Treatise of Three Conuersions of England from Paganisme to Christian Religion* (3 vols, [Saint-Omer], 1603).

Pettie, George, *A Petite Pallace of Pettie His Pleasure* (London, 1576).

Plutarch, *The Philosophie, Commonlie Called, the Morals*, trans. Philemon Holland (London, 1603).

Pollen, J. H., et al., *Miscellanea IV* (London, 1907).

A Poore Knight His Pallace of Priuate Pleasures Gallantly Garnished (London, 1579).

Prynne, William, *Histrio-Mastix: The Player's Scourge, or Actor's Tragedy*, with an introduction by Peter Davison (2 vols, New York, 1972).

R., J. G. [Minor Correspondence], *Gentleman's Magazine*, 2nd ser., 34 (1850), 234.

R., T., *A Confutation of the Tenne Great Plagues, Prognosticated by Iohn Doleta from the Country of Calabria* (London, [1587]).

Rankins, William, *A Mirrour of Monsters* (London, 1587).

Riche, Barnabe, *Farewell to Militarie Profession* (London, 1581).

—— *A Right Exelent and Pleasaunt Dialogue, betwene Mercvry and an English Souldier* (London, 1574).

Roberts, R. A., et al. (eds), *Calendar of the Manuscripts of the Most Hon. the Marquis of Salisbury* (24 vols, London, 1883–1976).

Robinson, Richard, *The Avncient Order, Societie, and Vnitie Laudable, of Prince Arthure* (London, 1583).

Rogers, John, *The Displaying of an Horrible Secte* (London, 1578).

Rogers, Thomas, *The Faith, Doctrine, and Religion* (London, 1607).

Rowlands, Samuel, *Hell's Broke Loose* (London, 1605).

Rudierde, Edmund, *The Thunderbolt of Gods Wrath against Hard-hearted and Stiffe-necked Sinnes* (London, 1618).

Rye, Walter (ed.), *Report on the Manuscripts of the Family of Gawdy* (London, 1885).

Sandys, Edwin, *Sermons* (London, 1585).

Scot, Reginald, *The Discouerie of Witchcraft* (London, 1584).

—— *A Perfite Platforme of a Hoppe Garden* (London, 1574).

The Second Report of Doctor Iohn Faustus: Containing His Apparances, and the Deeds of Wagner (London, 1594).

Bibliography

Shakespeare, William, *As You Like It*, ed. Alan Brissenden, The Oxford Shakespeare (Oxford, 1993).

—— *As You Like It*, ed. Richard Knowles, with a survey of criticism by Evelyn Joseph Mattern, A New Variorum Edition of Shakespeare (New York, 1977).

—— *Shakespeare's Sonnets*, ed. Katherine Duncan-Jones, The Arden Shakespeare, 3rd ser. (1997; repr. London, 2010).

—— *Twelfth Night*, ed. Roger Warren and Stanley Wells, The Oxford Shakespeare (Oxford, 1994).

Sidney, Philip, *The Correspondence of Sir Philip Sidney*, ed. Roger Kuin (2 vols, Oxford, 2012).

Smith, A. Hassell, Gillian M. Baker, and R. W. Kenny (eds), *The Papers of Nathaniel Bacon of Stiffkey, Volume 1: 1556–1577* (Norwich, 1979).

Smith, Henry, *Gods Arrowe against Atheists* (London, 1593).

—— *The Works of Henry Smith*, ed. Thomas Smith with intro. by Randall J. Pederson (2 vols, 1867; repr. Stoke-on-Trent, 2002).

Southwell, Robert, *An Humble Supplication to Her Maiestie*, ed. R. C. Bald (Cambridge, 1953).

The Statutes of Queen Elizabeth for the University of Cambridge. Translated from the Original Latin Statutes, Which Were Published by Mr. George Dyer, in 'The Privileges of the University of Cambridge', London, 1824 (London, 1838).

Stow, John, *Annales, or, a Generall Chronicle of England*, augmented by Edmund Howes (1607; repr. London, 1631).

Straunge Newes out of Calabria Prognosticated in the Yere 1586, vpon the Yere 87 (London, 1586).

Stubbes, Philip, *Philip Stubbes, The Anatomie of Abuses*, ed. Margaret Jane Kidnie (Tempe, AZ, 2002).

Stubbs, John, *John Stubbs's Gaping Gulf with Letters and Other Relevant Documents*, ed. Lloyd E. Berry (Charlottesville, VA, 1968).

Styward, Thomas, *The Pathwaie to Martiall Discipline* (London, 1581).

Tedder, William, *The Recantations As They Were Seuerallie Pronounced by Wylliam Tedder and Anthony Tyrrell* (London, 1588).

Tourneur, Cyril, *The Transformed Metamorphosis* (London, 1600).

Tymme, Thomas, *A Preparation against the Prognosticated Dangers of This Yeare, 1588* (London, 1588).

Tyndale, William, *The Whole Workes of W. Tyndall, Iohn Frith, and Doct. Barnes, Three Worthy Martyrs* (London, 1573).

Ulysses upon Ajax Written by Misodiaboles to His Friend Philaretes (London, 1596).

Vaughan, William, *The Golden-Groue, Moralized in Three Books* (London, 1600).

Venn, John, and John Archibald Venn (eds), *The Book of Matriculations and Degrees: 1544–1659* (Cambridge, 1913).

Vergilius, Publius Maro, *Vergil I: Eclogues, Georgics, Aeneid I–VI*, ed. H. Rushton Fairclough and trans. G. P. Goold (1999; repr. Cambridge, MA, 2006).

Verstegan, Richard, *An Aduertisement Written to a Secretarie of My L. Treasurers of Ingland* ([Antwerp], 1592).

—— *The Letters and Despatches of Richard Verstegan*, ed. Anthony G. Petti (London, 1959).

Viret, Pierre, *The Worlde Possessed with Deuils* (London, 1583).

Vitkus, Daniel J. (ed.), *Three Turk Plays from Early Modern England*: Selimus, A Christian Turned Turk, *and* The Renegado (New York, 2000).

Watson, Thomas, *The Complete Works of Thomas Watson*, ed. Dana F. Sutton (2 vols, Lewiston, 2006).

—— *An Eglogve vpon the Death of the Right Honorable Sir Francis Walsingham* (London, 1590).

—— *Thomas Watson: Italian Madrigals Englished (1590)*, ed. Albert Chatterley (London, 1999).

Webb, John (ed.), *The Town Finances of Elizabethan Ipswich: Select Treasurers' and Chamberlains' Accounts* (Woodbridge, 1996).

Webbe, William, *A Discourse of English Poetrie*, in G. Gregory Smith (ed.), *Elizabethan Critical Essays* (2 vols, Oxford, 1904), vol. 1, pp. 226–302.

Whetstone, George, *The Censure of a Loyall Subiect* (London, 1586).

—— *The English Myrror* (London, 1586).

Willet, Andrew, *Hexapla, That Is, a Six-fold Commentarie vpon the Most Diuine Epistle of the Holy Apostle S. Paul to the Romanes* (Cambridge, 1611).

Wither, George, *Britain's Remembrancer* (London, 1628).

The Wonders of This Windie Winter (London, 1613).

Woodes, Nathaniel, *The Conflict of Conscience 1581*, ed. Herbert Davis and F. P. Wilson, Malone Society Reprints (Oxford, 1952).

Wotton, Thomas, *Thomas Wotton's Letter-Book 1574–1586*, ed. George Eland (London, 1960).

SECONDARY SOURCES

Adams, John Charles, 'Gabriel Harvey's *Ciceronianus* and the Place of Peter Ramus' *Dialecticae Libri Duo* in the Curriculum', *Renaissance Quarterly*, 43:3 (1990), 551–69.

Adams, Simon, *Leicester and the Court: Essays on Elizabethan Politics* (Manchester, 2002).

Agnew, Jean-Christophe, *Worlds Apart: The Market and the Theater in Anglo-American Thought, 1550–1750* (New York, 1986).

Allen, Don Cameron, *Doubt's Boundless Sea: Skepticism and Faith in the Renaissance* (Baltimore, 1964).

Allison, A. F., and D. M. Rogers, *The Contemporary Printed Literature of the English Counter-Reformation between 1558 and 1640* (2 vols, Aldershot, 1994).

Almond, Philip C., *Adam and Eve in Seventeenth-Century Thought* (Cambridge, 1999).

Anderson, J. M., *The Honorable Burden of Public Office: English Humanists and Tudor Politics in the Sixteenth Century* (New York, 2010).

Anglo, Sydney, 'Reginald Scot's *Discoverie of Witchcraft*: Scepticism and Sadduceeism', in Sydney Anglo (ed.), *The Damned Art: Essays in the Literature of Witchcraft* (London, 1977), pp. 106–39.

Anstruther, Godfrey, *The Seminary Priests: A Dictionary of the Secular Clergy of England and Wales 1558–1850* (4 vols, Ware, 1969).

Archer, John Michael, *Sovereignty and Intelligence: Spying and Court Culture in the English Renaissance* (Stanford, 1993).

Bibliography

Armstrong, William A., '*Tamburlaine* and *The Wounds of Civil War*', *N&Q*, 203 (1958), 381–3.

Ash, Eric H., *Power, Knowledge, and Expertise in Elizabethan England* (Baltimore, 2004).

Aston, Margaret, *The King's Bedpost: Reformation and Iconography in a Tudor Group Portrait* (New York, 1993).

Auberlen, Eckhard, *The Commonwealth of Wit: The Writer's Image and His Strategies of Self-Representation in Elizabethan Literature* (Tübingen, 1984).

Aveling, J. C. H., *Catholic Recusancy in the City of York 1558–1791* (London, 1970).

Axton, Marie, *The Queen's Two Bodies: Drama and the Elizabethan Succession* (London, 1977).

Babb, Howard S., 'Policy in Marlowe's *The Jew of Malta*', *ELH*, 24:2 (1957), 85–94.

Bakeless, John, *Christopher Marlowe* (London, 1938).

—— *The Tragicall History of Christopher Marlowe* (2 vols, Cambridge, MA, 1942).

Bald, R. C., *Donne and the Drurys* (Cambridge, 1959).

Barber, C. L., *Creating Elizabethan Tragedy: The Theater of Marlowe and Kyd*, ed. with intro. by Richard P. Wheeler (Chicago, 1988).

Barber, Rosalind, 'Was Marlowe a Violent Man?', in Sarah K. Scott and M. L. Stapleton (eds), *Christopher Marlowe the Craftsman: Lives, Stage and Page* (London, 2010), pp. 47–61.

Barbour, Reid, *Deciphering Elizabethan Fiction* (Newark, DE, 1993).

Barish, Jonas, *The Anti-Theatrical Prejudice* (Berkeley, 1981).

Barker, Simon, *War and Nation in the Theatre of Shakespeare and His Contemporaries* (Edinburgh, 2007).

Barroll, Leeds, *Politics, Plague, and Shakespeare's Theatre: The Stuart Years* (Ithaca, 1991).

Barthes, Roland, *Sade Fourier Loyola*, trans. Richard Miller (Berkeley, 1977).

Bartram, Claire, '"Melancholic Imaginations": Witchcraft and the Politics of Melancholia in Elizabethan Kent', *Journal of European Studies*, 33:3 (2003), 203–11.

—— '"Some Tomb for a Remembraunce": Representation of Piety in Post-Reformation Gentry Funeral Monuments', in Robert Lutton and Elisabeth Salter (eds), *Pieties in Transition: Religious Practices and Experiences, c. 1400–1640* (Aldershot, 2007), pp. 138–43.

Bate, Jonathan, *The Genius of Shakespeare* (London, 1997).

Battenhouse, Roy W., *Marlowe's* Tamburlaine: *A Study in Renaissance Moral Philosophy* (1941; repr. Nashville, 1964).

—— 'Tamburlaine, the "Scourge of God"', *PMLA*, 56:2 (1941), 337–48.

Bauckham, Richard, *Tudor Apocalypse* (Oxford, 1978).

Bawcutt, N. W., 'Machiavelli and Marlowe's *The Jew of Malta*', *Renaissance Drama*, NS, 3 (1970), 3–49.

Bednarz, James P., 'Marlowe and the English Literary Scene', in Patrick Cheney (ed.), *The Cambridge Companion to Christopher Marlowe* (Cambridge, 2004), pp. 90–105.

Beier, A. L., *Masterless Men: The Vagrancy Problem in England 1560–1640* (London, 1985).

Beier, Lucinda McCray, *Sufferers and Healers: The Experience of Illness in Seventeenth-Century England* (London, 1987).

Bell, Gary M., 'Elizabethan Diplomatic Compensation: Its Nature and Variety', *Journal of British Studies*, 20:2 (1981), 1–25.
Bentley, Gerald Eades, *The Profession of Dramatist in Shakespeare's Time* (Princeton, 1971).
Bevington, David, *Shakespeare and Biography* (Oxford, 2010).
Biddle, Martin H., and John Summerson, 'Dover Harbour', in H. M. Colvin (ed.), *The History of the King's Works, Vol. 4, Part 2* (London, 1982), pp. 729–68.
Binns, J. W., 'William Gager's *Dido*', *Humanistica Lovaniensia*, 20 (1971), 167–254.
Birch, Thomas, *Memoirs of the Reign of Queen Elizabeth, from the Year 1581 till Her Death* (2 vols, London, 1754).
Birringer, Johannes H., *Marlowe's Doctor Faustus and Tamburlaine* (Frankfurt am Main, 1984).
Blacketer, Raymond A., *The School of God: Pedagogy and Rhetoric in Calvin's Interpretation of Deuteronomy* (Dordrecht, 2006).
Blomefield, Francis, *An Essay towards a Topographical History of the County of Norfolk* (11 vols, London, 1805–10).
Blunt, Wilfrid, *Sweet Roman Hand: Five Hundred Years of Italic Cursive Script* (London, 1952).
Boas, Frederick S., *Christopher Marlowe: A Biographical and Critical Study* (Oxford, 1940).
—— *University Drama in the Tudor Age* (Oxford, 1914).
Born, Hanspeter, 'Why Greene Was Angry at Shakespeare', in S. P. Cerasano (ed.), *MRDE, Vol. 25* (Madison, 2012), pp. 133–73.
Bos, Sander, Marianne Lange-Meyers, and Jeanine Six, 'Sidney's Funeral Portrayed', in Jan van Dorsten, Dominic Baker-Smith, and Arthur F. Kinney (eds), *Sir Philip Sidney: 1586 and the Creation of a Legend* (Leiden, 1986), pp. 38–61.
Botelho, Keith M., *Renaissance Earwitnesses: Rumor and Early Modern Masculinity* (New York, 2009).
Bourdieu, Pierre, 'The Forms of Capital', in John G. Richardson (ed.), *Handbook of Theory and Research for the Sociology of Education* (New York, 1986), pp. 241–58.
Boutcher, Warren, 'Pilgrimage to Parnassus: Local Intellectual Traditions, Humanist Education and the Cultural Geography of Sixteenth-Century England', in Yun Lee Too and Niall Livingstone (eds), *Pedagogy and Power: Rhetorics of Classical Learning* (Cambridge, 1998), pp. 110–47.
Bowers, Rick, and Paul S. Smith, 'Sir John Harington, Hugh Plat, and *Ulysses upon Ajax*', *N&Q*, 54:3 (2007), 255–9.
Boynton, Lindsay, *The Elizabethan Militia 1558–1638* (London, 1967).
Braunmuller, A. R., *Natural Fictions: George Chapman's Major Tragedies* (Newark, DE, 1992).
Bray, Alan, *The Friend* (Chicago, 2003).
Breight, Curtis C., *Surveillance, Militarism and Drama in the Elizabethan Era* (Basingstoke, 1996).
Brennan, Michael, 'William Ponsonby: Elizabethan Stationer', *Analytical and Enumerative Bibliography*, 7:3 (1983), 91–110.
Briggs, Julia, 'Marlowe's *Massacre at Paris*: A Reconsideration', *RES*, NS, 34:135 (1983), 257–78.

Briggs, K. M., *Pale Hecate's Team: An Examination of the Beliefs on Witchcraft and Magic among Shakespeare's Contemporaries and His Immediate Successors* (London, 1962).

Brink, Jean R., 'William Ponsonby's Rival Publisher', *Analytical and Enumerative Bibliography*, 12:3–4 (2001), 185–205.

Brinkley, Roberta Florence, *Arthurian Legend in the Seventeenth Century* (1932; repr. London, 1967).

Brooke, C. F. Tucker, *The Life of Marlowe and* The Tragedy of Dido Queen of Carthage (1930; repr. New York, 1966).

Brown, Georgia E., 'Gender and Voice in *Hero and Leander*', in J. A. Downie and J. T. Parnell (eds), *Constructing Christopher Marlowe* (Cambridge, 2000), pp. 148–63.

Bryson, William Hamilton, 'A Note on Robinson's Brief Collection of … Courts of Records', *TCBS*, 6:3 (1974), 181–7.

Buc, Philippe, *Holy War, Martyrdom, and Terror: Christianity, Violence, and the West, ca. 70 C.E. to the Iraq War* (Philadelphia, 2015).

Buckley, Emma, '"Live False Aeneas!" Marlowe's *Dido, Queen of Carthage* and the Limits of Translation', *Classical Receptions Journal*, 3:2 (2011), 129–47.

Buckley, George T., *Atheism in the English Renaissance* (1932; repr. New York, 1965).

Bushell, T. A., 'Scadbury Manor, Chislehurst', *AC*, 69 (1955), 219–21.

Caldwell, Patricia, *The Puritan Conversion Narrative: The Beginnings of American Expression* (New York, 1983).

Callaghan, Dympna, 'Marlowe's Last Poem: Elegiac Aesthetics and the Epitaph on Sir Roger Manwood', in Sarah K. Scott and M. L. Stapleton (eds), *Christopher Marlowe the Craftsman: Lives, Stage and Page* (Farnham, 2010), pp. 159–76.

Carey, John, 'Is the Author Dead? Or, the Mermaids and the Robot', in Takashi Kozuka and J. R. Mulryne (eds), *Shakespeare, Marlowe, Jonson: New Directions in Biography* (Aldershot, 2006), pp. 43–54.

Carleton, Kenneth, *Bishops and Reform in the English Church 1520–1559* (Woodbridge, 2001).

Carley, James, 'Polydore Virgil and John Leland on King Arthur: The Battle of Books', in Edward Donald Kennedy (ed.), *King Arthur: A Casebook* (New York, 1996), pp. 185–204.

Carrafiello, Michael L., 'English Catholicism and the Jesuit Mission of 1580–1581', *Historical Journal*, 37:4 (1994), 761–74.

Carson, Neil, *A Companion to Henslowe's Diary* (Cambridge, 1988).

Cavell, John, and Brian Kennett, *A History of Sir Roger Manwood's School Sandwich 1563–1963 with a Life of the Founder* (London, 1963).

Chadwick, Owen, 'Richard Bancroft's Submission', *JEH*, 3:1 (1952), 58–73.

Chalk, Brian, *Monuments and Literary Posterity in Early Modern Drama* (Cambridge, 2015).

Chambers, E. K., *The Elizabethan Stage* (4 vols, 1923; repr. Oxford, 1974).

Charlton, Kenneth, *Education in Renaissance England* (London, 1965).

Chartier, Roger, 'Intellectual History or Sociocultural History? The French Trajectories', in Dominick LaCapra and Steven L. Kaplan (eds), *Modern European Intellectual History: Reappraisals and New Perspectives* (Ithaca, 1982), pp. 13–46.

Chaudhuri, Sukanta, 'Marlowe, Madrigals, and a New Elizabethan Poet', *RES*, NS, 39:154 (1988), 199–216.

Bibliography

Cheney, Patrick, 'Biographical Representations: Marlowe's Life of the Author', in Takashi Kozuka and J. R. Mulryne (eds), *Shakespeare, Marlowe, Jonson: New Directions in Biography* (Aldershot, 2006), pp. 183–204.

Clancy, Thomas H., *Papist Pamphleteers: The Allen–Persons Party and the Political Thought of the Counter-Reformation in England, 1572–1615* (Chicago, 1964).

Clark, G. Kitson, *The Critical Historian* (New York, 1967).

Clark, Peter, *English Provincial Society from the Reformation to the Revolution: Religion, Politics and Society in Kent 1500–1640* (Hassocks, 1977).

Clark, Stuart, 'King James's *Daemonology*: Witchcraft and Kingship', in Sydney Anglo (ed.), *The Damned Art: Essays in the Literature of Witchcraft* (London, 1977), pp. 156–77.

Clifton, Robin, 'The Popular Fear of Catholics during the English Revolution', *Past & Present*, 52 (1971), 23–55.

Cole, Douglas, *Suffering and Evil in the Plays of Christopher Marlowe* (Princeton, 1962).

Collier, J. P., *A Bibliographical and Critical Account of the Rarest Books in the English Language* (2 vols, London, 1865).

Collinson, Patrick, *The Birthpangs of Protestant England: Religious and Cultural Change in the Sixteenth and Seventeenth Centuries* (London, 1988).

—— 'Ecclesiastical Vitriol: Religious Satire in the 1590s and the Invention of Puritanism', in John Guy (ed.), *The Reign of Elizabeth I: Court and Culture in the Last Decade* (Cambridge, 1995), pp. 150–70.

—— *The Elizabethan Puritan Movement* (1967; repr. Oxford, 1990).

—— 'John Foxe and National Consciousness', in Christopher Highley and John N. King (eds), *John Foxe and His World* (Aldershot, 2002), pp. 10–34.

—— *The Religion of Protestants: The Church in English Society 1559–1625* (Oxford, 1982).

—— *Richard Bancroft and Elizabethan Anti-Puritanism* (Cambridge, 2013).

—— 'Sir Nicholas Bacon and the Elizabethan *Via Media*', in *Godly People: Essays on English Protestantism and Puritanism* (London, 1983), pp. 135–53.

—— 'The Theatre Constructs Puritanism', in David L. Smith, Richard Strier, and David Bevington (eds), *The Theatrical City: Culture, Theatre and Politics in London, 1576–1649* (Cambridge, 1995), pp. 157–69.

Cooper, Charles Henry, *Annals of Cambridge* (5 vols, Cambridge, 1842–53).

Cooper, William Durrant, 'Notices of Anthony Babington, of Dethick, and of the Conspiracy of 1586', *Reliquary*, 2 (1861–62), 177–99.

Costello, William T., *The Scholastic Curriculum at Early Seventeenth-Century Cambridge* (Cambridge, MA, 1958).

Cox, Jacqueline, 'Trials and Tribulations: The Cambridge University Courts, 1540–1660', *TCBS*, 15:4 (2015), 595–623.

Cox, John D., *The Devil and the Sacred in English Drama, 1350–1642* (Cambridge, 2000).

Cozens-Hardy, Basil, and Ernest A. Kent, *The Mayors of Norwich 1403 to 1835* (Norwich, 1938).

Craig, John, 'The "Cambridge Boies": Thomas Rogers and the "Brethren" in Bury St Edmunds', in Susan Wabuda and Caroline Litzenberger (eds), *Belief and Practice in Reformation England: A Tribute to Patrick Collinson from His Students* (Aldershot, 1998), pp. 163–75.

—— *Reformation, Politics and Polemics: The Growth of Protestantism in East Anglian Market Towns 1500–1610* (Aldershot, 2001).

Craik, T. W., *The Tudor Interlude: Stage, Costume, and Acting* (1958; repr. Leicester, 1967).

Creaser, John, 'Jonson's *Bartholomew Fair* and Bancroft's *Dangerous Positions*', RES, NS, 57:229 (2006), 176–84.

Cressy, David, 'The Death of a Vice-Chancellor: Cambridge, 1632', in Mordechai Feingold (ed.), *History of Universities: Volume XXVI/2* (Oxford, 2012), pp. 92–112.

—— 'A Drudgery of Schoolmasters: The Teaching Profession in Elizabethan and Stuart England', in Wilfrid Prest (ed.), *The Professions in Early Modern England* (London, 1987), pp. 129–53.

Crewe, Jonathan V., 'The Theatre of the Idols: Theatrical and Anti-Theatrical Discourse', *Theatre Journal*, 36:3 (1984), 321–44.

Croston, James, *County Families of Lancashire and Cheshire* (London, 1887).

Curtis, Mark H., 'The Alienated Intellectuals of Early Stuart England', *Past & Present*, 23 (1962), 25–43.

—— *Oxford and Cambridge in Transition 1558–1642* (Oxford, 1959).

Cust, Richard, 'News and Politics in Early Seventeenth-Century England', *Past & Present*, 112 (1986), 60–90.

Cutts, J. P., *The Left Hand of God: A Critical Interpretation of the Plays of Christopher Marlowe* (Haddonfield, 1973).

Davidson, Nicholas, 'Christopher Marlowe and Atheism', in Darryll Grantley and Peter Roberts (eds), *Christopher Marlowe and English Renaissance Culture* (Aldershot, 1996), pp. 129–47.

Davies, S. F., 'The Reception of Reginald Scot's *Discovery of Witchcraft*: Witchcraft, Magic, and Radical Religion', *Journal of the History of Ideas*, 74:3 (2013), 381–401.

Davis, Alex, *Chivalry and Romance in the English Renaissance* (Cambridge, 2003).

Daybell, James, *The Material Letter in Early Modern England: Manuscript Letters and the Culture and Practices of Letter-Writing* (Basingstoke, 2012).

Deats, Sara Munson, and Lisa S. Starks, '"So Neatly Plotted, and So Well Perform'd": Villain as Playwright in Marlowe's *The Jew of Malta*', *Theatre Journal*, 44:3 (1992), 375–89.

Dennison, James T., *The Market Day of the Soul: The Puritan Doctrine of the Sabbath in England, 1532–1700* (Lanham, 1983).

Dessen, Alan C., and Leslie Thomson, *A Dictionary of Stage Directions in English Drama, 1580–1642* (Cambridge, 1999).

DiFonzo, Nicholas, and Prashant Bordia, 'Rumor, Gossip and Urban Legends', *Diogenes*, 54:1 (2007), 19–35.

—— *Rumor Psychology: Social and Organizational Approaches* (Washington, DC, 2007).

DiGangi, Mario, *The Homoerotics of Early Modern Drama* (Cambridge, 1997).

Dobin, Howard, *Merlin's Disciples: Prophecy, Poetry, and Power in Renaissance England* (Stanford, 1990).

Donaldson, Gordon, 'The Attitude of Whitgift and Bancroft to the Scottish Church', *Transactions of the Royal Historical Society*, 4th ser., 24 (1942), 95–115.

Donaldson, Ian, 'Matters of Life and Death: The Return of Biography', *Australian Book Review*, 286 (2006), 23–9.

Doran, Susan, 'Elizabeth I's Religion: The Evidence of Her Letters', *JEH*, 51:4 (2000), 699–720.
—— 'Juno versus Diana: The Treatment of Elizabeth I's Marriage in Plays and Entertainments, 1561–1581', *Historical Journal*, 38:2 (1995), 257–74.
—— *Monarchy and Matrimony: The Courtships of Elizabeth I* (London, 1996).
Dowling, Maria, and Joy Shakespeare, 'Religion and Politics in Mid-Tudor England through the Eyes of an English Protestant Woman: The Recollections of Rose Hickman', *Bulletin of the Institute of Historical Research*, 55:131 (1982), 94–102.
Downie, J. A., 'Marlowe: Facts and Fictions', in J. A. Downie and J. T. Parnell (eds), *Constructing Christopher Marlowe* (Cambridge, 2000), pp. 13–29.
—— 'Marlowe, May 1593, and the "Must-Have" Theory of Biography', *RES*, NS, 58:235 (2007), 245–67.
—— 'Reviewing What We Think We Know about Christopher Marlowe, Again', in Sarah K. Scott and M. L. Stapleton (eds), *Christopher Marlowe the Craftsman: Lives, Stage, and Page* (Farnham, 2010), pp. 33–46.
Drake, C. H., 'The Hospital of St Mary of Ospringe, Commonly Called Maison Dieu', *AC*, 30 (1914), 35–78.
Duthie, G. I., 'The Dramatic Structure of Marlowe's *Tamburlaine the Great, Parts One and Two*', *English Studies*, NS, 1 (1948), 101–26.
Eccles, Mark, 'Brief Lives: Tudor and Stuart Authors', *Studies in Philology*, 79:4 (1982), 1–135.
—— 'Chapman's Early Years', *Studies in Philology*, 43:2 (1946), 176–93.
—— *Christopher Marlowe in London* (Cambridge, MA, 1934).
—— 'Marlowe in Kentish Tradition', *N&Q*, 169 (1935), 20–3, 39–41, and 58–61.
—— 'Samuel Daniel in France and Italy', *Studies in Philology*, 34:2 (1937), 148–67.
Edelman, Charles, '"Shoot at Him All at Once": Gunfire at the Playhouse, 1587', *Theatre Notebook*, 57:2 (2003), 78–81.
—— 'Which Is the Jew that Shakespeare Knew? Shylock on the Elizabethan Stage', *Shakespeare Survey*, 52 (1999), 99–106.
Edgerton, William L., *Nicholas Udall* (New York, 1965).
Edwards, D. L., *A History of the King's School Canterbury* (London, 1957).
Edwards, Francis, *Robert Persons: The Biography of an Elizabethan Jesuit 1546–1610* (St Louis, 1995).
Eliot, T. S., 'Christopher Marlowe', in *Selected Essays* (London, 1951), pp. 118–25.
Ellis-Fermor, U. M., *Christopher Marlowe* (London, 1927).
Elmer, Peter, *Witchcraft, Witch-Hunting, and Politics in Early Modern England* (Oxford, 2016).
Enders, Jody, *Death by Drama and Other Medieval Urban Legends* (Chicago, 2002).
Erickson, Stacy, '"I do more confidently presume to publish it in his absence": William Ponsonby's Print Network', in John Hinks and Victoria Gardener (eds), *The Book Trade in Early Modern England: Practices, Perceptions, Connections* (New Castle, DE, 2014), pp. 45–60.
Erne, Lukas, 'Biography and Mythography: Rereading Chettle's Alleged Apology to Shakespeare', *English Studies*, 79:5 (1998), 430–40.
—— 'Biography, Mythography, and Criticism: The Life and Works of Christopher Marlowe', *Modern Philology*, 103:1 (2005), 28–50.

Estes, Leland, 'Reginald Scot and His *Discoverie of Witchcraft*: Religion and Science in the Opposition to the European Witch Craze', *Church History*, 52:4 (1983), 444–56.

Fairbank, Alfred, and Bruce Dickins, *The Italic Hand in Tudor Cambridge* (London, 1962).

Farley-Hills, David, 'Tamburlaine and the Mad Priest of the Sun', *Journal of Anglo-Italian Studies*, 2 (1992), 36–49.

Farmer, Richard, *Laurence Chaderton, D.D. Translated from a Latin Memoir of Dr. Dillingham with Notes and Illustrations* (Cambridge, 1884).

Feasey, Lynette, and Eveline Feasey, 'Marlowe and the Prophetic Dooms', *N&Q*, 195 (1950), 356–9, 404–7, 419–21.

Feingold, Mordechai, 'English Ramism: A Reinterpretation', in Mordechai Feingold, Joseph S. Freedman, and Wolfgang Rother (eds), *The Influence of Peter Ramus: Studies in Sixteenth and Seventeenth Century Philosophy and Sciences* (Basel, 2001), pp. 127–76.

Felsenstein, Frank, 'Jews and Devils: Anti-Semitic Stereotypes of Late Medieval and Renaissance England', *Journal of Literature and Theology*, 4:1 (1990), 15–28.

Ferguson, Arthur B., *The Chivalric Tradition in Renaissance England* (Washington, DC, 1986).

Festinger, Leon, Stanley Schachter, and Kurt Bach, *Social Pressures in Informal Groups: A Study of Human Factors in Housing* (1950; repr. Stanford, 1963).

Feuillerat, Albert, *John Lyly: Contribution a l'histoire de la Renaissance en Angleterre* (Cambridge, 1910).

Finlay, Roger, *Population and the Metropolis: The Demography of London 1580–1650* (Cambridge, 1981).

Firestone, Reuven, *Holy War in Judaism: The Fall and Rise of a Controversial Idea* (Oxford, 2012).

Fischer, Sandra K., *Econolingua: A Glossary of Coins and Economic Language in Renaissance Drama* (Newark, DE, 1985).

FitzGibbon, B., 'George Talbot, Ninth Earl of Shrewsbury', *Biographical Studies*, 2 (1953–4), 96–110.

Fleming, Juliet, 'The Ladies' Man and the Age of Elizabeth', in James Grantham Turner (ed.), *Sexuality and Gender in Early Modern Europe: Institutions, Texts, Images* (Cambridge, 1993), pp. 158–81.

Foster, Joseph, *Alumni Oxonienses* (4 vols, Oxford, 1891–92).

Fox, Adam, *Oral and Literate Culture in England 1500–1700* (Oxford, 2000).

Freeman, Arthur, 'Marlowe, Kyd, and the Dutch Church Libel', *ELR*, 3:1 (1973), 44–52.

—— *Thomas Kyd: Facts and Problems* (Oxford, 1967).

Frye, Susan, *Elizabeth I: The Competition for Representation* (New York, 1993).

Gardner, Helen, 'The Second Part of *Tamburlaine the Great*', *MLR*, 37:1 (1942), 18–24.

Gaskill, Malcolm, *Crime and Mentalities in Early Modern England* (Cambridge, 2000).

Gaumer, Matthew Alan, *Augustine's Cyprian: Authority in Roman Africa* (Leiden, 2016).

Gayley, Charles Mills, *Representative English Comedies* (2 vols, New York, 1912).

Bibliography

Gazzard, Hugh, 'An Act to Restrain Abuses of Players (1606)', *RES*, NS, 61:251 (2010), 495–528.

Ghose, Indira, 'Laughter and Blasphemy in the Shakespearean Theater', in John Pitcher (ed.), *MRDE, Vol. 16* (Madison, 2003), pp. 228–39.

Gibson, Jonathan, 'From Palatino to Cresci: Italian Writing Books and the Italic Scripts of Early Modern English Letters', in James Daybell and Andrew Gordon (eds), *Cultures of Correspondence in Early Modern Britain* (Philadelphia, 2016), pp. 29–47.

Gildersleeve, Virginia Crocheron, *Government Regulation of the Elizabethan Drama* (New York, 1908).

Gill, Roma, 'Marlowe's Virgil: *Dido Queene of Carthage*', *RES*, NS, 28:110 (1977), 141–55.

Ginzburg, Carlo, and Carlo Poni, 'The Name and the Game: Unequal Exchange and the Historiographic Marketplace', in Edward Muir and Guido Ruggiero (eds), *Microhistory and the Lost Peoples of Europe*, trans. Eren Branch (Baltimore, 1991), pp. 1–10.

Glenn, John Roland, 'The Martyrdom of Ramus in Marlowe's *The Massacre at Paris*', *Papers on Language and Literature*, 9:4 (1973), 365–79.

Godshalk, William Leigh, 'Marlowe's *Dido, Queen of Carthage*', *ELH*, 38:1 (1971), 1–18.

Goldberg, Jonathan, *Sodometries: Renaissance Texts, Modern Sexualities* (Stanford, 1992).

Grande, Troni Y., *Marlovian Tragedy: The Play of Dilation* (Lewisburg, PA, 1999).

Grantley, Darryll, and Peter Roberts (eds), *Christopher Marlowe and English Renaissance Culture* (Aldershot, 1996).

Gray, Austin K., 'Some Observations on Christopher Marlowe, Government Agent', *PMLA*, 43:3 (1928), 682–700.

Green, Ian, 'Career Prospects and Clerical Conformity in the Early Stuart Church', *Past & Present*, 90 (1981), 71–115.

Greenblatt, Stephen, *Renaissance Self-Fashioning from More to Shakespeare* (Chicago, 1980).

Greg, W. W. (ed.), *English Literary Autographs 1550–1650, Part 1, Dramatists* (Oxford, 1925).

Groves, Beatrice, '"They repented at the preachyng of Ionas: and beholde, a greater then Ionas is here": *A Looking Glass for London and England*, Hosea and the Destruction of Jerusalem', in Adrian Streete (ed.), *Early Modern Drama and the Bible: Contexts and Readings, 1570–1625* (Basingstoke, 2012), pp. 139–55.

Gurr, Andrew, *The Shakespearian Playing Companies* (Oxford, 1996).

Guy, John, 'The 1590s: The Second Reign of Elizabeth I', in John Guy (ed.), *The Reign of Elizabeth I: Court and Culture in the Last Decade* (Cambridge, 1995), pp. 1–19.

Hacket, Helen, *Virgin Mother, Maiden Queen: Elizabeth I and the Cult of the Virgin Mary* (Basingstoke, 1995).

Hadfield, Andrew, 'Tamburlaine as the "Scourge of God" and *The First English Life of King Henry the Fifth*', *N&Q*, 50:4 (2003), 399–400.

Halasz, Alexandra, *The Marketplace of Print: Pamphlets and the Public Sphere in Early Modern England* (Cambridge, 1997).

Hale, J. R., *Renaissance War Studies* (London, 1983).

Hamilton, Donna B., *Anthony Munday and the Catholics, 1560–1633* (Aldershot, 2005).
Hamlin, Hamel, *The Bible in Shakespeare* (Oxford, 2013).
Hammer, Paul E. J., 'The Earl of Essex, Fulke Greville, and the Employment of Scholars', *Studies in Philology*, 91:2 (1994), 167–80.
—— 'Essex and Europe: Evidence from Confidential Instructions by the Earl of Essex, 1595-6', *EHR*, 111:441 (1996), 357–81.
—— 'A Reckoning Reframed: The "Murder" of Christopher Marlowe Revisited', *ELR*, 26:2 (1996), 225–42.
—— 'The Uses of Scholarship: The Secretariat of Robert Devereux, Second Earl of Essex, c. 1585–1601', *EHR*, 109:430 (1994), 26–51.
Happé, Peter, 'The Protestant Adaptation of the Saint Play', in Clifford Davidson (ed.), *The Saint Play in Medieval Europe* (Kalamazoo, MI, 1986), pp. 205–40.
Hardin, Richard F., 'Marlowe and the Fruits of Scholarism', *Philological Quarterly*, 63:3 (1984), 387–400.
Harlan, Susan, *Memories of War in Early Modern England: Armor and Militant Nostalgia in Marlowe, Sidney, and Shakespeare* (New York, 2016).
Harris, Jonathan Gil, *Foreign Bodies and the Body Politic: Discourses of Social Pathology in Early Modern England* (Cambridge, 1998).
Hasler, P. W. (ed.), *The House of Commons, 1558–1603* (3 vols, London, 1981).
Hattaway, Michael, 'The Theology of Marlowe's *Doctor Faustus*', *Renaissance Drama*, NS, 3 (1970), 51–78.
Hawes, Thomas (ed.), *An Index to Norwich City Officers 1453–1835* (Norwich, 1989).
Healy, Thomas, 'Marlowe's Biography', in Emily C. Bartels and Emma Smith (eds), *Christopher Marlowe in Context* (Cambridge, 2013), pp. 334–45.
Helgerson, Richard, *The Elizabethan Prodigals* (San Marino, 1976).
Helmholz, R. H., *Select Cases on Defamation to 1600* (London, 1985).
Henderson, Philip, *And Morning in His Eyes: A Book About Christopher Marlowe* (1937; repr. New York, 1972).
Herford, Charles E., *Studies in the Literary Relations of England and Germany in the Sixteenth Century* (1886; repr. Abingdon, 1966).
Hibbard, G. R., *Thomas Nashe: A Critical Introduction* (Cambridge, MA, 1962).
Hicks, Leo, *An Elizabethan Problem: Some Aspects of the Careers of Two Exile Adventurers* (New York, 1964).
Hill, Christopher, *Economic Problems of the Church: From Archbishop Whitgift to the Long Parliament* (Oxford, 1956).
—— *Intellectual Origins of the English Revolution* (Oxford, 1965).
Hill, Tracey, *Anthony Munday and Civic Culture: Theatre, History and Power in Early Modern London 1580–1633* (Manchester, 2004).
—— '"He hath changed his coppy": Anti-Theatrical Writing and the Turncoat Player', *Critical Survey*, 9:3 (1997), 59–77.
Hilliard, Stephen S., *The Singularity of Thomas Nashe* (Lincoln, NE, 1986).
Hindmarsh, D. Bruce, *The Evangelical Conversion Narrative: Spiritual Autobiography in Early Modern England* (Oxford, 2005).
Holmes, Peter, *Resistance and Compromise: The Political Thought of the Elizabethan Catholics* (Cambridge, 1982).

Höltgen, K. J., 'Sir Robert Dallington (1561-1637): Author, Traveler, and Pioneer of Taste', *HLQ*, 47:3 (1984), 147-77.
Honan, Park, *Christopher Marlowe: Poet and Spy* (Oxford, 2005).
Hooks, Adam G., 'Making Marlowe', in Kirk Melnikoff and Roslyn L. Knutson (eds), *Christopher Marlowe, Theatrical Commerce, and the Book Trade* (Cambridge, 2018), pp. 97-114.
Horne, David H., *The Life and Minor Works of George Peele* (New Haven, 1952).
Hotson, J. Leslie, *The Death of Christopher Marlowe* (1925; repr. New York, 1967).
Houlbrooke, Ralph, *Death, Religion and the Family in England 1480-1750* (Oxford, 1998).
Houliston, Victor, *Catholic Resistance in Elizabethan England: Robert Persons's Jesuit Polemic, 1580-1610* (Aldershot, 2007).
—— 'The Lord Treasurer and the Jesuit: Robert Persons's Satirical *Responsio* to the 1591 Proclamation', *Sixteenth Century Journal*, 32:2 (2001), 383-401.
Howard, Jean, *The Stage and Social Struggle in Early Modern England* (London, 1994).
Howell, Wilbur Samuel, *Logic and Rhetoric in England, 1500-1700* (New York, 1961).
Hudson, William, and John Cottingham Tingey (eds), *The Records of the City of Norwich* (2 vols, Norwich, 1906).
Hughes, Charles, 'Nicholas Faunt's Discourse Touching the Office of Principal Secretary of Estate, & c. 1592', *EHR*, 20:79 (1905), 499-508.
Hunter, G. K., 'The Beginnings of Elizabethan Drama: Revolution and Continuity', *Renaissance Drama*, NS, 17 (1986), 29-53.
—— *John Lyly: The Humanist as Courtier* (London, 1962).
—— 'The Theology of Marlowe's *The Jew of Malta*', *Journal of the Warburg and Courtauld Institutes*, 27 (1964), 211-40.
Hunter, Michael, 'The Problem of "Atheism" in Early Modern England', *Transactions of the Royal Historical Society*, 5th ser., 35 (1985), 135-57.
Hutchings, Mark, 'Marlowe's Scourge of God', *N&Q*, 51:3 (2004), 244-7.
Ide, Arata, 'Christopher Marlowe, William Austen, and the Community of Corpus Christi College', *Studies in Philology*, 104:1 (2007), 56-81.
—— 'Corpus Christi College, Cambridge in 1577: Reading the Social Space in Sir Nicholas Bacon's College Plan', *TCBS*, 15:2 (2013), 279-328.
—— '*Doctor Faustus* and the Appearance of the Devil', in Yoshiko Kawachi (ed.), *Japanese Studies in Shakespeare and His Contemporaries* (Newark, 1998), pp. 11-24.
—— '*The Jew of Malta* and the Diabolic Power of Theatrics in the 1580s', *SEL*, 46:2 (2006), 257-79.
—— 'John Fletcher of Corpus Christi College: New Records of His Early Years', *Early Theatre*, 13:2 (2010), 63-77.
—— 'Nathaniel Woodes, Foxeian Martyrology, and the Radical Protestants of Norwich in the 1570s', *Reformation*, 13 (2008), 103-32.
—— 'Robert Greene *Nordovicensis*, the Saddler's Son', *N&Q*, 53:4 (2006), 432-6.
—— 'Tamburlaine's Prophetic Oratory and Protestant Militarism in the 1580s', in Yasunari Takahashi and Yasuo Tamaizumi (eds), *Essays on Shakespeare and His Contemporaries* (New York, 2000), pp. 215-36.

Ingram, Martin, *Church Courts, Sex and Marriage in England, 1570–1640* (Cambridge, 1987).

Jackson, MacDonald P., 'Francis Meres and the Cultural Contexts of Shakespeare's Rival Poet Sonnets', *RES*, NS, 56:244 (2005), 224–46.

Jacquot, Jean, 'Ralegh's "Hellish Verses" and *The Tragicall Raigne of Selimus*', *MLR*, 48:1 (1953), 1–9.

James, Mervyn, *Society, Politics and Culture: Studies in Early Modern England* (Cambridge, 1986).

Jantz, Harold, 'An Elizabethan Statement on the Origin of the German Faust Book', *JEGP*, 15:2 (1952), 137–53.

Jardine, David, *Criminal Trials* (2 vols, London, 1832–35).

Jardine, Lisa, 'Humanism and the Sixteenth Century Cambridge Arts Course', *History of Education*, 4:1 (1975), 16–31.

—— 'The Place of Dialectic Teaching in Sixteenth-Century Cambridge', *Studies in the Renaissance*, 21 (1974), 31–62.

—— and William Sherman, 'Pragmatic Readers: Knowledge Transactions and Scholarly Services in Late Elizabethan England', in Anthony Fletcher and Peter Roberts (eds), *Religion, Culture and Society in Early Modern Britain: Essays in Honour of Patrick Collinson* (Cambridge, 1994), pp. 102–24.

Jenkins, Harold, 'On the Authenticity of *Greene's Groatsworth of Wit* and *The Repentance of Robert Greene*', *RES*, OS, 11:41 (1935), 28–41.

—— *The Life and Work of Henry Chettle* (London, 1934).

Johnson, James Turner, *Ideology, Reason, and the Limitation of War: Religious and Secular Concepts 1200–1740* (Princeton, 1975).

Jones, Norman, and Paul Whitfield White, '*Gorboduc* and Royal Marriage Politics: An Elizabethan Playgoer's Report of the Premiere Performance', *ELR*, 26:1 (1996), 3–16.

Jorgensen, Paul A., 'Moral Guidance and Religious Encouragement for the Elizabethan Soldier', *HLQ*, 13:2 (1950), 241–59.

Jowett, John, 'Johannes Factotum: Henry Chettle and *Greene's Groatsworth of Wit*', *Papers of the Bibliographical Society of America*, 87:4 (1993), 453–86.

Kapferer, Jean-Noël, *Rumors: Uses, Interpretations, and Images*, trans. Bruce Fink (New Brunswick and London, 1990).

Kapitaniak, Pierre, 'From Grindal to Whitgift: The Political Commitment of Reginald Scot', *Études Épistémè*, 29 (2016), <http://episteme.revues.org/1263> [accessed 23 November 2022].

—— 'Reginald Scot and the Circles of Power: Witchcraft, Anti-Catholicism and Faction Politics', in Marcus Harmes and Victoria Bladen (eds), *Supernatural and Secular Power in Early Modern England* (Farnham, 2015), pp. 41–66.

Katz, David S., *The Jews in the History of England 1485–1850* (Oxford, 1994).

Keenan, Siobhan, 'Spectator and Spectacle: Royal Entertainments at the Universities in the 1560s', in Jayne Elisabeth Archer, Elizabeth Goldring, and Sarah Knight (eds), *The Progresses, Pageants, and Entertainments of Queen Elizabeth I* (Oxford, 2007), pp. 86–103.

Kelliher, Hilton, 'Francis Beaumont and Nathan Field: New Records of Their Early Years', in Peter Beal (ed.), *English Manuscript Studies 1100–1700, Volume 8: Seventeenth-Century Poetry, Music and Drama* (London, 2000), pp. 1–42.

Kellner, Leon, 'Die Quelle von Marlowe's *Jew of Malta*', *Englische Studien*, 10 (1887), 80–111.
Kelly, Erin E., 'Doubt and Religious Drama across Sixteenth-Century England, or Did the Middle Ages Believe in Their Plays?', in Jessica Dell, David Klausner, and Helen Ostovich (eds), *The Chester Cycle in Context, 1555-1575: Religion, Drama, and the Impact of Change* (Farnham, 2012), pp. 47–63.
Kelsall, Malcolm, *Christopher Marlowe* (Leiden, 1981).
Kendall, Roy, 'Richard Baines and Christopher Marlowe's Milieu', *ELR*, 24:3 (1994), 507–52.
Kenny, Anthony, 'Anthony Munday in Rome', *Recusant History*, 6 (1962), 158–62.
Kietzman, Mary Jo, *The Biblical Covenant in Shakespeare* (London, 2018).
King, Andrew, *The Faerie Queene and Middle English Romance: The Matter of Just Memory* (Oxford, 2000).
King, John N., *English Reformation Literature: The Tudor Origins of the Protestant Tradition* (Princeton, 1982).
Kingsley-Smith, Jane, *The Afterlife of Shakespeare's Sonnets* (Cambridge, 2019).
Kiséry, András, 'An Author and a Bookshop: Publishing Marlowe's Remains at the Black Bear', *Philological Quarterly*, 91:3 (2012), 361–92.
Knutson, Roslyn L., 'Marlowe, Company Ownership, and the Role of Edward II', in S. P. Cerasano (ed.), *MRDE, Vol. 18* (Madison, 2005), pp. 37–46.
Kocher, Paul H., 'Backgrounds for Marlowe's Atheist Lecture', in Baldwin Maxwell, W. D. Briggs, Francis R. Johnson, and E. N. S. Thompson (eds), *Renaissance Studies in Honor of Hardin Craig* (Stanford, 1941), pp. 112–32.
—— *Christopher Marlowe: A Study of His Thought, Learning, and Character* (1946; repr. New York, 1974).
—— *Science and Religion in Elizabethan England* (San Marino, 1953).
Kuin, Roger, 'Life, Death, and the Daughter of Time: Philip and Mary Sidney's Translation of Duplessis-Morney', in Catherine Gimelli Martin and Hassan Melehy (eds), *French Connections in the English Renaissance* (Aldershot, 2013), pp. 143–60.
Kuriyama, Constance Brown, *Christopher Marlowe: A Renaissance Life* (Ithaca, 2002).
—— 'Marlowe's Nemesis: The Identity of Richard Baines', in Kenneth Friedenreich, Roma Gill, and Constance B. Kuriyama (eds), *'A Poet and a Filthy Play-maker': New Essays on Christopher Marlowe* (New York, 1988), pp. 343–60.
—— 'Second Selves: Marlowe's Cambridge and London Friendships', in John Pitcher (ed.), *MRDE, Vol. 14* (Cranbury, NJ, 2001), pp. 86–104.
Lafont, Agnès, 'Multi-Layered Conversations in Marlowe's *Dido, Queen of Carthage*', in Janice Valls-Russell, Agnès Lafont, and Charlotte Coffin (eds), *Interweaving Myths in Shakespeare and His Contemporaries* (Manchester, 2017), pp. 195–215.
Lake, Peter, *Anglicans and Puritans? Presbyterianism and English Conformist Thought* (London, 1988).
—— and Michael Questier, *The Anti-Christ's Lewd Hat: Protestants, Papists and Players in Post-Reformation England* (New Haven, 2002).
Lamb, John, Masters, *History of the College of Corpus Christi* (London, 1831).
Le Goff, Jacques, 'The Whys and Ways of Writing a Biography: The Case of Saint Louis', *Exemplaria*, 1:1 (1989), 207–26.
Le Neve, John, *Fasti Ecclesiae Anglicanae* (3 vols, Oxford, 1854).

Leedham-Green, Elisabeth S., *Books in Cambridge Inventories: Book-Lists from Vice-Chancellor's Court Probate Inventories in the Tudor and Stuart Periods* (2 vols, Cambridge, 1986).

Levi, Giovanni, 'On Microhistory', in Peter Burke (ed.), *New Perspectives on Historical Writing*, 2nd edn (Cambridge, 2001), pp. 97–119.

—— 'The Uses of Biography', in Hans Renders and Binne de Hann (eds), *Theoretical Discussions of Biography: Approaches from History, Microhistory, and Life Writing*, rev. and augmented edn (Leiden, 2014), pp. 61–74.

Levin, Richard, 'The Contemporary Perception of Marlowe's Tamburlaine', in J. Leeds Barroll (ed.), *MRDE, Vol. 1* (New York, 1984), pp. 51–70.

Lewis, C. S., *English Literature in the Sixteenth Century Excluding Drama* (Oxford, 1954).

—— 'Hero and Leander', in *Selected Literary Essays* (Cambridge, 1969), pp. 58–73.

Loewenstein, David, *Treacherous Faith: The Specter of Heresy in Early Modern English Literature and Culture* (Oxford, 2013).

Loomie, Albert J., 'The Authorship of "An Advertisement Written to a Secretarie of M. L. Treasurer of England"', *Renaissance News*, 15:3 (1962), 201–7.

—— 'Philip II and the Printing of "Andreas Philopater"', *Library*, 5th ser., 24:2 (1969), 143–5.

MacCaffrey, Wallace T., *Queen Elizabeth and the Making of Policy, 1572–1588* (Princeton, 1981).

MacDonald, Michael, 'Religion, Social Change, and Psychological Healing in England, 1600–1800', in W. J. Sheils (ed.), *The Church and Healing* (Oxford, 1982).

MacLure, Millar, *The Paul's Cross Sermons 1534–1642* (Toronto, 1958).

Manning, Roger B., *An Apprenticeship in Arms: The Origins of the British Army 1585–1702* (Oxford, 2006).

Marcus, Leah, *Puzzling Shakespeare: Local Reading and Its Discontents* (Berkeley, 1988).

Marotti, Arthur F., 'Alienating Catholics in Early Modern England: Recusant Women, Jesuits and Ideological Fantasies', in Arthur F. Marotti (ed.), *Catholicism and Anti-Catholicism in Early Modern English Texts* (London, 1999), pp. 1–34.

Martin, Patrick H., and John Finnis, 'Thomas Thorpe, "W.S.", and the Catholic Intelligencers', *ELR*, 33:1 (2003), 3–43.

Martin, Richard A., 'Marlowe's Tamburlaine and the Language of Romance', *PMLA*, 93:2 (1978), 248–64.

Maslen, Robert W., 'Marlowe's Ghost: *The Second Report of Doctor John Faustus*', in Karin E. Olsen and Jan R. Veenstra (eds), *Airy Nothings: Imagining the Otherworld of Faerie from the Middle Ages to the Age of Reason: Essays in Honour of Alasdair A. MacDonald* (Leiden, 2014), pp. 1–23.

Massai, Sonia, 'Edward Blount, the Herberts, and the First Folio', in Marta Straznicky (ed.), *Shakespeare's Stationers: Studies in Cultural Bibliography* (Philadelphia, 2013), pp. 132–46.

Masson, David, *The Life of John Milton* (7 vols, Cambridge, 1859).

Masters, Robert, *The History of the College of Corpus Christi* (Cambridge, 1753–55).

Mateer, David, 'New Sightings of Christopher Marlowe in London', *Early Theatre*, 11:2 (2008), 13–38.

McCoog, Thomas M., '"Playing the Champion": The Role of Disputation in the Jesuit Mission', in Thomas M. McCoog (ed.), *The Reckoned Expense: Edmund Campion and the Early English Jesuits* (Woodbridge, 1996), pp. 119–39.

—— *The Society of Jesus in Ireland, Scotland, and England, 1541–1588: 'Our Way of Proceeding?'* (Leiden, 1996).

McCoy, Richard C., *The Rites of Knighthood: The Literature and Politics of Elizabethan Chivalry* (Berkeley, 1989).

McDonnell, Michael, *The Annals of St Paul's School* (Cambridge, 1959).

McGee, C. E., 'Puritans and Performers in Early Modern Dorset', *Early Theatre*, 6:1 (2003), 51–66.

McKim, Donald K., *Ramism in William Perkins' Theology* (New York, 1987).

McKisack, May, *Medieval History in the Tudor Age* (Oxford, 1971).

McMillin, Scott, and Sally-Beth MacLean, *The Queen's Men and Their Plays* (Cambridge, 1998).

McPherson, Miller, Lynn Smith-Lovin, and James M. Cook, 'Birds of a Feather: Homophily in Social Networks', *Annual Review of Sociology*, 27:1 (2001), 415–44.

Merriam, Thomas, 'Marlowe and Nashe in *Dido Queen of Carthage*', *N&Q*, 47:4 (2000), 425–8.

Mildenberger, Kenneth, 'Robert Greene at Cambridge', *Modern Language Notes*, 66:8 (1951), 546–9.

Millican, C. Bowie, 'The Supplicats for Spenser's Degrees', *HLQ*, 2:4 (1939), 467–70.

Minshull, Catherine, 'Marlowe's "Sound Machevill"', *Renaissance Drama*, NS, 13 (1982), 35–53.

Monta, Susannah Brietz, *Martyrdom and Literature in Early Modern England* (Cambridge, 2005).

Morgan, Victor, 'Cambridge University and "the Country"', in Lawrence Stone (ed.), *The University in Society: Oxford and Cambridge from the 14th to the Early 19th Century* (Princeton, 1975), pp. 183–245.

——, with a contribution by Christopher Brooke, *A History of the University of Cambridge, Volume II, 1546–1750* (Cambridge, 2004).

Mozley, J. F., *John Foxe and His Book* (1940; repr. New York, 1970).

Muldrew, Craig, *The Economy of Obligation: The Culture of Credit and Social Relations in Early Modern England* (Basingstoke, 1998).

Neill, Michael, *Issues of Death: Mortality and Identity in English Renaissance Tragedy* (Oxford, 1997).

Nelson, Alan, 'Contexts for Early English Drama: The Universities', in Marianne G. Briscoe and John C. Coldewey (eds), *Contexts for Early English Drama* (Bloomington, 1989), pp. 138–50.

—— *Monstrous Adversary: The Life of Edward de Vere, 17th Earl of Oxford* (Liverpool, 2003).

Nicholl, Charles, *A Cup of News: The Life of Thomas Nashe* (London, 1984).

—— *The Reckoning: The Murder of Christopher Marlowe* (London, 1992).

Nicolas, Harris, *Memoirs of the Life and Times of Sir Christopher Hatton* (London, 1847).

O'Day, Rosemary, *The English Clergy: The Emergence and Consolidation of a Profession 1558–1642* (Leicester, 1979).

Oliver, Leslie Mahin, 'John Foxe and *The Conflict of Conscience*', *RES*, OS, 25:97 (1949), 1–9.

Ong, Walter J., *Ramus, Method, and the Decay of Dialogue* (Cambridge, MA, 1958).
Orgel, Stephen, *The Authentic Shakespeare and Other Problems of the Early Modern Stage* (New York, 2002).
Owen, Dorothy M., *Cambridge University Archives: A Classified List* (Cambridge, 1998).
Paleit, Edward, *War, Liberty, and Caesar: Responses to Lucan's 'Bellum Ciuile', ca. 1580–1650* (Oxford, 2013).
Palliser, D. M., *Tudor York* (Oxford, 1979).
Paradise, N. Burton, *Thomas Lodge: The History of an Elizabethan* (1931; repr. Hamden, 1970).
Parker, Patricia, *Literary Fat Ladies: Rhetoric, Gender, Property* (London, 1987).
Parr, Johnston, 'Robert Greene and His Classmates at Cambridge', *PMLA*, 77:5 (1962), 536–43.
—— *Tamburlaine's Malady and Other Essays on Astrology in Elizabethan Drama* (Tuscaloosa, 1953).
Parry, Glyn, *The Arch-Conjuror of England: John Dee* (New Haven, 2011).
Patterson, Annabel, *Reading Holinshed's Chronicles* (Chicago, 1994).
Peacock, George, *Observations on the Statutes of the University of Cambridge* (London, 1841).
Peek, Heather, and Catherine Hall, *Archives of the University of Cambridge* (Cambridge, 1962).
Peel, Albert, *The Brownists in Norwich and Norfolk about 1580* (Cambridge, 1920).
Pelling, Margaret, and Charles Webster, 'Medical Practitioners', in Charles Webster (ed.), *Health, Medicine and Mortality in the Sixteenth Century* (Cambridge, 1979), pp. 165–235.
Phillips, Ellie, 'Account Rolles of the Great Hospital, Norwich, 1549–50 and 1570–71', in Ellie Phillips and Isla Fay (eds), *Health and Hygiene in Early-Modern Norwich* (Norwich, 2013), pp. 1–104.
Pinciss, G. M., 'Marlowe's Cambridge Years and the Writing of *Doctor Faustus*', *SEL*, 33:2 (1993), 249–64.
—— 'Thomas Creede and the Repertory of the Queen's Men 1583–1592', *Modern Philology*, 67:4 (1970), 321–30.
Pollmann, Judith, 'A Different Road to God: The Protestant Experience of Conversion in the Sixteenth Century', in Peter van der Veer (ed.), *Conversion to Modernities: The Globalization of Christianity* (New York, 1996), pp. 47–64.
Poole, Kristen, *Radical Religion from Shakespeare to Milton: Figures of Nonconformity in Early Modern England* (Cambridge, 2000).
Porter, H. C., *Reformation and Reaction in Tudor Cambridge* (Cambridge, 1958).
Pulman, Michael Barraclough, *The Elizabethan Privy Council in the Fifteen-Seventies* (Berkeley, 1971).
Purkiss, Diane, 'Marlowe's *Dido, Queen of Carthage* and the Representation of Elizabeth I', in Michael Burden (ed.), *A Woman Scorn'd: Responses to the Dido Myth* (London, 1998), pp. 151–67.
Questier, Michael C., *Conversion, Politics and Religion in England, 1580–1625* (Cambridge, 1996).
—— 'English Clerical Converts to Protestantism, 1580–1596', *Recusant History*, 20:4 (1991), 455–77.

Quinn, David B., and John W. Shirley, 'A Contemporary List of Hariot References', *Renaissance Quarterly*, 22:1 (1969), 9–26.

Rackham, Oliver, 'The Pseudo-Marlowe Portrait: A Wish Fulfilled?', *The Letter*, 93 (Corpus Christi College, Cambridge, Michaelmas 2014), 31–3.

Rackin, Phyllis, *Stages of History: Shakespeare's English Chronicles* (Ithaca, 1990).

Rapple, Rory, *Martial Power and Elizabethan Political Culture: Military Men in England and Ireland, 1558–1594* (Cambridge, 2009).

Rasmussen, Eric, 'The Black Book and the Date of Doctor Faustus', *N&Q*, 37:2 (1990), pp. 168–70.

—— *A Textual Companion to Doctor Faustus* (Manchester, 1993).

Rawcliffe, Carole, *Medicine for the Soul: The Life, Death, and Resurrection of an English Medieval Hospital St. Giles's, Norwich, c. 1249–1550* (Stroud, 1999).

Read, Conyers, *Lord Burghley and Queen Elizabeth* (London, 1960).

—— *Mr. Secretary Walsingham and the Policy of Queen Elizabeth* (3 vols, 1925; repr. New York, 1978).

—— 'William Cecil and Elizabethan Public Relations', in S. T. Bindoff, J. Hurstfield, and C. H. Williams (eds), *Elizabethan Government and Society: Essays Presented to Sir John Neale* (London, 1961), pp. 21–55.

Reagans, Ray, 'Close Encounters: Analyzing How Social Similarity and Propinquity Contribute to Strong Network Connections', *Organization Science*, 22:4 (2011), 835–49.

Reed, Robert Rentoul Jr, *Crime and God's Judgment in Shakespeare* (Lexington, 1984).

—— *The Occult on the Tudor and Stuart Stage* (Boston, 1965).

Reid, Lindsay Ann, 'The Spectre of the School of Night: Former Scholarly Fictions and the Stuff of Academic Fiction', *Early Modern Literary Studies*, special issue, 23 (2014), 1–31.

Reynolds, Matthew, *Godly Reformers and Their Opponents in Early Modern England: Religion in Norwich, c. 1560–1643* (Woodbridge, 2005).

Rhodes, Neil, *The Power of Eloquence and English Renaissance Literature* (Hemel Hempstead, 1992).

Ribner, Irving, 'The Idea of History in Marlowe's *Tamburlaine*', *ELH*, 20:4 (1953), 251–66.

Richardson, Brenda, 'Robert Greene's Yorkshire Connexions: A New Hypothesis', *Yearbook of English Studies*, 10 (1980), 160–80.

Ricks, Christopher, '*Doctor Faustus* and Hell on Earth', *Essays in Criticism*, 35:2 (1985), 101–20.

Riggs, David, 'Marlowe's Quarrel with God', in Paul Whitfield White (ed.), *Marlowe, History, and Sexuality: New Critical Essays on Christopher Marlowe* (New York, 1998), pp. 15–37.

—— *The World of Christopher Marlowe* (London, 2004).

Roberts, Peter, 'Christopher Marlowe at Corpus, 1580–87', *Pelican: The Magazine of Corpus Christi College Cambridge*, 26 (Easter 2014), 22–31.

—— 'Dr Robert Norgate, Master of Corpus, 1573–87', *Letter of the Corpus Association*, 86 (Michaelmas 2007), 12–22.

—— '"The Studious Artizan": Christopher Marlowe, Canterbury and Cambridge', in Darryll Grantley and Peter Roberts (eds), *Christopher Marlowe and English Renaissance Culture* (Aldershot, 1996), pp. 17–37.

Robertson, Jean, 'The Early Life of George Chapman', *MLR*, 40:3 (1945), 157–65.
Rosenthal, Robert, *Papers of Sir Nicholas Bacon in the University of Chicago Library* (Chicago, 1989).
Rostenberg, Leona, *Literary, Political, Scientific, Religious and Legal Publishing, Printing and Bookselling in England, 1551–1700: Twelve Studies* (2 vols, New York, 1965).
Roth, Cecil, 'The Jews of Malta', *Transactions of the Jewish Historical Society of England*, 12 (1928–31), 187–251.
Roth, Cecil, et al. (eds), *Encyclopaedia Judaica* (16 vols, Jerusalem, 1972).
Rothstein, Eric, 'Structure as Meaning in *The Jew of Malta*', *JEGP*, 65:2 (1966), 260–73.
Rowse, A. L., *Christopher Marlowe: A Biography* (London, 1964).
Russell, Frederick H., *The Just War in the Middle Ages* (Cambridge, 1975).
Rutter, Tom, 'Marlowe, the "Mad Priest of the Sun", and Heliogabalus', *Early Theatre*, 13:1 (2010), 109–19.
Ryrie, Alec, *The Gospel and Henry VIII: Evangelicals in the Early English Reformation* (Cambridge, 2003).
Sales, Roger, *Christopher Marlowe*, English Dramatists (Basingstoke, 1991).
Saunders, H. W., *A History of the Norwich Grammar School* (Norwich, 1932).
Schoenbaum, Samuel, *William Shakespeare: A Compact Documentary Life* (1978; repr. Oxford, 1987).
Scouloudi, Irene, *Returns of Strangers in the Metropolis 1593, 1627, 1635, 1639: A Study of an Active Minority* (London, 1985).
Seaton, Ethel, 'Fresh Sources for Marlowe', *RES*, OS, 5:20 (1929), 385–401.
—— 'Marlowe, Robert Poley, and the Tippings', *RES*, OS, 5:19 (1929), 273–87.
Shapiro, James, *Rival Playwrights: Marlowe, Jonson, Shakespeare* (New York, 1991).
—— *Shakespeare and the Jews* (New York, 1996).
Shapiro, Michael, *Children of the Revels: The Boy Companies of Shakespeare's Time and Their Plays* (New York, 1977).
Sharpe, J. A., *Defamation and Sexual Slander in Early Modern England: The Church Courts at York* (York, 1980).
Sharpe, James, *Instruments of Darkness: Witchcraft in England, 1550–1750* (London, 1996).
Shell, Alison, *Catholicism, Controversy and the English Literary Imagination, 1558–1660* (Cambridge, 1999).
Shenk, Linda, 'Gown before Crown: Scholarly Abjection and Academic Entertainment under Queen Elizabeth I', in Jonathan Walker and Paul D. Streufert (eds), *Early Modern Academic Drama* (Farnham, 2008), pp. 19–44.
Shepard, Alexandra, 'Contesting Communities? "Town" and "Gown" in Cambridge, c. 1560–1640', in Alexandra Shepard and Phil Withington (eds), *Communities in Early Modern England: Networks, Place, Rhetoric* (Manchester, 2000), pp. 216–34.
—— 'Legal Learning and the Cambridge University Courts, c. 1560–1640', *Journal of Legal History*, 19:1 (1998), 62–74.
—— *Meanings of Manhood in Early Modern England* (Oxford, 2003).
Shepherd, Alan, *Marlowe's Soldiers: Rhetorics of Masculinity in the Age of the Armada* (Aldershot, 2002).

Sheppard, Kenneth, *Anti-Atheism in Early Modern England 1580–1720: The Atheist Answered and His Error Confuted* (Leiden, 2015).
Sherman, William H., *John Dee: The Politics of Reading and Writing in the English Renaissance* (Amherst, 1995).
Shirley, Frances A., *Swearing and Perjury in Shakespeare's Plays* (London, 1979).
Shrewsbury, J. F. D., *A History of Bubonic Plague in the British Isles* (1970; repr. Cambridge, 1971).
Simkin, Stevie, *Marlowe: The Plays* (Basingstoke, 2001).
Sims, James H., *Dramatic Uses of Biblical Allusions in Marlowe and Shakespeare* (Gainesville, FL, 1966).
Sinfield, Alan, *Literature in Protestant England 1560–1660* (London, 1983).
Singer, Irving, 'Erotic Transformations in the Legend of Dido and Aeneas', *Modern Language Notes*, 90:6 (1975), 767–83.
Skalnik, James Veazie, *Ramus and Reform: University and Church at the End of Renaissance* (Kirksville, MO, 2002).
Skretkowicz, Victor, 'Chivalry in Sidney's Arcadia', in Sydney Anglo (ed.), *Chivalry in the Renaissance* (Woodbridge, 1990), pp. 161–74.
Slack, Paul, *The Impact of Plague in Tudor and Stuart England* (London, 1985).
Smith, A. Hassell, *County and Court: Government and Politics in Norfolk 1558–1603* (Oxford, 1974).
—— 'The Gardens of Sir Nicholas and Sir Francis Bacon: An Enigma Resolved and a Mind Explored', in Anthony Fletcher and Peter Roberts (eds), *Religion, Culture and Society in Early Modern Britain: Essays in Honour of Patrick Collinson* (Cambridge, 1994), pp. 125–60.
Smith, G. C. Moore, 'Marlowe at Cambridge', *MLR*, 4:2 (1909), 167–77.
—— 'Matthew Roydon', *MLR*, 9:1 (1914), 97–8.
Smith, Hallett, 'Tamburlaine and the Renaissance', in E. J. West (ed.), *Elizabethan Studies and Other Essays in Honor of George F. Reynolds* (Boulder, CO, 1945), pp. 126–31.
Solt, Leo F., *Church and State in Early Modern England 1509–1640* (New York, 1990).
Somerville, Robert, *The Savoy: Manor, Hospital, Chapel* (London, 1960).
Spence, Leslie, 'The Influence of Marlowe's Sources on Tamburlaine I', *Modern Philology*, 24:2 (1926), 181–99.
Stark, Adam, *The History and Antiquities of Gainsburgh* (London, 1817).
Steane, J. B., *Marlowe: A Critical Study* (Cambridge, 1964).
Stern, V. F., *Sir Stephen Powle of Court and Country* (Selinsgrove, 1992).
Stokes, H. P., *Corpus Christi* (London, 1898).
Stone, Lawrence, 'The Educational Revolution in England, 1560–1640', *Past & Present*, 28 (1964), 41–80.
—— 'The Size and Composition of the Oxford Student Body 1580–1910', in Lawrence Stone (ed.), *The University in Society: Oxford and Cambridge from the 14th to the Early 19th Century* (Princeton, 1975), pp. 3–110.
Strathmann, Ernest A., 'John Dee as Ralegh's "Conjurer"', *HLQ*, 10:4 (1947), 365–72.
—— *Sir Walter Ralegh: A Study in Elizabethan Skepticism* (1951; repr. New York, 1973).
Strickland, Ronald, 'Pageantry and Poetry as Discourse: The Production of Subjectivity in Sir Philip Sidney's Funeral', *ELH*, 57:1 (1990), 19–36.

Strong, Roy, *Gloriana: The Portraits of Queen Elizabeth I* (London, 1987).
Strype, John, *Annals of the Reformation* (4 vols, Oxford, 1824).
—— *The History of the Life and Acts of the Most Reverend Father in God, Edmund Grindal* (Oxford, 1821).
—— *The Life and Acts of John Whitgift* (3 vols, Oxford, 1822).
—— *The Life and Acts of Matthew Parker* (3 vols, Oxford, 1821).
Stump, Donald, 'Marlowe's Travesty of Virgil: *Dido* and Elizabethan Dreams of Empire', *Comparative Drama*, 34:1 (2000), 79–107.
Sullivan, Erin, 'Doctrinal Doubleness and the Meaning of Despair in William Perkins's "Table" and Nathaniel Woodes' *The Conflict of Conscience*', *Studies in Philology*, 110:3 (2013), 533–61.
Sullivan, Vickie, 'Princes to Act: Henry V as the Machiavellian Prince of Appearance', in Joseph Alulis and Vickie Sullivan (eds), *Shakespeare's Political Pageant: Essays in Politics and Literature* (Lanham, 1996), pp. 125–52.
Syme, Holger Schott, 'Marlowe in His Moment', in Emily C. Bartels and Emma Smith (eds), *Christopher Marlowe in Context* (Cambridge, 2013), pp. 275–84.
Symonds, Henry, 'The Mint of Queen Elizabeth and Those Who Worked There', *Numismatic Chronicle*, 4th ser., 16 (1916), 61–105.
Tannenbaum, Samuel, *The Assassination of Christopher Marlowe* (New York, 1926).
Tanner, J. R., *The Historical Register of the University of Cambridge* (1917; repr. Cambridge, 1984).
Taylor, E. G. R., 'The "Doctrine of Nauticall Triangles Compendious" I: Thomas Hariot's Manuscript', *Journal of the Institute of Navigation*, 6 (1953), 131–40.
Thomas, Keith, *Religion and the Decline of Magic* (London, 1971).
Thomas, Vivien, and William Tydeman, *Christopher Marlowe: The Plays and Their Sources* (London, 1994).
Thorn-Drury, G., 'George Chapman', *RES*, OS, 1:3 (1925), 350.
Thrush, Andrew, and John P. Ferris (eds), *The House of Commons 1604–1629* (6 vols, Cambridge, 2010).
Tittler, Robert, *Nicholas Bacon: The Making of a Tudor Statesman* (Athens, OH, 1976).
Todd, Margo, *Christian Humanism and the Puritan Social Order* (Cambridge, 1987).
Tosh, Will, *Male Friendship and Testimonies of Love in Shakespeare's England* (London, 2016).
Turner, Celeste, *Anthony Munday: An Elizabethan Man of Letters* (Berkeley, 1928).
Tydeman, William, and Vivien Thomas, 'One Play or Two?', in William Tydeman and Vivien Thomas (eds), *Christopher Marlowe: A Guide through the Critical Maze* (Bristol, 1989).
Urry, William, *Christopher Marlowe and Canterbury*, ed. with intro. by Andrew Butcher (London, 1988).
—— 'John Lyly and Canterbury', *Friends of Canterbury Cathedral Annual Report*, 33 (1960), 19–25.
—— 'Some Forgotten Schools in Tudor Canterbury', in M. H. A. Berry and J. H. Higginson (eds), *Canterbury Chapters: A Kentish Heritage for Tomorrow* (Liverpool, 1976), pp. 98–105.
Usher, Brett, 'The Fortunes of English Puritanism: An Elizabethan Perspective', in Kenneth Fincham and Peter Lake (eds), *Religious Politics in Post-Reformation England: Essays in Honour of Nicholas Tyacke* (Woodbridge, 2006).

Usher, Roland G., *The Rise and Fall of the High Commission*, with new intro. by Philip Tyler (Oxford, 1968).
Van Winkle, Kathryn Rebecca, '"Then Speak, Aeneas, with Achilles' Tongue": Ethopoeia and Elizabethan Boyhood in Marlowe's *Dido Queen of Carthage*', in David S. Thompson (ed.), *Theatre Symposium: A Publication of the Southeastern Theatre Conference, Vol. 23, Theatre and Youth* (Tuscaloosa, 2015), pp. 42–51.
Venn, John, *Biographical History of Gonville and Caius College 1349–1897* (3 vols, Cambridge, 1897).
Venn, John, and John Archibald Venn, *Alumni Cantabrigienses: Part I, from the Earliest Times to 1751* (4 vols, Cambridge, 1922).
Vickers, Brian, '"Upstart Crow"? The Myth of Shakespeare's Plagiarism', *RES*, NS, 68:284 (2017), 244–67.
Vogt, George McGill, 'Richard Robinson's *Eupolemia* (1603)', *Studies in Philology*, 21:4 (1924), 629–48.
Waith, E. M., *The Herculean Hero in Marlowe, Chapman, Shakespeare and Dryden* (London, 1962).
Walker, D. P., 'Ways of Dealing with Atheists: A Background to Pamela's Refutation of Cecropia', *Bibliothèque d'Humanisme et Renaissance*, 17:2 (1955), 252–77.
Walker, Jonathan, 'Learning to Play', in Jonathan Walker and Paul D. Streufert (eds), *Early Modern Academic Drama* (Farnham, 2008), pp. 1–18.
Wallace, Dewey D., 'From Eschatology to Arian Heresy: The Case of Francis Kett', *Harvard Theological Review*, 67:4 (1974), 459–73.
Walsham, Alexandra, '"Frantick Hacket": Prophecy, Sorcery, Insanity, and the Elizabethan Puritan Movement', *Historical Journal*, 41:1 (1998), 27–66.
—— *Providence in Early Modern England* (Oxford, 1999).
Warneke, Sara, *Images of the Educational Traveller in Early Modern England* (Leiden, 1995).
Watkins, John, *The Specter of Dido: Spenser and Virgilian Epic* (New Haven, 1995).
Webb, E. A., G. W. Miller, and J. Beckwith, *The History of Chislehurst: Its Church, Manors, and Parish* (London, 1899).
Weil, Judith, *Christopher Marlowe: Merlin's Prophet* (Cambridge, 1977).
Wernham, R. B., *Before the Armada: The Growth of English Foreign Policy 1485–1588* (London, 1966).
—— 'Christopher Marlowe at Flushing in 1592', *EHR*, 91:359 (1976), 344–5.
Westley, Richard, 'Computing Error: Reassessing Austin's Study of *Groatsworth of Wit*', *Literary and Linguistic Computing*, 21:3 (2006), 363–78.
White, B. R., *The English Separatist Tradition: From the Marian Martyrs to the Pilgrim Fathers* (Oxford, 1971).
White, Paul Whitfield, *Drama and Religion in English Provincial Society, 1485–1660* (Cambridge, 2008).
—— 'The Pammachius Affair at Christ's College, Cambridge in 1545', in Peter Happé and Wim Hüsken (eds), *Interlude and Early Modern Society: Studies in Gender, Power and Theatricality* (Amsterdam, 2007), pp. 261–90.
—— 'The Queen's Men in Elizabethan Cambridge', in Helen Ostovich, Holger Schott Syme, and Andrew Griffin (eds), *Locating the Queen's Men 1583–1603: Material Practices and Conditions of Playing* (Farnham, 2009), pp. 41–9.
—— *Theatre and Reformation: Protestantism, Patronage, and Playing in Tudor England* (Cambridge, 1993).

White, Peter, *Predestination, Policy and Polemic: Conflict and Consensus in the English Church from the Reformation to the Civil War* (Cambridge, 1992).

Wickham, Glynne, Herbert Berry, and William Ingram (eds), *English Professional Theatre 1530–1660* (Cambridge, 2000).

Wiener, Carol Z., 'The Beleaguered Isle: A Study of Elizabethan and Early Jacobean Anti-Catholicism', *Past & Present*, 51 (1971), 27–62.

Wiggins, Martin, 'When Did Marlowe Write Dido, Queen of Carthage?', *RES*, NS, 59:241 (2008), 521–41.

——, in association with Catherine Richardson, *British Drama 1533–1642: A Catalogue* (11 vols, Oxford, 2012–).

Wigmore, John H., 'The History of the Hearsay Rule', *Harvard Law Review*, 17:7 (1904), 437–58.

Williams, Deanne, 'Dido, Queen of England', *ELH*, 72:1 (2006), 31–59.

Williams, Franklin B., *Index of Dedications and Commendatory Verses in English Books before 1641* (London, 1962).

Williams, Penry, *The Later Tudors: England 1547–1603* (Oxford, 1995).

Willis, Robert, and John Willis Clark, *The Architectural History of the University of Cambridge and of the Colleges of Cambridge and Eton* (4 vols, Cambridge, 1886).

Wilson, John Dover, 'The Missing Title of Thomas Lodge's Reply to Gosson's *School of Abuse*', *MLR*, 3:2 (1908), 166–8.

Wilson, Richard, *Will Power: Essays on Shakespearean Authority* (Detroit, 1993).

Wind, Edgar, *Pagan Mysteries in the Renaissance* (1958; enlarged and repr. New York, 1968).

Wine, Celesta, 'Nathaniel Woodes: Author of the Morality Play *The Conflict of Conscience*', *RES*, OS, 15:60 (1939), 458–63.

Winkelman, Michael A., *Marriage Relationships in Tudor Political Drama* (Aldershot, 2005).

Winters, William, *Biographical Notes on John Foxe the Martyrologist, with an Account of His Family and Friends at Waltham Abbey* (Waltham Abbey, Essex, 1876).

Wolf, Lucien, 'Jews in Elizabethan England', *Transactions of the Jewish Historical Society of England*, 11 (1924–27), 1–91.

Woolfson, Jonathan, *Padua and the Tudors: English Students in Italy, 1485–1603* (Cambridge, 1998).

—— 'The Paduan Sojourns of Samuel and Simeon Foxe', *Quaderni per la storia dell'Università di Padova*, 30 (1997), 111–24.

Wootton, David, 'New Histories of Atheism', in Michael Hunter and David Wootton (eds), *Atheism from the Reformation to the Enlightenment* (Oxford, 1992), pp. 13–53.

—— 'Reginald Scot / Abraham Fleming / The Family of Love', in Stuart Clark (ed.), *Languages of Witchcraft: Narrative, Ideology and Meaning in Early Modern Culture* (Basingstoke, 2001), pp. 119–38.

Woudhuysen, H. R., *Sir Philip Sidney and the Circulation of Manuscripts 1558–1640* (Oxford, 1996).

Wraight, A. D., and Virginia F. Stern, *In Search of Christopher Marlowe: A Pictorial Biography* (Chichester, 1993).

Wrightson, Keith, *Earthly Necessities: Economic Lives in Early Modern Britain* (New Haven, 2000).

Yamada, Yuzo, *Writing under Influences: A Study of Christopher Marlowe* (Tokyo, 1999).
Yates, Frances A., *The Art of Memory* (London, 1966).
Youngs, Frederic A. Jr, 'Definitions of Treason in an Elizabethan Proclamation', *Historical Journal*, 14:4 (1971), 675–91.
Zagorin, Perez, Ways of Lying: *Dissimulation, Persecution, and Conformity in Early Modern Europe* (Cambridge, MA, 1990).

INDEX

Aaron 304–5, 306
Abbys, Christopher
  career 53–4
  as disseminator of rumour 113, 272
  eulogy to Butts 54, 101 n.38
  Norwich Scholar and Fellow 36, 40, 51, 54, 58, 358
  old-boy network with Greene 59, 62, 272
  supports the expulsion of Hickman 54, 105, 106–7, 109, 113
  tutorial relationship with Aldrich 76
Absalon, William 65–6, 83
Acerbas (Sychaeus) 156, 157
Adam 258
Adams, Simon 118
Admiral's Company 127, 128, 280, 281, 324
Aduertisement and Defence for Trueth against Her Backbiters, An 219
Aeneas 150, 159
  representation of 156–8, 160–1, 165, 166–73
Agazario, Alfonso 92
Alasco, Albertus, palatine of Sieradż 159, 160, 161
Aldrich, Henry
  antipathy to attaining degrees 52
  censures Parker 50
  Norwich Fellow 36, 39
  Norwich network 62
  one of the pro-Aldrich faction 42
  resignation of 40, 56
  tutorial payments to 76
Aldrich, John 40, 60
  and Norwich puritanism 45
  as patron of players 47
  recommends Harrison as schoolmaster 43, 50
  relationship with Sotherton 49
Aldrich, Simon 313
Aldrich, Thomas

allies 42, 45, 62
antipathy to attaining degrees 52
censures Parker 41, 50
Corpus's radical generation of 247, 251
faction against 42, 45
relationship with Parker 40–1
resigns mastership 41–2, 51
sympathy with Presbyterian movement 41
as writer of an academic play 46
Aldye, Villers 84
Allen, William
  activities 92–3, 213, 301
  An Apologie and True Declaration 297
  on atheism 299, 304
  criticized by Burghley 296
  Imprisonnement of Iohn Nicols 213, 223
  loathing for pamphlets 222–3
Alleyn, Edward 124, 128, 269
Amalekites 191, 192, 194, 195
anabaptist 256, 261, 297
Anderson, Anthony 194–5, 320 n.85
anti-Christ 150, 181, 195, 196, 197, 199, 201, 202
anti-Martinists 23, 110, 244
  basic policy of 254, 257
  smear campaign of 253
  See also Martin Marprelate
anti-theatricalism 209–10, 211, 215, 272, 279–80, 281, 288–9, 317–18, 322, 329, 332
apocalyptic vision 195–6, 198, 199, 200–1
Aquaviva, Claudio 92, 219
Archer, John 28
Arianism 258, 309
Aristotle 240, 242, 244, 258
  Analytics 239
  Natural Philosophy 238
  Organon 238, 245, 246

Index

Armada, The 157, 163, 195, 197, 201, 202, 220, 268, 276, 320
Arthington, Henry 252, 253, 261
Arthur, (legendary) King of Britain 179, 180, 181, 184, 197
Arthur, Thomas 229, 234
Arundel, Charles 305
Ascham, Roger 258
Aske, James 157
   Elizabetha Triumphans 157
atheists, atheism
   apologetics against 23, 29, 285–7, 294, 304, 306, 310
   cause of 299
   as defamatory term 270, 285
   definition of 285
   inventing 255–6, 305–6, 312
   recantation of 315
   threat of 26, 310, 312
Auberlen, Eckhard 283
Augustinus, St Aurelius 254, 255, 301
Austen, William
   Eastbridge Scholar 68, 361
   financial hardship 68–9
   friendship with Marlowe 72–3, 102
   pawns Marley's cloak to Hayes 67–8, 242
   seeks career out of the Church 99, 101
   trouble with Gee 71–2, 89
   tutorial relationship with Thexton 69, 75, 76
   autobiography 63, 282–3
   See also autobiographical hermeneutics *under* Robert Greene
Averell, William 222
Aylsham, Norfolk 38, 49, 51, 69, 74, 75, 76
Aylsham Grammar School 37, 43, 50, 247

Babington plot, plotters 216–17
Babraham, Cambridgeshire 103
Babylon 195, 196, 201, 202, 269
Bacon, Anthony 87, 122, 235, 307
Bacon, Edmund 38
Bacon, Sir Francis
   close associate of Fulbecke 205 n.79
   negative of Bancroft's strategy 254
Bacon, James 38
Bacon, Sir Nicholas, Lord Keeper

chamber plan of 1577 14–16, 17, 34, 35, 36, 37, 38, 74, 78
connection with Corpus Christi 16
'eye for detail' 16, 100
foundation for scholarship 14–16, 38–9, 97–8, 100
Baines, Richard
   atheism 213
   Baines Note 306, 308–11, 313
   espionage activities 25, 114, 134, 213
   hearsay about Marlowe 20, 25, 28, 29, 234
   hostility towards Marlowe 26, 132, 134
   monetary motivation of theatrics 213–14
   recantation 212
   theatrical dissimulation 212–13
   in Vlissingen 26, 131–2, 134, 213
Baines, Thomas 12
Bakeless, John 4, 295
Baker, John 301
Balaam, prophet 191–2, 204
Ballard, John 94
Bamford, James 321
   A Short Dialogve Concerning the Plagves Infection 321–2
Bancroft, Richard, Bishop of London
   criticism against 254
   ecclesiastical regime with Whitgift 53
   journalistic capacity 253–4, 255
   organizes anti-Martinists 110, 244, 251–2
   protégé of 236
   representation of puritanism 253, 254–6, 257
   Sermon Preached at Paules Crosse 254
   suppression of heresy 23
Barber, C. L. 189
Barbour, Reed 282
Barham, Kent 314
Barnard, Robert 129
Barrow, Henry 248, 250, 252, 253, 255, 256
Barthes, Roland 346
   'biographeme' 346
Basel, Switzerland 123
Battenhouse, Roy W. 184, 199
Bauckham, Richard 195–6, 260
Bawcutt, N. W. 209, 217, 226
Beadle, Samuel

400

accommodated in the storehouse   38,
     74
  Canterbury Scholar   360
  Marlowe's roommate   74–5
  master of Boston Grammar
     School   76–8
  from the parish of St George in
     Canterbury   37
  witnesses on behalf of Thexton   69,
     75, 76
Beard, Thomas   276, 335
  The Theatre of Gods Iudgements   335
Becket, William   59, 359
Beckwith, J.   343
Bell, Gary M.   129
Belleforest, François de   214–15
Belsavage playhouse   316
Benchkin, John   19, 73, 234
Benchkin, Katherine   10, 234
Benet College see Corpus Christi College,
     Cambridge
Bernard de Clairvaux   255
Bevington, David   293
Bible
  Acts 2   186
  Colossians 3   208 n.3
  II Corinthians 3   258
  II Corinthians 11   208
  Deuteronomy 18   186
  Deuteronomy 20   191
  Ephesians 6   187
  Joel 2   198
  Joshua 7   191
  2 Kings 18   151
  Numbers 22–23   192
  Numbers 24   192
  II Peter 2   192
  Psalm 14   294, 314
  Psalm 110   198
  Psalm 133   182
  Psalm 139   327
  Revelation 2   192
  Revelation 6   199, 200
  Revelation 16   201
  1 Samuel 15   190, 192
biblical analogy   195–7, 198
biography
  as critical methodology   1, 27–8
  microscopic approach of   3–4, 5, 12
  the new role of   2–3
Bird, Samuel   35
Blackfriars playhouse   152
Bland, Tobias   109, 246

A Baite for Momus   110
'A necessary Cathechisme'   109–10
blasphemy
  definition of   287
  against Diana   163
  divine retribution for   310–11, 316,
     317
  English gentlemen studying   301
  on stage   268, 278–9, 280, 288–9, 294,
     305, 313
Blount, Edward
  apprenticeship   336
  dedication of *Hero and Leander*   336
  description of Marlowe   7, 336
  friendship with Marlowe   337, 338–9,
     340
  one of the 'compeers by night'   345–6
  publication project   339, 341–4, 346
  relationship with patrons   338–9, 342
  taste for literature   336
Boas, Frederic S.   4, 163–4, 270–1
Boleyn, Anne, Queen of England   343
Bolton, Robert   209
Boston, Lincolnshire   77
Boston Grammar School   77
Botelho, Keith M.   20
Bowes, Thomas
  anti-atheist apologetics   286–7, 294
  on Robert Greene   287
  *The Second Part of French
     Academie*   286
Boyle, Richard, later 1st Earl of Coke   85
Braborne, Richard   38, 76, 356
Bradley, William   86, 125, 135
Braunmuller, A. R.   341
Bray, Alan   12
Bredwell, Stephen   248
Breight, Curtis C.   308
Bridgham, St Mary, Norfolk   52
Briggs, Julia   88
Bright, Arthur   53
Bristol   53
Brome, John   106
Bromley, Sir Thomas   182
Brooke, C. F. Tucker   4
Brooke, Sir William, 10th Baron
     Cobham   84, 115, 235
Brookes, Thomas   103, 104
Brown, Georgia E.   338
Browne, Robert   43, 51, 247, 248, 249,
     259
Brownists, Brownism   248, 251, 255
Brownrigge, Henry   99, 101, 360

Bull, Eleanor   135, 345
Bullinger, Heinrich   194
  Decades   194
Burghley, Lord *see* William Cecil
Burman, John   99, 362
Burton, Edward   94
Burton, Robert   119, 322
  The Anatomy of Melancholy   322
Burton, William   61, 209
Butcher, Andrew   3
Butts, Sir William   54 n.72, 100
Bynneman, Henry   240

Calvin, John   238, 301
Cambridge, city of   43, 52, 67, 77, 153, 247, 269
  Great St Mary's Church   95, 243
  St Bene't's Church   247
Cambridge University
  academic drama   21, 46, 149–52, 153, 155, 173–4
  'act verses'   297
  admonition to   65
  Catholicism   90, 92, 93, 95, 97, 150
  college *see individual colleges*
  college networks   4, 33, 57, 60, 62, 87–8, 272
  commencement   8, 73
  on the death of Elizabeth I   157
  disputatious atmosphere   24, 41, 95–6, 150, 159, 240–3, 246, 251, 258
  dress code   66–7
  everyday lives of scholars   64–5, 151–2, 238–9
  fellow *see separate entry*
  fellow-commoner   64, 65, 93
  humanist curriculum   239
  infected with emerging heresy   256, 258
  interests in religious matters   242–3
  'lewd wags' in   63
  'little ape' in   273
  pensioner   6, 68, 84, 94, 104, 245, 246
  Presbyterian movement   43, 243
  proctor   8, 18, 70, 112, 271
  questionist   8, 9, 11
  sizar   59, 62, 94
  social community   3, 12, 39, 93, 102, 242
  social role   97–8, 149
  social strata   64, 91, 94
  supplicat *see separate entry*

town and gown   67, 70
tutor   65, 67, 72
vice-chancellor's court *see separate entry*
Camden, William   260
Campion, Edmund   211, 218
Canterbury, Kent   3, 4, 19, 37, 66, 74, 77, 83, 85, 229, 234, 235, 250, 271, 317
  Eastbridge Hospital   68
  King's School *see separate entry*
  St George the Martyr   37, 74
  St Stephen   86
Carey, Henry, 1st Baron Hunsdon   114, 304
Carey, John   1
Cartwright, Thomas   41, 42, 46, 62, 243, 251, 252
Case, John   241
  Speculum moralium qvaestionum   241
Catholicism   49, 50, 90, 93, 95, 129, 132, 151, 217, 228
Cave, Henry   275
Cecil, John (alias Snowden)   123
Cecil, Robert, 1st Earl of Salisbury   80, 304
Cecil, William, 1st Baron Burghley   41, 42, 107, 108, 126, 131, 229, 254
  atheism criticized   299, 301, 304
  attends Halliwell's *Dido*   150, 158
  attitude towards Croft's peace negotiations   115
  chancellor of Cambridge University   9, 65, 114, 116
  commissions of English comedies   153
  The Copy of a Letter ... to Don Bernardin Mendoza   221 n.53
  The Execution of Justice in England   219
  hostility towards seminary priests   219, 296, 298
  as part of the 'inner ring'   118
  pursues Habsburg marriage negotiation   159
  recommends his protégé to fellowship   55–6, 105
  relationship with Marlowe   117, 134
  relationship with Walsingham   115
  on watchmen searching conspirators   217
Cecil, William (grandson of Lord Burghley)   123

Index

Cerne Abbas, Dorset 302
Chaderton, Lawrence 241
Chapman, Edmund 62
Chapman, George
   All Fools 340
   Batrachomyomachia 131
   The Blind Beggar of Alexandria 344
   case against Wolfall 130
   The Conspiracy and Tragedy of Charles Duke of Byron 339, 340, 341
   dedication to the Walsinghams 339, 340, 341
   financial distress 128, 130, 344
   Hero and Leander see under Christopher Marlowe
   An Humorous Day's Mirth 344
   literary reputation 130, 344
   Ovid's Banquet of Senses 344
   patronage of Sadler 130–1
   relationship with Thomas Walsingham 340–1
   as 'rival poet' 345
   Seaven Bookes of the Jliades 344
   The Shadow of Night 344
Charier, Benjamin 12, 71, 361
   memorial note 74–5
Charles II, Archduke of Austria 159
Chartier, Roger 5
Chatterley, Albert 125
Cheney, Patrick 291
cherem, the concept of 190–1, 193, 201, 202
Chester Cycle plays 305
Chettle, Henry
   authorship of *Groatsworth* 292–3
   financial dependency on Henslowe 128
   friendship with Greene 292
   Kind-Harts Dreame 292, 308, 330
   prejudice against Marlowe 294
   role in *Groatsworth* 293, 337
Chever, Robert 16, 111, 112
Children of the Chapel 152, 154–5
Children of Paul's 155
Cholmeley, Richard
   esteems his own wit 304
   hearsay report by 25, 28, 29
   invents atheists 304, 306–7, 308
   organizes atheists for conspiracy 303
   relationship with Marlowe 306
   religious opinions 304–5
   'Remembraunces' 303, 304, 307, 308

Christ, Jesus 26, 200, 203, 204, 228, 258, 304–5
Christ's College, Cambridge 12, 62, 149, 241
Church, Stephen 65–7, 83
   letter to Lord Burghley 65–6
Cicero, Marcus Tullius 159, 238, 240, 241
civic chivalry 176, 177, 179, 181–2, 184, 185, 188, 195, 197
Clapham, Henoch 191
Clare Hall, Cambridge 70
Clark, G. Kitson 27
Clark, Peter 85
Clarke, John 99, 363
Clifton, Robin 220
Clugston, George Alan 276
Clyomon and Clamydes 176
Cobler of Canterbury, The 270
Coke, Sir Edward 25, 27
Coldwell, John 228, 229, 234
Coldwell, Thomas 234
collective experience 2, 3, 5, 12, 17, 346
Collier, J. P. 315
Collinson, Patrick 247, 251
Confutation of the Tenne Great Plagues, A 275
Constable, Henry 128
Constantinople 119, 214, 325
conversion, changing religion 92, 96–7, 226, 282–3
Cooper, Elizabeth 49
Cooper, Thomas
   Thesaurus 74–5
Copcot, John
   death 109
   elected as master 106
   expels Hickman 104, 105
   henchmen of 106–7, 108–9
   prejudice against Hickman 54, 107–8
   relationship with Whitgift 107, 109, 113
Coppinger, Edmund 252, 253, 261
Corbet, Thomas 36, 75, 355
Corbold, Thomas 100, 362
Corkine, William 135, 235
Cornwallis, Sir William 80
Corpus Christi College, Cambridge
   'absentee' students 69, 71, 121
   academic plays 46, 153–4
   accommodation crisis 33–4, 35
   annuity of Great Hospital to 58
   Audit Book 11, 37, 68, 98

as Benet College   41, 77, 96
Buttery Book   71, 100, 248, 249
career choice   35, 80–1, 87–8, 98–101
chamber plans *see under* Matthew Parker and Nicholas Bacon
chapel project   54, 55, 56
Chapter Book   34, 39, 105, 112, 121
connection with Canterbury   33
connection with Norwich   18, 42–3, 45, 50, 57, 59, 249, 250
fellow-commoner   35
fellow *see separate entry*
frictions in   19, 29, 41–2, 55–7, 90, 103–4, 106, 108–9, 110, 246
influx of students   16, 33, 64, 239
interdependence of students   4, 12, 17, 73, 77, 90
library   13, 34, 74
local politics   12, 16, 17, 19, 39, 66
pensionary building   14, 15, 33, 34, 35
pensioner   56, 68
refurbishment   6, 13, 14, 33, 34, 36
regional units   7, 11–12, 16, 17, 19, 37–8, 39, 62, 74–5, 77
religious radicalism   40–1, 42, 50, 51, 57, 247
room allocation   7, 14–16, 17, 35–7, 38, 39
room swapping   36–8, 39, 74, 76
scholar *see separate entry*
sizar   65, 68, 248
social community of   3, 5, 12, 21
'the stoare house'   7, 15, 37–8, 74, 76, 78, 79
syllabus   238
tight-knit network   3, 19, 60, 73, 90, 102, 104, 242
tutorial system   69, 75–6, 78–9, 122
Cosin, Richard   260, 261
Cotton, Timothy   36, 37, 360
counterfeiting   26, 131, 132, 133, 208, 210, 214, 248, 262, 290, 309
Cranford, John   250
credit   41, 69, 72, 84, 90, 112, 113, 117, 118, 119, 128, 131, 136, 209, 212, 282, 293, 336, 339, 346
Creed, Thomas   276
Croft, Sir James   56, 114–15
cultural capital   3, 22, 80, 87, 88, 119, 282
Cupper, William   323
Curtain playhouse   124, 273

Curtis, Mark H.   69, 242
Cyprus   214–15

Dakyns, Edward   94
Dallington, Robert   54 n.72, 100
  A Booke of Epitaphes   54, 100
Danby, William   135
Daniel, Samuel   80, 129
David, King of Israel   26, 191
  as chivalric hero   181, 182
  and Elizabeth I   195
  as prophet   186
  prophetic song   198
  as shepherd   176
  vision of fraternal unity   182
Davidson, John   254
Davidson, Nicholas   28
Davidson, William   82, 118
Davies, Sir John   128
  Le Primer Report   128–9
Dawson, Ralph   102–3, 104
Deane, William   94
Deats, Sara Munson   210
Declaration of Great Troubles, A   220, 296
  'school points of sedition'   296–8, 300
Dee, John   302, 303, 307
  To the Kings Most Excellent Maiestie   302
Dekker, Thomas
  financial condition   128
  on Jesuits   220, 222
  on plague   319–20, 322
Dent, Arthur   201
Dering, Edward
  Two Godly Sermons   259
devil
  appearance   29, 316–17, 329
  conjuring   301, 314, 315, 316
  deceits   208
  as entertainer   326, 327, 328, 331, 332
  as God's instrument   317–18, 319, 322, 329
  as helper   322–3, 325
  incarnate   192
  and Jesuits   216
  and Jews   217
  on stage   316, 318, 330
  and theatre   209, 324
Diana   161, 162, 163
Dido, (legendary) Queen of Carthage   156–8, 159
DiGangi, Mario   26

404

Digges, Thomas   229, 230
  'Discourse of Sea-Ports'   229
dissimulation *see* theatrics
Dix, Barnabie   53
Dix, Dorrathie   53
Dix, John
  career   52–3
  eulogy to Butts   54, 101 n.38
  Norwich Fellow   51
  Norwich Scholar   36
  old-boy network with Greene   58, 59, 62
  oversea travel   121
  tutorial relationship with Thaxter   76
Dix, Thomas   53
Doleta, John   274, 275
Donaldson, Ian   1
Douay   92, 94
Dover   229, 234, 314, 315
Dover harbour construction project
  directors of   235
  engineering employed in   230–1
  launched by Henri VIII   229
  local associates involved in   22
Driver, Thomas   11
Dudley, Ambrose, 3rd Earl of Warwick   169
Dudley, Robert, 1st Earl of Leicester
  attends Halliwell's *Dido*   150, 158–9
  criticism against   92
  expedition to Low Countries   180
  faction of   22, 115, 162, 163, 172, 192, 196
  as Meleager   162
  militarism   161, 162, 163, 177–9, 196
  misogynistic sentiment   173
  as part of the 'inner ring'   118
  pro-Dudley plays   159, 161–3
Dunning, Michael   49
Duport, John   104
Dymock, Sir Edward   80

Eaton, Reginald   94
Eccles, Mark   85, 314
Edge, John   117, 119
Egerton, Edward   121
Elderton, William   219–20
Elizabeth I, Queen of England   41, 119, 129, 225, 300, 302
  ambassadors of   121
  ascension   150
  as Atalanta   162
  complaint against   151, 161, 162–3, 173
  conjurer of   303
  as David   195
  as Dido   156–7, 158, 160–1, 167–8, 173
  diplomatic policy   115, 152, 158
  dubbes Thomas Walsingham   343
  guard against dissidents   262, 310
  as Hezekiah   151
  informed of Marlowe's death   310–11
  mandate of   105, 106, 108
  marriage negotiation   151, 155, 158–9, 160–1, 168, 172, 173
  panegyric to   150, 158, 162, 164, 167–8
  progress to Cambridge University   150–1, 152, 155
  service to   85, 89, 114, 117, 118, 120, 133, 136
  stays at Scadbury   343
  supports Dover harbour construction   230
  under the threat of Catholic conspirators   219
  as Virgin Queen   157, 158, 160–1, 165
Ellis-Fermor, Una   187, 192, 294
Elwin, Edward
  College Foundation Scholar   357
  lawsuit against Marlowe   79
  succeeds Ninth Fellowship from Harris   78
  supplicat   11
  supports the expulsion of Hickman   106
  takes charge of Marlowe downstairs   79
Enders, Jody   318
English Church   52, 151, 237, 242, 243, 255
  Bullinger's influence upon   194
  career in   6, 18, 98, 99, 100–1, 110, 239
  ceremonies of   189
  decline of   298
  discontent with   92, 250
  of the elect   48, 49
  eliminates magic   322
  as false Church   248, 251
  fight against   201, 299
  holy war and   205
  hostility towards   54, 97, 256

Index

mouthpieces for 261
and plague 322
and prophecy 189–90
social role 321
threat to 252, 253, 258
traditional exegesis of 258
Erne, Lukas 20
Exeter, Devon 316
Exton, Brian 37, 71, 360

Fairbank, Alfred 9
Family of Love 233 n.90, 256, 297
Farley-Hills, David 268
Farnese, Alexander, Duke of Parma 115, 117
Faunt, John 81
Faunt, Nicholas
　connection with Manwood 82–5
　connection with Marlowe 78–80, 81, 112, 124
　Discourse Touching the Office of Principal Secretary 119
　oversea travel 121–2, 126
　as Parker's scholar 36, 37, 75, 81–2, 84, 99, 101, 360
　recruits Cambridge scholars 79, 87, 118
　religious attitude 82
　secretary to Francis Walsingham 37, 79, 82, 84, 85, 101
　stays in Padua 122
　supplicat 10
　tutorial relationship with Willoughbye 79, 122
　on Whitgift 235–6
Faversham, Kent 75, 234
Feasey, Lynette and Eveline 199
Feingold, Mordechai 241, 245
fellow
　appointed to lecture 112
　of College Foundation 36, 40
　complaints about 65
　election of 40, 42, 55, 105–6, 107
　exploits finances of scholars 79, 103
　of Ninth Fellowship 78
　Norwich Fellows 7, 17, 35, 39–40, 42, 44, 51, 52, 54, 75, 76
　outsider 104
　produces plays 46, 150
　tasks of 69, 70, 100, 121
Fernam, Abel 132–3
Ferrarius, Johan 184–5
Ferrour, William 59, 60

fiction-making
　employed to construct reality 20, 29, 251, 306, 333
　by the English government 25, 225–6, 236–7
　through literary discourses 28, 29, 225, 312–13, 315, 318
　in the process of heresy-hunting 22–3, 25, 28, 253, 312
　talent for 208
　and theatrics 210, 213
　as tool to invent nationhood 223, 225–6, 237
Field, John 249, 259, 273
　A Godly Exhortation 273
　reference to *Tamburlaine* 189, 259
Field, Thomas 102–4
Finch, John 12
Fineaux, John 314–15
Fineaux, Thomas 314–15
Fingley, John 94
Fischer, Sandra K. 207
Flacke, William 94
Fleetwood, William 273
Fleming, Juliet 174
Fletcher, Richard 42
Flushing *see* Vlissingen
Forman, Simon 277
　'A Discourse of the Plague' 320, 321
Fortescue, Thomas 192, 199
　The Forest or Collection of Historyes 192–3
Fowler, Moses 35, 36, 37, 359
Foxe, John 123, 205
　Actes and Monuments 47–8, 49, 50, 61
Foxe, Samuel 124
　notebook 123–4
　stays in Padua 123
Foxeian martyrology 47–50, 250–1
François, Duke of Anjou and Alençon 159, 161, 173
Fraunce, Abraham 336
Frizer, Ingram 135, 136
Fulbecke, William 174, 205–6
　close associate of Francis Bacon 205 n.79
　The Misfortune of Arthur 174
Fulke, William 192
Fuller, Thomas 259

Gabriel, angel 304
Gager, William

406

Index

alliance with Leicester 159–60, 162–3
asks for Peele's assistance 155
Dido
  and academic stage 155
  celebrates Virgin Queen 162
  for entertaining Alasco 159–61
  influence upon Marlowe 163–4
  political design 160–1
Meleager
  expresses militarist frustration 161–3
  as lesson to Leicester's household 161–2
  as panegyric to Elizabeth I 162
  performed before Leicester's faction 161
  popularity of 165
  represents Meleager as a symbol of militarists 162
  pro-war attitude 174
Galilei, Galileo 96
Gardiner, Stephen 150
Gaskill, Malcolm 132, 135
Gawdy, Bassingbourn 52
Gawdy, Philip 280
  reference to *Tamburlaine* 127 n.54, 280–1
Gayley, Charles Mills 276
Gee, Richard 73
  claim against Austen 71–2, 89
  deposition 72
George, Saint 197
Gibson, Abraham 195
Gibson, Jonathan 9
Gideon, judge of Israel 195, 197
Gifford, George 196, 255
Gilbert, Gifford 131, 133, 134
Gill, Roma 124, 165
Ginzburg, Carlo 5
Godfrey, Daniel 101, 354
Godfrey of Bullion 180
Godshalk, W. L. 170
Goffe, Christopher 68
Gold, Henry 36, 59, 76
Golding, Henry 36, 59, 76, 359
Gonville and Caius College, Cambridge 58, 59, 60, 83–4, 94
  Catholicism in 82, 93–4
  scholarships *see under* scholar
Gooch, Thomas 35, 39–40, 42
Goodman, Christopher 305
  'Notes of the absurdities & c' 305

Goodman, Paul 290
Gorboduc 151
Gorhambury, Hertfordshire 16, 100
gossips *see* rumours
Gosson, Stephen
  anti-theatricalism 273, 284
  Ephemerides of Phialo 271, 273
  at King's School, Canterbury 81
  as playwright 197
  pro-war attitude 197
  The Schoole of Abuse 172, 273
  on 'simplicity' 208
  supports militarist policy of Walsingham 172
  on Thomas Lodge 278
  'word and sword' 172, 174
Gostwick, Roger 191
Gouge, William 208
Graceborough, Mark 71, 360
Grande, Troni Y. 193
Gravet, William 195
Gray, Austin K. 73, 114, 115
Gray, Hugh 95
Gray's Inn 174, 205 n.79
Gray's Inn entertainment 151
Green, Ian 98
Greenblatt, Stephen 260, 291
Greene, Robert (father of the poet) 57, 59, 60
Greene, Robert 18, 104
  Biographical Events
    associates in Norwich 29, 57, 60, 62–3, 269, 272, 282
    on 'atheist' Tamburlaine 267–8, 269, 294
    comes to St John's, Cambridge 59, 104
    death 60, 282, 286, 337
    exhibition given to 58–60, 63
    formative years 57–8, 272, 295
    relationship with Marlowe 269, 271
    tribute to John More 60, 62, 282
    writes for Queen's Men 276
  Personal Characteristics
    as atheist 285–7, 291, 292, 295
    autobiographical hermeneutics 29, 290–2, 295, 313, 333
    blasphemous rhetoric 281, 287–90, 291, 294
    constructs 'atheist' Marlowe 188–9, 263, 270,

Index

294–5, 307, 311, 312, 319, 333, 335
conversion narrative   28, 63, 272, 282–4, 286–7, 290, 294
fashions himself as moralist   277, 280–1, 282–4, 290, 292, 294, 295
prejudice against Marlowe   18, 20, 28, 29, 63, 206, 271–2
psychological links to Norwich   28–9, 57, 63, 272, 283
sense of guilt   288, 290, 294
Works
  Alphonsus   267, 276, 278, 280, 291
  Francesco's Fortunes   269
  Friar Bacon and Friar Bungay   276
  Greene's Farewell to Folly   288
  Greene's Groatsworth of Wit
    authenticity   292–3
    autobiographical hermeneutics in   290–2, 295
    Chettle's role in   293
    as conversion narrative   28
    denounces Marlowe   268–9, 306, 308
    Greene's moralist project in   272
  Greene's Mourning Garment   277
  Greene's Vision   270, 284
  James IV   276
  A Looking-Glass for London and England   276
    collaboration with Lodge in   278, 281
    as counterattack on *Tamburlaine*   280, 281
    date   276–7
    guarantees Greene's moral integrity   272, 277, 280, 281, 289
    Rasni's blasphemy in   278–9, 289
    repentance framework   28, 277, 280, 281
    repertoire of Queen's Men   276
    and Sabbath-breaking   277
  Mamillia   267
  Menaphon   188, 269, 271
  Perimedes the Blacksmith   28, 188, 267, 268, 269, 270, 272, 276, 281, 291
  The Repentance of Robert Greene
    and anti-atheism apologetics   286–7
    as conversion narrative   28, 63

conversion at St Andrew's church in   61, 284–5
Greene's moralist project in   272
literary tactics   282, 285
offers new narrative identity   284
recourse to Norwich puritanism in   57
refers to Norwich puritan community   284
represents his former self as atheist   285, 290–1
Selimus   276, 291, 313
Spanish Masquerado   278
Greenwood, John
  arrest of   249
  debt to Browne   247, 248
  educated at Corpus Christi   51
  execution   250, 252
  intellectual milieu   247
  in London   249–50
  orientation towards Foxeian martyrdom   247, 250–1
  relationship with Marlowe   248–9
  representation of   253, 255, 256
Gresshop, John   81
Grey, Arthur, Lord Deputy of Ireland   180
Grindal, Edmund, Archbishop of Canterbury   243, 311
Grosse, John   96
Guilpine, John   118
Guy of Warwick   182, 184

Hacket, William
  insurrection at London   251, 252–3
  as Tamburlainean prophet   260, 261
Hadfield, Andrew   185
Hakluyt, Richard   128
Halasz, Alexandra   282
Hall, Peter   6,
Halliwell, Edward   151, 155, 158, 159, 164
  'a tragic poem of Dido and Aeneas'   150, 158
Hammer, Paul E. J.   136
Harborne, William   119
Harlan, Susan   166
Harriot, Thomas   234, 302, 307, 310
  'Doctrine of Nauticall Triangles Compedious'   302
Harris, Thomas
  italic script   11, 79
  roommate of Faunt   37, 38, 79, 112

408

Index

succeeds Ninth fellowship from Willoughbye 78, 96
tutorial relationship with Willoughbye 78-9, 122
Harrison, Robert 43, 50, 247, 249
Harrison, William 98
Harsnet, Samuel 236
Hartwell, Abraham 151, 158
  Regina Literata 151, 158
Harvey, Gabriel
  Ciceronianus 240
  criticism against Greene 292
  criticism against Marlowe 259, 337
  criticism against Nashe 258, 259
  elected fellowship at Pembroke 242
  enemies of 10, 242, 244
  as leading exponent of Ramism 240, 243
  Pierces Supererogation 258
  Ramist method 240-1
  supplicat 9-10
  as Tamburlainean orator 261
  Rhetor 240
Harvey, John 274
Harvey, Richard 274
  An Astrological Discourse 274
Hastings, Sir Francis 222
Hatcher, John 106
Hatton, Sir Christopher, Lord Chancellor 56, 84-5, 114, 115, 118, 156, 252, 253, 254
Hawkins, Henry 122
Hayes, Nevill 67, 70, 71
hearsay rule 25, 27
Heber, Richard 315
Helgerson, Richard 283, 290
heliotrope 21, 163
Henry I, Duke of Guise 204, 217-18, 245, 246
Henry VIII, King of England 179, 181, 229
Henslowe, Philip 128, 276
Herbert, Henry, 2nd Earl of Pembroke 161
Herbert, Mary, Countess of Pembroke 336, 337
heresy-hunting 20, 23, 25, 28, 29, 304, 312, 342
Hiarbas, King of Numidia 156, 157
Hickman, Anthony
  alliance with Norgate 106, 107, 111
  appointed to fellowship 104-5, 112
  career 104

  connection with Francis Walsingham 108-9
  dispute over 110
  expelled from Corpus Christi 54, 104, 106-8, 247
  puritan leanings 54, 107-8
  signs Nashe's supplicat 112-13, 271
  teaches rhetoric to Marlowe 112, 271
  will of 113
  witnesses on behalf of Norgate 111-12
Hickman, Henry 113
Hillarye, John 52
Hilliard, Stephen S. 257, 258
Hindmarsh, Bruce 282-3
Historie of ... Doctor Iohn Faustus, The 124, 325, 326
Hodiloe, Thomas 111
Holinshed, Raphael 160, 274
  Chronicles 230, 232
Holland, Henry 233, 322, 323
  Spirituall Preseruatiues 322-3
holy war theory 22, 184, 187, 194-8, 202, 205-6
homophilic tendency 12, 16, 36, 37, 79, 90
Honan, Park 6, 7, 152
Hotson, J. Leslie 4
Houlbrooke, Ralph 311
Howard, Charles, Lord High Admiral 304
Howard, Jean E. 272
Hull, John 221
Humberston, Robert 94
Hunter, G. K. 189
Hunter, Michael 23
Hymenaeus 113

iconophobia 151
Inner Temple 151
Ipswich, Suffolk 153
Israel
  beleaguered 196
  English Israel 189, 190, 195, 198
  as God's scourge 191, 196
  Israelites 181, 192, 305, 306, 320
  land of 191
  military leaders of 176, 180, 182, 184, 191
  prophets of 188
Israelization 182, 188, 194, 197, 198
italic hand 9-10, 11
Ive, Paul

Index

involved in Dover harbour project 235
The Practise of Fortification 235

Jackson, MacDonald P. 345
Jacquot, Jean 313
Jardine, Lisa 88, 239
Jegon, John 109
Jenkins, Harold 128, 292
Jesuits
  demonization of 25
  fiction-making strategies of 236
  identified with biblical models 216
  impersonation of 221
  mission 92, 218–19, 220, 228
  representation of 219–20
  theatrics of 208, 211 220-2
  threat posed by 211, 218, 220
  and 'witchmongers' 228–9
Jesus College, Cambridge 104
Jews
  and Jesuits 216–17, 236
  London community of 215
  prejudice against 216
  representation of 215–16, 217
Job 207, 210
John (disciple of Jesus) 26
John of Leiden 261
Johnson, James Turner 194
Jonah 275, 277
Jonathan (son of King Saul) 26
Jones, Edward 307
Jonson, Ben 133
  Alchemist 133
  Bartholomew Fair 257
  Sejanus His Fall 163
Joseph (husband of Virgin Mary) 305
Josephus, Flavius 156
  Jewish War 277
Joshua 182, 184, 193
Josselin, John 12, 13
  Historiola 12–13
Joyner, Ralph 99, 358
Judas Iscariot 216, 294
Judas Maccabeus 180

Kapferer, Jean-Noël 89
Keats, John 291
  'negative capability' 291
Kelsall, Malcolm 295
Kennet, Samuel 114
Kett, Francis 16, 38, 51, 56
  Arian heresy 51

King, Ros 124
King's College, Cambridge 151, 158
King's School, Canterbury 11, 17, 37, 38, 65, 66, 68, 69, 74–5, 77, 78, 81, 114, 123, 154, 234
Kirchmayer, Thomas 149
  Pammachius 149–50
Kiséry, András 338
Kocher, Paul H. 190, 268, 308
Kuriyama, Constance Brown 19, 126, 132, 135, 154, 249, 263, 268, 310, 337
Kyd, Thomas
  arrest of 120, 263, 311
  denial of friendship with Marlowe 342
  letter to Puckering 26, 227
  on Marlowe's favourite haunts 337
  shares room with Marlowe 263, 309
  slanderous report of Marlowe 20, 28, 29, 308
  untrustworthy witness 25

Lackingdon, Essex 51
Lant, Thomas 177
La Primaudaye, Pierre de
  The Second Part of French Academie 286
Łaski, Olbracht see Albertus Alasco
Lawse, William 36, 37, 38, 71, 76, 77, 361
Layer, Thomas 61
Legge, Thomas
  policy of tolerance 94–5
  provides religious asylum 93
  Richardus Tertius 113, 164
  as vice-chancellor 107
Le Goff, Jacques 1
Leicester, Earl of *see* Robert Dudley
Leicester's Commonwealth 92
Leipzig, Germany 123
Leland, John 179
  Assertio Inclytissimi Arturii 179, 182
Levi, Giovanni 1
Lewes, Henry 38, 42
Lewgar, Thomas 10–11, 74, 361
Lewis, C. S. 168, 341
Lewkenore, William 129
libel, libeller 23, 26, 109–10, 120, 216, 243, 247, 251, 254, 262–3, 295
Lightfoote, William 221, 362
  The Complaint of England 221
Lloyd, Lodowick 156

Index

Lloyd, Richard 182, 184
  A Briefe Discourse of ... the Nine Worthies 182-4
    chivalrizes Old Testament charismatics 182
    Israelizes chivalric tradition 184
Lodge, Thomas
  defence of the stage 278-9, 280
  financial distress 130
  friendship with Greene 278
  Honest Excuses 278
  A Looking-Glass for London and England see under Robert Greene
  on plague 320
  The Wound of Civil War 278
London 63, 132, 155, 174, 175, 280
  Aldersgate Street 63
  Bridewell Prison 250
  Cheapside 252
  civic culture of 21-2, 177, 181, 243
  Clifford's Inn 279, 280
  Clink Prison 250
  conventicles in 249
  Deptford 134, 136
  Dutch Church cemetery 216, 262
  fires that happen in 220
  Fleet Prison 130
  insurrection in 253, 262
  Jewish community in 215
  Merchant Taylors' Hall 181
  Miles End Green 181
  Newgate Prison 26, 128, 309
  as Nineveh 277
  Norton Folgate 124
  Old Bailey 86, 87
  plague in 235, 319, 321
  poverty in 126
  St Andrew Undershaft 53
  St Bartholomew-by-the-Exchange 53
  St Nicholas's Church, Deptford 339
  St Olave's School 248
  St Paul's Cathedral 53
  St Paul's Churchyard 337, 347
  St Paul's School 104
  sensation of *Tamburlaine* in 175, 268, 271, 272
  Shoreditch 332
  Southwark 248, 250
  theatres *see separate entry and individual playhouses*
  as turbulent 'ocean' 237
  Tyburn 250
Longworth, Adam 42

Lopez, Roderigo 215, 216
Low Countries 121, 133, 172, 180, 235
Lucan (Marcus Annaeus Lucanus)
  Bellum Civile 205
Lupton, Thomas 208, 216
  The Christian against the Iesuite 216
Lyly, John 66, 77, 80, 152, 155
  Euphues 271
Lyly, Peter 77
Lymbert, Stephen 43, 54, 58

Machiavelli, Niccolò 217, 294
Machiavellian 22, 25, 204, 209, 211, 215, 218, 221, 222, 225, 262, 263
Malta 22, 214, 215, 222
Malym, William 104
Manwaring, Richard
  Canterbury Scholar 37, 38, 77, 123, 360
  possibility of staying in Padua 123-4
Manwood, Sir Roger
  allegiance to Whitgift 236
  collaboration with Matthew Parker 83-4
  connection with Sir Francis Walsingham 82, 84-5, 234
  criticism against 83-4
  intellectual attitude 228
  marble monument 86-7
  Marlowe appears before 85-6
  MP for Sandwich 66
  recruitment of scholars 83, 84, 85
Marcus, Leah S. 21
Marley, John 67-8, 70, 242
Marlowe, Christopher
  biographical approach to 1-3, 5-6, 7-8, 11-12, 333
  localizing 2-3, 5-6, 7-8, 11-12, 17, 21, 29, 332-3
  Biographical Events
    absent from college 116, 121, 234, 249
    arrested for libel 263, 309
    autograph 10, 234
    career choice 78, 80-1, 88, 101-2, 119, 163, 270
    certificate from Privy Council 89-90, 116-17, 118, 119-20
    chamber-fellows 74-6, 79
    commencement 73, 98, 117
    connections with Francis Walsingham 4, 19, 21, 79-80,

411

88, 110–12, 113, 116–17, 126, 163, 173, 234–5
contact with religious radicals   248–9, 250
counterfeits coins   131–2, 133–4
death   28–9, 134–6, 309–11, 313, 316, 329, 330, 332–3, 335–6, 336–7, 344–5, 346
deposition to Richard Gee's allegation   72–3
detained on suspicion of the murder   85–6, 125, 128
donation to fund the college chapel   55
financial circumstances   6–7, 19, 22, 127–8, 131, 134–6, 237
John Parker Scholar   7, 22, 99, 101, 153, 206
local associates   18–19, 65, 72–3, 75–7, 78, 85, 86–7, 120, 234–5, 339, 346
as messenger   88, 120–1
patronage of Sir Thomas Walsingham   86, 126, 263, 336–7, 339, 340–1
portrait   5–7, 27, 346
possibility of staying in Padua   124
quarrel with William Corkine   135, 235
service to Privy Council   19, 78–80, 88, 114–15, 117–18, 120–4, 136
shares room with Baines   131
shares room with Kyd   263
and stationers   336–7
supplicat   10–12, 72, 79, 112
tutorial relationship with Elwin   78–9
tutorial relationship with Harris   78–9, 112
witnesses on behalf of Norgate   111–12
Personal Characteristics
anti-social tendencies   19, 20, 24, 90, 102
atheism   22, 23, 26–7, 29, 202, 268–9, 270, 310, 311, 312, 313
as atheist icon   308, 313, 333, 342
attitude toward Ramism   245–6
biblical knowledge   192, 198, 327
as conjurer master   29, 307–8, 332
'divine Musaeus'   344

empirical frame of mind   22, 227, 234, 235, 237
faithful dealing   73, 114, 116, 118, 119, 128
hearsay evidence against   2, 20, 23, 24, 26–7, 306, 308, 337
hostility towards   19, 26, 90, 132, 134, 135, 267–8, 269
indoctrinates people in atheism   306, 314, 315
interest in fortification technology   234–5
and Kentish intellectual milieu   86–7, 227–9, 229–37, 234–7
'Merlins race'   188, 267, 281, 291
'mighty lines'   24, 259, 268
militarist tendency   21–2, 163–4, 166, 173, 174
mythology of   20, 21, 23, 24, 27, 29, 295, 303, 306–7, 310–12, 313–16, 333
prophetic oratory *see under* Tamburlaine
reads atheist lecture   306–7, 308
religious beliefs   26–7, 202, 268, 272
rhetoric of violence   171, 246, 262, 263
rumours about   4, 19, 27, 29, 89–90, 101–2, 110–11, 113, 114, 271–2, 313, 333, 335
smear campaign against   25, 263, 270, 308–9, 335–6, 342–3, 344, 346
sociability   19, 24, 73
as social critic   22, 206, 226
sodomy   26, 294, 300, 309
and university drama   21–2, 113, 153–4, 155–6, 163–4, 165, 166–7
urban legends about   20, 27–9, 89, 272, 313–16, 319, 332–3
Works and Characters
Aeneas
emasculation of   168, 169–71, 173–4
militarist rhetoric   165–6, 168–9
'warlike' soldier   165, 168
Dido
masculinization   170–1, 173–4
misogynistic discontent with   171–2, 173
rhetoric of love poetry   168

412

Index

Tamburlainean rhetoric   171
Dido, Queen of Carthage   21–2, 335
   and conventions of the children's stage   171
   date   152–3, 155
   ethopoeia in   167–8
   Gager's influence upon   163–4
   gives voice to anxiety among militarists   173
   as panegyric to Elizabeth I   164, 165, 173
   as post-Tamburlaine play   154–5
   as pro-war burlesque   173–4
   and university drama   153–4, 155–8, 167–8
   Vulcan's net in   169
Doctor Faustus
   confounds illusion with reality   328–9
   on divinity   239, 242
   as entertaining hero   326–7, 332
   and Fineaux   314–15
   as perverted Christ   327
   superimposed on Marlowe   313, 319
Doctor Faustus   29, 66–7, 73, 127
   devil's appearance in   316–17, 318–19, 329
   hell on earth in   327–8, 329
   materialistic fantasy in   239, 325, 328–9
   novelty of   318–19
   offers escapist realm   325, 326–7, 328–9, 332
   performed by Admiral's after plague   324
   seeking devil for help in   322, 324, 325
   shows and entertainments in   210, 326–7
   sources of   325–6, 330 n.108
   urban legends about   316–17, 318–19, 329, 332
   utilized in constructing atheists   315, 332
Edward II   80, 218 n.40, 335
The First Booke of Lucan   205
Hero and Leander
   Blount's dedication of   336, 338–40, 342–4, 346
   on 'a bold sharp sophister'   243
   Chapman's sequence of   341–2
   literary rejoinders to   343, 344–6, 347
   material imagination in   168
   myth about scholars' poverty in   91
   Prideaux lost copy of   315
   publication of   338, 342, 344, 345
   and the strait of Dover   229
   written in Scadbury   340
In obitum honoratissimi viri Rogeri Manwood   85–7
The Jew of Malta   21
   anxiety about theatrical strangers in   22, 215, 262
   associates Barabas with conspirators   217–18
   'counterfeit profession' in   209
   Ferneze's power of theatrics in   223–4
   fiction-making in   223, 225, 236–7
   hooked nose of Barabas in   217
   and Jesuits   216–17
   juxtaposes England and Malta   222
   Marlowe's intellectual attitude in   227, 229, 234, 236–7
   metaphor of counterfeit coin in   208–9
   meta-theatrical Barabas in   210–11, 223–4, 225
   power of theatrics in   209, 210–11, 214, 223–4, 237
   providence in   224–5, 226–7
   refers to Paduan scholars   122
   represents Malta as beleaguered island   215, 222
   sardonic tone of   226–7
   'simplicity' in   207–8, 222
   sources of   214
   thirst for monetary power in   127, 207, 214
The Massacre at Paris   335
   and Aeneas' long narrative   166
   date   88
   representation of Guise in   204, 218
   representation of Ramus in   244–6
   sources   244, 246
Tamburlaine
   as apocalyptic agent   198–200, 201–2, 268

as atheist   28, 188, 267, 268, 269, 270, 272
and David   176, 186
death of   193, 203, 337
employed to represent religious zeal   190, 259, 261
as God's scourge   176, 187, 189, 193, 198, 202, 204
libeller's pseudonym of   262-3
militarist   166, 193
mimetic effect on radicals   190, 259-61
profane character of   161, 188-9, 267-8, 269-70, 280
as prophet   186, 200, 201, 202
prophetic oratory of   22, 24, 186-7, 188-9, 193, 200, 203, 251, 262, 268
and religious radicalism   187-8, 189-90, 251, 259
Tamburlaine the Great   21, 24, 28, 155, 260, 291
  accident during the performance of   280
  attribution to Marlowe   268 n.2
  branches of laurel in   260
  chivalric romance framework of   175-7
  colour sequence in   199-200, 259
  concept of holy war in   190-1, 193, 202, 204, 206
  contemporary references to   175, 188, 267, 269
  Greene's criticism against   188-9, 190, 269, 280
  'high astounding terms' in   174, 187, 188
  humanistic lauding of eloquence in   185-6
  imitators of   278, 289
  performed by Admiral's   127, 280-1
  questions legitimacy of holy war   203, 205, 206
  second part of   202-3
  self-justifying logic in   188, 190-1, 193, 200, 202, 263
  sense of election in   189, 193
  sources of   192-3, 205, 235
  swearing in   203-5
  word and sword in   187-8
Marlowe, John   234, 250

Marlowe, Katherine   229
Marprelate, Martin   24, 251, 297
  Certain Mineral and Metaphysical Schoolpoints   297
  cultural significance   254
  hypocrisy   256
  identity   243-4
  target of   107, 110
  way of writing   253
  See also anti-Martinists
Marten, Anthony   196-7
Martin, John (mason)   111, 112
Martin, John (Woodes's classmate)   42-3
Martin, Nicholas   103
Martin, Richard   132-3
Martyn, Thomas   124
Mary I, Queen of England   124
Mary, Queen of Scots   131
Mary, Virgin   304-5
Maslen, Robert W.   330-1
Massai, Sonia   338
Masters, Robert   34, 40, 96, 107
Mateer, David   79
Melton, John   318
Mendez-Nassi, Joseph   214-15
Meres, Francis   28, 335, 346
  Palladis Tamia   335
Mexia, Pedro
  Silva de Varia Lecion   192
microhistory   1, 5
Middleton, Thomas   332
  The Black Book   331
  Father Hubburd's Tales   64-5
Mihil, Henry   107, 359
Mildenberger, Kenneth   59
Miller, G. W.   343
millitarism   162-3, 172-4, 177-9
misogyny   157, 162, 172-3
Moabites   192
Mondeforde, Francis   94
Monta, Susannah Brietz   48
Morden, John   159
More, John   45, 61-2
More, Miles   61-2
Morley, Christopher   72
Mornay, Philippe de   285, 294, 305
Moses   191, 193, 194, 234, 304, 305, 306, 310
Mosse, Miles   69
Muhammad, Mahomet   187, 202, 203, 204, 205, 206, 279
Mulcaster, Richard   181

Index

Positions 181
Muldrew, Craig 112
Munday, Anthony
  anti-theatricalism 275, 284, 289, 290
  career 212
  dissimulation 212, 214
  The English Roman Life 212
  wins patronage of Privy Council 212
Musaeus 344
mythmaking *see* fiction-making

Nashe, Thomas
  admiration for *Euphues* 271
  Almond for a Parrat 244
  anti-Martinism 24, 243
  anti-Ramist attitude 243-4, 245
  apologetics against atheism 258, 285-6
  Christs Teares 200, 285, 304
  as contentious polemicist 24
  criticism against Harvey 10, 261
  criticism against Penry 244, 261
  as Cutbert Curryknave 256
  on Dover cliffs 229
  enthusiasm for singularity 244, 258-9
    See also singularity
  follows Bancroft's method 256
  friendship with Marlowe 113, 271, 344
  on intelligencer 212-13
  Nashes Lenten Stuffe 344
  Pierce Penilesse 256
  reference to *Tamburlaine* 200
  relationship with Greene 271, 292
  residence at St John's 271
  share in *Dido* 152-3
  supplicat 9, 112, 271
  way of representing separatists 256-7, 261
Naxos 214-15
Neville, Thomas 242
Nicholl, Charles 119, 125, 271, 311
Nichols, Josias 251
Nichols, Philip 34, 35, 36, 37, 38, 55, 56, 106
Nineveh 275, 277, 289
Norgate, Robert
  administrative policies 50, 51
  alliance with Walsingham 56, 109
  anti-Aldrich fellow 42
  attitude toward the stage 76, 153
  from Aylsham 38
  career 50-1
  chapel project 54
  compiler of college plans 15 n.43, 39
  consults Bacon about scholarship 15
  criticism against 34, 54-5, 106, 110
  death 106, 113
  expels Bland from college 110, 246-7
  faction against 55-6, 106, 109, 113
  financial mismanagement 34, 54-5, 57
  libel against 109-10
  memorandum 238
  nepotism 51, 55-6, 57, 105, 106
  political manoeuvrings 40-1, 51-2, 54, 55-7, 105-6
  preciseness 39
  refurbishes his room 34, 36
  relationship with Parker 42, 50, 51, 56
  secures fellowship for Hickman 104-6, 107
Norgate, William 38, 55
Northbrooke, John 273
Norwich, city of 18, 28, 39, 42, 50, 51, 53, 152
  aldermen 7, 17, 18, 36, 43-4, 49, 54, 59, 60, 100, 249
  Great (or St Giles) Hospital 43, 44, 57-9, 60, 61, 62, 63
  Mayor's Court 44, 45, 57, 59
  religious milieu 42, 49, 50, 61, 62, 63, 247, 249, 251, 272, 283-4
  St Andrew's Church 45, 60-1, 62, 282, 283, 284-5
  St George, Colegate 53
  St George, Tombland 58, 60
Norwich Grammar School 43, 44, 53, 54, 57, 59, 62, 63

Offley, Hugh 181
Oliver, Leslie Mahin 47
Orgel, Stephen 20
Ormes, Cicely 49
Orwell, George 347
  Nineteen Eighty-Four 347
Osburne, Edward 94
Ospringe, Kent 234
Ovid (Publius Ovidius Naso) 192, 340, 344
Oxford University 64
  Christ Church 155, 159, 161
  Corpus Christi College 81
  Trinity College 123, 153

Index

Oxinden, Henry 85, 314

Padua 122, 123, 124
   Basilica of St Anthony 124
Padua University 96
Palmer, John 9
Paris 96, 122, 125, 126, 129, 166
Paris Garden 273, 275, 331
Parker, John 7, 37, 99, 100
Parker, Matthew, Archbishop of
      Canterbury
   acquaintance with Absalon 66
   attentiveness to his scholars 13–14,
     16, 36, 100
   chamber plan of 1575 7, 15, 34,
     35–6, 37, 39, 79
   chaplain and physician of 234
   collaboration with Manwood 83–4
   collision with Aldrich brothers 41–2,
     45, 50
   connection with Norwich 40–1
   criticism against 13, 41–2, 50
   faction of 51
   fellowship *see under* fellow
   foundation of scholarship 13, 15, 37,
     39, 68, 81–2, 83, 97–8
   friendship with Bacon 14
   furnishes the storehouse 74
   'pope of Lambeth' 41, 50
   recommends Aldrich to
     mastership 41
   report about *Pammachius* 150
   requests production of
     Historiola 12–13
   scholarships *see under* scholar
   supports Norgate 51, 56
   as vice-chancellor 150
   will of 7, 37, 83
Parker, Thomas 41
Parkhurst, John, Bishop of Norwich 49
Parnassus plays
   *The First Part of the Return from
     Parnassus* 91–2
   The Pilgrimage to Parnassus 91
Parr, Johnstone 59
Parry, Glyn 303
Pashley, Christopher 37, 38, 74, 75, 77,
   362
Paul (Apostle) 48, 187, 258
Paule, George 253
Paulet, Sir Amias 229
Peck, Thomas 50
Peele, George 155

Pembroke Hall, Cambridge 69, 109,
   242, 246, 335
Penry, John 244, 261
Percy, Henry, 9th Earl of
   Northumberland 118
Perkins, William 233, 283
Perne, Andrew 67, 159
Persons, Robert
   arrival in England 211, 218
   A Briefe Apologie 303
   called 'a schoolman' 296
   criticism against Cecil 298–9, 304
   invents Raleigh's school 29, 299–301,
     306, 312, 313
   missionary activities 92–3
   on popular images of Jesuits 219
   reference to conjurer 29, 299, 301–3,
     307–8
   reports of 92–3
   reports to 250, 319
   Responsio 29, 298 n.7, 302, 303, 307
   uses school metaphor 298–9, 300–1
Peterhouse, Cambridge 104, 109 n.67,
   122, 159, 244
Philip II, King of Spain 115, 296, 297,
   300 n.20
plague
   in 1592–3 29, 235, 277, 319–20, 324,
     332, 340
   cause of 320, 323
   garment full of 256
   as God's scourge 176, 185, 199, 321
   impact on the populace 274, 276,
     322, 325, 327
   and playhouse 323–4, 329, 332
Plautus 46
player
   commits blasphemy 279, 288–90,
     317
   counterfeit profession of 209–10,
     212, 215,
   devises fictions 223
   prohibition of 323–4
playhouse
   cultural impact 175
   draws plague 323
   incurs the charge of blasphemy 288
   moral effectiveness of 277
   offers escapist realm 324, 325
   as 'Sathans pallaces' 323, 329
   social role of 197, 276
playwright
   amateur 21, 150

diffuses fictions   223
heliotropic tendency of   152
living standards of   128
manipulates people   225
resemblance to secretary   88
Plombe, Thomas   36, 40, 59, 76, 359
Poley, Robert   135
Pollmann, Judith   283
Poni, Carlo   5
Ponsonby, William   336, 337, 344
Poole, John   26, 309
Poole, Kristen   253
Poore Knight His Pallace of Priuate Pleasures, A   157
Pope, the   48, 195, 201, 212, 219, 221, 222, 326
Popham, Sir John   25
Porter, H. C.   14 n.39, 42
'positive capability'   291
Powle, Stephen   121
Poynter, James   37, 74, 75, 361
praelector   8, 11, 79, 112, 240, 242
Presbyterianism   41, 42, 189, 252, 254, 260
Privy Council
  certificate of   19, 90, 116, 117, 119
  channels of information   121–2, 236, 304, 306
  collaborative workings of   118
  function and administration of   114–16
  guard against dissidents   96, 218, 225, 262, 263, 310, 311
  mandate of   1, 117, 121
  messengers of   120–1
  misjudges political situation   218
  patronage of   19–20, 24, 119–20, 130–1, 134, 159, 212
  regulation of plays   273, 323–4
  relationship with Marlowe   22, 79–80, 89, 90, 136, 173, 309, 340
  slander against   25, 229, 300, 304
  supports Dover project   230
Proctor, John
  The Fall of the Late Arian   309
prophet, prophecy   186, 189–90, 195, 198, 206, 248, 252
  prophecy for 1588   200–1, 274
providential framework   29, 273, 275, 281, 310, 311, 329, 330, 335–6
Prynne, William   316, 317
Puckering, Sir John   23, 26, 227, 286, 307, 337

Pulman, Michael Barraclough   116, 118
puritan, puritanism
  in Cambridge   54, 69, 93, 95, 108, 244, 247
  constructing   23, 133, 190, 226, 245, 253, 257, 261
  conversion narrative   226–7, 284–5, 295
  denounces theatre for plague   323, 324
  exorcism of   233, 236
  as 'godly'   36 n.8
  as 'laie factious'   252–3
  in Norwich   29, 41, 45, 57, 61, 62–3, 282–3, 285
  and Ramism   244, 245
  on stage   113, 226, 253, 257, 261
Purkiss, Diane   158

Queen's College, Cambridge   151
Queen's Company   80, 154, 276, 280
Questier, Michael   97
Qur'an, the   187, 202, 203, 204, 269

Radclyffe, Henry, 4th Earl of Sussex   56, 118
Raleigh, Sir Walter
  conjurer of   234, 302, 332
  hearsay evidence against   24–5, 27, 312
  'hellish verses' of   312–13
  investigated at Cerne Abbas   301–2
  nationalist policy against Spain   300
  relationship with Marlowe   307–8, 310, 332–3
  school of atheism   29, 299–301, 303–4, 306, 312, 333
  trial at Winchester   24, 302
Ramism
  arouses rivalries in universities   241, 242
  develops religious confrontation   242–3
  enthusiasm for   240, 241, 246
  hostility towards   242, 244, 245
  and religious radicalism   242–3, 244
Ramus, Peter (Pierre de La Ramée)
  Ars logica   241
  attitude toward Aristotle   246
  criticism against   242, 244, 245
  Dialecticae libri duo   241
  method   240–1, 246
  representation of   243–4

417

Index

Rankins, William
   anti-theatricalism 273, 279, 280, 289
   'implicit dialogue' with Marlowe 279
   A Mirrour of Monsters 273, 279, 289
   superimposes character on playwright 290
Rasmussen, Eric 332
Read, Conyers 115
Read, William 56-7
Redgrave, Suffolk 100
Redman, William 228, 229, 236
Reed, Regina B. 189
repentance campaign 275, 319, 321
Rewse, Henry 106, 107 n.55, 363
Reynolds, Matthew 42
Rheims (Reims) 4, 19, 25, 92, 94, 95, 96, 97, 102, 114, 213, 218
Rhodes, Neil 186
Riche, Barnabe
   complains of Hermaphroditus 169
   Farewell to Militarie Profession 174
   A Right Exelent and Pleasaunt Dialogue 169
   on subjugation of Mars 169
Riggs, David 26, 86, 152, 260, 270
Robartes, Thomas 42, 45
Robertes, John 94
Roberts, Peter 116, 154
Robinson, Nicholas 150, 159 n.39
Robinson, Richard
   The Avncient Order ... of Prince Arthure 180
   Israelizes chivalric tradition 180, 182
   A Learned and True Assertion of ... Prince Arthur 179, 181, 182
   political attitude of 180, 195 n.58
   as Smith's protégé 180
   as sympathizer with militarism 179 n.10, 180
Rogers, John 258
Rogers, Thomas 253
Rome 26, 94, 95, 96, 97, 122, 123, 156, 165, 185, 201, 212, 296, 326
Romney marsh 232
Rose playhouse 324
Rowlands, Samuel 261
   Hell's Broke Loose 261
Rowse, A. L. 114, 117, 337
Roydon, Matthew 26, 130 n.67
Rugge, Francis 60, 62
rumours 20, 23, 25, 89-90, 94-5, 215, 303, 314

Sabbath-breaking 273, 274, 275, 277
Sadduceeism 233, 234
Sadler, Francis 99, 101, 359
Sadler, Sir Ralph 115, 130-1
Sadler, Ralph (grandson of Sir Ralph) 131
Saffron Walden, Essex 242
St John's College, Cambridge 57, 58, 59, 62, 91, 104, 112, 113, 149, 234, 271
St Mary's Church, South Walsham, Norfolk 42, 43, 44, 45, 47
Sandwich 66, 83, 84
Sandwich Grammar School 66, 83, 84
Satan *see* devil
Saul, King of Israel 190, 191, 192, 204
Savoy Hospital 66, 77 n.46
Sayer, Robert 40, 42, 55, 76, 354
Scadbury, Kent 250, 263, 340, 341, 343, 347
scholar 35
   Bible clerks 13, 36, 99, 101, 354-5
   Canterbury Scholars of the Westminster Foundation 36, 37, 38, 78, 82, 99, 123, 359-60
   College Foundation Scholars 37, 38, 99, 355-7
   definition 80, 293 n.79
   discontent of 91-3, 94, 97, 297
   Eastbridge Foundation Scholars 36-7, 38, 68, 71, 99, 360-1
   financial difficulties of 61, 64-7, 71, 90, 91-2, 102-3, 127, 246
   Joan Trapps Scholars 83-4
   John Mere Scholars 99, 357-8
   John Parker Scholars 5, 6, 7, 15, 22, 37, 50, 74, 78-9, 99, 101, 153, 361-2
   moral obligation to benefactors 13-14, 16, 62, 100-1, 102
   Nicholas Bacon Scholars 14, 38, 99, 100-1, 362-3
   Norwich Scholars 6, 7, 13, 15, 17, 36, 39, 44, 53, 54, 58, 59, 62, 75, 99, 100-1, 358-9
   Paduan scholars 122
   Parker Scholars at Gonville and Caius College 58, 59, 81-2
   requirements of 68, 71, 72, 87, 97, 100, 101, 153
   use of university attainments 87-8

Index

school of atheism *see under* Walter Raleigh
school of Christ   301
Scot, John   35, 42
Scot, Reginald
 allegiance to Whitgift   236
 The Discouerie of Witchcraft   22, 227, 228, 233, 234, 236
 empirical attitude of   227, 229, 233
 on miracles of Moses   306
 'note' in Holinshed's *Chronicle*   230, 232–3
 A Perfite Platforme of a Hoppe Garden   228
 philanthropic enthusiasm   228, 233
 praise for Manwood   228
 Sadducean mindset   233–4
 surveyor of Romney marsh   232
Scot, Sir Thomas   228, 230, 232, 233, 236
scourge of God   176, 180, 182, 187, 189, 193, 196, 198, 202
 concept of   177, 184–5, 191, 204, 236, 321
Seare, Robert   94
Sebastian, Saint   26
Second Report of Doctor Iohn Faustus, The   330
 collapse of the Theatre in   332
 represents Wagner as conjuring entertainer   330–1
 superimposes Wagner on Marlowe   331
Selim II, Sultan of the Ottoman Empire   214
seminary   4, 25, 91–3, 94, 96, 114, 213, 296–7, 298, 299, 304
seminary priest   92, 94, 95, 96, 97, 211, 212, 216, 218, 219, 220, 222
 See also Jesuits
Sennacherib   196
separatists, separatism   247, 248, 249, 251, 252, 253, 256, 258
Sethell, Matthew   106
Seton, John   149
 Dialectica   149, 238, 239, 244
Shakespeare, William   340
 As You Like It   344, 346
 biographical documents about   2
 career choice   80
 competes with Marlowe   340
 hommage to Marlowe   344–5, 346
 'negative capability'   291

representation of puritans   257
rival poets   345–6
Sonnets   345, 346
Venus and Adonis   340
Shelton, Sir Ralph   343
Shepard, Alexandra   70
Shepherd, Alan   173
Sherman, William   88
Sidney, Frances   125
Sidney, Sir Henry   180
Sidney, Sir Philip
 anti-atheist apologetics   285
 Arcadia   285
 attends Gager's plays   160, 161
 as chivalric hero   177
 funeral of   177, 181
 Gager's tribute to   162
 as Meleager's son   165
 militarist policy   161, 162, 163, 172, 179 n.10
 misogynistic sentiment   173
 Ponsonby publishes the work of   336
Sidney, Robert   26, 80, 131, 133–4
Sims, James H.   198 n.66, 327
Singer, Irving   171
singularity
 definition   256, 257–8
 employed to invent puritanism   255, 261
 Malvolio's 'trick of singularity'   257
 'new sects of singularitie'   256, 258
 Tamburlaine   190, 263
Skeres, Nicholas   130 n.67, 135, 136
Skretkowicz, Victor   176–7
Smith, G. C. Moore   4
Smith, Henry   98
Smith, Sophonius   38, 112
Smith, Thomas
 attends Sidney's funeral   177, 181
 finances Leicester's expedition   180
 holds the post of Prince Arthur   181
 as patron of Robinson   180, 182
Smyth, Robert   73, 101, 354
Smyth, Sir Thomas   242
Society of Prince Arthur
 activities   181–2
 origin   179, 181
 political purpose   182
 Robinson's celebration of   180
sodomy   20, 28, 294, 300
Sotherton, Leonard   49
Sotherton, Thomas   47, 49, 50, 60, 61, 62
Southwell, Robert   25, 220

419

Index

Humble Supplication to Her Maiestie   220, 298 n.8
Spenser, Edmund
   The Faerie Queene   174 n.81, 176
   Ponsonby publishes the work of   336
   as pro-war poet   174
Spinola, Baptista   82, 121
Stafford, Edward   116, 129
Stanley, Ferdinand, 5th Earl of Derby   132
Stanley, Henry, 4th Earl of Derby   115
Stapilton, Richard   95
Starks, Lisa S.   210
Stationers' Company   336
Stationers' Register   293, 308, 330, 342
Steane, J. B.   26, 210
Stephen (martyr)   197
Still, John   62, 153
Stone, Lawrence   64
Stone, Robert   37, 76, 77, 359
Strathmann, Ernest A.   300, 302
Straunge Newes out of Calabria   274
Stuart, Lady Arbella   300
Stubbes, Philip   273, 275
   The Anatomie of Abuses   273, 275
   The Second Part of the Anatomie of Abuses   273
Stubbs, John   172
   The Discovery of a Gaping Gulf   173
Stump, Donald   156
Styward, Thomas   166
   The Pathwaie to Martiall Discipline   167
Suckling, Robert   45, 60
Suffield, Walter, Bishop of Norwich   43
Sullivan, Erin   46
supplicat   8–9, 10–11, 72–3, 112–13
Sutterton, Henry   38, 356
Sutton, Dana F.   164
Swale, Richard   94
Swet, Robert   76
Sychaeus *see* Acerbas

Talbot, George, 9th Earl of Shrewsbury   123
Taleus, Audomarus   241, 245
   Rhetorica   241
Taylor, Richard   247
Tedder, William   123
Temple, John   38, 76, 357
Thaxter, John   35, 36, 39–40, 42, 51, 52–3, 56, 76, 358
Thaxter, Simon   11

Theatre playhouse   124, 273, 332
theatrics
   anxiety about   95, 211, 214, 219–20
   as critical component of society   211
   definition of   208
   of the English government   225–6
   makes things seem miraculous   227, 233–4, 236
   monetary motivation of   211–13
   power of   22, 24, 29, 237
Thetford, Norfolk   52
Thexton, Launcelot   50
Thexton, Robert
   attendance at a play   69, 76, 246
   as Austen' tutor   69–70
   friendship with Beadle   37, 76
   John Parker Scholar   361
   origin of   37, 50
   relationship with Marlowe   74, 75–6
   roommates of   38
Three Ladies of London, The   215
Thrush, Andrew   341
Tilman, Abraham
   Canterbury Scholar   99, 359
   at King's School   11–12, 74–5
   library   74 n.37, 74–5, 241
   supplicat   11
Timur   204, 205
Trinity College, Cambridge   9, 41, 60, 72, 95, 243, 314
Troy, New Troy   156, 157, 165, 166, 168, 169, 170, 172
Tucke, Christopher   101, 356
Tyrrell, Anthony   96

Udall, Nicholas   151
   Ezechias   151
'ugly decade'   23, 251, 304, 332, 342
Ulysses upon Ajax   125
Umberfield, Richard   250
urban legend   20, 28, 89, 220, 314–15, 317–18, 319, 332
Urry, William   3, 66, 77, 314

Vaughan, William   335
   The Golden-Grove   69, 335–6
Venice   122, 124
   St Mark's Basilica   124
Vere, Edward de, 17th Earl of Oxford   305
Vergil (Publius Vergilius Maro)   151, 154, 155, 156, 157, 158, 164, 166, 171, 172

Aeneid 154, 155, 158, 159, 160, 164, 165, 166
Verstegan, Richard
   An Aduertisement 297–8, 299, 302, 303, 307
   on Burghley's grandson 300
   The Copy of a Letter 225
   on plague 319
   on Raleigh's school of atheism 299, 303, 304
   on separatists 250, 252
vice-chancellor 8, 67, 73, 103, 104, 105, 106, 110, 116, 150, 153–4, 159, 247
vice-chancellor's court 18, 67, 72, 75, 95, 107, 112, 242
   Act Books 18, 19, 72, 243
   defamation cases in 90
   jurisdiction 18
   office 18, 90, 95, 103
violence, representation of 102, 166, 171, 246, 257, 262, 263
Vlissingen, Zeeland 26, 80, 131, 132, 134, 213,

Waferer, Thomas 84
Walker, Jonathan 151
Walsall, Samuel 157
   Threno-Thriambeuticon 157
Walsham, Alexandra 275
Walsingham, Lady Audrey 340, 342, 343
Walsingham, Sir Francis
   agents of 4, 37, 73, 79, 80, 82, 88, 120, 121, 122, 123, 126, 129–30, 274
   connection with Marlowe *see under* Christopher Marlowe
   criticism against 109, 110, 247
   death 21
   dedication to 194, 216, 235
   as director of Dover harbour project 232, 235
   elected consiliarius at Padua University 122
   employs Faunt *see under* Nicholas Faunt
   faction of 21–2, 163
   as God's scourge 184
   infirmities 115–16
   militarist policy 114–15, 163, 172
   misogynistic sentiment 173
   mobilization led by 22, 177–8, 194
   organizes Sidney's funeral 177
   as part of the 'inner ring' 118
   pays for information 214
   protégés in and around Corpus Christi 19, 56, 108, 109
   recommends Manwood as Chief Baron 84–5, 234
   relationship with Burghley 115, 217
Walsingham, Sir Thomas
   as agent for Francis Walsingham 126, 130
   dedications to 125, 336–7, 339–40, 342
   dubbed knight 343
   financial distress 130
   literary circle of 338, 341, 342–3
   as patron 136, 263, 342, 344
   stays in Paris 125
Walsingham, Thomas (son of Sir Thomas) 341
Watson, Thomas
   Amintae Gaudia 337
   Catholic sympathies 126
   as agent for Francis Walsingham 125
   detained on suspicion of the murder 85–6, 125
   An Eglogve 125
   employed as tutor 80
   friendship with Thomas Walsingham 124–6, 340
   Meliboeus 125, 340
Webb, E. A. 343
Webbe, William 166
   A Discourse of English Poetrie 166
Whetstone, George
   The English Mirrour 193, 199
   on Jesuits 221
White, Paul Whitfield 154
Whitehall 151
Whitehead, George 118
Whitgift, John, Archbishop of Canterbury
   allies of 53, 54, 107
   and Croft's peace negotiations 115
   demand for subscription to Prayer Book 235–6
   friction with Walsingham 108–9
   highly esteems Bancroft's talent 254
   makes peace with Browne 248
   orders to provide Bullinger's *Decades* 194
   organizes anti-Marprelate campaign 110
   political support of 113

Index

as Privy Councillor 114
protest against 235–6, 252, 259
Wigborough, Essex 53
Wiggenshall, Norfolk 78
Wiggins, Martin 45, 46, 154, 155, 276
Wilkes, Thomas 46
Willan, Robert 42
Willoughbye, Richard
   career choice 97, 122
   Catholicism 96
   elected consiliarius at Padua
      University 96, 123
   holds Ninth fellowship 78
   as intelligence provider 122, 124
   meets Samuel Foxe 123
   pupils of 78–9, 122
   relationship with Marlowe 126
   supports Norgate's line 40, 42
   tutorial payments to 78–9
Wilson, Robert 276
Wine, Celesta 43, 44
Wither, George 188
Wittenberg, Germany 331
Wolfall, John 130
Wolfe, John 342
Wonders of This Windie Winter, The 317
Wood, Edward 76, 355
Woodes, Nathaniel
   appearance in Mayor's Court 44–5

The Conflict of Conscience 18, 42, 45–6, 47–9, 50, 247
debt to Foxe 47–9
martyrdom mentality 48–9, 247, 251
matriculation 50
rapport with Norwich
     aldermen 43–5
as Reformation dramatist 45, 47
religious milieu 17, 42–3
religious orientation 45, 50
Woodford Hall, Essex 104
Woodleff, Drew 136
Woolfson, Jonathan 124
Wotton, Sir Henry 88
Wotton, Thomas 83, 230
Woudhuysen, H. R. 87, 164
Wraight, A. D. 114
Wright, William 292, 293
Wriothesley, Henry, 3rd Earl of
     Southampton 338, 340
Wrothe, John 123
Wymondham, Norfolk 37, 38, 74
Wymondham Grammar School 37

xenophobic movement 26, 120, 216, 263

Yemes, Henry 40, 76, 357
Young, John 10, 242

Studies in Renaissance Literature

Details of earlier volumes in the series can be found at
www.boydellandbrewer.com

Volume 20: *The Heroines of English Pastoral Romance*
Sue P. Starke

Volume 21: *Staging Islam in England: Drama and Culture, 1640–1685*
Matthew Birchwood

Volume 22: *Early Modern Tragicomedy*
edited by Subha Mukherji and Raphael Lyne

Volume 23: *Spenser's Legal Language: Law and Poetry in Early Modern England*
Andrew Zurcher

Volume 24: *George Gascoigne*
Gillian Austen

Volume 25: *Empire and Nation in Early English Renaissance Literature*
Stewart Mottram

Volume 26: *The English Clown Tradition from the Middle Ages to Shakespeare*
Robert Hornback

Volume 27: *Lord Henry Howard (1540–1614): an Elizabethan Life*
D. C. Andersson

Volume 28: *Marvell's Ambivalence: Religion and the Politics of Imagination
in mid-seventeenth century England*
Takashi Yoshinaka

Volume 29: *Renaissance Historical Fiction: Sidney, Deloney, Nashe*
Alex Davis

Volume 30: *The Elizabethan Invention of Anglo-Saxon England:
Laurence Nowell, William Lambarde, and the Study of Old English*
Rebecca Brackmann

Volume 31: *Pain and Compassion in Early Modern English Literature and Culture*
Jan Frans van Dijkhuizen

Volume 32: *Wyatt Abroad: Tudor Diplomacy and the Translation of Power*
William T. Rossiter

Volume 33: *Thomas Traherne and Seventeenth-Century Thought*
edited by Elizabeth S. Dodd and Cassandra Gorman

Volume 34: *The Poetry of Kissing in Early Modern Europe:*

From the Catullan Revival to Secundus, Shakespeare and the English Cavaliers
Alex Wong

Volume 35: *George Lauder (1603–1670): Life and Writings*
Alasdair A. MacDonald

Volume 36: *Shakespeare's Ovid and the Spectre of the Medieval*
Lindsay Ann Reid

Volume 37: *Prodigality in Early Modern Drama*
Ezra Horbury

Volume 38: Poly-Olbion: *New Perspectives*
edited by Andrew McRae and Philip Schwyzer

Volume 39: *The Atom in Seventeenth-Century Poetry*
Cassandra Gorman

Volume 40: *Pity and Identity in the Age of Shakespeare*
Toria Johnson

Volume 41: *John Cruso of Norwich and Anglo-Dutch Literary Identity in the Seventeenth Century*
Christopher Joby

Printed in the United States
by Baker & Taylor Publisher Services